INTEREST CONFLICT AND
POLITICAL CHANGE IN BRAZIL

INTEREST CONFLICT AND POLITICAL CHANGE IN BRAZIL

PHILIPPE C. SCHMITTER

STANFORD UNIVERSITY PRESS

STANFORD, CALIFORNIA

1971

Stanford University Press
Stanford, California
© 1971 by the Board of Trustees of the
Leland Stanford Junior University
Printed in the United States of America
ISBN 0-8047-0733-2
LC 78-93496

To Barbara qui s'est débrouillée

Acknowledgments

In the preparation of this book I have contracted a large number of personal and intellectual debts, the greatest of which I owe to those Brazilians who opened a *crédito de confiança* on my account and guided me through the labyrinths of their political life with intelligence, patience, and compassion. I have promised anonymity to those who responded to my questionnaires, and can therefore only thank them as a group; but fortunately I am under no such restraint in acknowledging the contributions of Brazilian scholars and friends.

To my colleagues at the Instituto de Ciências Sociais of the University of Brazil (now the Federal University of Rio de Janeiro)—Maurício Vinhas de Queiroz, Luciano Martins de Almeida, Ivan Gonçalves de Freitas, José Antônio Pessoa de Queiroz, Nilda Agueda Martinez Pita, Carlos Dório Gonçalves Soares, and Maria Stella Faria de Amorim—and to the Instituto's directors—Themístocles de Brandão Cavalcanti, Luiz de Aguiar Costa Pinto, Roberto Cardoso de Oliveira, and, especially, Evaristo de Moraes Filho and Marina São Paulo de Vasconcellos—I am indebted for encouragement as well as innumerable suggestions that saved me from many pitfalls in the collection of data. Several of these colleagues have subsequently suffered at the hands of an arbitrary and repressive regime, and I salute them for their courage and integrity. To my students at the Instituto I owe most of my orientation to the political language and customs of Brazil. Alexandre de Souza Costa Barros has made important contributions to this study, literally from its inception—first as my research assistant in Rio, then as a graduate student at the University of Chicago.

In São Paulo I was fortunate to be associated with the members of the Escola Libre de Sociologia e Política, especially with Professors Cyro

Berlinck and Vicente Marotta Rangel. Luis Washington Vita introduced me to *paulista* and *paulistano* life with sardonic good humor and great intellectual verve; his premature death has robbed Brazil of one of its most promising scholars. From Leôncio Martins Rodrigues, my predecessor in the analysis of *sindicalismo*, I learned much, thanks to his continuous and friendly collaboration.

In one case I feel I must violate my pledge to preserve the anonymity of my informants. José E. Mindlin has shared with me his deep understanding of Brazilian politics, in particular the dilemmas of industrialists working within this complex setting. He is of course not responsible for my evaluation of their political role—but that evaluation might not have been what it is without his knowledge and insight.

Other Brazilian scholars contributed to this manuscript in a variety of ways. I cannot thank them all by name here, but I hope that their intellectual contributions are adequately acknowledged in the footnotes. Special debts are owed to Hélio Jaguaribe, Candido Mendes de Almeida, Guerreiro Ramos, Fernando Henrique Cardoso, Simon Schwartzman, Celso and Betty Lafer, Amaury Guimarães de Souza, Antônio Octávio Cintra, and José Murilo de Carvalho, all of whom have read and commented on parts of this manuscript. I also admit to having brazenly exploited the talents of several Brazilian students at Chicago: Alexandre de Souza Costa Barros, Roberto Gambini, Cesar Guimarães, and Mário Machado. Without the initial encouragement of Gláucio Dillon Ary Soares, I might never have thought of doing research in Brazil—but neither he nor anyone else mentioned above should be held responsible for the result.

This study was first presented as a doctoral dissertation at the University of California (Berkeley), and reflects imperfectly the immense collective talent of its Department of Political Science. To Ernst B. Haas I owe a very special debt: he managed to convince me by his own example that political inquiry could be innovative, intellectually exciting, and just plain fun. David E. Apter, Seymour Martin Lipset, and William Kornhauser also served on my dissertation committee. Ralph Retzlaff made a special contribution by "turning me on" to aggregate data analysis, the impact of which has proved difficult to eradicate.

My stay in Brazil was financed by a generous grant from the Rockefeller Foundation, through the Department of Political Science at Berkeley. The Center for Latin American Studies, University of California, provided supplemental funding. On my return from the field, I was given a year away from job-hunting and teaching thanks to the generosity of the Studies in International Integration Project of the Institute of International Studies (Berkeley). Since 1967, when I accepted a position as an assistant professor at the University of Chicago, I have obtained important support from its Social Sciences Divisional Research Fund, and constructive intellectual criticism from my colleagues. The able editorship of John Daniel, formerly with Stanford University Press, has greatly improved the book, as have the comments of two fellow travelers on the Brazil route, Douglas Chalmers and Robert Packenham.

To my wife, who first suffered from the vagaries of the perpetual *bagunça* that is Rio de Janeiro, then from the burden of typing 900 pages of manuscript, I have dedicated this book.

PCS

Contents

Figures and Tables

Figures

Tables

Glossary of Brazilian Terms

ATESTADO DE ANTECEDENTES IDEOLÓGICOS. Certificate of political and ideological background demanded of candidates for syndical office.

ATO INSTITUCIONAL. A "constitutional" decree imposed by military rulers after the 1964 coup. Minor implementing decrees are referred to as "complementary acts."

AUTARQUIA. Semi-public government agency usually not subordinated to any ministry. Similar to *sociedades mixtas*.

BAHIANO. Resident of the State of Bahia.

BANCADA. Ensemble of representatives from a given state or region who act together in the legislature regardless of party.

CABIDE DE EMPRÊGO. Literally "a hat-stand for jobs." A sinecure organization whose members hold many jobs; also, an individual who holds many jobs.

CABO ELEITORAL. Ward heeler.

CARIOCA. Resident of the city of Rio de Janeiro (Guanabara).

CLASSE. Literally "class." Used in corporatist systems of representation to refer to sectoral interests, e.g., *a classe médica*.

CLASSES PRODUTORAS. Euphemism for propertied classes or bourgeoisie.

CLIENTELISMO. System of decision-making based on exchange of legal privilege, material favors, or immunity from sanction between political actors.

COBERTURA. Negotiated political support, often divided into *militar* and *civil*.

CORONELISMO. The system of political bossism by local notables (*coroneis*).

DEPUTADO CLASSISTA. Federal or state deputy considered accountable to specific sectoral interests.

DIÁLOGO. Literally "dialogue." Propensity for reaching a mutually satisfactory solution by extended conversation and negotiation.

EMPREGUISMO. Cooptation by means of offering jobs to one's supporters and/or opponents.

ENQUADRAMENTO SINDICAL. System of preestablished membership categories for syndical representation.

ENTIDADE CIVIL. Private representative association not officially recognized as a *sindicato*.

ESTADO CARTORIAL. Literally "notorial or sinecure state." A system of political domination based on cooptation, especially by means of public employment. See *empreguismo*.

ESTADO NOVO. The New State, a corporatist, quasi-fascist authoritarian state formally in existence from 1937 to 1945.

FAVELA. Brazilian city slum.

GAÚCHO. Resident of the State of Rio Grande do Sul.

GRUPO EXECUTIVO. High-level working group within the public administration, usually concerned with industrial promotion.

IMPÔSTO SINDICAL. Obligatory tax for the support of workers' and employers' syndicates.

JEITO. "Unorthodox way out of a difficulty. Close in meaning to 'Yankee ingenuity,' but [referring] not only to successful mechanical improvisation but also, like the French *se débrouiller*, to extricating oneself from man- and society-made trouble." (A. O. Hirschman, *Journeys toward Progress*.)

JUSTIÇA DO TRABALHO. System of special labor courts.

LIGAS CAMPONESAS. Peasant leagues.

MESOI. Greek term referring to those in the middle. Used here in preference to "middle class" or "middle sectors."

MINEIRO. Resident of the State of Minas Gerais.

PACTUALISMO. Propensity for making pacts or compromises, often at the expense of absent or unrepresented parties.

PANELINHA. Interpersonal or face-to-face clique of status equals.

PAULISTA. Resident of the State of São Paulo.

PAULISTANO. Resident of the city of São Paulo.

PAZ SOCIAL. "Social peace"—the slogan of the Dutra regime (1945–50) and of Brazilian conservatives in general.

PELÊGO. Professional syndical leader. Generally used to refer to workers' representatives, but sometimes applied to employers' representatives as well.

PETROBRÁS. Federally owned and operated oil industry.

PLURALISMO SINDICAL. Opposite of *sindicalismo único*. A system of representation with more than one organization per interest category.

PODER MODERADOR. The moderative power or capacity to intervene to restore "balance" to the political system. Originally exercised by the Emperor, usurped by military authorities after 1889.

REGULAMENTAÇÃO. "Regulation" or reinterpretation of laws to adapt them for bureaucratic implementation.

SALÁRIO MÍNIMO. Minimum salary levels fixed periodically by the federal government.

SINDICALISMO ÚNICO. System of representation that permits only one officially recognized organization per interest category.

SINDICATO. "Syndicate" or officially recognized representative association.

SINDICATO FANTASMA. Fictitious syndicate, usually fabricated for electoral-manipulative purposes. Also "drawer syndicate" (*sindicato de gaveta*).

TÉCNICO. Highly trained public administrator, often an economist.

TRANSIGÊNCIA. A spirit of mutual compromise.

PART I

ONE

Development, Political Groups, and Interest Politics

> Among the laws that rule human societies there is one which seems to be more precise and clear than all others. If men are to remain civilized or to become so, the art of associating together must grow and improve in the same ratio in which the equality of conditions is increased.
>
> TOCQUEVILLE

DESPITE its postulated clarity and precision, Tocqueville's "law" has never been put to a rigorous empirical test.[1] Nor, surprisingly, have contemporary scholars attempted to link systematically the concepts and hypotheses of interest group theory and those of political development. My intent here is first to analyze this relationship and present a number of middle-range hypotheses concerning it. I shall then go on to test these hypotheses in the light of the Brazilian experience from 1930 to 1965.

Tocqueville made an independent variable of societal development, which he defined as increased social equality. In this study, we shall follow Tocqueville in regarding changes in the nature and role of political associations as a consequence of development. But we shall also be concerned with the functional relationship between the two variables. In the concluding chapter the patterns of emergence, interaction, and influence of political associations will be considered briefly as active change agents, giving direction to the developmental process as well as being given direction by it. There is no logical reason why changes in the "art of association" should not in certain circumstances—especially when cultural diffusion is involved—precede structural changes in the economic and social spheres.[2] Indeed, there is every reason to assume that past patterns of interaction will decisively influence the course of future development.

The concept of societal development, as used in this study, is conceived as the "contrapuntal interplay between differentiation (which is divisive of established society) and integration (which unites differentiated structures on a new basis)."[3] This process of increased specialization in roles and their subsequent reincorporation into more diversified and complex organizations is itself made up of several component processes: urbanization, industrialization, commercialization, bureaucratization, agricultural specialization, and even migration and immigration.

We cannot assume that role differentiation leads inevitably to integration, or that the two together tend toward some sort of functional balance or political consensus. There are many possible outcomes of the exchange between the two, and many possible political consequences of these different exchanges. An important intervening condition appears to be a change in the normative context of action toward a specifically modern problem-solving type of rationality. In Fred Riggs's terms, such a change involves "a progressive narrowing or regulation of the range of consideration taken into account in social action," a process he calls "refraction."[4] Lucian Pye would make the capacity "to create more effective, more adaptive, more complex and more rationalized institutions" the hallmark of successful development and has stressed the need for actors to "relate themselves to each other so as to facilitate collective action."[5] This capacity to trust or empathize with one's fellow citizens in the pursuit of common objectives is an important component of Tocqueville's "art of association."

The payoff of a successful developmental interplay, we may hypothesize, is the building-in of an institutionalized capacity to absorb self-induced or externally introduced change. A developed society is not an end-state, a static configuration of perfected structures and values. Nor must all developed societies resemble some ideal model. Rather, they are dynamic systems in which change has become the norm.[6]

Political Development

Theoretical discussions of the structural implications of political development can be divided, broadly speaking, into two categories. On the one hand are those that emphasize the emergence of a permanent, depersonalized, and centralized set of institutions, "an organ distinct from the rest of society," engaged in authoritative decision-making and implementation.[7] On the other hand are those that equate political development with "politicization," or "increased participation or involvement of the citizens in state activities, in power calculations and consequences."[8] In fact, despite their obvious differences, these two views are not irreconcilable. Indeed, just as societal development can be seen as an interplay between role differentiation and structural integration, political development can be seen as an interplay between two distinctive but interdependent subprocesses, the one tending toward the centralization or concentration of authority and the other toward the dispersion or distribution of participation.[9] Theoreticians of the first school stress the consensual aspects of the development process, theoreticians of the second its conflictive aspects.

Political development is, then, the product of the contrapuntal, if not dialectical, interplay between concentration and dispersion. Its end product is a complex of structural and normative changes involving the emergence of highly differentiated but interrelated political structures and roles with a certain degree of self-sufficiency and a distinctive set of goals and orientations—in short, a political culture. Where some sort of viable combination of the concentration of authority and the dispersion of participation is achieved, the nation-state emerges as "the impersonal and ultimate arbiter of human affairs."[10] Citizens acquire a wider sense of group loyalties. Authorities acquire legitimacy, and can expect voluntary compliance with their acts. As with societal development, the ultimate payoff of political development is an enduring capacity for dealing with a continuously shifting schedule of supports and demands, and for generating and absorbing change as the political system moves beyond the conditions that determined its original configuration. In other words, political development is a success when the polity becomes a going concern. In the contemporary international environment, this means acquiring the effective power, as well as the formal legal status, of a nation-state.

The developed polity, like the developed society, is not a predetermined end-state; indeed, its chief characteristic is a constant tension between antagonistic trends. There seems to be no reason to believe that the process is unidirectional or irreversible, inevitable or even desirable. Some, as we have noted, would equate political development with the subordination of authority groups to autonomous political associations. Others stress the creation and dispersion of authoritative institutions exclusively. Still others seem to imply that only an "integration" or "balance" of component processes constitutes development. As far as I am concerned, any change that results in institutionalizing either political associations or authoritative institutions is a change in the direction of political development.* After the fact, one can always describe development in terms of increased political participation (by means of specialized intermediaries) and increased political control (by means of specialized institutions), and of the interplay between them. Thus, perhaps, one can predict the immediate future by extending observed

---

* Political development, as described here, is not necessarily a desirable outcome. I confess my personal preference for a developmental pattern in which authority groups are subordinated to independent associations, and I admit that this preference has led me to follow Tocqueville in concentrating on the activities of such associations. I hope that this bias has not prejudiced either my observations or my evaluations of the actual process of Brazilian political development.

trends. But the long-term outcome of development is predictable only to the extent that one can specify beforehand the conditions determining the predominance of one of the two component processes and its likely impact upon the other. Hopefully, empirical studies will contribute to the systematic specification of these conditions.

The intent of this study is much more modest; it deals systematically with only one part of the process just described. Following Weber's suggestion, recently elaborated by Reinhard Bendix, a distinction was first made between "formally instated authority typically entailing relations of command and obedience, and customarily or voluntarily established associations typically involving relations based on affinities of ideas and interests, or state and society for short."[11] The first type, authority groups, consists of "the direct agents of the legitimate use of force," those structures that specialize in making and executing policy for the society as a whole: presidencies, cabinets, police forces, legislatures, judiciaries, government bureaucracies, military establishments. In this study, these will be treated only indirectly, that is, to the extent that they are the objects of the demands and supports of the second general type of specialized political structure, political associations.

Development and Associability

To rephrase Tocqueville, development (functional differentiation and reintegration) stimulates the emergence of all associational forms of political activity. The relationship between development and associability* provides the first global hypothesis of this study. An increase in functional differentiation and specialization in role structures has a fragmenting impact on traditional, polyfunctional institutions. It also multiplies the number of potential interests and attitudes around which secondary groups can form, creates wider networks of communication, and provides these potential organizations with additional, previously uncommitted human and material resources. From the standpoint of the individual actor, the more specialized his various activities, the more likely he will be to join or support a greater variety of associations and the less likely he will be to have all his demands satisfied by a single primary group. As the affective bonds of kinship, tribal, and locality groups grow weaker, the actor develops a new capacity for social and psychic mobility. Earlier theorists of development feared that primary groups would be eclipsed. The citizen would become isolated, retreat

---

* As used herein, "associability" refers generally to the propensity of actors for forming, joining, or participating in permanently administered secondary groups that explicitly advance or defend a specific set of interests. See p. 10 below for the definition of "representative association."

into political apathy, and passively accept the domination of huge bureaucratic agencies or nationwide political machines. Associations were seen as a remedy for this problem as well. In the words of Durkheim, "A nation can last only if, between the state and the private citizen, there intrudes a whole series of secondary groups that are close enough to the citizen to pull him into their sphere of action and thus sweep him along in the general torrent of social life."[12]

Today this fear that separation and compartmentalization will result in a general withdrawal from politics has markedly decreased. Contemporary development takes place in an age of "faith in the miraculous powers of politics," not of faith in the beneficent powers of private initiative and activity.[13] Given this orientation, it seems certain that the extension of communication networks, the greater availability of physical and monetary resources, the proliferation of bureaucratic forms, and similar instances of differentiation will not only increase the number and variety of associations in the system, but also ensure that they will be politically oriented.

Development also increases the influence of political associations in the decision-making process. As Almond observes, secondary structures tend to penetrate and dominate primary-group structures;[14] premodern corporate groups are likely to be stripped of their direct economic and political functions by role specialization. But a degree of reciprocity, diffuseness, particularism, and ascriptiveness always remains. Primary-group relationships are not irrevocable obstacles to modernization and development, but can be utilized and incorporated within new institutional structures.[15] Where they are not, one can anticipate "unintegrated" sets of political groups with modern associations situated precariously among apathetic or antagonistic premodern tribes, clans, and cliques. Even the most thoroughly modernized and developed systems have a mixture of associational and nonassociational groups mobilizing support and articulating demands—although some are more mixed up than others.

Nevertheless, development provides groups of all kinds with the means to organize and continue in operation. In a developing system traditional allegiances lose their appeal, suffering the "disenchantment" of which Weber spoke. The distribution of political power is altered in favor of associations. Interests on the rise and interests on the wane alike resort to creating permanent, voluntarily recruited conflict groups. As organization begets counter organization, a cumulative process of transformation is begun; as previously unrelated groups are drawn into conflict with each other, they also come to participate in a network of mutual rights and obligations. Which types of associations—movements, parties, or representative associations—are most likely to benefit from this transformation will be discussed below.

Development has a peculiarly paradoxical or dialectical impact on the extent of conflict in the polity. Even when it is accompanied by a steady increase in system performance and per capita income (an unlikely event),[16] development both stimulates and moderates political conflict. On the one hand, it generates increased tensions by throwing potentially hostile groups into contact and by raising status and income expectations that are hard to satisfy; on the other hand, it generates the wherewithal to channel the new tensions and satisfy the new expectations. "These tensions result from the very success of modernization; they are the price paid for any substantial change."[17]

This is where a change in the nature of political groups has a crucial impact on the outcome. As Lewis Coser has pointed out, when cultural or historical conditions cause primary groups to remain prominent in the political process despite structural differentiation in other spheres, "conflict with other groups contributes to the establishment and reaffirmation of the identity and boundary lines of societies and groups." Thus he argues that "patterned enmities and reciprocal antagonisms conserve social divisions and systems of stratification." If this is so, increased tensions are likely to ossify existing social relations, precisely at a time when more mobility and flexibility are required. When, however, "groups . . . appeal only to a peripheral part of a member's loyalty, . . . conflicts are apt to be less sharp and violent than in groups wherein ties are diffuse and affective." Hence, conflict based on associations is likely to lead to mutual restraints, to the political socialization of both contenders, and to greater flexibility and adaptability to change, thereby facilitating further development. Under these circumstances, "the very multiplicity of conflict in itself tends to constitute a check against the breakdown of consensus."[18]

Beyond these very general expectations, it is obvious that political associations in societies at approximately the same level of differentiation and structural complexity vary considerably in relative influence, modes of action, and general type. Further independent or intervening variables must be specified if we are to make discrete predictions. In subsequent parts of this study it will be argued that government policy toward freedom of association strongly affects the way associations emerge and develop, that the nature and scope of authoritative decision-making are closely related to the way associations interact, and that political culture has a pervasive influence on both the emergence pattern and the interaction pattern.

Types of Associations

Tocqueville did not distinguish conceptually among the various politically active groups he had observed in America. To him the Anti-Tariff Convention of 1831, the myriad of local civic organizations, and the Democratic Party were all species of a common genus, the political association.[19] Before associations are fully developed—while they are still highly segmented[20] and organizationally unstable[21]—it may indeed be difficult to distinguish between different species; moreover, a given association may frequently shift in type. However, as the techniques of organization and successful influence become diffused and the pattern of emergence becomes consolidated, three distinct types of associations emerge: movements, parties, and representative associations. All are engaged in processing demands upon and marshaling support for authority groups. They differ in the nature of member identification, tasks performed, and organizational objectives.

Movements. A movement is a "social collectivity whose members voluntarily participate and for which the basic unifying factor is a psychological identification."[22] The intensity of personal identification is only one criterion, however. Equally important is the diffuse scope of the movement's objectives, which are aimed at changing substantial aspects of the existing order. Although movements differ considerably in the extent to which they have specialized decisional and administrative structures and stable systems of delegating authority, they do qualify as associations because of their voluntary membership and because each has a special purpose. They play a particularly dynamic role in the political process, and there is evidence that they act as catalytic agents in the creation of other types of associations.[23] As they become routinized, they tend to transform themselves into ruling authority groups, parties, or representative associations. Movements, then, are essentially transient phenomena that have a profound effect on the political system: they help the growth of representation by mobilizing previously apolitical groups, and they bring about a change in the nature of constituent units by becoming routinized and also by stimulating subsidiary and rival associations. They are not, however, the primary focus of this study.

Parties. A party is a political association whose principal objective is to control recruitment to major authority group positions. It does this either by presenting candidates for elections or by selecting occupants bureaucratically. For the member, participation in or identification with the party becomes a general standard by which he interprets (and misinterprets) political reality. In essence, the power of the party lies in its ability to elicit a diffuse and spontaneous commitment from its members—a flexible and partial commitment not as comprehensive or intensive as that to a movement or to the political community as a whole. Graham Wallas seems to have been the first to detect that the modern "associational" party, as distinct from traditional factions or "political connections," is rooted in enlarged participation and the need of "men in the mass" for some mechanism of emotional involvement and symbolic reference. Neil MacDonald has captured this well:

A party or party system is a kind of intermediary or intervening social formation that has created a minor or lesser loyalty . . . which is less absolute and rigid in its demands than is the loyalty required by the state, for example, and more comprehensive but not necessarily stronger or more compelling than the loyalty to family or to the neighborhood.[24]

The composite definition used here eschews the functionalist approach and instead emphasizes organizational structures, actor objectives, and concrete tasks; Gabriel Almond and others, however, have observed that parties are associations that specialize in "converting demands into general policy alternatives."

Representative associations. The objectives of party actors, though not as comprehensive or as system-challenging as those of movement actors, are less specific and exclusive than those of the third type of political association, the one that is the main concern of this study.[25] This is the representative association, a secondary group with voluntary membership, a permanent administrative structure, and a decisional hierarchy that explicitly advances or defends a specific set of attitudes or interests before political authorities. This may remind some readers of David Truman's definition of an interest group as "any group that, on the basis of one or more shared attitudes, makes certain claims upon other groups in the society."[26] But the representative association, as defined here, is a special type of interest group—almost identical, in fact, with what Almond calls the "associational" type. Membership in it is both instrumental and partial; recruitment tends to be impersonal and oriented toward achievement.[27] Its objective is not to capture authoritative posts (at least not by open competition or appointment), nor is it to effect broad societal changes. However, in order to be a representative association at all, it must be politically oriented, i.e., aimed "at exerting influence on the directing authorities of a corporate political group; especially at the appropriation, expropriation, redistribution or allocation of the powers of government."[28] This restriction excludes from our definition such voluntary associations as mutual aid societies, charities, fraternal orders, social and sports clubs—at any rate, to the extent that such organizations are politically quiescent. Also excluded are what Almond calls "institutional interest groups" (authority groups in the terminology of this study), even though, as he notes, they may indeed perform important input functions.

The sorting of groups into dichotomous categories—*gemeinschaftlich* and *gesellschaftlich*, primary and secondary, status and contract, mechanical and organic, sacred and secular, and the like—has become commonplace procedure in the social sciences. Fred Riggs has suggested that this procedure is useless for understanding transitional societies, which he regards as characterized by intermediary forms of social and political organization. He refers to the representative structures typical of such societies as "clects."[29] Clects are "poly-functional" in their objectives, they are "attainment-oriented" in their recruitment, and they deal "selectivistically" with authority groups.[30] Without questioning the descriptive validity of the concept, it does seem applicable only to a particular kind of developing society, one where the traditional order is differentiated into autonomous communities based on ethnicity, language, religion, regional loyalty, or lineage.[31]

The bulk of this study will be devoted to an empirical examination of two sets of hypotheses that relate development specifically to changes in the nature and role of representative associations. The first set concerns the pattern of their emergence; the second concerns the pattern of their interaction with authority groups. The former is directly inspired by Tocqueville's remarks on associability in general, as well as by the more recent literature on political development. The techniques of analysis are largely based on historical documentation and aggregate data. The latter set of propositions, dealing with the pattern of interaction with and influence upon authority groups, is more informed by the so-called group theory of politics. It is investigated primarily by means of interviews and the written accounts of those involved.

The Pattern of Emergence

Structural differentiation encourages the emergence of associational forms of interest and attitude expression. This is a rather broad orienting hypothesis. However, such emergence can be divided conceptually into four distinct but interrelated dimensions, three of which bear a hypothetically positive relationship to development and the fourth an indeterminate one. These dimensions are coverage, functional specificity, density, and plurality.

Coverage. This is the extent to which differentiated social groups in a given polity have available for the expression of their interests formal, specialized associations. Operationally speaking, coverage can also be described as the number of active representative associations together with their geographic and functional scope. Number implies that the sheer quantity of associations is likely to increase with development. Geographic scope implies an extension of their activity so that associations and hierarchies of associations—federations and confederations— formally represent interests and attitudes throughout the polity. Although the "organizationally rich" will presumably become richer, and the "organizationally poor" will presumably become poorer,[32] if development trickles down to the provinces, so will associability. Functional scope implies that an increasing variety of interests and attitudes, whether directly or indirectly affected by development, will be drawn into formal associations. At the start of a differentiation sequence, interests will be latent, unorganized, or informally organized; in a fully developed polity, theoretically, no interest will be without an association for its expression.

Functional specificity. This is the degree to which associations voluntarily restrict their activities to the defense and promotion of a narrow band of interests or attitudes. In the earlier stages of development, interests are likely to be broadly articulated: solidary groups such as "industry," "commerce," "the middle classes," or "the proletariat" demand, insist, request, beg, or threaten. At its most extensive, of course, the representative association transforms itself into a movement. But if development proceeds, creating more and more complex social organizations, one should be able to expect that associations will become accordingly more and more specialized. The demanding, insisting, requesting, begging, or threatening will be done by such groups as "the chemical industry," "sales managers," "employees of the Ministry of Finance," or "metallurgical workers."

Density. This is the degree to which members of a given social group actually join and participate in the associations that formally claim to represent their interests. The mere existence of more numerous, more widespread, and more specialized associations does not by itself guarantee that people will join them. Even less does formal membership in an association ensure active participation in its affairs. Density, however, implies both membership and participation.

Plurality. This is the extent to which members of a given social group are presented with alternative associational channels for expressing their interests or attitudes. In other words, plurality makes it possible for an authoritative decision-maker to be confronted with supports and demands emanating from different associations purporting to represent the same clientele.

It is my feeling that the availability of alternative associations claiming to represent the same cluster of social, economic, cultural, or political interests is more a function of political culture and the pattern of authoritative policy toward freedom of association than of the level or degree of structural differentiation. Plurality is not the same thing as pluralism. The former refers simply to the availability of alternative associations; the latter refers to a global pattern of political conflict among many autonomous groups. Nor does the existence of plurality guarantee that such a situation is democratic. Whether or not plurality results in democracy depends upon how the associations compete with one another, to what degree the leaders can be held accountable to their followers, the degree of government control over these groups, and the nature of the political norms acquired through associational participation.*

Plurality, it may be hypothesized, has a dual set of consequences. On the one hand, the existence of alternative associations makes the leaders of these associations more responsive to their followers' interests, forces them to work constantly in order to maintain coverage, and encourages high rates of member participation. Leaders who are themselves or who know their followers to be divided in allegiance will be more moderate and conciliatory. On the other hand, the presence of plurality implies that the political system as a whole will be saturated with differing reports about the level of support and the intensity of demand. When authoritative decision-makers as well as association leaders and followers become subject to cross-pressures, they begin to doubt their unilateral wisdom, and they vacillate, moderate, and eventually compromise.

Many North American theorists have suggested that plurality is an integral part of pluralism and that the conflicts arising from plurality result in a stable, democratic political process that guarantees the protection of individual freedoms. Whether or not this proposition can be said to apply to the United States, one must call attention to some of its more questionable assumptions. If the interests and attitudes of followers are, in fact, strongly antagonistic (and they are likely to be so in an asymmetrically developing society), the quest of leaders for authentic representation will lead them to adopt increasingly divergent positions.[33] If the system for exchanging information is as perfect and equalitarian as the model assumes (again, an unlikely occurrence in a developing system), the result of such a saturation of conflicting demands and supports could be immobilism rather than moderation. Decisional paralysis, in a setting where interassociational competition has been raising expectations, is more likely to lead to political instability than to political stability. The consequences of plurality, then, vary with the nature of

---

* One is reminded of Harry Eckstein's comment that although Weimar Germany was a pluralist paradise owing to its great multiplicity of associations, it was not a stable and thriving democratic polity.

emerging associational structures, the system's political culture, and the pattern of policy.

The four dimensions of the emergence pattern are clearly interrelated. In the succeeding presentation, however, it will not always be possible— or even desirable—to distinguish between them. For example, density and coverage might normally be expected to vary coterminously. Nevertheless, coverage may outrun density, especially in periods of innovation in associability; and in periods of organizational maturity, density may rise without an increase in the number, geographic scope, or functional scope of associations. Similarly, functional specificity can increase without any change in functional coverage. This is most likely to happen in the later stages of emergence, when virtually all the broader interests have been organized. A high degree of plurality ipso facto involves greater coverage, if only because the total number of associations is bound to be greater. Accordingly, one might hypothesize that plurality results in a higher overall density, as alternative groups compete for members, but in a lower specific density for any one association in a given category, since its occupants would be divided in their allegiance.

The Pattern of Interaction and Influence

The group theory of politics abounds in hypothetical statements about the relationship between representative associations and authority groups. Attributes of the associations such as size, density, resources, strategic position, prestige, internal cohesion, political skills, technical competence, and intensity of interest are combined with variables describing the structure of political decision-making and the scope of government activity. In this way users of the theory hope to predict the likelihood that certain channels of access will be adopted for influencing the course of public policy.

Unfortunately, the resulting abundance of hypothetical "leads" is rather deceptive. The concepts involved are often both too ambiguous and too ambitious; research hypotheses based on them are consequently vague and difficult to translate into the language of empirical research.[34] Political group theorists have not devoted much attention to constructing systematic conceptual frameworks or to testing "middle-range" propositions. The works of Bentley, Truman, Meynaud, Gross, Finer, Potter, Zeigler, and others consist largely of descriptive material interspersed with interesting, insightful, but elusive and empirically unexploited propositions. They conclude rather than begin with hypotheses.[35]

For the student of comparative politics, the group approach appears excessively culture-bound.[36] For the student of development, the approach offers little in the way of hypotheses relating changes in social structure and cultural values to changes in the nature of interest politics,* and even less in the way of verifying such hypotheses. Group theorists seem to have taken for granted not only the context of group behavior, but also the manner in which patterns of group behavior emerge. Nor has the group theory of politics been sufficiently exploited as an analytical tool for explaining political development.

The purpose of this study is to predict, by means of general "orienting hypotheses," the impact of development upon two distinct but related dimensions of the relationship between authority groups and representative associations. These are the direction and the influence of the interaction process. Given the differences in the rate and timing of structural differentiation, in political cultural attitudes, in government structures, and in the pattern of emergence of associations, it is not easy to advance and test hypotheses that are logically convincing and relevant for cross-national comparison. There are simply too many intervening variables. One is tempted to derive either very general and innocuous hypotheses or very specific ones that in effect "predict" only the Brazilian case. It is hoped that the "orienting hypotheses" used here avoid both pitfalls.

As we have seen above, the structural differentiation of society results in the multiplication of interests and attitudes around which associations may form. It also tends to result in the proliferation of government functions and tasks. As new types of productive activities appear, economic pursuits become monetary and commercial, large urban conglomerations form, transport and communications networks are created, individual citizens are mobilized into wider social and political participation, and the pressures upon authority groups to provide more services and to control previously unregulated or nonexistent activities increase.[37] These pressures are likely to be even stronger in late-developing societies and economies, whose sense of their own underdevelopment and whose desire for rapid emulation of the services and controls of more differentiated polities add a compelling urgency to the process. The result is likely to be both a physical expansion of the public bureaucratic establishment and an increase in its capacity for commanding and distributing scarce resources. Because the new social services and political controls require specialized technical skills that are often monopolized by bureaucratic elites, the decisional autonomy of these elites is enhanced at the expense of elected or politically appointed elites.† Not only do the

---

* I use the term "interest politics" to refer generally to all efforts by representative associations to influence public policy outcomes.

† A likely subhypothesis would be that the rate of expansion of services and controls influences the extent to which publicly elected officials are capable of preserving their power in relation to the bureaucracy. The faster the expansion, the more likely

trained bureaucrats gain considerable discretion in their allocation of resources, but they also provide the information upon which decisions are formally made elsewhere in the political system.[38] Fred Riggs, from a slightly different perspective, similarly concludes that "it is precisely in the prismatic [or transitional] situation that bureaucratic power is most likely to rise to unprecedented heights. . . . <u>Bureaucracies</u>—military more often than not—<u>have usurped in the name of 'tutelage' or popular 'guid-ance' the roles which, in a modern society, are played by legislators, elected executives and party leaders.</u>"[39] Regardless of whether they openly usurp control of public policy-making, their power vis-à-vis other authority groups does increase: they have more resources at their disposal, their tasks are greater, and they enjoy more decisional auton-omy. It follows, then, that because demands will seek out the distribu-tion of effective—not formal—decisional power, the direction of the activities of representative associations will increasingly focus upon the public bureaucracy.

It also follows from our hypothetical observations about the prolifer-ation of government services and controls and about the expansion in number, scope, and density of associational forms of interest expression that the significance of these associations in the political process is likely to increase with development. By significance is meant simply the fre-quency of interaction between representative associations and authority groups. However, "significance" is not synonymous with "influence." Al-though those groups that have more frequent contact with the govern-ment are more likely to be influential, especially when their demands are functionally specific,[40] significance cannot be considered a satisfactory operational measure of influence. For one thing, the rate of interaction is usually reported by the associations themselves and is hence subject to distortion. What one group regards as frequent contact another might consider as intolerably rare. Seldom is one actually able to tabulate the number of daily or weekly encounters. Moreover, even the most quan-titatively refined index of communications exchange leaves unmeasured the intensity of the relationship. A single visit a year may be sufficient for some groups to acquire all they need; others may petition the govern-ment daily for redress without satisfaction. In order to estimate the influence of such confrontations, one must also have some idea of the nature of interaction (consultation, negotiation, manipulation, co-opta-tion, pressure, violence, etc.). Finally, the reports of this sort of contact generally overlook (or deliberately ignore) informal, interpersonal ex-

---

it will be that decisional autonomy will devolve upon the bureaucratic elites. In the event of rapid expansion at the hands of a self-appointed revolutionary elite, greater "political" control is probably maintained.

changes of interest and attitude. The mass media and even the specialized press of the associations record only a fraction of the "public" exchanges and very few of the "private" ones. Although Brazilian interest groups are formal, often highly bureaucratized organizations, they do not hesitate to exploit all the channels of particularistic access available to them, as we shall see. Of course many of the private contacts between group leaders and decision-makers are in fact for private ends. But a good deal of associational business is also transacted in this intimate, interpersonal, and largely unrecorded manner.

It would seem to follow logically from the combined effect of the previous hypotheses that the global influence of representative associations in the making of public policy should increase as an indirect consequence of the structural differentiation of society. There are, however, some theoretical reasons for questioning this proposition and some very formidable practical reasons for doubting whether or not it can be convincingly tested by empirical methods. Many if not <u>most of the hypotheses concerning interest politics seek to predict the effectiveness or influence of a given group, i.e., its ability to initiate or veto a proposal for public policy.</u> Those whose patterns of demands most closely approximate the outcomes in terms of realized or frustrated government policies are held to be the most influential. For example, on this basis, anyone studying the general configuration of Brazilian public policy in the last few decades could "prove" by extrapolation that the influence of associations representing industrialists has increased while the influence of associations representing rural landowners has decreased. On a more sophisticated basis, one could, for example, match the pattern of pronouncements by leaders of the National Confederation of Industry (CNI) with that of policies adopted by the government and "prove" the great and increasing influence of the CNI. Since the overall scope of public policy has expanded enormously—roughly at the same time as have the number, scope, density, and functional specificity of representative associations—and since these new policies have generally favored the interests of an increasing variety of social groups, one could easily conclude that the global influence of representative associations has expanded correspondingly. This would be, to say the least, a spurious correlation.

One can easily imagine a situation in which the demands of an increasing number of denser, more functionally specific associations become more frequent, bureaucratically directed, and institutionalized, but remain confined to sectors or issues of relatively minor importance. The major public policy decisions continue to be made at a "macropolitical" level—by professional politicians and high-level administrators (técnicos)—on the basis of nationalist ideology, economic theory, pressures from the international environment, elite paternalism, desire for personal enrichment, immediate client satisfaction, or political survival. Representative associations may or may not be in a position to influence policy based on these criteria or to force policy-makers to use more "rational" (i.e., more pragmatic) criteria. Therefore, an increase in the influence of representative associations in the total political process is simply not deducible from the hypotheses already advanced or partially verified. Such an increase seems to depend primarily on qualitative changes whereby both sets of actors become more "operationally rational," and these changes in turn depend on numerous other variables— in fact on the total configuration of the political system.*

Thus it is impossible to predict that development will necessarily both result in the emergence of representative associations and also make those associations the most influential units in the political system. For this reason, some might respond that the group theory approach is irrelevant to the study of political development. This naïve position is based on the naïve pretense of earlier group theorists that all political activity could be explained by describing the dynamics of interaction between organized interests. This is certainly not the intent either of this study or of most recent monographs on interest groups. Used intelligently, there is no reason that the group theory of politics cannot predict associational impotence as well as omnipotence. Practically speaking, the group theory approach has the advantage of a more elaborate conceptual apparatus and a set of relatively more workable hypotheses than, for example, the class or elite approaches. It is also more discretely predictive. The fact that none of these approaches separately or even all of them together can completely explain the dynamics of policy-making in a transitional, developmental setting is lamentable, but it does not invalidate attempts at partial explanation.

Of course the above hypotheses are intended to apply only to the relationships between representative associations and authority groups. They do not apply, for example, to relationships between movements and authority groups. It should also be noted that certain other standard

---

* The core of the problem is in predicting the likelihood of mutual operational rationality. By "operational rationality" is meant the ability of actors to elaborate self-consciously long-range goals, to select appropriate means for attaining these goals, and to reevaluate performance on the basis of reliable, empirical evidence. When both representative associations and authority groups have this ability, there will be a convergence of interest in the exchange of information about performance and intentions. This is conducive to greater interdependence, regardless of whether the long-range goals of the two coincide. The rub, of course, lies in the complexity of conditions underlying the emergence of operational rationality.

hypotheses are absent or are treated incidentally. These include: (1) "Development tends to increase the autonomy of associational activity." For reasons that should become clear in the course of my exposition, I reject this hypothesis, or at any rate this form of it, as I do the classic Marxist view. The latter view can be formulated as follows: (2) "Concomitant with development, there will be an increasing polarization of associational conflict into two antagonistic, mutually exclusive clusters, one of which (the bourgeoisie) will dominate the other (the proletariat) and subordinate the authority groups (the State) in order to promote its interest." (3) "As a result of this, there will be an increasing tendency toward a radicalization and globalization of conflict relationships (e.g., toward the conversion of representative associations into movements), and, ultimately, the dominated cluster will triumph." All three of these hypotheses will be discussed in the concluding chapter.

TWO

The Development of Brazil Since 1930

REGARDLESS of the indices selected, the extent of social and economic change in Brazil since 1930 has been impressive. Indeed, knowledgeable observers, both native and foreign, have not hesitated to speak of a Brazilian Revolution.[1] Unlike other revolutions, however, the Brazilian one has not involved a definitive rupture with past political elites or with traditional political culture. In fact, there has been great change and ferment within a context of relative political continuity. This has led some to speak of a nonpolitical Brazilian Revolution. Can this concept be considered the operational equivalent of our analytical concept of development? The position taken here is that it cannot. As we have seen, a specific process, structural differentiation, lies at the core of development. It is this process that has a significant effect upon the emergence of a new type of intermediary political association. Moreover, development manifests itself not as a single process but as a series of related ones, not all of which necessarily have the same (or even compatible) political consequences. Even when one of these subprocesses appears theoretically significant, it may prove impossible to isolate its specific impact when collecting and testing data. Thus what the observer frequently calls the Brazilian Revolution may in fact be an aggregation of loosely related phenomena.

The same difficulty is encountered with the concept of structural differentiation. It can sometimes be demonstrated that the emergence of a given representative association was directly related to the formation of a totally new occupational group or to the subdivision of a single group into more specialized ones. But it is nearly always difficult to factor out the relative impact of other closely related phenomena: industrialization, bureaucratization, urbanization, social mobilization, and what Tocqueville called increase in the equality of conditions.

Industrialization clearly implies structural differentiation, since through it the functional specialization of labor is increased.[2] But the specialization of industrial labor is only one of many possible types of specialization. A preindustrial society may have a quite complicated division of labor and consequently many different occupational groups. The same may be true of modern agricultural economies. One could argue, for example, that although Argentina, Chile, and Uruguay are less industrialized than Brazil, because of the specialized nature of their agriculture and the greater diversification of their tertiary sectors they are more structurally differentiated in global terms. Thus one could expect to find more organized interest articulation in these three countries than in Brazil.

Commercialization, which usually precedes industrialization, is itself a type of differentiation, though it is rarely given as much attention. Brazil had a commercialized capitalist economy from an early period. At first it was based on the export of various primary products to world markets, and subsequently on the exchange of goods, especially draft animals and animal products, between regions.[3] It is hardly surprising, then, that chambers of commerce (*associações comerciais*) were the first representative associations to appear. In the absence of other sustained specialization processes, they remained virtually the only such associations for some years.

In the following treatment of Brazilian society we shall first consider the general changes in structural differentiation. Because it will prove difficult, if not impossible, to isolate the impact of this variable, we shall then turn our attention briefly to the concomitant developmental processes mentioned above: industrialization, bureaucratization, urbanization, social mobilization, and increase in the equality of conditions.

Structural Differentiation

Although aware of its materialist bias, I shall use as my operational indicator shifts in the pattern of social stratification occasioned by the creation of new or the subdivision of existing occupational categories. Except during its very earliest period of settlement, Brazil has always had a differentiated, nonegalitarian social structure based on occupational diversity, and this diversity has become even more important in recent years. Actually, the stratification system never rested "principally on social and political action," as B. J. Hoselitz has suggested of some African societies.[4] Even immigration of peoples and ideas, which has always been an important source of Brazil's vast diversity, is not as important as it once was.[5] Brazil's class and status systems are at present firmly based on the proliferation of specialized professions that do not follow ethnic or racial lines; hence the influence of these latter factors has also declined. This being so, the interest activities of political participation have tended to become more and more absorbed in protecting and advancing class or strata positions.[6]

Whether or not these differentiated strata tend to form broadly based conflict groups and establish relations of mutual antagonism is an issue that I shall discuss later. Here I am seeking only to demonstrate that such "developmental" indices as rise in gross national product, growth of per capita income, and increase in net capital accumulation are only surface reflections of more fundamental changes. The Brazilian economy did not become more wealthy or more productive simply because of aggregate increases in previous economic activities, better performances within existing structures, or greater demand for its traditional exports. Rather, it became so as the result of a structural shift toward a more diversified, more specialized, and consequently more productive labor force.

How much the occupational composition of the Brazilian population has changed is not easy to gauge empirically. Although national censuses were taken in 1872, 1900, 1920, 1940, 1950, and 1960, and all contain data on the distribution of the population over ten years of age according to fields of economic activity,* definitions of census categories vary widely from census to census,[7] and many of the figures are unreliable.[8] Thus simple, global comparisons are difficult to make and often misleading. After comparing the enumerations for 1872, 1900, and 1920, we can conclude only that they seem to indicate remarkable stability. Agricultural employment increased slightly from 61 to 62 to 69 percent. Shifts in other occupational categories were also slight; manufacturing employment, for example, varied only from 15 percent in 1872 to 13 percent in 1920. Until further analysis is performed, these figures must stand as the best we have. For the more recent period, however, we are fortunate to have the corrective efforts of Pompeu Accioly Borges and Gustaaf Loeb.[9] By rearranging the various categories in order to make them more comparable, and by introducing data from the agricultural

---

* Unfortunately, the census classification *ramo de atividade* (field of economic activity) is not equivalent to that of "occupation." For example, a doctor and a charwoman working for an automobile manufacturing plant would both be classified under the category "manufacturing industries." Only the 1950 Census collected data specifically on occupation, and the 1960 data are not yet entirely available. We are forced, for general purposes, to consider field of activity and occupation as synonymous.

TABLE 2.1
ECONOMICALLY ACTIVE POPULATION BY MAJOR OCCUPATIONAL GROUP,
1920–40, 1940–50, 1950–60
(percent)

Occupation	1920 & 1940[a]		1940 & 1950[b]		1950 & 1960[c]	
	1920	1940	1940	1950	1950	1960
Agriculture[d]	69.0%	65.1%	69.4%	62.5%	57.9%	51.6%
Mining	1.5	2.7	2.3	2.5	2.8	2.5
Manufacturing	13.0	14.0	8.2	12.3	13.1	12.3
Trade and commerce	5.4	5.5	4.7	5.3	6.3	6.7
Transport	2.8	3.4	2.9	3.5	4.1	4.8
Public administration	1.0	1.6	1.4	1.3	1.5	
Public security	1.0	1.1	1.0	1.2	1.5	9.9[e]
Liberal professions	2.3	2.1	1.7	2.6	3.0	
Domestic service[f]	4.0	4.4	3.3	3.3 ⎫	9.8[g]	12.1[g]
Miscellaneous services			5.1	5.5 ⎭		

SOURCE: Adapted from T. Pompeu Accioly Borges and Gustaaf Loeb, "Desenvolvimento Econômico e Distribuição da População Ativa," in Bernstein, pp. 38–40, Quadros A and B, Brasil,
IBGE, Anuário Estatístico—1965, p. 35.
NOTE: Columns may not add to 100 because of rounding.
   [a] 1940 data adjusted for comparability with 1920 data, notably through inclusion of repairmen
under Manufacturing.
   [b] 1940 data adjusted for comparability with 1950 data through inclusion of data from 1940
Agricultural Census; 1950 data adjusted for comparability with 1940 data through inclusion of
data from 1950 Agricultural Census.
   [c] Unadjusted data.
   [d] Includes cattle raising and forestry.
   [e] Combined data for Public administration, Public security, and Liberal professions.
   [f] Remunerated workers only.
   [g] Combined data for Domestic service and Miscellaneous services.

censuses of 1940 and 1950 to correct some errors of the general censuses
of those years, they have compiled a reasonably reliable record of shifts
among broad fields of economic activity from 1920 to 1950. These data
are presented in Table 2.1. To them I have annexed some figures recently
made available from the 1960 census.[10]

   Although it is difficult to compare such shifting categories, and although the categories themselves only indirectly reflect occupational
structure, the data do support the frequent observation that there have
been some fundamental changes. Most important, there has been a
marked shift out of agriculture in relative, if not absolute, terms. As Brazilians continue to find nonagricultural occupations, they are not moving en masse into a single category; rather, they are filling out a considerable variety of fields, especially those that display more internal
differentiation than do most such categories. The trend is most marked
toward the service, or tertiary, occupations. Except for the "domestic
service" category, which has declined in relative numbers, all the service headings have increased. Unfortunately, the 1960 data are not yet
broken down in sufficient detail. But for the combined category of gov-

ernment services, liberal professions, and social activities, the increase was 3.9 percent, the highest relative change except for the 6.3 percent decline in agricultural employment. The change for employment in manufacturing has not been so striking: the percentage has remained stable or decreased since 1950, depending on the figures used.[11] (Of course, these figures hide a great deal of change that has been occurring within the category itself, a matter I shall take up below.) I conclude, therefore, that the global differentiation process has been especially marked by a shift into the tertiary sector and that, although the secondary sector has increased greatly in absolute terms, relatively it has barely held its own.

The second major conclusion is that this differentiation has taken place only recently. The percentage of those employed in agriculture remained comparatively steady until 1950. There is even some indication that the importance of agriculture may have increased in the 1920–40 period. As shown by the 1920 and 1940 figures, the occupational structure continued more or less unchanged with some shifts into extractive industries, transport, and public administration. Greater positive and negative changes are shown by comparing the figures for 1940 and 1950, and for 1950 and 1960. Although certain important shifts in public policy and in the nature of ruling elites took place during the 1930's, we may infer that the impact of these changes, combined with the indirect consequences of World War II, did not begin to register on the pattern of social stratification until after 1945.[12]

The differentiation process for the entire national society is undoubtedly important, especially for a study that focuses on the emergence of national representative associations. But the impact of differentiation on the formation of interest groups, even at the national level, is likely to be less diffuse. Numerous economists have suggested that development tends to occur around certain "growth poles" or "core areas."[13] Presumably, then, differentiation, which by definition accompanies economic development, will also be concentrated initially in these areas of accelerated change. Only later can we expect to observe the "trickle-down" effects upon outlying regions. Many observers have argued that Brazil represents a particularly striking case of uneven development.[14] In order to obtain a clearer idea of the impact of our independent variable, therefore, we should break down the national occupational data by regions and states.

The occupational distribution of the population in different regions lends strong support to the economists' observations that regional inequality is based on disparities in aggregate share of national income and in per capita income. According to Table 2.2, the South was already more differentiated in 1940 than the Northeast was to become by 1960. In

TABLE 2.2

ECONOMICALLY ACTIVE POPULATION BY MAJOR OCCUPATIONAL GROUP
FOR SELECTED REGIONS, 1940–60

(*percent*)

Occupation	Northeast[a]			East[b]			South[c]		
	1940	1950	1960	1940	1950	1960	1940	1950	1960
Agriculture[d]	77.2%	74.9%	66.3%	65.9%	55.2%	49.3%	63.2%	50.9%	44.5%
Mining	2.5	2.3	3.1	2.1	1.9	2.0	1.1	1.6	1.3
Manufacturing	6.9	7.4	7.9	9.8	12.8	11.1	13.4	18.4	17.0
Trade and commerce	3.8	4.6	4.7	5.7	5.9	6.9	6.3	6.3	7.9
Transport	1.7	2.4	2.9	3.7	4.5	5.3	4.4	4.9	5.6
All other services[e]	8.0	8.5	14.1	12.8	19.5	25.4	11.6	17.8	23.6

SOURCE: Brasil, IBGE, *Recenseamento Geral—1940*, 1950; Brasil, IBGE, *Censo Demográfico—1960*.

NOTE: Columns may not add to 100 because of rounding.
  [a] Maranhão, Piauí, Ceará, Rio Grande do Norte, Paraíba, Pernambuco, Alagoas.
  [b] Sergipe, Bahia, Minas Gerais, Espírito Santo, Rio de Janeiro, Guanabara.
  [c] São Paulo, Paraná, Santa Catarina, Rio Grande do Sul.
  [d] Includes cattle raising and forestry.
  [e] Public and private, including liberal professions.

1940, 63.2 percent of the South's working population was in agriculture and 13.4 percent was in manufacturing. In 1960, the Northeast still had 66.3 percent in the fields and only 7.9 percent in the factories. The South had a 37.3 percent net shift during these two decades, of which 18.7 percent represented a switch out of agriculture. In the Northeast, on the other hand, 20.7 percent changed fields of activity, and only 10.9 percent left agriculture. The corresponding figures for the East were 33.4 percent and 16.6 percent. The sum of all percentage changes in occupational categories for each region can be used as a rough dynamic index of the extent of change in that region's structural differentiation. It is important to note, of course, that the productive bases of all the regions, including those of the North (Amazonas, Pará, and the territories) and the Center-West (Mato Grosso, Goiás, and the Federal District), for which recent data are not yet available, have become more structurally diversified since 1940. One should therefore find in all of them evidence of an increase in associational forms of interest representation. But regions do differ in degree of structural differentiation, and there is not much indication that these differences are decreasing.

Regions, as defined for census purposes, are not the most useful units for our analysis. The East, for example, contains Guanabara, where the per capita income is almost three times the national average, and Sergipe, whose per capita income is only 55 percent of the national average. The spread is not quite so extreme in other census regions, but none of them, except possibly for the South, forms a society with a single interdependent set of economic roles or an integrated system of social stratification. In order to isolate the core areas of greatest structural differentiation, we

TABLE 2.3

RATIO OF AGRICULTURAL WORKERS TO WORKERS IN MINING AND MANUFACTURING,
BY REGION AND STATE, 1950 AND 1960

Region and state	1950	1960	Region and state	1950	1960
North:			East:		
Amazonas	24.5	33.8	Sergipe	10.0	17.7
Pará	22.2	27.9	Bahia	38.6	43.5
Northeast:			Minas Gerais	17.4	15.9
Maranhão	43.7	76.7	Espírito Santo	35.9	28.6
Piauí	108.4	98.6	Rio de Janeiro	3.5	2.2
Ceará	26.7	42.5	Guanabara	0.1	0.1
Rio Grande do Norte	30.5	33.2	South:		
Paraíba	19.5	32.0	São Paulo	2.9	2.0
Pernambuco	10.7	17.6	Paraná	15.4	18.9
Alagoas	12.0	18.6	Santa Catarina	10.6	9.9
Center-West:			Rio Grande do Sul	10.3	9.7
Mato Grosso	26.9	22.6			
Goiás	96.4	71.4			

SOURCE: For agricultural workers, Brasil, IBGE, *Anuário Estatístico—1965*, p. 90. For industrial workers, Brasil, IBGE, *Anuário Estatístico—1964*, p. 93; *Anuário Estatístico—1955*, p. 132.

NOTE: These regions, with their component states, make up the whole country except for the state of Acre, and the various non-self-governing regions. Figures for 1950 and 1960 are not directly comparable because of a discrepancy in the classification of rural female employment. They do, however, provide a valid rank order for each year.

would do well to examine the states instead. Lacking full occupational data on each state for 1960, I have constructed an index of occupational diversity by calculating the ratio of manufacturing workers to agricultural workers in that year. As is shown by Table 2.3, the index varies enormously. In Piauí, there are 98.6 agricultural workers for each member of the industrial proletariat. In the city-state of Guanabara, there are ten industrial workers for each agricultural one. The degree of industrial concentration is well illustrated by the fact that only three states have ratios more "favorable" than the national average: Guanabara, São Paulo, and Rio de Janeiro. Variations within census regions run from 98.6 to 17.6 in the Northeast, 43.5 to 0.1 in the East, and 18.9 to 2.0 in the South.

In spite of the imperfections in these data, I conclude that a general process of structural transformation has occurred and continues to occur throughout Brazilian society. This process began rather slowly, but it has accelerated greatly since 1950. It has been more comprehensive and regular among males than among females, although the difference may have been exaggerated by inaccurate data collection. Of course, such differentiation has occurred in all parts of Brazil. But it has occurred very unevenly. States like São Paulo, Guanabara, and Rio de Janeiro have attained a relatively high degree of diversification and even of self-sustained occupational change. Others, such as Rio Grande do Sul,

Santa Catarina, Minas Gerais, and Pernambuco, are in an intermediary category with a definite tendency toward further differentiation. The remainder are as yet relatively undifferentiated and, except possibly for Bahia, without many signs of dynamism. These very considerable disparities in the rate and extent of structural transformation afford the observer an almost laboratory-like opportunity for testing the general hypothesis concerning development and occupational stratification.

Industrialization

With the collapse of external markets in 1929 and the subsequent policy of supplementing the coffee sector's money income with public funds, the growth of Brazil's internal market became the primary focus of economic attention for the first time. Consequently, "growing industrial production came to be the main dynamic factor in the process of income generation."[15] As Table 2.4 indicates, the relative share of industry (when calculated at constant prices) in the net national product has increased steadily, passing that of agriculture in the early 1950's.[16]

Pacesetter though it may be in terms of contribution to the net national product, industry—or manufacturing—is not absorbing larger and larger relative numbers of entrants into the labor force. Absolutely, of course, the number of those employed in manufacturing establishments has risen considerably, but the share of the total economically active population employed in manufacturing declined from 13.1 percent in 1950 (unadjusted figures) to 12.3 percent in 1960 (see Table 2.1). This phenomenon does not appear to be confined to Brazil; in fact, it has been occurring throughout Latin America in recent years. According to Z. Slawinski, these low proportions of manpower absorption by the manufacturing sector "are incompatible with the assumption that Latin America is engaged in an intensive industrialization process, although certain major industries are obviously developing rapidly and the growth of the industrial product seems to be satisfactory."[17] Celso Furtado has re-

TABLE 2.4
NET DOMESTIC PRODUCT BY MAJOR ECONOMIC SECTOR, 1939–63
(*percent, at 1939 prices*)

Sector	1939	1947	1951	1960	1963
Agriculture	33.3%	27.7%	24.5%	21.4%	21.0%
Mining and manufacturing	18.0	22.2	25.0	34.0	35.3
All other groups	48.7	50.1	50.5	45.6	43.7

SOURCE: For 1939, 1947, and 1951, Joint Brazil–United States Economic Commission, p. 290. For 1960 and 1963, "Evolução da Economia Brasileira 1940/1965," *Desenvolvimento Econômico*, X, 2 (Feb. 1966), 117.
NOTE: Columns may not add to 100 because of rounding.

cently argued that because of exchange rate policies that encouraged overmechanization and a social policy of artificially high wages for factory workers, "the major industrial investments realized in Brazil between 1950 and 1960 therefore never helped to alter the occupational structure of the population."[18]

Such strong statements deserve some modification. The low absorptive capacity of manufacturing does pose a serious social problem to Brazil and other latecomers dependent upon imported technology and subject to the rapid rise in consumer expectations. Nonetheless, Brazil's occupational structure did change considerably during the 1950's, and though this change may not be reflected directly in the aggregate importance of those employed in manufacturing, the indirect impact of industrialization on other sectors has been considerable. Moreover, changes within the occupational structure of the industrial sector itself have also been important.

The first major change might be termed the industrialization of the manufacturing process, i.e., the increasing role played by factories and series production. This might be evidenced by an increase in the average size of manufacturing establishments or by a decrease in the importance of artisan production. In fact, the number of workers in the average establishment has steadily decreased, not increased, since 1920. If we assume that establishments with fewer than four employees are organized on a nonspecialized-artisan basis, they still represented some 68 percent of the total number of industrial firms in 1960, more than they represented in 1950. Only when we calculate their share of total industrial employment and gross value added is there any evidence of a decrease.[19] In assessing the potential impact of Brazilian industrialization upon the development process, then, one should not overlook the existence of a large number of small workshops with a very low degree of internal division of labor. Their continued importance is a factor inhibiting the impact of the global process upon associability.

If, however, we compare the sectorial distribution of industrial employment in 1960 with that in 1950,[20] we may see more fundamental changes in the quality of industrialization. These data are presented in Table 2.5. New industries—those with the most internal division of labor and specialization of function—have greatly increased their share, not only of the total industrial output, but also of the total industrial labor force. Such industries include iron, steel, and metal products, machinery, electrical machinery and appliances, transport equipment, chemicals, pharmaceuticals, and plastics. They all have a high degree of specialization in terms of both product and means of production; together they employed some 26.3 percent of the total working population in 1960,

TABLE 2.5
MANUFACTURING: GROSS VALUE ADDED AND EMPLOYMENT,
BY INDUSTRIAL SECTOR, 1950–60
(*percent*)

Sector	Gross value added		Employment	
	1950	1960	1950	1960
Mineral products (exc. metal)	7.2%	6.7%	9.7%	9.7%
Iron, steel, and other metal products	9.4	11.9	7.9	10.2
Machinery (exc. electrical)	2.1	3.5	1.9	3.3
Electrical machinery and appliances	1.6	3.9	1.1	3.0
Transportation equipment	2.2	7.5	1.3	4.3
Wood products (exc. furniture)	4.2	3.2	4.9	5.0
Furniture	2.2	2.2	2.8	3.6
Paper and products	2.2	3.0	1.9	2.4
Leather and products	1.3	1.1	1.5	1.5
Chemicals (exc. pharmaceutical)	5.3	8.7	3.7	4.1
Pharmaceuticals	2.8	2.5	1.1	0.9
Perfumes, soap, candles	1.6	1.4	0.8	0.7
Plastic products	0.3	0.8	0.2	0.5
Textile spinning and weaving	19.6	12.0	27.4	20.6
Clothing (inc. shoes and accessories)	4.2	3.6	5.6	5.8
Food products (exc. beverages)	20.5	16.9	18.5	15.3
Beverages	4.4	2.9	2.9	2.1
Tobacco	1.4	1.3	1.3	0.9
Printing and publishing	4.0	3.0	3.0	3.0
Rubber and products	1.9	2.3	0.8	1.0
Miscellaneous manufactures	1.6	1.6	1.7	2.1
TOTAL	100.0%	100.0%	100.0%	100.0%

SOURCE: Adapted from Baer, *Industrialization*, p. 76.

as opposed to 17.2 percent in 1950. Perhaps most important, these new industries collectively accounted for most of the absorption of new employment in manufacturing during the 1950's. Thus although proportionally speaking more Brazilians are not entering the industrial sector, those who are seem to be entering areas in which occupational specialization is greater. However, in such traditional industries as textiles, food products, and clothing the relative decline in gross value added was greater than that in employment; the reverse was true of the new industries. As Werner Baer points out, this is evidence of the greater capital intensity (and therefore of the more specialized productive processes) of the latter.[21]

The relative importance of the semiartisan factory with a low capital intensity, a minimum of internal division of labor, and a preestablished, personal hierarchy of authority—the factory Juarez Brandão Lopes has aptly described as having "many personal relationships and a good dose of traditional behavior"[22]—is declining, at least in areas that have already experienced the initial stages of industrialization. Faced with a new work situation in which increased functional specialization is coupled with greater reliance on impersonal authority and channels of communication, Brazilian workers and employers can be expected to turn increasingly to specialized, formally organized intermediaries for self-protection and advancement.

Considered from the angle of production indices or shares in national income, Brazilian industrialization has been a more or less continuous process since World War I, with some periods of more rapid change and a noticeable recent tendency toward acceleration.[23] Viewed in terms of its impact on occupational structure, the pattern has been much less continuous. Prior to 1940, there was a lag during which social stratification remained fairly stable. From 1940 to 1950 the proportion employed in industrial firms rose very rapidly, industry being the primary absorber of new entrants into the labor market. During the period from 1950 to 1960, industry barely held its own quantitatively, although of course it expanded in absolute numbers. Qualitatively, on the other hand, there occurred a significant process of internal specialization, with the more differentiated, modern types of industrial production playing the leading role at the expense of such traditional industries as textiles and food processing. Since these more specialized industries are also more capital intensive, overall industrial employment lagged at a time when production continued to increase. Although no statistics are available to confirm it, the 1960's have probably witnessed an acceleration of the qualitative development of industrial production. At the same time, however, production itself has probably expanded at a lower rate. The Brazilian pattern of industrialization seems likely to have had little impact upon the creation of representative associations until 1940. There probably followed, according to our hypothesis, a period of more or less diffuse interest-group activity until the early 1950's. Finally, one might expect a marked increase in the activity of more specialized associations since about 1955. Let us now turn to other developmental processes, in order to determine whether they tend to reinforce or dissolve the pattern set by industrialization.

Bureaucratization

Bureaucratization, like industrialization, is a developmental process that contributes to a country's overall structural differentiation. As a theoretical concept, it implies the "gradual substitution of 'routine procedures in administration' for traditional practices."[24] It is a difficult concept to operationalize, partly because, as Weber pointed out, it involves both organizational and behavioral changes.

One possible global index of bureaucratization is the proportion of salaried employees in the occupational structure. The limited data available show that there has in fact been a rise in the percentage of salaried employees. In 1940, 43.3 percent of the employed population were salaried, 28.7 percent were self-employed, and 25.6 percent were working in family enterprises. By 1950, the number of salaried employees had risen to 45.2 percent, and that of employers had risen from 2.4 to 3.0 percent. At the same time, the percentage of those in other, presumably less bureaucratized, categories had declined.[25] Reinhard Bendix suggests that a more indicative, if still crude, measure of the rate of bureaucratization is the change in the proportion of salaried to production workers.[26] Unfortunately, the data we have for the employed population are not broken down in this way, and therefore calculations of this sort are impossible.

One could try to determine the amount of bureaucratization by calculating the ratio of tertiary to secondary employment. As we have seen, there has been a very marked increase in tertiary employment, especially since 1950. We can see in Table 2.6 that as industry lagged in absorbing new workers, services took up much of the slack. But this again would be quite misleading. For one thing, data are broken down by "field of activity," not by occupation. This means, for example, that the technical-administrative personnel of industrial or agricultural establishments are not registered in the service category. Moreover, the service category is itself made up of a very mixed bag of occupations. We are of course most interested in the nonmanual service employers and employees, the administrative, supervisory, managerial, and inspectorial people who tend to have a distinctive, middle-class, group self-assessment.[27] Unfortunately, this group is lumped in Brazilian census data (under the head-

TABLE 2.6
New Employment by Major Occupational Group, 1940–60
(*percent*)

Occupation	1950: new since 1940		1960: new since 1950	
	All employees	Male only	All employees	Male only
Agriculture[a]	18.4%	37.7%	32.8%	34.0%
Mining	3.9	4.4	1.6	1.7
Manufacturing	33.6	29.2	11.9	11.1
Trade and commerce	8.9	6.8	10.1	11.8
Transport[b]	8.3	7.2	7.1	9.3
Services[c]	25.9	14.7	36.5	32.1

SOURCE: For total employment, Brasil, IBGE, *Anuário Estatístico—1965*. For male employment, see the sources cited in Table 2.3 above.
NOTE: Columns may not add to 100 because of rounding.
[a] Includes cattle raising.
[b] Includes Communications.
[c] Public and private, including Liberal professions.

ing *"prestação de serviços"*) with a large number of manual workers—seamstresses, repairmen, waiters, etc., who are clearly not agents of bureaucratization. Finally, as Table 2.4 shows, the service sector's share of total national income has declined. In any other context, this would be surprising. But, as Slawinski points out, it has been happening all over Latin America. The sharp rise in tertiary employment is concentrated primarily in "miscellaneous services, including professional services and the numerous personal services and entertainment activities carried out both on a commercial scale and in the form of domestic services." Slawinski argues that it represents "disguised unemployment on a large scale."[28] In any case, given the decline in productivity and in relative income of the service sector, the enormous increase in numbers can hardly be cited as evidence of a massive and widespread bureaucratization process.

Certain sectors of tertiary employment can, however, safely be considered highly bureaucratized: public administration, public security, liberal professions,[29] and various social activities. Bearing in mind that this by no means covers everyone involved in the administration of routine procedures, changes in the ratio of this group to all industrial workers (even though some of the latter are administrators) can give us one indication of the rate of bureaucratization since 1920. The ratio of employees in mining and manufacturing to employees in public security, liberal professions, and social activities declined as follows:* in 1920, 3.0; in 1940, 2.0; in 1950, 2.2; and in 1960, 1.2. This indicates that bureaucratization increased rapidly from 1920 to 1940, during the period before the economy "took off" in the direction of fuller industrialization. The growth of bureaucratization (at least in comparison with that of industrialization) was not as dramatic during the 1940's, but during the 1950's, no doubt because of the process of internal specialization we observed within the industrial sector, the number of administrative service employees outside industry rose very fast, much faster than the increase in production workers.[30] This lends some support to those who see bureaucratization as the currently dominant developmental force.

When Brazilians comment on the tendency toward *burocratização* in their society, they are almost always referring to the growing size and role of public administrative agencies.[31] Although they apparently agree that the number and importance of public functionaries has increased enormously, this is not easy to confirm empirically. Fortunately, we do have available reliable and reasonably comparable data on federally employed civil servants. Empirical evidence bears out the many impressionistic observations about the growing size of the federal bureau-

* For these figures, see the sources cited in Table 2.1.

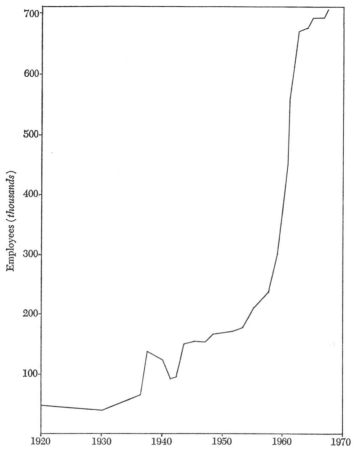

FIG. 1. EMPLOYMENT IN FEDERAL GOVERNMENT.
(Adapted from "A base da Reforma," *Visão*, Mar. 29, 1968.)

cracy. The number of its employees has increased steadily, as Figure 1 shows. There were especially steep rises in the 1930's and 1950's (both, incidentally, periods during which Getúlio Vargas was president). In 1920, one out of every 195 actively employed Brazilians was in the federal bureaucracy. By 1940 this ratio had changed to one out of every 132, and by 1960 it was one out of every 65. We cannot say whether or not state and municipal employment expanded in a similar pattern.[32]

More important than the increase in *funcionários* and *extranumerários* (temporarily employed functionaries) in the regular ministries is the very rapid increase in those employed by semipublic autarchic agencies and mixed companies like the Banco do Brasil, Petrobrás, Loíde Brasileiro, and the retirement and social welfare institutes. In his study of

Brazilian social mobility, S. Iutaka observed that there are an unusually large number of downwardly mobile individuals in these semipublic agencies. Because of the "pressure of people toward a participation in the public structure," and because the regular ministries can expand only so much, "one of the answers for preserving the system was the creation of semipublic enterprises."[33] Whatever the motivation or the systematic consequences of creating such a large number of semipublic agencies, one effect was to confirm an already established trend toward increased bureaucratization.

I mentioned above that one of the difficulties involved in measuring bureaucratization is that it is a behavioral as well as a structural phenomenon. The evidence of structural transformation is fairly conclusive, if incomplete. Evidence of behavioral transformation, on the other hand, is by no means conclusive. Costa Pinto stresses the importance during the 1930's of "systematic efforts . . . to make the recruitment of public employees less patrimonial and more rational,"[34] presumably implying that norms and behavior within the newly created bureaucratic structures changed accordingly. But other observers of Brazilian public administration have stressed the importance of the failure to rationalize recruitment.[35] Prebureaucratic norms continue to prevail in public agencies,[36] and resistance to routinized impersonal norms of recruitment and behavior seems only slightly less strong in private enterprises.[37]

A Brazilian sociologist has argued that the formal imposition of administrative structures

spread on an unexpected scale, reaching sectors, especially in the public administration, that did not require it for functional reasons. . . . On the other hand, it developed along with the survival of elements of the preexistent economic and social order, whose patrimonial techniques of administration (*coronelismo,** nepotism, favoritism, etc.) still persist to a large degree, even in highly urbanized communities.[38]

The result of these processes of structural overbureaucratization and behavioral underbureaucratization has been still another bottleneck impeding development.[39] Except in the case of scattered, better trained, and functionally specific groups, one cannot expect to find, at least on the public side, much evidence of an increase in associational forms of interest representation. Rather, one can expect relative stagnation coupled with protection of *positions acquises.* The important associational demands for change within this sector are most likely to come from without—from other social groups perceiving that resistance to change in this sector impedes further development in their own.

* A system of traditional political domination by local rural oligarchs.

Urbanization

Brazil, in keeping with its traditionally agrarian economy, has been a traditionally rural society. Even in 1960 over half of its population lived in the countryside. Nonetheless, urbanization has been since 1930 the most consistent and perhaps most impressive component of the Brazilian Revolution. More and more Brazilians are coming to the cities and becoming exposed to the more complex urban economy, the more differentiated social structure, and the norms of modern life.

Although census data prior to 1940 are deficient in this respect, Pedro Geiger estimates that until 1920 the urban population remained at a constant 10 percent of the total population.[40] By 1940, the urban percentage had increased threefold, and by 1960 it was seriously challenging the rural population for predominance. Growth of the cities has not only outstripped general demographic growth; it has far outstripped the rate of normal, or self-generated, urban growth, primarily because of massive internal migration. According to T. Lynn Smith, 60.1 percent of São Paulo's population growth from 1940 to 1950 was due to internal migration, only 37.6 percent to natural increase, and a mere 2.3 percent to immigration from abroad.[41] In the same decades during which urban population increased 46 percent (1940–60), the rural population did not decrease or stagnate, but maintained a steady 17-percent growth. But urban centers absorbed 61 percent and 69 percent of the total demographic increase in the same two decades.[42]

The distribution of this urbanization process was surprisingly broad. Of the 141 cities with more than 10,000 inhabitants in 1940, those with 10,000–20,000, 20,000–50,000, and 50,000–100,000 increased 42.3, 40.1, and 42.5 percent respectively in the following decade. Only the cities with populations over 100,000 grew faster (53.9 percent). Urbanization rates for backward, moderately backward and advanced areas were also rather similar: 47.6, 47.1, and 50.3 percent respectively.[43] In short, urbanization is affecting all sizes of towns and all regions of the country, regardless of their levels of economic development.

Important consequences stem from this broad distributional pattern. For one thing, as Waldemiro Bazzanella points out, urbanization and industrialization are not related in much of Brazil. In spite of the frequently made assumption that urbanization is the product of industrialization, cities in the nonindustrial regions of Brazil are growing about as fast as cities in the industrial regions. In "backward" areas the percentage increase in urban population greatly exceeds the increase in the proportion of those employed in manufacturing; the opposite is true for those areas where industrialization has already taken hold. This lack of correlation between the two developmental processes was probably especially true during the 1950's, when industry, as we have noted, began to absorb labor at a lower rate.

Increase in employment in the service sector is, however, closely associated with the rate of urbanization in all three areas. As a general trend, the larger the city and the greater the degree of prior industrialization, the greater the increase in tertiary employment. But the global relationship between urbanization and employment in the tertiary sector (as between urbanization and bureaucratization) holds. Unlike that in industry, the proportion in services tended to increase slightly faster than that of the urban population at all levels of economic development.

In the already developed urban areas, between 51.8 and 52.8 percent of the increased population find some employment. In the least developed areas, between 24.6 and 40.6 percent become economically active, depending on the size of the city. As we noted above, the tertiary sector contains a good deal of disguised unemployment; thus we can conclude that a substantial proportion of those entering the urban milieu do not become meaningfully integrated into a more diversified, functionally specific social and economic structure. They subsist on the fringes of the urban economy; real participation in it is not possible for them.[44]

Brazzanella convincingly argues that, given the rigidity of Brazil's agrarian structure, the desire for certain material and social benefits of modernization is more responsible for urbanization than the attraction of widening employment opportunities in the more differentiated occupations. If this is so, the impact of urbanization upon associability is likely to be less. Those who are imperfectly integrated into the more differentiated pattern of urban society may regard their stay as a temporary expedient. Whether they are resigned to their new locations or not, they are much less subject to the disciplinary effects of occupational specialization. This growing marginal group, to the extent that it finds any steady employment at all, finds it in undifferentiated, unskilled construction or in personal services.[45] According to our major hypothesis, we would not expect these groups to participate actively in representative associations. Presumably, the offspring of migrants will become more functionally integrated into the urban society. When that happens, they may furnish a more important impetus toward associability.

Communications Mobilization

Karl Deutsch has stressed the analytical importance of what he calls "social mobilization," which is a "recurrent cluster of consequences" within the global process of development. Except for bureaucratization, the concepts we have discussed so far involve material or structural changes that can be measured directly. Social mobilization, on the other hand, like Weber's concept of bureaucratization, involves an attitudinal change that must be inferred from primary material indices. It is "the process in which major clusters of old social, economic, and psychological commitments are eroded or broken and people become available for new patterns of socialization and behavior."[46]

Hypothetically, this new attitudinal availability can be expected to manifest itself in the creation of or participation in various types of political associations: parties, movements, or representative associations.[47] My argument is that structural differentiation makes a new political actor available for the specific role of participant in a representative association, whereas social mobilization simply makes him available for participation of any kind. Social mobilization, then, would be a necessary, but not sufficient, cause of increase in associability. I further hypothesize that where social mobilization occurs without structural or occupational differentiation—where, for example, the radio audience or the literate population increases in the absence of industrialization or bureaucratization—the result is more likely to be recourse to diffuse and emotional participation in mass movements than to the more specific and rational style of interest conflict offered by representative associations. Similarly, where the newly urbanized (and hence newly mobilized) are not functionally integrated into the society and its economy, one can expect more participation in movements than in representative associations.

According to the data presented by Deutsch, 52 percent of Brazil's population had been "exposed to modernity" by 1945 and 61 percent by 1955. His projected minimum levels for 1960 and 1970 were 66 and 76 percent respectively. For my purposes Deutsch's global index of "exposure to modernity" is a bit misleading, because it overlaps with two of the processes we have discussed above, urbanization and structural differentiation. (His variable "percentage of economically active population in nonagricultural occupations" is a crude index of structural differentiation.) By constructing a separate index using only communications variables, we can get a more specific idea of the extent to which, independent of other developmental processes, Brazilians are being drawn by the mass media into contact with modern values and behavior. Data of this sort are presented in Table 2.7.

I have chosen as a base 1940 or the first year after it for which data are available. The first and most immediately apparent finding is that these rates of change far exceed those of any of the other processes we have discussed, except for industrial production, which of course started from a very low level in 1940. Second, several indices are very

TABLE 2.7
COMMUNICATIONS AND POPULATION GROWTH, 1940–63
(*selected indices*)

Index	1945	1950	1955	1960	1963
(1940 = 100)					
Total population	112	126	142	172	188
In-school population[a]		124	164	252	
Number literate[b]		140		238	
Number voting		133	147	203	237
Radio receivers	163	698	978	1,276	2,081
Cinema attendance	127	208	358	365	
Hours of radio and TV	668	1,845	4,033	6,189	7,036
Newsprint consumed	112	126	142	172	188
(1950 = 100)					
Newspaper circulation			198	256	280
Books and pamphlets[c]			111	183	286
(1955 = 100)					
Television receivers				800	1,333

SOURCE: Brasil, IBGE, *Anuário Estatístico—1937–65*; UNESCO, *World Communications: Press, Radio, Film, Television* (Paris, 1964); Guerreiro Ramos.
[a] Excludes university students.
[b] Aged 14 and over.
[c] Number of copies printed.

clearly (and for obvious reasons) associated with that of literacy; newspaper circulation, books and pamphlets printed, newsprint consumption, in-school population, and size of electorate (only the literate may vote). All of these have more than doubled since 1940.[*] Third, it is clear that visual and audio communications media are expanding phenomenally and at a rate far beyond that of literacy. Whereas the mobilization of the print media is inhibited by the difficulties involved in rapid expansion of literacy, movies, radio, and television are reaching an ever-widening audience at a cumulative rate. In calculating the extent to which communications mobilization has exposed Brazilians to modernity, we must assume that an increasing percentage of this mushrooming audio-visual audience does not overlap with the more slowly growing category of new literates. If I assume that the literate portion of the population includes all the newspaper readers, book buyers, and voters, if I further assume that approximately one in four of the radio and television audience is illiterate, and if, as Deutsch suggests, I inflate the final proportion

[*] An index of urbanization with 1940 as the base year shows a very similar rate of increase: from 7 in 1872, to 9 in 1890, to 23 in 1920, to 100 in 1940, to 144 in 1950, to 240 in 1960. This suggests that, at least in the case of Brazil, there is a closely associated, "recurrent cluster" of phenomena involving urbanization, literacy, size of electorate, in-school population, and newspaper audience, but that the rate of expansion of the "newer" audio-visual media responds to different variables and transcends the limits imposed by urban literacy.

by 20 percent in order to account for "less formal ways of exposure,"[48] I get the following pattern of communications mobilization since 1900. Approximately 25 percent of the total population were exposed to modernity in 1900, and this remained constant until 1920. Two decades later, perhaps 40 percent had been drawn in. Thereafter the rate accelerated until by 1960 approximately two-thirds of Brazil's inhabitants constituted the national audience. A projection of current trends would increase the exposure to over four-fifths by 1970.

As anticipated, the pattern is roughly similar to that of urbanization, with aggregate figures running about 10 percent above those of total urban population and with the rate of increase also running consistently higher. If, as Deutsch suggests, his index underestimates the extent of exposure to modernity, and if, as I suggested above, the Brazilian census data on urbanization overestimate its importance, then the disparity between the two processes would be greater. Whatever its relation to urbanization, however, communications mobilization is affecting Brazilians faster than any other component process of the Brazilian Revolution.

Increase in the Equality of Conditions

As we have seen, Tocqueville made the art of association depend upon increase in the equality of conditions. My preference is for a different independent variable, namely, structural differentiation. Unlike Tocqueville, I am arguing that it is not increments in similarities, but increments in differences that create an increased desire and capacity for forming political associations. In other words, the more a society develops along equalitarian lines, that is, increases its internal division of labor in such a manner that material and status disparities constantly decrease, the less likely the actors in that society will be to resort to representative associations as a form of interest expression.* It has frequently been observed, for example, that a high rate of real or imagined social mobility, which presumably accompanies an increase in the equality of conditions, exerts a dampening effect on trade union activity.[49]

To some extent, my differences with Tocqueville may stem from a difference in the timing of our respective observations. Simon Kuznets has emphasized that development has a curvilinear effect upon income inequality.

---

* The development of Communist societies suggests a possible illustration of this dampening effect of equalitarianism. The role of independent representative associations is denied on the grounds that regime-enforced equality of conditions precludes their necessity. Interest expression is confined to a single, omnipotent *movement*, which in turn may create and control more functionally specific subgroups.

The scanty empirical evidence suggests that the narrowing of income inequality in the developed countries is relatively recent and probably did not characterize the early stages of their growth. . . . Indeed, they would suggest widening inequalities in the older countries where the emergence of the new industrial system has shattering effects on long-established preindustrial economic and social institutions.[50]

One could argue that Tocqueville observed a growing, but not a developing society. Before the period of accelerated structural transformation, increase in equality of conditions could produce the incentive for the formation of political associations, especially of the interclass, communitarian sort. And later, after such structural transformation has occurred, and as development begins to have a definite equalitarian impact, Tocqueville's hypothesis may again be valid. During the transformation itself, however, when capital is scarce and expensive, labor abundant and cheap, traditional societal values resistant to change, education still primarily for the elite, and industrialization running behind urbanization, the strong likelihood is an increase in material and status inequalities. It is this phenomenon that provides, I would argue, the impetus for the formation of new conflict groups, new political associations. If I am right, the types of associations that emerge and the means they use to express their demands depend upon a number of factors, most important of which is the degree to which structural differentiation, an increase in the functional specificity of the productive process, occurs concomitantly.

It is no easy matter to ascertain whether or not contemporary Brazil is more equalitarian than the preindustrial Brazil of thirty years ago. We must not confuse the very obvious overall increase in living standards with increased equality. Let us discuss, therefore, using the limited empirical materials available, three indicators of social and economic inequality: income, educational opportunity, and social mobility.

Income. Reliable data on the distribution of income in Brazil do not exist. Massive avoidance and underreporting make the use of tax data impossible. Only indirect (and therefore tenuous) computations are feasible.

One source of information is the national account statistics on the respective shares of urban national income going to "labor," "labor and capital," and "profits, interest, and rent."

To judge by these data, from 1947 to 1960, the functional distribution of internal income has been significantly modified, with an increase in the proportion absorbed by wage-earners from 56 to 65 percent and a reduction in that destined to the group composed of liberal professionals, business administrators, and owners of individual firms. The wage-earners, thanks to their political efforts, seem to have been the greatest benefactors of the process of economic development in the post-war period.[51]

TABLE 2.8

REMUNERATION OF LABOR (*L*) AND INDIRECT TAXES (*I*)
AS A PROPORTION OF GROSS NATIONAL INCOME (*G*), 1947–60

(*factor cost*)

Year	L/G	I/G	Year	L/G	I/G	Year	L/G	I/G
. . .			1951	.39	.13	1956	.45	.14
1947	.39	.11	1952	.40	.13	1957	.45	.14
1948	.40	.11	1953	.40	.12	1958	.45	.17
1949	.41	.12	1954	.39	.15	1959	.45	.19
1950	.41	.12	1955	.42	.13	1960	.44	.18

SOURCE: Calculations made by I. Kerstenetsky from data of the Fundação Getúlio Vargas, cited in Baer, *Industrialization*, p. 120.

However, government planners wisely go on to note that this conclusion is a hasty and misleading one. For one thing, it does not take into account the fact that the number of urban workers grew rapidly and disproportionately during the same period. Even with the increase of their percentage of the national income, their per capita income could have declined. Furthermore, the cost of living during this period increased more than the general price indicator implicit in the gross national income figures,[52] and the minimum salary set by the government has not kept pace with this rise.[53] As Werner Baer notes, <u>inflation has been a powerful reallocator of resources, transferring them from the consumer sector to the producer sector.</u> In particular, the government has used it to force a transfer of savings from the private to the public sector. Most important, indirect taxes have risen significantly since 1947. Table 2.8 shows the corrected figures as Baer has presented them. Here the statistical adjustment shows that there was comparatively little real increase in the remuneration of labor.

Baer concludes that in the urban sector,

even though real wages have increased, they often lagged behind the increase in real output. Since the rate of increase in the employment of new workers was usually smaller than the rate of increase of output due to the capital intensity of new firms, a lag of the increase in real income behind the increase in output of various industries is an indication that the share of labor in additional output is smaller than its share in the original total output. In other words, for a large proportion of urban workers inflation consisted of a redistribution of the increment in the real product to the producing sector. This means that workers did not necessarily suffer in their living standards but that the increase of the living standard was slower than the increase in the real national product.[54]

As for the rural sector, the preface to the stillborn Three-Year Plan of 1963 noted that

in per capita terms, real income in the agricultural sector has grown by five percent yearly, a rate far above that recorded for the population as a whole. However, there is no indication that the living conditions of rural labor have improved at the same rate. Hence, the most plausible conclusion is that the main portion of this income increase has been absorbed by the landowners and by the medium and high income businessmen.[55]

Thus, in spite of the increase in the standard of living and in spite of some increase in the real income of workers in urban areas, there is no overwhelming evidence of a trend toward income equality in the Brazilian population as a whole. In the face of severe inflation, the lower-income urban groups, although aided by various government policies (especially the minimum salary), seem at best to have held their own. The distributive gap was particularly great during the early 1950's and again in the middle 1960's, two periods during which the government exercised strong control over the labor movement. During the Kubitschek and Goulart regimes (1955–60 and 1961–64), when, as we shall see, government control over workers' associations was relaxed, the increase in real salaries tended to keep better pace with inflationary pressures. This suggests, hypothetically, that the increase in the equality of conditions following the transformation period may, in fact, depend on the performance of representative associations, whose pattern of formation has been set during the earlier period. Equality of conditions would then be the dependent variable, and the art of association the independent one—precisely the opposite of Tocqueville's formula.

Educational opportunity. Educational opportunity is another possible indicator of growing equalitarianism. An expansion of the relative number of students in school reflects structural differentiation that has already been accomplished, especially in the middle of the stratification pyramid. It also indicates to what extent the equality of conditions will increase as these newly educated people seek the higher-income posts for which they have been preparing.

As Table 2.9 shows, the proportion of eligible children enrolled in

TABLE 2.9
School Enrollment, 1907–60
(*number enrolled per 1,000 in age group*)

Year	Primary schools (ages 7–11)	Secondary schools (ages 11–17)	Higher education (ages 18–21)
1907	202		
1910			4
1920	291		
1930	430	17	6
1940	460	35	6
1950	554	60	11
1960	735	96	17

Source: Adapted from Havighurst and Moreira, p. 85, Table 6; p. 187, Table 27.

school has increased at all levels of education, especially during the 1950's. The increase in enrollment has been most spectacular at the secondary-school level. Nonetheless, the proportion of children enrolled in secondary school is still small compared with the proportion of those enrolled in primary school. And in view of the very substantial expansion in middle-status categories, "it appears . . . that most of the upward social mobility in Brazil has been achieved with no more than a primary school education."[56] For, if primary education has become customary, secondary education is still a long way from it, and this probably presents the greatest barrier to the attainment of middle-class status. It is even more obvious, with only 1.7 percent of the eligible age group going to the university, that the lack of higher education is not a rigid obstruction to the attainment of upper or upper-middle class status.

The general expansion at all levels of education, combined with the broader class and status composition of university students, reveals the equalizing impact of increasing educational opportunity. Nonetheless, the proportions involved are still so small in comparison with the needs generated by continuing structural change that Bertram Hutchinson seems justified in concluding that "the greater access to the educational system has not produced an increase in social mobility."[57] The new positions constantly being opened up by development are being filled by the self-educated, the naturally gifted, those with good connections, and the just plain lucky.

Social mobility. Brazilian sociologists and social commentators all agree that the traditional, two-class, undifferentiated social structure of the past offered little opportunity for mobility. Marriage, godparent and paternalistic relationships, the military, and the church were a few avenues by which one could improve one's status. The boom-and-bust economic cycles provided some sporadic opportunities, and, toward the end of the nineteenth century, immigration and new techniques of economic exploitation were beginning to loosen barriers in the South. But social mobility remained a rare phenomenon until as late as 1920, partly because access to the educational system was limited to so few.

The same observers also stress, however, that social differentiation has occurred in more recent years, and that this has created new occupational roles much faster than members of the former upper and middle strata have been able to fill them. It would be normal to assume that this increase in social mobility has had a very significant equalitarian influence on Brazilian society. But before doing so, let us first examine Bertram Hutchinson's excellent, detailed study of social mobility in the most differentiated region of the country, São Paulo.[58]

Having concluded that there has, indeed, been "a considerable degree of social mobility" in terms of intergenerational changes in status and that this has been related to important changes in occupational structure and opportunities (only 42.6 percent of the males interviewed had the same status as their fathers), Hutchinson notes that <u>upward mobility has been about twice as great as downward mobility</u>. This is compared to Great Britain, which has about the same aggregate rate of mobility, but whose downward mobility slightly exceeds its upward mobility. Hutchinson argues that the Paulista variety is different from the British because

it results from modifications in the structure of status, itself the consequence of economic development. The new status positions created by development mean that new opportunities for mobility are offered to the ambitious, and these are opportunities whose successful exploitation does not depend upon a corresponding movement of people. There is not, in other words, the exchange of positions which characterizes the pattern of mobility in a society with a stable structure.[59]

Furthermore, in spite of the new opportunities created by structural change, there "persists a comparatively rigid structure" that is made especially evident by the lower degree of mobility among members of Brazilian families as opposed to those of immigrant origin. "It is probable that the barriers imposed by a traditionally rigid system of status continue to be very strong among those born in Brazil."[60]

For our purposes, what is important is that this type of mobility need not have much of an equalitarian impact upon existing structures and values.

The fact is that in a society in the process of change, such as urban Brazil, social mobility is often obligatory. That is why it is essential, in any analysis of the phenomenon, to distinguish clearly mobility that is "normally" permissible given a pre-existing degree of structural rigidity (when the role of individual volition is of great importance) from that caused by the opening of new status positions and the closing of others following economic development. The latter form of social mobility may exist temporarily within the framework of an ordinarily quite rigid social structure; indeed, if it does not persist for too long, it may have little effect upon class permeability as this is ordinarily understood.[61]

If it can be shown that the newly differentiated occupations account for much of the mobility (46.7 percent in the Brazilian case, according to Hutchinson), and that they become filled by immigrants or internal migrants who are not bound by the traditional stratification system, we can expect to see very little reformulation within that traditional system. And assuming that this pattern of mobility is common to societies in stages of rapid development, we can also hypothesize that it will result in new forms of interest articulation. For if the original structure remains relatively rigid, those filling the newly differentiated occupations will find it especially difficult to gain influence over political decision-making by means of preexisting channels of family and friendship relations. Those representative associations that predate the rapid transitional phase may continue to recruit according to the rigid criteria of the intact traditional system and therefore resist or ignore the efforts of the newly differentiated to gain influence through them. Thus the migrants and immigrants will in effect be forced to search for new methods of interest expression. Conversely, we can reasonably expect that the leadership of these new associations will be likely to contain a relatively high proportion of outsiders: immigrants, internal migrants, and their descendants.

If we call Tocqueville's independent variable an increase in the equality of material conditions rather than an increase in the equality of aspirations, then we must conclude that there is no clear evidence that this has, in fact, occurred in Brazil in the last three or four decades. What information we have suggests that income has become more concentrated, not more widely distributed. Educational opportunities have expanded, but not enough to present an important equalizing factor. Similarly, although a great deal of social mobility has taken place, this has been, at least in São Paulo, the result of temporary structural changes, not of a general loosening of the status hierarchy.[62] Therefore, according to Tocqueville, we should not expect to encounter any significant increase in the art of association during this period.

Conclusion

In Brazil, structural differentiation shows up mainly as change in the nature and distribution of occupations within the society. It is essentially the product of two developmental processes, industrialization and bureaucratization. These two processes have an interesting but as yet unexplained inverse relationship with each other within the Brazilian developmental process. During periods when labor is being rapidly absorbed into the manufacturing sector, such as 1915–20 and 1940–50, the rate of bureaucratization lags. Between such spurts of industrialization, bureaucratization increases noticeably. As a result, an apparently smooth rate of overall differentiation is maintained. One could argue, on the one hand, that this is a system-changing characteristic and that prior to each industrial leap forward, the society accumulates administrative competence and equips itself institutionally for the impending change in the means of production. On the other hand, one could argue, as does S. Iutaka, that the slowing down of industrialization sets off pressures by elites whose sons and protégés are threatened with downward mobility caused by the decline in employment opportunities. These pressures focus on the bureaucracies, especially the public and semipublic ones, which are forced to open their doors to new (and sometimes unneeded) entrants. If this is so, the inverse relationship between the two processes is a system-maintaining, not a system-changing device. Perhaps both interpretations are correct. The manifest (if not publicly admitted) function—to provide employment for elites threatened with downward mobility owing to contraction of the industrialization process—is system-maintaining. Its latent consequence—to provide a pool of new or expanded institutions that may be called upon or take upon themselves to provide supporting services for industrialization at a later stage —is system-challenging. Regardless of their own dynamic interrelationship, these two processes make up the general process of Brazilian structural development.

It is noteworthy that both urbanization and communications mobilization have outpaced structural differentiation. It could be argued that they, especially the latter, are enabling factors, necessary but not sufficient conditions for associability. Given their rather different pattern of development, one could also argue that they are part of the process of *modernização*, i.e., of adherence to or desire for the values and products of a "modern" society; whereas industrialization and bureaucratization are part of the process of *desenvolvimento*, i.e., of structural differentiation. Modernization and structural differentiation combine, in unequal and varying proportions, to produce the Brazilian Revolution. Now we shall turn to the political consequences of this "Great Transformation."

So far, except for my remarks on the failure of behavioral changes to accompany changes in bureaucratic structure, I have not discussed whether or not, in the face of such structural transformations, Brazilians have come to act any differently. Have these material changes wrought a "violent change in . . . the mental structure of the country's traditional society," as Josué de Castro has suggested? Has the increasingly specialized nature of the occupational environment been translated into increasingly specific attempts to influence policy? Has the greater rationality of the productive process found any corresponding expression in political action? If so, has this resulted in a heightening or a diminishing of social and political tensions? Has it generated support for or threats against national integration? Obviously, an examination of the pattern of emergence and patterns of integration of one type of political association, the representative association, cannot provide the definitive answer to these questions. It can, however, contribute to our knowledge of the political consequences of social and economic changes in both the Brazilian and other transitional settings.

THREE

Political Enculturation

ALTHOUGH traditional political philosophers have observed repeatedly that different types of systems tend to be permeated by different collective "spirits" based on certain common or shared psychological attributes, only recently have "national character," "modal personality," and "political culture" become subjects for explicit conceptual formulation or objects of independent empirical analysis. The numerous efforts to define and describe political culture have not yet produced a satisfactorily operational paradigm.[1] I therefore had to devise one of my own.

I prefer the term "political enculturation" to "political culture" because it denotes a continuous process whereby actors acquire a set of predispositions to respond in a certain similar manner to stimuli perceived as politically relevant.[2] If it can be demonstrated that a given political system has a political culture, then we can expect its members to share common expectations about the nature of the politically ideal as well as the politically real. These expectations in turn give "meaning, predictability, and form" to the political process. Without a political culture, the individual actor does not know how to relate himself to the system or how to evaluate the performance of other actors.

As a singular noun, the term "political culture" unfortunately implies that one "pattern of orientation to political actions" is shared by all members of the system. Such coherence and unity cannot be taken for granted. In fact, the three most important general questions one can ask about the political culture of a given system are: is it homogeneous (is there some degree of coordination between elite subcultures or between elite and mass cultures);[3] is it coherent (are the norms inculcated at the different stages of the enculturation process compatible and mutually supportive);[4] and is it congruent (do the shared new political expectations support the existing formal political institutions)?[5]

My second innovation was to subdivide the concept operationally into three distinct and hypothetically sequential stages through which members of a system pass on their way to becoming fully-enculturated political actors.[6] In these stages, actors acquire (1) early and largely unconsciously assimilated basic attitudes or "primitive beliefs," (2) learned values and ideals about the ends and means of political activity, and (3) operational norms gleaned from personal experiences and reactions to actual participation in politics. Political enculturation, then, is the product of *political socialization, political indoctrination,* and *political experience.*[7] Thus it is the result of a continuous life experience; it is constantly being renewed and altered. Not only must each generation enculturate, consciously and unconsciously, each succeeding one, but the process of assimilating norms and expectations is never finished for any single actor, because he is continually being subjected to new political experiences. Young actors are not endowed once and for all with a set of political predispositions based on childhood socialization; old political dogs can learn new tricks and unlearn old ones. Unfortunately, the discussion of political culture to date, with its accent on basic personality and the immutable influence of time-honored traditions, especially those of child-raising, has greatly overemphasized static components.

With these introductory remarks, I have set up a simple conceptual scheme for ordering whatever empirical material on Brazilian political culture can be found. Unfortunately, there is not much to work with in the way of previous studies. Some insight is provided by travelers' accounts, the essays of native social thinkers, and a limited amount of recent survey research, but the only treatment of Brazilian political culture as such consists of a few not very enlightening paragraphs in a recent text on Latin American politics.[8] My study should therefore be regarded as an attempt to synthesize a wide body of descriptive materials into a set of tentative observations or hypotheses. Unfortunately, I have had to overstress the traditional, as opposed to the transitional, aspects of the political culture. Thus what I offer is more a guide to future investigation than a set of definitive conclusions from past research.

Political Socialization in Brazil

The structure of "primitive beliefs" or basic orientations in Brazilian society has been the subject of rather extensive commentary. Both nationals and foreigners have discussed the existence and nature of the Brazilian "national character."[9] With some exceptions, they tend increasingly to agree that this "first great attempt" to create a relatively autonomous and distinctive civilization in the tropics[10] has been a success, and that there has emerged a new synthesis that is basically Western but not strictly neo-European.[11] Its unifying "cultural baseline" was furnished by the Portuguese heritage,[12] but this has been deflected by different conditions of physical occupation and economic production[13] and modified by an intensive and intimate cultural exchange with native Indian and, later, African societies.[14] However they may disagree on the respective relative contributions of differing settlement patterns or of differing component cultures, most would agree with Charles Wagley that "Brazil is an immense nation of many contrasts and inner differences and yet it has achieved a remarkably homogeneous culture."[15] In fact, one of the most persistent themes in the discussion of the formation of Brazilian culture is its dialectical nature: Brazil has been described as "a melting pot for conflicting elements,"[16] "the coexistence of contradictory cultures in permanent conflict,"[17] and "this paradox of oneness enclosing many differences."[18] As we turn to the specific content of this fusion of differing elements, we are forewarned against expecting any monolithic unity.

"Individualistic, emotional, indolent, hospitable, tolerant, patient, affable, freedom-loving, moderate, erotic, broad-minded, gentle, peaceloving, and inclined to imitate foreigners" were the descriptions most frequently encountered by Dante Moreira Leite in the literature on the Brazilian national character.[19] Obviously, many of these traits have only very remote or very latent political relevance. It is important to note, however, that in the stereotype of the traditional Brazilian, positive characteristics far outnumber negative ones. During my interviews with associational, political, and administrative elites, I was surprised by how frequently the respondents spontaneously offered the reflection that "our people are good." This was often coupled with the reflection that the *bondade* (goodness) of the people has in fact been responsible for keeping the country from collapse. And perhaps Brazilians in general do have an ego-satisfying image of themselves. It is also possible—and certainly more important if true—that the elites have a very favorable impression of the masses. This would facilitate the latter's incorporation into and eventual participation in the political process.

It is also important to note that from this collection of traits one can perhaps abstract a relatively stable set of latent and manifest attitudes toward political activity. Here I have the support of Brazil's only—but very suggestive—theorist of political culture, F. J. de Oliveira Vianna.* In an attempt to study "the system of practical norms alongside our

---

* Oliveira Vianna's political oeuvre is not studied today, perhaps because of his association with racist and corporatist thought in the 1920's and 1930's. It is, however, full of both theoretical and descriptive insights. Among other things, he uses the "modern" concept of *cultura política* and even refers to Great Britain as having a *cultura cívica*.

written public law," Oliveira Vianna searched below the formalities of the political system for

those uses, customs, types, and conditions, forming the complex of our political culture, [that] penetrate . . . the psyche of our "citizens," principally in the rural areas, and constitute the determining motive of their daily conduct in public life, not only among the masses, but also among the ruling elites. These are not improvised and individualized creations, drawn from the minds of a few men, wise or corrupted. They form slowly under the impact of centuries [and] have a collective and social history.[20]

More clearly and insistently than any other Brazilian social thinker, Oliveira Vianna has stressed that the extraordinary continuity of the Brazilian political culture, as well as its very existence and nature, depend upon the persistent role of the major, almost unchallenged, agent of attitudinal socialization, the family, or rather (as he insists) the patriarchal clan. Gilberto Freyre, another major social thinker, stresses the same theme:

The family and not the individual, much less the State or any commercial company was from the Sixteenth Century the great colonizing factor in Brazil, the productive unit, the capital that cleared the land, founded plantations, purchased slaves, oxen, implements; and in politics, it was the social force that set itself up as the most powerful colonial aristocracy in the Americas. Over it, the King of Portugal may be said, practically, to have reigned without ruling.[21]

Portuguese control over the colony was kept to a minimum, settlement was dispersed, internal communications were poor, and, after the expulsion of the Dutch in the seventeenth century, there was virtually no need for permanent cooperation in collective self-defense. As a result, the family, with its virtual monopoly of economic, social, political, and defense functions, became the leading institution. "No institution has contributed more to the social structure of the country and to the establishment of a meaningful pattern of life for its inhabitants."[22]

The only institution that could hope to challenge the dominance of the family was the Church. No doubt "the solidarity of ideals or religious faith . . . made up for laxness of political or mystic ties and the absence of race consciousness"[23] and hence was important in maintaining national unity, especially against the threats of invading Dutch, French, and English Protestants. However, once the patriarchal clans won out over the Society of Jesus, "the church that affected our social development . . . was not the cathedral, . . . the isolated church, . . . [or] the monastery or abbey. It was the plantation chapel." Given this "privatization" of religious practice and the dependent position of the local priest, it is hardly surprising that Freyre should describe Brazilian Christianity as "lyrically

social, a cult of the family rather than a religion of the church or cathedral."[24] The school, where one existed, was similarly subordinate to the
casa grande.

Obviously, for the patriarchal clan to have been so predominant, it
must have consisted of more than just the nuclear family. It was, and to
a lesser extent still is, a vast set of interpersonal ties based not only on
consanguinity, but also on personal affinity (marriage, adoption, com-
paternity, and voluntary dependence). Oliveira Vianna sees the clan
as arranged in two dimensions. First, there was the "feudal clan," which
was made up of vertical relationships between the patriarch and his
household of economic dependents: slaves, servants, and laborers. Even
independent small farmers located near the patriarchal domain found
it necessary or prudent to declare their loyalty to the clan chief and to
accept his "jurisdiction."[25] Given the autonomy and self-sufficiency of
the large rural estate ("Each plantation nucleus is a social micro-
cosm"),[26] there was little opportunity for independent commercial or
communal organizations to develop, at least until well into the nineteenth century. The second dimension of the family Oliveira Vianna
called the "parental clan." It consisted of an inter-elite set of ties based
on consanguinity, marriage (heavily endogamous), adoption, and com-
paternity.[27] As a result of these two sets of relationships, one vertical
and interclass, the other horizontal and inter-elite,* a given member of
the dominant rural aristocracy found himself in a network that often
comprised hundreds of members throughout a large geographic area.[28]

The traditional patriarchal clan, which was omnifunctional and omnipotent, no longer exists in its pristine form. Gilberto Freyre's second
major volume, *The Mansions and the Shanties,* remains the classic description of how in the ninteenth century, "a period of deep differentiation," new social institutions and roles emerged to challenge the absolutism of the paterfamilias and the "towering dominance" of the *casa
grande.*[29] Overshadowed and counterbalanced by government, church,
bank, school, and factory, the patriarchal clan was forced to share or
give up many of its key functions. Nevertheless, it has proved to be extraordinarily tenacious.[30] Emilio Willems notes that whereas "in areas
of heavy foreign immigration the position of family oligarchies was not
strong enough to prevent the rise of a new economic and political
elite, . . . it also is true that the new elite has adopted the same patterns

---

* Oliveira Vianna suggests that both clans were combined and mobilized to produce
a third type, the "electoral clan," a necessity formally imposed by the extensive
franchise and majority criteria of the Imperial electoral system. These clans called
themselves parties and were weakly coordinated at the national level into two competing clans, the conservatives and the liberals.

of familism and nepotism which characterized the traditional power structure."[31] A recent empirical study of socialization patterns in São Paulo shows that, though its structure has been undermined, the normative consequences of that area's patriarchalism are still very much evident. Bernard Rosen summarizes the literature:

Virtually all of the Brazilians' close relationships are limited to family members. Persons outside the family are treated with a courteous reserve, mingled with suspicion, that makes intimate association with non-kinsmen difficult and very uncommon. Not having learned to enjoy or trust nonfamilial relationships, the Brazilian finds it difficult to enter into cooperative effort, economic or otherwise, with persons who are not members of his family.[32]

When he asked a sample of mothers of secondary-school children to respond to the statement "Nothing is worth the sacrifice of moving away from one's parents," 51 percent of those in metropolitan São Paulo and 45 percent of those in Rio Claro, a small town in the interior of the state, agreed. Only 11 percent of a comparable sample of North American mothers agreed. To the statement "A good son would try to live near his parents even if it means giving up a good job in another part of the country," 31 percent in São Paulo, 42 percent in Rio Claro, and 8 percent in the United States responded positively.[33] Unfortunately, the data on familism are not broken down by class, but the difference on the second question indicates a slightly lower propensity on the part of more urbanized groups.

The primary legacy of this tradition of strong family ties in the Brazilian political culture has been the privatization of the public order. Basic values and loyalties are lodged in and controlled by particularistic, extended kinship institutions. Political supports and demands are perceived in personalistic, paternalistic, and nepotistic terms. In vain have Brazilian social and political thinkers argued that the state is not "an amplification of the family circle"; that the individual must transcend the family and domestic order in his role as citizen, taxpayer, and elector; that he is in fact "eligible, recruitable, and responsible before the laws of the polis."[34] In vain have they decried "the tenuousness or weakness of our consciousness of the common good, of our sentiment of social solidarity and public interest, ... [and] the absence of comprehension of the power of the state as an organ of public interest [and not as] a force at their disposition to reward friends and their interests and to punish adversaries and their interests."[35] "The invasion of the public by the private, of the state by the family," and its consequences, "national disorganization," "lack of national consciousness," and "absence of communal or collective solidarity beyond that of the clan"—the literature is full of such themes.[36] Frank Bonilla observes that this is not merely the reflection of the perennial problem of conflict between local and national authorities or between "reason of family" and "reason of state." Rather, it is the product of "a competition between institutionalized systems of social organization."[37] It goes beyond the problems, more or less chronic throughout Latin America, of personalism, paternalism, and nepotism. The main issue is in fact whether there can emerge a fully differentiated political culture with a national or even trans-municipal base. So far, Brazilian society does not possess one.[38] Nestor Duarte expressed the dilemma particularly well:

In a history in which everything went against the state, favoring instead the victory and rejuvenation of other groups and principles of rule and organization, the political institution, in addition to having a precarious objective scope that failed to reach the centers of force and discipline of the community, . . . likewise lost its power to influence the spirit of that community and was incapable of implanting upon it distinctly and unequivocally a differentiated public spirit. Brazil is a new nation in that it has failed to complete the process of its political differentiation, and an old people, living under an old order.[39]

The dilemma of political culture in Brazil is thus rather different from that of the rest of Latin America. It is not the problem of creating a national synthesis capable of assimilating resistant native Indian subcultures. Tolerance, attitudinal flexibility, and "the lubricating oil of deep-going miscegenation"[40] gave the Brazilians, or more accurately the Portuguese colonists, the ability to assimilate a wide variety of Amerindian, African, and immigrant European cultures. Nor is it the problem of incorporating recalcitrant class subcultures. The observable discontinuities in values and expectations between elites and the masses are less structural than temporal. Almost all emerging social groups have tried to emulate preexistent elite values. Indeed, there is no distinctive set of revolutionary class values, for, in the subcultural sense, there is no bourgeoisie or proletariat. The Brazilian problem, then, is less one of assimilation than one of differentiation. Brazil has had difficulty replacing affective, familistic particularism with a distinctive set of universalistic, rational orientations toward the political process. To a certain extent, all Latin American polities share this problem, but the great strength and resilience of the traditional Brazilian patriarchal clan has created in Brazil a special disparity between what Oliveira Vianna called "the territorial march of society" and "the territorial march of power," between "the area of social expansion and the area of political effectiveness."[41] The gap in social control, in *herrschaft*, was filled originally by the patriarchal clan; it is now filled by the *parentela*. It is this omnipresent, omnipotent institution that has contained and assimilated dissident cultures, has furnished channels for the expression of conflict and for most of its resolution, and, in the process, in its fragmented decentralized manner, has held the country together.[42]

One can argue that this problem is much less serious than that of assimilating ethnic or class subcultures. One can also point to a number of signs indicating a definite shift in loyalties and identification toward national and other communal institutions. There is no question, however, that the basic, family-oriented, politically undifferentiated norms inculcated at this first stage of the enculturation process dominate the self-conscious attempts at political indoctrination and permeate the code and style of political experience. Similarly, there is no question that these norms severely inhibit the emergence of functionally specific, impersonally administered, rationally appropriate associations for interest expression.

The Brazilian national character. The colonial Brazilian seems to have been preoccupied with enjoying life and leisure.[43] His indolence,[44] his lack of regard for the commercial value of time, and his remarkable patience[45] have frequently been remarked upon. Presumably these qualities stemmed from a background of slavery and were reinforced by a very gradual process of social change. The accent was on the present and the past, rather than on the future;[46] consequently the Brazilians developed what nineteenth-century French diplomats identified as an institutionalized practice of delay, procrastination, and even nonchalance.[47] The colonial Brazilian regarded his environment with fatalistic acceptance. "Widespread lack of ambition for material gain or intellectual improvement was characteristic of Brazil of the colonial period."[48] Economic exploitation was considered a sporadic and spontaneous process of rapid enrichment,[49] not the result of careful planning and sustained effort.[50] As Bernard Rosen observes, the popular saying "God is a Brazilian" was an expression less of confidence in the benevolence of the environment than of mystical dependence on outside forces to pull one through.[51] But it was perhaps in his basic attitude toward society that the *homen cordial* was most distinctive among Latin Americans. Brazil's tradition of hospitality, courtesy, civility, tolerance, and "softness" (*doçura*) in social relations was noted by many observers and was usually attributed to the extraordinary social flexibility of the Portuguese colonialists, who are assumed to have been less obedient to fixed rules and regulations, less obsessed with uniformity and symmetry, and less possessed with a sense of racial superiority than their Spanish counterparts.[52] This propensity "to accommodate to the caprices of nature and to the law of least effort"—the very reverse of the Spanish sense of order and mission—gave Brazilian colonials a tradition of accommodation, compromise, and trust in political relations, at least among elite groups.

Sérgio Buarque de Holanda has argued that "the notion of natural goodness combines singularly well with our cordiality as described above. The thesis of a humanity bad by nature or of the war of all against all must seem to us extremely distasteful."[53] Thus the Brazilian was naturally trusting, sociable, and empathetic.[54] Oliveira Vianna, however, questions whether such trust extended to those outside the circle of family and friends, and claims to find only a precarious "sense of sympathy, beyond the sense of clan solidarity, for our fellow creatures."[55] It is perhaps possible to conclude that in traditional Brazilian culture the cordiality and sense of mutual trust was based more on friendship and familial relations than on a generalized and universalistic sense of empathy and common interest.

"In a radiant land live a sad people," begins Paulo Prado's classic essay. He considers the fundamental trait of the Brazilian character to be melancholia accompanied by a perpetual inferiority complex. The inferiority was felt not vis-à-vis the colonial mother country (as Freyre quips, the Portuguese left "a clinging tradition of ineptitude, stupidity, and salaciousness"),[56] but vis-à-vis Europe in general. Above all, the Brazilians' inferiority complex was brought about by their own failure to take advantage of the natural richness of their own land. An acute sense of racial inferiority further contributed to the melancholic image. Vianna Moog summarized these traits in his description of *mazombismo*,[57] the prime characteristic of which was "the absence of determination to be and satisfaction in being a Brazilian."[58] Overdrawn as these portraits may be, they do seem to indicate a lack of self-confidence, which in turn must have reinforced such other traits as the propensity for fatalism.[59] The writings of such social thinkers as Affonso Celso and Alberto Torres could be considered conscious attempts to counteract the prevailing negative self-esteem.[60]

The traditional Brazilian attitude toward authority came almost exclusively from the family system, which has been described as rigidly patriarchal and authoritarian. The stereotype of the Brazilian family consisted of "a morose father, a submissive mother, and terrified sons."[61] Authority was vested in the family patriarch, with lesser authority extended to the sons in the order of their births, and obedience to it was supposed to be unquestioning. Decisions affecting the whole family were made by its head in an entirely autocratic manner. Children were not consulted. Disobedience was met with physical punishment; in some cases, death was the penalty for transgressions. It is no wonder that numerous observers found the Brazilians humble, obedient, and easy to govern. As a colonial official put it in the eighteenth century, they "follow the commands they receive; yet, unless they be commanded, they often remain in a state of inaction, until they are reduced to the most extreme indigence."[62]

Freyre, in his now classic discussion of the evolution of the Brazilian family, stresses that patriarchal absolutism was modified by a variety of social attitudes and practices, including miscegenation, paternalism, respect for women, and religious belief. A certain reciprocity and emotional exchange existed between the omnipotent patriarch and his subordinates. Adoption and co-option—personal and paternalistic—created an intermediary status group of *mestiços*, "a middle race," and thus made "the hard social gradations" and despotic norms of patriarchalism less severe. Members of this *mesoi* group gradually infiltrated the ruling hierarchy, especially as the forces of urbanism began to predominate over those of agrarianism. The resultant authority pattern was "a combination of democratic [sic] and authoritarian tendencies,"[63] in which "the patriarchal tends to prolong itself into the paternalistic, in the sentimental and mystic cult of the father, still identified for Brazilians with the image of the protector, the man of destiny, the man indispensable to the good ordering of society."[64] In return for his exercise of noblesse oblige and favoritism, the *patrão* in this system expects unquestioning personal loyalty and voluntary compliance with his orders. The whole transaction involves close, warm, interpersonal ties; authorities and subordinates alike are treated with respect, "as individuals, not as members of a different group."[65] This faith that one's leaders will exercise their power for one's benefit but without one's participation, and that such an exercise will be personal and particularistic, is at the core of the traditional Brazilian attitude toward authority. Rosen reports the bitter comment of a Brazilian to the effect that "we depend upon the father when we are children and upon the government when we are adults."[66]

Given the settlement pattern, the poor communications, the degree of local autarchy, the familistic individualism, and the personal and paternalistic loyalties, it is hardly astonishing that a broad sense of community identification was slow in developing. In spite of the commonality of language, religious belief, and familial and economic organization, Brazil was accurately termed at the moment of Independence "an aggregate of families."[67] The French visitor, Saint Hilaire, has left a classic description of the state of community at this time: "A crowd of aristocratic patriarchies divided among themselves by intrigue, petty vanity, and selfish interests was scattered about on the surface of Brazil; but in the countryside, there was no society at all, and one would be hard pressed to find there any elements of sociability."[68] The collective expulsion of Protestant invaders, especially of the Dutch from the Northeast, and the periodic outbursts of violence against the Portuguese have been cited as evidence for a wider sense of community among

Brazilian elites. But, although the standing opposition of the rural patriarchs to the Portuguese commercial monopoly and to the memories of past abandonment by the Crown certainly increased their potentiality for later mutual responsiveness, their demonstrations were too sporadic and localized to create a lasting emotional or symbolic bond.

In 1822 the Portuguese Crown attempted to return Brazil to its former status as a colony. The free trading right Brazil had acquired in 1803 was retracted, and the Regent Dom Pedro was ordered to return to Lisbon. Pressured by his Brazilian advisors, however, Dom Pedro responded with the famous *fico* "I am staying," and Brazil slid into independence, with only scattered violence,[69] and without either a break in symbols of power or a change in social institutions. The ensuing Imperial period (1822–89), though by no means as tranquil as is commonly thought, contributed much to the creation of a national spirit among certain elites. The new aristocracy, *"os homens de mil,"* personally recruited by the Emporer and subject to the famous red pencil of his moral censorship, were, in Oliveira Vianna's words, "the first to behave like citizens of Brazil."[70] Even in 1914, long after this period of gradual elite formation, Alberto Torres could argue convincingly that Brazil remained a "new nation." It still lacked a "practical national spirit, a patriotic solidarity founded on the awareness of interests common to all political, religious, economic, geographic, commercial, and industrial groups." Presaging contemporary theories on nationalism, he then noted that "this solidarity . . . is the secular product of relations, exchanges, and mutual support."[71]

Even if the elites had a sense of higher communal identity, the masses obviously did not. Oliveira Vianna cites the case of some army recruits studied in a Rio garrison in the 1920's. In spite of their having come principally from the relatively politicized state of Rio de Janeiro, only 42 percent had any concept at all about Brazil as a nation, and 20 percent of these "couldn't mention any specific possibilities the country had to offer."[72] Marvin Harris, in his excellent monographic study of Minas Velhas, a *município* in the interior of Bahia, affords us some hint of how far national consciousness had advanced by the 1950's. The townspeople were "fully aware that they are members of a large national state," they knew its symbols, and they participated vicariously in its victories and defeats. In the rural zone (Serra do Ouro), by contrast, "the overwhelming majority of villagers [were] simply indifferent to the entire political process."[73] Somewhere between Minas Velhas and Serra do Ouro (the names are fictitious) ran the line between political subjects and parochials.

It is important to note here that the Brazilian solution to the identity problem has followed what Verba has called an "incorporative" path.[74]

Owing to increased communications mobilization, national awareness
is spreading, but it is not displacing the former parochial loyalties. My
hypothesis is that the Brazilian develops a sense of multiple identity,
and that he sees no conflict in being both a loyal bahiano, mineiro, or
gaucho and a loyal Brazilian. A difference in style, yes; a conflict of
loyalty, no. There are indications, however, that once a Brazilian does
develop a sense of national identity, he is likely to be proud of it. "For
all their realistic appraisal of their own faults, their pessimistic streak,
Brazilians have an almost mystical faith in their country and its future."[75]
Dante Moreira Leite found that Paulista secondary-school students
attributed more favorable characteristics to Brazilians than to North
Americans, English, or Japanese.[76] Needless to say, a favorable self-
image—that of a generous, kind, friendly people—can be a powerful
support for maintaining a community when system performance is low.

I have deliberately placed our excursion into the process of political
socialization in the past tense. To contemporary observers of Brazil my
comments may seem a bit old-fashioned. There is not a trait in the set of
traditional orientations to self and society outlined above that has not
been challenged by some recent observer. Many have noted a new sense
of urgency, activism, and demand for change; an increase in competitiveness, mistrust, and unscrupulousness; a decrease in familism and patriarchal dominance; and a more enduring commitment to national mission and identity. One author has gone so far as to announce the demise
of the *homen cordial* and his replacement by the *homen radical*.[77] Nevertheless, I submit that the traditional pattern did have a homogeneity,
a coherence with other stages, and a congruence with formal institutions
that formed a very resilient foundation for contemporary behavior. The
efforts of modernizing elements to undermine this foundation have
been only sporadically successful. As Florestan Fernandes warns, "It
is not always correct to assume that modernization absorbs archaic
influences. Sometimes the opposite occurs. Tradition absorbs the modernizing influences."[78]

Two recent surveys on basic attitudes tend, in fact, to support those
who would stress the continuity of traditional norms and expectations.
Bernard Rosen's work on child socialization patterns in São Paulo
demonstrates that indulgence, overprotectiveness, and authoritarianism—all traits of the traditional process—are still common, and that
they have an inhibiting impact on both achievement motivation and
achievement values. When matched with comparable North American
groups, Brazilian children scored markedly lower on such traits as activism, competitiveness, future-orientation, and individualism.[79] Joseph
Kahl's survey of career values among manual and nonmanual workers
in Rio and two small cities of the interior uncovered a traditionalist

syndrome that corresponded strikingly to many of the traits observed above: fatalism, differential access to personal opportunities, familism, preference for small-town life, community stratification, mistrust of outsiders, low work aspiration, and low contact with mass communications.[80] The correlation between urban residence and modernism was only .26. Social and economic status, with a correlation of .57, proved the more relevant predictive factor. Men of high status tended to have modern values regardless of residence, but medium and low status respondents in the two provincial towns were more traditional than their status equals in the metropolis. Since education was used as the measure of social and economic status, Kahl's findings imply that beyond a certain level of instruction, Brazilians are likely to move away from traditional values. The emergence of a new value syndrome is, therefore, closely linked to the performance of the educational system, something I shall take up in the succeeding section.

Political Indoctrination in Brazil

The most important general observation to be made about political indoctrination in Brazil is that there has been very little of it. The extent to which Brazilians are taught specific, differentiated values about the ends and means of political activity is very limited. Neither the traditional elites nor their opponents have tried very hard, at least until recently, to disseminate political ideologies or sets of doctrinal values. In fact, one of the most frequent laments of Brazilian intellectuals has been that most Brazilians neither have nor are susceptible to any ideology.[81]

A second general observation one could make is that those systems of political values which have played some historical role have been imitations of foreign models and have, perhaps consequently, not been rigidly adhered to.[82] João Cruz Costa notes, "to write an intellectual history of Brazil is to describe how foreign ideas have been imported and then modified."[83] According to Frank Bonilla:

Major social and political transitions in Brazil have in fact been achieved without the support of formalized political programs or bodies of doctrine and without the mobilization of mass opinion. The major turning points of Brazilian history—the establishment of the independent monarchy in 1822, the shift to republican form of government in 1889, and the Vargas revolution of 1930—were all ideologically unguided accommodations to underlying economic and social changes. . . . The relative smoothness of these transitions has been seen as a symptom of the small role played by ideas in the life of a nation given to drift and improvisation.[84]

The relative weakness of the political indoctrination process is a by-product of the failure of the education process in general. It also stems from the absence of other types of independent secondary associations that might have taught their members different political values. During the colonial period, there was no public effort at education. "Brazil's only focuses of intellectual culture for three centuries, and the basis of the formation of the first Brazilian elites," were the Jesuit schools, which were aimed exclusively "at the humanistic and Catholic training of the ruling class."[85] After receiving their "dogmatic and abstract" training at these schools, the sons of the wealthier plantation owners were sent to Europe—to Coimbra for doctorates in law and theology or to Montpellier for advanced degrees in natural sciences and medicine. "The university was not transplanted to Brazil. Political motives led the Portuguese colonizers, unlike the Spanish, to this act of pedagogic prudence. Thus we arrived at Independence without any press[86] and without any higher-level schools."[87]

The Imperial Constitution in 1824 bravely guaranteed universal, free primary education (as have all succeeding constitutions). In 1827 another law ordered the creation of primary schools in all cities, towns, and villages. Yet in 1889, at the proclamation of the Republic, only 3 percent of the population was in school. Anísio Teixeira observes that "during the entire Monarchy . . . we continued, as far as the expansion of the school system was concerned, cautiously and slowly. The ruling class, small and homogeneous, endowed with a lively awareness of European patterns, and extremely vigilant about its own preservation, seems to have intended to keep access to education restricted, especially at the highest level."[88] Furthermore, the Additional Act of 1834 transferred responsibility for elementary and secondary educational policy to the provincial governments, who kept it for almost a century. This decentralization impeded the establishment of the sort of "community of ideals and sentiments . . . indispensable to developing national feeling and increased the disparity in education between masses and elites."[89] The effects of this action were only somewhat counteracted by the creation of a national system of higher education.

The shift in sovereignty meant the loss of Coimbra as the center for higher education. Consequently, in 1827, four schools of advanced education were created in Brazil. These "nurseries of the aristocracies," especially the law schools in São Paulo and Recife (Olinda), became important centers, not only for training in their own disciplines, but also for the dissemination of new philosophical, literary, and political currents. The content of instruction and its formalistic nature and rhetorical mentality greatly influenced the Brazilian political style. The very existence of these schools was a "factor of mobility in a horizontal sense, . . . attracting individuals from different social environments . . . [and] submitting them all to a process of intellectual assimilation. These schools . . . played a worthy part, standing out as forgers of national consciousness." [90] In the new young educated and urbanized elite, indoctrinated into juridical formalism and imbued with the ideals of liberalism, the Emperor found an important counterweight to the older, more conservative rural aristocracy. The major conflict between the two elites was over the institution of slavery. When slavery was abolished in 1883, the delicate balance that had sustained the Empire was no longer viable. In 1889 the Republic was proclaimed.

During the Republic (1889–1930), the role of explicitly political values became more important than it had been during the Empire. Positivism among the military had been a factor in the downfall of the Empire, and its "cult of order, authority, hierarchy, and discipline" was an element in the consolidation of the new regime.[91] Anarchism began to appear among immigrant workers in the first decades of the twentieth century.[92] In the 1920's, the Brazilian Communist Party was founded.[93] Simultaneously, under Jackson de Figueiredo and Cardinal Leme, a Catholic revival began. Interestingly, this ideological fervor took place in the absence of any important changes in the system of formal education. In spite of a few reform bills and a widely expressed public desire for popular education to provide a stable basis for republican rule,[94] the school system remained virtually unaltered until 1928. Illiteracy, 67.2 percent in 1899, declined only 7.1 percent in thirty years![95] The new sets of political values were confined to small, but often strategically placed elites, and they were propagated by means of various new secondary associations: secret societies, Masonic lodges, military academies, literary circles, artisans' mutual aid associations, trade unions, clubs, study centers, etc.

Nationalism, or "nationalistic ideology"—"express bodies of political thought concerning what the nation was, is, and ought to be, the means to be employed for seeking national goals and for discriminating between state power and individual rights"—was another product of this period.[96] In the writings of Alberto Torres, for example, Brazilian history and character are evaluated, the causes of and obstacles to national unity and greatness are explored, and programs of national goals are suggested.[97] The Liga de Defêsa Nacional was created about 1915 to propagate national loyalty and symbols.[98] True, these isolated and largely literary attempts were premature. Nonetheless, they are evidence of a growing political consciousness and reliance upon sets of elaborated political values.

The breach between growing elite consciousness of national political ideals and goals and the resistant political structures of the decentralized

"Old Republic" became evident first in the military uprisings of 1922 and 1924[99] and again in the Revolution of 1930. Getúlio Vargas's extra-legal ascension to power is widely recognized as the beginning of the Brazilian Revolution, and his long period of direct authoritarian rule (1930–45) brought significant and lasting changes in the country's political culture.

Change in the formal educational system had already begun in 1928. The Escola Nova movement, heavily influenced by the teachings of John Dewey and led by a group of dynamic and educated young men, tried to broaden and popularize instruction. This ideal had important (and self-conscious) political overtones, as Roberto Moreira notes, because education was considered "a powerful instrument for social, political, and moral reconstruction, and for the progressive realization of greater democracy."[100] After initial successes in reform at the state level and in the Federal District, the movement encountered increasing resistance from the Church and from other groups interested in maintaining a more restricted, literary-oriented, and privately controlled system of education. The coup d'etat of 1937 put an end to the acrimonious debate and to the reform movement as well.

The installation of the *Estado Novo* did, however, bring with it a strong nationalization of the educational system. The 1934 Constitution had already given the federal government the right to fix a national educational plan and thereby set up directives for the state school systems. The 1937 Charter went further, making the central regime responsible for general guidelines on the "physical, intellectual, and moral training of youth" and suppressing state and local symbols by making the use of the national flag, hymn, shield, and coat of arms compulsory. The school curriculum was to include courses in civic and political education.[101] A youth organization was formed in 1939 to supplement and regiment this effort.[102] The radio was used extensively for political indoctrination, and a wide variety of government-sponsored journals appeared, one appropriately entitled *Cultura Política*. All the media were placed under the watchful and censorious eye of the Departamento de Imprensa e Propaganda (DIP). How effective these measures were in indoctrinating elites or masses with a new set of orientations is debatable. As late as 1961, for example, the Ministry of Education had to appeal to private firms in order to equip primary schools with the symbols of nationhood for the first time. Brazil's entry into World War II on the Allied side presumably put a damper on the inculcation of the more authoritarian, semi-fascist norms.

The official ideology of the Estado Novo was corporatism.[103] Although they never formed a coherent ideological movement as did the Communists and the Integralistas (fascists), whose revolts were easily suppressed in 1935 and 1938 respectively, the corporatists provided a sort of intellectual rationalization for Vargas's "experimental politics," much as fascism did for Mussolini. Critics have dismissed this doctrine of nationalistic, authoritarian, and centralized tutelage as merely another foreign fad followed by Brazil's alienated elites. In fact, Brazil was deluged with translations of Bonnard, Manoilesco, and the *Carta del Lavoro*. Oliveira Vianna argues, however, that the Brazilian version was significantly different, that it was closely related to the earlier positivist movement, that it had deep roots in Brazilian political culture, and that it provided a sort of transitional stage between privatistic patriarchalism and some future stage of participatory democracy.[104] It is hard to imagine that corporatism could have had such a lasting impact upon the structural and behavioral norms of representative associations, if it did not correspond in some way to underlying patterns of basic political socialization.[105]

The peaceful deposition of President Vargas in 1945 did not bring about any immediate major changes in the process of political indoctrination. Officially, of course, the corporatist-syndicalist trappings were replaced by those of liberal representative democracy. Nonetheless, most of the institutions created in the name of the former survived. The 1946 Constitution again made the federal government ambiguously responsible for legislating on "the directives and bases of national education," assigning the states a "supplementary and complementary role." But it took fifteen years for this provision to bear fruit, and in the meantime the formal educational system continued as before with private schools, both secular and religious, playing an increasingly important role at the critical secondary-school level. Illiteracy did decline, and an increasing proportion of the population was going to school, but there was no substantial innovation in the political-civic content of instruction, except, of course, for the halting of the corporatist-fascist indoctrination. The 1961 Educational Reform Bill, after a lengthy battle reminiscent of the 1928–37 struggle,[106] brought only one important change as far as this discussion is concerned. The Federal Council of Education created a new discipline, "Brazilian Political and Social Organization," which was designed "to prepare young people for the conscious exercise of democratic citizenship."[107] The textbooks so far offered for the course have been serious, rather objective, and surprisingly nonlegalistic.[108]

Associational indoctrination. By far the most interesting development in political indoctrination during recent decades has been the emergence and vigorous activity of new secondary associations with the self-appointed tasks of forging a new consciousness of national mission and of immunizing the nation against subversion and corruption. Some of these have focused their efforts on elites, others on the masses.

The best known of the elite-oriented associations was the Instituto Superior de Estudos Brasileiros (ISEB), an institution supported by the Ministry of Education to create an ideology linking nationalism and development.[109] A sort of combined graduate school and research facility, ISEB offered instruction in the social sciences, history, and philosophy to a select group of full-time students, most of them "middle-level government functionaries and military officers." It also offered a group of public evening lectures aimed at a wider, but still elite, audience. An extensive series of publications further extended ISEB's influence during the nine years of its existence (it was started in 1955 and was closed down by force after the coup of 1964). Since ISEB was never an ideologically monolithic group, it is not easy to summarize its line.[110] Although it later became more abstract and doctrinaire,[111] its attempt to use at least some of the tools of social science and objective analysis to pinpoint key obstacles and to publicize certain developmental goals "set an intellectual standard for nationalist theorizing that has strongly influenced both in content and style nationalist writing of whatever political aspiration in Brazil."[112] Other nationalist groups, such as that formerly associated with the *Revista Brasilense* and that now writing for *Revista Civilização Brasileira* and *Política Externa Independente,* whether they agree with the ISEB approach or not, have been compelled to make a similarly serious effort.

Perhaps second in public renown, but vastly more important in terms of its impact on government policy, is the Escola Superior da Guerra (ESG). Also an official body (under the General Staff of the Armed Forces) ESG has offered and continues to offer both a regular full-time, one-year indoctrination program and a series of public lectures. Most of the graduates have been military officers, but there have also been a select group of strategically important leaders from certain representative associations, administrators from government and semipublic agencies, and politicians. The ideology of ESG, like that of ISEB, is nationalistic: all social, economic, and political problems are viewed in terms of "the doctrine of national security."[113] Its ideology is more cohesive than ISEB's, but it has less qualitative depth, and it lacks imagination and ISEB's strong foundation in the social sciences. Furthermore, the ESG doctrine is not autonomous: it defines Brazilian security in terms of its military alliance with and dependence upon the United States. Unlike ISEB, which saw increased economic and political participation as one of the major obstacles to national development, ESG has focused on Communist subversion and internal corruption as the major impediments to national greatness. Thus it comes as no surprise that the two associations were regarded as antipodes, and that the latter was instrumental in closing down the former.[114]

An unofficial indoctrinating association active among businessmen was the Instituto de Pesquisas e Estudos Socials (IPÊS). A formally nonpolitical institute devoted to the "study of democratic solutions to problems posed by national development," IPÊS offered a series of courses, seminars, and public lectures at its branches in Rio, São Paulo, and Pôrto Alegre. It also printed and distributed a large number of propaganda leaflets aimed at a wider audience. Orthodox liberalism—private property as the foundation of political democracy—made up its basic ideology, tempered by the reformism of the Charter of Punta del Este and the Papal encyclical *Mater et Magistra*. The Rio group took an especially pragmatic attitude toward government intervention in the economic sphere, agrarian reform,* income redistribution, regional integration, and even the extension of the voting right to illiterates.[115] The group in São Paulo supplemented its direct educational and propaganda activities by lending financial and intellectual assistance to a number of other associations whose purpose was similar but who aimed their message at trade union leaders, students, women, or the general public. Since the "Revolution" of 1964 all branches of IPÊS have shed their subversive (or, to them, antisubversive) functions and plan to give their energies to the study of national and international problems along liberal lines[116] and to the "betterment of the civic and democratic consciousness of the people."[117]

To a certain extent, these efforts to indoctrinate elites were nothing new, though they gained somewhat in variety, scope, and intensity as ideological positions became more polarized in the late 1950's and early 1960's. What was a decided novelty were the attempts made to extend this political indoctrination to the masses. Except for civic education programs sponsored by a few right-wing and liberal groups like IPÊS and certain state governments, the indoctrination of the masses was left almost exclusively to left-wing, progressive groups. There now developed a general effort to inculcate in the masses some notions of group or class interest and some ideals about the role of the state and the desirability of certain national goals. This effort was known as *consciêntização*. The collective phenomenon on the part of both nationalist elites and the newly aware masses was termed the *tomada de consciência* ("gathering of consciousness"). Various organizations became involved in the process: the Church through the Basic Education Movement

---

* Its study of agrarian reform provided the basis for the Estatuto da Terra bill of 1964.

(MEB), the National Union of Students (UNE) through its Popular Center for Culture, the Ministry of Education and the state Secretaries of Education through their Commissions for Popular Culture and a variety of literacy programs.

In Brazil the right to vote is denied to illiterates. But literacy does not directly provide the citizen with the kinds of political sentiments and skills necessary for effective participation.[118] However, as progressive Brazilian educators discovered, if the teaching of literacy is combined with a concentrated effort at inculcating certain basic ideological values, the result can become a force for change that is powerful but also manipulable. The best example of this combination of literacy training and indoctrination (well illustrated by its title) was the MEB pamphlet *Lutar é Viver (To Fight Means to Live)*. Paulo Freire, one of the most effective practitioners of this program and the inventor of a new rapid technique for teaching literacy, noted among the objectives of his experimental work the development of students' "critical consciousness of their position and their task in its total context." His aim was to give them "an existential apprenticeship in democracy by replacing old cultural habits of passivity with new habits of participation and self-government."[119] The traditional elites naturally regarded these efforts as manifest attempts at Communist subversion (which may have been true in some cases), or at least as decided threats to the existing order (which they certainly were). *Lutar é Viver* was seized as subversive in early 1964. The literacy and popular culture movements were abruptly stopped after the coup of 1964, and only the pure literacy campaign has been revived since, and that hesitantly.[120]

How far has the process of political indoctrination gone in Brazil? How widespread is the *tomada de consciência?* To what extent have elites acquired a distinct set of national goals and political values—a nationalist ideology—and the masses a distinct set of national loyalties and political expectations—a national consciousness?

Elite ideology has clearly lost much of the homogeneity, based on common acceptance of foreign models and common experience in the law schools, that prevailed in the nineteenth century. Moreover, the growing ideological heterogeneity of this century has not been overcome by the emergence of a new elite based on any mutual acceptance of developmental goals or on a common educational experience. Although various elites identify themselves as "nationalist" (89 percent of the Brazilian national congressmen in Lloyd Free's sample did so), the programmatic content of this sentiment in terms of attitudes toward foreign capital, United States aid, neutralism in foreign policy, greater national independence, etc., is very diverse, if not self-contradictory.[121]

Frank Bonilla notes that even in the headquarters of the Nationalist Movement (ISEB) there was little evidence that its leaders were themselves "gripped by the powerful feeling of commitment." Brazilian nationalism has less of the "irrational fanaticism directed toward outsiders, the ingenuous tendency for self-glorification common to nationalism in other countries."[122] The attachment is more pragmatic and utilitarian.[123]

Only 7 percent of a national sample of the general urban public and 1 percent of the rural public were self-avowed nationalists.[124] Lloyd Free concludes that, "as a whole, the Brazilian people are not very much preoccupied with the question of nationalism," and that the indoctrination efforts noted above have not had much of an effect. Only 19 percent of the urban respondents and 6 percent of the rural ones indicated that they had "ever heard or read about nationalism in Brazil and the Brazilian nationalists." Among the small number who did know about the subject, only a minority (38 percent of the urbanites and 20 percent of the rural respondents) said they agreed with the nationalists.[125]

But the self-seeking nationalism of an elite is not to be confused with the far more widespread and generalized nationalism of a people that has succeeded in developing a common attitude toward the state as the impersonal and ultimate arbitrator of human affairs.[126] Empirical data on the extent to which Brazilians feel a sense of mutual empathy and voluntarily accept subjugation to national political authority are hardly plentiful. The very high percentages of "don't knows" in Free's national opinion survey are evidence of a general incapacity for perceiving or conceiving of political problems in personal terms. He concludes that "the rural population, by and large, is ignorant, inert, and unconcerned about issues involving nationalism or foreign affairs." Two-thirds of the sample could not even name the President of their country![127] "The urbanites as a whole are also too ignorant . . . and their horizons too limited for them to feel significantly strongly about such issues, by and large, even to attempt to bring pressure to bear upon their political leaders."[128]

TABLE 3.1

RESPONDENTS MENTIONING PERSONAL AND/OR NATIONAL ASPIRATION
FOR IMPROVED OR DECENT STANDARD OF LIVING

Region	Percent of urban public mentioning:		Percent of rural public mentioning:	
	Personal aspiration	National aspiration	Personal aspiration	National aspiration
Northeast	55%	24%	47%	19%
East	39	43	38	32
South	44	49	39	42

SOURCE: Adapted from Free, pp. 54, 62.

Table 3.1, which juxtaposes personal and national aspirations for improved or decent living standards, demonstrates considerable variety in the capacity to translate a widespread personal aspiration into something like a diffuse political demand. In the Northeast, and especially in its rural areas, the demand is translated at a considerable discount. In the intermediate developing areas of the East, only the urban group sees the issue in predominantly political terms. In the more developed South, both rural and urban sectors perceive the demand more in national than in personal terms—very impressive scalar evidence of the impact of development upon politicization.

Frank Bonilla, reporting on his and Kalman Silvert's unfinished study of "national identification" or "loyalty and confidence in the system," indicates an interesting relationship between this variable and social class. When managers, skilled workers, and *favelados* (slum dwellers) were compared, the first group scored significantly higher, as was anticipated. But the response of skilled workers was closer to that of the *favelados*, "despite the fact that [the former] were in terms of subjective class identification, values related to the sphere of work, and personal development values much closer to the managers than to the *favelados* to whom skilled workers are closer in origins and objective social situation." He concludes that the disparity in social and personal attitudes and values "was not matched by a significant shift or orientation toward the central political mechanism."[129] In short, social mobilization in this group, as in all groups sampled in Brazil, has not been accompanied by politicization.[130] On the other hand, the low level of information, lack of faith in political action, and cynicism toward those in authority is, according to Bonilla, balanced by faith in the potential for growth of the economy and in the imagined opportunities for mobility in the society.[131]

The evidence, both historical and contemporary, supports the conclusion that political indoctrination, the self-conscious process of teaching and learning differentiated manifest ideals concerning the ends and means of political action, plays a very weak role within the total process of political enculturation in Brazil.[132] Although most of the population has passed beyond a pure *parochial* status and has become aware of some larger community, a less substantial proportion has acquired competence in translating their personal aspirations and interests into the sort of politicized, public demands required for *subject* status. Of course, even fewer manage through actual experience to attain the capacity for effective *participation*. For the great bulk of the population, political loyalties and demands simply represent public projections of private orientations assimilated in the basic socialization process. Marvin Harris's anthropological monograph demonstrates this attitude:

In the eyes of the townspeople the principal duty of all governments is to produce "progress." . . . The prevailing attitude is, "we are too weak to help ourselves." *O Govêrno tem de dar o impulso* (the Government has to give the push). *O Govêrno,* in this case, refers to something beyond the country, but to no specific bureaucracy or agency. What the townspeople have in mind is the "boss" of super proportions embodied in the state and federal government. Everyone, from mayor and councilmen to artisan and storekeeper, is firmly convinced that herein lies the solution to Minas Velhas's problems.[133]

Political Experience in Brazil

By actually participating in politics or by learning of the activities of others, actors acquire a political memory, or an internalized set of perceptions of actual behavior and personal strategies for effective action. Methods perceived as effective in past cases of problem-solving tend to serve as models for future action. These accumulate, become habit or standard practice, and provide a sort of "hidden rationality" behind seemingly unconnected events. They may even find their way into formalized rules, such as constitutions and administrative regulations, although such documents are usually poor indicators or imperfect compilations of the content and form—the operational code and style—of the actual processes.

One may hypothesize that the fewer the participants and the more selectively they are recruited, the more informal and secret the code and style will be. At its extreme, public or societal decision-making becomes a private or family affair. As popular participation increases, the arcane element should decrease and the formalized component should increase. For Brazil, a polity of still restricted, though fitfully expanding participation, this hypothesis implies not only that the Constitution is not likely to be an informative guide, but also that little explicit discussion of the rules of the game exists. Indeed, attempts to penetrate the natural secrecy surrounding them may be considered crimes of lèse majesté. Another problem of particular relevance to Brazil is that "codebooks" and "style manuals" become rapidly outdated when demands and expectations are constantly shifting and new types of participants are continually entering the game. By the time one has codified the rules for one period (the Vargas dictatorship for example), they may well already have become passé. Brazil is not in such chaos that each succeeding politician must write his own text, but it does fluctuate enough for some politicians who have manifestly refused to go by the book, such as Jânio Quadros and Carlos Lacerda, to have been at least electorally successful.

These problems make the workings of the Brazilian political system difficult to assess. Furthermore, my experience with the system is limited to a few months of observation, and much of my knowledge on the subject has come from the outside. I advance the following observations, then, with considerable trepidation. Some rules are constantly changing, and the rate of change has been especially great since the 1964 coup. Also, different codes and styles may be used to solve problems at different levels of the system and in different areas of policy. My impression is that political experience is the stage of the enculturation process at which regional or subregional differences are greatest. My isolated comments are therefore confined to patterns of problem-solving and conflict resolution at the national level.

The operational code. The most prominent characteristic of the operational code of Brazilian politics, one commented on by innumerable natives and foreigners and frequently cited as both the product and the producer of the nation's remarkable political continuity, is a propensity for conciliation and accommodation. Many, like Gilberto Freyre, have argued that this genius for compromise is inherited from Portugal, that it is based essentially on racial tolerance and miscegenation and has been diffused throughout the society. According to those observers, the propensity for "the triumph of the process of composition over the process of opposition"[134] and its components—nonviolence, pragmatism, tolerance, co-optation, moderation, and temporization—are rules of the game shared by all. They are a product of basic socialization, and therefore are part of the general political culture.

I dissent from this view and hypothesize (i.e., I admit the fragility of the empirical evidence) that these norms of conciliation are in fact shared primarily by the elites, applied principally (if not exclusively) in inter-elite relations, and are adhered to by those elites mainly in the interests of self-preservation.[135] Whether or not those who practice the code are fully conscious of its conservative and self-preservative nature is perhaps debatable. Brazilian elites are probably aware that inter-elite discord, violence, and high levels of repression would easily threaten the cohesion of such a poorly integrated, hetereogeneous system. "Without internal peace, the Brazilian union would be a simple memory in less than half a century."[136] It is true that, as a result of socialization and indoctrination, non-elites can become convinced that these norms are generically Brazilian and may behave accordingly. But a cursory look at the historical record, at existing monographs on local politics, or even at the daily newspaper would demonstrate the inoperability of these norms in elite-mass relationships, or even in relationships between elites at the local level. Following my hypothesis, an empirical survey would show a strong tendency for these political values to "fall off" as one moves down the status pyramid and as one descends from the national to the local political arena. These norms are part of the national system's operational code, not its basic socialization process (which as we have seen is much more authoritarian and hierarchical). As such, they are restricted to relatively small numbers of adherents.

The historical origin of the code could be traced less to the basic tolerance and flexibility of the Portuguese colonialists than to their need for a spirit of compromise in order to survive and to overcome "the social and natural factors of dispersion and differentiation."[137] Brazil's first bishop wisely anticipated this need when he advised his superiors that in such a new land "many more things must be covered up than punished."[138] Whatever its historical origin, the Brazilian preference for negotiated solutions, often at the expense of principles and self-interest (though never at the expense of one's elite status) rests on a set of supporting norms and mechanisms.

The first and most basic of these is the tacit commitment that one should not eliminate by physical violence one's elite opponents or groups sponsored or protected by him, or react to a pacific defeat by recourse to armed violence.[139] As a corollary, one should also offer clemency to one's defeated opponents in the form of symbolic (but well-paid) positions or, in cases of extreme animosity, exile.* When recourse to violence is used, each party invariably protests that the other transgressed the norm first or was about to do so. Consequently, normal political conflict, although it can become verbally vituperative, takes place in an atmosphere of civility, mutual respect, and even ceremoniousness. Clashes are often referred to mediating third parties rather than fought out face to face and in public.

The second principle of the code is that elite actors must demonstrate considerable personal and pragmatic flexibility. In terms of Verba's dichotomous variables, their belief systems should be open, implicit, and instrumental, though not necessarily rational in any immediately perceptible way. Ideas and principles are not rigidly adhered to. Tractability and tolerance are the hallmark. Gilberto Amado gives us a well-drawn, if caustic, portrait of what was traditionally and conventionally called "good political character":

What we praise and prefer in the conduct of public affairs is the pondered temperament, serene and polished mediocrity, sure and average virtues; . . . the anonymous man, almost always without literary or artistic taste, who does not fight, have his own opinions, or take responsibilities, [but] who smiles gravely, compliments with austerity, attempts to earn his living without bothering others, managing in the shadow of an apparent smoothness to irritate as little as possible, who doesn't provoke a reaction, and who follows paths

---

* Getúlio Vargas's treatment of the insurrectionary Paulistas in 1932 was an important case of this.

already opened by others; . . . the man of the middle term, of the average cut, of reasonable proportion, of perfect equilibrium.[140]

One of the most popular political sayings is attributed to a contemporary congressman who, when asked if he supported a certain bill, replied, "Eu? Não sou nem contra, nem a favor. Muito pelo contrário" ("Me? I neither favor nor oppose it. Much to the contrary").* This institutionalized opportunism, malleability, and cynicism, though frequently the subject of intellectual and moral scorn, has played an important role in crucial periods of Brazilian political life, both as a consolidator of innovation and as a perpetuator of stability. For example, the *adesistas*, politicians of the Empire who recognized the permanence of the change to republican institutions, served the new regime loyally and effectively.[141] However, like so many other rules of the operational code, these reached their apex of expression and utility during the Getulian era.[142]

The third major item in the code, one closely associated with flexibility, is a notable capacity for co-optation. Phrased more cynically, it is the propensity to "corrupt rather than imprison"[143] or to "absorb rather than crush"[144] one's opponents. Getúlio Vargas is supposed to have said, "I never made any friends that I could not set aside, nor enemies to whom I could not draw closer."[145] Here we see illustrated not only the predominant role played by inter-elite friendship ties, but also how in order to be successful the astute politician must be able to manipulate those ties flexibly, improvising new combinations for the sake of expediency, and not be a prisoner of past friendships. In this process of abandoning old alliances and forming new ones, timing is a key factor. Put simply, the skillful Brazilian conciliator must co-opt his opponent before the latter can mobilize an independent basis of support. As Antônio Carlos, President of Minas Gerais, said in 1930, "We must make the Revolution before the people do it." The quality of paternalist co-optation—"the disposition to yield among groups at the top . . . more than the apparent pressures from below would reasonably demand"— coupled with non-elites' "disposition to accept small concessions . . . often out of line with the urgency of their need or their apparent power at given moments"[146] explains to some extent the evasiveness, the indeterminacy, the lack of apparent rationality behind policy pronouncements. The completely enculturated and system-perpetuating Brazilian politician is a master at anticipated reaction. He responds to overt and latent signals of threats to his position by accommodation and co-optation, rather than by repression or violence.

---

* This saying has been used to epitomize the ideology of the Partido Social Democrático (PSD). Indeed, most of my observations about the code and style are popularly associated with this, formerly the largest of Brazilian parties. The Partido Trabalhista Brasileiro's style was similar. Both parties were created by Getúlio Vargas.

The primary mechanism for co-optation is an institutionalized spoils system at all levels of the polity. During the Empire, this involved such relatively minor devices as offers of posts in the Guarda Nacional (hence the origin of the term *coronel*) and titles of nobility. With the Republic, the primary mechanism came to be offers of employment in the public bureaucracy in exchange for political support, and, during the *Encilhamento* of the early 1890's, the selective distribution of credit, licenses, and other economic favors. Both of these devices became fully institutionalized during the Getulian period, especially during the *Estado Novo* (1937–45), and easily survived the change of regime in 1945.[147] With the proliferation of semipublic agencies and autarchies and the steady increase in government revenues, the importance of controlling this machine for distributing rewards and punishments and the potentialities for using patronage to consolidate oneself in office have risen dramatically.

The fourth major item in the codebook is the need for a sense of proportion and balance. In a large and heterogeneous country like Brazil, this implies, first of all, a skill at striking a regional balance in the composition of cabinets, boards of directors, aid and development programs, etc.* Beyond this obvious and often purely symbolic talent, the successful Brazilian politician must develop a sense of internal proportion and balance, a self-limiting quality by which he voluntarily tones down the extremist content in his demands and moderates his own personal ambition. Not surprisingly, since self-limitation is not easily acquired or sustained, this item is the weakest in the codebook. For this reason, though probably not consciously, the system provides an institutionalized functional equivalent: *o poder moderader* (the moderative power). According to a formal provision of the Imperial Constitution, the Emperor could (and did) intervene on a personal, authoritarian basis to correct what he saw as imbalances or imperfections in the political process. In particular, he used his neutral power to enforce a certain rhythmic exchange of power between the two more or less identical parties, thereby preventing either from perpetuating itself.[148] The military inherited the role after 1889,† and it has continued to claim this justification for intervention ever since.[149] Of course the functional justification for this role in terms of the code, the need to provide an outside check on politicians' failure to limit themselves, depends on the role occupant's not

* The gentlemen's agreement to rotate the national presidency between São Paulo and Minas Gerais during the Old Republic was the most obvious example of such a regional proportional scheme. Its collapse in the 1930 election was an important factor in the ensuing revolution of that year.

† This was rather ambiguously legitimated by Article 177 of the 1946 Constitution, under which "the armed forces are intended to defend the fatherland and to guarantee the constitutional power and law and order."

becoming an active agent in the apportionment of favors and enjoyment of privileges. In this respect, the nature of the role has been altered radically, if not irrevocably, by the Brazilian military since the coup of 1964.

Finally, the operational code depends on procrastination and indecision.[150] Another of Getúlio's favorite maxims was "Leave things as they are so you can see how they stay." In other words one should hesitate and vacillate, in the hope that as passions and interests cool the problem will go away.[151] If it does not, then one should attack the problem, but using an avoidance pattern. For example, if one must do something about a given agency that has proven itself to be incompetent or disloyal, one need not abolish the agency. Rather, one should outflank it by creating a new organization staffed with "men of confidence." Then, by funding the parallel agency liberally and by cutting back financially on the original agency, one can keep the latter from posing any threat, even if it continues to exist for decades in a state of harmless vegetation. It will become what the *cariocas* call a "hatstand for jobs" (*cabide de emprêgo*). (Of course one's successor can always reverse the process, and is as likely as not to do so.)

Another standard practice in the decisional process is that of avoiding a "closure point," a point at which interest inputs are definitively converted into authoritative outputs. In line with the general desirability of procrastination, one should string out the decisional process as much as possible. And if a final decision must eventually be reached, it should contain within it a provision for the founding of a permanent representative or consultative body that will keep the decision under constant surveillance. This way the door is always open to a revision of the distribution of benefits and sacrifices in the light of new circumstances.* Thus no one feels permanently disadvantaged; one can always maintain the illusion that an unfavorable decision will in time be reversed.†

In a society like contemporary Brazil, marked by a strong sense of rapid social change, the propensity for making pacts between groups with divergent political conceptions is a frequent mode of adaptation and adjustment among discrepant positions. In fact, this style of leadership . . . coincides precisely with the profound alterations that have been shaking Brazil in the last decades.[152]

Manipulation of the code depends strongly on centralized leadership. This is perhaps why presidentialism is so often cited as the prime char-

---

* Also, if the actor is a national or state executive, this keeps the decision permanently within his realm of control, the administrative process.

† This standard pattern of indecision does not imply that no decisions are made rapidly and definitively. Many are, especially when a decision-maker feels pressed for time because he is sure his successor will not carry on the policy or when he feels that the momentary constellation of forces is appropriate.

acteristic of Brazilian political culture.[153] The leader need not be politically strong, but in order to control this kaleidoscopic policy process
he must be clever and experienced.* In Hirschman's terms, it is a mixture of "log rolling" and "shifting coalitions," with strong emphasis on
the former, based essentially on bargaining between regional *bancadas*,
or blocs. Succeeding decisions involve more or less covertly related
package deals based on the exchange of *cobertura*, or support.[154] The
central role is made all the more difficult by the presence of a self-appointed moderative power in the wings, which is prepared not only to
intervene periodically in the name of order, but also to act as a veto
group when its own interests are threatened. *Cobertura militar* is, therefore, the most important *cobertura* of all.

Given the enormous complexity of the top leadership roles, there is
a tendency to exhaust one's energies in survival tactics and to use the
position solely for self-preservation and enrichment. Getúlio Vargas
was perhaps so preoccupied with self-preservation that he had little left
for other goals, although his daughter has claimed that his basic conception of his role was that of tutoring the polity. Some other top officeholders, for example Adhemar de Barros, have been frequently accused
of being too concerned with self-enrichment. One cannot help admiring
the capacity of Juscelino Kubitschek, who not only survived, but succeeded in giving a sense of direction to the whole cumbersome policy
machine.†

These remarks point out another fundamental weakness in the code,
beyond its extreme dependence on skillful leadership. The system is
immoral or amoral. As Hirschman points out, these "reformmongering"
styles of decision-making are not morally attractive, nor are they usually
openly defended. The cynical justification "he steals but he gets things
done" may appeal to some, but the system is sure to produce indignant
(and probably intolerant and intransigent) groups who will protest
loudly. In Brazil, this protest has taken the institutional form of the
urban União Democrática Nacional (UDN) party.[155] Representing a
minority opinion, this party has had only local success at the polls. It

---

* Neither Getúlio Vargas nor Juscelino Kubitschek was strong at the onset of his
term of office, but both proved consummate manipulators of the code. Jânio Quadros,
who took office on the greatest wave of popular electoral support in Brazilian history, failed (perhaps deliberately) as a manipulator of the code. Interestingly, both
he and another recent political failure, João (Jango) Goulart, had had meteoric careers and had, therefore, missed the opportunity to acquire a deep knowledge of the
intricacies of political maneuvering. Jango, of course, took lessons from the master
himself, Getúlio, but the record seems to show that there is no substitute for experience—unless it is military strength.

† Some, of course, have charged that he also succeeded in the goal of self-enrichment, but such charges are speculative.

has therefore been most prone to appeal to the military in its effort to clean out pragmatism, laxity, and "historical opportunism."[156]

Recent years have seen an increase in public violence, a decrease in both ideological and personal flexibility, new limitations on the possibility of satisfaction through co-optation, a loss of the sense of proportion (especially because of a growing awareness of the disparities in regional payoffs), and political immobilism rather than tactical indecision. These trends have all tended to reduce the viability of an operational code based on compromise. One could argue that whatever remnants of it we find lodged in the politics of representative associations are just that: remnants of a decadent order and nothing more. Presumably, the new rules of the game are now being written under military sponsorship. The recent flood of official documents and regulations (for example the *Atos Institucionais, Adicionais e Complementares*) is perhaps a crude attempt to formalize and publicize these new rules, since, given the rapidity of events, the elite actors have not had time to assimilate a new code through actual experience.

The style. The content and form of the political process are obviously related, but the Brazilian case seems to indicate that they may in fact be related in paradoxical ways. The predominant style is formalism. In the administrative and legislative sphere, this formalism is expressed as an intense concern with legal phraseology, precision of expression, and rigidly designed, exhaustively contrived, and minutely detailed provisions and rules.[157] In the popular, electoral sphere, formalism shows up in the extensive use of stereotypic phrases and vague, demagogic promises of comprehensive, definitive, and simple solutions.[158] The types of formalism used in the two spheres may appear different, but they are both more or less calculatedly divorced from the complexity of real political and social processes. The administrator or legislator who painstakingly drafts a bill with hundreds of detailed provisions and the politician in the hustings who unhesitatingly promises to end all misery by expropriating the wealth of the rich both know that their measures will not obtain the proclaimed results (nor, one could say, do they really desire those results).

The historical origins of formalism, especially of the first type, lie in the Empire and in the early law schools. As Paulo Prado observed, "We attained [during the Empire] the highest point that the juridical conscience of people could reach. . . . Only one law was missing, . . . one that commanded that all the others be carried out.[159] This delicate and subtle style, "an instrument of precision designed to control and orient the tumultuous currents of popular opinion,"[160] began to run amok during the Republic as the basis for recruitment became less aristocratic. The demagogic type of formalism gained currency, especially after 1945 as elections became an important selection device. Demagogic, or juridical, formalism is designed, consciously for some and unconsciously for others, to cover up the less morally appealing aspects of the operational code. Beneath the formal façade, therefore, there is a second political style more in tune with the reality of the code. This style is captured by the expression *jeito*, "a short-term improvised and unorthodox way of either getting out of a difficulty or avoiding one altogether."[161] *Dar um jeito* (to find a way out) is an act neither legal nor illegal, but "paralegal."[162] Roberto Campos argues that the *jeito* is a generalized Latin style, produced by the expectation of unequal, particularistic treatment from authorities, by a rigidly codified, transplanted legal system of symbolic and unexecutable norms, and by the dogmatic intolerance of Catholicism. Without any formal modification of ethical values, this paralegal institution becomes indispensable for maintaining society. It keeps alive the convenient myth that there is always room for bargaining and maneuver, even in the face of formal defeat. In situations "where laws are reinterpreted, regulations and instructions of the government are already decreed with a certain previous calculation of the degree to which they will be carried out, where the people is a great filter of laws and where functionaries, small or powerful, create their own jurisprudence," it is not surprising that this informal jurisprudence "enjoys general approval, if it seems dictated by common sense."[163] Hardly surprising, then, that one of the most popular folk heroes of Brazil is Pedro Malasarte, a sort of Till Eulenspiegel who resolves all problems effortlessly, employing "craftiness, intrigue, calculation, and astuteness."[164]

Political experience, as synthesized in the code of compromise and the style of formalism and jeitoism, has until recently proved capable not only of considerable adaptability and of high (if wasteful) performance, but also of modifying and even channeling the basic orientations left by the socialization process. Given the general failure of indoctrination to provide a stable, deeply felt set of explicitly political values, an enormous burden rests on the few who actually experience political activity and learn from it. These elites, very often chosen because of their primary and particularistic loyalties, must overcome the privatism and authoritarianism inculcated in the context of these affiliations if the whole political system is not going to degenerate into a self-seeking free-for-all.

The Brazilian Political Culture: Concluding General Remarks

Viewed from a general historical perspective, the evolution of Brazilian political culture has been remarkably continuous. This continuity owes its existence to the ease with which the colonists' territorial rights were established, to the high degree of physical isolation and consequent absence of serious external threats (after the seventeenth century), and, most of all, to a very slow rate of social change. Changes in regime have happened gradually, problems have been solved one at a time, and basic national symbols have been maintained throughout Brazil's history. From an almost pure form of patriarchalism, the system passed through a long period of tutelary rule—a symbiosis between patriarchal family organization and monarchic and authoritarian political institutions.[165] Gradually, the basis of recruitment to top political roles broadened and the center of political gravity shifted to the cities. With the advent of the Republic, this compromise (usually called *coronelismo*) between the newly mobilized, ambitious urban elites and the stagnant, traditional rural ones was maintained, albeit uneasily.[166] Without the unifying presence of the Emperor, the system became a bargaining process between regional oligarchic blocs. The 1930 Revolution introduced (unintentionally) another long period of tutelary rule. National symbols, as opposed to regional ones, were reaffirmed, and a new national operational code and style (with, of course, important roots in past experience) were created. The criteria for recruitment again shifted, but the new elites were co-opted on the basis of their acceptance of the existing rules of the game.

After World War II, the basic requisites for political cultural continuity were missing, but this was somewhat hidden at first by the immobilism of the Dutra regime (1945–50). Brazil was no longer so isolated from imperialist and cold-war pressures and from subversive ideologies. Most important, an accelerated process of social structural change had begun. As a result, the previous homogeneity of elite political culture was undermined; the degree of coherence between the norms inculcated at various stages of the enculturation process declined, and more actors were becoming aware of the lack of congruence between values and expectations and the actual performance of institutions. In this state of confusion, observers began to write of anomie and of a premature mass society. As the techniques of political effectiveness and success became less obvious, actors experimented with new ones. Public morality and responsibility (never very high) declined. Political careers followed less standardized paths and became meteoric in some cases. The presence of so many uninitiated and inexperienced actors added further confusion to the political process. As predictability declined, so did mutual trust. Finally, the crisis in political culture was resolved by recourse to violence and the moderative power. The victors have since begun to experiment with a new and more authoritarian political culture.

FOUR

The Political Subculture of Associational Leaders

THE DISCUSSION in the previous chapter suggests two broad, tentative observations about the impact of Brazilian political culture and its component processes on the nature and role of representative associations. First, the historically prevalent pattern inhibits the emergence and maintenance of impersonal, functionally specific, and permanently administered interest groups. Second, because of its influence on values, perceptions, and expectations, the Brazilian political culture is likely to reinforce the associations' asymmetric dependence upon authority groups and thus limit the effectiveness of those associations. In short, association leaders in Brazil have to learn norms of moderation, self-limitation, and subservience.

As we have seen, the literature of national self-examination is full of laments about the "vacuousness, the lack of organization, the disunity, the absence of collective motivations, and the lack of any associative or team spirit" in Brazilian public life.[1] Similar observations were made by group leaders interviewed. Many causes for these failings have been suggested, some of which have been discussed: the dispersed settlement pattern; the role of familistic individualism and clan politics; the tendency to personalize all political and social relations; the distaste for sustained effort and continuous routine; jeitoism, or the reliance upon short-term improvisation and spontaneity; the lack of a sense of personal political competence in the face of complex and seemingly omnipotent governing forces; the expectation, characteristic of paternalist societies, that favors will be dispensed from above without effort on the part of the receiver; and the absence of any sort of external or internal challenge that might trigger a sustained, collective response.*

---

* This last observation suggests that the mere existence of a greater variety of more differentiated interests is unlikely to produce greater group consciousness and orga-

I have attempted to operationalize several of the attitudinal dimensions suggested by the qualitative, "para-sociological" literature discussed above. At the end of a lengthy personal interview, associational leaders along with several control groups were asked to fill out a two-page questionnaire made up of 26 Likert-scaled items. Although the sample was not randomly selected, it was quite comprehensive, and I believe that the distributions obtained more or less represent the existing population of associational leaders.* I have therefore occasionally used chi-square to test the significance of differences between subsamples.

Traditionalism

The first general hypothesis the items were designed to test was that associability and interest leadership tend to go along with a pattern of less traditionalistic values. Fortunately, a scale measuring traditionalism-modernism in basic social values had already been developed and applied in the Brazilian setting by Joseph Kahl.[2] I merely appropriated from his pioneering work the ten items that I found most applicable. Owing to Brazil's historical continuity, of course, leaders could not be expected to completely reject premodern values. But it was expected that they would score low on such characteristics as personalism, fatalism, familism, fear of impersonal aggregates, and a sense of social and personal immobility. In general, the hypothesis seems confirmed. Brazilian associational leaders reported predominantly modernistic values.

Before turning to the detailed breakdowns, however, I should introduce another major hypothetical proposition that all the questions were designed to test. This is the frequently made assertion that fully enculturated participants in Brazil share a relatively similar set of operational political values. The descriptive literature suggests that, regardless of sphere of interest, class represented, type of region, or density of association, etc., the leaders should display substantial agreement based on common socialization experiences and voluntary acceptance of certain continuous and predominant norms of legitimate political activity.

---

nization in the absence of some challenge, such as the threat of foreign invasion or sharp class conflict. These precipitating factors were long absent from the Brazilian system. Territorial control was secure after the expulsion of the Dutch, and a slavocratic caste system prevented the formation of a class-based system of stratification until relatively late. With the end of slavery, owing to growing commercialization and bureaucratization, a class system begins to emerge. However, its originally slow and discontinuous development, coupled with the asynchronous, belated nature of industrialization, inhibited or prevented the adoption of a distinctive mode of political action or complex of social values by a new "modernizing elite."

* For a detailed discussion of the sample, as well as a complete list of the questions in English, see Appendix B, p. 400.

They may differ widely on immediate substantive issues, but they should agree on basic orientations.* Hence, the more often cross-tabulations by discriminant variables fail to turn up significant differences, the more this hypothesis is confirmed. Let us begin by considering variables relating to the nature of the associations and then examine cross-tabulations based on the personal characteristics of association leaders.

Only one question, "Making plans only brings unhappiness because plans are so difficult to realize," results in a significant difference between leaders of semiofficial syndicates and those of private or civil entities.† The leaders of civil entities take a less fatalistic and hence less traditionalistic position. When the response pattern is dichotomized, the relationship becomes weaker, but persists. None of the other responses to traditionalism questions exceeds the .05 level of confidence, indicating insignificant differences between the populations. The limited number of cases makes it usually unfeasible to control for third variables. In the instance just cited, for example, there was no control for class or sphere of interest. However, if only the employer associations are considered and then separated into syndical and private organizations, inferences can be drawn. Using this breakdown, we find that two traditionalism questions show significantly different distributions: the one mentioned above and one related to familism ("When looking for a job, one should find a place near one's parents, even if it means losing a good opportunity"). Again, if the categories are collapsed, the difference is shown to be smaller.

The data on traditionalism, then, strongly support both general hypotheses. Both syndical and private leaders express predominantly modern ideas with equal intensity, except when it comes to personal relations, when both agree equally (and, one might add, realistically) on their importance in contemporary Brazilian society. Syndicalists prove to be a bit more traditionalistic (and a bit more realistic) than

---

* Of course, the fact that the interviews were all conducted in "postrevolutionary" Brazil (1965–66) from which "radical" and "subversive" leadership elements had been purged strengthened my expectations of homogeneity. I have some reason to expect (on the basis of the student control group) that the distribution of operational political values during the latter half of Goulart's regime would have been much more varied.

† The difference between publicly registered syndicates (*sindicatos*) and private or civil entities (*entidades civis*) will be discussed in detail in the next chapter. In short, the former are established under the provisions of the Labor Code, are subsidized directly by an obligatory tax, and are subject to a variety of authoritative controls. The latter are formed independently, and, although many are or were indirectly subsidized by the government, their processes of leadership selection and interest expression are not so strictly controlled. Almost all workers' organizations are syndicates; employers and liberal professionals often have both syndicates and civil entities at their disposal.

private association leaders, but no substantial attitudinal differences exist that might make mutual comprehension and adjustment difficult.*

Class is perhaps the crucial test for the validity of the general propositions, since differences in property can generate substantial subcultural discontinuities within societies. Presumably, these discontinuities should be reflected in the opinions of interest representatives. In fact, as far as tradition is concerned, the data show class to be a differentiating factor of no greater importance than legal status. However, the few questions to which members of different classes responded with different answers were not the same. Table 4.1 shows how association leaders of three classes responded to four traditionalism questions. Not surprisingly, workers' leaders were much less sanguine than employers' leaders about the prospects for mobility, although the difference shows up primarily in the reserved "agree a little" category. In general, workers' leaders scored consistently, but not dramatically, higher on the traditionalist end of the scale. On the need for personal confidence, the responses were similar, although workers' leaders were slightly more aware of the need for *pistolão* (pull). The most interesting deviations, however, came from the middle-sector representatives (although unfortunately my interpretation is strained because there were only 11 respondents). They were completely and evenly divided on the possibilities for worker mobility, yet elsewhere they were more modernistic than either of the other types of class representatives. (Again the exception occurred when it came to questions related to personalism. Not a single middle-sector leader disagreed with the statement that one can have confidence only in those one knows well). My tentative conclusion is that workers' leaders are consistently more traditionalistic than employers' leaders, but that the general responses of the two groups are similar (the significance of the differences never exceeded the .07 level). Representatives of professional and administrative groups have much less consistent and rather more extreme attitudes. They have more activist values; they are extremely mobility-oriented, and they would

---

* For five of the items testing traditionalism, the median score was "disagree very much"; for three others, it was "disagree a little." Two questions elicited traditionalistic responses, and both were related to personalism: "You can have confidence only in those you know well," and "One must have good relations with influential people in order to progress in one's profession." Of the interest leaders interviewed, 36 percent agreed very much with the former, and 35 percent agreed a little with the latter. The homogeneity of response between syndical and private leaders persists even when there are controls for class of representation. Leaders of employers' syndicates are a bit more inclined to perceive (or to admit to) a more rigid stratification of life chances and to the need for confidence to be based on personalist criteria than are private employers' leaders. However, the latter tend slightly more to feel that pull (*pistolão*) is essential for getting ahead in life.

TABLE 4.1
INDICATORS OF TRADITIONALISM, BY SOCIAL CLASS

Statement and response categories	Employers (N = 85)	Middle sectors (N = 11)	Workers (N = 29)
1. "The son of a worker does not have much chance of getting into one of the liberal professions."			
Agree very much	21%	[36%]	24%
Agree a little	15	[9]	41
Disagree a little	25	[9]	21
Disagree very much	39	46	14
2. "In general, life is better in small cities, because everyone knows every one else."			
Agree very much	11	[18]	31
Agree a little	37	[36]	24
Disagree a little	18	[18]	14
Disagree very much	35	[27]	31
3. "When looking for a job, one should find a place near one's parents, even if this means losing a good opportunity."			
Agree very much	2	0	10
Agree a little	6	0	7
Disagree a little	19	[18]	31
Disagree very much	73	82	52
4. "One must have good relations with influential people in order to progress in one's profession."			
Agree very much	9	[9]	21
Agree a little	38	[18]	31
Disagree a little	27	[9]	14
Disagree very much	26	64	35

NOTE: Columns for each statement may not add to 100 because of rounding. Brackets denote percentages based on fewer than five cases. All percentages and base figures exclude those who either did not answer or said they had no answer.

at least like to think that efforts are rewarded on grounds of merit alone. What we can gather from the small number of respondents suggests that the middle sectors seem to be more nonconformist and outright confused in their political culture than any other group.

One might expect to find dramatic differences in the degrees of traditionalism expressed by members of the agricultural sector and the traditional merchant groups and by members of the modern sectors of industry and urban bureaucracy. Thus the specific sphere of interest represented by the association provides a further test for the thesis of homogeneous modernism. In fact the rural and commercial leaders did tend to score a bit higher on traditionalist questions, but again, the differences were not statistically significant. If there are two Brazils with two distinctive cultural subsystems—one rural and archaic and the other urban and modern—the split is not reflected in the attitudes of those formally chosen to represent these different sectors. Furthermore, whether the association is formally national or regional in scope has no measurable impact on traditionalist attitudes. Nor does the geographical location of the association's headquarters alter the pattern of responses significantly, although the sampling criteria excluded those groups working exclusively at the local and state levels. It seems that once they are engaged in making demands in the national political arena, their regional subcultural differences become obliterated and a national elite consensus predominates. Finally, the age of the association also seems to have little effect on traditionalism: in general, leaders of newer associations are neither more modernistic nor more traditionalistic than leaders of groups founded before World War II or even before 1930.

So far, my operationalization of Brazilian political cultural values lies open to one major challenge: the questions could be considered either so innocuous or so self-evident that all those interviewed would respond in a roughly similar manner. However, by introducing as control groups three subsamples, each of which holds a different position in the sphere of interest politics, I can test my major assumptions by comparison. Table 4.2 shows the responses of three such control groups, along with the responses of elected and administrative leaders, to questions measuring traditionalism. The first group consists of higher civil servants in the federal bureaucracy. Of the three subsamples, this is the only one that has been fully enculturated. This group can be expected to have been exposed to similar enculturative experiences as the interest representatives and to have participated (on the other side of the table) in similar negotiatory processes and exchanges of information and influence. Indeed, most of these higher civil servants were nominated for the subsample by the interest leaders themselves. The second group (the pretest sample) is made up of social science students. Younger, with less exposure to the enculturation process, and coming mostly from the radical National Faculty of Philosophy,[3] they could be expected to deviate sharply from the prevailing norms of compromise and accommodation. The third group affords an even greater contrast. It consists of some thirty students at the Instituto Cultural do Trabalho (ICT) in São Paulo attending a trade union leadership training course financed and run by the AFL-CIO's American Free Labor Development Institute. These trainees are lower-level activists, their average age is in the lower twenties, and they presumably do not yet have much influence in the decision-making process. Moveover, since they come from all over Brazil, the data they provide could somewhat correct the strong metropolitan bias of the general sample. Also, they are being self-consciously socialized to a set of norms that are somewhat incongruent with those described above as predominant in Brazilian interest politics. Finally they are of lower social status and educational attainment than any of the other populations.

In eight of the ten questions related to traditionalism, statistically significant differences were found between the samples exceeding the .04 level of confidence. Important divergences between the patterns of response appeared for the first time and, as predicted, these divergences were due principally to the answers of the social science student and ICT trainee control groups. The higher civil servants, with few exceptions, conformed to the pattern already observed among associational elites. The sole question on which all samples agreed was the very one that differentiated most effectively between types of associational respondents: "You can have confidence only in those you know well."

The elected and administrative officials of representative associations are quite similar in their predominantly modernistic attitudes, and the civil servants, exactly as anticipated, tend to share the same basic norms as the interest representatives who are placing demands upon them. The data suggest that interaction between interest group personnel and public bureaucrats rests on a foundation of considerable homogeneity of values. The interaction between political system elites and university students, by contrast, promises to be more tumultuous. Students are more modernistic concerning conformity, urbanism, and familism and more traditionalistic concerning personal and political fatalism, the need for personal relations with influentials, and especially mobility opportunities. Student traditionalism centers on instrumental variables involving opportunities for advancement and the potential rewards for personal effort. This probably reflects cynicism and alienation more than any underlying conservative desire for a return to past values. The ICT trainees, recruited from a lower status and more geographically dispersed population, reported very markedly less modern values. On every question but one they agreed more with traditionalist propositions than the other groups. The only items upon which a majority of trainees reported modern values were those related either to mobility at the expense of family ties or to fatalism. Again, the peculiar item was the personal trust question. Although the differences were not statistically significant, this was the only area in which the trainees came out more modernistic than the other groups. One could argue that since they, like the students, are not yet fully enculturated, they only dimly perceive the great importance of the network of exploitable personal contacts in the Brazilian system.

TABLE 4.2

INDICATORS OF TRADITIONALISM: ASSOCIATION LEADERS AND CONTROL GROUPS

Statement and response categories	Association leaders		Control groups		
	Elected (N = 73)	Adminis- trative (N = 56)	Higher civil servants (N = 35)	Students (N = 44)	ICT trainees (N = 30)
1. "To be happy one should do as others wish, even if it means not expressing one's own ideas."					
Agree very much	[3%]	[2%]	[3%]	0%	[10%]
Agree a little	12	14	[6]	18	43
Disagree a little	21	16	17	14	17
Disagree very much	64	68	74	68	30
2. "The son of a worker does not have much chance of getting into one of the liberal professions."					
Agree very much	25	23	[9]	46	36
Agree a little	16	18	20	25	26
Disagree a little	26	21	23	[5]	23
Disagree very much	33	38	49	25	16
3. "In general, life is better in small cities, because everyone knows everyone else."					
Agree very much	22	11	12	[7]	23
Agree a little	28	36	29	14	47
Disagree a little	17	21	29	23	13
Disagree very much	33	32	29	56	17
4. "When looking for a job, one should find a place near one's parents, even if this means losing a good opportunity."					
Agree very much	[3]	[4]	0	0	[13]
Agree a little	[6]	[5]	[9]	[2]	23
Disagree a little	29	14	20	23	17
Disagree very much	63	77	71	75	47
5. "People in large cities are cold and hard to get to know; it is difficult to make new friends."					
Agree very much	[7]	[7]	[9]	11	45
Agree a little	25	25	37	11	29
Disagree a little	18	25	23	25	[10]
Disagree very much	51	43	31	52	16
6. "These days, as things are, an intelligent person should worry about the present without bothering about what should happen tomorrow."					
Agree very much	[3]	0	[6]	[5]	3
Agree a little	[3]	[5]	[6]	14	23
Disagree a little	[6]	11	17	[9]	[13]
Disagree very much	89	84	71	73	61

TABLE 4.2 (*continued*)

Statement and response categories	Association leaders		Control groups		
	Elected (N = 73)	Adminis-trative (N = 56)	Higher civil servants (N = 35)	Students (N = 44)	ICT trainees (N = 30)
7. "It doesn't make much difference whether the people elect one candidate or another, because nothing is going to change."					
Agree very much	0	0	0	[5]	[7]
Agree a little	[4]	11	[6]	[5]	[13]
Disagree a little	7	[7]	[9]	[9]	[10]
Disagree very much	89	82	86	82	70
8. "You can have confidence only in those you know well."					
Agree very much	36	38	40	28	31
Agree a little	22	27	26	33	31
Disagree a little	25	20	20	19	[10]
Disagree very much	17	15	14	21	28
9. "One must have good relations with influential people in order to progress in one's profession."					
Agree very much	12	13	14	11	39
Agree a little	29	39	34	48	39
Disagree a little	18	27	23	19	[10]
Disagree very much	41	21	29	23	13
10. "Making plans only brings unhappiness, because plans are so difficult to realize."					
Agree very much	0	[2]	[3]	0	[7]
Agree a little	[1]	[4]	[9]	11	21
Disagree a little	21	16	23	14	17
Disagree very much	78	79	66	75	55

NOTE: Columns for each statement may not add to 100 because of rounding. Brackets denote percentages based on fewer than five cases. All percentages and base figures exclude those who either did not answer or said they had no answer.

Turning to the personal attributes of association leaders, one again does not find strong differences. Lower-status respondents are less sanguine about the prospects of mobility, but the lower and higher status groups are both less inclined to move away from their families for good job opportunities. Older leaders gave more traditionalistic responses than younger leaders, but the difference was not statistically significant enough to justify any conclusions about generational discontinuities or trends toward more modern attitudes over time. The student control groups of roughly similar status and urban origin did show very considerable deviation, but this hardly warrants any expectation that their attitudes will remain divergent once they become active participants in occupational associations or political parties. Education does produce a marked effect on two questions. Those with only primary schooling are noticeably more disposed to small-town life and to living near their parents.[4] The regional origin of the respondent (independent of where the association is located) has no significant impact on traditionalism. Nor does belonging or not belonging to a political party or having other associational membership or leadership posts.

Authoritarianism

The descriptive materials on Brazilian political culture are curiously ambiguous on the subject of authoritarianism. On the one hand, they stress the absolutist nature of patriarchalism and the asymmetric relationships inherent in paternalism. On the other hand, they stress the high degree of tolerance, civility, and respect for others. With this ambiguity in mind, I introduced three questions to measure authoritarianism. These questions are presented in Table 4.3. Item 3, coded inversely, was also used to construct a measure of the respondent's propensity for nonviolent resolution of conflicts. The assumption was that faith in the possibilities for what Brazilian politicians call *diálogo* is a prerequisite for a nonviolent attitude.

The legal status of the association has no significant effect on the distribution of responses, even when there are controls for class. Breaking down the responses by class representation discloses some differences, but they are still not statistically significant. Employers' and workers' leaders tend to agree with the first two statements and disagree with the third in roughly similar proportions. The middle sector leadership once again demonstrates its attitudinal schizophrenia with a markedly bimodal distribution. Likewise, the sphere of interest causes change in a predictable direction, but again, the change is not statistically significant. The urban industrial and commercial leaders respond quite similarly. Those from service occupations are a bit more authoritarian and yet more inclined to trust *diálogo*. More rural than civic-religious leaders agree that obedience and respect for authority are cardinal virtues. Rural leaders also tend to see a more polarized world and to feel that it is less worthwhile to discuss issues with one's opponents. Whether the association is formally national or regional in scope, whether its headquarters are in Rio or not, whether it has direct or indirect membership, whether the respondent has been in office more than four years or not—none of these considerations have a significant impact on authoritarian values.

A very marked difference does appear when the control groups are introduced. Only in the case of the second question does the significance of differences arise above five chances in a hundred. Otherwise, as was the case with traditionalism, the difference between those in the system (elected and administrative associational leaders and higher civil servants) is negligible, but those on the outside aspiring to get in are either much less authoritarian (as is the case with the students) or much more (as is the case with the trainees).

Personal variables such as education, status, regional origin, or activity in party affairs do not appear to have a strong impact upon authoritarian values. Age, however, does have an influence: older respondents definitely regard obedience and respect for authority as major virtues; younger people tend to disagree with the existence of a polarized world and to agree on the need for a dialogue of opposing views.

The data from our limited sample tend to confirm the descriptive generalities about authoritarianism. On the one end, there is general agreement that obedience and respect for authority are important values in the socialization process. However, the milder reaction to the proposition that the world is sharply divided into polarized clusters with great disparities in influence demonstrates a weakening of authoritarian values. Consensus again emerges on the third question, but in a predominantly nonauthoritarian direction. It is possible that although authoritarian values are strongly inculcated during basic socialization, especially within the patriarchally dominated family, later exposure teaches Brazilians that, as one respondent said, "the world is full of weak men and strong men, but some are strong in some things and weak in others. No one is strong all the time." Moreover, sheer survival in such a complex polity as the Brazilian forces a certain sense of tolerance upon the actors. The limited data also confirm that, as we saw in our discussion concerning

TABLE 4.3

INDICATORS OF AUTHORITARIANISM: ASSOCIATION LEADERS AND CONTROL GROUPS

(*percent agreeing "very much" or "a little"*)

Statement	Association leaders		Control groups		
	Elected (N = 72)	Administrative (N = 55)	Higher civil servants (N = 35)	Students (N = 41)	ICT trainees (N = 20)
1. "Obedience and respect for authority are the most important virtues a child has to learn."	73%	75%	75%	30%	95%
2. "There are two types of people in the world, the weak and the strong; and the latter will always run things."	49%	55%	47%	25%	33%
3. "It is not worth the trouble to debate with people whose ideas are very different from your own."	39%	30%	34%	21%	58%

NOTE: Those who either did not answer or said they had no answer were excluded from the distribution before the responses were dichotomized.

traditionalism, there is a substantial measure of inter-elite normative consensus, modified only slightly by the nature of the interests represented or by the type of association. It is modified only slightly more by the personal status, age, or regional origin of the respondent. This consensus drops off markedly, however, when imperfectly enculturated groups are compared with active participants.

Religiosity

Brazilians have been described as a deeply spiritual people; but, as we have seen, numerous observers have also remarked on the institutional weakness of the Church in Brazilian society. Two items on religiosity were designed to determine how Brazilians feel about religious values as an integral component of social order and about the political activities of religious authorities. As hypothesized, the general distribution tended to agree that "religion is a force indispensable to social harmony" (69 percent agreed very much), but they also agreed that "religious authorities should not interfere in the political life of the country" (55 percent agreed very much). Very little intervenes to disturb this pattern. Legal status has no impact. Class has very little. Representing rural interests makes one more aware of the indispensability of religion and less in favor of keeping religious authorities out of politics. Otherwise, the only associational variable with any impact is regional location. Rio-centered groups are less convinced of the essential need for religion and more convinced that the Church should stay out of politics.

Again, the only dramatic difference appears when the control groups are considered. The students are decisively less religious, both socially and politically. The ICT trainees score higher than the norm on both dimensions. For once, elected and administrative leaders differ a little. Higher civil servants are more secular, although not as strongly so as the students. The personal variables of education, status, regional origin, party activism, and membership in other associations have no significant effect. Age, however, has a great impact. Only 27 percent of the association leaders under thirty think religion and social harmony are closely related, whereas 95 percent of those over sixty agree very much. On the other hand, a substantial proportion of the younger respondents (27 percent) disagree that the Church should not interfere in politics, owing perhaps to the activities of a number of progressive Catholic groups prior to 1964 and the several Bishops' manifestos since the coup that have counseled revolutionary moderation.

Nationalism

The qualities we have discussed so far—traditionalism, authoritarianism, and religiosity—are products of the basic socialization process in Brazil.

Nationalism, however, primarily reflects a planned program of political indoctrination.

Three items on the questionnaire were used to measure nationalistic attitudes: "Brazilians can do anything as well as foreigners," "Foreign capital brings only benefits to the country" (scored inversely), and "Brazil should be independent of other countries regardless of the cost." Syndical leaders tend to give more nationalistic answers than private association leaders. For the first time in the tables, the class represented becomes a significant predictor. Workers' leaders are more nationalistic than employers' leaders concerning the innate capacity of Brazilians and the desire for independence, but they are slightly more favorable to foreign capital than employers' leaders. Spokesmen for the middle sectors again present a confused pattern, either more unevenly or more bimodally distributed than the others. Employers' leaders are most consistent, but are definitely wary of foreign capital. The type of interest represented has less impact. Rather surprisingly, rural leaders come out every bit as nationalistic as their colleagues. Not so surprisingly, representatives of commercial interests are more favorable to foreign investment and less autarchy-minded than those who watch over industrial interests. In no case, however, do the responses run in opposite directions.

They do, however, when the control groups are introduced. Student attitudes toward foreign capital run almost diametrically opposite to those of elected and administrative group leaders. They also clash with those of the ICT trainees, who are in favor of foreign capital. For once we have an issue on which the civil servants differ from the association leaders—but only slightly. On the other two nationalist items, while intensities of agreement differ, all groups express great confidence in the inherent capacity of Brazilians and the desirability of national independence.[5]

Representative elites from regional associations tend to be slightly more nationalistic, especially concerning foreign capital, than those from national associations. One variable with a marked effect upon these attitudes is the date of foundation. The older the association the less nationalistic the attitudes of its leaders (although the desire for independence at all costs is shared equally by leaders of organizations founded during and after the Vargas era). The pre-1930 group officials score lower on all three measures of nationalism. Although there is no close association between them, the duration of one's term in elective or administrative office tends to vary inversely with the nationalistic variables, suggesting the relative recentness of the emergence of such attitudes.

It is not surprising then, that among personal rather than associ-

TABLE 4.4
INDICATORS OF NATIONALISM, BY REGION

Statement and selected response	North and Northeast ($N = 26$)	Center East ($N = 29$)	Center South ($N = 82$)	South ($N = 14$)
1. "Brazilians can do anything as well as foreigners." Agree very much	89%	89%	80%	80%
2. "Foreign capital brings only benefits to the country." Disagree very much	23%	[6%]	17%	0%
3. "Brazil should be independent of other countries regardless of the cost." Agree very much	39%	48%	39%	50%

NOTE: Brackets denote percentage based on fewer than five cases. Those who either did not answer or said they had no answer were excluded from the distribution before the responses were dichotomized.

ational characteristics of the respondent, age has the greatest impact on nationalism. Older people who have experienced the great transformation of the Brazilian society and economy tend to affirm strongly the capacity of their fellow citizens to do anything, whereas younger respondents seem to be losing their nerve. The oldest age group is strongly in favor of foreign investment, the youngest equally opposed to it. Attitudes toward national autarchy seem to be curvilinear, sagging for middle-aged respondents.*

Other variables—education, status, regional origin, and party participation—do not affect nationalism as consistently as age does. The more educated are less favorable to foreign investment, but also rather less enthusiastic about costly autarchy, than the less educated. The upper-middle and middle-middle classes are both less nationalistic, especially on the issue of autarchy, than the lowest or the highest status groups. It has been suggested that this convergence from opposite ends of the prestige scale on the subject of nationalism provides the sociological basis for populist movements.[6] Regional origin of respondents seems to have even more random effect upon nationalism. As Table 4.4 shows, national self-confidence is relatively evenly distributed, but lowest in the South and Center-South, where Brazilians have best proven their

---

* This curvilinear effect may be the product of a poorly drafted question. Qualitative remarks made during the filling-in of the questionnaire led me to conclude that, although younger respondents would agree, desiring to cut existing ties of dependency, older respondents would interpret the question formalistically with comments such as "Of course, I agree. After all, we have been independent for almost one hundred and fifty years."

capacity to become industrial men! Suspicion of foreign capital is great-est in the Northeast, where there is the least of it. Desire for autarchy is greatest in the Center-East and the South, the two regions perhaps least subject to the vagaries of shifts in international trade. For the first time, a difference between party activists and nonactivists is detectable: they are similar on the first two questions, but on the third only 37 per-cent of nonmembers agree with independence at all cost, whereas 62 percent of those who report party membership support the proposition.

Pactualismo

The propensity of Brazilians for preferring and seeking nonviolent means to resolve their differences has, as we have seen, been one of the most frequently discussed characteristics of the country's political culture. I have argued that this is less a product of basic socialization than of ex-perience gathered from inter-elite contacts, and thus it does not apply to elite–mass relationships. Unfortunately, our sample does not permit a meaningful test of that hypothesis, but it does permit us to compare different elites and aspirant elites (see Table 4.5). The reader is also reminded that I can offer no evidence specifically linking reported atti-tudes with actual compromising behavior in situations of conflict.

Legal status does, for the first time, seem to make a difference. I would expect civil entities, which are less incorporated within the system, to be more oriented toward conflict and violence than the semiofficial syndicates. This is only partially the case. In fact, leaders of civil entities report slightly more support for the proposition that "in politics it is better to compromise than to fight,"* although they are also more likely to disagree with the statement "Controversies should never be resolved by violence." The relationship remains the same when there are controls for class representation. Class once again separates out the middle-sector representatives, who are much more in favor of compromise and nonviolence and slightly more in favor of dialogue. Employers, for a change, differ a bit from workers and are very slightly less supportive of pactualismo. The differences are not statistically significant, however. Sphere of interest makes no difference, except that, as the answers to the obversely coded dialogue question suggests, rural leaders are less

---

* The Portuguese version of this question, *"Na política, mas vale se entender do que brigar,"* contains a double entendre that pretesting and prior discussion with col-leagues in Rio had failed to turn up, but that made the question all the more indica-tive. *Se entender* in this context could mean either "to come to an agreement or understanding" or "to make a deal." The latter definition carries the inference that the deal is made at the expense of someone not a party to it. Either way it definitely implies a voluntary foregoing of one's interests or principles for the sake of avoiding greater hostility. Needless to say, it was not usually possible to discern when the respondents interpreted the question in constant- or expanding-sum terms.

likely to see virtue in abstaining from violence. They are, however, equally in favor of compromise. Formal geographic scope, regional location, and type of membership have no effect on the general distribution.

The major finding of this whole series of political attitudinal questions is again reaffirmed: significant differences do not emerge until the control groups are included. First, as Table 4.5 shows, there is a steady erosion in the reported propensity for compromise as on passes from elected group officials to administrative group officials to higher government employees. Once the "agree a little" responses are included, however, the differences evaporate, and there is no major difference between the three categories on the other two questions. Second, the ICT-trainees stand out as being very much in favor of compromise but rather ambiguous about violence and dialogue. Looking at the student responses (which show the strong deviance one might expect by now), one can read between the lines and imagine their dilemma. The elite norms of the society clearly support compromise and nonviolence; yet, with the

TABLE 4.5

INDICATORS OF PACTUALISMO: ASSOCIATION LEADERS AND CONTROL GROUPS

	Association leaders		Control groups		
Statement and response categories	Elected (N = 73)	Adminis- trative (N = 56)	Higher civil servants (N = 35)	Students (N = 43)	ICT trainees (N = 31)
1. "In politics it is better to compromise than to fight."					
Agree very much	62%	43%	38%	38%	83%
Agree a little	25	39	50	21	[13]
Disagree a little	[7]	[8]	[9]	12	0
Disagree very much	[7]	10	[3]	29	[3]
2. "Controversies should never be resolved by violence."					
Agree very much	81	75	83	47	61
Agree a little	8	13	14	16	29
Disagree a little	10	[7]	[3]	23	0
Disagree very much	[1]	[5]	0	14	[10]
3. "It is not worth the trouble to debate with people whose ideas are very different from your own."					
Disagree very much	50	46	40	54	29
Disagree a little	11	23	26	26	[13]
Agree a little	25	20	20	14	23
Agree very much	14	11	14	[7]	36

NOTE: Columns for each statement may not add to 100 because of rounding. Brackets denote percentages based on fewer than five cases. All percentages and base figures exclude those who either did not answer or said they had no answer.

students' different values, for example on nationalism, they are unlikely to be satisfied by conforming to those norms. For this reason, the questions on pactualismo divide up what has heretofore been a fairly cohesive bloc of opinion. As many students as civil servants would very much rather compromise than fight, but it is also true that a great many students would prefer very much to fight. In the case of the utility of violence the division among students is also marked. In both cases, however, the modal response is the same as that of the general sample.

The personal variables are important in explaining differing attitudes toward conflict resolution in Brazil. The middle-middle-status respondents emerge as the strongest supporters of pactualismo. The lower-middle strata are less inclined both to value compromise and to restrain from violence. The virtual absence of lower-status respondents in the sample prevents any extension of this generalization downward, but the trend seems to fit my hypothesis about the stratified nature of Brazilian pacifism. Increasing age tends to be associated with increasing stress on compromise and decreasing willingness to talk things over— hardly a viable operational code. Younger leaders are less enthusiastic about the virtues of self-limitation, but more open to listening to all sides. Support for using violence to obtain one's interests increases up to fifty years of age and then declines. Regional origin is an interesting variable to examine given the frequent observation that the style of Brazilian politics is heavily influenced by mineiros and bahianos (Brazilians from the Center-East). Fortunately, there are enough of them in higher representative posts in Rio and São Paulo to permit comparison. And, in fact, on the first two questions they express greater agreement than their colleagues from other regions. They are also above the norm concerning openness to opposite opinions, though they are not as open as those from the Northeast.

Corporatism

The values grouped under this heading are less systematically interrelated than the values we have examined so far. They were drafted on the basis of my reading of the descriptive literature in an attempt to measure several traits of Brazilian political culture that are allegedly prominent but whose logical interconnection has remained obscure. These traits all relate to a world view that stresses a hierarchical and harmonious structure of distinct social groups. The social groups are linked vertically to the upper strata, or at least the governing authorities, who in turn have a special asymmetrical responsibility for the well-being of those below them. I have therefore called the aggregate of these traits corporatism, though I have not yet argued that it forms a cohesive value system. In terms of the enculturation process, these values are the most likely of any we have examined to reflect actual experience in political activity and formal indoctrination. Therefore, one might expect the distribution of responses to vary considerably. One might also expect it to be more conditioned by the nature of the social group or association represented than by the personal characteristics of the respondents. These have already been shown to be more important in predicting attitudinal differences inculcated earlier in the enculturation process. I have operationalized what I call corporatism with a set of six questions, which have been grouped into several subcategories: elitism, paternalism, and social, governmental, and constitutional corporatism. Each of these subcategories will be discussed independently.

Elitism. This is measured by a single question: "The political decisions in this country are always made by a small and closed group, and the average citizen never has much influence." Most of the association leaders agree with this statement; 41 percent agree very much, and 35 percent agree a little. Legal status has little effect, although when there are controls for class the private associational leaders are more inclined than the syndicate leaders to perceive the decisional system as restricted. Workers' representatives are much more likely to agree strongly than are employers' leaders, and the middle sector shows its customary schizophrenia (46 percent agree a little, 27 percent agree a lot, and 27 percent disagree a lot). Those who represent commercial and service interests and civic or religious attitudes are more likely to argue that the system is open than are those from either industrial or rural associations. The control groups again provide the major contrast. Students see access as quite limited; the trainees hardly differ from the norm. For once, administrative and elected leaders differ; the former are more conscious of restricted access than the latter. Regional scope, type of membership, date of foundation, and length of term in office do not seem to make one markedly more or less sensitive to political elitism. The location of the association's headquarters does, however. Faith in the common man's influence over politics is stronger in the more developed regions of the country than it is in the less developed regions. Personal variables also influence views on elitism. As education rises, so does the belief (or the self-deception) that the ordinary citizen's voice is heard. (However, those with higher vocational training—priests and military officers, for example—express the strongest elitist perceptions.) Similarly, increase in status makes one feel that the system is more open. Other personal characteristics have only a moderate impact, except for party membership. Being active in partisan politics apparently makes one less aware of the potential influence of ordinary folk than does participation in representative associations: 83 percent of the party activists, as contrasted with 71 percent of those denying membership in any party, felt that the common man hasn't much influence over elite decisions.

Paternalism. "More fortunate social groups have the duty to look after the well-being of the less fortunate" and "The government should help persons from less favored classes enter into occupations of higher prestige" are items designed to measure social and political paternalism respectively. Brazilian leaders are unquestionably paternalistic on the whole: 78 percent of the total associational sample agree with the former, 57 percent with the latter. Legal status has no effect on social paternalism, even when there are controls for class. It does, however, affect political paternalism: syndical leaders are definitely more in favor of public largess than are leaders of private associations. Workers and employers express similar support for both propositions; and, somewhat surprisingly, the middle-sector representatives come out the most paternalistic of all, both privately and publicly. The least socially paternalistic are the industrial leaders (only 69 percent agree very much); the most are the civic-religious and rural leaders (93 and 86 percent respectively agree very much). The representatives of commerce are socially paternalistic, but quite opposed to government intervention, as are the civic-religious leaders. Rural leaders are strong on both; industrialists are lukewarm on both. Die-hard opponents of welfare statism are hard to find: they make up only 13 percent of the industrial spokesmen and only 8 percent of the association leaders as a whole.

A comparison of association leaders and the control groups as presented in Table 4.6, shows the first break in the otherwise rather con-

TABLE 4.6
INDICATORS OF PATERNALISM: ASSOCIATION LEADERS AND CONTROL GROUPS
(*percent agreeing "very much" or "a little"*)

	Association leaders		Control groups		
			Higher		
		Adminis-	civil		ICT
	Elected	trative	servants	Students	trainees
Statement	($N = 72$)	($N = 56$)	($N = 44$)	($N = 35$)	($N = 32$)
1. "More fortunate social groups have a duty to look after the well-being of the less fortunate."	90%	89%	86%	47%	97%
2. "The government should help persons from less-favored classes enter into occupations of higher prestige."	83%	81%	83%	78%	93%

NOTE: Those who either did not answer or said they had no answer were excluded from the distribution before the responses were dichotomized.

sistently paternalistic facade. Association leaders, both elected and appointed, and senior civil servants agree with both these statements, although on the question of political paternalism the government employees agree a little less. The trade union trainees believe very strongly in both types of elite favoritism. Students, however, are less socially than politically paternalistic. Only about half of them agree very much with the first statement, and only 60 percent with the second—by far the lowest of all group responses.

Other associational variables modify responses only slightly. Leaders of the newer associations are more paternalistic than those of older ones. Leaders of groups with headquarters in São Paulo are less enthusiastic about welfare statism than leaders of groups with headquarters in Rio or in the interior. The personal variables, to my surprise, have a strong impact on both types of paternalist attitudes. Paternalism decreases steadily with education. Private paternalism is affected in a curvilinear manner by status: the lower and upper strata are more paternalistic than the middle. Public paternalism, however, is inversely related to status. Paternalism seems to increase with age and to decrease with the rise in the level of development of one's region of origin. Leaders from the Center-South, especially leaders of associations based in São Paulo, show a slightly more ruthless attitude toward the less favored. Party activists, on the other hand, are less tough-minded: 97 percent accepted the social obligation, and 90 percent accepted the political obligation. (Of the non-party-members tested, 90 percent agreed with the former, and 85 percent with the latter.)

Basically, corporatism is a belief in and acceptance of a natural hierarchy of social groups, each with its ordained place and its own set of perquisites and responsibilities. These "orders" have and accept voluntary restrictions on their autonomy and horizontal interaction. They are seen as linked by vertical lines of subordination directly to higher social institutions, which are conceded the right and the duty to intervene in intergroup conflicts for the sake of social peace.* Although corporatism stresses the immutability of the social and political order, it by no means precludes individual mobility or the participation of newly formed interest associations, provided such associations accept certain limitations on their autonomy and patterns of interaction. As an

---

* As Nestor Duarte and others have observed, this world view is rooted in the tendency of the actors to regard the political order as a sort of overgrown family or aggregate of families with essentially the same principles of authority and organization. As we have seen, Brazilian corporatism appears to be strongly associated with elitism and paternalism; and, through its deliberate confusion or obfuscation of the distinction between public and private, it seems to produce endemic nepotism and corruption.

effective, conservative ruling ideology, corporatism may minimize the impact of a more differentiated social and economic order, but it does not prevent its development.

Social Corporatism. "People are born into social groups, each of which has different capacities; for this reason, people should have different duties and rights." This question was designed to measure social corporatism. Viewed in retrospect, it seems poorly drafted. It is too long and intellectual, and too far removed from the subject matter of daily political discourse in Brazil. In short, it tended to create opinion rather than measure attitudes already salient. The question was also too extreme. Numerous respondents read it aloud, nodding in agreement until they reached the last word. The notion of formal political equality of rights seems very strongly ingrained. Had the proposition stopped at duties, it might have attracted many more favorable responses.

Nevertheless, the responses do indicate differential support in anticipated directions. For example, when there are controls for class of representation, 61 percent of the employers' syndical leaders disagree very much, whereas 79 percent of the private leaders disagree very much. Workers' leaders (virtually all syndicalist) favor social corporatism more than employers' leaders; middle-sector and civic interest officials recognize and favor greater inequality than do industrialist leaders. There are, as usual, few differences between elected and appointed association personnel, and the students are massively opposed. The civil servant sample again lies between these two, but closer to the interest officials. The ICT trainees—lower-status young people from small towns all over Brazil—are by far the most socially corporatist: 50 percent agree with the proposition. Representatives of associations that are formally national in scope and are headquartered in Rio de Janeiro support the proposition more strongly than those of regional associations whose headquarters are outside of Rio. The age of the association affects responses in an unanticipated way. Leaders of groups founded before 1931, when corporatism became the basis of public policy, tend to agree less than leaders of groups founded during the Vargas dictatorship; but those whose associations began their operations after 1945, when corporatism was officially replaced, tend to agree more strongly. Though this cannot be considered evidence of a cumulative political learning experience, it does indicate that there has been no weakening of corporatist ideals and no tendency for the newly formed groups to break radically with the past by opting for more liberal norms. Neither length of term in office nor the holding of prior positions alters the pattern of response: recent and less experienced actors seem to have the same values as the old-timers.

TABLE 4.7
INDICATOR OF SOCIAL CORPORATISM, BY AGE
(*percent agreeing "very much" or "a little"*)

	Age group				
Statement	20–29 (N = 11)	30–39 (N = 44)	40–49 (N = 49)	50–59 (N = 40)	60 + (N = 23)
"People are born into social groups, each one of which has different capacities; for this reason, people should have different duties and rights."	27%	25%	14%	20%	30%

NOTE: Those who either did not answer or said they had no answer were excluded from the distribution before the responses were dichotomized.

Personal variables influence social corporatism more noticeably. Those with a university or technical education are much less corporatist on this question. Likewise, rising status is accompanied by declining corporatism. The impact of age seems rather uneven, as Table 4.7 indicates. There is an interesting trough in social corporatism among those in their forties and perhaps early fifties. This is the age group that attained its political maturity immediately after the Estado Novo, and they could well have been affected by the anti-fascist and pro-liberal ideas of the postwar period. In any case their reaction seems to have been a passing phenomenon.

Governmental corporatism. This is measured by responses to the statement "The government should act as arbitrator between employers' associations and workers' syndicates in the interest of social harmony." This is no farfetched, opinion-creating question; it is in fact a restatement of the orthodox rationale behind the existing pattern of interest politics in Brazil, and to disagree with it is to disagree with a system of group interaction that has evolved over the last thirty-five years.

In fact, most respondents do agree with the proposition, and in all but a few categories they agree very much. For the first time, however, a significant difference emerges from the different legal types of associations. As Table 4.8 shows, syndical leaders are in favor of governmental intervention to keep things on an even keel, although 35 percent are a bit guarded in their enthusiasm. We might have expected this favorable response. We are surprised to find, however, that an even greater percentage of private leaders are very much in favor, although a significant minority is very much opposed. If only employers' leaders are considered, the difference in distribution is even more apparent. Government corporatism is also an issue that divides classes of representation: employers like the existing scheme very much, workers' representatives are almost equally divided between liking it very much and

TABLE 4.8

INDICATOR OF POLITICAL CORPORATISM, BY AFFILIATION

Statement and response categories	Affiliation	
	Syndical association (N = 78)	Private association (N = 60)
"The government should act as arbitrator between employers' associations and workers' syndicates in the interest of social harmony."		
Agree very much	58%	63%
Agree a little	35	17
Disagree a little	[3]	[5]
Disagree very much	[5]	15

NOTE: Columns may not add to 100 because of rounding. Brackets denote percentages based on fewer than five cases. All percentages and base figures exclude those who either did not answer or said they had no answer.

liking it a little, and the middle-sector leaders, as usual, include both strong proponents and strong opponents. A majority of all three categories, however, approve the proposition. None of the classes reject it so decisively as to make a really definite break with present practice. The sphere of interest also seems to influence responses. Tertiary-sector representatives are most in favor, followed by civic-religious leaders, industrialists, and agriculturists. The only sphere for which there is not a clear majority very much in favor of government intervention is the commercial sector. Only 42 percent of their officials took this position, and some 31 percent disagreed. None of the other associational variables—geographic scope, location of headquarters, type of membership, term in office, previous positions—are associated with a significant change in the pattern of response, except date of foundation. Table 4.9 suggests that officials of those organizations founded during the Estado

TABLE 4.9

INDICATOR OF POLITICAL CORPORATISM, BY AGE OF RESPONDENT'S ASSOCIATION

(*percent agreeing "very much" or "a little"*)

Statement	Period Association Founded		
	1930 or earlier (N = 22)	1931–44 (N = 36)	1945 or later (N = 73)
"The government should act as arbitrator between employers' associations and workers' syndicates in the interest of social harmony."	73%	94%	88%

NOTE: Those who either did not answer or said they had no answer were excluded from the distribution before the responses were dichotomized.

Novo are more likely to regard government corporatism as normal and desirable practice. The only personal variable that has any noticeable effect on official corporatism is regional origin (and even its effect is not statistically significant). Those from the Center-South are less strongly in favor of institutionalized intervention than those from the North, the Northeast, the Center-East, and the South.

The control groups, however, do make a difference. The civil servants come out very corporatist (80 percent agree very much), more than the administrative interest group personnel (66 percent) or their elected superiors (57 percent). The students are only lukewarm supporters of government interference, although a majority (53 percent) support it. However, one quarter of the students disagree very much with the idea. The ICT trainees are especially interesting on this question, since they were being instructed in a doctrine of interest-group activity that stressed relative official abstinence and independent collective bargaining between autonomous actors. This indoctrination seems to have been partially successful: 26 percent (the lowest of any subcategory by far) agree very much, 29 percent agree a little, 19 percent disagree a little, and 26 percent disagree very much. If these nonconformist attitudes persist once the ICT trainees have entered important positions in the universe of interest politics, there will be a discernible break in what are now homogeneous attitudes toward this aspect of the political process.

Constitutional corporatism. "The political process would be better if the representatives were elected by their occupational groups rather than by parties." This question, designed to measure constitutional corporatism, was of some immediate relevance, since existing political parties were abolished during the course of the interviewing. (The party system was not, however, replaced by a professional or corporatist system of representation.) On the other hand, the response pattern was somewhat marred by the tendency of older respondents to answer "But we tried that before," to which they occasionally added, "and it didn't work." The younger respondents, especially the student sample, tended to see the proposal in terms of a leftist syndicalist republic. There seemed to be no way of redrafting the question to prevent such a contrary ideological contamination, although an agreement in either case did in fact imply a manifestly corporatist position.

Overall, almost 50 per cent of the associational respondents disagree very much with the proposition, and 40 percent agree with it. Syndical leaders are about evenly split between support and opposition, whereas private association leaders as a whole are opposed, even when controls for class of representation are introduced. Perhaps the latter fear that corporatist representative positions would be restricted to officially certified organizations, as was the case in the 1934–37 experience. Workers' representatives are strongly in favor of their obtaining such a guaranteed position: two-thirds agree to the proposition. By contrast, only one-third of the employers' leaders and one-third of the middle-sector officials are in favor. Rural and service spokesmen are slightly more supportive than urban industrial spokesmen. National organizations are no more in favor than regional ones, although those in Rio de Janeiro agree more than those in São Paulo. (São Paulo, with its greater proportion of private associations and its greater distance from the centers of national decision-making, exhibits more liberal political values.) Federated organizations are no more manifestly corporatist than organizations with direct membership.

In spite of the fact that many of the respondents' organizations owe their existence and continued financial support to the earlier experiment with professional representation, a breakdown by date of foundation reveals an extremely even rate of response from all three categories. Length of term in office, however, does influence the response. Ex-leaders and those with less than two years on the job like the idea of changing the system of formal representation more than leaders who are now in at least their second term of office. This is a bit puzzling, since those with such tenure, especially the associational oligarchs with more than four years on the job, would be most likely to profit personally from such a change. Personal attributes of the respondent have a strong effect on his attitudes toward constitutional corporatism. Favorable response declines steadily and markedly with rise in education and status, but not with age. The youngest respondents are the least agreeable to the suggestion; the oldest are the most agreeable.

Again, the control groups provide the best test of the general homogeneity of attitudes toward the proposition. The civil servants are by far the strongest opponents of corporatist representation: only 14 percent agree even a little. This may be because they fear that such a system would threaten their job autonomy, security, or political representation, since government employees are prohibited from forming or joining sindicatos. Administrative and elected officials of the associations are, as usual, identical in their patterns of agreement; 38 percent of both favor the proposition. For the first time, the responses of the students and the ICT trainees are virtually identical, and both are easily the strongest supporters of manifest corporatism. The ICT trainees probably feel that such a scheme would open up new and attractive career opportunities for them. The student response is very likely due more to disillusionment with the party system than to enthusiasm about corporatism. Student corporatism may also be the by-product of their desire for what was loosely called a "syndicalist republic," in which certain progressive forces were to be granted direct and permanent access to the highest councils of government and to be used as agents in carrying out basic reforms. At any rate, the students, who have demonstrated the least support for social or government corporatism, and who in their performances on the political cultural questionnaire have scored low on traditionalism, authoritarianism, religiosity, and nonviolence, can find in corporatist representation a suitable political strategy for coping with their problems. This suggests that corporatism is indeed a flexible operative ideology. It cannot be considered exclusively left or exclusively right, exclusively traditional or exclusively modern. It seems to provide a lowest common denominator upon which a great variety of social groups can agree for a great variety of reasons.

An Overview

Analysis of the responses to individual questions about political culture has shown that to a remarkable degree the historical and descriptive literature led me to the correct anticipations. The major orienting hypotheses on both the content and the homogeneity of the responses stand confirmed, and (although the sample is admittedly not a random one) the dramatic contrast between the interest association leaders and civil servants on the one hand and the students and ICT trainees on the other provides additional comparative evidence of the significance of the findings. In order to summarize these findings, I have calculated an aggregate score or index for each of the attitudinal categories: traditionalism, authoritarianism, religiosity, nationalism, *pactualismo*, and corporatism. These scores have been in turn collapsed into "high," "medium," and "low."

At the conventional .05 level of confidence, few statistically significant differences in patterns of response emerge until the control groups are introduced. Even then, the civil servants differ from associational leaders only on corporatism (admittedly an important index): 38 percent of the elected and 30 percent of the appointed interest officials score high on corporatism, whereas only 17 percent of the civil servants are in that category. Different associational variables, of course, affect different attitudinal categories. The social class represented affects nationalism and corporatism: in both cases, workers' leaders score higher by some 20 percent than employers' leaders, and the middle-sector representatives are the most nationalistic of all, with 73 percent receiving a high score. The sphere of interest seems to influence corporatist attitudes: rural, service, and civic leaders get high scores (57, 53, and 64 percent respectively), whereas industrialists and merchants fall predominantly in the medium range (73 and 85 percent). Other differences are less important. Provincially located association leaders are a bit more religious than those located in Rio, and elected leaders are a bit more authoritarian than those they appoint. The longer the associational leader has been in office the less nationalistic he is likely to be. Interestingly, those who have been in office only one or two years and those who have recently retired or are temporarily among the outs report the most corporatist views.

Personal attributes seem to have a somewhat greater influence than associational characteristics on the political cultural values of respondents. Increased age makes them more authoritarian and definitely less nationalistic. Status, rather surprisingly, has little effect on responses, perhaps because of the unsatisfactory method used to assess that independent variable. Education tends to be associated with decreasing corporatism. Regional origin and study abroad have no significant relationship. What the respondent does outside his association clearly influences his political cultural values. Those with two or more jobs in addition to their associational position, for example, are significantly less traditionalistic. Those who have held at least one federal government position are more corporatist, but they also score lower on the propensity for nonviolence. Party membership has little effect, but leadership in additional associations goes with increased religiosity (if only because the additional associations are frequently religious ones).

The average associational respondent can be described as follows: He is strongly modernistic, and the only thing preventing him from becoming completely so is his abiding tendency to accord confidence on personal grounds and his continuing respect for the need to know influential people in order to get ahead. He is moderately religious: he believes that religion is necessary to society, but he would rather the Church stayed out of politics. His moderate authoritarianism is tempered by his strong belief in the virtues of nonviolent resolution of conflict and in the desirability of continuing dialogue between opponents. His nationalism is also tempered. Although he has great faith in the innate capacity of his countrymen, he is rather wary of the risks connected with going it alone in world politics. On the subject of foreign capital, his mind is especially divided. Although he is by no means a liberal pluralist, he does not overtly approve of differential political rights or of corporatist systems of representation. He does, however, concede the government a definite right to intervene in group conflict for the sake of systemic harmony. The average associational leader recognizes (although he may not like it) that popular influence upon societal decision-making is slight, and he somewhat makes up for this by his strong faith in private and public paternalism. He is, in short, very much the way those unsystematic, descriptive, and nonquantitative social thinkers had warned us he would be.

I shall conclude by describing how these various attitudinal scales

TABLE 4.10
RANK AND PRODUCT-MOMENT CORRELATIONS BETWEEN COLLAPSED
AND UNCOLLAPSED SCORES FOR SIX ATTITUDINAL SCALES

Attitudinal scale	1	2	3	4	5	6
			Gamma values (collapsed scores) above the diagonal			
1. Traditionalism		.399	.176	.148	− .057	.485
2. Authoritarianism	.336		.485	− .283	− .263	.485
3. Religiosity	.127	.344		− .373	.293	.240
4. Nationalism	.041	− .210	− .280		.156	.169
5. Pactualismo	− .102	− .094	.198	− .124		.051
6. Corporatism	.340	.311	.154	.143	.171	
		Product-moment values (uncollapsed scores) below the diagonal				

relate to each other, this time using the data from all respondents. On Table 4.10 the values above the diagonal represent the gamma ordinal correlations between the collapsed scores, and those below the line represent the product-moment correlations between the original, uncollapsed scores. The two measures show very similar relationships. Traditionalism is strongly related to authoritarianism and corporatism, as expected, but weakly related to religiosity and nationalism. The propensity for pactualismo varies independently of traditionalism. Authoritarianism correlates positively with corporatism and religiosity (and, as we have seen, with traditionalism) and negatively with nationalism and pactualismo. The more religious tend to be less nationalistic and more in favor of pactualismo. The high corporatists, besides being more traditionalistic and authoritarian, are also more religious and nationalistic. There is a surprisingly weak relationship between propensity for pactualismo and both traditionalism and corporatism, although the product-moment correlation between the uncollapsed scores does show a significant association between religiosity and corporatism.

The positive relationships just described are presented in Figure 2 in

FIG. 2. THE FORMATION AND MAINTENANCE OF CORPORATIST ATTITUDES.

a way that shows how the various political values help form and maintain Brazil's corporatist attitudes toward the political process. Traditionalism and religiosity would seem to be basic values relatively unrelated to each other. Both, however, are strongly associated with authoritarianism, which in turn is positively linked with corporatism. Nationalism is weakly associated with the other antecedent variables, but it seems to make an independent contribution to corporatism. Religiosity may also be linked to corporatism by way of its positive relationship with pactualismo. The fact that so many negatively correlated or unrelated attitudinal syndromes are in some way positively associated with corporatism hints at both its ideological inconsistency and its capacity for accommodating actors with diverse motives and values. This may explain why corporatism has had such a persistent impact upon the pattern of public policy.

FIVE

Public Policy Toward
Freedom of Association

Freedom of association may be a beautiful thing in principle,
but experience has shown that if taken too liberally it can do
more harm than good.   OLIVEIRA VIANNA

ALTHOUGH Oliveira Vianna apparently had read Tocqueville, there is
no evidence that the above quotation was inspired by the Frenchman's
observation, in his chapter on political associations, that freedom of
association was "la dernière qu'un peuple puisse supporter." Rather,
Oliveira Vianna was reflecting on his personal experience, both as a
social thinker and as a political activist. Faced with the emergence of
the new types of intermediary political associations, traditional ruling
elites tend to find the new freedom dangerous and subversive. For this
reason, they consciously and frequently use their control of the state
apparatus to modify the "free" rate of association formation and the
channels of permissible interest expression.

The pattern of a government's policy toward freedom of association
is most usefully treated as an independent variable that intervenes between development and associability. Such intervention by authority
groups can vary from outright control to complete permissiveness or
spontaneity. Between these extreme points is a policy of sponsorship,
whereby authorities in effect follow a mixed pattern, both facilitating
political associations and imposing limits on them. Basically, there are
two kinds of sponsorship: authorities can control freedom to create and
organize political associations; or, once such associations are formed,
authorities can control their freedom to make demands.[1]

Figure 3 is a matrix juxtaposing the degrees of control exerted by authorities over political associations and the two kinds of freedom that
the authorities control. The FF box represents the pure liberal, spontaneous pattern, more often discussed than experienced. In this type, the
structure of associations is likely to be decentralized and maintained by
competitive interaction. Political groups are freely permitted to organize and are given access commensurate with their representative

Ability to make independent demands

	Free	Controlled
Free	FF Spontaneous Liberalist	FC "Natural" Corporatist
Controlled	CF "Artificial" Corporatist	CC Controlled Collectivist

Ability to Organize

FIG. 3. AUTHORITATIVE POLICIES TOWARD ASSOCIABILITY.

strength and organizational capacity. In the CC box, or the pure collectivist pattern, an authority group—usually a revolutionary elite—controls very tightly the creation and activities of all political associations. The structure of associations is usually monolithic rather than dispersed, and different associations are held together by centralized coordination and coercion. Participation is permitted, even encouraged, but access is limited by the ruling group, which consequently enjoys a large measure of decisional autonomy. In studying the relationship between development and associability in such a system, this pattern of policy is the key variable. In the purely spontaneous one, it can be largely discounted. The two mixed boxes distinguish between two different policies of sponsorship. The FC box represents a pattern that I call "natural corporatism." Authority groups do not control the formation of political associations, but do place limitations on their access and participation. The reverse is true of "artificial corporatism," represented by the CF box: the state sponsors the creation of certain groups and then grants them a degree of internal autonomy and freedom of participation. In both corporatist types the associations become, in fact if not in law, semiofficial bodies, whereas in the FF model they are outside or private entities, and in the CC model they are fully official and public. The scheme represented by this matrix implies hypothetically that the pattern of policy adopted will have an important impact upon the structure of emerging associations and upon the patterns of interaction among them. In particular, policy will determine whether groups will be centralized or decentralized, and whether they will be related to one another in an atmosphere of competition or coordination.

Concrete policies rarely correspond exactly to the above simplified models. Frequently a given political system may apply all the patterns of policy at the same time. In the case of certain associations, literary societies and fraternal orders for example, it may abstain from any controls. Some preexistent representative associations, such as merchants' associations, it may co-opt and thereby at least partially control. To others, for example emerging employers' associations, it may give an initial helping hand in the hope of ensuring subsequent loyalty and later leave them unfettered. In particularly sensitive areas like workers' groups, the authorities may find it necessary for their own survival to create the new groups and continue to control their activities. Of course they may respond by exercising the strictest control possible, i.e. by suppressing incipient group formation altogether.

Government Policy Before 1943

The government policy toward representative associations in Brazil has been and continues to be quite eclectic. Although from time to time the extremes of both permissiveness and rigid control have been practiced, most of the policy has followed a mixed pattern. The federal republican Constitution of 1891 was the first in Latin America to grant unrestricted freedom of association and assembly.[2] Before this time there had been a few employers' associations and workers' mutual aid organizations, but society had been undifferentiated and work relations had been governed by the norms of slavery. Thus, though the Constitution of 1891 was a manifestation of liberal attitudes, no apparent need was felt for an explicit and detailed statement of policy until 1903. Disrupted by Abolition and hoping to attract foreign labor, the landowners met in a National Congress of Agriculture (1902) and petitioned the legislature for recognition of their right to organize. The resulting law, strongly influenced by Catholic ideology and French legislation, permitted the organization of rural associations, federations, and central unions.[3] Although the policy was designed to help create mixed owner-worker (*paritário*) organizations, in fact it benefited only landowners.[4] In 1907 the right of association in sindicatos* was extended to all professionals, including members of the liberal professions. Strongly influenced by the French Waldeck-Rousseau Law of 1884, this decree went further than that of 1903. It diminished the number of required formalities, guaranteed autonomy of activity, allowed voluntary membership, and placed no restrictions on the number of sindicatos representing the same profession or interest sector. The most interesting feature of the bill, in retrospect, was Article 8: "The sindicatos that

---

* In order to insist on the difference between this type of association and what is called in English a labor or trade union, I will refer to them throughout as sindicatos or syndicates.

establish themselves in the spirit of harmony between employers and workers, in other words those with permanent councils for concilia- tion and arbitration designed to settle disputes between capital and labor, will be considered legal representatives of the *whole class* of working men and, as such, will be consulted on all matters pertaining to the profession." (Italics mine.) In these provisions (which to my knowledge never produced any concrete results) one can already see the hallmark of corporatism: the exchange of a legal monopoly on rep- resentation and a guaranteed access to decision-makers in return for compliance with certain limitations on behavior.

Until 1931 there was no substantial legal change in the freedom to associate. There was, however, an important policy change. As we shall see, the first decades of the twentieth century were marked by an up- surge in working-class associability and combativeness of an anarchist sort, culminating in the first general strike in 1917. On the one hand, this resulted in a growing concern with "the social question," especially by humanitarian socialist legislators, and the passage of a few welfare measures.[5] Perhaps most important, it resulted in the firm establishment of the federal government's power "to legislate about labor."[6] On the other hand, the federal and state executives responded to the threat with repressive measures.[7] Various decrees were passed for the repres- sion of anarchists (1921) and Communists (1927). By contrast, there is no evidence prior to 1930 that any such controls were placed upon employers' associations.

From 1930 to 1937, the pattern of policy toward interest representa- tion in particular and toward "the social question" in general went through a period of experimental innovation and modification. From the Estado Novo coup of 1937 until 1943, it became increasingly con- sistent, culminating in the promulgation of the Consolidation of the Brazilian Labor Laws (CLT), the provisions of which continue to con- trol the system of semiofficial interest representation. The corporatist ideologues of this period loudly insisted that all this innovation in wel- fare legislation was purely the paternalistic personal gift of a benevo- lent leader to whom all should be duly thankful.[8] Recently, the truth of these claims has been increasingly questioned. Everardo Dias, a working-class militant of this early period, argues that almost all the so-called gifts of the Labor Code had already been won in earlier class struggles.[9] Evaristo de Moraes Filho, Brazil's foremost contemporary labor lawyer, in reviewing the parliamentary debates and the work of the Parliamentary Commission on Social Legislation, concludes that it would be a historical injustice to accept the official line that the Revolu- tion of 1930 entered an institutional vacuum. There was a tradition both of organized worker protest and of legislative concern. The new authoritarian regime merely continued, at first hesitantly, along preestablished lines.[10]

There was, however, an important difference. Authority groups began self-consciously to implement a policy that might be called "preemptive co-optation."

> The social problem in Brazil is not the consequence of a conflict between the workers on the one hand and governing classes on the other. Such demands as the workers may have put forward in the past have never been backed by an organized movement, grouping the majority of wage earners, and still less by a political party represented in Parliament and possessing adequate means to influence public opinion. Brazilian social legislation was not imposed out of fear of a subversive movement; it was introduced spontaneously by the Government, which realized its political and economic importance from the point of view of preserving social peace.[11]

This policy is an almost perfect example of what we have called "artificial corporatism." The state sponsors, creates, and supports the emergence of representative associations before they can emerge by themselves, for the reason that structural differentiation has not yet proceeded far enough. Out of gratitude for this gesture of preemptive co-optation, "instead of acting as a negative force hostile to public authority, [they] should become useful elements of cooperation with the ruling mechanism of the state."[12] Artificial corporatism by means of preemptive co-optation requires: the creation of a set of legal norms governing the formation of representative associations; a set of rewards and punishments to reinforce the norms; sufficient authority to administer the rewards and punishments; and a set of institutionalized channels of representation that will provide at least a simulacrum of access and accountability. It took some years for artificial corporatism to become fully established, but its success is evidenced by its subsequent resistance to further modification.

The first step came only a month after the Revolution with the creation of the Ministry of Labor, Industry, and Commerce (MTIC). As a result, "All labor matters came to rotate around a single organ."[13] In 1931 the first of the comprehensive syndicalization laws was decreed, replacing the liberal pluralist law of 1907 and setting the major lines of corporatist policy. Employers and employees were given permission to organize separately and in a parallel manner, although both types of organization were subject to extensive controls.* A group had to have a certain number of members to be recognized; it had to be free

---

* Public employees and domestic servants were denied the right to associate, but were promised a special statute.

of all sectarian, social, political, and religious ideologies; it needed prior approval of its constitution, and such approval was granted only for constitutions that met certain standards; it could not change its constitution without prior approval; it had to submit annual reports on its activities; it was prohibited from joining any international movements; and its leaders had to be Brazilian. To ensure compliance, delegates from the Ministry were to be assigned to attend meetings and to examine sindicato books quarterly. In addition, any member who felt wronged by his sindicato could appeal to the Ministry for an investigation. The punishments threatened ran from fines to dissolution of the association. Only one sindicato was to be recognized for each profession, although the definition of "profession" was not spelled out. Three sindicatos from any state were permitted to form a federation, and five federations could join together into a national confederation.* A number of incentives were offered. First, the recognized sindicatos were to be consulted about the social and economic problems concerning their class interests "always through the MTIC." Second, they alone were to participate in the "mixed or permanent councils of conciliation and judgment" for the resolution of labor conflicts. Third, only they could sign collective bargaining contracts with other sindicatos, firms, or individual people. Fourth, the sindicatos could apply to the Ministry for financial assistance. Finally, the right of association was protected by a provision forbidding the firing of employees for membership in syndicates or the involuntary transfer of syndical leaders.

This decree put an end to the incipient liberal pluralist pattern. "The sindicatos were still the spontaneous creation of the workers, but the first step had already been taken toward their control. From 1931 the professional associations began to become institutions linked to the state."[14] The provision that only one syndicate could be recognized for each profession created a split between those representative associations that accepted the new semiofficial juridical status of sindicato and those that for one reason or another remained outside the fold as civil entities (*entidades civís*).[15] The split has persisted to this day. It is important to note that civil entities were never persecuted; in fact Vargas later followed the "natural corporatist" policy of co-opting them.

Additional incentives for forming sindicatos were soon added. In 1932 the juntas of conciliation and judgment were created, and only union members could plead cases before them. Holidays were granted only to unionized industrial workers, and syndicalized firms were to be ac-

---

* The law specifically provided for the eventual creation of two peak associations: Confederação Brasileira do Trabalho and Confederação Nacional de Indústria e Comércio.

corded preference in state purchases. But the greatest incentive to the movement for both workers and employers was the innovation of professional representation. The Constituent Assembly of 1934 and the Constitution it drafted contained provisions that representatives from officially recognized representative associations make up one-fifth of the Chamber of Deputies. Somewhat ironically, the corporatists were not in favor of the measure, arguing that this should follow upon, not precede, the syndicalization movement. Oliveira Vianna pressed for a controlled, gradual process of group formation, working up from the município to the state and finally to the national level. He predicted that premature representation would result in the proliferation of "pseudo-sindicatos . . . representing not the classes and their interests, but only the interests and ambitions of a small group of profiteers."[16] Whatever the quality of the response, the provision for such representation greatly stimulated the creation of and interest in official representative associations, both of employers and of workers.[17]

The year 1934 brought a drastic though ephemeral modification in the policy toward freedom of association. Article 120 of the Constitution proclaimed that "the law will assure syndical plurality and the complete autonomy of syndicates." This radical change was strongly influenced by the revived Catholic movement.[18] However, the new clauses concerning sindicatos actually did not permit unbounded plurality, since they restricted recognition to syndicates having one-third of the professional category as members. "The técnicos [of the MTIC] received this transformation badly. . . . They attempted to minimize its impact on the existing syndical structure, at the cost of hard effort and long doctrinal discussions with the interested classes, especially the owners."[19] Although Article 120 and the provisions of the new syndical code of 1934 seemed to protect associations against intervention, Moraes Filho's study of the jurisprudence and departmental memoranda of the period leads him to conclude that there was no break in the Labor Ministry's bureaucratic control.[20] The established pattern of artificial corporatism through co-optation into *sindicatos únicos* continued unchanged.

The coup d'etat of 1937 and its "graciously granted" Constitution erased all ambiguity about future policy. Corporatism and unitary, controlled syndicalism were rigorously reinstated: "Professional and syndical association is free. However, only the syndicate regularly recognized by the state has the right to legally represent those who participate in any given category of production, to defend their rights before the state and other professional associations, to make collective contracts binding on all their members, to impose contributions and exercise functions delegated by public authority."[21] In addition to a wide variety of other social provisions (including an article prohibiting strikes as "an antisocial recourse . . . contrary to the superior interests of national production"), the document outlined a vast scheme for professional and functional representation in policy-making through the syndicates, culminating in a Council of National Economy. This, like many of the Constitution's provisions, went unimplemented. In the succeeding years of direct authoritarian rule (the Constitution had abolished all parties and suspended the legislature), a veritable avalanche of decrees and administrative rules were promulgated concerning social and syndical matters. In 1943, these were consolidated in a Labor Code proudly proclaimed as the most advanced in the world. Although since 1943 the Labor Code has been enriched by an extensive jurisprudence and a considerable number of executive decrees and ministerial instructions, and although the application of its rules has been inconsistent, its major legal dispositions continue to be valid. The 922 articles of the Consolidação das Leis do Trabalho (CLT)[22] regulate with exhaustive formality the working conditions of all but domestic employees, rural workers, public servants, and employees of semiofficial agencies and sindicatos.* Title five (Articles 511–610) sets the norms for the organization of employers' and workers' syndicates.

The Consolidated Labor Code of 1943

The broad outlines of the newly codified system were actually an intensification of those in the original syndicalization decree of 1931. The CLT upheld voluntary membership, *sindicalismo único* (limiting recognition to one sindicato for each profession), representation of professional categories rather than just the syndicates' associates, separate but equal treatment and parallel organization of workers and employers, and a series of government controls coordinating the activities of the associations and subordinating them to national interests.[23] To these were added four important innovations: a system of membership categories, a syndical tax, a comprehensive system of labor courts, and a minimum wage law.†

The syndicate. The basic unit of the system is the sindicato, composed of at least one-third of the workers and firms in a given occupational category. Only officially recognized representative associations can use the title, and only one such association may legally represent each category in the same territory (usually the municipality or county). Although an association may set up branches within its territory (e.g.

---

* Decree-Law No. 7,889 of August 21, 1945 (just before the elections of that year) permitted the employees of Lóide Brasileiro, a government autarchy, the right to organize syndicates.

† The last two innovations of the Estado Novo, though not directly part of the syndical organization, have affected it greatly.

factory locals), this has rarely been done by either employers' or workers' syndicates. Recognition of a syndicate's special status and legal representational monopoly depends upon having the proper convocation of a founding assembly, the proper statutes,[24] and the proper leadership.* The essential rewards of syndical status are: guaranteed access, or an absolute right to represent the category, to conclude labor contracts, and "to collaborate with the state in the capacity of a consultative and technical organ in the study and solution of problems concerning its respective category of profession"; guaranteed financial support, for example, the right to collect the syndical tax from the whole category and not just from its members; and guaranteed privileges, such as preference for syndicalized workers in employment in public enterprises and preference for syndicalized firms in competition for official concessions. In exchange for these guarantees, the sindicato assumes some heavy duties and accepts extensive government control. The three major official duties for both employers' and workers' associations are: "to collaborate with the authorities in the development of social solidarity"; "to maintain legal aid services for its members"; and "to promote the conciliation of labor disputes." Workers' groups must also promote cooperatives and establish and maintain schools and employment agencies.[25] Perhaps the sindicatos' most solemn duty is to abstain from "propagating doctrines incompatible with the institutions and interests of the nation," from interfering "with candidates for election to posts outside the syndicate," and from granting use of "its headquarters . . . to any organization involved in party politics." Until 1956 all syndicate officials were prohibited from accepting remuneration for their posts or for administrative posts in other syndical bodies.†

It is up to the Ministry of Labor to grant or withhold a syndicate's recognition in the first instance. Thereafter the Ministry must approve all candidates, all elections, and all changes in statutes. It may even send an agent to preside over meetings making such decisions. Each

* The necessary ingredients of proper leadership are Brazilian nationality, 21 years of age, a voting record from past elections, two years of activity in the profession, six months of membership in the sindicato, and a certificate of good conduct from the local police. According to the original ministerial *portaria* of July 31, 1940, to obtain recognition all directors had to furnish "proof that they do not profess ideologies incompatible with the institutions and interests of the nation, through documentation provided by the Special Delegation of Political and Social Security . . . or equivalent police authorities" (Art. III, Para. b). The same *atestado de antecedentes ideológicos* was reinstated during the Dutra administration and was not revoked until May 1, 1951. It was revived by the "revolutionary" regime of 1964. This provision applies also to eligibility to vote in syndical elections.

† An elected leader may receive a salary equivalent to his worker's salary, if his new post forces him to be absent from his job. The CLT does not prohibit such leaders from accepting paid positions in the government bureaucracy.

year the sindicato must present a budget for prior approval, as well as a record of the previous year's expenses.[26] Should any member successfully appeal any act or decision of the sindicato to the Ministry, or should the Ministry itself perceive any irregularities, it may penalize the association by fining it, by annulling the offending act, by suspending or permanently dismissing the directory, by closing the sindicato for six months, or by revoking its charter altogether. Penal action of this sort usually involves the appointment of an intervenor, who may be a member of the sindicato or an employee of the Ministry. Oliveira Vianna, the ideologue behind the syndical policy, has argued that "state control is necessary and should penetrate very deeply into the social life of these associations. It derives logically from the sum of powers of the state and the new 1937 Constitution."[27] The Labor Code provides for this penetration at all levels of the syndical structure.

The federation. The second link in the representational hierarchy is the federation. A minimum of five legally recognized sindicatos of the same category can decide to form a federation; and much the same norms regulate its recognition and control its functioning, although the statutes are slightly different. They provide for a council of representatives from member sindicatos. These representatives elect a board of directors, who in turn elect a president. Article 536 of the Labor Code hints that in the future new supervisory duties will be accorded to *federações*. The President of the Republic is empowered to force the creation of new federations (and confederations) and to establish the "nature and extent of their powers over the syndicates."[28]

The functional scope of the federations aroused great controversy in 1939. At that time the provisions concerning their organization were altered. Whereas existing representative associations at other levels either conformed to the system or remained outside of it, the Federation of Industries of the State of São Paulo (FIESP), in existence since 1929 and well organized and staffed, openly opposed the new provisions. Decree No. 1402 of that year would have split the syndical structure at the state level into as many federations as there were sindicatos, outlawing such omnibus federations as those representing "industry," "commerce," or "engineering" and making the the national confederations the only broadly aggregative representative bodies. The government, with Oliveira Vianna directing the effort, clearly intended to destroy the existing statewide associations and federations.[29] Each state would have had fourteen industrial, six commercial, and eight engineering federations![30] After an extensive debate,[31] the paulista industrialists won, and Article 573 permitted the President of the Republic to recognize at his discretion omnibus federations. As a result, the center of gravity of the system of representation shifted away from the excessively fragmented local sindicato and toward the state *federação*. (The national confederation did not exist at the time.) Most of the industrial interests and some of the commercial employers used federations as their normal channel of representation. As a rule, employees have continued to rely on local syndicates.*

The confederation. The highest stage in the official syndical hierarchy belongs to the employers' and workers' confederations, composed of at least three state federations. The confederations have headquarters in the national capital.† Their exact potential number (fourteen, or seven of each type) and even their exact names are set out in Article 535 of the CLT. Formally, they enjoy the same prerogatives and are subject to somewhat fewer and less clearly defined restrictions. In practice, however, it has been clear from the beginning that both the employers' and the workers' confederations enjoy (or suffer) a very special relationship with the President of the Republic. This has come about because of their prestige, their physical location (close to the centers of executive authority), their financial strength, and their extensive powers to name representatives to consultative posts in the ministries and semipublic agencies and to nominate judges to the Supreme Labor Tribunal. According to Oliveira Vianna, President Vargas intended to make the confederations

organs of general orientation for the broad productive activities they encompassed, higher agents for the coordination of these categories, through which the state, or better, the President of the Republic, could transmit the economic policy of the nation to lower-level associations. . . . In summary, in our syndical system, the confederations are essentially organs of the government's economic policy, instruments the President of the Republic uses principally to control and direct the national economy, as well as to define the general directives of his social policy. . . . This function logically implies one consequence— that the position of these institutions . . . must be one of close collaboration with the state, . . . [and] their leaders must have . . . a statist mentality.[32]

---

* In many states, the commercial employers' interests are fragmented into retail trade, wholesale trade, autonomous agents, and tourism, each with its own federation. Each state (except Mato Grosso and Acre) has a single federation of industrial employers' sindicatos covering the whole state.

Only a few states, especially in the Northeast, have omnibus federations of industrial workers. On the other hand, all commercial employees are grouped in a single federation for each of the most important states.

† In practice, this still (in 1966) means Rio de Janeiro. Legally committed to moving to Brasília, most have announced plans for the construction of headquarters there, and some have even purchased land; but none seem to be seriously contemplating the move in the near future.

The title of confederation, like that of federation and syndicate, can legally be used only by recognized entities. In practice, however, unofficial confederations have been formed. Two of the most prominent are the Confederation of Commercial Associations of Brazil and the National Confederation of Public Servants.

Because the leaders of these national peak associations must have the confidence of the President of the Republic, the open forms of intervention used on the fragmented local sindicatos and even on the state federations are rarely used on the national confederations. Pressure from above is generally applied more privately and subtly.

Innovations of the Labor Code. On the surface, the new dispositions outlining a set of professional categories around which employers and employees can organize do not appear particularly significant, except for the obvious prohibition against the founding of single trade unions and employer centrals (and in fact some of those have been formed, though unofficially). The case of FIESP's struggle in 1938–40 showed, however, that these provisions are crucial to determining at what level interests are going to be aggregated; it also showed how much pressure can be brought to bear on a given issue. The full subtlety of *enquadramento* (literally, framing), which was clarified by the 1943 Labor Code, becomes apparent when one realizes that all sorts of exceptions are permitted. This institutionalized flexibility is entrusted to the Comissão de Enquadramento Sindical, a commission with representatives from workers' and employers' confederations and from the Ministry of Labor. If, for example, a manufacturer is having difficulty with the leader of the workers' syndicate in his category, he may appeal to the commission for a change to another category where the leadership is less likely to oppose him.* A faction in another syndicate may request that the category be subdivided in order to weaken the opposition.[33] Perhaps more important, firms or workers in a small but important industry may attempt to gain recognition as a national syndicate or federation, and thus gain a more direct access to important centers of decision in the federal government.† This apparently minor and virtually invisible commission has the power to decide within certain limits who may bargain with whom in the name of what interests.

The second important innovation in the new system is the syndical tax (*impôsto sindical*).[34] For employees this consists of one day's wages

---

* The most important instance of this occurred with the emergence of the ship-building industry and the ensuing dispute over whether its workers were to be classified as metallurgical or maritime workers.

† The list of industries for which employers have gained the right to organize recognized national associations reads like a who's who of ownership concentration and established privilege: coal, matches, shipping, cement, beer, iron ore and basic metals, book publishing, movies, commerce of precious stones, insurance, and automobile manufacturers. The list for the workers and the self-employed is like another who's who of privilege, although the categories are different: stevedores, port workers, warehousemen, railroad workers, various categories of maritime workers, airline employees and pilots, journalists, truck drivers, customs agents, and private-school employees. Neither list is complete. If there is a "syndical aristocracy," these are its members.

a year; for employers it is a quota based on the registered capital of each firm.* Proof of prior payment is required for a variety of dealings with the government. The proceeds are deposited directly in the Banco do Brasil[35] and are divided among the three syndical levels: 5 percent goes to the confederation, 15 percent goes to the federation, and 54 percent goes to the syndicate. The Bank takes 6 percent for its services, and the remaining 20 percent goes to the Department of Employment and Salaries of the Ministry of Labor (before December 1964 it went to that Ministry's Social Syndical Fund).[36] When there is no sindicato for a given category, its share goes to the federation; when there is no federation, both shares go to the confederation; where there is no syndical organization at all, the entire amount goes to the Ministry. The amounts involved in the syndical tax are considerable, although the degree of inspection and control over its collection has varied.[37]

Many attacks have been launched against this "fascist" tax, but none have succeeded.† After the coup of 1964, the military regime seemed about to abolish it; instead, they ordered a commission of Labor Ministry officials and representatives from all the confederations to study the matter. The commission stated flatly, "Either there will be a compulsory contribution, or the present labor organization and its impact upon the understanding between classes will not be viable." To demonstrate the necessity of the tax, the commission's report cited figures on its contribution to total revenue among worker's organizations. These figures are presented in Table 5.1. The federations and confederations are by far the most dependent on the *impôsto sindical.* Only the so-called *sindicatos de praia* (beach syndicates) have monthly dues greater than the compulsory tax. When broken down regionally, a 70 to 77 percent dependence is consistently maintained.[38] No data were presented on employers' associations, but the National Confederation of Industry expressed its strong support for continuing the tax and cited a study made by the Federation of Industries of the State of São Paulo showing that all of its member syndicates approved of the tax, many of them admitting that they could not survive without it. The industrial and commercial federations and confederations of employers are in a less vulnerable position, since they receive an important part of their revenues from two other compulsory contributions, one that supports

---

* Because of inflation, the employers' quota has tended to decline in terms of real income and has been occasionally redefined by law. This was last done in January 1962. The tax going to workers' organizations follows the trend in wage negotiations and especially in minimal salary levels. It is, therefore, automatically adjusted to inflation, so to speak.

† The tax was rigorously opposed by Communist and non-Communist radicals until 1952. At that time they began capturing key leadership positions, and by the 1960's they had become the tax's strongest supporters.

TABLE 5.1
TOTAL INCOME DERIVED FROM SYNDICAL TAX BY WORKERS' FEDERATIONS,
CONFEDERATIONS, AND SYNDICATES
(*percent*)

Type of organization		Income from syndical tax
Confederations		99.2%
Federations		92.5%
Syndicates:		70.0%
Industrial workers	71.0%	
Commercial workers	74.7%	
Bank workers	69.0%	
Transport workers	62.2%	
Communications workers	52.3%	
Stevedores, warehousemen, and dock workers	27.3%	

SOURCE: Ministério do Trabalho e Previdência Social, "Relatorio da Comissão Instituida pela Portaria No. 439/65 de 24 de agosto de 1965" (mimeographed).
NOTE: Percentages have been rounded to one decimal place. Remaining revenues were identified simply as "Monthly Dues."

the Social Service of Industry (SESI) and the Social Service of Commerce (SESC) and one that supports the National Service of Industrial Apprenticeship (SENAI) and the National Service of Commercial Apprenticeship (SENAC). These taxes have also come under frequent attack.

Although the *impôsto sindical* provides the principal financial support for the official syndical structure and has attracted the most attention, it is by no means the only way government authorities at various levels can financially sponsor or subsidize a representative association. In Brazil an association that is not receiving or has not received some public funds is very rare. There are innumerable sources of financial backing: subsidies from the presidency or from various ministries and government agencies, many of which have independent sources of income (like the Fundo Social Sindical); credit facilities on favorable conditions from the Banco do Brasil or one of the welfare institutes; subsidies from individual deputies and senators;[39] government facilities for the publishing of journals or books. State and even some local governments follow similar practices, although these may be limited by their own dependence on federal funds. The extent of this informal financial sponsorship and its impact on the subsequent behavior of the associations cannot be determined. We can hypothesize, however, that sponsorship of this sort has helped bring about the subservience and generally pro-government orientation of many entities not manifestly dependent upon the regime or overtly regimented by the Labor Code.

The establishment of an elaborate system of labor courts (*justiça do trabalho*), from local conciliation and juridical boards to regional labor tribunals and the Supreme Labor Tribunal, has had a profound indirect impact upon representative associations. On the one hand, their compulsory jurisdiction (coupled with the prohibition of or severe restriction on the right to strike) has forced the bulk of worker protest into government channels. Even collective bargaining agreements made independently of the Ministry must be approved by a labor court in order to be valid for the entire professional category.[40] The process of obtaining a decision tends to be lengthy, if not tortuous.[41] Both types of sindicatos must maintain and operate extensive legal services. Much of the interaction between levels of the syndical structure consists of exchanges of legal expertise. This process is costly, it creates a larger bureaucracy involved exclusively in shuffling legal files, it absorbs most of the energy and resources of the syndicates (especially of workers' syndicates), and it reduces the incentive for rigorous independent organization and activity. Nevertheless, the labor justice system is believed to be widely accepted by employees as something that advances their interests.[42] (José Albertino Rodrigues even charges the employers with "systematically boycotting it.")[43] For one thing, the labor courts have afforded many workers' leaders attractive careers, since they are composed of both workers' and employers' representatives in equal proportions. The functional representatives are picked by the authorities from lists furnished by the sindicatos (for juntas, or boards), the federations (for the regional courts), and the confederations (for the Supreme Labor Tribunal). In the last two cases, the choice is made by the President of the Republic. Competion for these honored and lucrative posts can be fierce.[44] Occasionally, the nominating entities get together and rotate the privilege, in good Brazilian accommodating fashion.[45] Often, however, especially among workers' confederations, the struggle for these posts creates lasting enmities that prevent the contenders from acting together in making other demands.[46]

Virtually all of the detailed protective and welfare provisions of the Consolidated Labor Code have had an impact upon representative associations, if only by removing such matters as working hours and paid holidays from the list of group contentions before the interested groups could mobilize about them. As I have mentioned, the regime has taken much advantage of the voluntaristic and paternalistic aspects of this pattern of preemptive co-optation.[47] One innovation that has affected associational interaction greatly, although again indirectly, was the minimum wage (*salário mínimo*) provision.* In practice the minimum sal-

---

* Like many of the other features of the CLT, this one predated it by several years. The first minimum salary levels were decreed in 1940.

ary has tended to become the average salary in many spheres of the economy. Even for those groups that have managed to obtain "a professional salary," this is usually a multiple of the minimum one. In many sectors, therefore, wages are not determined by group interaction, even by group interaction through the Labor Ministry. According to the CLT, the minimum levels were to be set for periods of three years by 22 regional commissions, each with equal syndical representation, strictly on the basis of statistical data. As a rule, however, they have been decreed by the President, and the periods between readjustments have -varied from three months to four years. Leôncio Martins Rodrigues observes that, although pressure from salaried groups suffering from inflation is a factor in forcing readjustment, the industrialists do not usually resist the change very adamantly.[48] The current revolutionary regime has attempted to reintroduce the original, purely technical method of calculation, but it has centralized the authority in a National Council for Wage Policy. The purpose of this new body is not only to "rationalize" the minimum salary adjustments, but also to establish a limit to be enforced by the labor courts upon wage increases gained by collective bargaining.[49] This, of course, even further limits the autonomy of the syndicates in making wage demands. Oliveira Vianna, as always a sharp observer, has commented on the deadening impact of the minimum salary upon group solidarity: "It has become a sort of mystique in which the minimum salary appears to be some kind of panacea for social policy, solving all the problems of workers and industrialists."[50]

Developments Under Vargas

In his Manifesto to the Nation in 1930, Vargas proclaimed that both the urban and the rural proletariat needed tutelary management. With the CLT providing ample tutelage for the urban sector, he turned his attention belatedly to rural groups. Resistance to the idea of syndicalization among landowners was strong.[51] Vargas's Rural Labor Decree of November 10, 1944, closely paralleled the CLT provisions, tying the rural syndicates to the Labor Ministry. It had little effect; the rural employers had already formed a few associations of their own, and they displayed no enthusiasm for the proposed system. Less than a year later (October 24, 1945), two new measures permitted the landowners many of the advantages of syndicalization (unitary representation and guaranteed access, principally) without making them dependent on the Ministry of Labor. Instead, the rural associations were to become "technical and consultative organs" registered only with the Ministry of Agriculture, whose controlling powers were minimal. This deprived them of *impôsto sindical* funds, but they survived for a decade on assorted federal and state subsidies. In 1955 they were granted a sizable federal subsidy by Congress; the local associations received 80 percent, state federations received 15 percent, and national confederations received 5 percent.[52] Thus another set of representative associations had been sponsored, this one with fewer controls and covering only employers.

It would seem, then, that the pattern of Vargas's interest group sponsorship was exclusively that of artificial corporatism—that he sought to eliminate or chose to ignore preexisting, spontaneously created associations. For a short period, an attempt was made to eliminate nonconforming groups. I have already mentioned the dispute over the law in 1939 that would have fragmented or bypassed the Federation of Industries of the State of São Paulo. This same law also stated that "No act of professional defense will be permitted to an association not registered in the form laid out in this article, and none of its demands or representations will be recognized." In the declaration of intent prefacing the law, the motives of the Labor Ministry técnicos were clear: "With the institution of this registry, the entire life of the professional associations will gravitate around the Ministry of Labor: in it they will be born; with it they will grow; beside it they will develop; within it they will be extinguished."[53] The private entities apparently reacted, and one year later, another decree was passed, this one allowing the President of the Republic to grant "to civic associations constituted for the defense and coordination of economic and occupational interests" the status of "consultative and technical organs."[54] The first group to be so privileged was the Commercial Association of Rio. Many others followed. As a result of this policy of natural corporatism, a number of pro-Vargas leaders were elected to posts in these associations, and several of them gained permanent access to important government councils.* It is also perhaps interesting to note than many of these private entities, such as the Commercial Association of Rio, the Brazilian Press Association, the Club of Engineers, and the Association of Commercial Employees, built their impressive *sêdes*, or headquarters, during this period. It was not always necessary to be a syndicate to benefit from the regime's largess.

The partisans of "authoritarian democracy," with their preoccupation with organizing the people (before, I might add, the people could organize themselves) and for integrating them into the state, admitted that "in Brazil, there is no climate for a single-party system."[55] With "the multiple-party system dissolved and the single-party system not recom-

---

* The most important was João Daudt d'Oliveira, a childhood friend and schoolmate of Vargas, who was president of the Commercial Association of Rio from 1942 to 1951.

mendable, there was only one alternative possible for the authoritarian state: to search for the sources of democracy in organized classes."[56] This search for legitimation and information involved, as we have seen, tactics of both "artificial" and "natural" corporatism. But these efforts had to be supplemented by an attempt to link the co-opted entities to the state apparatus through which Vargas ruled. They had to be given at least a semblance of participation in decision-making. For this reason, "a considerable number of pre-legislative, administrative, juridical, and consultative institutions" were created with functional interest representatives from both semiofficial and private associations.[57] In the Ministry of Labor, Industry, and Commerce, a vast number of permanent commissions, such as those governing *enquadramento*, the *impôsto sindical*, the *salário mínimo*, and social welfare, as well as ad hoc working groups,[58] were established, usually with equal representation of workers and employers. The Labor Court system, as we have seen, was organized on a similar principle, as were the special Maritime Labor Delegations. The autarchic Retirement and Social Welfare Institutes for various categories of workers (IAPI, IAPM, IAPB, etc.) presently are governed by such tripartite councils.

Outside the Labor Ministry, a number of councils were established largely to treat economic problems generated by war conditions. These included the Coordination of Economic Mobilization, the Central Price Commission, the National Council of Industrial and Commercial Policy, the Textile Executive Commission, and many others. The most important of these was the Federal Council of Foreign Trade (Conselho Federal de Comércio Exterior), because it was instrumental in setting the guidelines of general economic policy.[59] At the end of the war a National Economic Planning Commission was created with a very wide mandate to review and coordinate the adaptation of the economy to peacetime conditions. On all these councils sat representatives of interest associations, though in most cases the representatives were from employers' groups only.[60] Although most of these councils were disbanded shortly thereafter, many have since been replaced by similar bodies with corporatist representation. Some of the more specialized ones, including the National Petroleum Council, the Executive Commission for Rubber, and the various professional orders and councils, have survived with altered functions. As we shall see, this system of institutionalized consultative bodies provides the associations, especially the employers' associations, with some of their most important channels of access. It also provides interest-group leaders with a series of attractive and prestigious posts: high executive positions in the Retirement and Social Welfare Institutes, important jobs in the administrative hierarchy of the Ministry of Labor (or the Ministry of Agriculture for rural leaders), and lucrative temporary appointments as Brazilian representatives to international conferences (especially those of the International Labor Organization). The attraction for workers' leaders has been particularly strong, given their lower-status origins and the formal prohibition against direct remuneration for their syndical jobs. One could argue that these personal incentives for participation in leadership roles have been more important in stimulating associability than the various incentives for ordinary membership.

Another distinctive product of this period was the creation of autarchic institutes for the control of specific commodities. These include the Brazilian Coffee Institute (IBC), the National Institute of Pinewood (INP), the National Institute of Maté (INM), the Institute of Alcohol and Sugar (IAA), and the Brazilian Institute of Salt (IBS). Individual states also began to maintain functional institutes for such commodities as tobacco, cacao, lard, wine, rice, and meat. Other commodities like wheat, rubber, cotton, fish, and even manioc have been regulated by administrative agencies that never developed into full-blown institutes. The provisions for interest representation to these bodies have varied. Some have only producers' representatives; others have workers' representatives as well. The more important (IBC, IAA, INP, for example) have, in addition to these, representatives from the governments of the states where the commodities are produced. They usually have virtually autonomous powers to set prices, wages, and quotas, distribute credit, and regulate foreign trade. Their respective revenues are also virtually autonomous, resting on an obligatory tax on production or exports. The producers accepted this degree of state penetration into their economic freedom partly because of the collapse of markets in the 1930's and partly out of fear of official reprisal; but they continued to cooperate mainly because they were granted ample subsidies and have been able to control policy-making in these autarchies.[61] "At heart, our autarchic institutes . . . are really cartels, or obligatory employer organizations."[62] Thus it seems that Vargas, unable to co-opt the rural sector voluntarily through syndicalism, co-opted its more specialized employer elements through institutes and commissions. These became de jure administrative agencies, but remained de facto representative associations. The full impact of this policy of granting decisional and financial autonomy would be felt later, when, in the interests of industrialization, other authority groups would attempt to force these commodity clienteles, these feudalities, to conform to their more general objectives.

Developments After 1945

The Estado Novo period has been inadequately studied and poorly understood. To the orthodox liberal democrat, it was simply an unfortunate aberration in Brazil's constant evolution toward representative democracy. To the orthodox progressive, it was simply a fascist interlude produced by the reaction of an alienated bourgeois elite to the world capitalist crisis. By concentrating on its personalistic and populistic aspects, observers have failed to notice the very profound changes that took place in the nature of intermediary political associations, the scope of government policy, and the interpenetration of the two.* They therefore assumed that with the deposition of Vargas in 1945 Brazilian political development would somehow resume its "natural" liberal democratic or progressive socialist course. The thought that corporatism or the mixed Getulian system might have struck deeper roots was rarely entertained. Liberals and progressives faced the new age with great hopes and expectations for renovation and change.

The Constitution of 1946 reaffirmed freedom of professional and syndical association, but qualified it (in Article 159) with government regulations about the form of the syndicates' constitutions, their legal power to make collective contracts, and the exercise of functions delegated by public authority. Although the amendment of 1934 on plurality was not repeated, legal commentators like Pontes de Miranda argued that plurality was implicit in its provisions.[63] Moraes Filho noted that the provisions were vague, permitting either plurality or *sindicalismo único* and leaving the choice to future legislation.[64] It was generally expected that the new Constitution would prove incompatible with many provisions of the Labor Code of 1943.† Nevertheless, "very few changes have been added to the 1943 syndical legislation, pending regulation of Article 159."[65]

What has changed frequently has been the disposition of authorities to apply the measures of control and repression to which they are legally entitled. With the "redemocratization" in 1945 and the formation of a party system, the syndicalized masses became an important source of electoral support. The Partido Trabalhista Brasileiro (PTB) was created by Vargas from the cadres of the Labor Ministry and the trade union movement, just as the Partido Social Democrático was composed of cadres from other branches of the federal and state bureaucracies.

---

* The ambiguity of the Vargas regime (and of populism) is well summarized in the popular carioca description of Vargas as *"pai dos pobres e mãe dos ricos"* ("father of the poor and mother of the rich").

† Its Article 159 declared: "The right to strike, whose exercise will be regulated by law, is recognized."

Under these conditions of increased competitiveness and impending elections, ministerial control began to loosen in 1944. A political amnesty was granted. The electoral process in the syndicates, frozen during the Estado Novo for the sake of "state security," seemed on the point of revival. The resurgence of new leaders, an increasing polarization into reformist and revolutionary ideologies, and a general belief that the major features of corporatist syndicalism were incompatible with the country's new status as a "social democracy" promoted an increase in associability and pluralism and a dramatic change in intergroup and group-government relations. The period of corporatism seemed to have provided the necessary leaven for breaking social groups out of their reliance on unstructured, individualistic, and personalistic channels of access into something approaching a structured, institutionalized pattern of access through secondary associations: parties, movements, and representative associations.[66]

Such pluralist expectations proved quite unrealistic. Because ministerial control was slipping and leadership was becoming more and more radical, and because of the external pressures of the cold war, a series of measures were taken in the name of *paz social* (social peace) by the new regime of E. Gaspar Dutra (1945–50) to reassert government hegemony, especially over the workers' associations. Syndical elections were postponed repeatedly. A formal "certificate of ideological antecedents" was demanded of both candidates and electors. In 1947 the principal, though unofficial, Communist-directed peak association, the Confederation of Brazilian Workers (CTB), was closed down along with several of its state federations, and heavy restrictions were imposed on syndicates and syndicate leaders who supported it. The Communist Party was also declared illegal at this time. Massive intervention was decreed, and juntas named by the Ministry took control of hundreds of workers' syndicates.[67] In addition to tightening direct executive control over syndical elections, finances, demands, etc., the regime began a longer-term campaign to mix indoctrination with social welfare services. Management of these campaigns was turned over to the employers' syndicates, and they were (and still are) financed by an obligatory payroll tax. The National Confederation of Industry and its constituent state federations run the Serviço Social da Indústria (SESI), and the National Confederation of Commerce and its federations run the similar Serviço Social do Comércio (SESC).*

---

* SESI and SESC are not to be confused with SENAI and SENAC, the industrial and commercial apprenticeship programs, also run by the patronal syndicates and financed by a payroll tax. In 1955 the SESI-SESC idea was applied to the rural sphere (Serviço Social Rural). However, this had a different control mechanism and also a different impact.

Sporadic but serious repression, combined with ideological enlightenment (*esclarecimento*), welfare paternalism, selected personal inducements, and other subtle forms of manipulation, turned the tide away from plurality and radicalism. The syndical leadership of long standing, closely associated with the bureaucracies of the Labor Ministry and the Retirement and Social Welfare Institutes and loyal to the idea of a paternalist reformist state as the protector and benefactor of the labor movement, retained its hold on the top posts. This class of association leaders became known as the *pelegos*. The term is accurately descriptive of their social role; it derives from the gaúcho term for a sort of hide blanket that absorbs the shocks between the horse and the saddle. The *pelego* is, therefore, a professional intermediary, an interest-group entrepreneur who makes a career of conciliating the conflicting interests of the Ministry, the employers, and the workers. He gets his cut from the negotiations, but he would argue that the cut is merely a broker's fee, and that the end result is less industrial violence and more "social peace" for all classes.* It is important to stress that *peleguismo* is not restricted to workers' associations. It is in the interests of authorities to have consistent, loyal, and conciliatory leadership in the employers' associations also, although the manipulatory devices used for selecting and keeping employers' leaders in line may be more subtle than those used on workers' representatives.

Syndical elections were held in 1950 for the first time in several years. The elections were strictly controlled, and a special propaganda agency was created in an attempt to overcome a prevailing apathy.[68] Vargas's return to power with strong worker support meant still another policy change. The infamous "certificate of ideological antecedents" was abolished, and controls over elections gradually loosened. While the formal

---

* Originally, *pelego* was a strongly pejorative term. In my interviews with some of the more prominent ones, however, I discovered that this was no longer the case. With their increased sophistication and experience, these leaders are more aware of the need for professional leadership cadres. This has become in their eyes a respectable middle-class position, demanding a certain commensurate income. Because the CLT denies them this overtly, they resort to various subterfuges, mainly employment in federal agencies. They are also no longer ashamed of their "shock-absorbing" role, which they apparently have come to regard as a socially important one. For a polemic but enlightening discussion, see D. Barreto, "Sindicalismo deve ser reformulado imediatamente no pais," *Jornal do Brasil*, May 20, 1962.

Pelegos are usually rewarded for their services by the employers, either directly through monetary compensations, or indirectly through *cobertura* for a desired government post. As one frank and cynical industrialist told me, "Don't think that the *pelegos* were created only by the government. We created them and we maintain them." He went on to point out that since the syndicates could not organize and support a strike in any case, this arrangement was of mutual benefit. After all, he claimed, "We will concede more benefits to workers represented by a *pelego*, because if we don't he may be replaced by some radical."

pattern of policy remained substantially unchanged in the succeeding decade, overt intervention declined.[69] The permanence of the PTB, with its unofficial hold on the Labor Ministry, as a partner in the ruling coalition, meant a continuation of the past policies of preemptive co-optation and paternalism.* The Labor Ministry functioned as a national trade union central. Covert manipulation of the right to associate and participate in both workers' and employers' associations continued and probably increased with the decrease in manifest intervention. As a Labor Minister said in 1951: "The workers must take over the syndicates, fight within their organizations to expel the Communists and their agents. In this struggle, they will be aided by the constituted authorities of the nation."[70] Loyalists in employers' associations received similar, if less obvious, assistance.

Nevertheless, beginning in 1952, the leadership of workers' syndicates began to diversify and become more militant.[71] Fernando Henrique Cardoso, a paulista sociologist, says the main cause for the change in syndical leadership and activity was the enormous expansion in the number of workers during this period. "Faced with the great masses of workers that exist today in the large cities, with the spontaneous and organized pressure [through parties] exerted by workers' groups on the syndical organization, and with appearance of leaders not linked to higher syndical circles, . . . it was not possible to maintain, after the so-called democratization of the country, the same type of official control over the unions."[72] The independent stance, militant activity, and ideological radicalism of the sindicatos in the later months of the Goulart regime made observers wonder whether the lines of dependency had become reversed, with the Labor Ministry becoming the agent of militant workers' leaders, rather than vice versa.[73] The widely diffused rumor that such a reversal of relationships was about to become formalized into something vaguely called a "syndicalist republic," in which leaders of workers' organizations would permanently have direct access to and control over key policy sectors, was an important factor in triggering the military coup of March 31, 1964.

Another modification in the pattern of policy toward representative associations that led conservatives to distrust Goulart's intentions was the Rural Labor Statute of March 2, 1963.[74] This extended to the rural

* This was not the case during the short term of Jânio Quadros (1961). President Quadros did not accept the time-honored tradition of permitting the PTB leadership, i.e., his Vice-President, João Goulart, to name the Minister of Labor. He unceremoniously sacked a number of ministerial employees and ordered investigations into irregularities in the Syndical Tax Commission, the Social Syndical Fund, and various welfare institutes. His Labor Minister, Castro Neves, declared his desire to extinguish the *impôsto sindical* and announced his unwillingness to support "careerist syndical leaders" (*O Estado de São Paulo*, Feb. 5, 1961).

sector both the corporatist-syndicalist and the paternalist-welfare provisions of the Consolidation of the Brazilian Labor Laws of 1943. *Sindicalismo único*, recognition by the Ministry of Labor, *enquadramento*,
preestablished hierarchy, union membership requirements,[75] limitations
on the electoral and administrative process, and the usual prohibitions
(especially those on strikes), duties (especially that of abstaining from
political activity), prerogatives (especially that of receiving the syndical
tax), and penalties (especially that of direct intervention) were all extended to the rural sector—to both employers' and employees' associations. A National Commission for Rural Syndicalization was established
(with corporate representation), and the Labor Ministry announced its
goal to be "the completion of the rural union organization with 2,000
unions distributed rationally throughout the country, according to the
criteria of demographic concentration."[76] Article 141 of the Statute
facilitated the conversion of the patronal *associações rurais* into *sindicatos rurais* within a certain time period. Goulart's agrarian reform
agency, SUPRA, became actively engaged in sponsoring this new round
of artificial corporatism.[77] It was cut short dramatically by the events of
March 31, 1964.

Public Policy Since 1964

The coup (to its opponents) or the revolution (to its proponents) that
deposed the Goulart regime brought about an immediate change in
policy toward representative associations. Massive direct intervention
was decreed. The new Labor Minister later admitted that 15 percent
of the country's syndicates had suffered intervention during this time.[78]
An undetermined number of leaders were arrested or forced to flee into
exile. New executives were appointed to all of the Retirement and Social
Welfare Institutes. The Ministry itself was not as severely hit by this
campaign to purge the syndical movement of "subversive and corrupt"
elements. The infamous Commission of Syndical Orientation and the
Syndical Tax Commission, the agents for the distribution of the Social
Syndical Fund,* were abolished "as an imperative of political and moral
order," and their money was incorporated into the ministerial budget.[79]
The charters of some of the syndicates were revoked, usually on the
grounds that the syndicates did not have enough members.† Usually
an intervenor from the Ministry was appointed and control was later
turned over to a ruling junta composed of "loyal" syndicate members.
In January 1965 new instructions on elections were decreed,[80] and by

* This fund amounted to 1.8 billion cruzeiros in 1964, or about one million dollars.
† Although the CLT requires one-third of the category to be members, one-tenth
was used as a more practical minimum. The rural workers' sindicatos were especially hard hit by the crack-down on "phantom entities."

1966 the status of most syndicates had returned to normal.[81] Most of the imposed juntas were elected, though the elections were tightly controlled. In the few cases where the intervenors lost the vote, the Ministry prevented their opponents from taking office, charging irregularities.

Many of the groups supporting the violent deposition of Goulart expected that one of its first products would be a drastic revision of the nature and role assigned by the government to representative associations. These liberalist apostles of "democratization" and "trade-union autonomy" were to become sorely disappointed.[82] The General Command of the Revolution and the new Labor Minister announced during their first week in power that the basic syndical rights would be maintained. With certain exceptions, the basic structure of the system remained untouched. Cardoso's assumption that increase in numbers and in group consciousness had made dependency on the Ministry unworkable proved partially unfounded. What did prove unworkable was the previous system of subtle co-optation by means of differential personal incentives and anticipated reaction. "Order" was reimposed, but only by the use of overt coercion, regular intimidation, and systematic bureaucratic control—somewhat reminiscent of the "social peace" imposed by the Dutra regime after 1947.

Some innovations were introduced. The right to strike was finally (after eighteen years!) regulated.* The restrictions imposed were considerable, but the measure was more liberal than the 1946 act it replaced. Certain categories, such as maritime, dock, and railroad workers' associations, lost most of their acquired privileges and guarantees. Steps were taken to unify the Retirement and Social Welfare Institutes under a single administration. Perhaps the most important innovation has been the Ministry of Planning and Economic Coordination, which has taken over areas that were formerly in the exclusive domain of the Labor Ministry and the labor courts. This new ministry controls the minimum wage and the permissible limits of salary increases by forbidding the labor courts to authorize wage increases above a preestablished maximum. The Ministry of Planning and Economic Coordination has also proposed a number of other changes in salary and employment policy, but its attempt to replace the CLT provisions on job stability by an unemployment fund failed, partly because of protesting workers. Nonetheless, relations between the syndicates and the Labor Ministry have been re-established in their traditional pattern of dependency; moreover, the

---

* The new (1966) constitution incorporates these "revolutionary" changes and prohibits strikes in "essential activities," which are left undefined in the text. Strikes have also been suppressed under the vague, omnibus provisions of the 1967 Law of National Security.

relations between that ministry, other ministries, and the presidency have altered in a new direction.* The Labor Ministry may still be the central syndical organization for the articulation and aggregation of workers' (and to a much lesser extent, of employers') interests within the system, but its bargaining position and role have changed greatly.[83] Whether this is a permanent change or one dictated by the current severe anti-inflationary policies is not clear.

Having taken control of so much in the sphere of interest politics, the new authorities were faced with a problem President Dutra had experienced, a diffuse passive resistance or general apathy toward the sindicatos. According to Roberto Campos, the syndicalization movement had "an excessive preoccupation with massive increases in nominal salaries." He charged that it was not interested in increasing educational opportunities or demanding a rationalization of government welfare services, that it was unequal, rewarding certain worker aristocracies inordinately, that it was egoistic, not interested in increasing investments or creating new jobs, and finally, that it had brought about "a dissolution of moral standards." In late 1965 and early 1966, the government tried to initiate a program called *novo trabalhismo* in order to combat these problems. Specifically, it would democratize opportunities; divert energies into the quest for education, better housing, and more rationally administered social services; expel the workers' aristocracies and spurious "leadership"; and develop concern and responsibility for public and private investment.[84] The only concrete manifestation of this effort was a program of cooperative housing construction. Another device to counteract lagging participation was a revision of the CLT making it obligatory to vote in syndical elections. A series of preferences were accorded to syndicate members in job competitions, housing credit, sale of urban or rural lots, acquisition of automobiles, scholarships, and admission to port services. Union contributions and dues were made tax-deductible. Whether or not these modest inducements can effect the desired change in attitudes and norms has not yet been determined. The problem remains: how restricted can a government keep the functions of representative associations and still expect those associations to function?

---

* The extension of the system to cover rural employers and workers has proceeded, although at a more cautious and controlled pace. In 1966, the first collections of the rural syndical tax were made. In 1968, discussion began on the issue of extending the labor court system to the rural area (*O Estado de São Paulo*, July 26, 1968).

PART II

I suggested in Part I that the structural differentiation of Brazilian society into more and more specialized and interdependent roles, combined with the political enculturation of the actors and the shifting policies of authority groups, has influenced and even determined the pattern of emergence of representative associations. We are now ready to examine this first set of dependent outcomes: changes in the number, coverage, functional specificity, and density of participation in this form of interest representation.

We have already observed that the Brazilian political culture as such does little to promote participation in impersonal secondary associations. The basic legal and political norms for forming and operating this type of unit were established by the late 1930's, and they have remained substantially unchanged since then. The major changes in Brazilian society did not occur until the mid-1940's, 1950's, and 1960's. Did the "art of association" change concomitantly? How and when did an increasing number and variety of social groups respond by forming associations to protect and promote their interests in such a dynamic setting? Equally important, can we prove there was a causal relationship between the two? In general, we cannot, although there are times when it may be possible—for example, when a respondent answers, "We formed because the CLT provisions decreed it" or, "Suddenly we realized there were enough of us with the same interests to support an association." Of course this sort of evidence tends to be strictly qualitative and confined to specific cases. For reasons discussed below, more systematic statistical techniques such as multiple regression are of limited use.

For these reasons I have resorted to a tactic already evident at several points in this study: eclecticism in both the collection and the analysis of data. Chapter 7 offers a quantitative overview of the extension of coverage and the changes in density of member participation using time series of aggregate data. In Chapter 8, the different types of associations, syndical and private, are discussed qualitatively in terms of functional scope and specificity. This rather lengthy historical and descriptive treatment also serves to introduce the major dramatis personae in Brazilian interest politics at the national level. But before discussing the modern period from these two perspectives, I must first describe briefly the associational base line bequeathed to the "revolutionaries" of 1930. This will be done in Chapter 6.

SIX

Representative Associations in Brazil
Before 1930

THE SHEER disarray of the Brazilian polity seems to have made quite an impression on the victorious "revolutionaries" of 1930. They reported finding not only an impoverished treasury and a disordered set of administrative structures, but also an impoverished and disordered set of representative associations. In the words of one observer,

The state [before 1930] lived at the margin of recognizing the existence of these associations. The failure of those decrees [encouraging the formation of syndicates] to be applied was due to the absence of associative spirit, the lack of agreement among the interested parties, the dearth of financial resources, and the disinterest of public authorities. It is no exaggeration to state that until the triumph of the Nationalist Revolution of 1930 we had no real syndicates. There were, of course, a few workers' associations, promoted by the solidarity of resistance to employers and by the workers' need to protect themselves. . . . The employers, imbued with a profound sense of individualism, avoided forming associations for the support of mutual interests.[1]

The new elite shrewdly perceived that a program of officially sponsored and controlled interest group formation would advance their plans to consolidate their hold over national institutions and to introduce substantial changes in the scope of national policy-making. By adopting the policies reviewed in the preceding chapter, they raised representative associations from "the most complete and painful anarchy" to the status of keystones in maintaining the existing order.

The anarchy of national interest politics was perhaps particularly apparent to the revolutionaries because so many of them were gaúchos, citizens of Rio Grande do Sul. This state had, in the period following World War I and more specifically during Getúlio Vargas's term as governor, undergone something of an organizational revolution. The state government sponsored the creation of a number of commodity producers' sindicatos to regulate (essentially by cartelization) markets in rice, dried beef, lard, and wine.* Whether the new policy of promoting syndicates and commodity institutes was inspired by the success of this scheme or, as so many of its critics have charged, by the success of Mussolini's *Carta del Lavoro*, or both, it was to leave an enduring impression upon representative associations and upon the political process as a whole.

Living as they did in a period of creative political intrepreneurship, the innovators had some reason to exaggerate the anarchy of the old order, even if this meant deriding or ignoring the existing associations. Official propaganda cultivated the erroneous impression that representative associations emerged only after 1930 and that those associations were the exclusive product of Vargas's corporatism. It can be argued, if not conclusively proven, that Brazil had in the late 1920's a network of institutionalized interest groups more or less commensurate with the level of its economic and social development. They were not very numerous, but neither were the sources of interest differentiation. In terms of their willingness to oppose the regime or to oppose each other, they were more active before 1930 than they were for thirty years thereafter.[2]

Brazil did not inherit from Portugal the rich and complex system of guilds, corporations, and *grêmios* (societies) that have played such an important role in the latter's historical development. There was no equivalent in the New World of the famous Casa dos Vinte e Quatro, a corporatist, semireligious chamber of guild leaders, through which "technicians and artists exerted a palpable influence over the city administrations."[3] In colonial Brazil, slaves performed many of the manual trades, there were relatively few skilled workmen because of the official prohibition on the creation of industries, and those that did exist were spread out all over the country. Foreign visitors, including Saint-Hilaire, Eschmege, and Denis, were astonished by the great geographic and occupational mobility of the Brazilian populace. Sérgio Buarque de Holanda notes that few of the Portuguese settlers spent their lives in any single profession, and that it was rare for a family to stay in the same trade for more than one generation.[4] "No one here tries to follow the natural course of his indicated career; rather, each tries to leap to

---

* Even today, Rio Grande do Sul has a reputation for associability. When asked who participates most, several leaders of national representative associations volunteered the impression that gaúchos were particularly association-minded and were active beyond the restrictions imposed upon them by geography and economics. An explanation for this, following our three major variables, would stress the relatively differentiated nature of the social structure, especially the more equalitarian distribution of land and income, the cultural role played by a large, mostly Germanic immigrant population, and the policy of the state government toward associations.

profitable positions and jobs. . . . To have five or six occupations at the same time and not practice any is not unusual."[5] João Capistrano de Abreu, the father of modern Brazilian historiography, summarizes the societal arrangement in colonial Brazil as follows:

> The mechanical trades never formed professional societies as they did in Europe. There were too few of them; moreover, although one could live from a single occupation in the big cities, in the less densely populated areas one needed seven trades to make a living. Even in the cities, they had to compete with enslaved officials. . . .
>
> The lack of grêmios was evident in other classes. They continued to exist in a historical sense, but their activity, already weakened by the vastness of territory, dwindled away until a leveling absolutism ignored their privileges. Except for some religious brotherhoods and such charitable associations as the almshouses, which were always worthy and active,[6] gatherings were always transitory: house-raisings, fishing trips, roundups, fairs, and novenas. Between the state and the family were interposed no coordinators of energy or formers of tradition, and there was no definitive progress. . . . Social life did not exist, for there was no society.[7]

Buarque de Holanda asserts that this institutional impoverishment distinguished Brazil from the Spanish-American colonies, presumably implying that differences in present-day associability can be traced to this factor.[8] It seems doubtful, however, that the guild tradition provided the basis for modern representative associations, even in societies where that tradition was strong.[9]

Workers' Associations

The Companhia de Prêtos Trabalhadores para o Serviço da Alfândega da Capitânia de Pernambuco, founded in Recife in 1812, has been called the first workers' association in Brazil.* On closer examination, it appears to have been more a novel attempt by local authorities to regulate the working conditions of dock-working slaves than a modern (i.e. voluntary) association. There is little evidence that associability among workers increased until the emancipation of the slaves in 1888 and the proclamation of the Republic the following year. Aziz Simão says there were a few mutual benefit societies, especially within the German colony.[10] Evaristo de Moraes Filho describes two "pressure groups formed by free workers with the aim of making demands," the Liga Operária founded 1870, and the União Operária, founded 1880, both in Rio.[11] What must be the oldest workers' association with a continuous existence, the Association of Commercial Employees of Rio, was also found-

---

* The National Federation of Workers in Warehousing (Comércio Armazenador), founded in 1939, claims to be the direct descendant of the Companhia dos Prêtos of 1812. I got this information from an unpublished manuscript kindly furnished by the present president of the Federation.

ed in 1880. By 1930 this association existed in 46 cities and claimed to
have a membership of 38 thousand.[12]

The important changes of 1888 and 1889 were followed by a period
of intensive development, innovation, and speculation. This period,
known as the *Encilhamento*,[13] was accompanied by a rise in immigration and a sharp increase in associability on the part of workers.
Numerous leagues, centers, "societies of resistance," unions, and syndicates were formed in the first decades of the twentieth century to serve
the workers in certain territories, plants, and industrial categories.[14]
Some of the names of the associations (e.g. Círculo Socialista Enrico
Ferri, Allgemeiner Arbeiterverein, Federação Espanhola, Liga Operária
Italiana, and Liga Anti-Clerical) and of their publications (e.g. *O Grito
do Povo, Avanti, La Propaganda Libertária, Volksfreund,* and *A Guerra
Social*) attest to the importance of immigrants and of anarcho-syndicalist ideas in this early period.[15] Regional peak associations soon appeared,
the first and most important of which was Federação Operária Regional
Brasileira of Rio, founded in 1903. Three years later, the first national
workers' congress was held. Representatives from 30 associations and
seven states attended.[16] In 1908, as an outgrowth of this congress, the
Brazilian Workers' Confederation (COB) was created with a German
immigrant printer, Edgar Leuenroth, as its president. That same year
the COB organized "a tremendous protest demonstration [in favor of
peace], in which about two hundred workers' associations from Rio
plus delegations from other states participated, forming a procession of
more than ten thousand people."[17] Exaggerated though these figures
may be, they do indicate an impressive outburst of spontaneous organization in the first decade of the twentieth century.

As we have seen, the initial response of authority groups to the expansion of associability was to legalize the situation by offering registered
syndicates certain limited rights and privileges. Preventive co-optation
seems to antedate by several decades the more extensive use made of
it during the 1930's. One example of this deeply rooted and persistent
national style was the way the authority groups handled the Fourth
National Congress of Workers in 1912. This meeting of 187 delegates
from 71 associations was the high-water mark of the early stage of
worker organization.[18] Interestingly, the congress was held in the Palácio Monroe, seat of the Brazilian Senate, and all the expenses of workers' representatives, including maritime passages, were paid by the authorities. The organizer of the congress was Mário Hermes, a federal
deputy and the son of Marechal Hermes da Fonseca, President of the
Republic. Observers have traced to this meeting the policy of government sponsorship and paternalism in workers' organizations, and have
called Mário Hermes the first in a long line of national *pelegos*.[19]

Except for a period of renewed activity during and shortly following the spurt in industrialization caused by World War I, the dynamism of the Brazilian workers' movement declined during the 1920's. Ideological conflicts over who would control the movement, coupled with sporadic police repression, weakened and fragmented its organizational impetus. The COB and several of the more important regional federations folded. Leôncio Martins Rodrigues argues that the gradual shift in the recruitment of the labor force from external immigrants to internal migrants contributed to a decrease in the militancy and associability of members or potential members.[20] During this time, the newly founded Communist Party gradually extended its control over the divided movement. It set up parallel federations and syndicates, especially in São Paulo, Santos (the Brazilian Barcelona), and Recife and attempted in 1929 to set up a national central, the General Confederation of Labor of Brazil (CGT). The period immediately prior to the revolution saw a rise in worker militancy—there were lengthy strikes in São Paulo and Rio—and in repression by authorities. The Communist Party was declared illegal in 1928, and the CGT was prevented from holding its convention in 1930.

The influence of workers' organizations in the 1930 revolution was slight, if not nil.[21] The victors had relatively little difficulty in establishing strict limitations on workers' participation in political and associational life. They controlled the terms under which associations could form or reform, forced employers to accept the representative status of recognized workers' syndicates, and deprived the latter of their anticapitalist pretensions. The facility with which the new rules of the game were imposed does not confirm, however, the revolutionaries' claim that they found workers' groups in a state of "most complete and painful anarchy." A tradition of associability had existed among Brazilian workers before 1930, a tradition of "associations created spontaneously by worker militants who were strongly embued with collective ideologies and who saw syndical organization and economic and salary demands less as an end than as a means, as an instrument designed to prepare and organize the working class for the economic and political struggles that would end in the abolition of private property and in the collectivization of the means of production."[22] In terms of the conceptual apparatus outlined in Chapter 1, the pre-1930 groups were movements. The net effect of the Vargas sponsorship policy was to persuade or force them to accept the role of representative associations.

Employers' Associations

Although employers' associations in Brazil before 1930 probably had less relative coverage and density than workers' associations, a considerable number—even a national network—of formal organizations represented the collective interests of merchants, rural landowners, and industrialists.

Commercial associations. The oldest representative association in Brazil with a continuous historical existence is probably the Associação Comercial of Bahia, founded in 1811, shortly after the Portuguese crown lifted its commercial monopoly by opening the ports to foreign ships.[23] This association was followed by numerous others during the Empire.[24] They were formed in the port cities to represent a small number of importers, mostly foreigners. They then expanded gradually to include merchants engaged in internal trade, industrialists, bankers, and various professional people; but they had difficulty casting off the image produced by their origins.[25] Until well into the twentieth century, these commercial associations served as the sole aggregators of the interests of the conservative classes, or, as they now prefer to call themselves, the "productive classes" (*classes produtoras*). Even today, in small, undifferentiated communities, the only local employers' association may be called "Associação Comercial Industrial e Rural de . . . ." The Commercial Association of Bahia, for example, is divided internally into the same three categories in an attempt to maintain "the unity of the conservative classes."[26] As we shall see, the organizational unity of many such associations had been broken and more specialized associations had appeared by 1930. This process whereby the commercial associations lost their representational near-monopoly was greatly accelerated, however, in the 1930's and 1940's.

The best known of the commercial associations is that of Rio de Janeiro. It very soon became important because of its proximity to national decision-making centers.[27] From its creation as the Sociedade dos Assinantes da Praça in 1834 under Imperial sponsorship, the AC-Rio has played a role in virtually all the major events of imperial, republican, and dictatorial Brazil. According to its official history, it had a key role in such diverse events as the creation of the Banco do Brasil, the promotion of the first railroads,[28] the laying of the first submarine telegraph cable, the drafting of the Commercial Code, the establishment of the first system of coffee classification, the Paraguayan war and the assistance given to its veterans, the abolition of slavery,[29] and the proclamation of the Republic. In 1912 the AC-Rio joined with fifteen other commercial associations to form the Federation of Commercial Associations of Brazil, the first formal national peak association in the country. The president of the Rio Association was made the permanent president of the Federation, and the latter appears never to have had an independent organizational existence.[30]

The First Congress of Commercial Associations of Brazil was held in

Rio in the fall of 1922. By that time the network of such associations had grown to 68, with almost every state represented. In addition to these, 29 other "class institutions" attended, most of them from Rio itself. Already some more specialized organizations had formed, e.g. Centro de Fiação e Tecelagem de Algodão, Centro da Indústria de Calçados e Comércio de Couro, Centro Comercial de Cereães, Centro de Navegação Transatlântica, and Liga do Comércio Importador. Also present were a large number of foreign chambers of commerce: Portuguese, French, Spanish, Belgian, North American, and British. Two similar conventions of employers' groups met four years later in São Paulo and made recommendations to the president of the state and to the President of the Republic. Oliveira Vianna observed these conferences and was favorably impressed with the directness of their action, especially with their having bypassed "unauthentic and unresponsive parties." He considered them "the first step toward the permanent constitution of consultative organs of our economic classes attached to public authorities."[31] Another of Brazil's early sociological essayists, Gilberto Amado, could claim in 1928 that "the example of other class associations, of the commercial associations for example, is characteristic. In no other country do the merchants talk so much and show themselves to be so vigilant in the defense of their interests as they do in Brazil, especially in the Federal Capital. They obtain what they want from Congress, some things justly desired, other things favorable only to themselves."[32] All this is hardly evidence of organizational anarchy. On the contrary, it is evidence of a gradual process of institutionalization, extension of coverage into new areas, coordination into national organizations, and politicization with ever more active participation in national policymaking. The plurality among workers' associations was rarely duplicated among employers' associations. The specialized centers and foreign chambers of commerce mentioned above seem to have functioned alongside and sometimes within the AC-Rio, instead of offering a competitive alternative.

The commercial associations never had a popular image. The official history of the AC-Rio frequently laments the misunderstandings, attacks, and scapegoating to which commercial associations were subjected and glowingly reports their paternalistic but futile attempts to improve their image. One obvious problem was that they represented the wealthy; merchants are particularly subject to charges of illicit gains in an inflationary economy. Moreover, the commercial associations also suffered from their foreign image: until 1867 the directorate of the AC-Rio consisted of two Brazilians, two Englishmen, one Portuguese, one Frenchman, one North American, one Spaniard, and one German. A report in 1944 stated that they were still known popularly as "the old

Portuguese associations."[33] This diffuse, unpopular, anti-national image, plus the fact that they had backed the deposed President in 1930, made them obvious targets for revolutionary reform. When the directors of the AC-Rio presented themselves at the Catete Palace to pay their respects to Getúlio Vargas, they were refused an audience. One month later, an emergency election was held and an associate of Vargas was elected president of the organization.[34] A new era had dawned in the relations between public authorities and "the old Portuguese associations."[35]

Rural associations. Gilberto Freyre comments that Brazilian *fazendeiros*—planters, farmers, and ranchers—are "least given to acting together in combination," and that only the coffee growers "eventually learned to cooperate."[36] A brief history of associations active in this sector bears out this observation. During the Empire, a number of regional institutes and societies were formed under official sponsorship, each "with the aim of cultivating, creating, and diffusing agricultural information by maintaining a model farm."[37] After 1888 more of these regional associations were formed, and in 1897 the Sociedade Nacional de Agricultura (SNA), the first with formal national coverage, was created. In addition to sponsoring many technical innovations and holding numerous expositions and national congresses, the SNA is credited with initiating the 1902 syndical law, with creating sixty similar associations in various states by 1908, and with sponsoring and staffing the Ministry of Agriculture in 1906.[38]

Of the regionally based associations, by far the most important has been the Sociedade Rural Brasileira (SRB), with headquarters in São Paulo. In spite of its title, the SRB recruits primarily within the state of São Paulo and primarily among large, traditional landowners.[39] Its organizational structure was modeled on that of the Sociedade Rural Argentina,[40] and its original objective was "to orient and stimulate cattle-raising in São Paulo and all of Brazil," probably because of a postwar crisis in the export market for meat. Coffee, however, soon became its major concern. As a paulista newspaper stated, "General Coffee has definitely installed his headquarters in the SRB."[41] The SRB takes credit for having set up the official Instituto de Café de São Paulo,[42] and from its members have come most of that organization's executives, as well as most of the secretaries of agriculture of the state of São Paulo. It later vehemently opposed the Conselho Nacional do Café and its successor, the Departamento Nacional de Café (DNC), in spite of the fact that one of its directors was also a DNC director.[43] The position of the SRB and of coffee growers in general vis-à-vis the role of official autarchies charged with regulating the coffee sector is well summarized in the following quotation: "The SRB has always recognized the necessity for a state organ of national scope that would watch over the coffee economy ... but has always opposed an entity that would serve the interests of the government and be subordinate to the Ministry of Finance."[44] Such a policy more or less foredoomed the Society to constant conflict with public authorities.

The SRB, it should be stressed, has not restricted its activities to the defense of coffee interests. It not only has absorbed other agricultural associations,* but has been a fertile producer of specialized associations for stockmen, citrus fruit growers, poultry farmers, cotton growers, etc. Nor is the SRB strictly a regional organization, since it has served and continues to serve as a point of aggregation for agrarian interests from other states than São Paulo. It is true that in the period before 1930 the interests of São Paulo received most of the SRB's attention (and apparently the SRB did not participate in the SNA, which was much less coffee-oriented), but the Society nonetheless did represent a broad set of organized institutions. In its Annual Report of 1929, the SRB could proudly state: "Although completely stripped of any political character, the SRB maintained with public authorities the most cordial of relations."

Industrial associations. Brazilian industrialists, although definitely latecomers to the differentiation process, early demonstrated a certain superiority in the art of association. The Viscount of Mauá reportedly said in 1851, "The spirit of association, gentlemen, is one of the strongest elements of prosperity of any country; it is, so to speak, the soul of progress."[45] He was, of course, referring primarily to the industrial or financial joint stock company; but one could hypothesize that the early industrialists' awareness of the need to combine their resources in joint ventures was likely to spill over into an awareness of the mutual advantage in cooperating vis-à-vis public authorities.

The first industrialists' association, the Auxiliary Society for National Industry (SAIN), was founded in 1828. "Endowed with a semiofficial existence, living off the favors of the state," SAIN, in spite of its title, actually grouped "members of the most diverse *classes cultas* of society" and was greatly weakened by the "dispersion of their ideas" and "the differences in their designs."[46] Sporadically active throughout the nineteenth century, SAIN was unable to provide the collective strength necessary to force a revision of the predominantly liberal and fiscally oriented tariff.[47]

Dissatisfied with their failure to obtain a protectionist tariff revision in the 1870's, and bothered by the constant opposition of commercial

---

* For example, it absorbed the Sociedade Paulista de Agricultura and the Liga Agrícola Brasileira in 1931 and the Associação de Lavradores de Café do Estado de São Paulo in 1951.

interests, a group of industrialists from the Associação Comercial do Rio founded in 1880 the first representative association exclusively for industrial interests, the Associação Industrial.[48] The new association immediately set about collecting statistics, placing articles in the press, and sending representatives to the Ministry of Finance and the Senate. The organizational effort seems to have been somewhat premature. The association's first president resigned to become a federal deputy, and its first directorate complained that attendance at assemblies suffered because of a "lack of practice and associative experience." Moreover, although the association had representatives of such conventional industries as textiles, hats, candles, chemicals, foundries, and naval construction, there were also a great many artisans: boilermakers, locksmiths, tinsmiths, tailors, carpenters, and cabinetmakers. "It must not have been easy to bring together such heterogeneous elements," comments Nícia Vilela Luz.[49] In 1881, tariff rates were reduced in spite of the Association's efforts.[50] At this point, just prior to the proclamation of the Republic, Luz stops mentioning the Associação Industrial, presumably because it had ceased to exist.

Its campaign was taken up with added vigor in 1902 by the newly created Centro Industrial do Brasil (CIB), the first nominally national industrialists' association. Formed of a fusion of the dormant SAIN and the more specialized Industrial Center of Thread and Textile Manufacturers of Rio, the CIB carried the fight for industrial protectionism throughout the difficult wartime period. It provided its members and government authorities with technical information, planted articles in newspapers, offered conferences for the benefit of the general public, and held national congresses for the various industrial categories.* Its statutes clearly announced its intention not only to promote "the desired economic independence of the country" by advancing the cause of industrialization, but also to become the center of a new network of representative associations by promoting "the development and prosperity

---

* The Brazilian pattern suggests that in a large, heterogeneous country, representative associations find it difficult to establish national associations without prior organizational preparation. Where there is no widespread network of preexistent regional associations, one way of stimulating a national interest consciousnessness is for one constituent unit (usually the one in the national capital) to sponsor sporadic national congresses or conventions. Frequently these meetings end with a resolution to create a new national association. It is also a means by which a polyfunctional association can "spawn" more functionally specific ones. This observation suggests a modification of Tocqueville's hypothesis that the art of association would spread from local to regional and finally to national associations. The formation of national associations along the path of Tocqueville's model is, of course, encouraged by the legal norms of the Labor Code. But few of Brazil's private national entities have taken this route. Many were created as the result of national conventions called by preexisting associations or government agencies; not a few were created *de toutes pièces* without any prior organizational consolidation.

of diverse branches of industry, assisting whenever possible in the formation of kindred associations in the states in order to establish with security a federation of industrial interests in Brazil."[51] There is no evidence that the latter objective was attained; participation in the CIB seems to have remained largely restricted to Rio. Humberto Bastos claims it had 338 member firms in its founding years. If so, this would have been a rather high density, since the Industrial Census of 1907 counted only 3,258 industrial establishments in all of Brazil.

The new political and social forces liberated by the impact of abolition and republican government resulted in a policy change in favor of tariff protectionism and accelerated public credits for industry.[52] During this time, however, consumers from both the rural and the urban sectors were complaining about the rise in prices, and the industrialists, especially of the CIB, found it necessary to become defensive in order to conserve their position. Campaigns were mounted for tariff liberalization in 1909–10, 1913–15, and 1919–20; the CIB, under the leadership of Jorge Street, fought each of these initiatives successfully. But the issue boiled up again in the late 1920's. The growing group of industrialists in São Paulo began to feel more strongly the need for a more independent form of organization. Until then they had worked within the Commercial Association of São Paulo, which, unlike that of Rio, had taken a more protectionist, pro-industrialization line.[53] In 1928 a small group, mostly men of immigrant extraction, founded the Centro das Indústrias do Estado de São Paulo (CIESP).[54] The inaugural speech was given by the group's vice-president, Roberto Simonsen; it left no doubt that the industrial class had found a new and dynamic leader and the creator of a persuasive ideology of national independence through industrialization. The major points of his speech show the degree of ideological and theoretical sophistication that had been attained by that early date.

First, Simonsen argued that, although the basic structure of Brazilian society rested on agriculture, only by having an important industrial plant could Brazil gain her economic independence and the prestige and power accorded to a great nation by other world powers. Those who were resisting the development of industries were, consciously or unconsciously, aiding those who would keep Brazil dependent on foreign producers. Second, he denied that industrialization was responsible for high prices. This was the product of an indiscriminate tariff and insufficient income and productivity. More industrialization, not less, could help lower prices. Third, he argued that industry was not "a monopoly favoring half a dozen privileged individuals," but an important factor in opening up society by providing social mobility. Seen in this way, industrialization and industrialists had an important social function: to minimize the class struggle. Fourth, he denied that industry was incompatible with agriculture; the two were, according to him, complementary by nature. Industry was in no way responsible for a shortage of manpower in the fields, since only 3 percent of the population worked in industry. Fifth, he returned to the international field by noting that Argentina was outdistancing Brazil. This, he said, had important consequences for national security. Finally, presaging what was to become a fundamental theme of the ECLA doctrine in the 1950's, he observed that Brazil's balance of payment difficulties were due to the unequal movement of the terms of trade favoring industrial producers over raw materials suppliers.[55] Simonsen's speech was a virtuoso performance; it marked the beginning of a new ideology of industrialization. In spite of resistance from within the ranks as well as from without, this ideology gradually became the orthodox nationalist position. In Simonsen, the Brazilian industrial class found its most articulate spokesman and its most active interest-group entrepreneur.

Both Simonsen and CIESP's president, F. Matarazzo, deftly attempted to avoid an open break with other interest sectors. The accent was on the natural harmony among the specialized components of the "productive classes." CIESP announced its intention to become a focal point for preexisting industrial-class associations and to assist in the formation of new ones, and it invited the other interest groups to send representatives to its Consultative Council. The attempt at harmony failed somewhat when the AC-Rio accused Simonsen of trying to alienate commercial interests[56] and the SRB labeled his speech "ultra-protectionist."[57] In the next few years, many a protestation of faith was made, and many a congress was held in an attempt to demonstrate the essential harmony of the "productive classes." The representatives of the various employers' interest sectors made herculean efforts to be accommodating and to avoid open public confrontations and disagreements. On issues that might have driven them apart, such as the distribution of public credits, foreign investment, exchange rates, and export policy, the disagreements were expressed discreetly, almost privately; and when there were bitter conflicts within the productive classes, they were not between sectors, but between different associations claiming to represent the same sectorial interests. Nonetheless, and in spite of this superficial public harmony, the founding of the CIESP in 1928 marks the moment at which these interests took separate courses once and for all. Structural differentiation had asserted itself in associational form.

Middle-Sector Associations

The middle sector, that amorphous cluster of professional and technical employees, had also begun to find associational means of interest expression prior to 1930. The oldest of these is probably the Institute of Brazilian Lawyers (IAB), founded in 1843. The Clube de Engenharia in Rio had played an active role in introducing technological innovations and pressuring for industrialization since 1880.* By far the best known middle-sector associations of the late Empire and Old Republic period were the military clubs: the Clube Naval, founded in 1884, and the Clube Militar founded in 1887. Mixtures of social club, welfare agency, and representative association, these two, especially the latter, played a role in virtually every major political crisis during the period. One of the Military Club's first acts was to declare that military units would no longer consent to being used for hunting down runaway slaves. Another prominent institution, also a combination of social club and representative association, was the Brazilian Press Association, created in 1908. Its perennial fight for the protection of press freedom continued into the dictatorial period. In 1917 accountants organized their first syndicate in Rio de Janeiro; in 1927 physicians did likewise. The *Correio da Manhã* for the years 1929–31 contains scattered references to other associations, especially to clubs and unions of public employees. Apparently none of these survived, at least not under their original titles.

Where the Brazilian art of association was especially poorly developed was in the field of what S. E. Finer and Allen Potter have called "promotional groups." Unlike "interest" or "spokesman" groups, promotional groups do not press for their own sectorial, material interests; rather, they espouse causes, or what they consider the more general goals of society.[58] Few associations based on religious, confessional, civic, racial, communitarian, or even ideological attitudes were evident before 1930. There was a Catholic renaissance during the 1920's, led by Jackson de Figueiredo and Tristão de Athayde of the Ação Católica. This same period also witnessed the beginning of racially based protest associations and feminist groups like Sra. Berta Lutz's Federação Brasileira pelo Progresso Feminino, formed in 1922. The Associação Brasileira de Educação began promoting educational reform at the national and state levels in the early 1920's.[59] But, as so many of Brazil's historical and sociological thinkers have observed, the great changes in policy and regime were not accomplished under the influence of political ideologies or with the support of organized masses of people. Independence, abolition, republicanism, even the revolution of 1930 did not leave a heritage in the form of promotional representative associations. Of course, the Masons and the Positivists lingered on in their lodges and clubs, but they failed to play a consistent role as interest articulators or aggregators.

* The São Paulo equivalent of the Clube de Engenharia is the Instituto de Engenharia, which was also active before 1930.

Conclusion

In terms of the dimensions discussed above—coverage, density, functional specificity, and plurality—the associational base line of the late 1920's was far more elaborate than the revolutionaries of 1930 imagined or admitted it was. There were formal organizations for most of the urban interests and for some of the more specialized, export-oriented rural ones.* Functional specialization of these groups was low, but it was increasing rapidly: they were already divided among the rural, commercial, and industrial sectors. Although most of the associations were in Rio, São Paulo, and a few of the coastal cities, there were national associations linking outlying regions to common interests. The limited data available indicate that the density of membership was moderate.[60] Plurality existed primarily among workers' organizations and to a limited extent in the overlap between commercial and industrial associations.

This associational base line limited the new political elite somewhat in their efforts to impose their syndicalist-corporatist model of interest representation during the 1930's and early 1940's. Prerevolutionary associations usually managed to survive if they had an independent financial base, a sufficient degree of membership participation, and a fairly elaborate administrative and decision-making structure. Some of them even succeeded in forcing important concessions and compromises upon the emerging syndicalist-corporatist framework. In the end they were co-opted and made semiofficial, but they kept substantive control over their internal organization and their external activities. The poorly organized, low-density, and weakly financed associations put up only feeble resistance to the new policy and either disappeared or became dependencies of authority groups. As a rule, the line of survival ran along class lines. Most employers' and professional associations survived; virtually all employees' and workers' associations succumbed in the early 1930's.

---

* One must note that the legitimacy accorded this form of interest expression was differentially distributed and that workers' associations were subjected to sporadic repression. This factor, a product of government policy and paternalistic-authoritarian political culture, contributed to an uneven associational life among workers. The pattern of employer and professional associations was more regular and cumulative. Presumably, then, the numerous observations on the "most complete and painful anarchy" referred only to workers' associations.

SEVEN

The Pattern of Emergence: A Quantitative Analysis

As a consequence of their corporatist policies of active sponsorship, Brazilian authorities became more concerned after the revolution of 1930 with collecting information on the number, geographic locale, functional scope, and membership of representative associations. Hence, the pattern of emergence from the early 1930's until the present can be documented with some completeness and reliability from records kept by the Ministry of Labor.[1] After 1952, the Ministry of Agriculture began issuing similar information about the rural associations.* The number, variety, and membership of the civil entities have not been reported or collected by any official body. Occasionally, such data can be obtained from association publications or interviews. But because this information has been incomplete and obtained episodically, it has not been added to the syndical data. Since the pattern of emergence of the private groups differs markedly from that of the semipublic ones (for reasons to be discussed in Chapter 8), the following quantitative analysis is necessarily distorted. It underestimates the increase in coverage and density that has occurred during the 1960's.

Coverage

The most obvious indicator of an extension of organized interest expression is an increase in the overall number of associations. Figure 4 shows that the total number of syndicates has indeed increased as hypothe-

---

* Rural associations, though legally recognized by the Ministry of Agriculture, are not subject in practice to the same controls as syndicates. However, given their semi-official status and financial dependency, I have included them in the corporatist system of representation. At several points in the analysis their membership is merged with that of urban workers, employers and professionals. Since 1964, and especially since 1965, these rural associations have been converting themselves into *sindicatos rurais*.

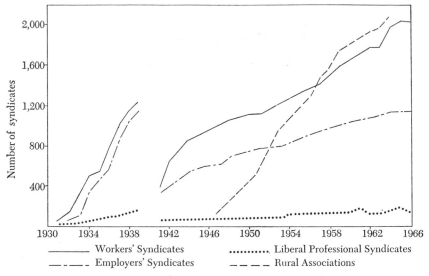

FIG. 4. NUMERICAL EXPANSION OF SYNDICATES AND RURAL ASSOCIATIONS, 1930–65.
(Adapted from Brasil, IBGE, *Anuário Estatístico—1937/38–67.*)

sized. According to the latest available census (1967), there were 3,290
sindicatos in all: 2,018 representing workers, 1,150 representing employers, and 122 representing the liberal professions. In addition, there
were some 1,975 rural associations (in 1965). The total in 1930 for all
types of interests combined probably did not exceed 500.

These gradients of associability, viewed globally, do not resemble
closely the curves related to structural differentiation as described in
Chapter 2. They are not steep enough or exponential enough to accompany the rise in mass media exposure or urbanization during the 1950's
and 1960's. Nor do they reflect the rate of industrialization: the stagnation in the 1930's, the steep rise in the 1940's, and the subsequent falling
off in the 1950's. The global configuration of syndicate formation conforms most closely to the rates and rhythm of bureaucratization: a
sharp rise in the late 1930's, a slowing down in the 1940's, and a rapid
cumulative takeoff during the 1950's and early 1960's. It is interesting
that both developmental processes twice suffered relapses at the same
times, in the early 1940's and again in 1964. Thus the rate of official association formation in Brazil responds more immediately to political incentives and inhibitions than to basic societal changes. The latter provide the necessary precondition; the former provide the sufficient precipitating events. It might be argued that the rapid numerical expan-

sion in the 1930's represents the delayed impact of repressed interests from an earlier period, but this argument is untenable when the emergence pattern is examined in detail. For example, in 1938 Ceará, with an industrial manpower of 6,972, a commercial work force of 15,878, and an urban population of 475,028, had almost as many syndicates as the city of Rio de Janeiro, with an industrial work force of 110,443, a commercial employment of ·72,210, and an urban population of 1,500,000! Clearly some factor other than structural differentiation was playing an important role.[2]

The pattern of emergence, then, is by no means continuous or linear, and it does reflect the importance of intervening political variables. The abrupt break between 1939 and 1941 marks a period during which data collection was suspended pending a change in registration procedures and a drastic revision in the *enquadramento* provisions of the CLT. Not until fifteen years later did the number of workers' organizations reach the 1939 peak. The sheer quantity of employers' and liberal professional syndicates has never attained the height of fragmentation of this previous, unregulated period. Rural associations began late, grew very fast, and overtook the workers' groups by 1956.

The most dramatic demonstration of the impact of political conditions is obtained by juxtaposing the annual rate of association formation against changes in government policy toward associability (in 1931, 1934, 1937, 1940–43, 1947, and 1964) or against changes in national chief executives (in 1945, 1950, 1954–55, 1961, and 1964). In most cases, until the mid-1950's, both employers' and employees' syndicates responded coordinately and simultaneously, whereas the liberal professional associations remained stagnant and unaffected throughout. The employers and the employees both seized the advantages of the new legal status of 1931 and of professional representation in 1934, although the employers' response was more sustained. The coup of 1937 had a greater impact on workers' associability—the number of new sindicatos dropped from 145 to 73—whereas employers barely flinched at the new, more authoritarian corporatism, dropping only from 141 to 135. The ouster of Vargas in 1945 sent the employers' rate plunging; workers responded favorably to the first two years of "democratization." From 1947–51 repressive controls were reinstituted and worker associability fell; there were only 21 new syndicates in 1950–51. Employers responded favorably to these controls at first, but after 1948 their rate of formation also fell. With the removal of the "ideological certificates" and the freeing of syndicates from intervention in 1951, both types of syndicates increased steadily in number until the suicide of Vargas in 1954. After a short interregnum, workers' organizations began to climb from 47 to 58 and finally to 93 a year in the relatively benign climate of the Kubitschek regime when João Goulart controlled the Labor Ministry. Employers' associations went into a peculiar and unaccountable series of two-year organizational cycles, rising and falling rhythmically. The accelerating inflation and executive instability of the early 1960's drove the rates down drastically (they were actually negative for workers' associations in 1963). But as a result of the plebiscite, with parliamentarism discarded and Goulart's political position apparently consolidated, the association rate for workers climbed dramatically to 185 during early 1964 (this presumably includes the beginning of the rural syndicalization movement), and the employer rate climbed only slightly less impressively—to 58 for the year.

Of course the number of associations and the rate at which they were formed is only one dimension in which associational coverage expanded. Functionally, the distribution of workers' syndicates in the late 1930's showed a heavy concentration in the field of transport and communications, especially in maritime transport. In the ensuing twenty-five years, the numerical importance of transport syndicates declined. Rural interests came to be represented by a different associational hierarchy, and the functional base of urban representation broadened. Throughout this period, however, industrial workers and commercial employers were the most active in forming syndicates. From 42 percent in 1936 to 57 percent in 1961 of all workers' syndicates were in the industrial, construction, and mining sectors. Almost one-half of all employers' syndicates are accounted for by tradesmen and merchants, despite the existence of a vigorous and numerous set of "parallel" private associations representing the same categories.

Regionally, the expanding network of interest representation gradually lost its initial strong concentration in Rio and São Paulo. This industrial area's hegemony declined from 45 percent of the total in 1936 to only 33 percent in 1963. The shares of both the Northeast and the Extreme South have increased markedly. Again, this pattern of variation seems to be related to the developmental process that has belatedly extended to these peripheral areas. It also reflects, of course, the legal restrictions on plural forms of representation and the organization maturity of areas that have already attained high levels of occupational complexity. This gradual shift in locale from the central to the peripheral regions suggests that in Brazil the organizationally rich are not becoming organizationally richer and are unlikely to do so under conditions of corporatist control and sponsorship. This in turn suggests possible consequences for national federations and confederations, namely, that they will tend to be dominated by provincial traditionalists. However, as I shall explain, the process of national leadership selection does not respond easily to changes at the local level and is very sensitive to manipulation from above by authority groups. This somewhat counterbalances the provincializing tendency of the corporatist system. Nonetheless, there is a long-term trend in the outlying areas toward greater participation in syndical activity.

The diffusion of representation through rural associations has, for some reason, proceeded inversely. In this case, the area of initial concentration was the Northeast, and an increase in the aggregate number of associations has shifted their distribution southward. The Center-East, with the transitional states of Minas Gerais and Bahia, and the South, with its more rationalized agricultural techniques, have grown proportionately the most. Rural associability in the industrial Center-South remains relatively fixed, partly because of the especially urban status of Guanabara.

Density

Presumably, where there is a sufficiently differentiated set of interests and attitudes, some entrepreneurs will be intrepid enough to try to regiment them into formal organizations. We are now interested in observing who uses these new channels of expression. As operationalized here, the measure of density is purely quantitative: how many occupants of a given category are members of the association that purports to represent it?* Again, to answer this question we must rely on data made available by the Labor Ministry and the Agriculture Ministry on semipublic organizations and on what occasional information I have been able to glean from published sources and interviews.

As Figure 5 demonstrates, the formally tabulated membership in all types of syndicates has increased. Brazil had only 389,000 registered workers, employers, and professional people at the time the system was being changed in 1938; by 1946 there were 880,000, and by 1966 there were over 1,856,000. Moreover, we can assume that certain entities did not report.† If we ascribe to them the average size of the reporting syn-

---

* In Chapter 9 I shall discuss the qualitative aspects of density, i.e., I shall describe member participation in associational activities.

† The percentage of nonrespondents to the Labor Ministry's questionnaire has been remarkably constant. Globally speaking, it varies from 30 to 35 percent. Although there is no way of ascertaining whether or not the delinquent syndicates remain the same (liberal professional syndicates, for example, are particularly poor respondents; over half of them consistently neglect to answer), the proportional constancy does suggest the presence of a relatively fixed quotient of inoperative "phantom" syndicates in the system. Correcting for this certainly results in an overestimate of

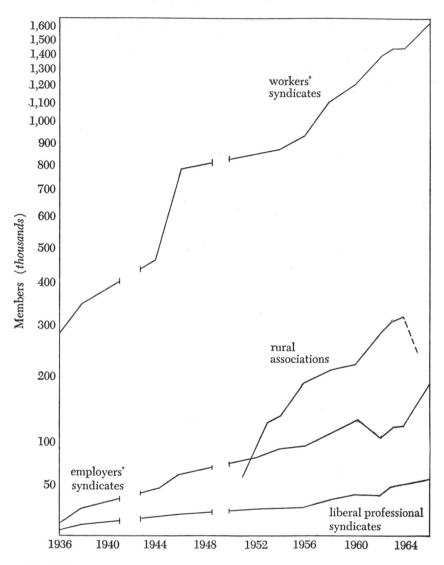

Fig. 5. Expansion of Membership in Syndicates and Rural Associations, 1936–66.

dicates, the total for 1966 is increased to approximately 2,200,000.[3] Also some of the annual irregularities observable in the graphed raw data can be removed by this corrective procedure. For example, the membership decrease in 1960–61 in employers' associations is partially imputable to measurement error.

Earlier we noticed an interesting peculiarity of Brazilian corporatism. Worker and employer syndicates tended to respond more or less coordinately to changes in public policy; increases in the total number of one type were accompanied, often after a slight time lag, by increases in the total number of the other. We also observed, however, a weakening of this concomitant variation in the late 1950's and 1960's. Now we can see that, at least for a certain period, total membership figures behave in somewhat the same way. Both employers' and workers' syndical participation increased sharply after 1944 and proceeded more gradually after 1946. Together both also took off again in 1956 at a sharply accelerated rate. Then in 1960, something had a very disparate impact on the two types of syndicates. Among workers, membership began to soar and continued to expand unabatedly until 1964. Among employers, on the other hand, it declined absolutely and subsequently remained stagnant. This phenomenon is still apparent when corrected totals are used. Nothing we have so far observed in the developmental pattern would lead us to anticipate this. Only the influence of short-term vicissitudes in public policy toward associability helps explain it: the election of Jânio Quadros, his resignation after eight months in office, and the ensuing regime of João Goulart. Clearly, Goulart's demagogic, or populist, manipulation of the Labor Ministry did stimulate worker participation—which included the rural sector for the first time—and made employers wary about using and being used by this semipublic system of interest articulation. As we shall discuss in the next chapter, employers did not withdraw from associational channels altogether; rather, they shifted increasingly to private entities. Membership in rural associations seems to follow a dynamic of its own. Membership in liberal professional syndicates shows only slight signs of growth, largely because, as we shall see, the major middle-sector categories—lawyers, doctors, and civil servants—were organized outside it.

---

the total, since nonrespondents are credited with the same average membership as respondents. There exists no visible incentive or sanction attached to increases or decreases in membership for syndicates. Their financial support is fixed by the total size of the category, and the law requiring that one-third of the relevant category be members has not been enforced.

It is impossible to correct rural association memberships. Incidentally, in this case, both government subsidies and voting strength in peak associations were proportional to reported membership, providing an important incentive for overreporting.

TABLE 7.1

SYNDICAL MEMBERSHIP, POPULATION GROWTH, AND SOCIOECONOMIC
CHANGE, 1940–60

(Selected indices; 1940 = 100)

Index	1950	1960
Total population	125	172
Urban population (in cities over 10,000)	161	305
Economically active population	113	147
Total industrial employment	160	214
Literate population	139	237
Contributors to Retirement and Social Welfare Institutes	167	237
Uncorrected syndical membership	144	213
Uncorrected syndical and rural association membership	165	247
Corrected syndical and rural association membership	207	331

SOURCE: Brasil, IBGE, *Recenseamento Geral — 1940, 1950, 1960*; Brasil, IBGE, *Anuário Estatístico—1958, 1961, 1965.*

Table 7.1 compares the rate of expansion in syndical membership since 1940 with that of other economic and social populations. By corrected or uncorrected calculations, with or without the rural associations, the rise in formal participation in these types of representative associations definitely has outstripped the general demographic increase and the rise in the economically active population. The uncorrected totals show a rather striking similarity to the patterns of increase in industrial employment, literacy, and contributors to the Retirement and Social Welfare Institutes. Only the phenomenal rate of urbanization seems to have outrun syndicalization (the index of corrected membership is undoubtedly an overestimation).

Thus not only the number of syndicates and their total membership but also the density of Brazilian associational life has increased over the past two decades. The total (corrected) membership in syndicates and rural associations combined rose from 4.3 percent of the economically active in 1940, to 6.5 percent in 1950, to 8.0 percent in 1960. Deducting the agricultural sector from both sets of data, 16.4 percent of the urban employed were formally registered as of 1940, 17.9 percent in 1950, and 25.4 percent in 1960. Although these corrected figures certainly include a number of "phantom" entities, it seems safe to say that between one in four and one in five Brazilians employed in the urban secondary and tertiary sectors in 1960 were members of one of the three types of syndicates.[4] Obviously, if memberships in the burgeoning number of private entities could be included, even discounting for overlap, the global density would be even more impressive.

Before passing out congratulations to the corporatists, however, we should observe that Brazil's performance is hardly impressive, even by the modest standards of Latin America. Using figures from *América en Cifras—1965* (used above in connection with total membership in Brazilian syndicates in 1966) and controlling for total population, Cuba, Venezuela, Argentina, Colombia, Chile, Uruguay, Mexico, Peru, Bolivia, and Paraguay have higher densities of trade union membership than Brazil.[5] Correlating these global estimates of worker organizational density with an indicator of labor force diversification proposed by Marvin Olsen,[6] the product-moment coefficient across nineteen Latin American polities in 1960 is a highly significant .597. Brazil emerges with a slightly negative regression error, indicating a poor performance, but one more or less consistent with the regional norm for its level of structural differentiation. Of course, the density of associational life should vary by occupational category and geographic locale, and global estimates can be misleading for a society as diverse and as unevenly developed as Brazil's.

Brazilian census data do not facilitate—to put it mildly—the quest for reliable indices of membership density by occupational groups, especially because confirmation rests partially on adequate time series information, as well as on information aggregated into appropriate categories. The absolute values expressed in Table 7.2 should therefore be considered approximate. We can, however, be fairly confident about the direction of change and the rank order of categories. Although, as we observed above, the overall proportion of those registered has increased, the density of certain specific occupational categories has not. Commercial employers, for example, seem to be participating less in syndicates (and participating more in other types of representative associations). Manufacturers and larger farmers have been more prone to join syndicates.[7] Among workers, the industrial proletariat shows the highest increase in density. Almost one-half were formally enrolled in syndicates in 1960. Land transport workers (truckers account for most of them), bank employees, and maritime workers all show a decrease, although in the latter two cases the total levels are relatively high.[8] As a rule, Brazilian corporatism provides a more complete system of representation and control for workers than for employers; at least, their density of participation is generally greater. Of course, one reason for this is that employers (and middle-sector professionals) have at their disposal other, i.e. private, organizational channels for expressing their demands.

The logic of the differentiation-associability argument leads one to anticipate, as an auxiliary hypothesis, that the more functionally specific or occupationally specialized the group, the greater the density of asso-

TABLE 7.2
Syndical Membership of Employers and Workers in Selected Economic
Sectors, 1950 and 1960
(*percent*)

	Members of syndicates	
Economic sector	1950[a]	1960
Employers from		
Industrial firms	17.9%	20.4%
Commercial firms[b]	13.3%	11.7%
Rural establishments[c]	9.8%	11.9%
Workers in		
Industry	38.4%	45.8%
Commerce[d]	32.7%	39.0%
Banking	45.3%	43.7%
Maritime transport	102.4%	65.1%
Land transport	14.4%	14.3%

Source: Data on number of firms and rural establishments are from the General Censuses of 1950 and 1960. The specialized sectorial census of industry and commerce furnished the data on workers. Populations in banking and transport were calculated on the basis of membership in their respective Social Security Institutes.
[a] Membership data (uncorrected) for 1952.
[b] Includes hotels.
[c] Excludes establishments with fewer than ten hectares.
[d] Does not include hotel workers.

ciational participation is likely to be. The global data presented seem to confirm this: the lower densities are in the less differentiated fields of agriculture, commerce, and land transport. Of course the categories used are too crude to permit a reliable conclusion. For a detailed test of the proposition, it is necessary to shift levels of analysis and to consider only the industrial workers' syndicates in the municipality of São Paulo. Such information is presented in Table 7.3. It does appear that in 1961 the more traditional industries—food, textiles, clothing, leather goods, and construction—have proportionately fewer syndicalized workers. Public utilities must be considered something of a special case. Otherwise workers in the dynamic, modern sectors of industry seem more inclined be members. The data reported for 1964 show a markedly different pattern, however. This study of the paulista syndical network is based on responses to a written questionnaire in which leaders were asked for the number of active associates. Perhaps because of discrepancies in their respective definitions of active membership, or simply because of inadequate knowledge about it, some dramatic rank order reversals occurred.* The construction trades, well known in Brazil for their irra-

---

* Having asked a similar question in my interviews, I discovered that association leaders are usually ill-informed about the size of their *classe* and frequently even unaware of the exact number of their members. Incidentally, about half of the syndicates admitted to having less than the one-third of the category required by law.

TABLE 7.3

SYNDICAL MEMBERSHIP OF INDUSTRIAL WORKERS IN SELECTED INDUSTRIES,
SÃO PAULO, 1961 AND 1964
(*percent*)

| | Members of syndicates | |
Industry	1961	1964
Public utilities	79.9%	75.9%
Toys and instruments	——^a	59.7%
Chemicals	——^a	49.5%
Rubber products	49.2%	51.5%
Paper and cardboard	45.0%	45.9%
Metallurgy	41.1%	18.7%
Printing	——^a	36.2%
Food	35.2%	47.1%
Leather goods	31.7%	52.6%
Textile spinning and weaving	28.5%	20.1%
Clothing	26.0%	28.5%
Construction	20.1%	79.2%
Glass and crystal	——^a	14.9%

SOURCE: For 1961, Brasil, Servico de Estatística, *Cadastro Sindical—1961*; SENAI, *Relatório de 1961*, as cited in "A Situação Económico Social da Classe Trabalhadora em São Paulo," *Revista de Estudos Sócio-Econômicos* (São Paulo), I, 7 (Mar.-Apr. 1962), p. 28. For 1964, Rabello, p. 178.

^a Data not available.

tional production methods and high use of illiterate, unskilled rural migrants, move from last place to first! The Syndicate of Metallurgical Workers of São Paulo—which frequently vaunts itself as the largest workers' organization in Latin America—falls from a respectable (and anticipated) above-average 41 percent to 19 percent.[9] The other changes are less marked, but the overall configuration of these self-reported densities does cast some doubt on the assumption that the differentiation and associability interact at all levels of the social and political system.

The density of business and professional groups is even more difficult to assess on a systematic comparative basis. As we have seen, employers' syndicates generally have a lower proportion of membership than workers' syndicates. There are exceptions, and some of the most important come from the National Syndicates. This small, privileged set of interests, which has been permitted to form direct channels of formal syndical representation, bypassing the state federations and national confederations, consists primarily of economic sectors in which the structure of ownership is quite concentrated. Hence, these sindicatos frequently include all the firms operating in the sector, or at least all the larger ones.*

* In interviews the following densities were reported: coal, 100 percent; cement, 97 percent; automotive manufacturers, 100 percent; airline companies, 98 percent;

The low density of the average employers' syndicate is, no doubt, related to the existence of alternative channels of formal as well as informal interest expression, channels that are not available to most workers' groups.* A recent North American observer has claimed that ideological resistance to the corporatist system plays a key role.[10] In my interviews, I did observe that employers' leaders strongly resented some of the restrictive and manipulative aspects of their semipublic status as well as the dubious authenticity of certain syndical leaders. The prevailing mood, however, was one of pragmatism and even opportunism, rather than dogmatic liberalism. They expressed a clear willingness to use both the semiofficial and the autonomous private channels of formal interest articulation. My previous discussion of the political subculture of associational leaders demonstrated a remarkable degree of agreement among representatives of various social classes on the issue of government intervention in interest politics.

A recent public opinion poll in the major capital cities asked respondents, "What is your opinion concerning sindicatos?" Sixty-eight percent answered, "There should be freedom, but it should be controlled to prevent the infiltration of subversive elements." Despite the vague wording of the question, and despite some possible reluctance to be frank given the nature of the regime at that time, this response does represent rather strong urban support for existing interventionist policies. Eighteen percent opted for "complete syndical freedom, even renewing the risk of Communist infiltration." This proportion varied from a high of 35 percent in Salvador and 25 percent in São Paulo to a low of 9 percent in Belém and Fortaleza and 10 percent in Guanabara and Brasília. Since these figures are not broken down by class, status, or occupation, they do not rule out the possibility of intense resistance to corporatism in specific sectors. But they do seem to suggest that the attitudes of associational leaders are not very different from those of the urban populace.[11]

A more immediate explanation for their low density is simply that classified as industrial and commercial firms are a vast number of arti-

---

maritime companies, "all the large firms and many small ones"; matches, "all"; cinema producers, "all but a few insignificant ones"; iron ore, "all the major ones"; public contractors, "the most important ones." It was not possible to interview anyone in the beer industry or the book publishers' syndicates, but they do not appear to deviate from the norm.

* One should not, however, underestimate the membership performance of employers' syndicates. For example, in 1961, 8,480 of São Paulo's industrialists were members of FIESP-affiliated syndicates. With 25,521 industrial firms then in existence in the state, this produces an approximate density of 32 percent, which compares favorably with the 46 percent for industrial workers in the same state.

san establishments and small owner-operated shops.* According to the *enquadramento* provisions that set the formal functional scope of representation, a one-man electrical appliance repair shop and a factory producing refrigerators are equally entitled to membership and participation in the same syndicate. Whether or not the repairman is likely to feel any bond with the large manufacturer, he simply does not have time to participate. The large manufacturer, at the other end of the scale, has the resources to employ an exclusive, full-time representative to the political authorities. If his resources are sufficient and his network of personal contacts adequate, he can afford to bypass the syndicate.† Although there are exceptions, employers' syndicates tend to recruit from and to be led by a disproportionate share of small to medium-sized concerns.

The new private associations are not so handicapped. They can, so to speak, predetermine their own density. Where the number of firms is large, as, for example, in the food processing or trucking industries, the objective is frequently not to encompass all of them, but only those with the greatest volume of production or business. For example, the Brazilian Association of the Electrical and Electronic Industry has about 15 percent of the category as members, but this amounts, according to my informant, to 95 percent of the production. In interviews, the lowest reported density (in terms of output) of any private employer entity was the Brazilian Association of Public Contractors (ABEOP), with 50 percent. The highest was the Bahian Association of the Cacao Industry, which embraces 100 percent of both producers (of which there are seven) and production. Usually, density varied between 70 and 80 percent. On the commercial side, density is harder to judge, since the number of sales managers, finance executives, and retail merchants is not easy to estimate, but density appears high. A few groups, such as the Association of Credit, Investment, and Finance Companies (ADECIF), even have a waiting list of prospective members. The Association of Authorized Automobile Dealers claims that 1,937 of Brazil's 2,183 eligible dealers are in its ranks.[12]

Middle-sector professionals by themselves are neither great founders nor great joiners of representative associations. They are obliged to belong to the various orders, but—except for accountants, for some reason—they are not active in syndicates. Some of the private professional

---

* For example, in São Paulo in 1963, 70 percent of the industrial establishments had less than five employees.

† This is especially likely to happen when the syndicate is perceived as too heterogeneous, too dominated by medium-size firms, or too dependent upon authority groups.

associations draw a larger clientele. The Medical Association claims that slightly over one-half of Brazil's physicians are members.[13] The Military, Naval, and Air Clubs, the Institute of Architects, and the Club of Engineers all draw sizable contingents of those active in such professions. Government employees' associations, especially those of the municipal and state workers in São Paulo, have large and relatively dense memberships.[14]

Again, the validity of the general observation can be illustrated by a deviant case. The Syndicate of Professional Journalists of the State of Guanabara had, at the time of the 1964 coup, some 9,500 members. This very large membership was not unrelated to the fact that journalists in Brazil enjoy a number of legal, financial, and fiscal privileges: special courts, exemption from income and several other taxes, half fare on air travel, easier credit for the purchase of automobiles and apartments, etc. A subsequent inquiry disclosed that a large number of senators, deputies, public officials, businessmen, industrialists, military officers, bankers for the *jôgo do bicho* (numbers racket), and even Rio's best-known peddler of smuggled goods were members of the syndicate, holders of journalists' identity cards, and therefore beneficiaries of the profession's corporate privileges. After the purge, only a little more than one thousand "legitimate" journalists were left.[15] This was probably the only syndical category with a density greater than 100 percent, and it was certainly the only one with a density of 900 percent!

Quantitative Analysis

The extraordinarily diversified human ecology of Brazil, coupled with its political subdivision into 23 territorial units for enumerative as well as constitutional purposes, affords an opportunity to compare intranationally changes in the structure of social and economic activities and increases in the art of association. Unfortunately, the aggregate data are neither perfectly reliable nor entirely valid. Nevertheless, though correlational analysis alone cannot provide final proof of the supposed relationship, it can provide some supplementary evidence.

Before looking at the data, however, four basic methodological problems should be discussed. The first is the danger of committing what W. S. Robinson calls the "ecological fallacy."[16] There is no doubt that my interest here is in the propensity for a given person in a given structural setting to join and participate in a formal, politically-oriented, secondary association. There is equally no doubt that, given the properties of the variables examined, "ecological correlations [cannot] validly be used as substitutes for individual correlations."[17] Therefore, my conclusions are limited to generalizations about the relationships between the collective properties of units. Rather than proving that, because a given unit (i.e. a Brazilian state) is more urbanized, the urbanized people within it are more likely to be syndicate members, I am restricted to concluding that a more urbanized community is likely to be more articulated as a whole in terms of representative and other types of political associations.

The second major problem concerns the reliability of the aggregate data. This type of data is notoriously inaccurate, even though the quality of Brazilian census materials is certainly above the international norm.[18] Some of the difficulties are avoided by using intranational data, although unfortunately the quality of collection has varied considerably, as have the categories to which the information has been assigned. A special problem is posed by the fact that, although most of the economic and social background data come from the Brazilian Institute of Geography and Statistics (IBGE), various other government agencies have also collected data. These agencies have presumably had varying margins of error. The reports on the dependent variable, total membership in syndical organizations and rural associations, come from two different sources, the Ministry of Labor and the Ministry of Agriculture. The Labor Ministry's data present some special difficulties: enumerations of syndical membership were not available for precisely the three time periods selected—1940, 1950, and 1960. The data for 1940 therefore come from the 1938 Syndical Census and cannot be corrected to account for syndicates that did not report. Since the reliability of reporting in later years declines regularly with physical distance from Rio de Janeiro, these figures probably underestimate membership in the North, the Northeast, and the Extreme South. Data for 1950 were not available, so an interpolation was made between the 1953 and the 1947 figures. In 1953 it was possible for the first time to obtain information on the number of registered but nonreporting syndicates. For that year and for the 1960 data, corrections were introduced. An average size for each type of syndicate (worker, employer, and liberal professional) for each state was calculated and added to the reported figures. For states where less than half the syndicates reported in 1960, data from 1959 or 1961 were introduced. In one case, Paraíba, this was impossible, and I derived an estimate on the basis of comparison with other Northeastern states. Unlike the case for 1938–40, these corrective procedures definitely result in an overestimation of the density of syndical membership in the least developed areas of the country. This presumably had the effect of lowering the correlations with predictor variables. Membership in rural associations is reported by the Ministry of Agriculture, and no indication of nonreporting associations is given.

This type of semipublic interest group did not exist in 1940. The first membership figures became available in 1952; they are used here in lieu of 1950 data. In all cases the enumerations on membership were reduced to proportions by dividing by the total population of the state for that period. It could be argued that controlling for the economically active population would have been preferable, but such figures are not yet available for 1960. The statistics on all but one of the independent variables—industrialization, urbanization, rural employment, literacy, size of industrial firm, and communications participation—come from the national censuses of 1940, 1950, and 1960. The voting information is taken from the presidential elections of 1945, 1950, and 1960, as reported by the Supreme Electoral Court in the *Anuário Estatístico do Brasil—1961*.

The third major methodological problem concerns the validity of the variables as indicators of the concepts discussed above. Syndical membership, even when combined with membership in rural associations, by no means exhausts the total participation in representative associations. However, as mentioned, there are no available systematic data for membership in private associations. I am assuming that membership in them tends to follow the same distribution as membership in the semipublic variety, and that the latter is therefore a valid indicator of the art of political association. Industrialization is measured by the proportion of the total population employed in manufacturing establishments (*indústrias de transformação*). This excludes those in mining enterprises (a very small percentage) and includes workers, salaried administrative personnel, and owners. The measure for urbanization is the proportion of the total population living in cities and towns with more than ten thousand inhabitants. Literacy is measured by the proportion that is able to read and write according to census standards. No data are yet available for 1960. The average number of workers employed per establishment is used as the measure of the size of industrial firm. Communications participation, or exposure to mass media, is measured by the average number of cinema and theater admissions per capita. Data on radio or television audience or on newsprint consumption or newspaper distribution might have been preferable, but they were not available. In any case, the *World Handbook of Political and Social Indicators* asserts that on a global scale these communications indices are highly correlated.[19] Voting, or electoral participation, is measured not by the percentage of the total population voting, but by the percentage of those eligible and registered. This proportion is a better indicator of voluntary participation in national politics.

Finally, there is the special problem of how to consider statistics on the state of Guanabara (GB). Guanabara is a city-state. It was formerly the federal district, and it is made up of the city of Rio de Janeiro and very little else. Given its very special ecology, its presence in the distribution greatly increases the range and standard deviation of most variables. This, plus the fact that it has by far the highest syndical density (a fact that confirms my general hypothesis), tends to give a very

TABLE 7.4

SELECTED PARAMETERS OF DEVELOPMENTAL VARIABLES, BRAZIL
(WITH AND WITHOUT GUANABARA), 1940, 1950, AND 1960

Developmental variable	Mean		Standard deviation		Range	
	With GB	Without GB	With GB	Without GB	With GB	Without GB
Industrialization						
1940	15.3	12.9	14.8	10.4	1.2—62.4	1.2—42.2
1950	18.6	16.2	17.1	13.5	1.9—66.5	1.9—57.9
1960	16.8	14.9	16.1	14.1	3.2—63.6	3.2—63.6
Urbanization						
1940	15.6	11.7	19.1	6.6	2.2—94.2	2.2—31.3
1950	19.1	15.3	19.5	8.5	3.3—96.0	3.3—40.1
1960	26.9	23.3	19.7	11.5	7.8—97.5	7.8—52.8
Rural employment						
1940	27.4	28.7	7.6	4.7	1.2—36.1	19.9—36.1
1950	21.3	22.4	13.7	4.6	.7—31.7	12.1—31.7
1960	23.9	25.0	8.5	6.7	.6—37.3	7.1—37.3
Average size of industrial firm						
1940	17.3	16.7	8.9	8.7	6.7—41.8	6.7—41.8
1950	12.9	11.9	7.5	6.2	4.6—32.1	4.6—24.1
1960	12.0	10.9	7.6	5.9	3.4—33.6	3.4—23.6
Communications participation						
1940	1.5	.8	3.6	1.3	.0—16.2	.0— 6.2
1950	2.8	2.0	3.8	1.6	.4—17.8	.4— 7.1
1960	3.5	3.0	2.8	1.7	.4—13.6	.4— 7.9
Literacy						
1940	29.8	27.8	13.1	9.7	15.6—69.3	15.6—45.9
1950	32.3	30.3	13.7	10.6	16.8—71.2	16.8—50.7
1960	——	——	——	——	——	——
Voting participation						
1940	82.2	81.8	4.8	4.5	68.8—90.5	68.8—87.7
1950	71.6	71.5	5.6	5.8	60.7—89.4	60.7—89.4
1960	76.4	75.6	10.7	10.3	54.1—91.74	54.1—90.2

NOTE: GB stands for Guanabara. Reasons for excluding it are given in text, pp. 167–68. No literacy data were available for 1960.

skewed distribution to the variables and, one suspects, to make the degree of association seem artificially high. Rather than perform a log-arithmic transformation bringing Guanabara back into the fold, I have decided to give two sets of statistics for each index, one including Guanabara and one excluding it. Not only should this solution provide a clearer picture of Brazilian development and associability in general, it should also indicate the influence of Guanabara over the total ecology.

Table 7.4, giving descriptive statistics on the developmental variables, confirms the general pattern we examined earlier, although the exact figures differ because of the different corrective measures taken. Indus-trialization hit a peak in terms of employment in 1950; urbanization has been rising rapidly and continuously; rural employment is declining (the trough in 1950 is caused by a change in enumeration techniques); the average size of industrial firm is declining; exposure to mass media and literacy are steadily increasing. The initially high electoral partici-pation is merely a statistical illusion, since elections were not held until 1945 and the 1940 population was used to convert it to a proportion. More than half the variables show increases in both standard deviation and range, indicating a trend toward ever greater disparities between the states in these areas of development. Industrialization, urbanization, rural employment, and voting are getting more and more concentrated. Only the size of the industrial firm is showing any tendency to even itself out. Nevertheless, the range of variation is enormous—probably as great as or greater than the variation between entire Latin American countries. Thus it provides an excellent opportunity to compare the im-pact of these variations across geographical units as well as across time.

Table 7.5 presents descriptive statistics on membership in syndicates and rural associations. Although the absolute magnitudes are quite low (in 1960 only 2.27 percent of the entire population was registered in either type of organization), the range of variation is again great, and the standard deviations tend to increase over time. Like development, associability is very unevenly distributed over the Brazilian social land-scape. It is also important to note that the numerical contribution of employers' and liberal professional syndicates to raising the mean level of association membership is quite modest. The emergence of a large number of rural associations during the 1950's does have a more pro-nounced impact upon the global mean; however, at most this raises it only about one-third of one percent. Associability has been increasing, but it is still far from being a mass phenomenon. Only in Guanabara are more than 10 percent of the total population formally enrolled in these types of associations. The second-place finisher, São Paulo, is a long way behind with 4.6 percent.

TABLE 7.5
SELECTED PARAMETERS OF ASSOCIATIONAL VARIABLES, BRAZIL
(WITH AND WITHOUT GUANABARA), 1940, 1950, AND 1960

Associational variables	Mean		Standard deviation		Range	
	With GB	Without GB	With GB	Without GB	With GB	Without GB
Total syndical and rural association membership (*per capita*)						
1940	.87	.37	2.29	.31	0—10.8	0—1.6
1950	1.81	1.27	2.61	.88	.20—12.6	.26—3.3
1960	2.27	1.72	2.76	1.07	.52—13.4	.52—4.6
Total syndical membership (*per capita*)						
1940	.87	.37	2.29	.31	0—10.8	0—1.6
1950	1.81	1.17	2.61	.85	.20—12.4	.20—3.2
1960	1.95	1.38	3.03	1.01	.19—14.4	.13—4.4
Total workers' syndical membership (*per capita*)						
1940	.79	.34	2.05	.28	0— 9.6	0— .95
1950	1.54	1.07	2.31	.78	.16—11.0	.16—2.7
1960	1.76	1.25	2.45	1.92	.08—11.4	.08—3.8
Total rural association membership (*per capita*)						
1940	0	0	0	0	0— 0	0— 0
1950	.10	.10	.10	.10	.01— .38	.01— .38
1960	.32	.33	.24	.24	.11—1.20	.11—1.20

NOTE: GB stands for Guanabara. Reasons for excluding it are given on pp. 167–68.

A first glance at the zero-order correlation matrices presented in Table 7.6 shows many very high rates of covariance. Even given the propensity for data aggregated in large units to produce high correlations, the figures are impressive evidence of the interrelatedness and degree of concentration of the different developmental processes in Brazil. For a case base of twenty, correlations over .520 are significant at the .01 level. According to Karl Deutsch and others, a ratio of .380 is significant at the .05 level;[20] by this "modest standard," there is almost no bivariate relationship in Table 7.6 that is not at least minimally significant. Even voting participation, which starts out with a weak relationship to average size of industrial firm in 1940 and a generally weak relationship to all other variables in 1950, has recuperated so that by 1960 it is a significant part of the developmental process.

As we might have anticipated, the inclusion of Guanabara in the matrix results in a dramatic increase in the degree of covariance among almost all variables. Only the impact of the size of industrial firm re-

TABLE 7.6

ZERO-ORDER CORRELATION MATRIX: DEVELOPMENTAL AND ASSOCIATIONAL VARIABLES, 1940, 1950, AND 1960

Variable	A. With Guanabara							B. Without Guanabara						
	1	2	3	4	5	6	7	1	2	3	4	5	6	7
1. Industrialization														
1940														
1950														
1960														
2. Urbanization														
1940	.868							.788						
1950	.847							.819						
1960	.821							.803						
3. Average size of industrial firm														
1940	.610	.432						.611	.504					
1950	.794	.771						.674	.705					
1960	.791	.902						.695	.847					
4. Communications participation														
1940	.856	.976	.370					.712	.809	.295				
1960	.843	.970	.739					.814	.830	.618				
1950	.859	.959	.832					.867	.877	.682				
5. Literacy														
1940	.778	.805	.119	.780				.554	.634	−.115	.515			
1950	.794	.784	.477	.806				.647	.604	.158	.678			
1960	...	...	...	...				...	...	...	...			

	L1	L2	L3	L4	L5	L6	L7	R1	R2	R3	R4	R5	R6	R7
6. Voting participation														
1940	.490	.389	.219	.372	.401			.322	.056	.120	.013	.193		
1950	.279	.155	.279	.122	.090			.326	.270	.270	.195	.081		
1960	.633	.514	.513	.642	...			.572	.452	.417	.675	...		
7. Rural employment														
1940	−.759	−.859	−.317	−.806	−.822	−.386		−.435	−.550	−.153	−.305	−.621	−.131	
1950	−.594	−.795	−.631	−.805	−.613	.158		−.248	−.480	−.374	−.517	−.273	.274	
1960	−.668	−.859	−.726	−.844	...	−.562		−.510	−.771	−.566	−.732	...	−.483	
8. Total syndical and rural association membership														
1940	.791	.970	.346	.954	.745	.404	−.826	.764	.815	.497	.642	.635	.105	−.503
1950	.836	.965	.748	.956	.746	.218	−.731	.916	.786	.741	.710	.527	.536	−.217
1960	.786	.942	.813	.936	...	.523	−.733	.929	.838	.731	.841	...	.607	−.510

NOTE: Literacy data not available for 1960.

mains approximately the same, and this is because carioca establishments are not appreciably larger than the national average. Nevertheless, one observation of major importance is that the global pattern of relationships between variables is basically the same whether or not Guanabara is included. Thus we may conclude that development proceeds along roughly the same lines throughout the country, although, as we noted above, the disparity between developed and underdeveloped states is increasing.

One very noticeable result of using all twenty-one states is a remarkable constancy of certain patterns of relationships between developmental variables over the three time periods considered. In each of the cases shown in Table 7.7 (except for the relationship between industrialization and urbanization), the twenty-state universe showed rather steady growth tendencies, while with Guanabara included the relationships remained virtually unaltered. Since the absolute values of the variables changed considerably, one is tempted to cite these constancies as evidence of the good quality of the data. Such an outcome could hardly be due to chance or to radical changes in the reliability of the data. However, it might well have been a reflection of the relative excellence of information collected in the city of Rio de Janeiro itself.

Let us look at the bivariate correlations with the independent variable, total membership in syndicates (of all three types) and in rural associations. These figures appear in Table 7.6. The first and obvious observation is that, with one exception, the developmental variables individually are very significant predictors of associability. With Guanabara included, urbanization is the most highly correlated variable. Com-

TABLE 7.7

PEARSON *R* COEFFICIENTS FOR SELECTED PAIRS OF DEVELOPMENTAL VARIABLES,
WITH AND WITHOUT GUANABARA, 1940, 1950, AND 1960

Developmental variables	With Guanabara			Without Guanabara		
	1940	1950	1960	1940	1950	1960
Industrialization and Urbanization	.869	.847	.821	.788	.819	.803
Urbanization and Communications participation	.976	.970	.959	.809	.830	.877
Industrialization and Communications participation	.856	.843	.859	.713	.814	.867
Industrialization and Literacy	.778	.794	. . .	.554	.647	. . .
Communications participation and Rural employment	−.806	−.805	−.844	−.305	−.517	−.732

NOTE: Literacy data not available for 1960.

munications participation (itself highly linked with urbanization) is also a good predictor; so is industrialization, though less consistently so. Rural employment is strongly and negatively correlated with associability, and its declining strength is probably a reflection of the increase in rural association membership. The average size of industrial firm, insignificant in 1940, rises dramatically in 1950 and 1960 (despite the fact that the average size of firm is itself decreasing) until it becomes a very good predictor. Voting participation is the least related variable, although it, too, picks up considerably in 1960.

The deletion of Guanabara provides a crucial test for my hypotheses. With by far the highest scores on both the independent and the dependent variables, Guanabara alone might have been enough to distort the pattern of response. As Table 7.6 shows, although the magnitude of the associations has generally declined, developmental variables continue to be highly significant predictors of associability in the remaining twenty states. Nevertheless, some very important changes have occurred. In 1940, urbanization was still the most highly correlated indicator. Communications participation lost some of its potency, and second place was taken over by industrialization. Also, average size of industrial firm in 1940 is more closely related to associability in the provinces than in the entire country. These hints of a reduced role for urbanization and social mobilization once the exceptional case of Rio is excluded are confirmed by the 1950 and 1960 data. Industrialization becomes easily the best predictor; urbanization drops to second in 1950 and third in 1960. Communications participation, a rough equivalent of social mobilization, rises rapidly, surpassing urbanization in 1960. Voting, which in 1940 (or 1945) is unrelated to associability, becomes even more important in the provinces than in Rio by 1960. The other variables, particularly rural employment, decline in significance without the distorting presence of the former national capital.

These figures demonstrate convincingly that development has stimulated the emergence of associational forms of interest expression. More specifically, development is seen to be associated with increase in the density of member participation in representative associations. The pattern of bivariate correlation suggests that differentiation variables (industrialization and size of industrial firm) will have a greater impact on associability than mobilization variables (urbanization and communications participation)—at least, if one discounts the abnormal influence of Rio. This hypothesis, however, cannot be adequately tested by bivariate, zero-order correlations alone. In order to determine the independent relationship between a single variable and a given outcome, holding all other specified variables constant, the appropriate technique is partial correlational analysis. In order to determine the independent relative impact of a change in a single variable upon change in a given outcome, holding the relative impact of all other specified variables constant, the appropriate technique is multiple regression analysis.[21] Both were applied to the data.[22]

Two things are immediately apparent from Tables 7.6–9. On the one hand, the multiple correlation techniques definitely improve our ability to predict the density of association membership. From the already high degree of association demonstrated by single developmental indicators, the level of predictability comes close to unity when we measure the linear additive effect of all the indicators. With Rio included, urbanization alone correlates .970 with associability in 1940 (see Table 7.6). Moreover, the coefficient of multiple determination climbs as high

TABLE 7.8
MATRIX OF PARTIAL CORRELATIONS: DEVELOPMENTAL VARIABLES
UPON ASSOCIABILITY, 1940, 1950, AND 1960

Developmental variable	With Guanabara			Without Guanabara		
	1940	1950	1960	1940	1950	1960
Industrialization	.008	.119	−.208	.019	.787	.683
Urbanization	.685	.546	.615	.073	.039	.570
Literacy	−.396	−.252	...	.406	.139	...
Size of industrial firm	−.362	−.143	−.316	.337	.314	−.209
Voting	.296	.204	.235	−.156	.677	.515
Rural employment	−.103	.188	.606	.062	−.338	.429
Communications participation	−.061	.429	.239	.091	−.373	−.274

NOTE: Literacy data not available for 1960.

TABLE 7.9
MATRIX OF STANDARDIZED BETA COEFFICIENTS: DEVELOPMENTAL VARIABLES
UPON ASSOCIABILITY, 1940, 1950, AND 1960

Developmental variable	With Guanabara			Without Guanabara		
	1940	1950	1960	1940	1950	1960
Industrialization	.006	.077	−.110	.025	.808	.607
Urbanization	1.258	.652	1.199	.119	.024	.763
Literacy	−.258	−.131	...	.590	.066	...
Size of industrial firm	−.181	−.072	−.209	.474	.165	−.123
Voting participation	.069	.056	.102	−.089	.294	.271
Rural employment	−.045	.086	.401	.043	−.139	.253
Communications participation	−.074	.479	.324	.104	−.243	−.270
MULTIPLE R	.982	.974	.969	.872	.965	.961
MULTIPLE R^2	.960	.950	.940	.760	.930	.920

NOTES Literacy data not available for 1960.

as .982 (Table 7.9). In 1950 it rises from .965 to .974, a more modest improvement, although at these high levels of relatedness it represents a considerable gain. In 1960 predictability increases from .942 (Table 7.6) to .969 (Table 7.9). Without Rio, the multiple correlation in 1940 rises to .872, compared with a bivariate correlation of .815 (Table 7.6). In 1950, industrialization best predicts association membership outside Rio (.916). However, when the other components of development are considered, the correlation becomes .965, which predicts some 93 percent of the total variance. In 1960 the improvement is less striking (from .929 with industrialization alone to .961). It is interesting to observe that for the twenty-one-state, complete sample the regression equation declines during the period considered, whereas for the twenty-state sample it increases from 1940 to 1950 and then retains its predictive power until 1960. This I would interpret as additional evidence of the contrived nature of early syndicalization—its concentration in Rio, its lack of connection with prior differentiation of social and economic structures, and its essentially political motivation. Subsequently, what was originally a creative, co-optive, preemptive maneuver on the part of political authorities began to lose some of this artificiality. Membership became less concentrated in Rio as industry grew and agriculture declined in other areas of the country, particularly in São Paulo. Therefore, multiple correlation becomes less predictive over time when Rio is included and more predictive when it is excluded.

The second obvious conclusion is that the partial correlations and standardized beta coefficients are not interpretable. It is manifestly implausible, for example, that literacy in the same year (1940) could have a strong negative impact with Rio included and a strong positive impact with it excluded, or that in the space of ten years the independent contribution of voting participation could change from slightly negative to strongly positive. The pattern for the beta weights is similarly confused and illogical. The reason is obviously the high degree of interrelatedness of the independent variables—or, in statistical jargon, multicollinearity. This violates the basic causal model assumed by both these techniques, that the predictor variables be independent of each other. Therefore, one variable tends to get all the credit and those correlating heavily with it are made virtually insignificant. Occasionally, as in the case of urbanization and communications participation in 1950 (with an intercorrelation of .970), the two variables will get approximately equal credit. Usually, however, one receives a high partial correlation or beta weight and those related to it are reduced to impotency. Since the independent variables are so related and since the relationships shift slightly over time, the principal variable shifts very dramatically.

Multivariate analysis does seem to support my hypothesis concerning the roles of the mobilization and differentiation variables. However, such support must be considered very tentative at this point, given the rather erratic effect of the other variables and the high degree of interrelatedness between all supposedly independent conditions. For this reason, both the partial correlation and the multiple regression were run again with only two ecological variables. The findings are presented in Table 7.10. Despite the considerable degree of interrelatedness between urbanization and industrialization, it may still be useful to examine their relative predictive contributions in isolation from the other more erratic and occasional variables. Although we can be sure that one of the two will dominate the other to some degree, it is crucial to my hypothesis to find out whether there is a definite shift in the relationship between them. Using the full sample, urbanization gets virtually all the credit, although the magnitude of its predictive influence declines rather steadily. Industrialization is reported as having a negative impact on associability in 1940 and almost no impact in the two succeeding periods. As before, the total capacity for predicting the multiple correlation declines. For the universe excluding Rio, the equations tell a very different story. In 1940, urbanization and associability covary more than industrialization and associability, although industrialization makes a considerable positive contribution. By 1950 the tables have turned. Industrialization in the provinces is getting all the credit, and its importance is even greater in 1960. Urbanization, after its poor showing in the interim period, is also a strong contender in 1960. Nevertheless, even in the last period for which we have data, a 10 percent increment in industrialization would be related to a rise in associability of some 7 percent, whereas an equivalent proportional rise in urbanization would have only a 2.5 percent impact. It is also interesting to note that without

TABLE 7.10

PARTIAL CORRELATIONS AND BETA COEFFICIENTS: IMPACT OF INDUSTRIALIZATION
AND URBANIZATION ON ASSOCIABILITY, 1940, 1950, AND 1960

Measure of correlation	With Guanabara			Without Guanabara		
	1940	1950	1960	1940	1950	1960
Partial *R*'s						
Industrialization	−.417	.135	.067	.339	.768	.788
Urbanization	.932	.879	.839	.537	.156	.416
Standardized betas						
Industrialization	−.205	.067	.039	.319	.827	.722
Urbanization	1.147	.908	.909	.563	.109	.258
MULTIPLE *R*	.975	.965	.942	.839	.918	.942
MULTIPLE *R*²	.950	.930	.890	.700	.840	.890

Guanabara the multivariate capacity for prediction climbs continuously. By 1960 it exactly equals the figure for the twenty-one-state universe.

I think it is permissible to infer from this evidence that the basis of Brazilian associability has indeed shifted since 1940 as my hypothesis suggests. When the city-state of Guanabara is included, the mobilization variables—urbanization, in particular, but also its closely related partner, communications participation—continue to be the best predictors of associability. When this highly politicized special case is removed, however, we discover another pattern of relationships in which structural differentiation, as measured by industrialization and by size of industrial firm, plays the more prominent role. In the one case, modernization provides the major impetus to a restructuring of political group activity along associational lines; in the other case, development, or increase in the division of labor and emergence of a class-based stratification system, seems to be behind the process. What the future course of the art of association will be in Brazil—with the former process increasing at steady, exponential rates and the latter still faltering—is difficult to predict.

EIGHT

The Pattern of Emergence:
A Qualitative Description

In Chapter 7 the emergence and diffusion of the "art of association" were examined in strictly quantitative terms. Aggregate data were broken down, built up, cross-tabulated, graphed, and correlated in a variety of ways to test the relation of associability to changes in economic, social, and political conditions. In most cases, covariance occurred in the anticipated direction. In several respects, however, the analysis was a failure. For one thing, it ignored associations not registered in the official syndical system, and these associations, as we shall see, have played an increasingly important role. It also failed to give the reader a concrete grasp of all that goes into association formation. In an effort to fill this gap, this chapter presents a descriptive and, unfortunately, fragmentary historical survey of associations active in Brazilian national interest politics since 1930.

Syndical Organizations

According to corporatist principles, the sindicato's territorial preserve is restricted to the município, or county. Although a given policy issue may propel a local syndicate into national relevance,* the Brazilian system is explicitly designed to minimize such direct articulations of interest and to channel demands through a set of intermediary federations and confederations. Therefore, in discussing nationally relevant groups, I am excluding most syndicates from detailed consideration.

---

* A particularly dramatic instance of this occurred when a group of navy and marine noncommissioned officers barricaded themselves inside the headquarters of the Rio Metallurgical Workers' Syndicate, providing the final precipitating incident for the April 1964 coup.

As with so many other features of the system, exceptions are permitted at the discretion of authority groups, and they tend to become the rule. A recent study revealed that only 46 percent of the workers' syndicates in São Paulo had a strictly municipal or county jurisdiction; 30 percent were state-wide, and 24 percent were at least intermunicipal.[1] Employers have been even more successful in avoiding local confinement at the sindicato level. Especially important to Brazilian interest politics as well as to this study are the few national syndicates (*sindicatos nacionais*). By special dispensation, certain categories of workers and employers have been permitted to bypass the limitations of territorial scope and intermediary aggregation imposed by federations and confederations. All the national workers' syndicates represent transport workers: twelve represent various types of merchant seamen and officers, and two represent airline personnel. All but two were formed before 1946. The fourteen employers' categories given the privilege of forming national syndicates are characterized by industrial power, concentrated ownership, and protectionist privilege. They are the iron ore, coal, matches, beer, and cement industries, the shipping and airline companies, the publishers and movie producers, the automobile manufacturers, the merchants dealing in precious stones, the prospectors, and the public works contractors.* Except for the last two, they all have few members simply because they are fields dominated by single firms or by small numbers of firms.[2] They also depend greatly on government protection and assistance. Since most of these syndicates were established after, not before, the special status and privileges had been acquired by the categories, I assume that becoming a national employers' syndicate is a product of or reward for having attained special access and favors, rather than a means for attaining them. Like the workers' national syndicates, most of these interests acquired their special status early in the syndical movement. According to informants who got theirs late (automobile manufacturers and public works contractors), it takes a lot of *pistolão*, or political pull, to accomplish this now. No new ones have been permitted to form since the early 1960's. At any rate, some of the most important interest sectors, especially in industry, do have direct, specialized channels of access through the syndical system.

Most sectors, however, have depended for the expression of their interests at the regional and national levels on the process whereby lower-level organizations are consolidated into federations and confedera-

---

* Reference was found to a national syndicate of railroad companies; but because most of these companies were nationalized after the war and because efforts to locate the syndicate failed, it is presumed to have folded.

tions.* The formation of semiofficial peak associations has followed a more orderly pattern than that of syndicates, although the rate of formation is affected by policy changes from year to year. There are currently 123 workers' federations, 75 employers' federations, and eight national confederations. Associability at these upper levels seems to depend on high levels of development even more than does associability at the syndicate level: 39 percent of all federations (and only 27 percent of the syndicates) are based in Guanabara or São Paulo.

Employers' associations. By far the best known of the state federations is the Federation of Industries of the State of São Paulo (FIESP). FIESP is a convert to official syndicalism. It existed before the policy modifications of the 1930's as the private Center of Industries of the State of São Paulo (CIESP). It voluntarily became an official syndicate (changing its name in order to include syndicates as well as individual firms), and in 1942 it was recognized as the exclusive official spokesman for the industrialists of São Paulo. The change was not made painlessly, however. In fact, from 1934 until 1941, because of personal rivalries and conflicting political ambitions, three industrial federations coexisted.[3] Roberto Simonsen was president of two of them: the Federation of Industries of the State of São Paulo and the Paulista Federation of Industries. To my knowledge, this marked the first use of an organizational tactic that later was to become common, especially in São Paulo—that of maintaining parallel representative associations. With an overlap in leadership, this technique permits exploitation of the advantages both of a private, financially and politically autonomous organization with individual membership and of a semiofficial, financially secure, sponsored organization with indirect membership and guaranteed access. In 1939, under the pressure of the new *enquadramento*, with its unitary corporatist measures, the rival Federation of Employer Syndicates of Industry of the State of São Paulo, led by Horácio Lafer, merged with the Paulista Federation of Industries, which in turn merged with FIESP. The former title Centro das Indústrias was revived to baptize the new, parallel private entity, CIESP. FIESP and CIESP have continued side by side to this day, sharing executives, administrative personnel, office space, and objectives.

Similar federations grouping industrial syndicates have been formed

---

* Again, although federations are "normally" statewide, exceptions are permitted. Some very important categories have been granted direct, exclusive, and specialized national representative roles. Employers are represented by associations of insurance companies, banks, and private schools; professionals by associations of journalists, dentists, and customs agents; and workers by associations of railroad workers, truck drivers, printers, stevedores, port workers, warehousemen, gas station attendants, maritime workers, and telephone and telegraph workers.

in every state but Mato Grosso and Acre.[4] Two are also converts of a sort: the Federation of Industries of the State of Guanabara (FIEGA), which claims to be a descendant of the Centro Industrial do Brasil, and the Federation of Industries of the State of Rio Grande do Sul (FIRGS), a syndical version of the Centro da Indústria Fabril. Both of these are in turn linked to state-wide, private parallel associations, or *centros industriais*. The state federations of commerce, although relative latecomers, are more numerous now than the industrial federations (there are 34 of the former and 20 of the latter), and they cover all 23 states.* They seem to have been sponsored originally by the preexistent commercial associations. The first directories of the São Paulo and Rio federations overlapped completely with those of the corresponding commercial associations.[5] Indeed, parallel groups often occupied the same quarters. Unlike the parallelism of the industrial federations and the centros industriais, however, that of the commercial interests broke down, and in the 1950's separate and frequently warring directories were chosen. The syndical hierarchy was and still is more oriented toward domestic trade, the commercial associations more around problems of export and import. As we have seen, rural associations began to multiply in the early 1950's. Encouraged by the Ministry of Agriculture and helped initially by generous federal subsidies, these associations rapidly formed state federations. By 1955, all states had federations of rural associations. Some, but by no means all, began transforming themselves into *federações de agricultura* under the financial and political guidance of the Ministry of Labor by 1965. The most active of the rural federations are in São Paulo, Minas Gerais, and Rio Grande do Sul, regions of advanced agricultural development.

As we have seen, some national representative associations had already been formed by 1930, but the new decrees accompanying the revolution promised a more elaborate system of national interest representation. There were to be fourteen confederations, a variety of specialized advisory boards, and a National Economic Council with corporate representation. Not all of this promise was fulfilled. The industrialists were the first—and until 1946 the only—occupational group to take full advantage of the corporatist opportunities. In 1933, the Industrial Confederation of Brazil (CIB) was formed with the participation of the state federations in São Paulo, the Federal District (now Guanabara), and Rio Grande do Sul (the federation in Minas Gerais joined

---

* They are more numerous because in some states there are specialized federations for retail commerce, for wholesale commerce, for tourism, or for salesmen. Guanabara and Rio Grande do Sul have four federations each, Piauí has three, and Pernambuco, Rio de Janeiro, and Paraná have two each.

these three in 1935). Its objective, as stated in Article 2 of its statutes, was to "represent in the Federal District the federations and those syndicates and associations of the states lacking federations." More evidence that the CIB was to have an essentially passive role comes from its first circular, which pleads with the members to send "their requests and representatives by way of this confederation." Furthermore, it was plagued by financial troubles and a "hostile environment."[6] But it was strengthened by its role in coordinating the industrial representation to the 1934 Constituent Assembly and by its official recognition in the same year. In 1937 Roberto Simonsen became its president. The CIB's reaction to the coup of that year and to the innovations in social legislation of the late 1930's was a resolution "to lend our decided support and our solidarity to the constituted powers at all times. . . . The industrial employers' institutions have taken great care to cooperate with the central government in the good execution of [its] numerous social measures."[7] In 1938, the CIB, "to give unity to the defense of its interests within the directives of the prevailing syndical legislation," changed its title to the Confederação Nacional da Indústria (CNI). This new title and this purpose have remained the same since then.

The first and only president of the CNI until 1954 was Euvaldo Lodi, a mineiro by origin and an engineer by training. Lodi had important industrial interests (iron, coal, textiles, and road construction) in several states, he had participated in the 1930 revolution, he had been a member of the October Third Club, and he was a close advisor and intimate friend of President Vargas.[8] Simultaneously president of the CNI and of the Rio Federation,* Lodi collaborated with Roberto Simonsen of São Paulo in virtually creating from scratch the system of semiofficial, national industrial representation. By the time he stepped down in 1954, all but four Brazilian states had industrial federations, and the CNI had become the most prominent representative association in the country.

Once the tide of war had turned against the Axis, it became increasingly obvious that some substantial changes in the nature of the regime were in the offing. The days of official syndicalism seemed numbered, as did the whole panoply of paternalistic corporatism. Shortages were manifold; wages had been frozen; prices and expectations had risen. In the new climate it no longer seemed possible to maintain the heavy restrictions on worker organizational autonomy or the lavish favors that had been bestowed on employers' associations. There was a widespread fear that the Communists, driven underground in 1935 but not destroyed,

---

* The Rio or Federal District Federation was more or less unofficially fused with the CNI and did not have an independent administrative existence until Lodi was deposed in 1954.

would profit from the dissatisfactions and capture the loyalties and organizations of workers. In this climate of uncertainty and apprehension, faced with the probability that their postwar role would have to be redefined, the employers' associations began to hold national conventions and congresses. The most important of these was the First Conference of the Productive Classes of Brazil, held in Teresópolis in May 1945. Almost six hundred rural, commercial, and industrial associations from every state in the country attended the five-day meeting, called jointly by the Federation of Commercial Associations of Brazil and the National Confederation of Industry.

The resulting Economic Charter of Teresópolis was something of a milestone in Brazilian interest politics. Its slogans, "Fight against Pauperism," "Increase in National Income," "Development of Productive Forces," "Economic Democracy," and "Social Justice" were and still are endlessly repeated. Its Declaration of Principles was by no means a simple rewording of liberal capitalist orthodoxy. Rather, it was a fascinating and rather original—if not always consistent—fusion of diverse ideologies. It began with the inevitable association of freedom and private enterprise, but immediately admitted that this must be restrained "by the precepts of justice and . . . the unavoidable limitations imposed by the fundamental interests of national life." It recognized the necessity of "a certain degree of interference by the state" and the importance of the "harmonious development of all regions and equal opportunities for all individuals," "the guarantee for men from the city and from the country of a real salary permitting them to live with dignity." and "the necessity for economic planning."[9] It also recommended that public authorities be given an increasing role in conservation, in agricultural development, in the production of energy and expansion of transport, in tariff protectionism, in developing basic industries, in preventing the formation of cartels, in import controls, and in stimulating but controlling foreign investment. At least on the verbal level, the "productive classes" seem to have understood that for postwar Brazil to have a "political democracy it must also have a corresponding economic democracy." They openly but cautiously proclaimed their willingness to compromise in the construction of a new social democratic order.

On the issue of the future configuration of representative associations, the Charter offered a very subtle package deal. The main features of the existing system would be maintained: "The state [should] guarantee freedom of association, without other restrictions *except those dictated by the common good,* and [should] consequently favor the syndical movement. For this end, it should assure the regime of *syndical unity,* giving the organs so constituted the prerogative of representing their respective categories . . . before the state and in the signing of collective agreements . . . and the *right [of the syndicates] to the contribution of all those in their respective categories* . . . subordinated to official fiscal control." (Italics mine.) Not only should the corporatist props remain—unity, monopoly of representation, the syndical tax, and the labor courts—but they should be extended to cover the rural areas.* What, one may legitimately ask, were the workers to get from this package deal labeled "social peace"? First, their existing leaders would get the assurance of organizational continuity and financial security, which reversion to a pluralist system would have jeopardized. In addition, "administrative freedom with complete autonomy to control social funds, and elect and impeach directories by the free will of the members" was promised, although "the official fiscal control" was to be maintained. Labor courts were to be improved. Most important, there was to be a massive increase in social welfare services, including medical assistance, sanitation measures, education, subsidized foodstuffs and clothing, cooperatives, colonization and even land redistribution, fairer minimum salary levels, better social security, accident insurance, and longer holidays—all without increased cost to the workers. What was not clear in the Teresópolis Charter was the organizational form these promised benefits were to take.

The paulista industrialists, led by the fertile mind of Simonsen, were already at work on this problem. In fact, the groundwork had unknowingly been laid in 1942. Faced with a decree from Vargas requiring all factories above a certain size to operate apprenticeship schools, Simonsen had ingeniously turned the impending obligation into a political asset by convincing Vargas to impose an obligatory surtax of 1 percent on all industrial payrolls and to entrust the CNI and its member federations with the management of a National Service of Industrial Apprenticeship (SENAI). SENAI quickly became and has remained a model institution of its kind (and one imitated elsewhere in Latin America). The CNI received a new and economically vital task, added public prestige, and, not incidentally, an important source of income. During 1945 and early 1946, a period of rising labor unrest and political tensions, FIESP-CIESP privately called upon its members to contribute voluntarily to two related efforts, the establishment of "Commissions of Efficiency and Social Well-Being" to dispense certain immediate welfare

---

* The recommendation added that in the regulation of rural associability "the peculiarities of the economic stage of the agrarian zones and the normal process of assembly" should be respected. In practice this meant subordinating the new syndical hierarchy to the friendly and weak Ministry of Agriculture and ensuring the prior formation of employers' associations.

services and sell foodstuffs and clothing at cost,[10] and the creation of a "Commission of Relations with the Public . . . to defend the most important interests of paulista industry."[11] The voluntary response was disappointing, but the SENAI precedent suggested a compulsory way to attain the same twin objectives: the immediate response to workers' demands through various paternalistic services and the longer-term modification of these demands by means of public relations and indoctrination. On June 25, 1946, newly elected President Eurico Dutra, in response to the personal urging of Roberto Simonsen and Morvan Dias de Figuereido, signed the decree creating the Serviço Social de Indústria (SESI) and authorizing an obligatory tax of 2 percent to be administered by the CNI and its federations.[12]

The decree was short and ambiguous concerning the specific objectives of SESI: "to study, plan, and execute, directly or indirectly, means that contribute to the social well-being of workers in industry and similar activities."* But other phrases hinted at its more specific functions: to provide various paternalistic benefits to aggrieved workers ("to distribute social assistance and better conditions of housing, nutrition, and hygiene") and to dampen political protest of workers ("by stimulating the sentiment and spirit of social justice between the classes"). In short, it was aimed at combating the resurgence of Communist strength among workers. Certainly this political objective was paramount in Simonsen's mind. Although the immediate problem was to lower the cost of living and to provide workers with a sense of personal progress, the long-term goal was nothing less than to lay the attitudinal and ideological basis for a capitalist industrial society. This involved, on the one hand, the "social education" of workers in small groups, "giving all citizens a clear comprehension of their duties before the community" and showing them "the possibility of a profound betterment of their economic, social, and moral conditions . . . without the necessity of a revolution or a break in the traditions of our Christian civilization." On the other hand, it involved the social education of employers "to explain to them the social function of private property, to habituate them to the understanding of modern conditions of life in which economic power, like political power, must suffer limitations for the realization of democracy."[13]

The concept was original, daring, and certainly not understood by most industrialists. For Simonsen did not limit his efforts to civic and moral indoctrination. Workers must also be instructed in their rights

---

* It was silent on the very important issue of how these potentially enormous and tax-free funds were to be controlled. Except for a representative of the Labor Ministry in the National and Regional Councils of SESI, the CNI was to be responsible only to itself in accounting for how the funds were spent.

under the labor laws; lawyers must be put at their disposal in order that they might assert their rights; workers' leaders must be taught organizational techniques and their associations be financially assisted. Only a strong, well-organized, well-informed labor movement could ensure the kind of social peace Simonsen envisaged as the basis of an industrialized Brazilian society. The industrialists' associations, the federations and confederations, were conceived of almost as mediators that brought the workers and the employers together, educated both in their obligations, and instilled in both a belief in the industrial future of the country.[14] With their vastly expanded financial resources and functions, the FIESP and the CNI were scheduled to become, in Simonsen's eyes, major societal institutions responsible for maintaining class harmony and for creating a new economic and political elite.

After Simonsen's death in 1948 the global sense of purpose faded. The secondary, emergency objectives became primary and permanent. The two-edged social education program became single-edged, and eventually even that became oriented toward filling in certain wide gaps in the public school curriculum with courses in literacy and home economics. Although it has continued some of its policies (now unilateral) of support for and interference with proletarian organizations, especially in São Paulo, it is perhaps best known publicly for such activities as holding a Worker Olympics, choosing worker beauty queens, and conducting mass marriages. Except for a short period in São Paulo, it has never functioned as its imaginative creator had anticipated. Nevertheless, SESI has left a very deep imprint on both the pattern of emergence and the pattern of interaction of both employers' and workers' associations.*

Merchants were not far behind the industrialists in perceiving the potential benefits of a social service scheme run by "class" leaders rather than by politicians. Since 1942 the Commercial Association of Rio had been led by João Daudt d'Oliveira, the third member of the interest group triumvirate surrounding Vargas. Daudt was a gaúcho, a military school classmate of Vargas, and reputedly "the man who modernized the commercial associations, giving them a new, more national and progressive image."[15] He vastly expanded the membership of the AC-Rio and tripled the number of commercial associations affiliated with the Federation of Commercial Associations of Brazil, which he also headed. He encouraged merchants to form parallel but more specialized sindicatos and led the Rio Commercial Association to become the first "tech-

---

* The number of industrial employers' federations tripled from 1946 to 1952. When asked why he had formed his association, the president of the federation of industries from one of the poorer Northern states replied candidly, "We get more SESI funds this way."

nical and consultative organ of the government," an integral part of the Getulian policy-making apparatus. By 1945 he could report that the AC-Rio had 122 affiliated entities, many of which were official syndicates.*

It was Daudt who called the Teresópolis Conference. As we noted, this conference accepted a number of progressive resolutions quite at variance with the orthodox liberalism that had previously characterized the Commercial Associations (and that would again characterize them after Daudt's death in 1952). Like Simonsen, Lodi, and Dias de Figuereido, Daudt saw the necessity for a distributional change and a positive response to the upsurge in worker demands and expectations, although he staunchly supported the existing structure of interest representation. In September 1945 he founded the Confederação Nacional do Comércio (CNC), the official syndical peak association of commercial employers' federations.[16] In 1946, the CNC was empowered to set up an apprenticeship system (SENAC) similar to that of SENAI, and five months later it got a decree from President Dutra to create and administer the Serviço Social do Comércio (SESC), which had an extensive program of welfare services, especially in the fields of medical assistance, recreation, social work, and education.†

The Confederação Rural Brasileira (CRB), the last of the major national employers' associations, was established in 1951 by Iris Meinberg, another member of the inner circle of personal advisors to President Vargas.‡ Like the CNI and the CNC, it groups federations from all the states. But, although it can claim the greatest number of affiliates

---

* By linking the AC-Rio to Mauá and by stressing its role as leader of the "productive classes"—an epithet he made up—Daudt sought to make it into the peak association for all the urban employer interests. Daudt himself, unlike the previous leaders of the Commercial Association, was primarily an industrialist.

† SESC was clearly patterned on SESI. But with only about one-third of SESI's resources, it never had that organization's strongly ideological objectives. As was true of the industrialists' associations, the postwar surge of interest in commercial syndicates can be traced in part to the generous funds given to SENAC and SESI.

‡ Actually, a Confederação Rural Brasileira was created in 1928 under the sponsorship of the Sociedade Nacional de Agricultura. It was still operating in 1936 (when it held a national cattle raising conference), but it apparently folded thereafter.

Formally, the present CRB represents all Brazilian agriculture—all 3 million proprietors, of all sizes, incomes, types of crops, and degrees of rationalization of production. In fact, however, the CRB tends to represent only larger, commercialized proprietors, especially in crops grown for the national market. Meinberg himself is a cattleman. The interests of the major specialized producers of export crops, especially coffee, cacao, and maté, and of such domestic crops as sugar and wine have their own means of interest articulation. The CRB is also oriented toward and run by the agriculturists with a higher level of technical training—more of an agronomists' than a latifundists' association. A special clause in the enabling decree permits agronomists, veterinarians, etc. who are not proprietors to participate in rural associations.

of any Brazilian peak association (2,069 in 1965) and the widest degree of functional coverage, the CRB has remained a weak institution and has never attained the prominence of the CNI or the CNC. It has been very closely linked with the unimportant Ministry of Agriculture (many of its leadership cadres are ministerial employees) and dependent on federal subsidies. A rural imitation of SESI and SESC, the Serviço Social Rural (SSR), was created in 1957, but it never became fully operative, and the CRB never gained the control over it that the CNI and CNC have had over their respective welfare agencies.[17] Attempts to set up a national service of rural apprenticeship failed.

Harassed by President Goulart, who cut off its subsidy, and fearful of the upsurge in rural worker associability, the Brazilian Rural Confederation decided in September 1963 to "syndicalize" itself and to encourage its member associations to do likewise.[18] The CRB was caught in the rather paradoxical position of accepting Goulart's organizational offer at the same time that it was strenuously opposing the regime's agrarian reform policy, and the response to this decision was hardly enthusiastic.[19] The CRB's claim that "the problem of syndicalization has always received the favorable attention of the rural class" was hardly a convincing one.[20] The coup of 1964 made the idea of conversion much more appealing, however. In 1965 the CRB became the National Confederation of Agriculture (CNA), and by May of the next year 237 rural associations and thirteen state federations had been recognized by the Ministry of Labor.[21] The new CNA managed to alter the basis for collection of the rural syndical tax in its favor, and its officials estimate their potential income at roughly one billion cruzeiros (500,000 dollars).[22] With these new resources and in conjunction with its own federations, the National Confederation of Agricultural Workers, and the government's Instituto Nacional de Desenvolvimento Agrário, the CNA intends to stimulate the creation of one employers' and one workers' syndicate in each município (of which there are approximately 3,700).[23] It is hoped that the new corporatist scheme will eventually cover eighteen million persons and be "the largest syndical congregation in Latin America." It is still a long way from that goal.

Urban workers' associations. The process of regional and national consolidation of employers' interests was partly a response to a similar process that seemed to be occurring among workers' associations in the mid-1940's. In the climate of postwar redemocratization, it appeared briefly that, under the leadership of the rapidly growing Communist Party, workers would organize themselves outside the official system. In April 1945, three hundred syndical leaders from thirteen states formed the Unifying Movement of Workers (MUT). This was complemented by the emergence of state-wide syndical unions in Minas

Gerais, São Paulo, and the Federal District (now Guanabara). The following year a tumultuous First National Workers' Congress was held. Leaders loyal to the Labor Ministry walked out on the issue of creating an extralegal, national peak association and announced their intention to follow the official *enquadramento* and to set up separate confederations. The remaining Communists and some of their Getulista allies decreed the formation of the Confederation of Workers of Brazil (CTB).[24]

The CTB expanded rapidly. When it was dissolved by executive decree one year later (1947), four hundred, or 45 percent, of the then existing syndicates were intervened on the grounds that they had joined or supported the illegal institution.* With the legal dissolution of the CTB and of the Communist Party, the attempt to establish an independent and politicized labor movement was checked. Those loyal to the Labor Ministry, sometimes called the "yellow *pelegos*," meanwhile went about forming the officially recognized confederations: the National Confederation of Industrial Workers (CNTI) and the National Confederation of Commercial Workers (CNTC) in 1946;[25] the National Confederation of Land Transport Workers (CNTT) in 1953; the National Confederation of Workers in Credit Establishments (CONTEC) in 1958; the National Confederation of Workers in Marine, River, and Air Transport (CNTFMA) and the National Confederation of Workers in Communications and Publicity (CONTOP) in 1960. The organizational drive faded after the first three and was not revived until the repressed ideological forces were liberated. The three original confederations joined the anti-Communist Inter-American Regional Organization of Workers (ORIT) and the International Confederation of Free Trade Unions (ICFTU), but did little to expand their organizational coverage in Brazil.

Beginning with the revocation of the "ideological certificates" in 1951, the nature of worker syndical leadership started to change, although it was a while before this change showed up in the national organizations. Frustrated in their attempt to establish an independent, parallel system of representation, the Communists began to work from within the official system, capturing positions at the syndicate level.[26] In 1954, when Goulart was Labor Minister, there was again a brief flurry of activity aimed at creating a national central, tentatively named the General Union of Workers (UGT). There was also an attempt to form state centrals such as the Pact of Syndical Unity (PUA) in Rio. Goulart's firing, Vargas's suicide, and the renewed policy of ministerial intervention under provisional President Café Filho put an abrupt end to these attempts.

Two years later, with the benevolent abstention of President Kubi-

---

* See p. 228 for a definition of "intervention."

tschek and the active sponsorship of Vice President Goulart and the Labor Ministry, the new ideological forces began to find organizational expression. A series of national worker congresses was held for specific categories in 1956 and 1957. These continued into the 1960's and became a frequent, if sporadic, feature of syndical life. In 1958, some twelve statewide meetings of workers in all categories were convened. The number increased to fourteen in 1959 and sixteen in 1960.[27]

Beginning in 1959, national congresses of syndical leaders took up where they had left off thirteen years before. The Third National Syndical Conference in 1960 was of particular importance in deciding the future organizational configuration of the workers' movement.[28] Before the Conference, the leadership of the CNTI, CNTC, and CNTT distributed a joint May Day Manifesto, sometimes referred to as the "Manifesto of Independence." They announced their intention of creating a mixed commission of their three presidents—a sort of diplomatic peak association—and called for sweeping revisions in syndical legislation: greater political autonomy, extension of the right to organize to rural workers and public employees, an untrammeled right to strike, increased collective bargaining, creation of union locals in places of work, and, most surprisingly, a gradual end to the syndical tax and its replacement by a voluntary check-off system.[29] Three weeks later the "Big Three," apparently having thought over the implications of their decision more thoroughly, issued a much milder statement calling for an "actualization" rather than a "drastic revision" of the system and avoiding any mention of abolishing the syndical tax.[30] Nonetheless, it was obvious that, as a Communist commentator put it, "the syndical movement is conflicting even more with certain aspects of the actual syndical structure."[31] With several years of unprecedented internal autonomy behind them, during which new cadres had replaced the conformist, bureaucratic types at the lower level, and with the uncertainty of an impending presidential election before them, the leaders of the syndical movement's various factions—Ministerial, Democratic, Communist, Renovating, Nationalist, and Catholic—converged upon São Paulo for their Conference. The Conference was hopelessly divided.[32] The "yellow *pelego*" group withdrew on the issue of establishing a syndical central and joining international organizations. The Communists and Nationalists pressed for the above and for a pro-syndical tax plank; the Catholic and Renovating factions strongly opposed these demands. The Syndical Council of Workers of São Paulo regarded the proposed national organ as a threat to the autonomy of the new state-based centrals. An open rupture was unavoidable. National workers' congresses and meetings of syndical leaders became a regular yearly feature of the 1960's, but never again with the presence of all factions.

The whole dynamic of association formation had shifted from its traditional corporatist basis, i.e., the interaction between the policy aims of authority groups and structural differentiation, to a pluralist basis, i.e., the interaction between the associations themselves and structural differentiation. True, the government remained an important and omnipresent actor rewarding loyal friends and penalizing dissidents, but it no longer exclusively controlled the process or successfully dictated the rules of the encounter. The result of this new competitive dialectic was an outburst of associational expansion in the 1960's and a significant change in the techniques of demand-making, first among the workers and subsequently among the employers. The regional and national meetings began to bear organizational fruit. Pacts, councils, commissions, forums, and commands sprang up in almost every state, linking workers horizontally across previously unconnected categories. Some of these, like the Conselho Sindical of São Paulo, were associations of specialized federations;[33] some, like the Forum Sindical de Debates of Santos, were of lower-level syndicates; some, like the Pacto de Unidade e Ação among Rio transport and dock workers, were of restricted functional categories; and still others, like the Comissão Permanente de Organizações Sindicais (CPOS) in Rio, linked only national entities. The capstone of the edifice of emerging unofficial associations was the General Workers' Command (CGT). Although it never formally constituted itself as an omnibus national workers' confederation, the CGT in its heyday certainly commanded the allegiance of the majority of the confederations and national federations. According to "research" conducted in mid-1963, the CGT dominated three confederations (the CNTI, the CONTEC, and the CNTFMA) and 425 syndicates—29 percent of the 1,453 for which data were collected.[34] No data were given on national federations and syndicates, but virtually all those in the transport and industrial sectors were members of the CPOS, itself part of the CGT "scheme." The CGT operated within the CNTI, using the latter's physical facilities and funds.[35] And although it never gained official recognition (an abortive attempt was made in 1963), it unquestionably received the political and financial support of the Goulart regime.[36] Because of the comprehensive nature of its demands, and because it never seems to have had much of an administrative structure of its own, it was more a movement than a representative association.*

After the break at the 1960 Conference, unofficial workers' groups were formed to oppose the growing Communist and radical nationalist

---

* Its original name was the General Strike Command (also CGT), and it was founded in 1961 as a vehicle for calling a general strike to ensure Goulart's succession to power after Quadros's renunciation. It seems to have maintained the original ad hoc organizational structure.

predominance. The Movimento Sindical Democrático (MSD), formed in 1961, was particularly strong among commercial employees. It took a moderate line opposing government control and the syndical tax and also attempted to create a so-called Democratic Syndical Central for Brazilian Workers, although this idea was never put into practice.[37] The União Sindical dos Trabalhadores (UST) was formed in 1962. It was based on the São Paulo industrial workers' federations and more specifically on the large Metallurgical Workers' Federation. The UST shunned a distinctive political or ideological coloration and took instead a generally militant but reformist line. It vegetated during the crises of 1962, but it was abruptly revived the following year when Goulart, his full presidential powers now reestablished, decided to support it as a ploy against the growing power and obstreperousness of the CGT. Goulart's purpose attained—a loyal supporter of his became president of the CGT—he sponsored a gentleman's agreement between the two groups and supported both.[38] At the time of the coup in 1964, there were three rivals in the top echelon of the workers' movement: the MSD, made up essentially of commercial workers, the CGT, having mainly transport workers, and the UST, composed mainly of industrial workers.

Of course these were not the only groups active in syndical affairs. A number of associations operated and continue to operate as "orienters"; they are, in effect, fifth columnists within the workers' movement. They range from organizations like the Movimento de Orientação Sindicalista, supported by businessmen's contributions, to organizations with a religious orientation such as the Movimento Renovador Sindical and the Frente Nacional do Trabalho. They also include the Instituto Cultural do Trabalho (ICT), sponsored by the American Institute for Free Labor Development (AIFLD), which is itself sponsored by the AFL-CIO and USAID. These groups all run congresses and seminars and occasionally even give full courses of indoctrination and leadership training.[39] Some also provide legal and financial assistance. By far the oldest indoctrinating association, and for years the only one that could compete with the socializing efforts of the Labor Ministry, is the Brazilian Confederation of Christian Workers (CBTC). Catholic labor groups had begun appearing after World War I and had gained momentum in the early 1930's with the formation of *círculos operários* (workers' circles). These were consolidated in 1937 along with other Catholic labor organizations into a National Confederation of Catholic Workers (CNOC). In recent years, the CNOC has used the more ecumenical title of "Christian Workers."* The movement was investigated and somewhat persecuted

---

* The CBTC does not appear to be organizationally distinguishable from the National Confederation of Workers' Circles (CNCO). It is loosely associated with the Latin American Confederation of Christian Trade Unions.

during Vargas's Estado Novo. Its membership was estimated at 100,000 in 1943.[40] When interviewed in 1965, an officer of the CBTC claimed 500,000 adherents in 540 workers' circles. There are Federations of Christian Workers in seventeen states.[41] In 1961, the São Paulo Federation alone claimed to have 74 circles and 250,000 members.[42]

These are not the only Church controlled or Church linked organizations active as "orienting" institutions among workers. Catholic Worker Youth (JOC) is active among younger Catholics and is a recruitment mechanism for future leaders in the CBTC. The Frente Nacional do Trabalho of São Paulo, founded in 1960, is a more militant para-Catholic organization. Engaged in coordinating legal and strike protest among workers, it, too, has worked within existing official syndicates. It is much more independent of the Church hierarchy, although it has received the approval of the Archbishop of São Paulo.[43] Ação Popular (AP), a radical offshoot of the Catholic University Youth (JUC), in alliance with the Movimento de Educaçáo de Base (MEB), played an important role in the organization of rural syndicates. It was, however, primarily concerned with student politics.[44]

The military coup of March 1964 abruptly changed the policy setting within which the above described associational expansion and ideological polarization operated. Parallel organizations defined as radical or subversive were dissolved by force, their leaders imprisoned or driven into exile, and their activities investigated in lengthy (if inconclusive) military inquiries. Those identified as "democratic," including the MSD and the UST, disbanded themselves. Once ministerial control over the syndicates, federations, and confederations was reaffirmed and the necessity for opposing subversive elements was no longer felt, the development of a genuinely autonomous set of worker organizations was no longer possible. The dismissal and suppression of *corruptos* and *subversivos* opened up a large number of vacancies in leadership posts. These were filled partially by recalling the loyalist *pelegos* voted out during the previous decade and partially by appointing younger elements from the Democratic, Autonomist, and Catholic factions. The associations whose tasks were primarily orientation or leadership training either went underground (if they had been labeled as subversive, as was the Ação Popular),* changed functions (as did the Frente Nacional do Trabalho), or continued their activities with somewhat less intensity (as did the Movimento de Orientação Sindical, the Instituto Cultural do Trabalho, and the Confederação Brasileira de Trabalhadores Cristãos). The net result—from the perspective of workers' organizations—

---

* According to newspaper accounts in 1968, Ação Popular (AP) had successfully gone underground and was playing a leading role in coordinating opposition to the military regime, especially among students.

has been a complete reversal of the pluralist pattern of emergence and a return to the manipulated unitarism of official corporatism, coupled with a decline in associational autonomy and activity. Geographical and functional coverage has not declined,* but participation in syndicates and their use as channels of interest expression are presently at their lowest point since the early 1950's.

Private Associations

In the latter half of the 1950's, developmental conditions began to change. Structural differentiation, which had been so rapid and chaotic in the 1940's, began to taper off; one could argue that the process had reached a point of moderate maturity. Recruitment to various occupations had become more regular. People began to expect to occupy the same occupational role for some time, and consequently a new kind of group consciousness emerged. The pattern of policy toward representative associations reinforced group consciousness, granting greater autonomy to organized groups.[45] This, in turn, began to affect the political culture. Kubitschek's very success in remaining in office and in peacefully passing on the mantle of authority to his successor, as well as his open, tolerant, and consensual personal style of ruling during a period when opinion was being mobilized into broad movements, probably reaffirmed in Brazilians a new confidence in the viability of the democratic pluralist process. In response to these new conditions there came a marked increase in the functional specificity of representation, a rapid extension of associational coverage, and experimentation with new forms of interest organization.

Employers. Employers reacted to this challege of liberalization and incipient pluralism by retaining their support for corporatism, but also by creating a new, parallel system of private interest representation. One of their first responses in the mid-1950's was to revive existing "class associations." With the dismissal of Euvaldo Lodi from the joint presidency of the National Confederation of Industry and the Federation of Industries of the Federal District in 1954, the two groups separated both administratively and politically. The new president of the Federa-

---

* Few syndicates had their charters of recognition revoked outright. The only cases of dissociation encountered—other than those involving the semilegal *pactos, conselhos, comandos, frentes,* etc.—occurred in the rural sector, where hundreds of "phantom syndicates" had been established. Another case of forced dissociation was the dissolution of the União dos Portuários do Brasil, which had enjoyed a special, but non-syndical, status. The Federação Nacional dos Portuários was intervened but was not dissolved. The newspaper *O Estado de São Paulo* complained that the "revolutionary" regime had been too lenient and published a fascinating and detailed exposé of one urban phantom syndicate. As a result that syndicate was later dissolved.

tion of Industries of the Federal District, Zulfo de Freitas Mallmann, also revived that group's moribund parallel organization, the Industrial Center of Rio de Janeiro. A similar revival of interest occurred in the Center of Industries of São Paulo. In the succeeding years parallel industrial centers with voluntary membership were established in Rio Grande do Sul, Paraná, Pernambuco, and Ceará.* An identical shift in leadership and organizational vitality occurred within the Commercial Association of Rio; when João Daudt d'Oliveira failed to impose his hand-picked successor in 1952, a new group seized control. São Paulo followed suit shortly thereafter, when Brasílio Machado Neto lost his bid for reelection. Throughout Brazil during the 1950's the commercial associations changed as the oligarchies of aging (often Portuguese) merchants were replaced by a more aggressive, younger group of entrepreneurs who were less narrowly tied to export and foreign commercial interests. The commercial association promoted itself as "a house open to any entrepreneur who feels his rights are menaced or to any suggestions, which will be promptly referred to the competent [government] organs."[46] The new leaders tried to give the commercial association the image of a private and independent peak association representing the general interest of all the "productive classes" and of the people as a whole, an image that ran counter to the more stratified and differentiated concept of interest inherent in the corporatist approach. The moribund Federation of Commercial Associations of Brazil was revived by the victorious opposition in the Commercial Association of Rio, and in 1963 its name was changed to the Confederation of Commercial Associations of Brazil (CACB). Meanwhile the number of commercial associations had grown steadily, in spite of the competition from official syndicates, from 77 in 1942, to 122 in 1945, to 180 in 1951. When the CACB was set up, its president, Rui Gomes de Almeida (who was also the president of AC-Rio), claimed that it aggregated the interests of 1,340 associations and that it was "the largest network of similar associations in the country." All the rival CNC network could muster was a hundred or so.[47] A more or less open hostility soon broke out between the private and the syndical organizations concerning who authentically represented which class interests.†

* The federations of commerce have not adopted the strategy of parallelism for the simple reason that they already have the private hierarchy of commercial associations at their disposal. However, the Federation in São Paulo did create an "independent" Centro do Comércio in 1964.

† The conflict was strongest between the Commercial Association of Rio and the CNC and was punctuated with frequent accusations of scandal and mismanagement, especially over the use of SESC funds. It had its parallel in the agricultural sector in the exchanges between the SRB on the one hand and the FARESP on the other.

The net result of these changes in organizational vitality and leadership was the emergence of a set of interest-group leaders definitely less committed to the sponsored corporatist conception of interest representation and to the social democratic, welfarist conception of the role of the state. These new and revived associations loudly proclaimed their own independence, their private status, and their implacable opposition to any increase in state power.* The delicate balance between innovation and conservatism that had characterized the Vargas regime, as well as the prevailing tone of accommodation and conciliation, had disappeared, or had been replaced by a new aggressiveness. Expressions of doubt in the goodwill of one's interlocutor, intransigent defense of rights and principles, and threats of noncooperation and sanctions became more common. These changes both reflected and caused changes in political culture and were rooted in underlying shifts in the organizational structure and leadership of representative associations—both bourgeois and proletarian. Attempts were made to override these organizational differences within the "productive classes" by means of a broad coalition of employer interests around some common set of principles. This is reminiscent of the Teresópolis Conference of 1945 and its follow-up at Araxá in 1949. Starting in 1957, these "plenary reunions" and "conclaves of the productive classes" met, drafted long lists of demands and complaints, faithfully proclaimed "the perfect identity of thought among the country's businessmen," and invariably had little or no impact either on more permanent forms of class cooperation or on public policy. All they could agree upon was that the situation was deteriorating, that the image of the entrepreneur was getting worse, and that the need for "campaigns of public enlightenment was great."[48]

In 1955, during the interregnum between Vargas's suicide and the inauguration of Kubitschek, the employers' associations of São Paulo banded together to form the first regional, eclectic peak association, the Council of the Productive Classes of São Paulo (CONCLAP-SP). The Council apparently had no formal organizational or bureaucratic structure. In fact, rather than an electoral process, it had only a three-month rotating presidency. Both syndical and private entities participated. It took a moderately nationalistic "developmentalist" line in a series of memoranda to Presidents Kubitschek and Quadros. Early in Goulart's term, CONCLAP-SP manifested its support for the new parlia-

---

Among industrialists, the tension between private and syndical forms of representation did not materialize in the same manner. Overlapping leadership has kept it "within the family." The CNI and its state federations have, however, contested the commercial associations' right to speak for all employer interests.

* Even though their present financial independence is often based on revenue from property given or financed for them by the Vargas regime.

mentary institutions, but generally avoided taking polemic and public stands on political issues. It seems, however, to have furnished a cover for clandestine conspiratorial activities. Nonetheless, on the very eve of the coup, its members maintained their support for reform within the Constitution and their readiness to admit state intervention and greater political participation by working-class groups.[49] In marked contrast to this publicly conciliatory attitude were the opinions expressed by the Superior Council of the Productive Classes of Rio (CONCLAP-Rio). From its foundation in 1959, CONCLAP-Rio sent forth a stream of overtly violent manifestos against the regime. Composed exclusively of private groups, it even had a worker (a commercial employee) as its president for one year.* Its steady invective against Communism, corruption, and lesser evils was very much out of tune with the prevailing style of interest expression. Its intransigent defense of free enterprise, financial and monetary stability, and foreign capital and its implacable opposition to price control, the right to strike, job stability, and government ownership of virtually anything undoubtedly seemed a bit extreme even to most members of the "productive classes."[50] Shortly before the coup, CONCLAP-Rio called for the formation of a "General Command of Productive Forces," and in a "Message to the Brazilian People" it openly incited them to rebellion against the government. Goulart's response, never made effective, was to threaten the Commercial Association of Rio, where the meeting was held, with intervention.[51] Intransigent polarization and outright rejection of the "System" was never, however, the response of more than an active minority of the "productive classes." The more predominant response has been an accommodative compromise and increased attention to private associations. Ordinarily, relations between these private associations and the parallel official syndicates are publicly harmonious, even when their leaders are different, although there have been rare incidences of both temporary and permanent discord.†

---

* The AC-Rio and the CIRJ were its strongest supporters. It operated for a while from within the Commercial Association. Leaders from official national confederations (CNI, CNC, and CRB) did not participate; nor did many prominent local syndical leaders. It never attempted to become numerically large.

† When asked why they have set up private, parallel associations, the participants almost invariably respond, "Because it permits us to do things we cannot do in the syndicate." When they are asked, "What can you do that you could not do otherwise?," their answers are more scattered (and more evasive). In general, the advantages are multiple. (1) They have greater freedom to engage in public relations campaigns, which may include some "political investing." (2) They can form national, functionally specific representative associations and seek direct access, thus bypassing the cumbersome and eclectic federations and confederations. This is of particular advantage in those sectors too numerous or geographically dispersed to

One of the first of the new wave of specialized private associations was the Brazilian Association for the Development of Basic Industries (ABDIB), founded in 1955.[52] The ABDIB was initially a purely technical organization designed to coordinate various national manufacturers in the supply of equipment to the national petroleum company, Petrobrás. Its membership is small (about fifty), but dense, made up of representatives from "all but a few of the small firms." In spite of its private, unofficial status, it has achieved excellent access to authority groups (it even has a permanent membership in one of the most important executive groups) and can cite a large number of successful policy initiatives to prove it.[53] During the 1960's, scores of national associations of this sort were created to represent specific industrial sectors.* Typically, they have small but very dense memberships, and their headquarters are in São Paulo, not in Rio.† Some openly state that their primary aim is to

---

qualify for national syndical status. (3) They can represent the *classe* internationally (seven of the new private associations interviewed reported that the prime motivation for their creation was the need to participate in sectorial meetings of the Latin American Free Trade Area). (4) They have greater flexibility in internal processes because they do not have to adhere to an annual "approved" budget; thus they are permitted to engage in profit-making activities and to purchase property and securities. (5) They can raise funds; this is an especially significant advantage during periods when inflation diminishes the real income derived from the syndical tax. (6) Finally, parallel associations provide an additional line of defense in the event that either the Ministry of Labor should be taken over by "subversives" or the corporatist system should be abolished altogether. Another motive, which I inferred although it was never cited directly, is that the private associations can set their own membership criteria and electoral procedures. By a variety of formal and informal means they can determine the composition of participants and the stability of leadership more precisely than they can under the "universalistic" standards of the Labor Code.

* Some are very functionally specific indeed, for example the Brazilian Association of Tin Can Manufacturers, the Brazilian Association of Instant Coffee Producers, the Brazilian Association of Machine Tool Manufacturers, and the Brazilian Association of the Packaging Industry (all in São Paulo). Others cover wider sectors: the Brazilian Association of the Chemical Industry and the Brazilian Association of the Food Industry (also in São Paulo). Occasionally an association will be formed explicitly to bridge the corporatist gap between industrial and commercial categories. For example, the Commercial and Industrial Association of Real Estate Owners of Rio de Janeiro was created in 1966 partly to bring together the syndicates of the real estate agents with those of the building contractors. Still other associations are perfectly "parallel" to the official *enquadramento*: the Brazilian Association of the Pharmaceutical Industry (Rio) and the Brazilian Association of the Electrical and Electronic Industry (São Paulo).

Some of these associations antedate the 1960's. For example, the National Association of Paper Manufacturers (Rio) traces its origin to 1919, but has only recently been revived. The Association of Radio, Television, and Electronics Manufacturers (São Paulo) was founded in 1952.

† For example, the Brazilian Association of Aerosol Bomb Manufacturers, founded in 1966, has only eleven members. Two make the gas, three make the valves, and

"defend the common interests of their associates" and to "cooperate with public authority in the study and solution of problems relating to industrial interests"; others say their main intention is to "refine the competitive conditions of price and quality in this sector of the industry through cooperation, market studies, and the rationalization and technical development of production."

Tradesmen and merchants, with their more liberal ideology, had long extolled the virtues of autonomous association—even if, in practice, they had reaped the benefits of co-optation during the Estado Novo. As we have noted, their *associações comerciais*, foreign chambers of commerce, and centros are among the most venerable of Brazilian institutions. Even so, in the last decade the polyfunctional pretensions of the commercial association have been challenged by the emergence of new, more specialized private associations. Typically, these have recruited from among the more dynamic and technologically advanced sectors of the commercial *classe*, and their organizations have been important foci for the introduction and standardization of new techniques of marketing, cost accounting, and banking.

The first of these, the National Association of Machinery, Vehicles, Accessories, and Pieces (ANMVAP), was founded in 1952 to protect the interests of importers whose existence was believed threatened by the impending national integration of the automobile industry. It has since accepted this national integration as a fait accompli, and it operates as "an organ of equilibrium between merchants, industrialists, and exporters" for its 250 members.[54] Although ANMVAP maintains a branch in São Paulo and offices in Recife, Curitiba, and Brasília, the first of these specialized associations to establish a genuinely national network was the Club of Retail Merchants (CDL), which was started in São Paulo in 1953 and in Rio de Janeiro in 1955. As of 1965 there were 60 clubs in 42 of the major cities of the country.[55] They promote an annual national convention (seven had been held as of 1967) honoring various authorities and presenting them with an extensive set of demands. The clubs seem to work closely with the local shopkeepers' syndicates, but they seem to have no institutionalized contact with the CNC. There is a considerable overlap in leadership with the Commercial Association of Rio (the president of the local *Clube* is a director of the Commercial Association), but elsewhere there apparently has been friction between the two private entities.[56] In Rio there is an even more specialized retail

---

six make the containers. Its density is 100 percent. Associations covering a wider sphere of interests naturally have more members, but the number rarely exceeds two hundred. The largest by far seems to be the Brazilian Association of the Electrical and Electronic Industry (ABIEE), with 281 members.

merchants' association, just for those engaged in the sale of electrical appliances (ACADE, formed in 1952). Another commercial entity with something approaching a national network is the Federation of Associations of Sales Executives of Brazil. It has member associations in São Paulo (the original one, founded in 1957), Rio de Janeiro, Pôrto Alegre, Belo Horizonte, Curitiba, Londrina, Presidente Prudente, and Fortaleza. Similar new associations that have not yet expanded beyond São Paulo are the Association of Financial Executives and the Association of Executive Directors, both founded in 1965. In each case the membership is very specialized, technically well trained, and from large firms, and the organization is designed not only to represent interests, but also to mold them through courses and conferences on marketing, cost accounting, management techniques, etc.

Shifts in government policy, as I have shown several times above, can be a powerful indirect as well as direct incentive for an extension of associational coverage. The decision of authority groups to modify a given tax law, to regulate a given profession, to control a determined sector of economic activity, or to join a regional free trade area may activate a latent group consciousness. Rarely did an informant answer the question about the motive for foundation by saying "Nothing specific; it just suddenly occurred to us that there were enough of us to sustain a separate association."[57] Of course, the new, more specialized associations rest on a more differentiated group consciousness, but interests may lie latent for some time until authoritative policy precipitates their articulation. Local Centers of Coffee Exporters have existed since the turn of the century, but they did not form their national peak association (CONSECAB) until 1962, when a change in the Brazilian Coffee Institute's policy forced them to. Stock markets have existed for some time, but not until a bill appeared in 1965 reforming them did the brokers establish a National Association of Capital Markets. Factory authorized automobile dealers have existed for years, but it took the threat of government regulation to bring into being a national representative body (ABRAVE). I have already mentioned above that the signing of the LAFTA Treaty (1960) indirectly led to the foundation of several industrial associations. The new government concern with diversification of exports was an important factor in the creation of the National Association of Exporters of Industrial Products (ANEPI) in 1964 and the National Association of Cereal Exporters (ANEC) in 1965. The Association of Credit, Investment, and Finance Companies (ADECIF) was formed in 1962 in response to a tax reform bill that threatened the existence of investment companies dealing in bills of exchange.[58] Started by fourteen members in 1962, it quickly grew to almost sixty, when a decision was made to restrict further entrants. ADECIF's success in establishing professional standards and in publicizing its image was such that membership in it had become a distinct commercial asset. By 1966, all existing firms in Rio de Janeiro had at least applied for admission, as had a few from São Paulo.* The creation of a parallel syndical body (a novelty, since private bodies usually arose out of dissatisfaction with public ones) was considered, but ADECIF's success in coordinating its competitive members and in legitimizing itself as an authentic representative of the sector persuaded most firms that there was no urgent need for a more official status.[59] As we shall see, ADECIF is perhaps emblematic of a new type of representative association emerging in Brazil: purely voluntary and characterized by a high rate of member participation, a great deal of autonomy in dealing with public officials, a high level of technical expertise, and a pervasive sense of public responsibility and self-limitation. There are very few analogous associations in Brazilian interest politics. One is tempted simply to write ADECIF off as a deviant case and explain its voluntaristic, pluralistic behavior by referring to the fact that so many of its members are trained in the United States or in the international financial community.†

Other types of employers have recently turned to private associational representation. Two are worthy of special mention. The National Association of Road Cargo Transporting Firms (NTC) is an interesting case of a very active association that grew up spontaneously in opposition to a preexisting syndicate.[60] Like most of the new associations covering a large category, it recruits almost exclusively from among the large, more rationally administered firms. In three short years, it has organized an impressive number of member services, installed regional branches in four areas and agents in 43 cities, popularized its emblem as a symbol of reliable trucking service, and, in the process, managed to ensure for itself an important place in transport policy-making. The Brazilian Association of Radio and Television Stations (ABERT) is a child of crisis. In 1962, President Goulart vetoed 52 articles of a draft National Telecommunications Code. By suggestive coincidence, the vetoes fell almost

* An equivalent organization covering the same interest sector (ACREDIF) had existed in São Paulo prior to the founding of ADECIF, but it has been much less active. In 1965 a duplicate of ADECIF was established in Minas Gerais (AMECIF), and another was established in 1966 in Rio Grande do Sul (AGECIF). As yet there exists no national peak association, and ADECIF handles most of the interest expression before the national government.

† Informants in ADECIF agreed with my general observation that their organizational behavior was aberrant by Brazilian standards, but they strongly denied that this had anything to do with foreign training. They tended to explain it by reference to the high cultural or status level of members.

exclusively on the articles that were to benefit the stations.[61] The stations banded together under the leadership of João Calmon, a federal deputy and executive manager of the Diários Associados radio and television chain. In three days, they managed to get the Congress to override every one of the 52 presidential vetoes. In the immediate wake of this success, ABERT was founded with Calmon as president. When it became organized the following year, it grew rapidly from 172 to 502 members representing between 60 and 70 percent of the category.*

Changes in the rate and nature of associability have been much less evident in the last decade among agrarian interests than among industrial and commercial interests. This is probably a reflection of the lower rate of structural differentiation in this sector. The number of rural associations continued to rise, and, as I noted above, the associations are now converting to syndicalism. The traditional rural entities, such as the Sociedade Rural Brasileira, the Sociedade Mineira de Agricultura, the Sociedade Rural do Triangulo Mineiro, and the Sociedade Auxiliadora da Agricultura de Pernambuco, have, however, remained active. In addition, several specialized associations have been founded among such groups as coffee growers, cattle raisers, poultry raisers, and wine growers. But the most important organizational change in the rural sector has been the rapidly increasing representational role played by cooperatives. There are specialized cooperatives for the producers of such products as wool, maté, rice, wheat, milk, cacao, sugarcane, and citrus fruit. Some of the mixed producers' cooperatives are quite large, e.g. the Cooperativa Agrícola de Cotía with over 8,000 members and the Cooperativa Central Agrícola Sul-Brasil with 4,000. They often play a direct representational role, although they tend to work through cooperative peak associations and state federations of rural associations. Cooperatives among coffee growers have been increasing by leaps and bounds since 1958. They tripled their memberships by 1960 under the sponsorship of the Brazilian Coffee Institute, which sees this as a means for improving the quality of the product.[62] Some of the larger ones in São Paulo and Paraná are exporting directly, in spite of the opposition of the Centros do Comércio de Café. In 1960 the Brazilian Federation of Coffee Cooperatives was founded in São Paulo. It currently has 29 member cooperatives.

The organizational hierarchy of the cooperative movement bears a

---

* Most Brazilian associations recruit either individuals and firms or other representative associations. ABERT is an unusual case in that most of its members are television or radio stations and some of them are state associations or *federações*. To some extent, ABERT is a parallel association. Calmon is also president of the Syndicate of Broadcasting Firms of the State of Guanabara.

strong resemblance to that of the corporatist syndical movement.[63] The local *cooperativas* are clustered into state or functional federations.[64] The only difference appears at the top: a single confederation, the National Union of Cooperative Associations (UNASCO), represents the movement at the national level.* UNASCO was founded by five state unions or federations in 1956. It now has eleven. As I shall show later, the cooperative movement has benefited greatly from authoritative patronage, and it maintains an extensive network of political contacts, administrative and legislative.

Middle-sector professionals. Although they supply the technical and professional skills that sustain the entire structure of representative associations, the middle sectors themselves have not demonstrated any remarkable capacity for self-organization. Their participation in the syndical system has been minimal. The number of local sindicatos remains more or less stable (there were 120 in 1962). Only four federations have been formed. In 1953 the National Confederation of the Liberal Professions was created, but it has never become an active spokesman for the middle sectors.[65] The failure of syndicalism is perhaps less related to a low propensity for associability on the part of these groups than to the existence of private associations on the one hand and official government professional "orders," or councils, on the other. There is a whole network of regional and national councils for lawyers, physicians, accountants, engineers and architects, social workers, and librarians. Membership in them is obligatory for practitioners, and they play a regular role as interest articulators; they also serve to "regulate and moralize" the professions. Leaders of both syndical and private professional associations claim that obligatory membership in the councils makes individuals reluctant to participate in other entities.[66] Nevertheless, these same leaders expend a great deal of their political effort to obtain seats in these councils.

Some of the private associations are quite old and have already been mentioned, for example the Institute of Brazilian Lawyers (IAB), the Engineering Club of Rio, the Institute of Engineering of São Paulo, and the military clubs. Others, like the Institute of Architects and the Association of Brazilian Judges, are newer, but nonetheless have been quite

---

* Apparently there is a competing peak association, the Brazilian Alliance of Cooperatives (ABCOOP), but I was unable to locate its headquarters. There is a great deal of controversy and factionalism within the cooperative movement. In São Paulo an important group of agricultural producers' cooperatives recently broke off from the Union of Cooperatives (UCESP) and set up a separate, more specialized association (ACAPESP). From scattered press accounts, the competition between UNASCO-UCESP and ABCOOP-ACAPESP seems to parallel that between the SRB and the CRB.

active in defending members' interests. The largest and most vociferous of them is the Brazilian Medical Association (AMB), founded in 1951. The AMB is actually a federation of members of 22 state medical societies, which have a total of about 20 thousand members. Its headquarters are in São Paulo in the building of the Paulista Medical Association, with which it has an especially close relationship. Also affiliated with it are a large number of scientific societies in the various medical specialties. The AMB seems to have been founded primarily in opposition to the growing trend of state control over the medical practice, and it has since been the promoter of several vigorous campaigns.[67] It and its member associations became the scene of fierce internal battles over the attitude to be adopted vis-à-vis public medical services, especially those of Retirement and Social Welfare Institutes. Since 1962 it has been in the hands of the privatist group, and it greeted the 1964 military coup with undisguised glee.[68]

The largest bloc of middle-sector actors has been at a severe organizational disadvantage. By law, public employees are denied the right to form syndicates and the right to strike. This has not prevented the emergence of associations representing the interests of municipal, state, and national government employees, but it certainly has delayed it. Even before 1930, numerous associations had been founded in Rio and the major state capitals, but these were and still remain essentially social clubs or mutual aid societies. Some are restricted to single agencies, such as the Athletic Association of the Bank of Brazil (AABB); others, like the Union of Welfare Workers (UPB) and the Association of Consumer Tax Agents, are for categories of employees; still others are open to all public employees. The largest of the latter is the Association of Civil Servants of Brazil (ASCB), which presently has 160 thousand members and branches in several states. These entities may and do engage in interest representation, but that is a decidedly secondary function for them.[69] The first national representative association for all public employees, the National Union of Public Servants (UNSP), was established in 1952. It was followed eight years later by the Confederation of Civil Servants of Brazil (CSCB), a more comprehensive body congregating state federations and national unions.* The UNSP was successful in promoting the very favorable Statute for Federal Public Employees

* Current (1966) members of CSCB's council are "eclectic" federations from Guanabara, Pernambuco, Minas Gerais, and Pará, two from São Paulo (one for state, the other for municipal employees), the Association of Civil Servants of Santa Caterina, the UPB, the UNSP, the National Union of Civil Servants of the Naval Ministry, the Association of Employees of the Ministry of Labor, Industry, and Commerce, and the Association of Employees of the National Department of Rural Epidemics.

only a few weeks after its inauguration.[70] Since then, militant associations have led campaigns for higher pay, for Christmas bonuses, for readjustment of job classifications, for retirement after thirty years' service, for the right to form syndicates,[71] and for pay and benefits equal to those of military employees. These campaigns have become a regular feature of Brazilian interest politics.

Students. Student associations can hardly be called typical middle-sector organizations, although they recruit primarily from those social groups.[72] In transitional societies and developing polities, structural contradictions—primarily role confusion and career ambiguities—seem to combine with discontinuities in political cultural values to produce a widespread syndrome of radicalism and total rejection of prevailing patterns of social and political behavior. Brazil is no exception.[73] *Radicalismo* is so characteristic of Brazilian student organizations that they are perhaps closer to movements than to representative associations. In spite of attempts by authority groups to compel them to accept the self-limiting role of representing only immediate group interests, student leaders have continued to concern themselves with making their followers and also the people at large conscious of national political issues. Often these policies of politicization and globalization of demands tend to cause internal strains—an increase in inter-elite factionalism and a growing disparity between leaders and followers.

Organization of students at the national level began as recently as 1929, when the House of the Student of Brazil (CEB) was founded.[74] The Casa offers services to students; its function is mainly cultural. In 1937 the Estado Novo helped create a national representative association. The following year the new organization became independent of the Casa and took the title of the National Union of Students (UNE). The UNE began as a sponsored peak association without constituent subunits. During the 1940's, previously organized *grêmios* were transformed into *centros*, or *diretórios acadêmicos*, and new centers and directories were created. These units (there were approximately five hundred of them by 1963) are organized within individual faculties or schools. They, in turn, are affiliated with a *diretório central*, which represents the entire student body of a university. At the next level, the central directories belong to state unions of students. The most prominent of these has been the Metropolitan Union of Students (UME) in Rio. For years it shared offices with the UNE, and its newspaper, *O Metropolitano*, served as a mouthpiece for the student movement as a whole. At all levels, the directories, central directories, and unions are quite independent and may refuse to follow UNE policy line. The UNE is one of the few Brazilian associations that have managed to hold regu-

lar, large national conventions, in spite of the fact that these have occasionally been faction-ridden, even tumultuous, affairs.[75]

The UNE has taken a stand on almost every major political issue of
the past twenty-five years. Beginning in 1958–59, it began systematically
adopting a more and more comprehensive set of demands covering such
issues as educational and university reform, inflation, foreign capital,
imperialism, independent foreign policy, support of Cuba, solidarity
with striking workers, literacy campaigns, agrarian reform, and technical assistance to the rural syndicalization movement.[76] Thus the UNE
became an integral part of the nationalist front. This made it and its
younger brother, the National Union of Secondary School Students
(UBES), a likely target for repression by the "revolutionary" authorities of 1964. Its headquarters were burned on the day of the coup, and
many of its leaders were arrested or driven into exile. In November 1964,
the regime promulgated a new law disciplining the system of student
representation.[77] The UNE and the state student unions lost the legal
monopoly they had acquired in 1942 and the relatively liberal statute
of internal autonomy guaranteed them by the Café Filho Law of 1955.
They were legally replaced by a National Student Directory (DNE) and
by state student directories specifically prohibited from engaging in "any
action, manifestation, or expression of a political nature as well as [from]
inciting, promoting, or supporting any collective absences from school."
The DNE was to have headquarters in Brasília, not Rio, and it was to
have plenary meetings only during school holidays and only when con-
voked by the Minister of Education. It was to be subsidized by the
Ministry of Education, but its accounts were subject to fiscal inspection
by the Federal Education Council. Candidates for office at every level
had to register before corresponding authority groups, and the elections
themselves were to be controlled by the university administrations.

In a sense the previous system had been a form of unbalanced corporatism. Authority groups had conceded the monopoly of representation and the guarantee of financial support without the corresponding
imposition of strict controls on leadership selection, interest articulation, and budgetary allocation. What the "revolutionary" regime did was
simply to reassert the logic of corporatist representation and demand,
in very strong terms, the requisite quid pro quo for official sponsorship.
Student leaders were faced with the choice of accepting the tutelage of
corporatism or risking the uncertainties of plurality. The UNE and most
of the state unions, central directories, and academic centers chose the
latter course. Most refused to modify their constitutions to conform with
the new restrictions. A few created "free" parallel associations. Although
the new law makes voting in student elections a prerequisite to taking

exams, many of the directory elections were boycotted.[78] The formation of state directories to replace the state unions was partly frustrated by the refusal of many recognized directories to participate. Nevertheless, the authority groups calmly went ahead with the formation of the National Student Directory in January 1966. Endowed with ample funds and control over the distribution of subsidies to its recognized affiliates, enjoying a formal representational monopoly, and supported by an obligatory vote and a captive membership, the DNE had everything going for it—except the allegiance of university students.[79]

Leaving nothing to chance, the regime formally abolished the UNE a week before the DNE elections.* Previously, authorities seemed convinced that the UNE represented only a small activist minority, and that it would collapse without its representational monopoly and its domestic and foreign subsidies.[80] Instead, the UNE registered itself as a civil entity and remained very active. Most of the directories and virtually all of the unions publicly proclaimed their allegiance to it. Even when it was abolished as a legal entity, prevented from raising funds through subscriptions, and ejected from its provisional office, it refused to give up and managed to hold its general congress in Belo Horizonte in July 1966. It is uncertain what will become of student representation. Authorities continue to regard the UNE as illegal, criminal, and subversive. At its 1965 convention, the UNE adopted a moderate program concerned with immediate student problems,[81] and after 1966 it returned to being more a movement than a representative association. Harassed by the military and forced to meet secretly in a convent, it declared its complete opposition to the regime and its intention to sponsor a Movement Against Dictatorship (MCD).[82] Its legal replacement, the DNE, failed to demonstrate any representative legitimacy and quietly faded away. In July 1967, in response to renewed militancy on the part of students, the regime hinted that it would sponsor still another national student organization.[83]

Lower-status groups. The degree of associational coverage tends to fall off gradually as one descends in socioeconomic status, but it plummets very markedly when one gets below the middle-sector level. Lower-status groups have almost no access to self-organized, self-run associations for the formal articulation of their interests. Occasionally, well-intentioned or politically ambitious men from the middle sectors will speak for them, as they have done through such groups as the various housewives' associations, welfare agencies, and charitable organizations.

---

* The state unions of Minas Gerais and Guanabara were also forcibly closed down or suspended.

An interesting example of this pervasive pattern of elite co-optation, control, and manipulation of lower-class interests is the Alliance of Solidarity and Protection for Renters (ASPI) of Rio. Although it has claimed to have 400 thousand members, it is made up, in fact, of a single lawyer and his staff and clientele.[84] By combining legal services with his own particularistic set of political contacts, this interest entrepreneur extends associational coverage and emerges as the popular leader of an unprotected segment of society. This is done from above with the connivance of authority groups and without the active participation of the interested parties, who appear to be dependent plaintiffs and grateful recipients of paternalistic favoritism.[85]

Not all the gates to lower-class protest are guarded by sponsors from the middle and upper classes. There exists a vast network of social clubs, sports groups, mutual aid and improvement societies, spiritualist circles, samba schools, *macumba* and *umbandista* cults, fraternal orders, religious brotherhoods, musical societies, community centers, religious and charitable institutes, fundamentalist sects, first aid stations, medical assistance posts, and even communitarian self-help and development organizations. Little is known about the influence of these groups, but they are organized and run by their own members, and they certainly play an occasional role as interest articulators.[86] In keeping with the general pattern, however, these organized groups are usually not self-supporting, and they depend on subsidies from political authorities.[87] Before any election, the newspapers are full of reports of generous grants given by those in control of the pork barrel to "deserving" and strategically placed associations; this amounts to a lower-class equivalent of the syndical-corporatist sponsorship given to upper and middle groups. An example of how this system operates is the case of the *favelado* (slum dweller) associations of Rio and their regional federation, FAFEG. According to one of their current leaders, "Governor Lacerda stimulated the development of these associations [in the early 1960's] to create a political clientele for himself."[88] Their number expanded rapidly as they became the focus of various competing political factions. By 1965 there were 120 in FAFEG "representing" some 680,000 slum dwellers. The fortunes of the local associations and of the federation ebbed and flowed with their relative success in obtaining a political patron and, through him, financial support. Authorities intervened in elections with promises and threats, and members were quick to dump a leader who had become visibly *queimado* (burned out), i.e., without a political patron. The current administration of FAFEG was seeking to steer a less partisan course, but it too remained dependent upon official patronage and the advice of middle-class professionals, especially lawyers, architects, and students. Breaking out of the syndrome of financial and political dependence is a difficult task in an environment so pervasively paternalistic.*

Rural workers. Ironically, this occupational sector, for which associational coverage is the least extensive, is the one about which the most has been written. In retrospect, the avalanche of comment by both nationals and foreigners seems to have greatly overestimated the degree to which the Brazilian peasant had obtained access to formal channels of interest expression. The prospect that fifteen million "parochials" might suddenly be catapulted into "citizen" status through participation in political groups—representative associations, parties, or movements— set off waves of revolutionary enthusiasm and conservative fear.

The rapid emergence of associability in this sector presents a rather serious challenge to the differentiation hypothesis. In global terms, there is little evidence in the rural structure of the kind of extensive structural changes that had occurred and were occurring in the cities. Except for certain isolated sectors where there had been technological innovation, shifts in the type of production, or changes in the nature of ownership (particularly as the result of wartime conditions), one would not have predicted on the basis of the hypothesis alone any marked rise in associability. To the extent that the increase resulted in the formation of representative associations, one is tempted to explain it by reference to another variable: the diffusion of organizational techniques, ideology, and leadership from other sectors. In cases where it resulted in movements, one could seek an explanation in the difference between rates of communication mobilization and structural differentiation—in people becoming mobilized by exposure to modern values in the media but not becoming assimilated into specialized roles in the occupational structure.

The first attempt by authority groups to stimulate associability was in 1903, and it was directed to the rural sector. In 1944 a rural syndicalization bill was decreed. Ten years later, Goulart, as Labor Minister, revived the theme, but it was cut short by the implacable opposition of rural employers. According to a survey conducted in 1961, the net result of these 58 years of sporadic sponsorship was six recognized syndicates of rural workers![89] In 1955, the leaders of the Sociedade Agropecuária e dos Plantadores de Pernambuco (SAPP) approached a young lawyer and newly elected state assemblyman, Francisco Julião, himself the son of a landowner but a member of the Socialist Party, for legal assistance.

---

* Nor are authority groups always so accommodative. For example, Associations of Domestic Servants were formed in São Paulo (1962) and Rio de Janeiro (1965) without much difficulty—or success, for that matter. An attempt to found a similar association in Minas Gerais was regarded as subversive and was suppressed by local authorities.

A new chapter in rural associability began to unfold. The SAPP, which had been founded as a mutual assistance burial society, turned to legal recourse when the owner of the plantation instituted eviction proceedings against 180 of its sharecropper members.[90] Julião shrewdly perceived the political potentiality of the demand and was instrumental in getting a bill passed expropriating the Galileia plantation and two others, dividing them among the threatened workers. The response was unanticipated. *Ligas camponêsas* (peasant leagues), as they were disparagingly baptized by local conservatives, grew rapidly, if in a disorderly fashion.[91] At their peak, membership was estimated at a hundred thousand, concentrated in the states of Pernambuco, Paraíba, Ceará, Piauí, and Alagoas.[92] Most of the recruits came from a narrow strip of humid plantation land, Zona da Mata, and from a single social group, sharecroppers and tenant farmers (*forreiros* and *arrendatários*). Julião himself was quite frank about the difficulty of extending recruitment to other groups and of organizing either small subsistence farmers or salaried proletarians.[93] In a thoughtful if partisan study, four explanations for the success of the peasant leagues are advanced.[94] First is "the fundamental and decisive role played by the legal character of the movement." The law was the great regimenting banner, and the provincial lawyer (like Julião) became the key figure in the movement.[95] Second, the *ligas camponêsas* were created and run from the cities.[96] The guidance of a corps of urban activists was of crucial importance, even though ideological differences between those activists would weaken the movement internally and make it externally dependent upon the political fortunes of various factions. Third, the rapid spread was facilitated by the ease with which the leagues could be legally registered as "civil entities." (The formation of rural syndicates depended upon a lengthy recognition process.) Finally, they dispensed free welfare services in addition to legal protection as a means for retaining the loyalty of members.

Even where they enjoyed the patronage of local authorities, the leagues were "a fragile organization." Julião was quoted as complaining, "To agitate is a beautiful thing. To organize is what is difficult."[97] As a consequence of this haphazard attitude toward administration and of ideological factionalism, the various state and local associations never formed a coherent national political force obeying a single command.[98] Nor were the leagues alone in attempting to provide associational coverage to the rural worker. In November 1961, the First National Congress of Rural Laborers and Workers was held in Belo Horizonte.[99] Julião's very success had attracted competitors, and the Congress was marked by factional strife.[100]

Except for their short venture in the 1940's, the Communists had not paid much attention to rural workers. Their Union of Agricultural Laborers and Workers of Brazil (ULTAB) had been founded in 1954 and had never become very active. Most of its strength was in São Paulo, where its headquarters were located. By 1961, it was claiming 9 state federations, 122 associations, and 35 thousand members. The Movement of Landless Farmers (MASTER) was an organization sponsored by Leonel Brizola, ex-governor and brother-in-law of João Goulart, in Rio Grande do Sul. Communists were also active in infiltrating the peasant leagues and rural syndicates.[101]

Of course, in 1961 there were only six rural syndicates to infiltrate. But the Church had already begun to take an interest in the matter. The bishops of Natal in Rio Grande do Norte and Aracajú in Sergipe had been conducting leadership training courses, and the former had some eight rural syndicates pending recognition.[102] Fathers Paulo Crespo and Antônio Melo in Pernambuco picked up the drive with renewed vigor and in direct competition with the peasant leagues. In spite of the noticeable reluctance of the ministerial authorities to recognize them, the Catholic-sponsored syndicates expanded rapidly, and the first statewide Federation of Rural Workers was founded by the Catholics in 1962.[103]

So far the political potentiality of "covering" rural worker interests had attracted three patrons: Julião, the Communists, and the Catholics. In late 1962 and early 1963 they were joined by a fourth, the Goulart regime itself. Its intentions were clear: to play the competing factions off against each other, to extend the existing system of welfare legislation and associational sponsorship to the unprotected, unco-opted rural proletariat, and, in the process, to create a vast new clientele group for *trabalhista* politicians, especially for Goulart himself.[104] It was intended as a repetition of the co-optive act that Getúlio Vargas had so skillfully performed in the 1930's with the urban syndicalization movement. It had the same, basically conservative, end in mind: "We hope through agrarian syndicalism to find, finally, the instrumentality capable of lessening the growing social unrest that already has begun to express itself in the country districts."[105] In March 1963 the Rural Workers' Statute was passed by Congress, and, one month later, the process of massive official recognition began. The number of recognized rural syndicates leaped from six in 1961 to 270 in late 1963, with some 557 recognitions pending. Ten official federations existed, and some 33 more had been formed.[106] The announced intention of the regime was to create two thousand "rationally distributed" syndicates by the end of the year.[107] In December 1963 the National Confederation of Agricultural Workers

(CONTAG) was formed, and the Communists (ULTAB), in alliance with the Catholic Popular Action group, defeated the Christian Democratic faction for control of it.

The "revolution" of 1964 radically altered the perspectives of the rural workers' movement. Peasant leagues, ULTAB units, and other "subversive" organizations were disbanded or forced underground. The CONTAG, most of its federations, and hundreds of rural syndicates were intervened. In some areas peasant leaders were assassinated in cold blood.[108] Despite its perception of the rural syndicalization movement as subversive and its protestations of liberalism, Brazil's new military regime did not abandon the idea of extending sponsored coverage to rural workers. With its support (and its strict controls) the syndicalization movement was permitted to revive itself. The interventions were gradually lifted, and by mid-1965 there were five hundred "regularly functioning and legally recognized" rural workers' syndicates,[109] three hundred of which had been recognized since April 1964.[110] The recognition of rural syndicates is handled by a special commission in the Labor Ministry.[111] The syndical tax is now being collected to support the new sponsored entities, and the National Institute of Agrarian Development (INDA) has been supporting regional and national meetings of syndical leaders. After some hesitation, the regime has gone ahead with the extension of welfare services to rural workers.* Despite this cautious corporatism and gradual paternalism, there are widespread indications that the provisions of the Rural Workers' Statute are not being fulfilled, either because the rural syndicates are powerless to ensure compliance or because authority groups are reluctant to prosecute violators.[112] In good measure, this is more the result of resistance at the local level than of a conscious policy on the part of national decision-makers.[113] At any rate, the future of the rural workers' movement is presently unpredictable. It remains suspended between uncertain and cautious support from above and sporadic resistance and indifference from below.

Foreign, regional, and ethnic groups. Three types of interests are surprisingly quiet in Brazilian political life, even though the society is quite differentiated in these dimensions. They are associations based on immigrant background, regional identity, and racial origin. There are many organizations that congregate Brazilians of foreign origin—Italian Circles, Portuguese Associations, Syrian and Lebanese Clubs, German *Schutzenvereine*, Jewish Societies, Japanese Cultural Societies and Nisei

---

* Such services had been stopped on April 11, 1964. In November 1965 a directive was signed permitting rural workers access to the medical services.

Youth Groups—but these seem to restrict themselves to social and mutual aid tasks.[114] Immigrant interests in an earlier period were often expressed by anarcho-syndicalist organizations; these days they are usually expressed by other types of associations (the Japanese, for example, operate from within the cooperative movement). The contemporary ventures of the immigrant associations into politics are infrequent and primarily confined to receiving ambassadors, promoting mutual trade, or ensuring favorable foreign policy support for the home country. This has been particularly true of the Portuguese Associations and their support for Portugal's colonial policy.

Rio de Janeiro has a number of organizations, such as the Associação Goiana, the Casa da Bahia, the Centro Paulista, and the Sociedade Sul-Rio Grandense, that seem to provide a home away from home for provincials living in Rio.* Some, like the Santa Catarina beer festival, engage in the promotion of local products, but none have attained any political prominence. The promotion of regional interests is accomplished largely through the *bancadas* (benches) of state representatives in Congress, through sporadic conferences of state secretaries of finance, education, labor, etc., through audiences with the President and other federal authorities, through appeals to ministers and other high officials from one's home state, and through the everyday use of regional *panelinhas* (cliques) composed of prominent public and private figures. State governments also maintain permanent offices in Rio.

Brazil is one of the world's most racially diversified countries. In spite of the well-publicized theme of racial democracy, all the many empirical studies point to the existence of substantial racial prejudice throughout Brazil.[115] But, although there is differential treatment based on racial stratification, there are no racially based associations presently active in Brazilian politics. Several exist either as social clubs or as cultural societies; others seem to be quiescent political associations in a state of suspended animation.

There were two periods, 1927–37 and 1945–50, during which representative associations of Brazilian blacks (*prêtos*) and mulattoes were very active in promoting an improvement in their collective status. Florestan Fernandes calls this outburst of associability an attempt at "a revolution within the order," a self-limited mobilization of effort aimed at achieving assimilation into Brazilian society without attempting to overthrow or even to alter drastically the basic premises of that society.[116]

---

* São Paulo even has a club whose purpose is to unite socially representatives from all the states: the Club of the Twenty-one Brother Friends.

Fernandes records in some detail the extent of social disorganization prevailing among blacks and mulattoes prior to the 1920's, their complete "incapacity for cooperation toward the attainment of collective ends," and their total "political inexperience."* In delineating the causes for the emergence of associations—first in São Paulo, which did not have the greatest concentration of blacks—he notes that "the intensive and rapid urbanization set off a chain of profound changes in the style of social life, in human relations, and in the mentality of men, converting the city of São Paulo into the principal center of technological and institutional modernization, of secularization of thought, of the propagation of new ideologies, of social agitation, and of the gradual democratization of political behavior."[117] The industrialization spurt concomitant with World War I reinforced the differentiation process begun by urbanization. Racial associability, then, was an indirect consequence of differentiation elsewhere, which had had the double impact of changing the behavior of aspirant groups and of weakening the traditional patterns of paternalist, authoritarian power—including racial dominance.

A second, independent but related, variable was the growing social and economic success of the new immigrant groups, especially the Italians. They introduced new behavioral patterns and forms of collective organization. By imitation, blacks and mulattoes began to acquire these new techniques of social control and organization. This case of transmission of associability from one group to another approaches Truman's hypothesis of waves of organization and counterorganization, except that the two were not locked in direct conflict.

Perhaps more important than "this complex apprenticeship" was the occupational differentiation that was beginning to produce a set of intermediary "middle-sector" positions blacks and mulattoes could realistically expect to attain. "Previously, 'to climb' meant to become the equal of the '*doutor*,' the '*senhor*,' the 'noble.' . . . In this epoch [they] commenced to perceive that they could 'climb' by performing modest services and that the end of the path demanded tenacity, gradations, and previous sacrifices."[118]

The first organized responses to these stimuli began in 1924, but the economic crisis of 1929 and the revolution of 1930 seem to have been the precipitating factors. The greater economic hardship and exaggerated belief that the coup signified "the dismantling of the oligarchy that dominated the country" shifted the basis of associability from a narrow cultural elite to a broader group of socially and economically deprived

---

* It should be remembered that the Abolition Movement was not the result of a slave revolt or even of a collective effort on the part of the slaves.

citizens. Blacks and mulattoes in São Paulo, and later in Rio de Janeiro and Bahia, began to congregate in large numbers around the banner of "the racial question," challenging the dominant elites' insistent theme that "the Negroes have nothing to demand." The Brazilian Negro Front (FNB), founded in 1931, grew rapidly to a membership of thousands of dues-paying and militarily regimented members.[119] It, and several other associations at this time, maintained a lively press and a fairly comprehensive indoctrination effort. However, already weakened by internal strife and on the verge of converting itself into a political party, the FNB was dissolved by force in 1937. In 1944, with the National Congress of the Negro, racial political organization began to revive. However, in spite of a brief period of activity, it gradually faded out—just when associability elsewhere was increasing.

One certainly cannot argue that racial protest did not emerge because there was no objective reason for it. The means whereby the system first ignored, then repressed, and finally de-fused racial protest merits detailed attention. One can hypothesize that it was the result of a deviation of interest consciousness from the racial to the occupational, itself stimulated by the emergence of new, more assertive channels of working-class protest in the late 1950's and early 1960's. This only partially explains the phenomenon. It must also be due to what I have described frequently above as the typical reaction of dominant Brazilian groups to emerging protest organizations: preemptive co-optation, or assimilation based on elite responsiveness via the granting of special favors (for example, protection against immigration in the 1940's) and financial support (for example, subsidies to representative associations and increased welfare benefits).[120] Just as it had absorbed rather than crushed emerging workers' associations in the 1930's, the system quietly, imperceptibly, and perhaps even unselfconsciously absorbed the racial question in the 1950's. It may, of course, be revived again if the ruling formula is changed or if it becomes financially impossible to maintain this policy. But for the moment, racial associations have only a latent political importance.[121]

Religious and ideological groups. Ideas and ideologies, religious or secular, have not played a prominent role in Brazil's historical development. This, as I argued above, partially accounts for the relative lack of associations based on shared values. The situation began to change during the 1950's, as did so many other aspects of Brazilian associational life. Brazilians were becoming more aware of the interest conflict caused by structural changes and also of the level of their development with respect to that of the rest of the industrialized world. As a result, they were forced to consider their position in terms of wider systems of meaning. Crude empiricism and improvisation began to give way to something approaching "the great lines of matured thought and great clashes of interests" that Bello found so lacking in past Brazilian history.[122] Ideological groups formed, recruited, indoctrinated, drafted, manifested, demonstrated, threatened, and even plotted with increasing frequency until they forced a military confrontation in March 1964.

"The Church had not become a highly effective social force in the Empire, partly because of the moral and intellectual mediocrity of its servants, mainly because of its subordination to the State."[123] When the yoke was finally lifted by the Republic, ecclesiastical and lay Catholics began slowly to correct this moral and intellectual mediocrity. But the more important attitudinal and organizational changes did not come until the 1950's. In 1952, the Brazilian Catholic Church created the National Conference of Brazilian Bishops (CNBB).* In addition to a secretary-general and numerous national secretaries, the CNBB has eleven regional councils.[124] Particularly when Dom Helder Câmara was its secretary, the CNBB played a very active public role. The pastoral letters it issued in 1962 and 1963 supporting basic reforms, especially land reform, created a considerable stir.[125] In 1962, with the personal encouragement of John XXIII and the promise of foreign financial support, the CNBB began to devise first a two-year Emergency Plan and then a more comprehensive four-year Pastoral Plan. It is hoped that this measure will provide a rationally integrated system of policy control and facilitate the rapid implementation of the Council's reforms in Brazil.[126] According to the claim of a bishop from the state of Bahia, the CNBB is beginning to have an impact: "The bishops are working every day more within the National Conference and less in isolation; they have managed to create a national pastoral plan that does not exist outside of Latin America, even in the most traditional Catholic countries. . . . The CNBB has managed to change the mentality of the people, thanks above all to the courageous work of its younger and more dynamic advisors."[127] It is significant that the CNBB was the first and for some time the only representative association to speak out against the abuses the "revolutionary forces" were committing against individual rights.[128]

Associated with the ecclesiastical authorities at both the national and the diocesan level are a considerable number of lay organizations with various attitudes. Foremost of these is Catholic Action with its affiliated youth groups of workers (JOC), young farmers (JAC), secondary-

---

* The Protestant peak association, the Evangelical Confederation of Brazil, antedates the CNBB by eighteen years. Created about the same time as the CNBB was the Conferência dos Religiosos do Brasil, a peak association for Catholic religious orders and congregations.

school students (JEC), and university students (JUC). Catholic Action took a very elitist corporatist position in the 1930's; more recently it has made reformist mass appeals.[129] There are a number of conservative family-oriented groups: the Christian Family Movement, the Confederation of Christian Families, the Crusade of the Rosary in Family, and the Legion of Social Defense. These have become particularly vocal whenever divorce legislation has been under consideration. Catholics have consistently been active in and concerned about educational policy, and the Association of Catholic Education aggregates these interests. For journalists there is a National Catholic Press Union, and for the military there is a Catholic Military Union. The Association of Catholic Business Managers (ADCE) is a recently founded entity modeled on a similar French body. It has an impressive Christian Social ideology that stresses the familiar Brazilian theme of *paz social* in a new garb and offers a comprehensive program of managerial training courses.[130] A unit of Opus Dei was established in São Paulo in 1965, and by the following year it had three university centers functioning, with plans for expansion into other states.[131] I have already discussed the involvement of the Church in workers' organizations: the National Confederation of Workers' Circles and the Brazilian Confederation of Christian Workers. In areas not specifically covered by a Catholic organization, the Church may act through other entities. For example, several of the women's groups to be discussed below reported that they worked closely with Catholic worker organizations. The Federation of Favelado Associations was also receiving assistance from Catholic sources.[132]

The Brazilian Association of Municipalities (ABM) is an attitude group initially founded to plead the cause of decentralized rule before the Constituent Assembly of 1946. Its adherents claim to have a comprehensive ideology and a historical tradition going back to 1828.[133] Its demands, however, are principally oriented around the immediate goal of obtaining the maximum amount of fiscal revenues and government subsidies for local government with the minimum amount of budgetary and political control. The ABM has three kinds of members: state federations of municipalities (of which there are about a dozen),* municipal governments (of which there are over three hundred), and experts, technicians, and professors of municipal government and administration.[134] Control of the ABM has increasingly passed from a group of administrative technicians to a group of professional politicians: councilmen, prefects, state assemblymen, federal deputies, and senators.[135] Their national congresses (five have been held since 1950) draw impressive sup-

---

* One of these, the Paulista Association of Municipalities, seems to be better organized and staffed than the ABM itself, especially as far as technical and legal assistance to its affiliates is concerned.

port from governors and even from the President of the Republic himself.[136] The ABM's activities are supported by generous federal and state
subsidies; and the government pays for its mail, for its members' trips
to international conferences, and for the printing of its publications.[137]
This impressive demonstration of public support for an ostensibly private association is hardly surprising when one considers the role of the
municipality in Brazilian politics.[138] It is the basic unit of the electoral
system; it is where most political careers start, where the rules of the
game are inculcated, where electoral support is consolidated, and where
debts are paid off. It would be only a slight exaggeration to call the
ABM the representative association of Brazil's professional politicians.[139]

The gradual lifting of police controls on freedom of expression in the
1950's began to be reflected in associational expressions of attitudes as
well as of interests. Communists, Socialists, nationalists, and leftist
Catholics, as well as democrats, spokesmen for free enterprise, and de-
fenders of Christian civilization all competed for the control of existing
syndicates, federations, confederations, military clubs, professional institutes, and societies. In the process they also began to form new attitude associations. Some, like ISEB, IPÊS, and the Superior War School,
set themselves the task of indoctrinating elites; some, like the MEB and
the Campanha de Educação Cívica (the popular culture movement of
UNE), tried mass indoctrination. Other organizations emerged and
began through a variety of more direct pressure tactics to attempt to influence public policy.

By far the best known of these was the Brazilian Institute of Democratic Action (IBAD), established in 1959 for the rather general and
ambiguous purpose of "defending democracy." In its first years, it seems
to have functioned primarily as a public relations enterprise and, in the
Northeast, as a welfare agency dispensing propaganda along with medical services and food.* It provided funds and some coordinating services
for a wide variety of other "democratic" attitude groups, such as the
Movimento Sindical Democrático (MSD) among workers and the
Movimento Estudantil Democrático (MED) among students.[140] IBAD
gained national prominence in 1962 when by means of a parallel association, the Popular Democratic Action or ADEP,† it intervened in the
elections of that year with massive campaign contributions to "deserving" candidates. The size and direction of the funds prompted accusa-

---

* SESI in its earliest period under Simonsen similarly combined paternalism and
political guidance in an effective manner. Here, however, the similitude ends, and
no evidence was discovered linking SESI and IBAD in the Northeast—or anywhere
else.

† IBAD and ADEP shared offices, presidents, and administrative personnel. Nonetheless, the president of both vigorously protested that they were unrelated.

tions of electoral corruption and aroused considerable suspicion concerning their national origin. The following year a congressional investigation was held on IBAD's and IPÊS's activities, and IBAD was dissolved by presidential decree.[141]

Estimates of the amount of funds involved in campaign subsidies alone vary from a proven minimum of one billion cruzeiros (US $2,500,000) to a maximum of five billion (US $12,500,000)—in either case a very considerable sum, especially in an inflationary, cash-hungry economy.[142] ADEP admitted to aiding 450 candidates for federal deputy, 850 for state assemblyman, and a few senators and governors.[143] In his testimony two weeks later, the president of ADEP-IBAD stated that the latter alone assisted 220 federal deputies, 660 state candidates, two governors, and various senators, prefects, and municipal councilmen. Even discounting for exaggeration and overlap, that represents quite a massive display of interest.

Of the hundreds of other associations engaged in "democratic" and anti-communist propaganda, none achieved as much public notoriety as the IBAD. The variety in terms of both ideological orientation and tactics of influence, however, is considerable.[144] They range from organizations like the Brazilian Anti-Communist Crusade, wholly preoccupied with military conspiracy and counterconspiracy, to the Brazilian Society for the Defense of Tradition, Family, and Property (TPF), a descendent of the Brazilian monarchist tradition, complete with heraldic symbols and ultra-Catholic ideology.[145]

Women made up a previously unrepresented sector to which associational coverage was extended during this period of ideological mobilization. There had been a brief flurry of feminist associability in the mid-1920's and early 1930's, but the 1934 Constitution had contained provisions favorable to women's rights and had thus effectively absorbed the emerging protest.[146] Women, of course, have been active in a variety of important charitable organizations. But the manifestly political women's association is a product of the last few years, beginning with the Movement of Feminine Regimentation (MAF). The MAF began in 1954 as an organization protesting the rising cost of living and the lack of civic education in public schools. In an increasingly radical political environment, the MAF found itself devoting increasing effort to "combating Communism and corruption." It currently has some five thousand members, most of whom live in the city of São Paulo, although it has eight "nuclei" in the interior of the state. Although the *Mafistas* proudly proclaim that any woman who is not Communist is eligible, their directory is composed exclusively of members of very high-status, traditional paulista families. Its president is the sister of the owner of

O Estado de São Paulo, perhaps Brazil's most prestigious newspaper. As is the case with all the women's attitude associations interviewed, there is behind the directory of the MAF a group of male advisors, and many of these are connected with the newspaper.[147]

A more recently formed group of paulista women is the Feminine Civic Union (UCF), whose members are younger, more engaged in professional life, and perhaps not so restricted to traditional families. It started in 1962 with an immediately political objective, "to awaken the civic consciousness of women." It has fewer members than the MAF but a more extensive network of "nuclei," including a few in the neighboring state of Paraná. Before the coup of 1964, the UCF devoted itself exclusively to propaganda campaigns against subversion. Not until after the victory of the conservative forces did it begin to occupy itself with welfare (favela social work) and consumer protection (a campaign for voluntary price controls). One of its current tasks is to maintain an Archive of Politicians, with personal biographical data as well as information on their voting records. To my knowledge this is the only such attempt in Brazil. It is also running a campaign to register women voters.[148]

Rio's equivalent of the UCF is the Woman's Campaign for Democracy (CAMDE), certainly the best known women's association in Brazil.* The CAMDE owes its prominence to its very active promotional programs, to its rapport with important political and military elites and with the national press (especially *O Globo*, a conservative Rio newspaper), to its proximity to national decision-making centers, and to its having been singled out by the foreign press as the primary civilian power behind the 1964 coup.[149] The CAMDE carried on a steady campaign of *esclarecimento* (enlightenment) before the coup, sponsoring lectures for its members on the peril of subversion, giving out pamphlets, holding public meetings, collecting signatures on protest petitions, putting up posters and banners during the election campaign urging citizens to "Vote for a Democrat so that tomorrow I may still be free," and appearing on television with a great variety of political, religious, and social personalities.† It worked in collaboration with sister associations in São Paulo and elsewhere and also with the Democratic Syndical

---

* Groups similar to UCF and CAMDE exist in Minas Gerais (the Democratic Women's League), Recife (the Democratic Feminine Crusade), and Pôrto Alegre (the Democratic Feminine Association).

† Both CAMDE and UCF have been accused of being partisan, i.e. party-linked. Their having both been formed just prior to the 1962 elections lends some substance to this, although both strongly deny such a link. They have also been perceived as Church-linked, but CAMDE officials stress that it is a purely secular organization even though it operates from the offices of the Ipanema parish.

Movement, the National Confederation of Christian Workers, the IPÊS-Rio, the AMB, and the AC-Rio. It was instrumental in the seizure of the "subversive" MEB literacy pamphlet. During Goulart's mass meeting of March 13, 1964, CAMDE urged Rio's women to stay home and place candles in their windows.

But the culmination of the efforts of these women's associations came six days later at the "March of the Family with God for Freedom" in São Paulo. An estimated 500 thousand people turned out to counter-protest the leftist *comício* of March 13. The paulista women's groups were not alone in organizing the march. The idea itself seems to have come from a Catholic sister, a federal deputy, and a high official of the CNC. The actual organization of the march took place in the Brazilian Rural Society with the assistance of members of the Commercial Association, the Federation of Industries, the Federation of Rural Associations, the Club of Retail Merchants, and other associations of the "productive classes." In the official album commemorating the march, it was claimed that 112 representative associations took part, including the Association for Combating Cancer, the Association of Veterans of 1932, the Federation of Workers' Circles, the YMCA, the Commodities Exchange Market of São Paulo, the Federation of Parent-Teachers' Associations, and the Urban-Rural Christian Friendship Fraternal Society! Most of the credit, however, fell to the MAF, the UCF, and a few smaller women's associations.[150] This march, followed by lesser ones in Santos, Belo Horizonte, Curitiba, and Pôrto Alegre, may have provided the legitimation the military legions were awaiting, although most of the evidence that has come to light since suggests that the military plans had been established for some time beforehand. In fact, it might be more accurate to say that the impending military coup triggered the march rather than vice versa.[151] The CAMDE in Rio had planned another march for April 1, but quietly called it off when told beforehand it would interfere with the coup.[152] Instead they held a gigantic (estimates run as high as a million participants) victory celebration two days after it.

Conclusion

This annotated directory of nationally relevant representative associations active in contemporary Brazilian politics has been neither systematic nor complete, though I believe all the major organizations have been discussed at least briefly. As I have surveyed the universe of Brazilian interest politics by written questionnaire, personal interview, and publicly available documentation, I have constantly encountered new national associations of whose existence I was previously ignorant. This continued high rate of activity—of creation and demise—is an important (if frustrating) finding in itself. It is evidence, as David Truman has observed, of a developing political system.[153] The pattern of emergence is strongly affected by the presence of an officially sponsored and protected system of interest expression. Directly or indirectly, corporatism conditions the activities and indeed the very existence of all Brazilian representative associations, even those that refuse or are denied its privileges.

The art of association among workers, first urban and more recently rural, has been particularly influenced by these authoritarian policies. In effect workers have been denied the right to establish other, less dependent, forms of representation. In the 1930's their spontaneous and plural organizations were destroyed or assimilated. Subsequently, every time government controls have been relaxed, workers have tended to respond by creating more militant and politicized "para-syndical" groups alongside and even superseding the semiofficial ones. But in each case the burst of suppressed associability has been halted by the eventual reassertion of authoritarian control, and the new units have been disbanded or driven underground.

The response of propertied individuals and firms has been somewhat different. For these clients, corporatism has offered more positive rewards than negative sanctions. Despite some initial reluctance, employers took ample advantage of the syndical opportunities during the 1930's. They did not, however, disband their previously created private associations, toward which the government adopted a permissive, even supportive attitude. Their continued loyalty to the system just after the war was due no doubt in part to their desire to control and profit from the very substantial resources so enticingly offered them by the SESI, SESC, SENAI, and SENAC programs.[154] This new feature of the system simultaneously reinforced the viability of a paternalistic labor-management arrangement and undermined worker associability by offering free (or almost free) services comparable to those their own syndicates could offer.[155]

In the late 1950's and early 1960's the political and social contexts changed. Employers responded either by reviving moribund private entities or by creating new ones. There was no wholesale desertion of the former channels of representation in favor of aggressive liberalism, although the rate of formation of new sindicatos lagged, as did membership in older ones.* Instead there ensued a sustained outburst of

---

* The lack of dynamism in employer syndicalism in the last three years in particular is somewhat hidden in the aggregate statistics by the large number of former rural associations that have been transforming themselves into sindicatos and *federações*.

activity in the creation and use of parallel private organizations and new, more functionally specific ones. To some extent, this can be attributed to the differentiation process and specifically to certain qualitative changes within Brazilian industry, finance, and commerce. Speculatively, it can also be related to changes in the nature of the policy-making process in general. During this period, the process was becoming increasingly bureaucratized and, to a degree, more instrumentally rational. The raw experimentalism and strong personalism of the Vargas dictatorship were giving way to forces of routinization. Vast numbers of working committees, consultative councils, advisory boards, executive groups, and mixed commissions were created and often had considerable decisional autonomy delegated to them. The experts' role in policy-making became more important, as did the need for accurate, detailed information for predicting the outcome and measuring the consequences of new government programs. Sectorial and comprehensive planning efforts were initiated. Of course, personal and particularistic channels of access permeated these efforts and remained important, but alongside them developed formal, institutionalized subsystems of representation.

PART III

What determines the form and direction of interaction between representative associations and authority groups? Why do interest spokesmen use certain tactics and forego others? Why do they focus on some decisional targets and ignore others? Such theorists of interest politics as Arthur Bentley, David Truman, and Jean Meynaud have suggested that the internal characteristics of the association, above all the extent to which members actively participate in its activities, provide the determining factors. Tocqueville's hypothesis involves greater indirection. Through their participation in such intermediary bodies, citizens or potential citizens learn operative rules of political behavior. They will naturally generalize upon these private experiences and apply such generalizations to their attempts to influence public policy-makers. In this way a certain set of predispositions and norms—the political culture of the more comprehensive system—is either reinforced or weakened, and this will determine the nature of the interaction pattern. Recent excursions into interest group analysis have partially inverted the original set of causal relationships, which treated policy outcomes exclusively as dependent variables, with or without the mediating impact of political culture. Harry Eckstein, among others, has suggested that the reverse may be true—that the nature of public policy-making may determine the form, intensity, scope, and significance of interest politics. "If interaction among politically active groups produces policy, policy in turn creates politically active groups."[1]

Both hypothetical perspectives agree, however, that there usually exists a stable and predictable relationship between associability and public policy. This will be discussed in Part III. Chapter 9 will inquire into the modalities and norms of participation within Brazilian associa-

tions and how this influences their attempts to influence authority groups. Chapter 10 will examine the process of policy-making for clues as to why associations tend to concentrate on certain institutions and segments of the decisional cycle. Chapters 11 and 12 will deal with interaction in the legislative and partisan, executive and bureaucratic forums.

NINE

Participation and Plurality

CORPORATISM, as practiced in Brazil, does not encourage active participation at the grass roots. In one of the few sociological studies that have examined the role of workers' syndicates, Juarez Brandão Lopes concludes, "The syndicate is not seen as something made by them, but as something done by others for them. When they mention the syndicate, workers do not use the pronoun 'we,' but 'they.' Just as they use the Welfare Institute [IAPI] or SESI to obtain services, they use the syndicate or ignore it depending on whether those services are satisfactory or not."[1] Among these services are legal protection, short-term loans, medical and dental treatment, in some cases subsidized food, and occasionally even barber shop services. The worker may pay his dues when he needs the services or attend meetings on the rare occasions when collective wage agreements are being discussed, but the syndicate remains an "outside" institution.[2] As far as the syndicates themselves are concerned, drives to acquire new members are rare because there is little financial payoff (the monthly dues are strictly nominal) and because there is a certain risk involved: one cannot be sure that the newcomers will not upset the leaders' dominance. Moreover, the Syndical Tax guarantees the syndicates an adequate income completely without regard to density of membership or intensity of participation. "Brazilian syndicalism is a syndicalism that lives outside the factories."[3] Accordingly, there are few incentives for establishing locals.

Many factors inhibit grass-roots participation, but the most frequently cited and creditable one, in my opinion, is the omnipresence of authority-group interference. With no guarantee that ministerial officials will not intervene to nullify the results of an election on behalf of the defeated

TABLE 9.1
DEGREES OF OLIGARCHY BY TYPE OF ASSOCIATION
(*percent*)

| Degree of oligarchy | Employers' ass'ns | | Workers' ass'ns ($N = 21$) | Liberal-professional ass'ns ($N = 10$) | Civic and religious ass'ns ($N = 11$) |
	Syndical ($N = 27$)	Private ($N = 38$)			
High[a]	44.4%	28.9%	14.3%	30.0%	63.6%
Medium[b]	14.8	13.2	33.3	40.0	9.1
Low[c]	14.8	5.3	19.1	20.0	9.1
Stable but shifting[d]	22.2	34.2	14.3	10.0	9.1
No answer	3.7	18.4	19.1	0.0	9.1

NOTE: Columns may not add to 100 because of rounding.
  [a] No leadership change or organized electoral opposition in last ten years or since foundation.
  [b] One leadership change or opposition candidacy.
  [c] More than one leadership change or opposition candidacy.
  [d] Regular rotation in office between parties or factions (*rotativismo*).

party, it is not surprising that voting particpation is low.[4] Under the current "revolutionary" restrictions, officials intervene even earlier to prevent the nomination of candidates they consider untrustworthy. The low participation—high interference syndrome is a circular one. The Labor Code requires that a quorum of two-thirds of the paid membership be present and voting. Failure to meet this quorum or lower ones in successive by-elections gives the Ministry or its regional delegate a legal excuse to intervene. Intervention after a financially exhausting and time-consuming series of elections discourages future participation, which in turn encourages or facilitates future interference.

As a result, syndical elections are rarely *concorrida* (competitive). In my interviews with association leaders, I solicited information on internal electoral processes.* In Table 9.1 the responses are coded and cross-tabulated against the type of interest represented. The apparent finding that employers' associations, both public and private, are more oligarchic than those of workers is somewhat misleading. A substantial number of the workers' syndicates that reported at least one leadership change or opposition ticket (one-third of the total) had lost their oligarchic purity by imposition, not by voluntary competition, and had been subjected to more or less disguised government intervention. Private entities representing propertied interests tend to be less dominated by single cohesive ruling groups, but they have a marked propensity for *rotativismo*, a fixed system of leadership rotation, often between different regional representatives. In workers' syndicates there is considerable evidence that membership is kept down to a restricted number of "activ-

* For a discussion of the sample, see the Appendix.

ists" who can be relied upon to provide the necessary support. Thus a stable and professional bureaucratic oligarchy (*peleguismo*) develops. The consolidation of its dominance depends to some extent on electoral manipulation, but more on the direct or indirect support of authority groups. Few major changes in control occur without the connivance of someone in an authoritative position. Favored leaders are assisted by means of various slush funds, of which the best known is the Social Syndical Fund. Authorities can enhance the prestige or influence of a given leader or group by public demonstrations of affection, grants of important consultative, administrative, or judicial posts, invitations to represent Brazil at foreign conclaves, etc. (Such favoritism is called *prestigiar*.) On the other side of the coin, followers are quick to observe when their leader is *queimado* (burned out, that is, cut off from easy and intimate access), and usually can be relied upon to respond accordingly.

Employer's syndicates are different in degree, but not in kind. Government interference in internal elective and deliberative processes is less omnipresent and more subtle. Expressions of favor and disfavor are less public. Fernando Henrique Cardoso, in his study of industrialists, reaches a conclusion concerning their view of syndicates that is rather similar to the observations of Brandão Lopes on workers' syndicates:

> In general, and this observation stems from the almost unanimous testimony of those interviewed, the industrialists see their representative associations as something foreign to them. "They only take care of the private interests of their leaders while speaking in the name of *classe*" and so forth. It matters little if the observation is correct or not; it expresses a type of reaction that has very negative implications for the possibilities of success of the type of leadership institutionalized in employers' syndicates. . . . Frequently, access to the leadership [of industrial class associations] is the safest means for solving the problems belonging to the firms of the "class leaders" rather than a type of struggle for common interests. Nevertheless, the criticism directed against them also expresses the effects of the heterogeneity of the industrial group in another sense: Participation in syndical activities necessarily imposes a political dimension to behavior, and political activity is looked down upon by the bulk of industrialists. . . . The first impulse is not to participate in any undertaking that escapes their usual sphere of action and control. Feeling out of place before the political mechanisms that orient syndical activity, they tend to deny any positive significance to this type of activity, which they consider wasteful, if not a total imposition on them.[5]

Cardoso's second major observation is that leaders of industrial syndicates tend to be recruited disproportionately from what he calls "the captains of industry." These entrepreneurs, "devoid of capital but often well connected in government circles, try in many ways to influence decisions that facilitate their obtaining loans and official concessions. If they can, they become politicians and leaders of professional categories.

At the head of patronal syndicates and federations, 'professional' industrialist leaders proliferate and eventually become real entrepreneurs."[6] In contrast with this type of industrialist, who is preoccupied with exploiting government favoritism for the maximum short-term return, is the *homen-de-emprêsa*, a sort of organization man who is more concerned with rationalization of production, who accepts competition, and who has a wider vision of the developmental process. This latter type is less likely to participate in syndical life and less likely to go through traditional channels of influence, i.e., "personal contact, friendship, subservience, and graft." His concern is more with industry as a whole, with the role of the productive classes, with defending democracy and free enterprise, and with "modernizing" the working class and increasing its standard of living.

My interviews neither definitely confirm nor contradict Cardoso's generalizations.* For one thing, I did not seek to interview industrialists systematically to discover how they viewed the activities of their syndicates. Although I heard numerous accusations, often accompanied by rather convincingly detailed examples, that leaders were using their associational position for personal gain, I would hesitate to call that the rule. Questions designed to elicit information on motivations for participation were not productive. Concerning the type of industrialist most active in syndical affairs, my interviews were restricted to nationally relevant associations. Nevertheless, with certain important exceptions, I would agree with Cardoso that employers' syndicates do recruit more from patrimonially oriented and merchantilistic entrepreneurs than from capitalistically oriented *homens-de-emprêsa*.[7] One frequently hears the complaint, especially from administrative personnel within the associations, that the "real industrialists" are not participating. By "real industrialists," most are referring to the size of the firm, but some are referring to role conception. In either case, the two are correlated.

One of Cardoso's generalizations I can support unequivocally: employers' syndicates are dominated by active minorities. Elections are generally uncontested. The same leaders rule for lengthy periods. However, the dynamics of patronal oligarchy differ from those of worker oligarchy. Outright manipulation, overtly fraudulent electoral practices, and open government interference are rare, though not unheard of. Tenure is ensured because leaders have enough time, financial resources, personal friends, contacts, and knowledge of the rules of the game, and because most of the members under them simply don't care who's on top.

---

* I might add that Cardoso does not substantiate his observation with specific quantitative breakdowns, although his study of industrialists was based on fairly rigorous stratified sampling in several regions of the country.

However, interaction between leaders and followers is much more frequent in employers' syndicates than in workers' syndicates. This is largely because of SESI and SENAI and a variety of government administrative regulations that are processed by the syndicate. The interaction is also helped by the fact that much more of the associations' revenue comes from voluntary contributions by members and that firms must take part in order to regulate competition and supply of materials. Brazilian syndicates are far from the corporatist ideal of self-regulation, but there is enough exchange of views and favors to encourage participation, especially among those who lack the resources to obtain these services elsewhere.

Federations

In general, all of the above comments on the quality of member participation in syndicates apply to federations as well. It should be noted, however, that workers' federations do not have a very clearly defined role in the Brazilian corporatist system. A few federations in São Paulo have assumed some limited functions as bargainers and as dispensers of welfare services, but for the most part the principal task of the workers' federation is to provide a base for confederational elections. Employers' federations, on the other hand, have acquired functions not originally assigned them by the Labor Code. By resisting fragmentation and by insisting on maintaining their eclectic scope, entities like the Federation of Industries of the State of São Paulo (FIESP) have become very significant aggregators and articulators of interests for the region as a whole. The creation of SESI, SESC, SENAI, and SENAC in the 1940's meant that the regional federations were vested with control over very substantial sums of money. Most of these funds go into various welfare and educational programs, but some are diverted to pay for federation administrative expenses and technical services. FIESP and FIEGA, for example, maintain large staffs of economists, lawyers, social workers, statisticians, and accountants who perform important professional services for member syndicates and individual industrialists. This gives them a rather exceptionally high rate of contact.

Some employer federations also make a deliberate effort to bridge the gap in participation. Any industrialist is welcome to attend FIESP's regular weekly meetings, listen to speakers who frequently are top government officials, and express his opinions. FIESP also sponsors a yearly Convention of Industrialists of the Interior as a means of involving those outside the capital in federation affairs. The Federation of Agriculture of São Paulo (FARESP, now FAESP) performs a number of important discount commercial services for members, regularly promotes gatherings in the interior of the state, and for a while showed weekly movies at its headquarters in order to stimulate the interest of its members. These are, however, exceptions. Most of the federations are institutions remote from the immediate preoccupations and interests of those they purport to represent.

Elections in federations present an element of added peculiarity beyond those present in lower-level elections: the "phantom syndicate." All legally recognized syndicates have one vote, regardless of size or density of membership. An enterprising leader can sponsor the creation of new syndicates or the subdivision of existing ones in a way that will ensure him a reliable bloc of supporters. Both incumbents and challengers can play the game, but it normally depends on ministerial favor. Like the phenomenon of *peleguismo*, phantom syndicates are often believed to exist only among workers. However, there are many among employers as well, and the consolidation of an enduring electoral alliance within employers' federations is further facilitated by the incumbent's control over the distribution of SESI funds, which can be used to reward supporters and punish opponents.*

In spite of these imperfections in representational and electoral forms, competition does occasionally break out. Although the process is slow, opposing tickets are formed and oligarchies are deposed. One characteristic way such conflicts are resolved is by means of a *prévia*, a sort of informal primary in which opponents size up each other's electoral strength. When a challenger has accumulated sufficient strength to force the issue into the open, he or some of his supporters are co-opted into a compromise ticket. Sometimes this is neatly taken care of by passing a constitutional amendment increasing the number of offices, so that everyone can participate.† When all else fails and strengths are even, a third party is often selected by both contending parties to effect the transition. Rarely does anything approaching stable factionalism exist;

---

* For example, the Syndical Census of 1961 records that 20 of FIEGA's 58 affiliates are located on the same floor of the same building—which is the address of FIEGA itself. The Federation of Industries of the State of Minas Gerais has 25 of its 35 members sharing its offices. This is not conclusive evidence of their being phantom syndicates, however. It has long been a policy of FIESP to encourage its affiliates to install themselves in the same locale. At one time, it was even a statutory obligation. FIESP currently has 39 of its 98 members sharing its building. In this case, however, most (though not all) of them sustain distinct corporate existences with separate offices and personnel; and the physical propinquity probably reinforces the degree of member participation and shared activity of the federation level. Where quarters are cramped and a single corps of functionaries handles the correspondence for dozens of syndicates, one wonders about the authenticity of their existence.

† The ultimate example of this occurred in the National Confederation of Industry when the number of offices to be filled was more than half the number of voting representatives. This made it physically impossible to form an opposing ticket.

even more rarely does control of the association pass from one distinct set of incumbents to a distinct set of challengers by means of an open vote. When such dramatic turnovers occur, they are usually caused by pressures from outside the association.

Confederations

"Poor confederations," to paraphrase Porfirio Díaz, "so far from their clients and so near the regime." The propensity of authorities for interfering in syndical elections and policy-making seems inversely proportional to the association's distance from Rio and directly proportional to its position in the syndical hierarchy. Hence syndicates in Rio are more restrictively controlled than those in São Paulo, and confederations, national federations, and national syndicates (whose headquarters with one exception are all in Rio) are more closely watched than state federations or local syndicates. When a longtime oligarchy like the one that controlled the CNTI is broken, it invariably involves the connivance of authorities—the ministry or occasionally the President of the Republic himself.

The employers' confederations, that is, the CNI, the CNC, and the CRB (now CNA), like the employers' syndicates in general, are not as directly or overtly dependent upon authoritative sanction as the workers' confederations. They all tend to show remarkable stability in upper-echelon elective positions. This is because (as was true of the federations) members do not show much interest in participating; because there is an equalitarian voting system in which each federation gets one vote regardless of size and operability; and because the incumbent has discretionary control over a number of subsidies.* The contin-

---

* Confederations have sporadically attempted to increase their contacts with the "base." The CRB has held a series of "Regional Encounters" and "National Congresses" of *ruralistas;* the CNI sponsored several "Plenary Reunions of Industry" in different parts of the country and "Investors' Congresses" between Northeastern and Southern industrialists; the CNC even had a floating national directory that met periodically in different state capitals. As a rule, however, association business is transacted in Rio and contacts with member federations are restricted to short biannual conferences of representatives. Some exchange is made directly with local syndicates and even with individual firms, but there exists a vague gentlemen's agreement to use the federations as intermediaries. The national syndicates and federations operate independently from the confederations.

The CRB had an electoral system with votes partially weighted according to the number of members in each state. This helped the long tenure of a paulista in the presidency. Otherwise, it is difficult for a paulista to be elected to such high office, despite the fact that his federation is likely to be the largest and most active, owing to the resentment of smaller states against São Paulo's prominence.

The weaker and less operative the federation, the more dependent it is upon confederationally allotted subsidies and, hence, the more likely it is to support the candidate who controls that allotment.

uity of executive control, strongly supported by internal structures and processes, is threatened usually only by an external condition: the presidents of the major confederations must be acceptable to the President of the Republic. This can be interpreted with some latitude, running roughly from a tacit assurance of passive acquiescence to an overt manifestation of personal friendship. Given sufficient flexibility, a confederation leader can, as one expressed it candidly to me, "get along with any President—provided he is democratic, of course."[8] Some have managed to obtain considerable tenure. The Brazilian Rural Confederation and the National Confederation of Land Transport have had the same presidents since their foundations, fifteen and nine years ago respectively. Being close to the President has its advantages, but it also places rather strict limits on one's tenure in office. In the CNI, for example, where personalism is still more important than institutionalization, the presidency has changed hands almost every time there has been a change in the national presidency. Three times, twice in 1961 and once in 1964, this came as the result of open government intervention.*

Of course such tactics can be rather destructive to the public prestige of the associations, and they are used rarely. But various regimes have not refrained from using less obvious methods of influencing the Confederation's leadership selection. For example, following the 1964 coup, two opposing tickets were presented in a CNI election (this had never happened before in the CNI's history). One of them dutifully presented itself to the President of the Republic for approval. Castelo Branco, seeing that his old schoolmate, General Macedo e Soares (the former director of the National Steel Company and current president of Mercedes-Benz do Brasil) was in one of the vice-presidential slots, suggested that his friend deserved a better position and refused to endorse the ticket. The opposition, hearing this, promptly offered the General the top spot on its ticket, which he accepted. On the day of the election, the General's ticket was down ten to nine. A few minutes after the elections had begun, the government stepped in to intervene in one of the Northern federations on grounds of electoral irregularities. This threw the election into a tie. Several months later, in a rematch, the General won handily.[9]

Private Associations

The quality of member participation in the private entities is rather different, suggesting that associational structure and the pattern of gov-

* In all three cases, the intervention was requested by industrialists within the CNI who saw such direct action as the only means for ensuring the selection of a president more compatible with the national executive.

ernment policy are at least as important determinants as "the lack of an associative spirit." Private associations are also oligarchic, especially the older ones. They tend to have large, stable directories and fairly well-defined channels of access to the inner executive circles.* But they have substantially more interaction between leaders and followers than do the public associations. Rank-and-file intimacy is helped by frequent plenary sessions, a well-developed system of committees and working groups of volunteers, and extensive legal, administrative, welfare, educational, and even commercial services for members.† Because the associations depend upon contributions by members and on income from services performed for members, the leaders have a direct incentive for expanding or at least maintaining the number of associates. On the other hand, members seem to be more concerned with controlling group expenditures than in the case of syndicates, where contributions are official and involuntary. The result of these factors, plus the relative freedom from government interference, is a generally more lively internal political process, both electorally and in the formulation of group demands. Although private association leaders complain often in interviews about member disinterest and lack of associative spirit, compared to most of the semiofficial syndicates they are hives of member activity. Not surprisingly then, their elections tend to be more openly contested, and in some of them something like a pattern of stable factionalism develops. One product of this, as we saw in Table 9.1, is *rotativismo*, or regular rotation between two leadership groups (often representing Rio de Janeiro and São Paulo), a solution very characteristic of the operational code of Brazilian political culture.‡

The most closely and publicly watched elections among all Brazilian

---

* The private entities have a means that is not available to syndicates for sustaining a ruling minority in office: weighted voting according to plant size or production. Also, many of them have their headquarters in São Paulo and are run by paulistas. In this way, the paulistas seem to be compensating for their relative underrepresentation in the syndical hierarchy.

† Some private associations, like the Retail Managers' Club and ADECIF, hold well-attended weekly luncheons. Several associations run social clubs and restaurants in the center of town where members congregate frequently and speakers are invited. The armed services clubs, the Engineering Club, and the Press Association combine the functions of social club and representative association. The American Chamber of Commerce and ADECIF are especially active in the provision of services by volunteers.

‡ This, of course, is a contemporary, private replica of the "policy of the governors," which rotated the national presidency between the state governors of São Paulo and Minas Gerais during the old Republic. Although in most cases the associational presidency is exchanged alternately, sometimes the top office remains constant and other positions are rotated to give an opportunity to representatives from different regions, firms of different sizes, or different branches of activity.

representative associations are those in the Clube Militar. They are also the most democratic elections in the country—at least they involve free and open competition between stable clusters of contenders representing distinctive points of view.[10] Other professional, middle-sector associations are the scene of lively electoral competition. The AMB, the various state medical associations and especially the Medical Association of Guanabara (AMEG), the Order of Physicians, and even the Syndicate of Physicians of Rio de Janeiro are divided into factions favoring public and private medical practice.* Elections are close and frequently accompanied by charges of fraud and threats of judicial recourse. Slightly less tumultuous but quite competitive are the elections in the Institute of Architects and several lawyers' associations. Once again we find evidence of the fragmented, ideologically inconsistent nature of the Brazilian *mesoi*. As for the many private associations of industrialists and businessmen that have been formed in the past decade, it is probably too early to assess the extent of their oligarchic tendencies. They do have unusually high rates of member participation, but, so far, there is little evidence of electoral competitiveness.

Associational Activity and the Political Culture

One expects to find oligarchy and differential participation in representative associations. Brazil, perhaps, somewhat overfulfills these expectations, but this is not what is surprising or distinctive about the quality of member participation. What is surprising is the lack of evidence that the divorce between the active minority and those whose interests are being represented generates any social or political tensions. Outwardly, there is tranquility and harmony in the relations between the rank and file and their leaders, which might lead one to conclude that comprehension and accountability are high. The more one penetrates the milieu of interest politics, however, the more one encounters private (in interviews) and public (in the media) doubts about the "authenticity," the "energy," the "image," and even the personal honesty of association leaders. Nevertheless, followers seldom revolt and leaders seldom change. When they do, more often than not it is as an indirect result of government intervention or the dimly perceived consequence of a power play at the summit. A certain but undeterminable amount of "voting with one's feet"—of leaving an association because of dissatisfaction with its electoral or policy process—probably happens, but the syndical tax guarantees formal survival until the Ministry decrees otherwise. The *enquadramento* system does not freely permit component associations

---

* The AMEG was expelled from the AMB shortly after the coup of 1964 for its "subversive" and "socialist" views.

to protest by shifting their allegiance to other peak organizations. On rare occasions, however, federations or syndicates may refuse to participate in their formally assigned peak associations, take public stands against them, or even try to have authorities intervene and appoint new directories.*

The answer lies, one can hypothesize, in the complex interrelation between participation in secondary associations and the general political culture of the system as I have described it. The rank-and-file member learns (or rather is taught) to regard his syndicate or association as a dependent recipient of public favors from a patrimonial order rather than as an independent producer of demands upon a competitive social order. The association or syndicate is to be exploited, along with a variety of other official and semiofficial redistributive agencies, as a conduit for paternalistic (and often particularistic) largess. It is not to be used as a channel for the aggressive expression of collective interests. There are exceptions, of course, even within the syndical hierarchies. The emerging and increasingly vital private representative associations provide a few sectors of the population not only with an alternative channel for the expression of collective interests, but also with the opportunity to learn new participatory norms in a setting of greater autonomy and competitiveness. This brings us to a discussion of plurality in Brazilian society.

Plurality. Whether they like it or not (and most observers, foreign and domestic, have concluded that they do), Brazilians live in a de facto pluralist society.[11] But this is social or ethnic pluralism, not associational pluralism or plurality. As we have seen, Brazilian national elites have succeeded in preserving a substantial measure of continuity in political cultural norms and in enforcing a policy that discourages the proliferation of alternative associations. Hence the apparent paradox of a pluralist society and a unitarist system of interest representation.

Many "interested parties" find themselves without formal, specialized associational representatives at all. To the extent they manage to make themselves heard, they must do so by means of a *patrão*: a populist politician, a government welfare agency, the Church, a spiritualist or *umbandista* cult, a *despachante*,† an employer or relative with political connections. Most urban subjects have only a single formal associational

---

* For example, the Syndicate of Textile and Thread Manufacturers of Rio de Janeiro publicly withdrew from FIEGA in 1954 to protest its president's policies; the Federation of Industries of the State of Guanabara (FIEGA) publicly opposed the CNI on several occasions during 1965; and in 1959 several commercial employers' syndicates petitioned the government for intervention in the CNC, alleging mismanagement of SESC funds.

† Literally, a customs agent. These are hired brokers, middlemen who specialize in transactions of all sorts with public authorities.

channel at their disposal. Of course, they, too, can and do use particularistic, informal channels. High-status actors are likely to have important informal means of access. In recent years they have also had more opportunities to choose between parallel associations. However, only a very few sectors are presented with a genuinely plural choice between different organizations with competing purposes or between stable competing factions within the same organization. Characteristically, these are sectors marked by polarized discord within as well as between conflicting associations, emotional and uncompromising demands, bitter accusations of fraud and lack of good faith, threats to appeal to authorities for legal or political redress, and, consequently, relative impotence before authority groups. These conditions prevail especially between and within certain middle-sector groups. But there is no better example of this brand of Brazilian plurality than in the coffee sector.

Brazil has no equivalent of Colombia's highly organized, unitary Federación Nacional de Cafeteros. The representation of Brazil's coffee growers' interests is divided, first, into regions producing different types of coffee and, second, into different types of associations in each region. There are the traditional agricultural societies like the SRB, specialized producers' associations (usually in league with the former), semiofficial rural associations and their state federations, and finally, in recent years, cooperatives of coffee growers and their federation. Not only is there universal discontent with virtually every aspect of the government's coffee policy, but the diverse representative associations of producers have remained divided among themselves and divided before authority groups.[12] Nor has this plural competition resulted in particularly high levels of density; leaders complain bitterly about lack of member participation and interest.[13]

On the basis of the limited experience of the few sectors for which something approaching an organizational alternative exists, it would appear that associational plurality in Brazil does not produce the consequences generally anticipated of it. From the perspective of the "interested party," it does not result in higher rates of participation, greater group autonomy, more leader accountability, or increased influence. From the perspective of the "System," it does not produce more carefully elaborated, moderate, and conciliatory demands. This finding by no means disproves the pluralist hypotheses. It merely suggests that pluralism or plurality in a predominantly corporatist setting will have different consequences from the phenomenon in a liberal setting.

By 1964 many specialized private associations had emerged, and the workers' organizations were gaining in autonomy. It is tempting to see in this a delayed pluralist reaction to industrialization. The truth is, however, that all such changes depended on the sanction and connivance of authority groups, even though these groups seem to have lost control of the situation in the final stages before the coup. What association leaders sought was not maximum autonomy with respect to authority groups, but maximum penetration of them—not the creation of competing alternatives, but exclusive channels of representation.

The emergence of private industrialists' and businessmen's associations represents a further deviation from the corporatist norm. Such associations are more eager for independence than pure corporatist associations, in terms of both internal processes and demand-making techniques. They are definitely more voluntaristic, have higher rates of member participation, and are readier to accept competition. Nevertheless, there has been no massive rejection of the preexisting corporatist system. People shuffle back and forth from private to syndical organizations and see no inconsistency in doing so.* The two systems of representation are perceived not as competing or incompatible, but as alternatives to be used as the occasion demands. In the right circumstances, private leaders do not hesitate to seek and accept corporatist positions, although several reported refusing official subsidies.[14]

My interviews with interest and attitude leaders permit an examination of plurality and its consequences from yet another perspective. Asked if they were members of other representative associations, a substantial majority (70 percent) answered affirmatively. Elected leaders were noticeably more likely to have multiple memberships, although for some reason administrative leaders were markedly reluctant to answer the question. As might have been anticipated, more private association leaders than syndical leaders reported multiple memberships; this is because many private associations were created by or alongside preexisting syndicates. Relatively few syndical leaders were also active in the older private associations, such as the commercial associations. The major exception is industrial leaders in São Paulo, virtually all of whom are also members of the Centro Industrial.

Workers' leaders reported fewer multiple memberships. As many as 37 percent belonged only to the workers' association of which they were leaders. The corresponding proportion for employers' leaders was 12 percent, for liberal professionals 8 percent, and for civic activists 13 percent. Plurality is a phenomenon largely confined to propertied groups.

The overlap in membership tended, as one might have anticipated, to follow class lines. Of the employers reporting multiple memberships, 35 percent were active in other employers' organizations. Similarly, 37 per-

* In the interviews some leaders referred alternately to their *"vida associativa"* and their *"vida sindical."*

cent of workers' leaders were members of other workers' groups, none belonged to employers' groups, and some 17 percent participated in various middle-class, civic, military, or religious associations. The liberal professionals showed the highest rate of secondary memberships, 75 percent of them in associations of the same general category. As we have seen, this is the category with the greatest degree of fragmentation and internal conflict. Civic leaders reported the greatest variety of secondary memberships, slightly over half of them in similar organizations.

The relatively high incidence of multiple membership among all types of leaders suggests that associability is a cumulative social phenomenon. Once a leader has learned the advantages and techniques of expressing his interests by associational means, once he has attained sufficient modernity and psychic mobility to join with others in a formal voluntary organization, he is likely to seek to repeat his initial experience by joining additional associations. Also, since such leadership skills are not widely disseminated in the earlier stages of political development, those who have them are more likely to be invited to lead other associations—just as the shortage of certain occupational and technical skills promotes multiple job-holding on a large scale. One might therefore expect the emergence of an associational elite, if not an out-and-out oligarchy, with a relatively small number of leaders in control.

The evidence from my interviews tends to confirm this expectation to some extent. Two-thirds of the leaders with multiple memberships reported that they held leadership positions in one or more of the other associations as well, and several listed an extraordinary variety of elective and administrative posts in representative associations. The champion was a man in Rio who simultaneously held elective or administrative positions in different associations representing industrial, commercial, and banking interests and a fascinating variety of leadership posts in social clubs, charitable societies, and civic associations. In all, this titan of associability occupied 29 leadership positions, of which eight were presidencies.

A possible test of the proposition would be to examine whether multiple membership in representative associations is correlated with a pro-

TABLE 9.2

MULTIPLE ASSOCIATIONAL MEMBERSHIP AND POLITICAL PARTY ACTIVISM

Political party membership	Multiple associational membership		
	Yes ($N = 105$)	No ($N = 25$)	No answer ($N = 19$)
Yes	20.0%	16.0%	15.8%
No	71.4	80.0	57.9
No answer	8.6	[4.0][a]	26.3

[a] Brackets denote percentage based on fewer than five cases.

pensity for other forms of political associability, e.g., political party activism. As Table 9.2 indicates, the anticipated relationship is positive, but the evidence is hardly conclusive. If a qualitative control were inserted, the relationship might get stronger, since it was apparent from the comments that accompanied the question that many respondents saw their secondary memberships as a pure formality or a matter of personal expediency having nothing to do with a desire for participation on their part. Most of the lawyers, accountants, and economists active in employer and worker organizations felt that their membership in the respective order or syndicate was merely a matter of professional necessity and carried with it no propensity or desire for participation. The same seemed to be the case for the very substantial number of participants in the Syndicate of Journalists, who had obviously joined exclusively for the perquisites and privileges membership conferred.

I have already questioned the applicability of the hypotheses relating associational plurality to increased accountability, density, and participation. Responses to the political-culture questionnaires administered to group leaders raise further questions on this score. It will be recalled that the questionnaire contained two clusters of three statements each concerning *pactualismo*, or readiness to compromise (see Table 4.5) and corporatism (see Tables 4.8–9). In Table 9.3, the responses in-

TABLE 9.3

MULTIPLE ASSOCIATIONAL MEMBERSHIP AND READINESS TO COMPROMISE

(*percent*)

Statement and response categories	Multiple associational membership		
	Yes	No	No answer
1. "It is not worth the trouble to debate with people whose ideas are very very different from your own."			
Agree very much	9.1%	34.8%	[5.9%]
Agree a little	28.3	[4.3]	17.6
Disagree a little	15.1	[4.3]	29.4
Disagree very much	47.5	56.5	47.1
2. "Controversies should never be resolved by violence."			
Agree very much	79.8	82.6	58.8
Agree a little	9.1	[4.3]	29.4
Disagree a little	9.1	[8.7]	[5.9]
Disagree very much	[3.0]	[4.3]	[5.9]
3. "In politics it is better to compromise than to fight."			
Agree very much	51.8	60.0	37.5
Agree a little	30.1	25.0	56.2
Disagree a little	10.8	0.0	[6.2]
Disagree very much	7.2	[15.0]	0.0

NOTE. *N*'s as follows: Statements 1 and 2, Yes 99, No 23, No answer 17; Statement 3, Yes 83, No 20, No answer 16. Columns for each statement may not add to 100 because of rounding. Brackets denote percentages based on fewer than five cases.

dicating a preference for discussing problems, for nonviolent resolution of conflict, and for compromise are classified according to plurality of associational membership. That members of only one association disagree more with the first statement and agree more with the second and third indicates a mild tendency on their part toward being more conciliatory than members of more than one association. If the answers are dichotomized, however, the relationship virtually disappears. There could be no clearer indication of the very substantial political cultural homogeneity of Brazilian associational elites.

Table 9.4 gives percentages of agreement and disagreement with

TABLE 9.4

MULTIPLE ASSOCIATIONAL MEMBERSHIP AND PLURALIST ATTITUDES

(*percent*)

Statement and response categories	Multiple associational membership		
	Yes	No	No answer
1. "People are born into social groups, each one of which has different capacities; for this reason, people should have different duties and rights."			
Agree very much	11.3%	27.3%	0.0%
Agree a little	10.3	[9.1]	[18.8]
Disagree a little	12.4	13.6	[25.0]
Disagree very much	66.0	50.0	56.2
2. "The government should act as arbitrator between employers' associations and workers' syndicates in the interest of social harmony."			
Agree very much	58.6	60.9	70.6
Agree a little	27.3	26.1	23.5
Disagree a little	[3.0]	[4.3]	[5.0]
Disagree very much	11.1	[8.7]	0.0
3. "The political process would be better if the representatives were elected by their occupational groups rather than by parties."			
Agree very much	17.7	27.3	[6.2]
Agree a little	19.8	22.7	31.4
Disagree a little	13.5	[9.1]	[6.2]
Disagree very much	48.9	40.8	56.2
4. "The political decisions in this country are always made by a small and closed group, and the average citizen never has much influence."			
Agree very much	61.7	39.1	58.8
Agree a little	22.3	34.8	29.4
Disagree a little	7.3	17.4	[5.9]
Disagree very much	8.5	[8.7]	[5.9]

NOTE: *N*'s as follows: Statement 1, Yes 97, No 22, No answer 22; Statement 2, 99, 23, 17; Statement 3, 96, 22, 16; Statement 4, 94, 23, 17. Columns for each statement may not add to 100 because of rounding. Brackets denote percentages based on fewer than five cases.

three statements relative to corporatist attitudes and one relative to the perception of political elitism. As pluralist theory would lead one to expect, members of a single association tend to express corporatist atttitudes, especially concerning the advisability of professional as opposed to partisan representation (third statement), although they tend to perceive the political process as less elitist than do members of more than one association. Again, however, none of the differences are particularly marked, and the homogeneity of elite values is more striking than their heterogeneity. It does not appear, then, that multiple associational membership (and presumably multiple allegiance) has a strong, differentiating impact on political values. To be sure, these are only attitudes, not indicators of actual behavior; it may be that in actual group interaction plurality works its hypothetically virtuous influence, crisscrossing the society with mutually canceling conflicts and preventing polarization along a single line of cleavage. From all appearances, however, Brazilian interest politics achieves a measure of nonviolence, vacillation, and compromise without relying on the cross-pressures of competing autonomous associations.

Conclusion

Our principal working hypotheses concerning the pattern of emergence of representative associations have been supported, if not completely confirmed, by the evidence presented above. The sectors whose interests are served by permanently administered secondary groups have expanded, albeit unevenly and incompletely. There are still many "parochials" and "subjects" whose demands are articulated not collectively but through complex networks of paternalistic or familistic ties—if they are articulated at all. Not a few "citizens" prefer to rely on personal relations rather than associations despite the growing impersonality of high-level decision-making.

The number of associations has risen consistently, and extensive networks of interest aggregation have been formed, some with branches in every state in the nation. Functional specificity has increased, owing at first to the filling out of the syndical *enquadramento* and more recently to the creation of ever more specialized organizations.

Membership in representative associations has also risen, faster than either Brazil's population as a whole or the populations of differentiated sectors. The qualitative change in density has been much less remarkable. Except in a few of the new associations, Brazilians seem no more disposed than ever to seek active, voluntary participation in formal interest organizations. They continue to regard such organizations more as conduits for favors from above than as channels for expressing their own demands.

Whether or not development would result in a plural or pluralist pattern of emergence and interaction was left indeterminate in our hypothesis, although it was suggested that the country's political culture and pattern of authoritative policy would go far toward determining what pattern prevailed. So far, the Brazilian Revolution has not produced a multitude of crisscrossing, competing, alternative associations, independent of each other and of authority groups; on the contrary, the political culture and public policy have so far been successful in confining group protest to corporatist channels. By a complicated schedule of rewards and sanctions, authorities have organized the country's main interests into unitary hierarchies of noncompetitive, almost noninteracting associations organizationally linked with and financially dependent on the government. While there are definite signs of tension in this system of interest representation and some organizational and behavioral changes have occurred, they scarcely suggest that Brazil is on the verge of a delayed pluralist reaction. Nor do they offer us any reason to believe that if such a reaction were to occur, it would have the consequences generally imputed to pluralism in developed systems.

TEN

The Process of Policy-Making

PUBLIC policy in Brazil has been a relatively continuous process that has shaped existing interest groups as much as they have shaped it. Indeed they have tended to accommodate themselves to the existing political pattern, to exploit its ambiguities and contradictions, making only minor incremental adjustments rather than attempting to reshape its basic configuration. Only in those Latin American countries that have experienced a revolution, a sudden and irrevocable change in the structure and legitimacy of authority groups, is one likely to encounter politics in which the form as well as the content of public policy is determined exclusively by clashing vectors of associational activity—where these groups can control not only who gets what and when, but how he gets it. Brazil is not one of these revolutionary countries; therefore, the global configuration of its policy-making process is a crucial independent variable determining patterns of interaction and influence.

"Economic policy-making in Brazil is a fairly decentralized and, at times, disorganized process." Werner Baer's carefully studied understatement would seem to apply equally to other arenas of decision as well. Regardless of where one looks in the policy-making matrix, one is first struck by the proliferation of agencies with overlapping jurisdictions and interests, the complicated and lengthy processes of negotiation, the apparent lack of continuity and coordination, and the sheer indirection and indeterminacy of outcomes. Nevertheless, and despite the fact that authority groups seem to be pursuing an ever increasing number of often mutually incompatible objectives, the resulting global configuration of policy has not been chaotic or even irrational.[1] Major decisions have been made, precedents have been established, mistakes have been corrected, priorities have been set, and policies have been implemented. Behind the chaos at the lowest levels and the discontinuities at the top, there has been a surprising degree of consistency in Brazilian policy since World War II, and it has had a profound impact on the pattern of development.

From the perspective of an interested party, two characteristics of the policy process stand out most prominently. The first is simply that it is increasingly difficult, if not impossible, to resolve internal disputes and satisfy external demands privately without recourse to public control or support. As Tables 10.1 and 10.2 make clear, authority groups have been commanding a steadily increasing share of the country's scarce resources; the total government share of gross domestic product has risen constantly and substantially since 1947, when the national account statistics begin. The figures in Table 10.1 do not include current expenditures or investments of the numerous "mixed government enterprises," one of which, Petrobrás, is the largest firm in the country.[2] The second table corrects this deficiency partially and tells an even more striking tale of expanding government activity. According to the higher APEC statistics, authority groups controlled 60 percent of the gross capital investment in 1958. Even according to the lower figures, their relative participation has more than doubled since 1947.

Admittedly, this is an indirect and imperfect index of the degree to which the role of authority groups in Brazilian society has changed in recent decades. Therefore it cannot be a perfect index of the degree to which representative associations find themselves forced to politicize their activities—i.e., devote increasing attention to public policy-makers. Sheer quantitative expansion of government resources certainly suggests rising incentives for such a concentration of effort on the part of rep-

TABLE 10.1
EXPENDITURE OF THE PUBLIC SECTOR, 1947–60
(*percentage of Gross Internal Product*)

Expenditure	1947	1955	1960
Consumption expenditure	10.7%	13.6%	14.2%
Compensation of employees	6.2	6.8	7.0
Purchases of goods and services	4.5	6.8	7.2
Current transfers to households	3.6	4.7	5.3
Subsidies	0.1	0.2	0.7
Gross fixed capital formation	2.7	3.4	5.7
Inventory changes	0.0	0.5	2.3
Purchases of existing capital	0.6	0.1	0.8
TOTAL	17.7%	22.5%	29.0%
Federal government	9.9	12.6	18.0
State and municipal government	7.8	9.9	11.0

SOURCE: Fundação Getúlio Vargas, as cited in Baer, p. 88.

TABLE 10.2
PARTICIPATION OF THE PUBLIC SECTOR IN FIXED CAPITAL FORMATION
(*percentage of Gross Fixed Capital Formation*)

Year	Government	Mixed government enterprises	Total	Year	Government	Mixed government enterprises	Total
1947	15.8%			1954	24.3%		
1948	23.3			1955	24.0		
1949	29.4			1956	24.8	3.1%	28.2%
1950	35.1			1957	37.0	4.7	42.1
1951	25.0			1958	40.8	5.5	60.0
1952	26.8			1959	32.3	6.0	41.3
1953	29.4			1960	38.2	8.0	48.1

SOURCE: Government and mixed government enterprises from Baer, p. 84; totals from *A Economia Brasileira e Suas Perspectivas: Maio 1963* (Rio: Edições APEC, 1963), p. 11. Although the two do not seem to agree on total participation (the APEC figures are consistently higher), both cite as their original source the Fundação Getúlio Vargas.
NOTE: Data not available for mixed government enterprises, 1947–55.

resentatives, but only hints at possible qualitative transformations.[3] The role of the state apparatus in Brazil has grown from almost nothing before 1930 to include a vast variety of functions. Public authorities in Brazil currently own all, or at least a substantial proportion, of the maritime, river, and railroad transport, petroleum, steel, and alkali production, mining of atomic minerals, and electric power generation. They intervene directly through institutes or indirectly through the Bank of Brazil in the commercialization of coffee, sugar, rubber, cacao, rice, maté, pinewood, salt, cotton, beans, corn, soybean, wheat, manioc flour, and other products; they produce and export most of the country's iron ore; they regulate mining rights, communications and transport concessions, exchange rates, and insurance; they fix (or attempt to fix) prices on basic goods, interest rates, minimum salaries, rents, and minimum agricultural prices; they provide much of the country's short-term and virtually all of its long-term credit; they finance and control directly port facilities, storage areas for agricultural products, and major housing projects. In addition, of course, they have the usual sorts of government controls over monetary, fiscal, investment, educational, health, national security, and foreign policy. What is surprising is not the extent of the list, but the fact that so many of these areas of policy concern have been added only in the last decades. Formal *estatização* (statism) is perhaps the most notable characteristic of the institutional development process in recent years.

If representative associations find it increasingly difficult to avoid appeals to authority groups, they are also finding it increasingly possible to appeal to a multitude of decision-making centers. For the second

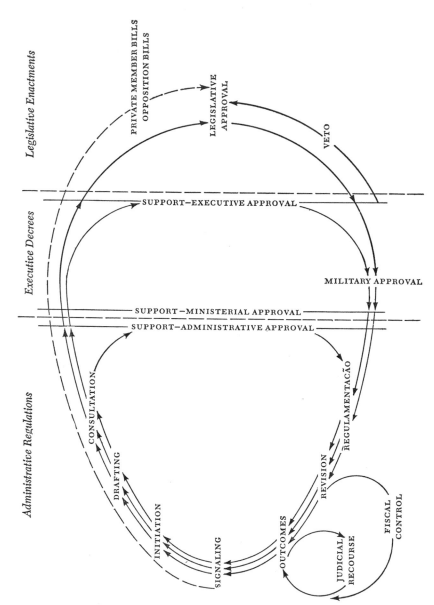

Legislative Enactments

PRIVATE MEMBER BILLS
OPPOSITION BILLS

LEGISLATIVE APPROVAL

VETO

Executive Decrees

SUPPORT—EXECUTIVE APPROVAL

MILITARY APPROVAL

SUPPORT—MINISTERIAL APPROVAL

SUPPORT—ADMINISTRATIVE APPROVAL

Administrative Regulations

CONSULTATION

DRAFTING

INITIATION

SIGNALING

OUTCOMES

REVISION

REGULAMENTAÇÃO

JUDICIAL RECOURSE

FISCAL CONTROL

Fig. 6. A Sequential Model of Federal Policy-Making.

major characteristic of the Brazilian policy process is its dispersion or polycentrism. For a variety of reasons, it has appeared either unnecessary or politically unfeasible to accompany the proliferation of controls and services with a corresponding effort to consolidate or coordinate decision-making.[4] Although the Constitution of 1967 severely curbs it, federalism is still effective in Brazil. State governments, and even a few municipal governments, have considerable financial strength and some financial autonomy.* The structure of the federal government affords even more points of access and centers of decisional autonomy. Jurisdictional overlaps, vaguely defined competences, framework legislation, delegated authority, permanently earmarked funds,[5] special clientele relationships, unequal distribution of technical skill and reliable information, interagency rivalries and jealousies—all these combined with the absence of strong party structures or party discipline, of an operative cabinet, of effective budgetary or fiscal controls, or of any overpowering, cohesive sense of national purpose—produce a very flexible decisional process, the keynote of which is bargaining, either by shifting alliances or (more commonly) by logrolling. The President of the Republic is, of course, at the center of the decision-making process, but in most negotiations he is no more than primus inter pares.

There is yet another dimension of this system of multiple access. Policy characteristically passes through several stages of elaboration from initiation to outcome, any one of which may provide an attractive possibility for a given representative association to press its demands. Although not all policies follow the full elaborative cycle or the same decisional sequence, there seem to be three different general sequential cycles: administrative regulation, executive decree, and legislative enactment.† The entire process is represented graphically in Figure 6. It begins with signaling. A problem is "politicized," or called to the attention of public policy-makers, and thereby transformed into an issue. The likelihood that a given "neglected problem" will become a "privi-

---

* As Table 10.1 shows, public expenditure in GIP on the part of state and municipal authorities has increased substantially (if not as much as federal spending). Perhaps more resources are controlled by state and local governments in Brazil than in any other Latin American country. The new Constitution reorders the tax-sharing scheme between levels of government and grants federal authorities enhanced powers to intervene in the states. For example, Article 10 makes it illegal for a state "to adopt measures or execute economic or financial plans contrary to the directives established by the union."

† Administrative regulations are usually called *regulamentos, circulares, portarias,* or *instruções*; executive decrees are called *decretos, atos institucionais,* or *atos complementares*; legislative enactments are called *leis*. However, these terms are flexible, and the formal title is no sure indication of what sequential path the policy has taken.

leged" one, to use Albert Hirschman's phraseology, depends partly on the nature of the problem itself and partly on the nature of the political actors in the system. Brazil has no shortage of chronic and obvious malfunctions, some externally imposed (such as decline in export earnings, wartime import shortages, balance of payments difficulties, drought in the Northeast, and floods in the South), some internally generated (such as low per capita income, chronic unemployment and underemployment, regional disparities in development, decline in political legitimacy, and disintegration of the party system).[6] In order for signals to become policy initiatives, they must be received and supported by politically relevant actors. North American empirical studies and even some theories of comparative politics lead one to expect that all such initiatives are products of peaceful, articulate demands of representative associations, or at least of spokesmen for victimized groups. In fact, as I shall discuss later, such interest representatives are not very important as policy initiators in the Brazilian political process. Much more important are (1) professional politicians (políticos) whose tenure may be threatened by decentralized violence, potential revolutionary movements, decline in electoral strength, or insufficient displays of visible progress; (2) economic administrators (técnicos) whose ideology stresses modernization through import substitution and planning; (3) intellectuals whose ideology accentuates the need for greater national independence and the acquisition of world power status; and (4) military officers (militares) whose ostensible primary concern is with national security and greatness. Whether a given signal will be received and converted into an initiative depends upon the nature of the actor affected by it. The effect need not be direct or manifest. As Hirschman has pointed out, the ideological actors (técnicos, intellectuals, and militares) will "build in" linkages between the new signal and their own problem (or act on their own problems autonomously and in the absence of any strong signals). The weakness of Brazil's organized interest representatives in converting signals into initiatives partially explains why so many problems go neglected, why so few are treated until they reach a crisis, and why decentralized elite-mass violence remains such an important signaling device.[7]

The initiative next goes to the drafting stage. Although some project-drafting is done by representative associations and by legislative commissions, most is done within the public administration in ad hoc working parties, inter-ministerial commissions, permanent consultative councils, and executive groups. Once drafted, it appears that most major projects then undergo an extensive process of consultation and negotiation. The numerous permanent consultative bodies, various inter-ministerial committees, and unofficial cabinets provide the institutional framework. Authorities sometimes request formal statements by various representative associations, and, if the policy has a sufficiently large public or has been ideologically linked, the mass media may conduct a public debate. For some projects, higher administrative and ministerial approval is sufficient and they proceed directly to the regulation phase.*

Others continue on in the policy sequence. Executive decrees acquire presidential support and approval simultaneously and thereby convert projects into legally binding obligations instantaneously. During the Vargas regime from 1937 to 1945, such decrees represented the most elaborate and definitive sequence of authoritative decision-making, Congress having been abolished. Article 86 of the 1946 Constitution granted the President extensive authority to issue decrees implementing existing legislation, and this provision has been interpreted very loosely. The de facto limits seem to be imposed primarily by the necessity for military approval, not fear of legislative protest or judicial annulment.[8] The First Institutional Act of April 9, 1964 considerably extended the presidential decree power. According to an editorial in the *Jornal do Brasil*, during the regime of Castelo Branco (1964–67) 19,259 decrees, 312 decree-laws, four institutional acts, and 36 complementary acts were promulgated by the national executive! During the first two and one-half years of this period, the executive branch drafted and sent to the legislature 733 bills, eleven constitutional amendments, and, ultimately, a new constitution.[9] In addition, there were 467 *portarias*, 99 *circulares* from the Finance Ministry, 58 general *circulares*, and 41 *resoluções* from the Central Bank.[10] The circumstances were of course unusual, but the figures (which by no means include all formal administrative decisions) more than demonstrate the crucial role played by executive initiatives and decrees in the policy-making process. Since the new Constitution of 1967 permanently incorporates many of the provisions of the institutional acts,† there is every reason to anticipate that most of the important policy initiatives will continue to originate and become converted into authoritative policy at this end of the elaborative cycle.

A restricted number of projects take the full circuit and are referred to the federal legislature. Some are introduced directly into the circuit

* Potential impact or political significance does not always determine which of the three types of decisions will be required. For example, the most important decisions in Brazil's import substitution drive since World War II have been the *instruções* of SUMOC relative to exchange policy. These certainly required presidential support and approval. Formally, however, such decisions are taken by an inter-ministerial council and are not subjected to legislative approval.

† For example, Article 58 permits the President "in cases of urgency or of relevant public interest" to decree laws relative to national security and public finance.

through the legislature, either as the result of pressure by the victims or their ideological allies, or as the result of anticipatory reaction by professional politicians responding to real or imagined threats on their tenure. Most of the projects considered by the Senate and Chamber of Deputies, however, have undergone the process of official drafting, consultation, and negotiation and bear the presidential or ministerial seal of approval. The 1946 Constitution granted the President exclusive power to initiate bills concerning federal employment and the military establishment. Since 1964 the institutional acts and since 1967 the new Constitution have extended this power to include all bills that "treat financial matters," "create positions, functions, or public jobs," "increase salaries or public expenditures," or "fix or modify the size of the armed forces." Article 54 of the same Constitution gives the Congress 45 days to make up its mind about an executive proposal before it automatically becomes a law.[11]

However, despite the President's authority to decree and his constitutionally exclusive powers of initiative in key arenas, his superior sources of information and expertise, his role as the major dispenser of patronage, his authority based upon nationwide popular suffrage (although the 1967 Constitution makes the election of the President indirect), and his usual status as leader of one of the major parties, the Congress has not been powerless. Formally, it has the power to withhold approval of a presidential request for a state of siege, federal intervention in the states, negotiation of international treaties, and presidential appointments to some administrative posts.* Moreover, in extreme cases, it can impeach and try the President, Vice-President, or Cabinet ministers for crimes against the Constitution. Informally, the lack of a disciplined party majority backing the President, the inoperability of the Cabinet, the unwieldiness and internal competitiveness of the bureaucracy, the President's relative impotence in dictating his successor (the 1946 and 1967 Constitutions limit the President to a single term of office and make his relatives ineligible to succeed him), and, most important, the restraints imposed upon him by an independent military all afford the Congress some room for maneuver. Granted that most of the decision-making process bypasses it, it nevertheless has some residual decision-making autonomy.

It can exercise this autonomy by passing member bills, by rejecting executive proposals, by overriding presidential vetoes, by deliberately delaying crucial measures, by instituting parliamentary commissions of

---

* Under the brief parliamentary regime from August 1961 to January 1963, the entire Cabinet of course depended upon congressional approval. Currently, ministers can be required to appear before Congress for questioning.

inquiry embarrassing to the regime, by refusing to lift the legal immunity of congressmen the regime wishes to punish, etc.* Before 1964, its greatest power was its control over the budget and supplementary appropriations.[12] In the haggling over the budget, congressmen could strike up temporary coalitions not only with the interested parties (regions, industries, firms, occupations, or individuals), but also with the fragmented and competitive administrative agencies dependent upon these appropriations. Attempts to cut back expenditures, to abolish agencies, or to subordinate one agency to another met with fierce resistance. Certain agencies became widely acknowledged political fiefs of individual congressmen or regional *bancadas*.[13] The new "revolutionary" rules of the game have sharply curtailed this mutually advantageous bargaining between autonomous administrative agencies and congressional factions. Stripped of their power to tack on additional expenditures or to initiate any bill resulting in added expenditures, the houses of Congress now have a scant 45 days each to consider, modify, and approve measures coming from the executive branch. If no action is taken in the prescribed time, the bill automatically becomes a law. Moreover, the two-thirds vote required for constitutional amendments before 1964 has been reduced to a simple majority. To make the issue all the more certain, the President is now empowered to take away the mandate or remove the political rights of anyone "in the interests of peace and national honor."[14] It is still too early to speculate whether the Legislature's new function as an electoral college and legitimizer of presidential authority will compensate for the decline in its former functions of consolidating local support and maintaining loyalty to the system through patronage and clientelistic payoffs.

After legislative enactment, the policy is subject to executive approval. The Brazilian President may, within ten days, veto a bill entirely or partially. In the past such a veto was frequently overridden by a two-thirds vote of a joint congressional session; since the 1964 coup only minor measures have made it over formal executive disapproval. The President must also issue decrees implementing legislative enactments, and these may substantially reinterpret the original legislative bill. Or the President may simply stall or refuse to act, thereby making the law inapplicable.†

* This sort of Congressional obstreperousness seems to have been a crucial factor in President Jânio Quadros's resignation (which the Congress joyfully accepted) and in forcing President João Goulart to resort to the promulgation of provocative reform decrees. In 1968 the Congress's refusal to remove the immunity of a leading opposition deputy led to the Fifth Institutional Act and the closing of Congress.

† President João Goulart hesitated for over a year before signing the *decreto* regulating the controversial remittances of foreign profits law. President Castelo Branco

A subject about which little is known but much has been speculated is the nature of military approval (*cobertura militar*). At what stage in the process it is necessary to negotiate for it and what institutional form this takes is unclear. For some major policy innovations, the National Security Council (CSN), composed of the President, the Vice-President, all ministers, all Chiefs of Staff, and all commanding generals of major commands, has played the multiple role of initiator, negotiator, and approver.[15] In other instances the support of the General Staff of the Armed Forces (EMFA), ministers of the individual military services, regional commanding generals, or even local garrison heads has been necessary in order to make policy authoritative.* The President of the Republic is only nominally Commander in Chief of all armed forces. It is widely believed that actual command is exercised by the respective military ministers, who have traditionally been high-ranking officers, and that they have unrestricted veto over matters of direct concern to them. Little is known of the scope of their policy interests, the modalities of their participation, or their patterns of coalition formation.

With the formal approval of the President, the informal agreement or indifference of the military, and the signature of the minister concerned, the policy innovation, now a legal document, goes into the particularly critical phase of regulation, or *regulamentação*. The measure must be translated into administratively enforceable procedures.† In the elaboration of these *regulamentos, resoluções, portarias, instruções,* and *circulares,* a considerable amount of discretion can be and is exercised, even though the major guidelines have been preestablished. As was the case with the planning and negotiation of the original project, this may be accomplished within a permanent executive group, an administrative junta, a commission, a council, or, especially in cases where the issue is not repetitive, a temporary ad hoc working group. These regulations become legally binding when approved by the respective minister, the president of the *autarquia* or *instituto,* or even the executive secretary of the executive group.

---

sent to Congress an executive draft of a new Press Law in 1967. After some debate and a great hue and cry in the media over its strict and rather arbitrary provisions, the Congress returned for his signature a modified version. The President signed the congressionally revised bill with virtually no reservations and then coolly decreed a new National Security Law one week later with most of the repressive provisions of the original Press Law.

* The Military Club and the Superior War School (ESG) have been important policy innovators and negotiators, but they do not seem to have the sort of institutionalized veto power of the CSN or the EMFA.

† The President's decree powers are formally based on his right to regulate existing laws. In fact, most Presidential decrees must themselves be regulated.

Nor is the process yet terminated. One of the distinctive features of the Brazilian policy-making style is, as I noted in Chapter 3, the desire to avoid a definitive point of closure. Among the institutional devices for assuring this, and a device well in keeping with the general propensity for paternalistic corporatism, is a provision for the establishment of a permanent advisory or consultative group. This group has the task of continuous revision and renegotiation of the original policy and usually includes representatives of the interested parties. The Brazilian public administration has hundreds of these *conselhos, comissões, juntas,* and *grupos executivos.* Some offer only symbolic satisfaction and an opportunity for co-optive manipulation by authority groups; others have considerable decisional autonomy, but are dominated either by professional politicians or by técnicos; still others are dominated by appointed outside representatives (from syndicates, civil associations, or state governments) and are capable of either altering or resisting changes in existing policy.* Regardless of their decisional autonomy and the role of their respective representatives, these consultative commissions are important institutional mechanisms for the capturing of new signals, the drafting of future proposals, and the negotiation of new projects.

Tentatively, then, the Brazilian policy process can be described in terms of three parabolic sequences leading to three general types of decisions: the administrative regulation, the executive decree, and the legislative enactment. To a limited degree, they are even substitutable or interchangeable. Although stages may be bypassed or prolonged for a given specific decision, the general pattern of elaboration appears to have remained fairly constant over the past decades—with the obvious exception of the legislative cycle, which was suppressed from 1937 to 1945 and which has just recently undergone some important modifications. Regardless of changes in role occupants and periodic attempts at administrative or executive reform, the basic process by which decisions are made is essentially the same: polycentric, uncoordinated, competitive, lengthy, inchoate, dispersed, and occasionally self-contradictory. The points of access are multiple but of limited efficiency; the points of authoritative concentration are few and also of limited efficiency. In such a process, it is relatively difficult to get a policy initiative going, almost impossible to get it completely consummated (unless one resorts

* As rule of thumb, the symbolic ones are found in the weak Ministries of Agriculture, Health, and Education; the técnico-dominated ones in the Ministries of Finance and Planning; the político-dominated ones in the regional agencies and the Ministry of Labor; the interessado-dominated ones in the production institutes. An interesting case study in these relationships would be that of the gradual subordination of the Junta Administrativa of the Brazilian Coffee Institute to its presidency and the subordination of the latter to the técnico-dominated Central Bank.

to dictatorial measures), but relatively easy to get minor adjustments made in ongoing policy, and very easy to prevent major reforms in established procedures and policy outcomes. Policy in Brazil changes by accretion rather than by substitution.

From the point of view of representative associations, the specific target structure has changed in recent years, although the general pattern of decision-making has remained relatively constant. The number of decisional actors has increased enormously; their interactions have become more formalized (although informal contact remains important); and the relative importance of different types of political actors as signalers, drafters, negotiators, supporters, approvers, vetoers, regulators, and revisers has changed. The whole process has become so cumbersome and lengthy that only through the use of extralegal circuits and procedures (often referred to as *jeitos* or *soluçãozinhas*) can innovations be made or ongoing policies be rendered effective. Paradoxically, one can argue that, whereas there is a surprisingly persistent and standardized process of national policy-making, the only way to get things accomplished is by devising particularistic and opportunistic means for short-circuiting it. In short, there is a stable general pattern for deciding things and a stable general pattern for avoiding that pattern for deciding things.

ELEVEN

The Pattern of Interaction:
Legislative and Electoral Arenas

A QUESTIONNAIRE was mailed to some 225 representative associations throughout Brazil requesting them to report, among other things, how often they made contact with a number of authority groups and other institutions. Table 11.1 records the distribution of the 59 responses received.* In general, the hypothesis concerning the importance of the bureaucracy to Brazilian representative associations seems to be confirmed. Among government organs, the concentration of attention upon federal administrative agencies is most marked: 46 percent of the respondents reported frequent contact with the ministries; 36 percent with such semipublic and autarchic agencies as the production *institutos*, the Retirement and Social Welfare Institutes, the Bank of Brazil, the Central Bank, etc.; and some 33 percent with a catchall category including such agencies as the Price Control Commission (SUNAB), the Economic Advisory Council (CNE), and others not linked to a specific ministry. The proportion reporting occasional contact with these organs is also consistently high. At the state level, reported frequent contact with administrative bodies exceeded contact with executive and legislative ones, although in all other categories of interaction more executive contact was reported. Municipal administrations appear to be weak and unattractive targets, but this probably reflects a sample bias.

Frequent direct access to the President of the Republic is a privilege reported by few.† About one-third report occasional contact, but slightly

* For a discussion of the sample, see the Appendix.

† Of course frequency of contact is assessed by the actors themselves, and different actors may vary on how they define "frequent." One might add that President Castelo Branco was generally considered an uncommunicative and personally reserved man, whereas his deposed predecessor was often publicly criticized for being excessively informal and accessible.

TABLE 11.1
FREQUENCY OF INTERACTION WITH AUTHORITY GROUPS AND INSTITUTIONS

Authority group or institution	Frequently	Occasion- ally	Rarely	Never	No answer
Chamber of Deputies	20.7%	46.5%	20.7%	6.9%	5.2%
Senate	17.2	43.1	19.0	15.5	5.2
Individual congressmen	24.1	41.4	19.0	10.3	5.2
Parliamentary commissions	12.1	29.3	24.1	29.3	5.2
President of the Republic	13.8	32.8	34.5	12.1	6.9
Ministries	46.5	39.7	3.4	5.2	5.2
Semipublic agencies and autarkies	36.2	29.3	13.8	12.1	8.6
Other federal administrative organs	32.8	17.2	13.8	20.7	15.5
Political parties	0.0	1.7	13.8	72.4	12.1
State legislature	17.2	29.3	20.7	22.4	10.3
State executive	17.2	32.8	29.3	13.8	6.9
State administration	20.7	29.3	24.1	17.2	8.6
Municipal administration	17.2	13.8	17.2	36.2	15.5
Other representative associations	53.4	25.9	6.9	5.2	8.6
Universities and research institutes	19.0	34.5	22.4	13.8	10.3
International associations	41.4	25.9	8.6	13.8	10.3

NOTE: Rows may not add to 100 because of rounding.

more seem to feel they rarely see or write to the President. The image projected is of a moderately accessible president who keeps some distance from organized interests but does grant them periodic audiences. The figures do not tell us how these audiences are negotiated or how many demands for presidential access are referred downward to administrative elites. Contacts with state-level executives are slightly more frequent, but they present a very similar general pattern. Legislative contacts, though lower in general than administrative ones, are nonetheless reasonably frequent. The Chamber of Deputies seems to be a mildly more attractive target than the Senate. The prime target, however, seems to be the individual congressman. Parliamentary commissions are of only moderate interest. A substantial proportion of the reporting groups have never participated in them. In general, the image is one of sporadic and individual attempts to influence legislative outcomes, especially through the Chamber of Deputies. Nevertheless, an important percentage follows the proceedings with assiduous attention and either sends regular statements to Brasília or invests in the costly trip there. The state assemblies also seem to have their steady followers and hangers-on, but the frequencies are rather consistently lower than those of the state executives and administrations. The most striking (but

TABLE 11.2

DIRECTION OF ASSOCIATIONS' MOST FREQUENT CONTACT WITH AUTHORITY GROUPS

(*percent*)

				Reported contact with:				
Association	Legis-lature $(N = 9)$	Executive and adminis-trative $(N = 79)$	Judi-ciary $(N = 1)$	Executive and legislature equally $(N = 11)$	Executive and judiciary equally $(N = 3)$	Judiciary and legislature equally $(N = 1)$	All groups equally $(N = 1)$	No answer, Don't know $(N = 3)$
Type								
Employers'								
Syndical	11.1%	77.8%	0.0%	7.4%	0.0%	0.0%	3.7%	0.0%
Private	0.0	84.2	0.0	10.5	2.6	0.0	0.0	2.6
Workers'	9.5	66.7	4.8	4.8	9.5	0.0	0.0	4.8
Liberal-pro-								
fessional	30.0	40.0	0.0	20.0	0.0	10.0	0.0	0.0
Civic	9.1	63.6	0.0	18.2	0.0	0.0	0.0	9.1
Membership								
Indirect	12.8	66.7	2.6	10.3	5.1	0.0	2.6	0.0
Direct	5.8	76.8	0.0	10.1	1.4	1.4	0.0	1.4
Geographic scope								
National	9.9	64.8	1.4	14.1	4.2	1.4	1.4	2.8
Regional	5.6	88.9	0.0	2.8	0.0	0.0	0.0	2.8

NOTE: Rows may not add to 100 because of rounding.

not unanticipated) finding concerns political parties: 72.4 percent report that they never have any contact with parties, and another 13.8 percent have had only rare contact. Finally, associations report high rates of interaction among themselves: 53.4 percent said they were in frequent contact with other representative associations, and 41.4 percent with international associations. Universities and research institutes (presumably including the Getúlio Vargas Foundation, which produces some of the most reliable and comprehensive economic statistics) are not important foci of interest. Here, the reported contact may amount to no more than the exchange or receipt of publications.

In personal interviews with a somewhat different sample, a more direct approach to patterns of interaction was used and then followed by qualitative probes.* Leaders were asked not the frequency of their contacts, but simply, "Do you have more contacts with legislative, executive-administrative, or judicial organs?" Their responses are shown in Table 11.2. The executive-administrative focus so apparent in the writ-

* The sample included 149 interviews with elected and administrative leaders of 108 nationally relevant representative associations. The written questionnaire was sent to most of these same associations, as well as to others judged to be locally relevant. There was an overlap of 30 between the two samples. For a more extensive discussion, see the Appendix.

ten responses reappears even more impressively. In every single category, it is the most frequently cited target. Private employers' associations report a particularly high concentration of effort there. Equivalent
syndical organizations and especially middle-sector and civic associations seem to distribute their efforts a bit more widely between the executive and legislative branches. Probing revealed that the juridical contacts reported by workers' organizations involved the prosecution and
defense of cases before labor courts, an activity many other respondents
may have classified as administrative. Peak associations with indirect or
federative membership seem to have a greater tendency for dispersed
effort than do those with individual members. The same remark applies,
respectively, to formally national and regional entities. The more national the association, the further away it is from individual members,
the further up it is in the syndical hierarchy (and, consequently, the
less functionally specific), the more likely it is to have some legislative
as well as administrative contacts.

Theorists of interest politics have frequently suggested that the global
pattern of interaction between representative associations and authority
groups is one of the most reliable indicators of the distribution of power
in a political system. The fact that the two samples of actor perceptions
cited above agree with and complement each other so well tends to
confirm this hypothesis. The map they draw of the political system suggests a concentration of power at the federal level and, more specifically,
in the federal executive and administrative offices, although there are
significant reserves of decisional autonomy at the state level and in the
national Congress. Political parties, as such, emerge as weak targets and
presumably weak actors, but individual politicians figure importantly.
The high reported rates of inter-associational contact hint at the role
of alliances. The relative frequency of international contacts suggests
that the Brazilian system is not politically autarkic and that external
interests and attitudes play a significant role in domestic politics.

Although this general distribution in no way conflicts with other observations of the system, one should be wary of the supposition that a
high frequency of interaction with a given authority group (or a given
cluster of authority groups) implies that this group possesses greater
decisional autonomy. For example, representative associations may seek
out contacts with individual congressmen in an effort to produce favorable responses that will be made elsewhere in the system—in the
bureaucracy, for example. The limited direct access to the President
does not imply that he is not an extremely important and, to a degree,
autonomous decision-maker. Virtually every decision in the system, at
some time, crosses his desk, although to reach him it may be advisable
to go through an intermediary. The high concentration of effort on direct

interaction with administrative elites, though certainly in part a reflection of their decentralized decisional autonomy, can also be explained in terms of indirect attempts to enlist their support on behalf of decisions made nearer the executive center. In short, the Brazilian decision-making process may be as much an "executive-centered coalition" as a network of "independent sovereignties with spheres of influence."[1]

The Legislative Arena

Evidence from a variety of sources indicates that association leaders see the legislature as a target of only secondary significance. Only about 8 percent of those interviewed reported legislative bodies as their primary point of political contact, although some 24 percent of those answering the mailed questionnaire said they had frequent contact with individual congressmen. These general configurative findings were followed up with more specific probes. First, they were asked, "Under the present conditions, is it necessary or indispensable for an association like yours to have in Congress one or a few deputies who are ready to defend the group's interests and inform it about what is going on there?" The answers to this question are presented in Table 11.3. The similarity in response between employers' and workers' sindicatos is striking. In

TABLE 11.3
DESIRABILITY OF LEGISLATIVE CONTACT

	Yes			
Association	Indispensable or necessary	Desirable	No	No answer
Type				
Employers'				
Syndical (N = 27)	29.6%	[11.1%]	37.0%	22.2%
Private (N = 38)	47.3	26.3	10.5	15.8
Workers' (N = 21)	38.2	14.3	42.9	[4.8]
Liberal-professional (N = 10)	60.0	0.0	[30.0]	[10.0]
Civic (N = 11)	45.5	[9.1]	18.2	27.3
Geographic scope				
National (N = 71)	42.3	16.9	25.3	15.5
Regional (N = 36)	41.7	[11.1]	30.6	16.7
Membership				
Indirect (N = 39)	46.1	[7.7]	41.0	[5.1]
Direct (N = 69)	39.1	20.3	18.8	21.7
Leadership				
Elective (N = 60)	43.4	13.3	30.0	13.3
Administrative (N = 39)	43.6	17.9	17.9	20.0
Intervenor (N = 8)	[25.0]	[25.0]	[50.0]	0.0
Legal status				
All syndical (N = 48)	33.3	12.5	41.7	12.5
All private (N = 60)	48.4	18.3	15.5	18.3

NOTE: Rows may not add to 100 because of rounding. Brackets denote percentages based on fewer than five cases. Normally, N equals 108. However, when subclassification proved ambiguous, individual cases were removed.

approximately the same proportion, they are the most likely to find it dispensable, unnecessary, and not even particularly desirable to have a man in Congress. (This finding conflicts somewhat with my earlier observation that syndical organizations were more likely to report frequent legislative contacts than were private ones. It may mean that sindicatos are less willing to make the effort to place their men in elective positions—or less willing to admit it, since such activity could be considered illegal.) The liberal professionals and the civic-minded find it most indispensable, although a good proportion of the latter avoided the question. Leaders of private employers' associations are the group least inhibited by the apolitical norms governing Brazilian interest politics: only 10 percent responded negatively to the hypothetical opportunity. Being in a formally national or a regional association does not seem to affect one's perception of the desirability of having an inside man very much. Type of membership seems to have its strongest impact upon the propensity for evading the question. Although administrators are slightly more in favor of the strategy, they are definitely more in favor of not answering. The low number of intervenors makes generalizations hazardous, but they do not seem to see much mileage in having a deputy or senator.

The role of legislative decision-making in interest politics was explored in yet another dimension. Respondents were asked to list their major campaigns. These were subsequently coded to distinguish campaigns that at some stage or another had involved an active effort on their part to influence the legislature. As Table 11.4 shows, slightly over one-half of the association leaders could not come up with a single campaign involving an appeal to the legislature. The syndical entities, employer and employee, again emerged as poor performers in this respect. However, those employers' syndicates that had tried were likely to have

TABLE 11.4
CAMPAIGNS INVOLVING LEGISLATIVE DECISION-MAKING

Type of association	Two or more campaigns	One campaign	No campaign	No answer, inapplicable
Employers'				
Syndical ($N = 27$)	32.1%	0.0%	64.3%	[3.6%]
Private ($N = 38$)	26.3	21.0	50.0	[2.6]
Workers' ($N = 20$)	[4.0]	[16.0]	60.0	[20.0]
Liberal-professional ($N = 10$)	50.0	[30.0]	[20.0]	[0.0]
Civic ($N = 11$)	[18.2]	[9.1]	54.5	[18.2]
TOTAL ($N = 106$)	23.9%	14.2%	54.0%	7.9%

NOTE: Rows may not add to 100 because of rounding. Brackets denote percentages based on fewer than five cases.

done it more than once, whereas many of their private equivalents reported only a single attempt. Workers were proportionately the least likely to have approached the Congress, and the middle-sector professionals were by far the most likely.

So far, legislative contacts have been discussed exclusively from the perspective of the interest leaders. How do the congressmen themselves perceive this activity?* The first finding is that congressmen will talk willingly and frankly about their contacts with representative associations, even though, as I shall note below, these associations are not particularly salient in their political consciousness. They are decidedly reluctant, however, to talk about their contacts with "economic groups"—individual firms or clusters of firms. They tend to differentiate this type of individualized exchange of interest and support from the collective expressions of "class" interest. This willingness is, I suggest, evidence of the fundamental legitimacy of this collective way of making demands. Some observers have suggested that the Brazilian legislator considers himself a spokesman for the seamless general will à la Rousseau and is consequently impervious to the functionally specific demands of special interest groups.[2] On a very superficial, verbal level—regarding "economic groups"—this may be the case. Regarding representative associations, I found no evidence of it, although again, as I shall discuss below, congressmen do express reservations about the quality of associational activity. Unfortunately, I was unable to administer the attitudinal questionnaire to them, but I venture to guess that they hold the same corporatist-patrimonialist world view as the associational leaders and civil servants.

The second general finding is that representative associations of either employers or workers are not perceived as very salient actors in the legislative process. The congressmen knew they existed, generally agreed that their role had been increasing, and received their publications and policy pronouncements. But almost all felt that they were not very important in parliamentary life. No one perceived them as being regularly and systematically engaged in influencing individual deputies or the Congress as a whole; most felt that they were sporadically active and not particularly effective on specific issues. This low saliency was reflected in the inability of congressmen to rank associations as especially

---

* The empirical basis for the following generalizations rests on interviews with some 35 congressmen, most of them deputies. The interviews lasted from 15 to 90 minutes and did not follow a preestablished itinerary. Interviewees were from 14 states, with the central, industrial states slightly overrepresented, and from six parties, with the major three and their principal factions all included. The interviews were conducted in Brasília during a three-day period of intensive legislative activity.

efficient or influential. Few could name more than three or four; several gave vague answers like "the confederations" or "employers"; many shrewdly noted that influence was both regionally and functionally specialized and hence depended on the issue at stake.*

One hypothesis leading me to select certain questions was the expectation that deputies and senators from the more developed regions of the country would be more aware of and receptive to associational forms of interest expression. In fact, deputies from São Paulo, Guanabara, Rio de Janeiro, Minas Gerais, and Paraná were more association-conscious than those from the North, the Northeast, and the Interior. They could cite more groups, they found them more influential, and they could offer more concrete and specific examples of associational intervention. On the other hand, elected representatives from relatively developed states were also more likely to be critical of existing associations and often mentioned their dependence upon administrative and executive authorities, their lack of imagination and dynamism, their predominant negativism, and their patterns of oligarchic domination. Merely being more aware of and receptive to associational activities does not necessarily entail being more approving of how these activities are actually carried out.[3]

Of course this correlation between representing a developed area and being association-conscious is by no means perfect. It fails to explain the great amount of variation encountered among deputies from developed areas and the few cases in which associational activity was rated very important by representatives of underdeveloped states. (It should also be noted that there was no residence requirement at the time; thus a deputy or senator was not always actually from the area he represented.) The key intervening condition seems to be role conception. The congressman who sees himself as a "conscientious legislator" is, regardless of regional origin or electoral base, more likely to be aware of

---

* An important exception to this overall pattern was the situation prevailing during the latter part of the Goulart regime. A mobilization of associational pressures on a broad range of issues was focused intensively and consistently upon the Congress. National conferences were held in Brasília; truck loads and caravans of workers descended on the Congress; the galleries were packed with vociferous supporters; deputies were frequently accosted by representatives urging the passage or rejection of "basic reforms" and threatened with sanctions for noncompliance. The congressmen interviewed regarded this outburst of lobbying as decidedly abnormal and illegitimate. They saw the mobilization of workers' organizations as sponsored and manipulated by the executive as a deliberate attempt to coerce the Congress. The gathering of conservative forces (rural groups, women's associations, Catholic associations, and some employers' federations and councils) was seen as a temporary, expedient reaction to these forces. Since the 1964 coup, the associations have reverted to their former pattern of specialized and sporadic attention to the legislative process.

and to appreciate the appeals and suggestions of representative associations. The conscientious legislator has a sort of craftsman's attitude toward legislation. He is jealous of the rights, prerogatives, and institutional independence of the Congress as a whole. His concern for well-drafted and realistic legislation may lead him to seek out, deliberately and actively, the opinions of affected groups. Such action also partially frees him from an otherwise complete dependency upon government sources of information. On the other hand, he by no means sees himself as dependent upon associational support. He is often the most critical of existing associational contacts, since their poor quality contributes little to his twin goals of legal realism and institutional independence. He is anxious to avoid identification as a *deputado classista* (a representative of a single class or social group) and considers himself a sort of generalist who should be accessible to all groups in society.*

Since this type is relatively common and plays such an important role in the Brazilian legislative process, perhaps the following case study from a lengthy interview will be instructive.[4] M. is a relative newcomer to politics, having been a deputy for only a single session. However, he has already been recognized as a particularly hard and conscientious worker. The associational infrastructure of his home state, a southern, moderately developed one, is primitive, and formal groups played no role in his campaign, the essential units being the "courthouse crowd," or local municipal machine. In the Câmara, M. has been the *relator* (rapporteur) of several important bills and is a permanent member of two major committees. Nevertheless, his contacts with representative associations have been few. He claims that when reporting a bill he actively solicits information and opinions from formal groups but rarely even gets an answer to his request. A rather prolific speechmaker, M. sends copies of his speeches to whatever associations exist in his home state, even though he never hears back from them. When asked if this was intended to produce a later payoff in the form of financial support or votes, he replied candidly that these groups are simply not "electoral forces." M. himself belongs to no "class" associations and volunteered no other group affiliations.† In an attempt to compensate for the lack

* The role conception is clearly linked to the legalism (*bacharelismo*) of Brazilian political culture. It differs from the Rousseauesque conception in that the constituency is viewed as a constellation or hierarchy of social groups, each of which has a distinct role to play and hence distinct interests to represent. The role of the legislator (and this is clearly linked to patrimonialism) is not to become subordinate to any one of the groups but to dispense rewards from above on the basis of independent judgment. In short, his is a Burkean, not a Rousseauesque conception of representation.

† Another orienting hypothesis in the congressional interviews had been that professional politicians would tend to be "joiners" and to use the multiple memberships

of associational interaction with his constituency, M. makes frequent trips back home and consults his clientele directly. He is pleased that he is well publicized on the nightly radio program, "A Voz do Brasil,"* as an active legislator and speechmaker.

The case of M. summarizes conveniently a variety of aspects of the electoral-legislative arena of Brazilian politics: the prominent role of municipal machines; the virtual absence of "party" as a means of selection, financial support, or interest aggregation; the legalism (M. is a lawyer) and corporatist patrimonialism of the political culture; the impoverished role of formal associations in general and representative associations in particular; the great importance attached to informal, face-to-face contacts on the one hand and to the mass media on the other; a feeling of dependency on executive information and initiative. Yet, in spite of the associational vacuum in which he lives and campaigns, M. is aware of the need for this kind of formal interest linkage and receptive to the few associational contacts that have come his way, although he is also critical of the general quality of these associations and of their dependency upon executive authority, especially upon the Ministry of Labor. He is, in short, a sort of "proto-pluralist" whose political culture and role conception incline him to accept associational demands as legitimate and even necessary, but whose actual political experience with them is both minimal and deceiving. In the case of conscientious legislators from the more associationally developed areas, the subjective and objective factors reinforce each other, and one finds even greater awareness and acceptance of the activities of formal interest and attitude groups.

Although most of the congressmen are generalists of this sort, the Brazilian parliament does have its *deputados classistas*.† They are well

---

for electoral purposes. With the exception of a few paulista deputies, this expectation was not confirmed. Few deputies belonged to more formal associations than one might have predicted on the basis of their professional background alone. Although few mentioned it—and it was awkward to probe further in such a personal area—politicians do seem to join many recreational societies and social clubs that may provide them with an important electoral clientele.

* A radio program produced by the government and carried by all stations from 7:00 to 8:00 every evening. According to M., the Congress is allotted twelve minutes of the broadcast time.

† The electoral system, which makes each deputy (and senator) run on a proportional basis from his state as a whole, rather than from a smaller district, would seem to enhance "class" representation, as would the fragmented party system. In such a large constituency, with such a large number of parties to choose from, it would seem possible for any sizable social group to have at least one of its own leaders elected. Nevertheless, such congressmen are definitely in the minority. This is further evidence of the preponderant role played by the multiclass municipal machine and personalism in Brazilian electoral politics.

known to their colleagues, and their role in the legislature is somewhat marked by that knowledge.[5] There are two types of "interested" deputies. The first, and by far the most common, has connections with an individual firm or economic group through family ties, direct professional interest, or indirect financial support. As the cost of campaigning has skyrocketed and as ideological polarization has threatened their position, economic groups have begun to invest more heavily in electoral support.[6] Most of the major firms have their *testas-de-ferro* (figureheads) or even one of their executives in the Congress. Some of Brazil's largest industrialists have run directly for public office and won. The presence in the parliament of such interested parties does not however necessarily redound to the benefit of their respective representative associations. For example, B., a deputy from an industrialized state, is widely recognized as the spokesman in the Chamber for one of the most important manufacturing industries. He makes no attempt to hide the fact that he is on the board of directors of one of the major producers (a North American firm); indeed, he is openly proud of his "pioneering" role. However, he is a little annoyed at being classified as a "class" deputy and protests that he represents the state as a whole. He has never been an officer in the sindicato or in the private associação representing that industry. When asked "What are your contacts with the syndicate?" and "Has it helped you in your legislative job?," he answers, "Very little. They take much too long to answer, and when they do it is too bureaucratic and statistical. Electorally and financially, they are unimportant. I already know what the industry thinks. If I don't know on a specific issue, I pick up the phone and talk to a few of my friends and associates. The association itself has no expression here."

In the case of this first type of "class" deputy, one could in fact argue that their presence in the Congress, far from being helpful to the respective representative association, provides convenient, personalistic circuits for bypassing it. The sheer presence of more industrialists or more coffee growers (or their *testas-de-ferro*) in the parliament does not necessarily increase the influence of the CNI or the FIESP or the CNA, the SRB, or the FARESP. On the contrary, the collective expression of sector interests is thereby fragmented into individualized support for and dependency upon competing politicians, parties, or political machines. As the individual firm or grower's capacity to ensure policy favorable to his interests goes up, the collective capacity of the *classe* goes down.

The second type of *deputado classista* consists of prominent members or leaders of representative associations. From 1934 to 1937, of course, one-fifth of the seats in the Chamber were reserved for corporatist representatives. Again in 1945, for reasons I shall discuss shortly, a relatively large number of association leaders were elected. In the ensuing years, as the local municipal machines and the state parties consolidated their hold on the nominating and electoral processes, the number of corporatist candidates declined. The 1962 elections saw a resurgence of *deputados classistas*, but most of these had their mandates removed and their political rights taken away by the 1964 coup. Nevertheless, the major employers' associations have usually managed to have at least one of their leaders or employees in the Chamber.* On the employee and professional side, transport and maritime workers, government functionaries, radio announcers, journalists, architects, engineers, lawyers, and physicians can usually count on having at least one or two of their "class" leaders in parliament. Even in these more direct cases of corporatist representation, however, the consequences in terms of associational influence are by no means obvious. In answer to the question about the desirability of having a representative in Congress, a number of association leaders—workers, employers, and liberal professionals—volunteered the aside that, although it was advantageous to have one there, it was self-defeating to support such a candidate openly. Moreover, once elected, associational representatives were difficult to control.

Two tenets of Brazilian political folklore are shared by association leaders and congressmen: that the Brazilian will not vote for a leader of his own *classe*, and that too close an identification with any class association costs a candidate more votes than he could possibly gain. H. is a deputy from one of the industrialized southeastern states and is also the president of a trade union.[7] Although the sindicato was useful in providing "voluntary" personnel for fund raising and campaigning (in short, it provided him an organization base), H. insists that he did not run as a class candidate and that he deliberately avoided too close an association with the syndicate. He admits that his appeal was directed toward the working class in general, but feels that too much emphasis on his syndical activities would have cost him votes. He notes that the same holds true for industrialist and business leaders.[8] "The public is just not attracted by class candidates, even candidates from their own class." As a deputy, H. says he does not consider himself the spokesman

---

* The political activities of the higher-level employers' syndicates are facilitated greatly by the availability of SESI and SESC funds. Even if they are not used directly to finance campaigns (and they certainly have been in the past), they can be used to distribute patronage and create the local paternalistic benefits that are the basis for most successful political careers in Brazil. In short, SESI and SESC give their respective confederations and federations an opportunity to use the traditional, clientelistic style of politics. These funds can also be used to hire or retain candidates after they have been elected. A number of state and federal congressmen receive such supplementary salaries. Some are even long-time SESI employees.

for his *classe* or even for organized labor as a whole. In fact, he claims to listen willingly to the demands and suggestions of employers' representatives as well.

By and large, the attempt by associations to provide themselves with more or less permanent, de facto corporatist representatives in the parliament has been largely unsuccessful. By themselves, the associations have proven incapable of exclusively sponsoring and then retaining the services of candidates. Class leaders who have managed to get elected usually have had to play down their associational connections and seek support elsewhere; that is to say, they have had to make the appropriate alliances with professional political machines. In so doing, they are no longer exclusively dependent upon their *classe* for support and must aggregate the interests of a wider, interclass clientele. The association becomes merely one among many competing clients. Once leaders are elected and in control of some of their own political resources, further opportunities arise for shifting alliances and recombining support in order to maximize autonomy and electoral security.

This system of patronage and machine politics (*clientelismo* in the Brazilian political jargon) clearly favors individualized political investments and payoffs, and fragments attempts by distinct social groups to capture control of the legislative process. Representative associations seem to have learned this lesson. Except during the resurgence of workers' *deputados classistas* in the 1962 parliament (and this was the result of attempts by Goulart and others to build a national machine), the number of corporatist congressmen has tended to decrease. Attempts to influence legislative proceedings through recruitment have been left either to the more or less covert activity of individual firms and economic groups or to massive, collective efforts such as IBAD.[9] Individual representative associations have increasingly confined themselves to lobbying activities—to providing information and pleading for special favors. And even this activity is carried on only sporadically and unsystematically. Very few national associations maintain important permanent staffs in Brasília, and those that are there are essentially agencies for gathering information, rather than for disseminating it.

Of course, as we have seen above and will see in further detail below, one reason representative associations do not concentrate their energies in the legislative arena is that the major channels of interest expression run directly between the associations and the administrative agencies. Deputies are fully aware and not a little resentful of this. They often volunteered, when asked about the activity of associations in the Congress, "Of course they pay much more attention to the executive and administrative branches than to us."[10] They added that most of the syndicates were virtual wards of the state and that since they depended upon the administration, especially the Ministry of Labor, for their survival it was rather natural that they should concentrate their efforts upon it.[11] One deputy believed that during the long Vargas dictatorship social groups had become accustomed to addressing the executive exclusively and had simply never learned to make demands before the Congress.[12] Another talked of a systematic campaign on the part of the executive to undermine the Congress's prestige. This has made social groups believe that the Congress is powerless and unresponsive to popular pressures.[13] Several mentioned that the remoteness of Brasília tended to isolate the parliament from popular pressures, and this had contributed to its declining prestige. Interestingly, not a single deputy or senator explained this universally acknowledged fact of concentration upon the executive branch by noting that it is there that decisions are effectively made.

Only two groups are consistently and primarily active in the legislature: the government employees and the *municipalistas*. Both are groups whose interests directly coincide with those of the professional politicians in the Congress. A very substantial proportion of the deputies and senators are public employees,* and virtually all of them use the distribution of public employment to consolidate their political support. Their deep solicitude for the living conditions and well-being of this social group is illustrated by the fact that 350 amendments were proposed to the last salary increase for government employees.[14] As a *classe*, the civil servants are not only numerous, but also have a very high and concentrated rate of voting participation. We have described the ABM as virtually "a professional association for professional politicians." It is the only representative association that has been successful in sponsoring and maintaining a functionally based, interparty faction within the Congress, the *bloco municipalista*. Attempts to form *blocos* of landowners or industrialists have been initiated, but have never succeeded. From this position of strength, the *municipalistas* accomplished a sort of legislative coup. In the chaos surrounding the implantation of the parliamentary regime of 1961, they unshelved a constitutional amendment that had been lying around since 1958. The amendment radically altered the distribution of fiscal revenues in favor of municípios. In addition to other measures, it transferred the Rural Territorial Tax to local authorities, thereby crippling President Goulart's proposed agrarian reform, since a great deal of reliance had been placed upon a progressive land tax as a means for encouraging productive use

* A retired employee of the Senate estimated that in 1966 some two-thirds to three-quarters of the senators were themselves professional public employees.

and sale of land. The ABM victory was Pyrrhic. The "revolution's" Agrarian Reform Law of 1964 transferred the rural land tax to the federal government (it had formerly been a state tax), where it was even more likely to be collected and less likely to be redistributed in favor of local government.

Most Brazilian representative associations approach the Congress as outsiders, although they all may (and most do) have friends on the inside who can keep them informed and occasionally intercede on their behalf. With the exceptions noted above, few have made a concerted effort to influence legislators. Even fewer are able to mobilize enough support to put through an important initiative or to override a presidential veto. The major national associations maintain a consistent, if not insistent, contact with the parliament. Their publications are usually sent to all the deputies. Most have permanent administrative departments charged with "accompanying" legislative proposals, and these emit a steady flow of *pareceres*—formal statements of position on a given bill.[15] When the issue directly affects their interests, a more concentrated technique may be used. One of the most frequent targets is the *bancada*—all the deputies who sit in Congress for a given state, regardless of party affiliation. Industrialists may confine their efforts to representatives from the more industrialized states, maritime workers will approach all the representatives from states bordering on the sea, etc. Another key target is the permanent commission and, more specifically, the committee member assigned as rapporteur for the bill in question. Again, however, the interaction is largely formal. Personal appearances by leaders from major national associations before the permanent commissions or ad hoc investigatory commissions are infrequent.

I have explained the failure of Brazilian representative associations to influence the recruitment and electoral success of congressmen and, subsequently, their inability to control significant blocks of legislative support in terms of some of the general characteristics of the political system. The failure of these associations to act as effective lobbyists is less readily explainable. Interviewed deputies, particularly those from the more developed states, are receptive to associational expressions of interest.[16] Although they are generally hesitant to be linked to or dependent upon any single interest group, their Burkean role conception, their ideological flexibility, their partisan indiscipline, their low level of technical skills, and their resentment of exclusive dependence upon the government for information makes them at least potentially attractive targets for associations that can provide the appropriate type of supports and demands.[17] The few associations that have perceived or have been forced to perceive this potentiality have reaped considerable, if incremental, benefits from it. Other not so strategically placed associations have been successful in their lobbying activities, once they have devoted adequate talent and resources to the job, and many can claim a legislative victory or two.[18] The point, however, is not that such attempts are frequent (they are not), but that it is possible for collective, aggregated expression of group interest to get a hearing and be acted upon favorably, although the system of elected representation clearly favors the use of more particularistic, personalistic, and private channels of support and demand. The fact that associations do not exploit these opportunities more often and more systematically is due less to the characteristics of the legislative subsystem itself than to the perception by association leaders that the major decisions concerning their interests are not made in that subsystem.* The parliament is the place to go for initiating minor measures or for making minor modifications in officially sponsored bills. The real action is elsewhere.

The Party and Electoral Arenas

For some countries of Latin America party membership, loyalty, and discipline act as powerful organizers of associational activity. Many students of Latin American interest politics have tried to analyze how and why such patterns of dependency emerge and persist between parties and representative associations.[19] At any rate, this sort of dependency is not at all common in Brazil. Of the associations responding to the mailed questionnaire, 72 percent claimed never to have any contact with political parties, and a scant 14 percent reported rare encounters. Not one had frequent contact, and only 2 percent had occasional encounters (12 percent did not answer the question). In the personal interviews, association leaders were asked, "Do you think it is a good tactic for an association to ally itself with a political party?" As Table 11.5 shows, not a single respondent answered affirmatively.† A fairly significant proportion would advocate a party alliance if it were legal: almost one syndical leader in three might try it if the CLT sanctions were lifted. Workers' and employers' leaders seem to agree on this

---

* This situation may be changing. The National Confederation of Commercial Associations has begun to mount what seems to be the first intensive, permanently organized legislative lobby in Brazilian interest politics.

† The question was badly phrased, and there was a fairly obvious reluctance on the part of leaders to respond. For syndical organizations such alliances are prohibited by the Labor Code, and many of the private entities have clauses in their constitutions against any form of partisan activity. In effect, most of the respondents were being asked if they would have liked to engage in prohibited activity.

TABLE 11.5
DESIRABILITY OF ALLIANCE WITH A POLITICAL PARTY

Association	Yes	Yes, if legal	Not with one, but with all	No	No answer, Don't know
Interest					
Employers' (N = 65)	0.0%	21.1%	0.0%	66.6%	12.3%
Workers' (N = 21)	0.0	25.0	[5.0]	70.0	0.0
Liberal-					
professional (N = 10)	0.0	[40.0]	[10.0]	[30.0]	[20.0]
Civic and					
religious (N = 12)	0.0	[18.1]	0.0	45.4	27.3
Legal status					
Syndical (N = 60)	0.0	30.2	[4.7]	60.5	[4.7]
Private (N = 48)	0.0	18.5	0.0	63.0	18.5
Geographic scope					
National (N = 71)	0.0	21.5	3.1	63.1	12.3
Regional (N = 36)	0.0	28.5	0.0	59.4	12.5
Leadership					
Elective (N = 78)	0.0	31.5	0.0	57.4	11.1
Administrative (N = 60)	0.0	13.3	[4.4]	64.4	17.8

NOTE: Rows may not add to 100 because of rounding. Brackets denote percentages based on fewer than five cases.

issue, although the latter are more inclined to duck the question. Formal geographic scope has no discriminating effect. Elective leaders, as one might expect, would be more willing to take the chance. Administrative leaders were rather noticeably reluctant to answer this and other overtly political questions. For approximately two-thirds of the association representatives interviewed, however, interest politics and party politics should be kept apart.

This observation corresponds well with the findings on party membership of interest leaders as presented in Table 11.6. The extent to which leaders are also party activists does not seem to vary greatly according to type of interest or association, except for employers, who are noticeably less partisan. Otherwise, one leader in five reported some sort of party link. Legal status has little effect, except perhaps to make *sindicalistas* a bit reluctant to answer the question. Globally speaking, roughly the same percentage reports no party membership as believes that party alliances are undesirable for interest groups.

The desire of Brazil's corporatists to link emerging and to co-opt existing associations into a direct relationship with the state apparatus independent of party politics seems to have been consummated.[20] Not only are there formal, legal barriers to forging lasting links with parties, but most association leaders do not perceive such tactics as being in

TABLE 11.6
PARTY MEMBERSHIP OF ASSOCIATION LEADERS
(*percent*)

Association	Members of a political party	Not members of a political party	No answer, Don't know
Interest			
Employers' ($N = 65$)	14.1%	75.0%	10.9%
Workers' ($N = 21$)	26.6	66.6	[6.6]
Liberal-professional ($N = 10$)	25.0	58.3	16.6
Civic and religious ($N = 12$)	[28.5]	71.4	[7.1]
Legal status			
Syndical ($N = 60$)	18.3	69.5	12.2
Private ($N = 48$)	19.4	73.1	7.5

NOTE: Rows may not add to 100 because of rounding. Brackets denote percentages based on fewer than five cases.

their best interests. Alliances with parties do not augment the association's potential influence; nor do they provide access to channels of influence otherwise closed. This generalization does not mean that associations do not acquire a "partisan coloration" (*coloração partidaria*) or that they do not participate in electoral politics in support of individual candidates or slates of candidates. For example, workers' syndical leaders were instrumental in dissuading Vargas from his original intention of creating a single party in 1944–45 and convincing him to throw his support behind a separate labor party, the Partido Trabalhista Brasileiro (PTB).[21] The leadership of the party, however, was dominated, not by the workers' leaders or *pelegos*, but by officials from the Ministry of Labor and from 1948 to 1954 by the personalism of Vargas himself. After his suicide, many members defected, and minor competing labor parties were established. In 1960, the syndicalist leadership made an abortive attempt to alter the relevant provisions of the Labor Code to permit "the active and permanent participation of the workers in the administrative and political direction of the PTB."[22] The PTB National Convention approved the initiative and even introduced a bill in Congress to that effect. The proposal was strongly opposed within the syndical movement, however, and it was never brought to a vote. During the Goulart period (1961–64), several prominent syndical leaders became members of the party's state and national directories, and some even became intimate advisors to the President himself. However, these relationships were informal and personalistic. At no time did they amount to the kind of institutionalized interdependency that characterizes the relationship between the British Labour Party or the Peruvian APRA and their respective trade union movements.[23] What linked the workers' syndicates and the Brazilian Labor Party was their common dependency upon similar parents, the Ministry of Labor and the Retirement and Social Welfare Institutes, and their mutual admiration for a common godparent, Getúlio Vargas. As long as the positions in the Ministry of Labor, welfare institutes, and labor courts were distributed through PTB channels, the party could maintain a modicum of unity, and it was expedient, if not indispensable, for syndical leaders to support it.* When, as during the short reign of Jânio Quadros or the much longer reign of Castelo Branco, control of these key patronage and decisional centers passed into the hands of another set of actors, the marriage of convenience between the PTB and the sindicatos was threatened. The partisan coloration of workers' organizations either changed or faded away.

Workers' syndicates are not the only representative associations with a party coloration. Politicians active in the commercial associations tend to be from the União Democrática Nacional (UDN) party. Euvaldo Lodi, Roberto Simonsen, Augusto Vianna, Lídio Lunardi, Haroldo Corrêa Cavalcanti, and Gen. Edmundo de Macedo Soares—men active in the leadership of the National Confederation of Industry—were all officeholders under the label of the Partido Social Democrático (PSD) at one time or another. Similarly, most of the politicians in the Brazilian Rural Confederation have been from the PSD. When queried about this in interviews, the respective association leaders claim that this is merely a coincidence, point out that they have other members and leaders linked to other parties, and strongly deny that there is any deliberate intent, formal or informal, to support a single party.† It is not at all uncommon for such leaders to protest (in the same breath) that their organization is strictly apolitical and that it gets along with all parties. This was confirmed in questions about parliamentary activity. Both con-

---

* The special case of São Paulo partially confirms this generalization. São Paulo had the largest syndicalized mass of workers in the country. Because the PTB had virtually no strength in this state, Vargas' political expediency dictated an alliance with the personalist, populist machine of Ademar de Barros, the Partido Social Progressista (PSP). In this case, presumably, the PTB had less control over the welfare system, the labor courts, and the regional delegation of the Labor Ministry; consequently, the paulista workers' syndicates developed less of a PTB coloration.

† This, of course, is the reverse consequence of the multiclass composition of Brazilian parties. Because leaders and members may belong to more than one class, no one party can adopt too exclusive a class position. And, because the associational leadership may have men of different party persuasions, no association can support a single party exclusively.

The timing of the creation of the Rural Association Movement (1945) and the original legislation controlling it strongly suggest an attempt by Vargas to use these associations to provide an organizational infrastructure for the PSD, just as he saw the syndicates as providing the basic support for the PTB. This is, however, only conjecture on my part.

gressmen and association leaders testified that approaches were not confined to a single party. Although the interested groups do not waste much time trying to convince recognized enemies, they are likely to find their friends scattered over several parties.

A change in the relationship between representative associations and parties may be in the offing. The "democratic revolutionary" regime of 1964 has enacted several measures reforming the "Organic Law of Political Parties," the electoral code, and, finally, in the new Constitution, the entire electoral system. In the fall of 1965 all thirteen parties were abolished and the regime set about establishing and maintaining a two-party system. The Aliança Renovadora Nacional (ARENA) is the party in power; the Movimento Democrático Brasileiro (MDB) is the party of the loyal opposition.* In establishing its national directory, the ARENA set an interesting precedent. Posts were given to a number of prominent association leaders (including the presidents of the CNI and the CNC, the president of the Commercial Association of São Paulo, the president of the ABM, a prominent official in the veterans' association, a leader of the metallurgical workers, and a leader from the commercial workers), although by far the majority went to professional politicians from several of the former parties. The MDB directory was composed exclusively of politicians.[24] The subsequent selection of ARENA and MDB candidates was dominated by President Castelo Branco and the military. The ostensible motive for these measures was to promote greater popular participation in and control over party decision-making on the one hand, and to ensure greater coherence and discipline in party performance on the other. To the extent that these objectives are fulfilled, parties may become more attractive targets for interest politicians. But it is still too soon to tell.†

Despite the lack of permanent, or even stable, links with parties themselves, representative associations are not completely absent from the electoral process. Pronouncements by such entities as the Military Club and the Commercial Association of Rio have always been a fairly com-

---

* The irreverent Brazilians promptly labeled the two *"o partido do sim"* (the "yes" party) and *"o partido do sim, senhor"* (the "yes, sir" party). The loyalty—and the minority position—of the MDB has been ensured by periodic purges.

† The initial results are scarcely encouraging. Except for those linked to persecuted *subversivos* and *corruptos* (Goulart, Brizola, Arraes, and Ademar de Barros, to name the most prominent), few of the local and state electoral machines seem to have disintegrated. There has been no massive shift in partisan loyalties or ideological consolidation around the new national parties. These have been the object of considerable factional conflict, some of which was "resolved" by the creation of *sublegendas* ("subtitles") at the local level. Without the polarizing impact of popular national presidential elections, it seems doubtful that the present artificial two-party system can be maintained.

mon feature of electoral life. Open, public endorsements of candidates by associations have become less and less frequent, with the important exception of the civic groups. Newspapers, walls, trees, and sidewalks are covered with public endorsements from various social groups, but these usually carry the name of a given individual leader rather than of his association. One is simply expected to know that he is a syndical leader, the president of a local favelado association, a member of the directory of the medical society, a prominent official of a sports club, or the general secretary of a civil servants' association.[25] For most lower and middle status associations, this is the extent of their electoral participation. In the words of one informant, they are used as "electoral nurseries" (*viveiros eleitorais*).

The basic unit of electoral politics is the ward boss, or *cabo eleitoral*,

a local leader who disposes of a few dozen or at the most a few hundred votes—not enough to permit him to win elective office himself. He is a sort of administrative lawyer for his community, which could be a small town, a favela, . . . a recreational club, . . . a spiritualist tent, an *umbandista* center, a Protestant church, or a Catholic parish. The *cabo eleitoral* takes care of the interests of those he "represents," mainly before public authorities. . . . His prestige is maintained or grows if he is capable of fulfilling a good proportion of their demands. If he fails, a more successful rival may replace him. Therefore he must be able to count on protection "from above," which he obtains precisely by contributing to the election of aldermen or deputies.[26]

This, then, is the broker or intermediary through which the immediate and specific demands of individuals and primary groups and the vague promises and short-term payoffs of actual or aspiring decision-makers are exchanged. The demanding groups need someone who can interpret their problems and transmit them through the appropriate network of personal contacts and relations; the supplying politicians need someone who can translate their promises into appealing popular terms and who has enough local prestige and authority to ensure that the votes contracted for will, in fact, be forthcoming.

How do formal representative associations plug into this diffuse and sporadic process of interest articulation? In some cases the *cabo eleitoral* is himself an association leader who can command enough votes personally to get himself elected. But because of the low degree of member participation and the distortions in leadership selection discussed in the previous chapter, the capacity of association leaders to command sizable blocks of votes seems limited. Deputies agreed in general that, because of the lack of internal cohesion and class-consciousness, the role of such formal organizations in the electoral process is minimal, and that they are not "electoral forces." The result is, as I have already noted, a paucity of corporatist, "classist" congressmen and a relative abundance of generalists.*

Employers' associations have other special resources to contribute to the electoral process: money, physical plant, organizational capacity, prestige, ideology, etc. However, in spite of frequent and vague allegations,[27] both their leaders and the professional politicians interviewed denied that they were heavy investors. Private representative associations and syndicates do not participate in the same way as individual firms and government agencies. Several associations admitted they drew up lists of worthy candidates and encouraged members to contribute to their campaigns; others encouraged members to run for office, but would not support them openly.

In recent years the conservative press, especially *O Estado de São Paulo*, and the new elite-indoctrinating organizations, especially IPÊS, have been exhorting industrialists and businessmen to participate more actively in politics. They have charged that, whereas the working class has acquired a mounting sense of group consciousness and has forged new instruments for political action, the "productive classes" have remained collectively reluctant to engage in the dirty politics of the electoral process. Now, they claim, it has become a matter of class self-preservation; the former methods of uncoordinated support for individual candidates are obsolete and self-defeating. One product of this revised tactical thinking was the Instituto Brasileiro de Ação Democrática (IBAD), and the Ação Democrática Parlamentar (ADP) with their massive attempts to sponsor a whole bloc of conservative, "democratic" candidates in the 1962 national election. "For the first time, all the peak [employers'] associations, civil and syndical," issued a joint manifesto announcing their sponsorship of an "enlightenment campaign" in support of those candidates who would "preserve our Christian heritage and maintain intact those institutions that signify the continuity of our national life and the defense of our sovereignty."[28] This, of course, was not an official or public entrance of associations into the political arena; the national employers' syndicates and private associations were never directly linked to IBAD or ADP.† About ths time, the Centro Industrial do Rio de Janeiro conducted a confidential survey of its members concerning electoral tactics.[29] Of the 427 members, 395 responded to a written questionnaire. Asked "Should industry have representatives

---

* The clientelistic system of representation favors those whose profession provides them with a "natural" clientele: physicians, lawyers, teachers, priests, and dentists. In the Guanabara state assembly, physicians and lawyers alone accounted for 43 percent of the deputies. All of the above accounted for 62 percent.

† It was charged, but never proven, that the CNC had allowed its offices to be used for IBAD purposes.

in Congress?," 94.8 percent said yes, 2.4 percent said no, and 2.8 percent expressed indifference. Asked "Can a layman without first-hand knowledge of industry represent industry?," 95.5 percent said no; but when asked "Have you already participated in some political party?," only 4.8 percent admitted that they had, and 6.2 percent gave indeterminate answers. More specifically, queried about what sort of elective office they had held, the survey turned up only one ex-governor, one ex-federal deputy, and one *deputado classista* from the 1930's. Several mentioned, however, that they had partners who held elected public positions. Finally, the respondents were asked to suggest the names of industrialists who merited their personal confidence as group representatives. In response, 587 suggestions were made concerning 261 possible candidates. This confirms some of my earlier observations about the activities of associations in the Congress: the diffuse desire for corporatist representatives, the distrust of unreliable professional politicians, and the low rate of actual participation.

IBAD was only the most ambitious and best financed of the electoral front organizations. The first was apparently the Liga Eleitoral Católica (Catholic Electoral League), founded in the early 1930's and reorganized in 1945. Its tactic was to "orient the electorate" by indicating those candidates who were unacceptable to the Catholic hierarchy.[30] The candidates were asked to adhere publicly to a document of Catholic principles, and those who were found lacking on grounds of immorality or Communism were denounced. Condemnations of whole party slates were rare. The LEC was disbanded in 1958 under charges that its selections had been influenced by political bargaining as well as moral principle.[31] In March 1962 it was replaced by a new Catholic electoral organization, the Aliança Eleitoral Pela Familia (ALEF). Instead of condemning candidates, the ALEF studied them, their party doctrines, and their "electoral possibilities" and indicated a selected number as worthy of Catholic support.[32] Although the group claimed half a million registered members and conducted an aggressive publicity campaign, the deputies queried (including one priest-deputy who had run with its support[33] and one secular deputy who is the Chamber's most celebrated *divorcista*[34]) were unanimous in their opinion that the ALEF did not represent an important electoral force.

Catholics are not the only sponsors of electoral fronts. As we have seen, most attempts by employers' associations have been ephemeral and ineffectual.* In 1945, however, employers played a major role. At that time, the Brazilian polity faced its first election in over a decade.

---

* For example, mention was encountered of a Liga Eleitoral do Comercio (1950) and a Liga Eleitoral Agrária (1954). In 1948 various rural associations discussed (and apparently rejected) the idea of forming a separate Partido Ruralista.

Parties were embryonic, candidate selection was chaotic, and, most important, voter lists were completely outdated. In this setting of uncertainty, Vargas pulled one of his more subtle political maneuvers. He announced his intention to permit the holding of elections and by decree automatically registered all voters who were government employees, members of syndicates and welfare institutes, and workers in semipublic enterprises. In short, he enfranchised ex officio his own clientele. Other sectors of the population had to register themselves voluntarily. The "productive classes" of São Paulo saw through the maneuver and organized the Paulista Commission in Favor of Registration. With the joint effort of the Commercial Association, the Federation of Industries, the Catholic Electoral League, and the Catholic Workers' Circles, over 300,000 voters were registered. Partly as a result of this effort and partly because of the chaotic state of party organization, a substantial number of association leaders were elected to public office in that year. In subsequent elections, as the local political machines consolidated themselves, the number of these corporatist politicians declined, as I noted above.

Voter registration is the major justification for the participation of civic associations in the electoral process. However, these associations often mix voter registration with candidate endorsement and partisan propagandizing, all in the name of democracy, motherhood, and Christianity. This is not regarded by their leaders as partisan activity. It is considered a simple response to one's civic duty, nonpolitical because it is not consistently linked to a single party or political personality. I had the rare treat of seeing this attitude demonstrated during the 1965 election in Guanabara. Waiting in the outer office of a civic association for an interview, I watched a volunteer pick up the telephone and answer, in response to queries about whether or not that night's rally was sponsored by the association, that it was not, that the association was strictly nonpolitical. However, she went on to say that all the directorate would be there on the platform and that the member's presence would be appreciated. As she spoke, she was turning the crank on a mimeograph machine that was reproducing handbills accusing the opposing candidate of being a *corrupto* and of consorting with Communists. That the definition of "political" is subject to interpretation was even more graphically demonstrated to me in an interview with the president of one of the feminine civic associations in São Paulo, who insisted in all seriousness, "We are so apolitical that we even sponsored our own candidate in last year's municipal elections"!

It is easy and a bit gratuitous for an outside observer to be cynical about this sort of objective "misrepresentation." However, associational leaders are, as a rule, genuinely sincere in their belief that they are not engaged in political activity, by which they mean partisan, electoral politics. This is a messy, relatively corrupt, and definitely uncertain arena in which even initial success does not guarantee the investor a continuous and reliable profit—i.e., a relatively fixed capacity to influence authoritative policy. Leaders of formal associations prefer, if at all possible, to avoid this indeterminate and risky arena and to devote their attention to the more stable, predictable arenas of executive and administrative decision-making.

TWELVE

The Pattern of Interaction:
Administrative and Executive Arenas

STUDENTS of Brazilian society have suggested that the principal focus of the political struggle there has been to gain control over the administrative apparatus of the state.[1] Once obtained, this control was not exercised as a means for molding or transforming the society according to the image of some cohesive social elite, nor was it exercised simply to provide that elite with immediate material or status rewards. It was used primarily as an instrument of political accommodation or conciliation for indirectly maintaining the status quo. "The essence of this system consisted in a bargain whereby patronage was accorded in return for the promise of support. The State served to foster and protect the existing regime, and at the same time provided the necessary number of sinecures to ensure the political support which the ruling class would otherwise have lacked, and which was needed in order to preserve its economic and political control of the country."[2] This arrangement of mutual convenience, by which the emerging urban middle class and leading elements of the working class were tranquilly co-opted into the preexistent social order, has been termed the *Estado Cartorial* (Sinecure State).[3] "The ruling class indirectly subsidizes the idleness and marginality of the middle class by incorporating it within the Estado Cartorial, and the middle class returns this tax by supporting clientelistic politics and the semicolonial and semifeudal [social] structure."[4]

The inevitable by-product of the accommodative process was the creation of a resistant stratum of many marginal and unproductive government employees.[5] Beyond self-support, its principal function was to provide minimal services: police, health, sanitation, and especially tax collection (most of which was used for the payment of salaries). Beginning in the 1930's, political leaders began to conceive of using the public bureaucratic apparatus as more than a source of parasitic sinecures.

New functions were successively added: regulation of commodity markets, provision of transport and energy, and direct public intervention in basic industries. In the 1950's some administrative policy-makers began to try using government controls over foreign trade and exchange policy to deliberately foster industrialization through import substitution. Concomitantly, but more hesitantly, there emerged a concern with coordinating these dispersed policy areas according to some set of national priorities.

The principal characteristic of this process of administrative change is that it occurred by sedimentation, not by metamorphosis. Traditional clientelistic agencies continue to exist, more or less unaltered, alongside new rational and efficient ones.[6] The new functions were acquired not by transforming or modernizing preexistent administrative bodies, not even by adding new departments to them, but by creating totally new agencies. As Octávio Ianni has aptly put it, "A technocracy was created alongside a bureaucracy."[7] A secondary but important characteristic of the process is the failure of these very differently staffed and administered agencies to have been consolidated into a manageable decision-making hierarchy.[8] There has been no institutionalized center for setting global performance standards and priorities consistent with available resources, much less for enforcing such standards. Certain serious issues may have given certain agencies a sort of de facto preeminence; for example, balance of payments difficulties and inflation may have emphasized the Superintendency for Monetary Coordination (SUMOC—now the Central Bank), the Bank of Brazil, the National Development Bank (BNDE), and the Ministry of Finance.* In spite of the predominant position of these técnico-dominated agencies, however, they lacked coordination with respect to policy. "Each instrument functioned in its own field of action, in accordance with its own special criteria, almost always conservative and implicit, and at times incompatible with those serving as a basis for other public policy sectors."[9] The third major characteristic, as we might expect, is the persistence of political criteria in the selection of higher administrative personnel. "All appointments to key positions in the public service have to be discussed and agreed with the ruling political forces, in other words, with the traditional ruling class."[10]

Several observers have stressed a somewhat contradictory theme: the

---

* Formally, the Administrative Department of Public Service (DASP) elaborates the budget, but in fact it merely compiles separate agency proposals. This, plus the clientelistic initiatives of congressmen, makes the final budget unmanageable. The Finance Ministry handles it with considerable autonomy. Also, as mentioned above, inflation hopelessly outdates the original provisions, and the necessary supplementary credits are allocated by the Finance Ministry.

recent emergence of a cadre of professional economic administrators. These técnicos, with their greater expertise, performance orientation, and reputation for probity in public office, have become virtually indispensable as the administrative process has become more technical and instrumental. They, so the argument goes, have acquired greater job stability and more authority to initiate new policies. Consequently, they are less dependent on regional or national political clienteles. Small in number, but with similar educational backgrounds and considerable group consciousness, they have avoided a distinctive partisan identification and can be expected to serve various national regimes indiscriminately. Although their influence is felt in relatively few agencies, it is spreading—even to some agencies that have been notoriously clientelistic in the past—and is concentrated in such prominent organs as SUMOC, the Bank of Brazil, BNDE, the Ministry of Finance, and the Ministry of Planning.[11] As we shall see, association leaders are very much aware of the growing influence of this elite group of cadres and model their demands in terms of it. As Furtado notes, however, the appointments of these técnicos are still subject to political bargaining. So, presumably, is their tenure in office. For example, when in 1967 President Costa e Silva retained his predecessor's policy of appointing técnicos to higher administrative posts, he did not retain his predecessor's appointees; rather, he appointed men of his own confidence.[12] Often this meant no more than transferring them from one agency or department to another, but the point was clearly established: the técnicos, whatever their decisional autonomy once in office, hold that office at the discretion of the political elite of the moment. Even in cases where an agency is supported by earmarked funds and thus has a guaranteed measure of financial autonomy, it is not fully protected from shifts of political fortune.

The Administrative Arena

It is not easy to generalize about standard patterns of access and interaction with such a patchwork quilt of ministries, autarchic institutes, mixed (public-private) corporations, superintendencies, commissions, and public banks—formed at different times and for very different reasons, recruiting their employees by different criteria, rewarding them at different rates, and possessing very different degrees of decisional autonomy. There are, of course, points of general concentration in those polyfunctional agencies that deal with a wide variety of interests. The rule, however, is decentralization and specialization—discrete and relatively self-contained subsystems of mutual influence. Specific patterns of interaction between representative associations and administrative units thus vary greatly according to the characteristics of both. Let us now see how the sample of association leaders perceive the administrative target structure.

From both the written questionnaire and the personal interviews, the federal bureaucracy stands out unequivocally as the primary focus of Brazilian interest politics. It seems safe to say that, to the extent that they are organized to place demands upon or give support to political decision-makers (and most are or they would not have been in the sample), representative associations try to make themselves heard mainly by trying to influence administrative elites. Channels of access to other decision-makers are, of course, exploited, but for most these are worthy of only incidental or sporadic attention.

The Brazilian public administration is, as we have seen, far from being a uniform and well-coordinated unit. On the supposition that different types of associations would seek out and report different patterns of interaction, respondents were requested to list the administrative agencies with which they had the most frequent contact. These answers were subsequently coded and a separation was made between the primary and secondary contact (see Tables 12.1 and 12.2). The most important primary contacts for employers' associations are the Ministry of Finance and the Ministry of Planning, followed by the assorted specialized ministries. Even at the level of secondary contacts, the Ministries of Finance and Planning predominate. Given their importance as centers of interest conflict, it is surprising that the Bank of Brazil, the Central Bank, and the BNDE are not frequently cited as first contacts, although their importance picks up in the second round.[13] This is a reflection of the extent to which demands in these forums are handled directly by individual firms and economic groups rather than by representative associations. The low initial score for the Ministry of Industry and Commerce indicates the limited influence and status of that recent ministry, although as a secondary target it becomes more prominent, owing to the numerous industrial *grupos executivos* attached to it. As we might have expected, workers' organizations are virtually excluded from these forums of economic policy-making. For them the primary and for many the only point of contact with the administrative system is the Ministry of Labor and the Retirement and Social Welfare Institutes. The syndical employers' associations, predictably, have much higher primary and secondary contacts with those administrative bodies than do private employers' associations.* Liberal professional organizations, many of

---

* The few reported contacts of private associations may be due to the fact that some of the interviews with leaders of parallel organizations were coded as "private," not syndical, when the private group of which the respondent was a leader was national and the leader's syndicate was regional. Such "parallel" leaders do not always differentiate between their two roles, and in reporting the primary contact they may have been thinking of their syndical activities.

which are syndicates, also focus upon the Labor Ministry and the Institutes. Civic associations have a very distinctive interaction pattern, although the small number of respondents makes generalization hazardous. They have less contact with the financial and planning organizations than employers' associations, but are not completely absent from these arenas. They alone have rather important primary and secondary contacts with the military ministries. The relatively intensive interaction with the regulatory agencies reflects the efforts of the feminine associations to find a new role for themselves in consumer protection in postrevolutionary Brazil. They report more frequent meetings with the President of the Republic than any other type of group. Contact with the President seems to be an important second line of defense for workers' and liberal-professional groups, who initially address most, if not all, of their appeals to the Ministry of Labor. In the event of failure, they turn directly to the president. Employers' groups seem to have multiple lines of defense and report only scattered secondary contacts with the presidency.

TABLE 12.1

DIRECTION OF ASSOCIATIONS' PRIMARY CONTACT WITH EXECUTIVE
OR ADMINISTRATIVE AGENCY

(*percent*)

Agency	Employers		Workers ($N = 21$)	Liberal-profes-sional ($N = 10$)	Civic ($N = 11$)
	Syndical ($N = 27$)	Private ($N = 38$)			
President of the Republic and advisors	3.7%	0.0%	0.0%	0.0%	18.2%
Ministry of Labor and Social Welfare Institutes	14.8	2.6	85.7	60.0	9.1
Ministry of Finance and Ministry of Planning	40.7	34.2	0.0	10.0	18.2
Bank of Brazil, Central Bank, and BNDE	3.7	7.9	0.0	0.0	0.0
Ministry of Industry and Commerce and executive groups	0.0	5.3	0.0	0.0	0.0
Ministries of War, Navy, and Air Force	3.7	0.0	0.0	0.0	9.1
Other ministries[a]	22.2	26.3	0.0	10.0	18.2
Regulatory agencies[b]	0.0	13.2	0.0	0.0	18.2
Autarchies and institutes[c]	7.4	7.9	14.3	0.0	0.0
All other[d]	3.7	2.6	0.0	20.0	9.1

NOTE: Columns may not add to 100 because of rounding.

[a] Ministries of Transport and Public Works, Foreign Affairs, Justice, Education, Health, Mines and Energy, and Agriculture.

[b] SUNAB, CADE, Juntas Comerciais, and CONTEL.

[c] Petrobrás, IBC, IAA, Loide Brasileiro, etc.

[d] Inapplicable, Don't know, No answer, or No other administrative contact.

TABLE 12.2

DIRECTION OF ASSOCIATIONS' SECONDARY CONTACT WITH EXECUTIVE
OR ADMINISTRATIVE AGENCY

(*percent*)

Agency	Employers		Workers $(N = 21)$	Liberal-profes-sional $(N = 10)$	Civic $(N = 11)$
	Syndical $(N = 27)$	Private $(N = 38)$			
President of the Republic and advisors	3.7%	2.6%	9.5%	10.0%	9.1%
Ministry of Labor and Social Welfare Institutes	14.8	5.3	4.8	0.0	0.0
Ministry of Finance and Ministry of Planning	25.9	26.3	4.8	0.0	0.0
Bank of Brazil, Central Bank, and BNDE	11.1	13.2	0.0	0.0	9.1
Ministry of Industry and Commerce and executive groups	14.8	15.8	0.0	0.0	0.0
Ministries of War, Navy, and Air Force	0.0	0.0	0.0	0.0	9.1
Other ministries[a]	11.1	15.8	38.1	30.0	9.1
Regulatory agencies[b]	7.4	5.3	4.8	10.0	18.2
Autarchies and institutes[c]	3.7	0.0	9.5	0.0	0.0
All other[d]	7.4	15.8	28.6	50.0	45.4

NOTE: Columns may not add to 100 because of rounding.
[a] Ministries of Transport and Public Works, Foreign Affairs, Justice, Education, Health, Mines and Energy, and Agriculture.
[b] SUNAB, CADE, Juntas Comerciais, and CONTEL.
[c] Petrobrás, IBC, IAA, Loide Brasileiro, etc.
[d] Inapplicable, Don't know, No answer, or No other administrative contact.

Tables 12.3 and 12.4 show the same answers coded in terms of geographic scope and type of membership. The formal geographic scope of the association does not seem to have a very significant impact on its pattern of primary interaction. The only exception is that regionally based organizations see a bit more of the Ministries of Finance and Planning. This distinction persists at the level of secondary contacts, but other distinctions appear as well. The Bank of Brazil, the Central Bank, the BNDE, the executive groups, autarchies, and institutes also see more of the regional groups than of the national ones. On the other hand, the latter definitely interact more often with the assorted specialized ministries. The type of membership has a very decided influence on the interaction pattern. Peak associations with indirect membership have many more primary contacts with the Labor Ministry and secondary contacts with the President of the Republic, the various banks, and the assorted specialized ministries. Groups that directly represent member interests approach the Ministries of Finance and Planning and other

TABLE 12.3
DIRECTION OF ASSOCIATIONS' PRIMARY CONTACT WITH EXECUTIVE OR
ADMINISTRATIVE AGENCY ACCORDING TO GEOGRAPHIC SCOPE
AND TYPE OF MEMBERSHIP
(*percent*)

Agency	Geographic Scope		Type of Membership	
	National ($N = 71$)	Regional ($N = 36$)	Indirect ($N = 39$)	Direct ($N = 69$)
President of the Republic and advisors	2.8%	2.8%	2.6%	2.9%
Ministry of Labor and Social Welfare Institutes	28.2	25.0	59.0	10.1
Ministry of Finance and Ministry of Planning	18.3	38.9	17.9	29.0
Bank of Brazil, Central Bank, and BNDE	4.2	2.8	0.0	5.8
Ministry of Industry and Commerce and executive groups	1.4	2.8	0.0	5.8
Ministries of War, Navy, and Air Force	2.8	0.0	0.0	2.9
Other ministries[a]	19.7	16.7	10.3	23.2
Regulatory agencies[b]	7.0	5.6	0.0	10.1
Autarchies and institutes[c]	9.9	2.8	7.7	7.2
All other[d]	5.6	2.8	2.6	2.9

NOTE: Columns may not add to 100 because of rounding.
   [a] Ministries of Transport and Public Works, Foreign Affairs, Justice, Education, Health, Mines and Energy, and Agriculture.
   [b] SUNAB, CADE, Juntas Comerciais, and CONTEL.
   [c] Petrobrás, IBC, IAA, Loide Brasileiro, etc.
   [d] Inapplicable, Don't know, No answer, or No other administrative contact.

ministries more often in the first instance. Unfortunately, the limited number of responses makes further breakdown tenuous. These general observations on the differential concentrations of effort on the part of various types of associations are further confirmed by another manner of arranging the materials. The responses on the question of administrative contacts were subsequently coded according to the total number of contacts cited.* The resulting data are presented in Table 12.5. What was already beginning to appear in the earlier tables, the ability of the employers' associations to maintain a wide set of contacts and the confinement of workers' and middle-sector organizations to a relatively few agencies, now stands out dramatically. Syndical status seems to help in increasing the number of administrative contacts. This complements

* Coding posed one serious problem. Some respondents gave very detailed answers and mentioned numerous specific agencies. Others merely cited ministries. Given the autonomy of many of the agencies cited, I decided to code the detailed answers. This penalizes the vaguer respondents, who may actually have more contacts than they are credited with here.

my previous finding that private associations report more activity in the legislature. Perhaps this is because they are at least partially shut out of the administrative policy nexus.

Interviews were held with 38 higher administratve officials in most of the principal ministries, institutes, councils, commissions, regional development organizations, and public banks in an attempt to ascertain how they perceived the efforts of associations to influence their decisions. As the coding of the first question indicates (see Table 12.6), the civil servants were not exactly overjoyed with the performance. Slightly over one-fifth expressed their unqualified approval and some 16 percent their unqualified disapproval. More than half of the administrators gave mixed answers, indicating varying degrees and motives for dissatisfaction.

The most common complaints concerned the general lack of technical competence of the associations. "They are not equipped to represent the interests of the sector" was a rather typical statement. With few ex-

TABLE 12.4

DIRECTION OF ASSOCIATIONS' SECONDARY CONTACT WITH EXECUTIVE OR
ADMINISTRATIVE AGENCY ACCORDING TO GEOGRAPHIC SCOPE
AND TYPE OF MEMBERSHIP

(*percent*)

Agency	Geographic Scope		Type of Membership	
	National ($N = 71$)	Regional ($N = 36$)	Indirect ($N = 39$)	Direct ($N = 69$)
President of the Republic and advisors	5.6%	5.6%	10.3%	2.9%
Ministry of Labor and Social Welfare Institutes	5.6	8.3	7.7	5.8
Ministry of Finance and Ministry of Planning	14.1	22.2	12.8	18.8
Bank of Brazil, Central Bank, and BNDE	7.0	11.1	10.3	7.2
Ministry of Industry and Commerce and executive groups	8.4	11.1	2.6	13.0
Ministries of War, Navy, and Air Force	1.4	0.0	0.0	1.4
Other ministries[a]	23.9	13.9	25.6	17.4
Regulatory agencies[b]	8.4	5.7	7.7	7.2
Autarchies and institutes[c]	1.4	5.6	7.7	0.0
All other[d]	23.9	16.7	15.4	26.1

NOTE: Columns may not add to 100 because of rounding.
  [a] Ministries of Transport and Public Works, Foreign Affairs, Justice, Education, Health, Mines and Energy, and Agriculture.
  [b] SUNAB, CADE, Juntas Comerciais, and CONTEL.
  [c] Petrobrás, IBC, IAA, Loide Brasileiro, etc.
  [d] Inapplicable, Don't know, No answer, or No other administrative contact.

TABLE 12.5

NUMBER OF REPORTED CONTACTS WITH GOVERNMENT AGENCIES
BY TYPE OF ASSOCIATION

(*percent*)

| | Employers | | Other types | | | Total | |
| | | | | Liberal-profes- | | | All | All |
Number of contacts	Syndical ($N = 27$)	Private ($N = 38$)	Workers ($N = 21$)	sional ($N = 10$)	Civic ($N = 11$)	Syndical ($N = 47$)	Private ($N = 60$)
One	3.8%	7.9%	28.6%	30.0%	27.3%	12.8%	16.7%
Two	11.5	10.5	23.8	10.0	18.2	14.9	13.3
Three	7.7	10.5	14.3	20.0	0.0	12.8	8.3
Four	15.4	18.4	0.0	10.0	18.2	8.5	18.3
Five	15.4	15.3	4.8	10.0	0.0	10.6	11.7
Six	11.5	15.3	14.3	0.0	9.1	12.8	11.7
Seven	7.7	0.0	0.0	0.0	0.0	4.3	0.0
Eight or more	23.1	18.4	14.3	0.0	9.1	19.1	13.3
No answer, Don't know, Inapplicable	3.8	2.6	0.0	20.0	9.1	4.3	6.7

NOTE: Columns may not add to 100 because of rounding.

ceptions, the administrators agreed that the government was better
informed, both specifically and generally, than the associations. Certainly it did not depend on information supplied by the associations,
which was often characterized as "of a low intellectual level," "lacking
in real substance," "short-sighted," and "regionally distorted."[14] This
perception, however, appears to be changing; several respondents mentioned that the specialized industrial syndicates were increasing in both
dynamism and technical capacity. But the more general the association

TABLE 12.6

HIGHER CIVIL SERVANTS' OPINIONS OF REPRESENTATIVE
ASSOCIATIONS' PERFORMANCE

(*percent*)

Question	Yes, without qualification ($N = 9$)	Yes, with qualification ($N = 14$)	No, with qualification ($N = 6$)	No, without qualification ($N = 6$)	No answer, Don't know, Inapplicable ($N = 3$)
"Reflecting on the representative associations that have approached you, would you say they represent accurately and authentically the social sector they purport to?"	23.7%	36.8%	15.8%	15.8%	7.9%

is, and the higher it is in the syndical hierarchy, the less likely its advice is to be appreciated by administrators.[15] Respondents were virtually unanimous in agreeing that the exchange was unsatisfactory at the confederational level. Many cited the fact that the economic research departments of the national confederations had declined in capacity and authoritativeness. A high official in the Ministry of Finance noted that in the CNI the industrialists insisted on controlling not only the Economic (Research) Department but also all the official representations in the bureaucracy—with damaging results. Unless the representative was discussing an issue in his immediate branch of industry, he tended to be poorly equipped to understand, much less to control, what was being decided. He also pointed out that most of the CNI's formal representative posts were filled by men from the Federation of Industries of the State of Guanabara (FIEGA), not usually the largest or most authentic industrialists in the country.

The second most frequent complaints involved the type of demands made by associations: "too specific," "concerned only with small measures," "mere movements without substance," "too many palliatives," and "too many special favors." Associations at all levels were repeatedly criticized for their immediatism, i.e. their unwillingness or inability to take a longer or broader perspective. As one official in the Central Bank phrased it, "They don't anticipate; they only react."[16] In the words of a técnico in one of the industrial *grupos executivos*, "They don't use any sort of preventive medicine."[17] Several respondents accused the associations of being excessively short-sighted, not only in the substance of their demands, but in the way the demands were handled. "They tend to get demoralized very fast and run screaming to the newspapers."[18] This tactic of attempting to bypass or override the técnicos by recourse to public opinion or higher political authority is resented by the técnicos, who stress the desirability and possibility of working out such conflicts without bringing in outsiders. One official in the Ministry of Industry and Commerce related to me in some detail an initiative he had voluntarily made to simplify commercial procedures. He requested the collaboration of a number of the national and local businessmen's associations, syndical and private, inviting them to join a ministerial working group. He received no answer from them, and, when he went ahead with the study, he was attacked in the press—at, he felt, the instigation of these "threatened" associations.[19]

Some of the sharpest criticisms were leveled at the quality of leadership in the associations. Several respondents pointed out that most of the class leaders were secondary figures in their respective fields and that the most capable and representative ones were too busy to participate. The top echelons of the semiofficial workers' and employers' associations had been taken over by "the professionals of syndicalism," men who had no authority and who were not above defending their personal interests before those of the sector they represented. Again, the administrators recognized that the situation was changing and that a new generation of leaders was emerging, especially in the private associations. The administrators seemed to welcome these new leaders, whom they considered more genuinely concerned with their sectors and less timid and dependent upon the government.

The fact that associational leadership is not accepted as representative and authoritative makes it difficult for the técnicos to gauge the real or potential impact of their policies. The associations themselves have no institutionalized means for assessing and interpreting the opinions of entire sectors. The result, as one respondent put it, is that the leadership abdicates its responsibility and permits the association to be used to express the views of an adversely affected minority of its members. The majority, which may be favorably or neutrally affected, remains silent. The associations therefore appear in the decision-making context as almost perpetually negative and far more conservative than their members actually are. One suspects, although the interview evidence is inconclusive on this point, that higher administrators, aware of this representational distortion, tend to resort to informal contacts with individual members whom they regard as representative of the affected sector in order to gauge the intensity of reaction to their policies. Factionalism, either within an association or between associations in the same sector, also weakens the influence of associational demands.* Personalistic leadership, especially when used for *promoção pessoal* (personal advancement—economic, social, or political), has tarnished the image of many associations in the eyes of administrators.

As was the case with the congressmen, however, the observer should not confuse dissatisfaction at the actual performance of representative associations with a rejection of the legitimate role of these associations in the decision-making process. The administrators were asked the following open-ended question: "What do you feel should be the relations between representative associations and public agencies?" Their answers were coded and recorded as shown in Table 12.7. Respondents who stated that the government should be free to select those interest representatives it regarded as authentic or that associations should be

---

* Several administrators cited the "confusion" created by splits between the various industrial federations and between them and the CNI. Others mentioned the long-standing feud between the CNC and the Commercial Association of Rio. Internal factionalism has also weakened the potential role of the rural associations, according to other administrative informants.

TABLE 12.7
ADMINISTRATORS' PHILOSOPHY OF ASSOCIATIONS

Type of philosophy	No. of administrators	Percent
Pure liberalism (freedom of action without guaranteed access)	7	18.4%
Liberal corporatism (freedom of action with guaranteed access)	17	44.8
Corporatist liberalism (restricted freedom of action without guaranteed access)	5	13.2
Pure corporatism (restricted freedom of action with guaranteed access)	7	18.4
Individualism (special interests should not participate or be consulted)	1	2.6
No answer, Don't know	1	2.6

independent of the government and permitted to seek access wherever they desire were coded as "pure liberalists." This point of view was well captured by the following response: "Yes, associations have asked for a permanent seat in the agency [an industrial *grupo executivo*], but I advised them against it. They would only be compromised by its decisions. Also, I prefer to listen to whomever I please. I like them on the other side of the counter, so to speak."[20] The "liberal corporatists" were those who felt that the associations should be free to run their own affairs and make the demands they saw fit, but should be brought into the administrative process in a more institutionalized manner. This point of view was well expressed by the administrator of another *grupo executivo*, who said, "These entities should assume part of the responsibility for government decisions. . . . I worked hard to get class representatives in the *grupo*. Before they were outside and merely complained. Now they participate and cooperate. The system has worked well."[21] The "corporate liberalists" are the most difficult group to categorize. With varying degrees of intensity, they recognized the desirability of controlling the "special interest" activities of associations in the name of the common good, but were unwilling to grant these groups any special, privileged access to their deliberations. Respondents in this category were particularly anxious to restrict associational activities to the defense of immediate interests and to restrain members from taking part in movements or campaigns aimed at attaining broader societal objectives. Like the "individualists," they do not seem to value the supports and demands of associational activities as important components of the political process. Unlike the individualists, they accept the need for such special interest congregations as instruments of social control. The "pure corporatists" in the sample were as numerous as the pure liberalists. To them, the associations should be sponsored and controlled by the government, either because sponsorship and control were needed for any associations to exist at all or because their activity, if not curbed, would endanger the common good. This policy, they claimed, was legitimated by Brazil's political culture ("We have traditionally been dependent on the center, on a single leader. ... we are not accustomed to deciding things for ourselves") or by political expedience ("In São Paulo any sort of solution for sindicalismo would work, owing to the higher cultural and educational level, but in the rest of Brazil, the *coronel* runs things, and he would take over if the state did not intervene; if not, the Communists and Catholics would fight it out and the associations would disappear").[22] Only one respondent in the sample expressed the pure "individualist" point of view that the government should not listen to such secondary sources of opinion, but should consult those individuals and firms directly affected. None took the anticipated pure "collectivist" view that government officials had no business listening to such special and selfish interests, but should consult only their consciences or the people as a whole.

The small number of respondents makes breakdowns according to type of agency, age, regional origin, or educational background rather meaningless. As a rule, however, it would appear that those with a legal or literary background tended to be older and tended to cluster in the corporate liberalist and pure corporatist categories. The younger and more technically trained tended to be liberalists or liberal corporatists. This two-dimensional distinction also tended to coincide with administrative position. The Ministry of Labor seems to have older people with a legal background who are decidedly (and understandably) corporatist; whereas the Ministry of Planning, the public banks, the executive groups, and the Ministry of Industry and Commerce seem to recruit younger people with more liberalist views on associational interaction. In between are those from other ministries and the production institutes, who make up the bulk of the corporatist liberalists and some of the liberal corporatists. The only individualist came from the Ministry of Justice and Internal Affairs, which has little formal contact with organized interests. These generalizations are tentative, however, and should be the subject of future research and reformulation.

Despite the great disparities among them, Brazilian administrators as a whole seem to be rather open and receptive to collective expressions of interest and attitude,* although they are often critical of the quality of these expressions. They definitely have more experience with and

---

* This, of course, confirms some of my earlier observations on their role subculture and its fundamental similarity to that of the association leaders.

knowledge about associational activities than the congressmen. They too, however, vary considerably in the degree to which they consider these associations influential. Some administrators saw them as well organized and aggressive, with an authoritative leadership capable of regimenting and aggregating sectorial opinion, important and prominent factors to be dealt with in any decisions relative to their interests. This perception was concentrated in the production institutes (coffee, maté, sugar and alcohol, and pinewood) and in certain agencies charged with regulating prices and conditions in a specialized sector, such as the National Petroleum Council (CNP), the National Council on Telecommunications (CONTEL), the Merchant Marine Commission (CMM), and the Planning Commission for National Coal (CPCN). In these specialized, vertical agencies, some of which have important foreign participation, the administrators dealt (often at a disadvantage) with articulate, technically skilled, collective spokesmen.[23]

Other administrators, those in the new sectorial executive groups and in the horizontal, polyfunctional agencies charged with budgeting, planning, tax collection, credit and monetary policy, and general price control, consider the associations much less formidable either as collaborators or as opponents. These agencies are dominated by técnicos who are much more consciously concerned with the national interest and with global rational economic performance. Thus they tend to find the associations badly organized, internally fragmented, led by unrepresentative figures, and poorly equipped technically. Nevertheless, they by no means regard collective expressions of special interest as illegitimate.[24] They are aware of the need for accurate information and lament the fact that so many associations are incapable of providing it: "The government wants to listen to the demands of the class associations, . . . especially in my field [foreign trade policy], but it is impossible to hear all of them. Therefore, it must depend on the confederations, which unfortunately don't always represent the general interest of their sectors."[25] Also it occasionally became evident during the interviews that técnicos resented the fact that the associations were not very reliable or enthusiastic supporters of the government agencies acting in their behalf. In the interagency and interministerial squabbles over competences and credits, they could not always count on assistance or *cobertura* from excessively dependent and timid representative associations.[26]

The technically competent and performance-oriented Brazilian administrator is, by and large, disappointed with the performance of the representative associations that have approached him. To the extent that they impede his progress, they do so largely by sins of omission rather than by sins of commission. The técnico is accessible to groups, but his conception of the ideal role for these organizations is rather restricted. He is quite certain he does not want the well-organized, aggressive, and independent interest representative enshrined in the pure liberal model of pluralist politics. Nor does he want him to be an unrepresentative, dependent, inhibited, and conformist actor of the pure corporatist model. He wants a group actor who will not only provide reliable information on demands and consistent demonstrations of support for agencies operating in his interest, but also will moderate these demands in terms of a broader national interest and will anticipate crises and offer preventive medicine. In short, the técnico wants the associational actor to behave as he imagines himself to behave.[27]

The efforts of associations to influence public policy made in the administrative sphere are much more frequent, regular, and concerted than those used to influence legislative behavior. In one major aspect, however, the efforts are similar. In neither case are the associations in a position to command favorable decisions or threaten sanctions for noncompliance. With few exceptions, they come as clients, consultants, negotiators, plaintiffs, or defendants—not as owners, bosses, judges, or even arbitrators of public policy.[28]

As was the case with the legislature, associations have not been markedly successful in directly determining the selection of administrative personnel. Some prominent industrialists, businessmen, and bankers have been appointed to high office, and a few of these had previously been active in their representative associations. Asked, "Have any of your leaders or members held important public office?," many employers' and professional associations could reel off a name or two. However, when probed, the respondents usually revealed that the association had not named the appointee for the job, nor had it even played a major supporting role.[29] As a rule, appointed high officials are much less dependent upon representative associations than the latter are upon the former. Indeed, there is nothing quite so pathetic and hopeless as an interest leader who knows or suspects that the minister, secretary (or minister at the state level), executive director, or regional delegate with whom he must deal is unsympathetic to him personally or to his cause—unless it is the leader who is persona non grata to the President of the Republic or the Governor of the state. Such publicly "burned" leaders are usually dumped by their followers without ceremony. Nor have associations been noticeably successful in causing modifications in the administrative structure designed to facilitate their own interests. Almost every Brazilian group has at least one function it would like to see transferred to another ministry or one agency it would like to see created, made more independent, or destroyed.* The Ministry of Agriculture does seem to have been created at the insistence of the National Society of Agriculture (SNA), as I mentioned above. After thirteen years of pleading, the "productive classes" managed to get Industry and Commerce separated from Labor, but they failed to get the control of the activities of employers' syndicates transferred at the same time. They must still report to the Labor Ministry, just as the workers' syndicates do. Medical and pharmaceutical associations have been trying unsuccessfully for years to get welfare services switched from the Ministry of Labor to the Ministry of Health.†

Frontal attacks by representative associations on various government agencies with charges of inefficiency, politicking, corruption, and subversion have rarely succeeded. One might have supposed that the "revolution" of 1964 would have afforded an opportunity to those groups supporting it to settle old scores. However, very few agencies were actually destroyed, and such prime targets as the Price Control Commission (SUNAB), the Coffee Institute (IBC), the regional development agencies (SUDENE, SPVEA, Fundação Brasil Central), the Drought Control Department (DNOCS), and the petroleum monopoly (Petrobrás) survived without so much as a name change. The extensive administrative reform bill and numerous decrees of the last months of the Castelo Branco regime did reshuffle a number of functions and abolish some of the most manifestly derelict agencies, but there is no evidence that this was done in response to the prompting of affected representative associations.

The efforts of associations to influence the selection of administrative personnel is generally felt at a lower level, through a tactic confidentially referred to by their leaders as *infiltração* (infiltration). At its simplest, *infiltração* involves providing a poorly staffed or poorly equipped agency with a needed secretary, typewriter, mimeograph machine, or, that most inaccessible piece of equipment, a telephone. More important and much more frequent is the practice of loaning out technical personnel to government agencies for extended periods of time. These economists, statisticians, engineers, accountants, and lawyers continue to receive their associational salaries as well as their new official ones.‡ It is difficult to

* In the words of one interviewed leader, "The ideal would be for every association to have its own government agency to look out for its interests."

† It is hardly any wonder that one of the interviewees in the Labor Ministry observed bitterly, "We have to be wary here. This is the most contested ministry in the entire government."

‡ The Federation of Industries of the State of Guanabara had the good fortune to find that one of its staff economists was the son-in-law of the man unexpectedly

estimate the payoff of this tactic in terms of public policy. A check of the payroll of one of the major national confederations revealed a substantial number of employees on loan to government agencies, some for as long as several years. When queried about the effect of this practice, most association leaders claimed that it was primarily a matter of courtesy, that when a particular man was asked for it was impolite (and impolitic) to refuse, but that they did not go about soliciting such contacts. Furthermore, they denied that this gave them any particular leverage on policy; these men were técnicos and did not take orders from the association. They did admit that it was useful to have a man on the inside who could keep them well informed and who could see that their *processos* were passed along to the proper sequence of authorities.

Associations also have other inside men. Employees of both workers' and employers' associations frequently supplement their income and their status with government jobs. As I mentioned above, authority groups have made a more or less systematic practice of co-opting and rewarding loyal trade union leaders by offering them public employment. For employers' leaders, such opportunities are less attractive, although a substantial number also have held jobs in the federal, state, and local bureaucracies. Opinion was divided among the leaders concerning the usefulness and effectiveness of inside men. Once a very large proportion of the associations' employees were simultaneously working for the government they tended to adopt its career perspectives and work habits. An association that overly encouraged or proved incapable of preventing double employment would find itself becoming a parasitic *cabide de emprego* (hatstand for jobs).*

Pantouflage, or the transfer of civil servants to important positions in corresponding representative associations, is practiced a bit differently in Brazil than in France. In France, they resign in order to take up their new private positions. Brazil maintains no such rigid distinction between the public and the private, and the co-opted civil servant usually keeps his government job while he works part time for a representative association. Also, a substantial number of the higher administrative personnel in the associations are retired government employees who pre-

---

named to the presidency after the 1964 coup. He received full pay during the entire Castelo Branco regime as special advisor to the President of the Republic, and FIEGA enjoyed unparalleled access.

* Associations varied considerably in their willingness to discuss the extent to which their leaders, members, and employees had penetrated the public administration. Some, like the National Union of Cooperatives, are openly proud of the large number of their supporters throughout the Ministry of Agriculture; others are a bit reluctant to admit any sort of *infiltração*. The number of infiltrated supporters is no sure index to potential influence. Some associations, e.g. the Association of Christian Managers (ADCE), have single, highly placed advocates who can be counted on to intercede on their behalf elsewhere in the system.

sumably retain their personal contacts and intimate knowledge of the agencies from whence they came. Several interviewees mentioned a growing propensity for both firms and economic groups as well as representative associations to hire retired military officers. But I personally observed only a few cases of this—all in the transportation and communications fields, which the Brazilian military have traditionally controlled.

Most of the contact between representative associations and the public administration consists of routine transmission and exchange of information. Syndicates, of course, must make several reports a year in order to maintain their special status. They are also called upon to furnish information on prices, employment, production, investment intentions, etc. Associations of all types serve as advisors, "administrative lawyers," and *despachantes* for their affiliates or individual members, helping to file *processos* and guide them through the bureaucratic maze. It is in this routine activity that it is most useful to have an inside man. Only he can be expected to know the course that the flow of paperwork will take and where a given *processo* will be at a given time. Only he can know what additional incentive may be necessary to get a document "unfrozen" or an approval signed. As LaPalombara has observed, "interest groups thrive in administrative situations that are muddy and confused."[30] The association with a reputation for being able to cut through the unbelievable complexity of the Brazilian administrative process has a valuable asset to offer its affiliates and members. Of course, they have no monopoly on this function. Specialized classes of labor lawyers, administrative lawyers, and *despachantes* are available to those who can pay, and large firms often purchase the exclusive services of such specialists.

With few exceptions, employers' representative associations have not maintained extensive staffs for the planning and drafting of specific investment projects and requests for long-term credit. This work is largely performed by specialized firms, the most famous of which is CONSULTEC. Again, the associations find themselves cut out of a potentially influential activity. On the other hand, the syndicates and, to a certain extent, the private entities are frequently used by administrative groups for the dissemination of "authoritative coordinations" to individuals and firms. During World War II, not only were they used as conduits for the transmission of government policies, but they were also charged with helping administer many of these policies, such as rationing, price control, industrial mobilization, and regulation of imports and exports. Gradually, these tasks were either dropped altogether or transferred to the exclusive competence of government bodies. Even in performing this communications function, syndicates, federations, and confederations have no monopoly. They are used often, but public agencies have on occasion addressed themselves directly to interested individuals and firms. Quite frequently, they bypass the peak associations and deal directly with the specialized groups.* At any rate, this process of exchanging information affords associations many possibilities for exerting some influence on the modification of existing policies, if not for initiating or vetoing policies. In areas like price control, where government resolve is weak, it may be possible to alter the policy drastically, either by denying collaboration or by becoming the exclusive furnisher of that information. In other areas where criteria are ambiguous (for example in preferential exchange rates and protection against import competition), the provision of information may become an instrument for the modification of policy. For example, since 1911 national producers have gained more and more protection on goods registered as nationally produced in "sufficient quality and quantity." In the 1950's one could get not only increased tariff protection, but also a specially disadvantageous foreign exchange treatment for goods so registered. Lincoln Gordon points out that "the precise meaning of 'sufficient quality and quantity' of production required to justify registration as a similar has always been flexible, and subject to a great deal of administrative discretion" and that "the law of similars has been a most powerful incentive."[31] Ordinarily, determination of the fulfillment of these criteria is the subject of confidential and discrete negotiations between the interested firm and the Council on Tariff Policy (CPA), with the respective industrial syndicate, the federation, and the CNI playing key roles,[32] and the issue is rarely taken beyond that forum.†

This process of exchanging information and opinion through perma-

* In fact, several técnicos mentioned that the industrial employers' syndicates resented being informed through the CNI or state federations and insisted on direct communication. As I mentioned above, técnicos tend to have a much more favorable opinion of the representativeness and capacity of these lower-level entities than of the peak associations. Some associations, e.g. those representing cement, coal, iron ore, textiles, machines, automobiles, auto parts, petroleum distribution, pharmaceuticals, and acceptance companies, are seen as providing quite reliable and virtually exclusive data on their respective sectors. In these sectors, the syndicates or associations are better informed than the government and can use that information to gain influential leverage.

† Once this issue of sufficient production did get a "public hearing." The agency directly involved was not the CPA but the CACEX, the foreign trade section of the Bank of Brazil. The national tin can manufacturers, with the assistance of their syndicate and industrial peak associations, ran a strong and successful press campaign against favorable treatment for the importation of machinery for the American Can Company. Presumably, it took the issue to the wider forum because it feared it could not control the outcome at the discrete administrative level. Normally, however, the industrialist respondents felt that such decisions were "mutually satisfactory."

nent representatives on consultative councils, commissions, and executive groups will be discussed below in greater detail. It is not, however, the only or the most efficient channel of interaction between the two sets of actors. I have already noted that there are three points of concentration in the policy-making process: the drafting of a proposal, the executive approval, and the regulation of a law or decree. Most proposals initiate with the public bureaucracy, and, as we shall see, direct access to the President is sporadic and rather unpredictable. Since all measures must ultimately be interpreted and converted into specific obligations and administrative competences, *elaboração* and *regulamentação* are very strategic points of attempted penetration. They are also points at which the influence of the técnico is greatest. Some drafting and even more regulation is done in permanent consultative bodies. But most of both goes on behind closed doors in inconspicuous ad hoc working groups. All associations want to be informed when a decision has been made to sponsor an initiative in their area of interest, so that they can have one of their men appointed to the drafting and regulating groups. As one business leader put it, "Once we're there, our influence becomes invisible. The proposal then goes out as an executive project . . . that is sure to pass without question."[33] Association leaders admitted that access to the drafting state is the most advantageous, but added that it is also the most difficult. Técnicos, they felt, resisted this penetration of their prerogatives.[34] The regulating stage is, association leaders conceded, easier to reach and currently the most productive point of influence.[35] Precisely because projects are drafted "in closets," discussed only by incompletely informed técnicos, jammed through a subservient legislature at high speed, or decreed by a trusting President immediately, the resulting laws are frequently "inapplicable, unrealistic, and contradictory." Consequently, it is often possible to play off one ministry or agency against another at the regulation stage, or to get substantial modifications made on the grounds of feasibility and practicality.[36]

The key to successful participation in this informal setting is *confiança*, or confidence on the part of the drafting or regulating administrators in the personal integrity, authenticity, and conscientiousness of the interest representative. Of course he must also be able to furnish reliable information on the opinions, intensities, probable responses, and moods of his followers. In these subtle consultations and negotiations, legal formal recognition is no guarantee of access or influence; leaders from private associations are just as likely to be invited to participate as syndical leaders. Those associations that manage to inspire the most confidence in high administrative personnel possess and exercise the most influence over policy outcomes relative to their interests. Nevertheless, it bears stressing that the terms of the encounter are usually set by the administrative elites—by their professional and technical standards, by their ideological leanings, by their concept of the public good, or by their clientelistic political dependencies. They are not determined by the organized, functionally specific interests of the society and the economy, as the more simplistic versions of the group theory of politics would have it.

The Brazilian public administration is characterized by a weak centralized executive control, by a large number of functionally specialized and autonomous agencies, by the low prestige and performance motivation of its civil servants,* by an increasing number of government services and regulations, by the limited capacity of authorities to control policy implementation uniformly, and by the imperfect sources of information and poor means of communication within the system. This, combined with the special status accorded to syndicates, would seem to provide the perfect conditions for what Joseph LaPalombara has called a *clientela*, a relationship in which "an interest group, for whatever reasons, succeeds in becoming, in the eyes of a given administrative agency, the natural expression and representative of a given social sector, which in turn constitutes the natural target or reference point for the activity of the administrative agency."[37] Yet associational *clientelas* of this sort are relatively scarce in Brazil. There are few policy areas in which a government agency confronts a single, well-organized, technically efficient and functionally authoritative association perceived as aggregating those "interests strongly affected by [that] agency's activities and the principal source of [its] political support and opposition."[38] Brazilian government agencies do have their surrounding clienteles, but most of them are not associationally based. Some, like the Amazon Valley Superintendency (SPVEA), the Foundation for Central Brazil, the National Department of Works against Droughts (DNOCS), and the San Francisco Valley Commission (CVSF), consist of an agency and a regional political machine or a coalition of regional interests; others, like the national institutes for coffee (IBC), sugar and alcohol (IAA), maté (INM), salt (IBS), pinewood (INP), and rubber (Comissão Executiva da Defêsa da Borracha), consist of an agency and a cluster of individually organized growers, processors, and merchants. In these cases the clienteles are not organized into single entities, but are scattered in numerous associations, firms, families, and factions. The multiplicity of supporting and opposing organizations and the conflicts among them

---

* I am reminded of the sign I saw over a broken telephone in a bar near one of the ministries: "Não funciono, sou funcionário público" ("I don't work, I am a public employee").

have given the administrators of even the more clientelistic agencies a certain margin of autonomy. As a técnico in the IBC remarked during an interview, "In this sector, only by dividing can we expect to control the situation."

Why, if they seem to have so much going for them hypothetically, have these associational *clientelas* generally failed to take hold in Brazilian interest politics?* Despite the widespread prevalence of over-simplifications to the effect that the Brazilian public bureaucracy is a veritable *chasse gardée* for coffee growers, cattlemen, merchants, *comprador* industrialists, and foreign investors, the organized actors on both sides hardly see it that way themselves. LaPalombara makes a very shrewd observation that furnishes a clue: he notes that when an association is too thoroughly dependent upon the public administration, there will be no *clientela*, because there is no bargaining between independent actors.[39] In a *clientela* relationship, both parties must have a distinctive basis of influence (wealth, status, strategic location, legitimacy, numbers, etc.) and hence be capable of providing each other with some resource they could not gain more easily elsewhere. Put simply, most Brazilian representative associations have too little to offer the administration. This, of course, is because of the low density and lack of participation of their memberships, their oligarchic or unrepresentative leadership, and, especially for syndicates and federations, their subservience to authority groups.† The succession of manipulated elections, retractions from policy statements in the face of government pressures, subservience in exchange for personal rather than collective gains, and overt ministerial intervention have served to undermine the prestige

* This inevitably brings up the issue of "conjunctural political circumstances"—more specifically, the fact that during the entire period of the interviews Brazil was being ruled by a military dictatorship. I deliberately avoided asking direct questions concerning the immediate regime. Questions concerning actor perceptions were prefaced with "in general," "in your experience," "since you came to office," etc. Nevertheless, I was bound to pick up some conjunctural "static." Although from the administrative perspective surprisingly little had changed, at least in terms of general interaction patterns, the Castelo Branco regime was clearly seen as an exceptional one—overly technocratic and not very responsive to dialogue. Time and again, in private interviews and in public pronouncements, complaints were made that the *classes* were not being consulted, especially that they were not being consulted prior to the formal presentation or decreeing of executive projects. It is possible that the "estrangement" I detected between the associations and the técnicos was more related to these conjunctural circumstances than to long term trends, although I doubt it.

† One might add here that the syndical *enquadramento* often fragments interest representation excessively. Government planners prefer their data aggregated on a broader functional and geographic basis. It is rather difficult to consult all the 120 or more syndicates representing employers in the food processing industry or even the eighteen in the textile industry simultaneously.

of both worker and employer associations. This last factor undermines the loyalty of members and the respectability of the organization in the eyes of administrators, for whom contact with a syndical leader is often not rewarding in terms of status. Moreover, the associations in general have not kept up with the government's expanding capacity for technical analysis and information-gathering. One can understand, then, why técnicos fail to consider the existing representative associations their natural and legitimate clienteles. Some associations are seen as such distorted entities that they are not even regarded as meaningful channels for the downward flow of explanations about already elaborated public policy, much less for the upward transmission of demands.

There are also impediments on the side of administrative decision-makers to the establishment of lasting associational *clientelas*. For one thing, the agencies that have become important as a result of the policy changes of the 1950's and 1960's have tended to interact with a wide spectrum of interests. Conversely, the broad penetration of such government bodies as the Bank of Brazil, the BNDE, and lately, the Ministry of Planning make it increasingly difficult for a representative association to confine its activities to a single specialized agency. Furthermore, the practice of shunting técnicos about from one agency to another, and of appointing new department heads and executive secretaries with changes at the higher executive level[40] prevents the administrators from acquiring an independent power base and makes it difficult to establish long-lasting relationships of mutual influence.

I have repeatedly stressed the concentration of Brazilian representative associations upon incremental modifications in established policies and their relative incapacity or inactivity as far as the initiation or blockage of new policies is concerned—first in connection with the legislature, and later in connection with the public administration. The scarcity of stable *clientelas* between independently organized interests and autonomous government agencies is both evidence of this and a factor reinforcing it. For many of the same structural reasons impeding the emergence and maintenance of *clientelas*, the associations tend to define their objectives exclusively by short-term criteria. Inflation is a powerful reinforcer of this tendency. Immediate credit, wage increases, tax relief, favorable import rates or foreign exchange treatment, exemptions from social security charges, and price controls become the overriding preoccupations—matters of status survival—for interest leaders and their followers. Even though the tone of public debate may occasionally be set by fervent insistence upon and fanatic resistance to basic, long-term reforms, the substance of Brazilian interest politics consists overwhelmingly of demands for short-term, incremental satisfactions.[41] This naturally leads the associations to concentrate on those decisional centers where such demands can be immediately met—namely, the public administration.

As long as administrative elites themselves were solely preoccupied with their own short-term survival by means of immediate clientelistic satisfactions, there was an obvious mutual convergence of interest. However, with the emergence of a small group of reform-mongering técnicos and the conscious use of government policy to regulate the economy and effect development rather than to help maintain existing structures, and later, with the beginnings of intersectorial planning and administrative coordination, bureaucratic elites began asking for and accepting demands and supports that were more consistent, aggregative, representative, technical, and impersonal.

There seems to be a certain estrangement and misunderstanding in the relations between associations and administrative agencies. Interest representatives, although they were obviously used to greater access and receptivity in the past and are finding it increasingly difficult to establish mutually satisfactory relationships with higher government officials, do not seem aware (or will not admit their awareness to a prying outsider) of the degree of dissatisfaction with their activities prevalent in técnico circles. True, some have "retooled" themselves to handle the new standards imposed by the técnicos. Moreover, the pattern of interaction is in a state of transition, and the Brazilian public administration has become a difficult and confusing target for interest politicians. Although such técnico-dominated agencies as the Central Bank and the Ministry of Planning have expanded their influence, large sectors of the administrative process remain faithful to the tradition of the "sinecure state."[42] A given representative association, obliged to plead its case before several agencies, has to adapt its tactics and style to appeal to a very heterogeneous group of decision-makers. As one newspaper editorial said, it has become a *ponto pacífico*—an incontrovertible fact—that the performance of the public administration is grossly inadequate and requires drastic modification. "It does not help much to plan better and better for a machine that works worse and worse," lamented the administrator who was to become Costa e Silva's Minister of Planning.[43] The final legacy of the Castelo Branco regime was an ambitious scheme of administrative reform, and it is too early to assess whether it will suffer the same fate as its numerous formalistic predecessors.

The crystallization of interaction between formal interest groups and government agencies into something resembling *clientelas*, a pattern frequently characterized as neocorporatist, depends on internal changes within both sets of actors. If the associations acquire higher member participation, more representative leadership, greater technical capacity, and increased independence from the control of authority groups, and if the performance-minded técnicos in government agencies expand their sphere of policy control and acquire a greater sensitivity to the need for independent information and support, there may well be such a convergence. However, the probability of such a dual process of change depends also on the response of another very important actor in the system, the President of the Republic.

The Executive and Presidential Arenas

Since the "redemocratization" of 1945, only two Brazilian presidents have filled out their legal terms of office. Getúlio Vargas, in his famous suicide note, blamed his frustration and incapacity to rule on "the forces and interests against the people . . . newly coordinated and raised against me. . . . An underground campaign of international groups joined with national groups revolting against the regime of workers' rights." Seven years later, Jânio Quadros abdicated, accusing those "whose only goals are to subject the general needs of the nation to some ambitious groups and individuals from inside and also from outside. . . . Terrible forces came forward to fight me and to defame me by all their means, with the excuse that they were only trying to collaborate."[44] These accusations by occupants of the role itself conflict somewhat with the observations of outsiders to the effect that the Brazilian presidency is an office of great power and authority, the freewheeling hub of the entire political system, unchecked by higher juridical authority or by party or parliamentary discipline, independent of state or local authorities and of rigorously observed constitutional precedents.[45] Those in or close to the presidency tend to see it as possessing enough severe structural and situational limitations to reward its occupant with virtual impotency and grave frustration; those observing it from without tend to see it as possessing enormous structural and situational advantages that afford the successful petitioner a virtual guarantee of complete satisfaction.

The Brazilian President is, first and foremost, at the center of an enormous patronage system. Whether by conscious design on the part of the President himself or because the decision-making style minimizes the propensity for taking responsibility at the lower levels and maximizes the reluctance of higher personnel to delegate authority,[46] the most minute decisions must cross the President's desk. Applications for credit, tax exemptions, social security benefits, and special import treatment, as well as all government purchases, contracts, and appointments to employment, must be approved by him.[47] Because clientelistic politics and inflation contribute to make these the principal demands on the system, the politician or interest leader with good and direct access to the President is in an enviable position.

The Brazilian President is also at the center of an enormous communications network. In a society characterized by poor inter-elite communication and by regional and class discontinuities in the transmission of messages, the President is one of the few actors who is simultaneously receiving information from all over the system.[48] He is also an important producer as well as a consumer of information. The plebiscitary prominence of his office, his control over the national news agency, the subsidies and favors he systematically grants to owners and operators of the mass media, and the potential sanctions he can bring to bear for non-compliance combine to give the Brazilian chief of state a substantial capacity for news management. His capacity for determining the issue content of public debate, for planting desirable issues, and for suppressing undesirable ones is not unlimited, but it is formidable.*

Normally, the President is also the head of one of the major national parties. This advantage is somewhat lessened by the fact that no Brazilian chief executive since 1945 has been elected with the support of a majority party. However, by manipulating the twin networks of patronage and communications, he can usually construct and maintain a ruling coalition without having to resort to the use of force and police repression. Quadros was hampered by not being a party leader and also weakened because he sought to upset some of the standardized patronage systems. He quickly found that the halo of office was not enough to ensure that his hundreds of little notes (*bilhetinhos*) would be converted into effective policy. Goulart was a leader, but of a badly divided party. In seeking to reconcile the increasingly polarized factions of his own party (PTB), he lost the support of his coalition partner, the PSD, especially as elections approached. In his indecision and frustration, he belatedly turned to the decree-making power in order to circumvent the inviability of his legislative coalition. He also used threats of federal intervention in order to suppress the conspiratorial activities of the state governors. Castelo Branco, backed by the "revolutionary" authority of the First and Second Institutional Acts and by a fairly cohesive military organization, resorted frequently to autocratic measures in the face of

* Under Goulart the whole business got out of hand—as did so many other aspects of the political process. Brizola, his brother-in-law, had his own plebiscitary base, his own radio station (owned by the Ministry of Labor), and even his own periodical. On the right wing, state governors, elite indoctrination groups (e.g. IBAD), and attitude associations (e.g. CONCLAP), were massively subsidizing the media. Other politicians, especially the state governors, and some interest group leaders are also in the news manipulation business.

any real or imagined threats to his authority.[49] He dissolved the existing parties by decree and created a new coalition, the ARENA, which he has since passed on to his successor.

Representative associations do not appear to play a significant role in the selection of presidential candidates. It is true that at one time no fewer than three employers' association leaders were considered possible candidates: Euvaldo Lodi of the CNI, Roberto Simonsen of the FIESP, and João Daudt d'Oliveira of the Rio Commercial Association.* But this was because of the general uncertainty and the embryonic state of party organization prevailing in the late 1940's. Since then no potential presidential candidate has emerged from these sources, and nomination is the exclusive province of professional politicians and the military. Nor, as we have seen, are the associations important contributors to campaign chests (*caixinhas*) or manipulators of bloc votes. Most are likely to be split between several candidates, and few come out openly in favor of or against any particular one. The usual tactic is either to seek accommodation with all candidates or to abstain and then to declare after the election that they are willing to cooperate with the winner. Candidates appear before assemblies of interest groups, accept their petitions, and even publicly espouse group positions. But the dynamics of Brazilian electoral competition force candidates to appeal to a wide variety of regional and functional groupings, making the productivity of such gestures of support for specific groups rather problematical.† We have already seen that when it comes to making appointments to higher administrative office, the President is more accountable to regional political machines or to technical administrators than to specific interest associations.

Again we find representative associations, even those at the highest national level, on the outside looking in—pleaders for special treatment rather than commanders of general policy.‡ One of the rules of Brazilian

---

* Interviews with associates of the three confirmed that all had in fact considered the possibility of running. Simonsen, in fact, had already begun his move when death struck him down.

† Since the coup of 1964 the electoral process has become increasingly circumscribed. Elections are "postponed"; candidates are declared ineligible; nominations are overtly controlled by military leaders; elected officials are purged to ensure regime dominance. The principal "plebiscitary" contests have been made indirect, with election by the legislative body. This prolonged moratorium on democratic competitiveness might enhance the role of interest representatives, were it not for the fact that the military has tightened its control over their activities as well.

‡ The one functionally specific clientele group that does command policy in its sector and appointments within it is the military. However, its representative associations, the Military, Naval, and Aeronautical Clubs, are not the principal aggregators and articulators of this control. The military ministers are selected by their respective corporate hierarchies.

corporatism is that the leaders of the national employers' and employees' confederations must be acceptable to the President of the Republic. If not, either they are *marginalisados* (in Brazilian political jargon, sent to the margin, where they are expected to remain quiet and unobtrusive) or, should they actively oppose his policies, they are *afastados* (forced to resign). The confederation leader who seeks to make opposition to presidential policy his electoral platform will almost surely find himself manipulated out of contention.[50] When the "President's candidate" in these major class elections loses, as he did in 1964 in the CNTI and in 1952 in the Military Club, it is widely (and accurately) interpreted as a weakening of the President's authority.

The *confiança* of the chief executive in the leadership of a particular national confederation is by no means a guarantee of access and favorable response. When the leader already possesses considerable authority among the members, acquires a special prestige in the eyes of the President, and has his own political base (as did Euvaldo Lodi, for example), the relationship undoubtedly confers upon the association a degree of influence in public policy that it could not attain on its own. Where, however, the leader owes his associational position not to his "natural" representativeness within the class, but to his having been handpicked by the President, and where he has no political support of his own (as was the case with Haroldo Corrêa Cavalcanti, president of the CNI from 1962 to 1964), then the association tends to lose whatever influence it might have exerted independently.

The case of General Macedo Soares, the president of the CNI during the Castelo Branco regime, illustrates the ambiguous payoff of the mutual confidence relationship. The General is a highly respected former military classmate of Castelo Branco. Under the circumstances described above, he owed his election to the manipulations of the national President. Yet Macedo Soares was also a man of considerable *projeção* in industrialist circles—the builder of the Volta Redonda Steel Works, the president of Mercedes Benz do Brasil, and a vice president of the FIESP. He also had a political following of his own as ex-governor of the state of Rio de Janeiro, a former member of the PSD, and, subsequently, a member of the national directory of the ARENA. This combination of resources gave him a facility of direct access and what the Brazilian jargon calls *atendimento* (attention) not shared by any other national class leader. Nevertheless, on two occasions when the CNI, under pressure from industrialists and his own technical staff, produced statements sharply criticizing the regime's economic policy, the General had to back down and eventually disown them. By exerting pressure on individual industrialists and on member federations (especially the

FIEGA), the government was able to force a public withdrawal that had very demoralizing effects on the aggrieved parties. It is true that some of the industrialists' demands were met (rather surreptitiously) and some policy modifications were introduced as a result of the exchange. Nevertheless, the example demonstrates that a relationship of personal confidence between a national association leader and the President of the Republic is a two-way channel of influence, or, to use another metaphor, a double-edged sword honed in favor of the latter.[51]

Frequent direct contact between associations and the President is not widespread. Table 12.8, compiled from information also found in Tables 12.1–4, provides data on the interaction patterns of various types of associations. Only the civic associations, especially the right-wing feminine ones, seem to have enjoyed unparalleled direct access. Employer syndical entities seem to have greater intimacy with the chief executive than do corresponding private ones, simply because the former are closer to the policy-making process. The frontline contact for workers' organizations is unquestionably the Ministry of Labor and the Social Welfare Institutes, but the relatively high rate of secondary contacts reported indicates the extent to which the President is called upon to resolve directly and personally wage conflicts and disputes over the Labor Code. Similarly, middle-sector associations report frequent secondary contact. This consists in large part of civil servants' organizations pleading for salary increases to the President, who alone has the power to initiate such a move. Rather surprisingly, formally national associations are no more likely to have their primary contact with the President

TABLE 12.8
ASSOCIATIONS' FIRST AND SECOND CONTACTS WITH THE
PRESIDENT OF THE REPUBLIC
(*percent*)

Association	First contact	Second contact
Type		
Employers' ($N = 65$)	1.5%	3.1%
Syndical ($N = 27$)	3.7	3.7
Private ($N = 38$)	0.0	2.6
Workers' ($N = 21$)	0.0	9.5
Liberal-professional ($N = 10$)	0.0	10.0
Civic ($N = 11$)	18.2	9.1
Geographic scope		
National ($N = 71$)	2.8	5.6
Regional ($N = 36$)	2.8	5.6
Membership		
Indirect ($N = 39$)	2.6	10.3
Direct ($N = 69$)	2.9	2.9
TOTAL ($N = 108$)	2.8	5.6

than are formally regional ones, although this finding is distorted by the relatively high frequency reported by civic associations, which are regionally based. Federations and confederations score higher on the second round, but in terms of primary contacts, the type of membership does not appear to be a differentiating factor. Globally speaking, the interaction pattern is one of infrequent and sporadic contact with the President, even though such access is highly prized and much sought after. The problem is that most Brazilian associations can get to the chief executive only by negotiating for a formal audience.[52] According to statistics released by the Office of the President, during the first one thousand days of his regime Castelo Branco granted 1966 audiences to congressmen, approximately 600 to his military ministers, 325 each to the Minister of Planning and the Minister of Justice, and only 84 to workers' organizations and 74 to student groups.[53]

Another way of reaching the President is by written correspondence. The Brazilian chief executive received some 80,000 letters in the twelve months following the 1964 coup[54] and 105,000 by November 1965. However, only 3,128 came from private associations, syndicates, federations, and confederations. Table 12.9 shows the geographical distribution as well as the institutional source of this mail. The developed states of São Paulo, Guanabara, and Minas Gerais have a disproportionate share. One-third of the mail from private associations and syndicates comes from paulistas; one-third of the mail from peak associations comes from Rio.

TABLE 12.9

SEVENTEEN MONTHS' LETTERS TO THE PRESIDENT OF THE REPUBLIC,
BY REGIONAL AND ASSOCIATIONAL SOURCE

Region and selected states	Private associations ($N = 1,610$)	Syndicates ($N = 925$)	Confederations and federations ($N = 593$)	Total ($N = 3,128$)
North	4.3%	3.0%	4.6%	4.0%
Northeast	14.3	21.5	14.0	16.4
Pernambuco	3.9	6.7	4.2	
Bahia	3.0	4.4	2.0	
Center-East	56.7	59.1	62.6	58.5
Minas Gerais	14.1	10.5	7.1	
Rio de Janeiro	3.9	4.2	1.3	
Guanabara	7.3	10.9	33.7	
São Paulo	30.7	33.4	18.9	
South	20.3	12.9	16.5	17.4
Paraná	8.6	1.7	7.1	
Santa Catarina	5.9	5.1	1.3	
Rio Grande do Sul	5.8	6.0	8.1	
Center-West	4.3	3.3	2.4	3.7

SOURCE: Personal correspondence from Dr. Luis Navarro de Britto, Gabinete Civil, Presidência da República, Dec. 17, 1965.
NOTE: Columns may not add to 100 because of rounding.

The Northeast is quite underrepresented, with 16 percent of the associational correspondence and 32 percent of the population. The North, South, and Center-West all manage to hold their own. These observations confirm my earlier data on the greater number of associations in the developed areas and the greater degree of member participation. By percentaging Table 12.9 along its horizontal axis one discovers that, surprisingly, the private associations (including the semipublic rural associations) sent Castelo Branco 51.4 percent of his associational mail, whereas the syndicates contributed only 29.6 percent. Only in a few Northwestern states did the syndical requests outstrip the private ones. The category "confederations and federations" is preponderantly syndical, although there are enough private entities with that title to make generalizations hazardous. Globally speaking, the peak associations supplied 19 percent of Castelo Branco's associational mail. One might hypothesize that the nationally relevent syndicates and peak associations usually possess intermediaries who will intercede directly on their behalf.

The role of direct interaction between representative associations and the President has varied over time, just as the political atmosphere has varied from the personalism and informality that characterized the Vargas and Goulart regimes to the isolation and authoritarianism of Quadros' brief reign. Viewed in historical perspective, however, the offices of the President have become increasingly bureaucratized, and the exchange of demands and supports surrounding it have become more and more formalized. The variety and scope of interests seeking direct access have expanded, though in recent years something like a rationalization and simplification of relations has occurred. A number of administrative agencies that formerly reported directly to the President have been, at least theoretically, subordinated to some intermediary authority, usually a ministry.* A super-ministry has begun to emerge, that of Planning and Economic Coordination. This provides a sort of intermediary stage for the examination, selection, and preliminary processing of demands that formerly went directly to the chief executive. Another variable affecting the desirability of direct contact as far as association leaders are concerned is the President's relations with his ministers and higher administrative officers. Brazilian presidents have varied considerably in the autonomy and discretion they have permitted their ministers. As we have seen, there is a clearly discernible trend toward selection on the basis of technological skills. However, this has not brought an increase in administrative autonomy; técnicos seem to depend a great

* In fine Parkinsonian fashion, the number of ministries has increased steadily to its present 23.

deal on the personality and political career of the President. One can certainly hypothesize that should the former trend persist, the extent of decentralized decisional autonomy would increase, and the importance of access to the President would decrease.

My data on interaction patterns suggest that the Brazilian political system is characterized by a greater multiplicity and variety of points of access than has commonly been assumed. Despite its populist predominance, its substantial capacity to determine the nature of issues, the content of public debate, and the outcome of public policy, the presidency is by no means the only or even the most frequent point of contact representative associations have with the political system. The bulk of their satisfactions and dissatisfactions are treated elsewhere. One of the most remarkable characteristics of the system is its decentralized and uncoordinated capacity for absorbing conflict. A wide variety of arrangements, some institutionalized like the labor courts and the consultative councils, others more erratic and informal like the patronage systems and the ad hoc drafting and regulating committees, operate to resolve problems by co-optation and conciliation—before they can become the objects of group mobilization and dramatization at the national level.[55]

The system does not work perfectly, needless to say, and the performance of recent years seems to demonstrate that it is under considerable strain. Once a group conflict breaks into the open and threatens a rupture in the usual norms of conciliation or a possible outbreak of violence —and this occurred with increasing frequency in the early 1960's—the President of the Republic must intervene directly. Thus one finds him sporadically initiating and decreeing a new minimum wage (when legally this should be handled by a technical commission), traveling to a remote area to sign personally a collective labor agreement to end an illegal strike (which should have been resolved by a labor court sentence), calling the planters and processors of sugar into his office to force an agreement (which is properly in the domain of the Sugar and Alcohol Institute), decreeing the export regulations for coffee (when this is a matter delegated to the Coffee Institute), etc. Failure to intervene or persistent incapacity to resolve such public conflicts undermines his authority and, perhaps, his tenure in office. But the rule is certainly to avoid such personal involvement and responsibility and to leave these matters to other important decision-makers as much as possible.

A deviant case may serve to illustrate the point. Abelardo Jurema, in his insider's account, provides the clue to an important weakness in the Goulart presidency. First, he observes that Kubitschek owed the relative social tranquility of his regime—the limited extent and short duration of strikes, for example—to the fact that his vice-president, João Goulart, was in control of the Ministry of Labor.

The same could not happen in Goulart's government, because he, as President of the Republic, did not have a president of the PTB who could speak coarsely and frankly to his coreligionists. He himself had to resolve all the disputes, wasting himself first among the workers. It is difficult for the President of the Republic and president of the PTB to coexist peacefully and profitably in the same person. The one who demanded the maximum would be up against the one who could only concede the possible; the one who acted in the name of law and order would clash with the one who led the masses in the name of better living standards; the one who interacted with employers and employees would conflict with the one who was already partial as the leader of a workers' movement; the one who asked for something would emerge as the same one who would have to say no. Evidently President Goulart had no Jango Goulart—the labor leader the government of Kubitschek had enjoyed.[56]

The norm of the political process, then, is to protect the President as much as possible from frequent and direct exposure to the unprocessed demands of group conflict. His role is that of an ultimate arbitrator, a last resort when the panoply of other decentralized and relatively autonomous subsystems of conflict resolution have failed to function. When, as in the case of Goulart, he cannot be so protected, the office loses autonomy, and the occupant's tenure becomes unstable.

PART IV

Unlike voting studies, where electoral performance is an important and obvious dependent variable, or elite studies, where career patterns (ending in membership in some prestigious clique or powerful political group) provide an adequate and easily available indicator, studies of interest politics begin to become interesting only after one has described the pattern of emergence, the patterns of internal conflict resolution and decision-making, and the pattern of interaction with authority groups. The payoff comes in assessing the capacity of politically active social groups to make public policy conform to their own interests and attitudes. And yet, this is where instruments of observation and measurement are weakest.

The reader is reminded that the intention of this study is not to analyze (explain and predict) the political influence of all social groups in Brazilian society. Rather, it is to assess this capacity as wielded by a specific set of social groups, representative associations—i.e., those formally and permanently constituted in order to advance and protect the interests of a functionally or attitudinally differentiated group of the society. Nor, as will become readily apparent, is it the contention of this study that all or even most decisions in the Brazilian political process can be attributed to or explained by the activities of this type of secondary association.

THIRTEEN

The Pattern of Influence

MY PRELIMINARY explorations on the topic of Brazilian influence patterns were discouraging. Not only has little been written on the political activities of representative associations, but most students of Brazilian politics are often not even aware that these groups exist. However, in my informal conversations with sociologists, economists, politicians, industrialists, journalists, lawyers, students, and personal friends I was exposed to what might be called the folklore of the Brazilian system. In particular, I became impressed with the frequent reappearance of two quite different "models," or "syndromes," of how influence is exercised, supports exchanged, and values authoritatively allocated in such a complex decisional process. The first I labeled the "informal-irrational-particularistic-corruptible" syndrome. It tends to attribute decisive influence in the political process to small, face-to-face groups of status equals, variously referred to in the Brazilian political jargon as *turmas, grupinhos, camarilhas, panelinhas, cliques, igrejinhas, grupãos*. Each of the participants has his own *projeção* (personal prestige), his own material basis of support, his own contacts, and his own clientele or surrounding cluster of followers. With their polyfunctionalism and their overlapping networks of clients, friends, and relatives, these cliques act as mutual aid and self-promotion societies for their intimate members on a wide spectrum of issues and contexts. The national policy-making apparatus is a complex and mutually interdependent hierarchy of such informal groups, cutting across formal institutional hierarchies and culminating in the President and his *turma*. Influence is exercised by the horizontal and vertical transmission of demands and supports from one clique to another. The allegiance of nonelites is maintained by means of clientelistic payoffs to those who attach themselves to members of cliques.

The second syndrome I labeled "formal-rational-universalistic-incorruptible." This type is much more recent in vintage and much less widely held, although, for reasons that will become apparent, it predominates among economists. It attributes decisive influence in the policy process to teams of well-trained, professionally minded technicians and administrators. These cohesive groups of técnicos dominate the key sectors of policy-making and to a large extent operate independently of both professional politicians and the affected parties. Decisions are arrived at by means of an impersonal calculus based on economic theory and a set of vague national goals. Influence is exercised by the exchange of calculations, predictions, information, and available resources between the formal institutions that provide the técnicos with their power base. In this model the allegiance of nonparticipants is maintained partly by payoffs in terms of the selective distribution of credit and other facilities, but principally by an overall increment in national production.[1]

Neither the intention nor the data-collection methods of this study allow one to determine which of the two "syndromes" comes closest to describing the reality of Brazilian policy-making. In fact, there is no reason to regard the two as mutually exclusive. A convincing case could be made that the presence of the informal group structure at certain levels and in certain areas of decision-making facilitates the autonomous activity of formal groups at other levels and in other areas. The two syndromes are, at least theoretically, complementary rather than antagonistic.[2] What is immediately relevant to my argument is that neither of the "folkloric syndromes" assigns a role to formally organized, functionally specific associations. Except where their leaders can penetrate an influential clique or where their técnicos can infiltrate an important agency, representative associations would appear to be left out of the policy-making process altogether. So I began interviewing, collecting data, and observing participants with these syndromes in mind and attempted to find out whether or not association leaders themselves shared these perceptions. Did they see themselves as influential? If not, who was? And what did the formal interest representatives feel they could do about it? Obviously, I also wanted to know if the reputed marginality of formal associations was a fact. Were there not less visible channels of influence that they could exploit? Had they perhaps been more influential in the past? Were they conjuncturally influential? Were they likely to be more influential in the future?

The major problem with predicting influence or the lack of it is less conceptual than operational. As one of its most prominent students has observed, "No matter how precisely one defines influence and no matter how elegant the measures and methods one proposes, the data within

reach even of the most assiduous researcher require the use of operational measures that are at best somewhat satisfactory."[3] There are
several unsatisfactory solutions to this problem. One can rely on actors'
estimates of influence. In Brazil, however, given the lack of communication between sectors and regions as well as the specialization and absence of coordination in the decision-making process itself, actors from
both the interest groups and the authority groups tend to be very poorly
informed about associational activity outside their immediate policy
sphere. As we shall see, perceptions of relative influence are highly specialized and intersectorial comparisons very difficult, if not impossible,
to make. Another unsatisfactory or incomplete solution is to concentrate
only on extreme manifestations of influence, namely the power to initiate
a new policy, to veto a proposed one, or to bring down one that is already
in progress. But this tactic overlooks the vast area of incremental modifications and mutual adjustments within the context of a general policy
line. For various reasons, some imposed by authorities and some chosen
by the associations themselves, Brazilian representative associations devote most of their energies precisely to exerting this type of more subtle
influence.

My approach to the elusive concept of influence is three-layered. First,
I shall discuss the reputational variety—the perception of interest and
attitude leaders, politicians, and public administrators of the role of
representative associations. Second, I shall take up the situational context of influence—the differential pattern of access to decision-makers
enjoyed by different types of associations. Third, I shall examine the
inferential aspects of influence—the degree of correlation, positive and
negative, observed between the demands of associations and public
policy outputs. Alone, none of these three layers of explanation and
description would be adequate. To the extent that the evidence from
all three is consistent, one can make a fairly convincing case for the
relative degree of influence wielded by a given group in a given policy
area.

The Reputation for Influence

In what has now become a rather standard operating procedure in interest group studies, I requested the respondents to the written questionnaire to "List in approximately the order of their importance the
ten or twelve representative associations that you think are the most
influential." Those participating in the personal interviews were asked,
"Of all the representative associations in Brazil, which are the most influential; that is to say, which manage to protect and advance the interests of the sectors they represent with the greatest efficiency?" The ques-

tions were intended to be a bit different. One suggests that there is a definite number of such associations and leaves the criteria of selection open. The other leaves the number open, but suggests some evaluative criteria for inclusion. Although I was a bit taken aback by the responses to these questions, I believe after reflection that they are very indicative of the present state of Brazilian interest politics. In a word, the pattern of response to both the written questionnaire and the personal interviews was chaotic. No definite consensual hierarchy emerged from either set of data. So many different associations were named that the task of coding and enumerating the answers seemed hardly worth the effort. I settled for a few qualitative observations.

The first general finding is that no single representative association or "class" cluster of associations emerges as dominant. The most frequently cited first-place finisher was the National Confederation of Industry—on about one-fifth of the responses. However, a substantial percentage did not mention the CNI at all; moreover, those who knew it best—including many of its own leaders and employees—were the least likely to name it as the most influential. The CNI owes its prominence in good measure to its formal position as representative of industrialists in an industrializing economy, not to its actual performance in that position. Several respondents went out of the way to say that the CNI was "a façade organization" and to warn me not to pay too much heed to it. The Commercial Association of Rio and the National Confederation of Commerce were each mentioned by a few as the most influential, but neither with any marked frequency. Among respondents who were directly involved, FIESP and FIEGA were often mentioned. The other responses were distributed over a wide number and variety of employers' and professional associations. No workers' organization was cited as being at the top of the hierarchy.*

One could certainly interpret this spread as supplementary evidence of the lack of a cohesive ruling elite in Brazilian politics or of what Dahl has termed "covert integration by economic notables." To the extent that the decisional elites of professional politicians and administrators are consistently held accountable to any economic and social elites, they seem to be responsive to a considerable variety of them—regionally, functionally, and attitudinally. Only a badly informed or ideologically deformed observer could attribute to coffee growers, merchants, large landowners, or industrialists a general dominance over the policy-making process. Even Brazil's own Marxian interpreters do not infer from the

---

* Several respondents did volunteer the opinion that under Goulart the CGT and some of the transport workers' syndicates were the most influential associations in the country.

fact that Brazil is industrializing as a capitalist society that the CNI or the FIESP or any combination thereof is the most influential interest group in the country and that it in turn is dominated by national (or international) monopoly capital.

The second finding is that no definite national rank order emerges from the ratings. Of course, some ordinal rankings remain fairly constant: the CNI is more influential than the CNC, with the CRB and other rural associations usually a poor third; the Commercial Association in Rio is more influential than that of São Paulo; the CNTI is more influential than the CNTC; employers' associations in general outrank workers' associations, with middle-sector organizations somewhere in between.* But beyond such general relationships, there was no clear hierarchy. This could be interpreted as supplementary evidence of the low saliency and general impotency of representative associations in Brazilian interest politics. I suggest, however, that it can also be explained by the actors' inability to make relative assessments of each other's activities. This in turn is related to the relative absence of interaction between associations; i.e., Brazil does not yet have an autonomous subsystem within which mutual influence is exerted and exchanged. Associations, especially conflicting ones, still interact indirectly, through intermediary government institutions. The fact that so few decisions are made as a result of direct interassociational bargaining and confrontation makes it difficult to assess relative influence. Other features of the responses tend to confirm this interpretation. For one thing, in the open-ended question of the personal interview, the number of associations named was usually limited to three or four, and was rarely more than seven. When probed, respondents excused themselves by saying that they could not think of any more. Direct questions about the activities of other associations were unproductive, partly because respondents were reluctant to criticize their rivals, and partly because they were generally ignorant about each other. In the written questionnaire very few took the opportunity to fill in all twelve of the rankings.

It was also interesting to see how often association leaders would divide up their hierarchies. Workers' leaders would often give a pyramid of workers' organizations and a separate one for employers and insist that it was impossible to compare them. Employers occasionally did this, but more frequently offered a "syndical plane" and a "civil plane." At

---

* This pattern strongly suggests that respondents tended to assess relative influence not on the basis of their perception of the specific efficiency of the association, but on the basis of their perception of the global performance of the class or status group the association purported to represent. Thus what I got from many respondents was their version of the influence of social stratification, not the influence of associations.

the head of one might be the CNI or the FIESP and at the head of the other the AC-Rio or the AC-São Paulo. The two were held to be non-comparable.

The third finding is that hierarchies of influence do exist within specialized sectors. Respondents who were leaders in more functionally specialized associations tended to give very specific and more or less repeatable orderings. For example, the leader of an association of paper manufacturers might cite the Syndicate of Newspaper Owners, the ABI, the Journalists' Syndicate, and the Printers' Syndicate; the leader of an association of road-builders would name a set of engineering institutes, clubs, and societies; the president of a civil servants' organization would list only other associations of public employees. Leaders of organizations with headquarters outside Rio de Janeiro tended to offer regionalist hierarchies, either with no national, Rio-based associations or with a few symbolic ones about which little was known. In interviews in São Paulo, Belo Horizonte, and Salvador da Bahia, I discovered much more standardized reputational hierarchies in which regional actors would agree on the prominence of the FIESP, the Commercial Association of Minas, and the Commercial Association of Bahia, followed by a number of less important groups. Although the number of interviews, especially of the regionalist sort, makes generalization hazardous, the data do suggest that Brazilian interest politics is characterized more by a series of virtually independent subsystems of influence differentiated in terms of region or functional specialization than by a single, cohesive national subsystem dominated by relatively few associations.

The fourth general finding is that leaders rarely rate their own interest associations among the most influential.* Only sixteen out of more than one hundred placed their own names in the reputational hierarchy, and much fewer put themselves at the top. Of course this was occasionally the product of simple modesty. Elsewhere in the interview, the same leaders were not the least bit reluctant to claim resounding successes in determining public policy. My interpretation of this is simply that they do not consider themselves very influential. But since it is scarcely feasible or productive (except in cases where one has unusually good personal rapport) to ask an interest leader point-blank if he has been successful in his job, the conclusion that they are by and large a frustrated and disappointed lot must be considered speculative.

I have already mentioned that to federal congressmen representative associations are not very salient political forces. Perception of associa-

---

* The only category in which groups frequently named themselves was the civic associations. These "democratic, anti-Communist" groups are inclined to regard themselves as very important forces in contemporary Brazilian politics.

tional activity tended to vary, as predicted, with the level of development of the state represented and, as discovered, with the role conceptions of the legislators. Even more than interest leaders, the deputies were unable to cite many specific associations as outstandingly efficient or influential and often gave such vague responses as "the confederations" or "employers" or such negative answers as "the confederations are less important than the syndicates," They, too, often volunteered the aside that it was difficult to select the single most influential, since influence was specialized according to the issue at stake and the region of the country. Several deputies commented that some groups like the rural associations were *inexpressivo* on the national level but carried a lot of weight in local politics. They were also aware that influence tends to vary over time and that the coup of 1964 resulted in some very dramatic reversals of position.

Higher civil servants clearly considered associations more salient forces in their political environment than did congressmen. They reported much more contact and were more familiar with the activities and even the intimate details of the national associations. This, of course, only confirms the interaction pattern I have described above. When probed, however, they did not report a high degree of associational influence, although they seemed most impressed by the effectiveness of the specialized industrial syndicates and new private associations of businessmen. Specifically, they were asked, "Can you cite any case in which the efforts of a representative association impeded the formulation of a policy that you considered to be in the general interest?" A few—all of them in the commodity production institutes—answered unequivocally "yes" and could furnish examples. Several—most of them in development banks and regional organizations—reported varying degrees of harassment and unwillingness to cooperate. But the overwhelming majority felt that the associations in their area of activity did not have the capacity to veto a "desirable" measure. I think their consensus was well expressed by the secretary general of one of the executive groups, who said, "They may manage to alter a few of the details, but the essence remains."[4] An official of the Central Bank went so far as to say, "I think we use them more than they use us."[5]

The response patterns of the three sets of informants on reputational influence are roughly concordant, or at least highly complementary. All agree on the absence of a single, dominant association or cluster of associations, on the absence of an independent, well-articulated subsystem of associations with a definite internal hierarchy of influence, on the specialized nature of influence, and on a generally low estimate for the global influence of representative associations in Brazilian policy-making—at least as far as their capacity to initiate or veto proposals autonomously is concerned. The disparities reported reflect the low interaction among associations, the prominence of the functionally, regionally, and temporally specific nature of influence, and the shifting criteria used by interest representatives, politicians, and administrators to evaluate influence. For most, high social status, position in the syndical hierarchy, and formal title are enough to confer a vague reputation for influence. For others, the personal prestige of the association's leader is the overriding concern, although those better acquainted with the system may be more impressed by the leader's authenticity, i.e. the fact that his followers really chose him. Sheer size and membership density seem to be the most relevant criteria for workers' associations, although the strategic position of transport workers gives them a special reputation. Among administrators and employers' leaders, the capacity to gather and process reliable information is increasingly perceived as the key to effective control over public policy. Several association leaders mentioned proximity to Rio as an important factor, although paulistas disputed this, feeling that their relative distance from federal authorities gave them greater freedom from authority group interference and put them in closer contact with their members.* Regardless of the criteria used, few actors or observers of Brazilian interest politics would dispute the generalization that, save in a few specialized areas, representative associations—singly or collectively—do not possess the autonomous influence to command or dictate policy outcomes. Their impact is felt more subtly in signaling new issues, modifying initiatives, altering projects and regulations, and reexamining established policies.

The Situation for Exerting Influence

Since David Truman's now classic work on interest politics, access, or the capacity for carrying one's case to decision-makers, has been recognized as the primary "facilitating intermediary objective of political interest groups."[6] It is often assumed that an association with access has an assured influence over policy outcomes. This is not, operationally speaking, a very satisfactory hypothesis. Curiously, the concept of access has gone unrefined and unexamined since Truman's original and speculative observations. The subleties involved are often simply glossed over by referring specifically to effective access. Let us consider briefly what is implied in the hypothetical statement "He who has access has influence." First, the significance of the relationship will depend on how frequently the decision-maker and the demanding party interact. Second, it is

---

* Paulistas also claimed that it is impossible to run an efficient bureaucratic organization in Rio: there are too many distractions, the climate is too poor, and there is too much of a behavioral spillover from the notoriously inefficient federal bureaucracy.

likely to depend on the degree of institutionalization, or the regularity and predictability of their mutual relationship. Third, the influence will be greater the more the two parties recognize the legitimacy of each other's goals and activities. All else being equal, an association whose access to authority groups is frequent, predictable, and legitimate will be in a more favorable position to influence public policy than one whose access is sporadic, fortuitous, and corrupt. One could imagine exceptions, but for the most part the conversion of access into influence would seem to be predictably related to the above three dimensions.[7]

Significance, institutionalization, and legitimacy have been discussed above on several occasions, and it hardly seems necessary to repeat what has already been said on the differential access of various associations. I have argued that both the political culture and the pattern of government policy toward associability have tended to legitimate participation of organized groups in policy-making at the same time that it has imposed restrictions on the autonomy of that participation. The corporatist ideology does not differentiate between workers, employers, and professional people: they are all *presumed* to have equal access in matters concerning them. In general, I have found that most associational interaction takes place with the public bureaucracy. The significance, regularity, and predictability of contacts with the legislature, the parties, and the presidency are all considerably lower. In specific terms, the employers' associations definitely have the situational edge in that they report higher frequencies of interaction with a wider variety of government agencies. Within that category, syndical organizations seem to have the edge on private ones. The access of both workers' and liberal-professional associations is to a great extent channeled exclusively through the Ministry of Labor and its assorted professional orders.

As we have seen, Brazilian associations tend to try to influence public policy by altering initiatives introduced by other political actors or by modifying current policies. The key institutional mechanisms for this are formal participation in a wide variety of working groups, mixed commissions, ad hoc committees, and consultative councils at the ministerial or interministerial levels, and informal contacts between national confederational presidents and high executive and administrative officials or between associational técnicos and their counterparts in the public bureaucracy. It is difficult to gather reliable comparative material on the informal contacts. However, the interviewees were asked about their formal participation in permanent consultative councils at all levels of Brazilian government: federal, state, and local. Since the sample was confined to nationally relevant associations, participation in federal councils predominates, although a few employers' groups manage to do

TABLE 13.1
MEMBERSHIP IN CONSULTATIVE COUNCILS
(*percent*)

Type of association	Federal councils only	State councils only	Local councils only	Federal and state councils	State and local councils	Federal, state, and local councils	None	No answer, Don't know
Employers'								
Syndical (*N* = 27)	37.0%	11.1%	3.7%	3.7%	7.5%	14.8%	22.2%	0.0%
Private (*N* = 38)	31.6	7.9	2.6	0.0	0.0	0.0	58.0	5.3
Workers' (*N* = 21)	23.8	9.5	9.5	0.0	4.8	0.0	52.4	0.0
Liberal-professional (*N* = 10)	10.0	0.0	10.0	0.0	0.0	0.0	80.0	0.0
Civic (*N* = 11)	27.3	0.0	0.0	0.0	00.	0.0	54.5	18.2
All syndical (*N* = 48)	31.3	10.4	8.3	2.1	6.2	8.3	33.3	0.0
All private (*N* = 60)	28.3	5.0	1.7	0.0	0.0	0.0	58.3	6.7

NOTE: Rows may not add to 100 because of rounding.

TABLE 13.2
WHO INITIATES ADMINISTRATIVE CONTACTS?

Type of association	Association initiates	Administrators initiate	Initiation is equal	No answer, Don't know, Inappropriate
Employers'				
Syndical ($N = 27$)	33.3%	3.7%	44.4%	18.5%
Private ($N = 38$)	50.0	2.6	36.8	10.5
Workers' ($N = 21$)	71.4	0.0	4.8	23.8
Liberal-				
professional ($N = 10$)	50.0	0.0	30.0	20.0
Civic ($N = 11$)	9.1	9.1	63.6	18.2
All syndical ($N = 48$)	45.8	2.1	31.2	20.8
All private ($N = 60$)	45.0	3.3	38.3	13.3

NOTE: Rows may not add to 100 because of rounding.

double and even triple duty, as is shown in Table 13.1. In general, associations of this category participate in more councils than do workers' organizations, the official rhetoric of equality notwithstanding. Employers' syndical groups enjoy an especially favorable situation in this type of access, although again, legal norms notwithstanding, a sizable proportion of the private associations are formal members of federal councils. This certainly understates their participation, since the question was directed to memberships permanently allocated to specific associations and hence did not include either elected consultative posts (such as those on the Deliberative Junta of the IBC or the various regional and national medical councils) or appointed consultative posts, the occupancy of which depends entirely on the discretion of the President or a minister. Private associations are well represented in both these types of positions. At any rate, viewed globally, only one-third of the employers' syndical entities are without the type of guaranteed access measured here, whereas 58 percent of the private ones are shut out. About half the workers' organizations and civic associations have no formal and permanent consultative positions.

Respondents were then asked if they considered such consultative councils useful for the purposes of their associations. Not a single leader from any category felt that they were harmful or that they were simply manipulatory devices of the government. Of the 32 employers' associations that were formal members of these councils, 81 percent found them definitely useful; workers' leaders were only slightly less enthusiastic. The next question the leaders were asked was whether they initiated most of the contacts themselves, whether the administrators took the first step, or whether it was about equal. Those who report that authori-

TABLE 13.3
PERCEIVED LEGITIMACY OF POLITICIANS, PUBLIC EMPLOYEES,
AND PUBLIC OPINION ($N = 58$)

Question	Yes	No	Some-times	Depends	No answer, Don't know, etc.
1. "Do politicians generally recognize the role and importance of representative associations?"	40.3%	7.0%	29.8%	14.0%	8.7%
2. "Do public employees recognize them?"	48.5	3.5	19.3	17.4	10.5
3. "And public opinion in general?"	49.1	7.0	17.5	20.9	5.2

NOTE: Rows may not add to 100 because of rounding.

ties contact them first are in an unusually good position to exert influence, because they must have some special information or skill that the public bureaucrats require. As Table 13.2 shows, there are not very many associations in this enviable position. One could suppose that those who report that they must go to the administrators first either initiate the contact in order to command a favorable response or initiate it as plaintiffs or pleaders for special treatment. As I have shown, I interpret the data as indicating the latter type of response, but this is an inference, not a firm conclusion.

The legitimacy of associational attempts to influence public policy is not an easy quality to measure directly. I have already discussed the view administrators have of interest activity. In both samples of association leaders, I tried to gather perceptions of this relationship from the other side. In the written questionnaire, the respondents were asked a series of questions relating to how they felt politicians, public employees, and the general public regarded their activities. Table 13.3 indicates a rather strong sense of acceptance by all three categories, especially by the public at large. The attitude of the bureaucracy seems to vary according to level and ministry, and a fair proportion of the associations feel that politicians make for rather irregular allies. The size of the sample does not permit more detailed breakdowns.

In the personal interviews, I was particularly interested in the reception interest and attitude groups felt they were getting from the federal bureaucracy. I asked them, "Do you think public employees accept your association as the most authentic and influential interpreter of your sector of society?" As is clear from Table 13.4, this was one question in

TABLE 13.4
PERCEIVED LEGITIMACY OF PUBLIC EMPLOYEES, BY ASSOCIATION LEADERS

Type of association	Yes	No	Sometimes	No answer, Don't know
Employers'				
Syndical ($N = 27$)	85.2%	0.0%	3.7%	11.1%
Private ($N = 38$)	73.7	13.2	0.0	13.2
Workers' ($N = 21$)	38.1	14.3	14.3	33.3
Liberal-professional ($N = 10$)	40.0	10.0	20.0	30.0
Civic ($N = 11$)	54.5	18.2	0.0	27.3
All syndical ($N = 48$)	64.6	2.1	8.3	25.0
All private ($N = 60$)	63.3	16.7	3.3	16.7

NOTE: Rows may not add to 100 because of rounding.

which the legal status of the organization had a very noticeable effect. Syndical employers demonstrate great self-confidence. Their formal legal monopoly seems to provide them with a secure feeling of legitimate access. Many of them considered the question a bit ridiculous. In the words of one, "Of course they accept us. We are the legal representatives of the *classe*." Workers' leaders, almost all from syndicates, are not so self-confident. Despite the legal monopoly and the formal equality of access supposedly guaranteed them, they definitely feel rather shut out. The same remark applies to the liberal professional groups. In considerable measure this may be a reflection of the military regime of the time, which did not show much willingness to listen to workers, civil servants, or students. Civic associations, as they do in so many of the interviews, show a pattern of their own—of both acceptance and rejection. The most interesting finding is that private employers' associations, though they are less convinced of the legitimate acceptance of their efforts than are their syndical equivalents, apparently do not feel rejected to any large degree. One could argue that this shows how successful the policy of natural corporatism through co-optation has been. It could also suggest that a more diffuse type of corporatism is loose in the political culture, legitimating the efforts of functionally or attitudinally specific groups to gain access to decision-makers. At any rate, private associations are by no means excluded from policy-making, although they probably must struggle harder than employers' syndicates to gain an equivalent position of legitimate access.

The final question in the interview concerned equality of access. The corporatist ideology stresses this insistently, and in practice a number of councils (though by no means all) have tripartite systems of representation. The respondents were asked, "Do you think that all representative associations, those of employers as well as of workers, have equal access to public employees and ministers? If not, which would have privileged access?" From the data already presented one could easily guess the objective answer to this question. What I was fishing for was the reaction of actors to a situation in which the operative code of the political process and its indoctrinated norms clash head on. The pattern of response is given in Table 13.5. As might have been predicted, the leaders of employers' syndicates, federations, and confederations are most likely to report that access is equal. Nevertheless, almost a fifth of them are willing to concede that they have a better foot in the door than the workers. Again in keeping with the political cultural observations, private associational leaders were more prone to admitting inequality, although a substantial percentage were reluctant to admit the disparity. Twenty-four percent of the workers' leaders reported feeling they had the same access as their counterparts, but 62 percent felt relatively deprived. Liberal-professional associations, as they did consistently throughout the interview, scored in a middle position between employers and workers. The number is small, but they were the most likely to see differences between ministries in the granting of access.

TABLE 13.5
EQUALITY OF ACCESS TO THE PUBLIC ADMINISTRATION

Association	Access is equal	Access is greater for employers	Access is greater for workers	Access varies according to ministry	No answer, Don't know, inappropriate
Type					
Employers'					
Syndical ($N = 27$)	44.4%	18.5%	3.7%	3.7%	29.6%
Private ($N = 38$)	23.7	28.9	2.6	6.7	39.5
Workers' ($N = 21$)	23.8	61.9	0.0	0.0	14.3
Liberal-					
professional ($N = 10$)	20.0	40.0	0.0	10.0	30.0
Civic ($N = 11$)	9.1	9.1	18.2	0.0	63.6
Leadership					
Elected ($N = 60$)	33.3	26.7	5.0	3.3	31.7
Administrative ($N = 39$)	20.5	30.8	2.7	2.6	43.6
Intervenor ($N = 8$)	12.5	75.0	0.0	0.0	12.5
Class status of leader					
Upper ($N = 29$)	37.9	13.8	6.9	3.4	37.9
Upper-middle ($N = 38$)	21.0	26.3	5.3	5.3	42.1
Middle and lower-					
middle ($N = 40$)	26.3	52.6	0.0	0.0	21.1

NOTE: Rows may not add to 100 because of rounding.

The Assessment of Influence by Inference

Inferring influence from a juxtaposition of policy outcomes and associational activities is a risky enterprise. Of course if an organized interest exclusively initiates and drafts a policy proposal that later becomes authoritative, or if it singlehandedly opposes a measure that subsequently fails to become authoritative, the risk is not so great. In the more common situation, however, where associations act in coalition, the risk is heightened, although one can still be relatively secure if the interest being examined is consistently on the winning side. When one begins calling an association influential just because it wins more than it loses, alone or in coalition, one is in danger of being far off base. Without a demonstrable causal link between the group stimulus and the government response, one cannot make reliable inferences.

What about associations that do little or no initiating or vetoing but are instrumental in bringing overlooked or deliberately ignored problems to the attention of policy-makers, that support or oppose issues brought up by other political actors or that seek to adjust and modify proposals or policies rather than to block or repeal them? Do these incremental participants lack influence? And what about the organized interests whose objective is to prevent a given issue from even being considered or becoming controversial? What about those who are satisfied with the status quo? Are these defensive, conservative participants necessarily less influential than the initiators? Since Brazilian representative associations most commonly use these incremental and defensive strategies rather than the more aggressive ones, are we therefore to conclude that they are incapable of influencing public policy? Or might we not conclude just as easily that their very invisibility is proof of their influence, proof that they have been successful within their restricted objectives and that they do not need to mobilize a wider public or threaten policy-makers with sanctions?[8]

Let us begin by examining the personal interviews for evidence of a combination of reputed and inferred influence. The respondents were asked to name the most important campaigns and demands that their associations had made or were then making. These were subsequently coded. An association's activity was classified "initiative" if the leader cited a single specific project that it had elaborated and pressed upon authority groups, whether or not it had been successful. It was called "collaborative" if the campaigns cited involved support for projects initiated elsewhere, mainly by authority groups. It was "protective" if the activities cited were attempts to block or repeal initiatives of other actors. It was "vegetative" if no campaign at all was cited. And it was

TABLE 13.6

PRINCIPAL CAMPAIGNS OF REPRESENTATIVE ASSOCIATIONS

(*percent*)

Principal type of campaign	Employers' associations		Workers' associa- tions (N = 21)	Liberal- profes- sional associa- tions (N = 10)	Civic associa- tions (N = 11)	All associa- tions (N = 108)
	Syndical (N = 27)	Private (N = 38)				
Initiative	29.6%	39.5%	19.1%	50.0%	36.4%	33.3%
Collaborative	22.2	7.9	23.8	10.0	9.1	14.8
Protective	33.3	31.6	4.8	20.0	0.0	22.2
Vegetative	11.1	7.9	9.5	10.0	18.2	11.1
Remonstrative	3.7	7.9	42.9	10.0	36.4	16.7

NOTE: Columns may not add to 100 because of rounding.

"remonstrative" if the activities were devoted either to diffuse protest against the government or to regularized protest against other social groups. Table 13.6 shows how the association readers responded. The professional associations of the middle sectors come out as the most frequent initiators. However, it is important to note that three of the ten respondents were medical associations who claimed to have initiated the same measures, and two were public employees' associations who reported identical successes. Otherwise, private employers' organizations emerge as the most active initiators, followed closely by civic interest groups. Syndical entities of both employers and workers seem more inhibited in this field and are the most likely to have engaged primarily in collaborative activities—a finding that confirms some of my previous generalizations about the role of corporatism. One workers' organization in five claimed an initiative of some sort; approximately one in four reported supporting mostly the initiatives of others. The propensity for acting essentially in a protective capacity resisting change is not as affected by legal status as it is by sphere of interest. Not too surprisingly, roughly one-third of the property-owning groups spend most of their efforts resisting the efforts of other groups to undermine their acquired positions. Workers' organizations are understandably less preoccupied with such efforts. Vegetative status—sheer inactivity—is rather evenly distributed among all types of groups, with civic associations contributing a bit more than their fair share. The strong protesters, again not astonishingly, are the workers and the civic-minded. The nature of the remonstrances, of course, differs considerably. Neither the employers' groups nor the liberal-professional ones engages in a great deal of this sort of diffuse protest activity.

The differential impact of the corporatist form of organization is well

TABLE 13.7
CORPORATISM AND THE NATURE OF ASSOCIATIONAL CAMPAIGNS
(*percent*)

Principal type of campaign	All syndical associations (N = 48)	All private associations (N = 60)
Initiative	25.0%	40.0%
Collaborative	22.9	8.3
Protective	20.8	23.8
Vegetative	10.4	11.7
Remonstrative	20.8	13.3

NOTE: Columns may not add to 100 because of rounding.

illustrated by Table 13.7. The voluntary, member-supported private associations emerge quite clearly as more assertive in their group political behavior. They are much more likely to be engaged in pressing new demands on policy-makers, and they are slightly more likely to be protecting their already acquired positions. When one considers that virtually all of the syndicates' remonstrative activity consists of salary demands made by workers in an attempt to keep up with galloping inflation, whereas the private entities mainly protest the government's "subversive" or "socializing" initiatives, the distinction becomes even more marked. As Brazil acquires more of these independent, functionally specific private associations, its interest politics are likely to get increasingly aggressive and full of open conflict. The reactive passivity and conformity associated with the corporatist pattern of interaction is likely to decrease in global importance. Under these conditions one would predict an increase in the influence of representative associations as development continues and as the control of authority groups over the patterns of emergence and interaction decreases. This is a matter we shall take up again in the concluding chapter.

The responses to another of the interview questions shed some additional light on the aggressiveness or passivity of interest representatives. In my preliminary readings and observations, I thought I had detected a certain reluctance on the part of associations, private and syndical, to take policy stands that openly conflicted with government intentions. In case after case, if an association's interests were obviously being challenged by actual or impending public policy, it either made only a symbolic protest or announced its intention to collaborate with authority groups in order to better but not defeat the measure.* Given the nature

---

* One of the more aggressive interest leaders interviewed poured scorn on this style of "protesting," noting the propensity of most Brazilians for "criticizing by clapping their hands and giving banquets."

of the regime at the time I made these observations, I could not be sure whether or not this was merely due to fear of reprisals. So I asked the leaders, "Was there ever a case in the past in which your association confronted the government in an important matter?" Although the angle of approach is a bit different, the spectrum of responses (presented in Table 13.8) fully confirms my previous findings on the degree of initiative and its distribution: 42 percent of the private employers' groups reported they had opposed the government on some issue, whereas only 30 percent of their syndicates could claim likewise. The former are also more likely to report success. The civic associations reappear with their remarkable and reportedly successful aggressiveness—most of which was directed against the Goulart regime. All in all, one-half of the interviewed associational leaders could remember or claim credit for the exhilarating but risky experience of locking horns with authority groups.

Influence over Outcomes and the Policy-Making Process

As we have seen, the process of producing public policy outcomes involves elaborate sequences or cycles of decision-making. Associations (or individuals, for that matter) rarely seek to influence policy in all decisional forums, and when they do they are rarely equally successful in all of them. This suggests that representative associations, both in general and in particular, tend to concentrate upon certain stages of policy elaboration. Their effectiveness depends not only upon region or issue area, but also upon their relative strength and weakness in specific decisional forums: signaling, initiation and drafting, consultation and negotiation, approval and veto, and regulation, revision, and renegotiation.

Signaling. Representative associations use signaling to make a ne-

TABLE 13.8
PROPENSITY FOR CONFRONTATION WITH THE GOVERNMENT

Type of association	Yes, and was successful	Yes, and was not successful	Yes, with indeterminate results	No	No answer, Don't know
Employers'					
Syndical ($N = 27$)	14.8%	3.7%	11.1%	59.3%	11.1%
Private ($N = 38$)	21.1	2.6	18.4	47.4	9.5
Workers' ($N = 21$)	4.8	4.8	4.8	57.1	28.6
Liberal-					
professional ($N = 10$)	10.0	10.0	20.0	40.0	20.0
Civic ($N = 11$)	54.6	0.0	9.0	36.4	0.0
All associations ($N = 108$)	18.5	3.7	13.0	50.0	14.8

NOTE: Rows may not add to 100 because of rounding.

glected problem into a priority issue, to show the intensity of their clients' attitudes and interests on an issue already being treated, or, in cases where policy is exclusively the product of organized group interaction, to determine the selection of issues for public debate. Virtually all active representative associations emit such signals, though their efforts vary in frequency, intensity, consistency, and veracity. Signals are sent by means of the associations' publications, the mass media, and a myriad of types of informal contacts with decision-makers.* Often the association responsible for the signal is identified; often the signal is planted anonymously. As a rule, these demands are designed to appear compatible with the public interest or even indispensable for "preserving our Christian heritage," "promoting national development," "attaining social justice," "preventing industry from becoming denationalized," or "maintaining the size of the national market."[9] Organized groups rarely ask for what they want simply on the grounds that it would benefit them. It is not clear whether this deference to the public interest is merely verbal or whether it is part of a genuine moderation of demands. Several association leaders insisted that the rules of the game precluded the militant pushing of self-serving demands. Such behavior would be self-defeating, because the association would soon lose the confidence and respect of the higher administrative elites. Although data on this were not collected expressly, I would venture from a number of asides made that neither politicians nor bureaucrats are particularly convinced of the public-mindedness of interest leaders. Some associations definitely have a special reputation for *idoneidade* and *seriedade de propósito* (a combination of informational accuracy and self-imposed moderation),† but most are regarded as a bit too preoccupied with promoting their own immediate interests independent of their impact upon the larger community. This image certainly hampers their signaling capacity and perhaps explains why so much signaling is disguised or informal.

Although they are often accompanied by predictions of the dire con-

---

* The major employers' associations maintain veritable "stables" of journalists in their employ. I was told in several interviews that the purpose for this was mainly to prevent unfavorable items from appearing, but the journalists themselves freely admitted that they also plant favorable ones. Industrialists' associations used to subsidize newspapers directly—a practice still common among many authority groups. The famous "Sea of Mud" scandal, which culminated in the suicide of Vargas in 1954, began with Carlos Lacerda's disclosure that the CNI had been heavily subsidizing virtually every newspaper in Rio with SESI funds, and that Euvaldo Lodi, the CNI president, with the industrialist Francisco Matarazzo, had financially sponsored the founding of the pro-Vargas, leftist daily *Ultima Hora*.

† One association that has been especially noteworthy in this regard, having achieved a substantial penetration of financial policy-making circles in a short time, is ADECIF.

sequences of an unfavorable response, signals made by Brazilian associations rarely contain overt threats of disobedience or violence. They are presented as suggestions or information "out of our desire to collaborate with public authorities," not as militant demands that must be met or else. In the early 1960's, one of the clear signs that the conciliatory style of politics was beginning to break down was a growing militancy and a threatening tone in associational signals. Workers' organizations aired the threat of general strikes in the cities and land seizures in the countryside; employers' associations announced their refusal to pay "illegal" taxes or to observe "illegal" controls; civic associations challenged the very legitimacy of the President and openly called upon the military to intervene. Since the coup of 1964, the tone of signaling has returned to its previous norm of nonviolent collaboration, except for some of the most frustrated extreme-right civic and military associations.

Some of these signals seem to have become routine, standardized components of the Brazilian political environment. The commercial associations complain year after year about port congestion; the coffee growers perennially inveigh against the government's coffee policy; industrialists are eternally grumbling about the lack of a consistent policy of support for industrialization and, more specifically, the lack of easily available public credit; businessmen's associations continually denounce the discriminatory activities of price-controlling and commodity-stocking agencies; workers' organizations are perpetually pointing out the necessity for decreeing a new minimum wage; civic groups are forever decrying the imminent danger of subversion by atheistic Communists, whom they see everywhere; and all organized interests gripe about inflation, bureaucratic inefficiency, and the poor communications system.

There are, of course, special campaigns, sporadic and intense attempts to single out immediate issues for treatment by authority groups. Also, associations or clusters of them periodically seek to render their signaling efforts more consistent. At various national congresses long lists of general and specific demands are compiled, most commonly by representatives within a given specialized sector. The function of these numerous Charters, Declarations, and Manifestos is essentially to overcome regional, social, functional, generational, and ideational differences within the sector, to increase member participation, and to create some sort of group consciousness. They serve as the basis for routine signaling thereafter, and the demands made on specific issues are often "legitimated" by reference to them.

How influential is this signaling by representative associations? The fact that it is often so repetitive and routine suggests that the decision-making elites, especially the administrative ones, are not very attentive, prefer to set up their own priorities, and resist being forced to examine issues. The most severe restriction placed upon signaling in Brazilian interest politics is the relatively limited autonomy of the political process as a whole. The caricature would have it that all Brazilian policy has been imposed by a cabal consisting of the U.S. State Department, the Pentagon, and the International Monetary Fund. Exaggerated as this may be, it is true that national policy-makers are not entirely free to select and ignore issues. In particular, the persistent crisis in the balance of payments has been a most important and insistent signal and one that has set priorities and raised limitations throughout the political process. This situation of dependence upon imposed problems (and, to a lesser degree, upon imitation of foreign solutions) makes it difficult for national interest representatives to command the exclusive attention of *políticos* and *técnicos*.

Moreover, associations are far from alone in their signaling efforts, even at the national level. They must compete with individuals and firms who feel under no obligation to process their demands indirectly and who do not hesitate to approach authorities to advance their own causes. Brazil also has a lively and independent group of intellectuals who specialize in pinpointing national problems and nationalistic solutions and who enjoy easy access to the mass media and to the advisory staffs of decision-makers. Within the government, the *técnicos* are active not only in the administration of existing policies, but also in propagandizing for new ones.

Despite such formidable competition, the associations might still be able to influence the content of the discussion of policy if the quality of their signals were high enough. However, because of the deficiencies noted above in member participation and leadership selection, most of the national groups, and especially the peak associations, are not likely to be in very close contact with the sector they purport to represent. Consequently, they are not likely to be very well informed about its activities and opinions. Nor are their leaders likely to exercise an authoritative command over the sector's reaction to public policy.

Nevertheless, there definitely have been cases where associations have affected public policy by the use of signaling. The persistent ideological efforts of Roberto Simonsen, Euvaldo Lodi, and their associates in the FIESP and the CNI, for example, probably did much to help convince the elites that there was a viable alternative to Brazil's remaining an essentially agricultural society. Whatever their direct or immediate impact, through signaling they kept the idea alive and provided a useful rationale to policy-makers once they had decided on their own.[10]

Initiation and drafting. Whereas signaling is frequently overlooked as an area of potential influence, the capacity to introduce and mold a new policy measure is usually considered the hallmark of influence. Yet this is where Brazilian representative associations are at their weakest. The general posture of associations is defensive, not offensive. Rather than acting aggressively to improve their status by pressing for new advantages, most organized interests react, positively or negatively as the case may be, to initiatives taken by the government. Even workers' organizations, which we might expect to take the lead in challenging the system, are largely involved in protecting and making effective their existing rights under the Labor Code. This may be partly a culturally conditioned response, a combination of the tendency to rely on the goodwill of higher authorities, the feeling that "o Govêrno tem que dar o impulso" (the government should take the initiative), and the general lack of a sentiment of collective social responsibility among private groups. It may also be based on a very realistic assessment that it would be a waste of an association's resources to stake too much of them on aggressive initiatives when the dice are so loaded in favor of authority groups.

The reactive-adaptive strategy is all the more appropriate when the interest leader feels that the initiatives taken more or less autonomously by professional politicians or técnicos are likely to be beneficial. When the industrialist believes that economic policy-makers are committed to furthering industrialization and protecting private enterprise, when the worker believes that Ministry of Labor officials are genuinely interested in maintaining and advancing the purchasing power and standard of living of employed groups, and when the private banker believes that public financial administrators are sincere in their desire to create an efficient and reliable securities market, why should their respective interest representatives knock themselves out trying to introduce new measures? I once commented to an industrialist leader that the CNI seemed strangely inactive during the Kubitschek administration, when the rate of industrialization was booming. He replied, "And why not? Why should we have risked upsetting the gravy train [*trem de alegria*]?"[11] Or, as an advisor to the CNI directorate put it, "When this country had no industrialists and no industrial policy, the CNI was a real power. Now that it has industrialists and something like an industrialization policy, the CNI is inexpressive."[12] From this perspective, it is the lack of initiative on the part of the association that becomes the hallmark of success for the sector it represents.

Another characteristic of postwar Brazilian policy-making that rather inhibited direct initiation by interested parties was the skillful way political elites used, stretched, and distorted the preexistent legal framework. Very substantial modifications and innovations emerged almost surreptitiously from a variety of administrative agencies and interministerial councils in the form of *instruções, regulamentos, portarias, circulares,* and *decrêtos.* Many of these were imposed by short-term, emergency conditions, without regard for their side effects, and were retained thereafter with important indirect and often unforeseen consequences.[13] In this "underworld" of manipulated exchange rate privileges, tariff and quota protection, selective exemption from duties and taxes, and government subsidies and credits, it has not been easy to mobilize outside, large-scale collective pressures for innovations. The context encourages individualistic scrambles for benefits. From the end of the Estado Novo until the Basic Reforms discussions of the Goulart regime, very few major policy decisions were given what could be called an intensive public hearing. None of the debates that did take place—concerning the taxing of extraordinary war profits, controls on the abuse of economic power (antitrust measures), the creation of a government petroleum monopoly, the formation of SUDENE, the building of Brasília, controls on the remittance of foreign profits, and comprehensive national economic planning—were the result of initiatives or project drafts by representative associations.

This does not mean that representative associations are completely absent from the initiating and drafting stages of policy-making. One occasionally finds associations presenting new and comprehensive *projetos* for authoritative approval. On closer examination, however, many of these turn out to be little more than lists of vague and unspecific demands, more like what arises from the diffuse process of signaling. Some are counter-initiatives, alternatives to the initiatives of políticos and técnicos, such as the Confederation of Bank Workers' Banking Reform Proposal of 1963. Others may be "invited" initiatives, for example the *Anteprojeto de Lei* drafted by the National Syndicate of Book Publishers in 1962 granting them tax exemptions and favorable credit treatment. Few associations seem to have enough intellectual and physical resources, group consciousness, information on members' attitudes, aggressive leadership, proper associational allies, and, above all, independence from authority groups to allow them to exercise a decisive influence upon policy initiation or drafting. Although approximately one-third of the associations claimed in the interviews to have made some initiative, most of these involved minor matters (however essential they may have seemed from the association's perspective). Often they concerned issues about which government officials were undecided or indifferent. On the few occasions in which they have played a prominent role, such as the CNI involvement with the Tariff Revision Bill, it has been because authority groups have invited them to do so. I encountered no case in which a formally organized national interest or attitude group created from scratch, either single-handedly or with the aid of other organized groups, a major policy innovation in the face of opposition by important authority groups.

There has been some participation in the drafting of initiatives made elsewhere, but again it has been dependent upon government discretion. Invitations to join those unobtrusive executive groups, ad hoc committees, interministerial discussions, and consultative councils in which político and técnico initiatives are converted into specific proposals for executive or legislative approval are highly coveted, but they cannot be commanded. There are some indications that authorities use them as a way of rewarding loyalty and quiescence. Association leaders frequently and rather bitterly remarked that the price for access to these inner circles was subservience to government objectives. Whatever the criteria or ulterior motives involved, the participation itself more closely resembles what I have called consultation and negotiation than the more independent activity I have called drafting.

Consultation and negotiation. The liberalist pattern of influence focuses on the group's capacity for initiation and veto; the corporatist on its capacity for consultation and regulation. The former is based on the dynamics of conflict between independently organized interests and the state, the latter on the active intervention of the state, which institutionalizes the relationships in such a way as to ensure that organized interests will collaborate with authority groups. Recent North American theorists of neocorporatism have been preoccupied with the effects of such representation upon the subversion of public decision-makers,[14] but in Brazil the concern is somewhat reversed. There, the success and persistence of the system has rested upon the ability of the government to co-opt interest representatives prematurely, so to speak, and to give them a semblance of effective participation without losing its own control over the general configuration of public policy. The fear is that authority groups have been too successful and that interest groups have been too dependent upon them.

In the corporatist system, it is essential that authorities guarantee organized interests a chance of exerting their influence upon policy before it is authoritatively approved; that is, they must give recognized associations the right to prior consultation and negotiation. The interest representatives, in turn, agree to modify their demands in the "public interest," i.e. to follow the government's initiative, and to refrain from recourse to such "illegitimate" forms of protest as violence or even vituperative public-opinion campaigns. In its pure form, the rhetoric of corporatism seems to imply the capacity to negotiate—the right of organized groups to prevent decisions from being made contrary to their interests within their recognized sphere of legitimate concern. In its most advanced or pure form, corporatism promises the associations a virtual symbiosis with authority groups through joint participation and control over autonomous functional "corporations." Brazil, of course, does not have and has never had a purely corporatist system of interest representation. There are numerous and increasingly important elements of liberalism, and there have been periodic expressions of collectivism. Nevertheless, the predominant rhetoric and practice is corporatist; hence the central importance of consultation and negotiation in Brazilian interest politics.

Administrative and executive elites directly solicit the views of associations far more now than they did before 1930. Consultation became especially important after the proclamation of the Estado Novo in 1937. Employers' interest representatives began to play an important consultative and probably negotiative role in the commissions, which from 1937 to 1943 drew up such important innovations in social legislation as the Labor Court system, the social security measures, the minimum salary arrangements, the job stability provisions, the new guarantees on working conditions and holidays, and, most important, the corporatist syndicalization scheme. Interest representatives also participated in most of the major economic policy councils. Octávio Ianni, a sociologist who has studied this period in some detail, concludes that the experience, though "predominantly verbal," was important in determining both the direction and the nature of future policy-making. On the one hand, the "productive classes" came to accept the direct participation of the state in both production and planning; on the other hand, the government actors came to accept the direct participation of interest representatives in their deliberations. Thus, in spite of their differences, the técnicos and the interessados reached a level of general agreement and mutual respect.[15] During this period it became standard practice for both sides to exchange demands and supports through the myriad of permanent councils, mixed commissions, committees, juntas, and executive groups.

In the postwar period, the tendency toward mutual *entrosamento* (interpenetration) through consultation continued. The functional representatives remained within the juntas of the various commodity institutes, the commissions of the Labor Ministry, and the tribunals of the Labor Court system. The principle of corporatist representation and administrative control was permanently extended to the Retirement and Social Welfare Institutes when they were reformed in the late 1950's. The omnibus economic policy councils of the Estado Novo were largely disbanded and replaced by specific agencies, but these commissions for sectorial planning in such fields as rubber and coal also provided for permanent representatives from the respective syndicates. President Kubitschek created numerous sectorial planning agencies in order to bypass the traditional ministerial bureaucracies. Although in many cases associations were not (and still are not) formally members of these *grupos executivos*, their success largely depended on a climate of mutual understanding and confidence between government técnicos and interest representatives.

Gradually (it is difficult to pinpoint a specific crisis or even a general period) the climate of mutual understanding and confidence became less dependable. Organized interests had never been very successful in consultative penetrations of the monetary and credit arenas. As organizations like the Superintendency for Money and Credit (SUMOC), the Foreign trade (CACEX), the Industrial and Agricultural Credit Section (CREAI) of the Bank of Brazil, and the National Development Bank (BNDE)—none of which had permanent forums for the exchange of opinions—became increasingly preeminent, associations found themselves being progressively shut out of the policy process and being caught unaware by government initiatives. They also discovered that the sectors in which they enjoyed easy access and had sufficient *entrosamento* were gradually being subordinated to those major policy centers with which they did not have such cordial relationships. In these latter forums they appeared as special pleaders and clients alongside an increasing number of lobbying specialists, administrative lawyers who represented individual firms or economic groups and who often had better inside contacts. Under Goulart, these trends, combined with a vague distrust by employers' associations of the President's ulterior motives and a growing suspicion of the intimate consultative status he was according certain workers' leaders, brought about a disintegration of the corporatist quid pro quo. Leaders of organized employer interests began to resort more and more to other channels of demand and protest.

The change of regime in 1964 has not had as much of an impact upon consultative relationships as one might have anticipated. The Castelo Branco regime moved quickly to delegate to técnicos a degree of autonomy they had never enjoyed before. This frequently caught representative associations off guard. There were complaints that their views had not been properly solicited and that many of the decrees, laws, and administrative regulations were therefore inapplicable. My interviews, however, gave me the impression that mutual confidence has been repaired and that consultative channels have been unclogged. The corporatist arrangement, with its limited but secure role for interest representatives, is being revived. Even workers' organizations were consulted on one government initiative that vitally affected their acquired rights, the attempt by the Ministry of Planning to do away with the CLT provisions guaranteeing workers permanent job stability after ten years of employment. They were also granted prior consultative opportunities on several other initiatives: the unification of the Retirement and Social Welfare Institute system, the new collective bargaining law, and the splitting up of the Christmas bonus (although one suspects that these concessions were largely a formality). Employers' associations observed with approval the creation of a number of new and potentially very important consultative councils.

Except possibly for some of the commodity agencies, most participants agree that the government still has the whip hand in these formal and informal exchanges of demands and opinions. Interest representatives could cite cases when theirs had been a minority vote, but were unable to cite many cases in which they had been able to gang up with other private members against the government. Indeed, one suspects that such an alliance would violate the very purpose of these councils, which is not to defeat the authorities, but to get them to accommodate to the specific, "realistic" demands of interested parties. This is simply another way of saying that organized groups have a consultative capacity but rarely a negotiative one. The situation will vary, of course, according to the type of association, its technical skills, and its internal cohesion, sense of group purpose, and solidarity. Moreover, it varies according to whether the council is deliberative (i.e. its decisions are binding) or consultative (i.e. its activities offer only personal prestige or a vague satisfaction of government concern), and according to whether the government's resolve is firm and its technical and administrative cadres united. But even under the most favorable circumstances, organized groups find it difficult to convert consultations into negotiations. Within the limits imposed by dependent corporatist representation, elite ideological objectives, and general economic conditions, they may and often do reach a mutually satisfactory understanding by which government policies are modified, but rarely can they command conformity to their interests.

The criteria for selecting interest consultants has shifted significantly in recent years. Article 547 of the Labor Code states flatly: "Any official representation of an economic or occupational category that makes decisions for the entire group . . . is restricted to members of a syndicate." In other words, guaranteed access to these inner councils is supposed to be the exclusive privilege of recognized syndicates, federations, and confederations. Of course, during the 1930's and early 1940's, when these had not yet been formed, certain private associations consented to being naturally co-opted and were granted the status of "technical and consultative organ of the government." Thus they obtained seats on the numerous advisory bodies then being created, and many of them, including the Commercial Association of Rio, still have these seats.* But the general practice until recently was to favor syndical organizations in this way. Thus the CNI, the CNC, the CRB, and the workers' confederations monopolized at least formal access to this part of the policy process. The private associations, especially the commercial associations, were increasingly impeded from exerting influence at this level, unless they could smuggle one of their men into an equivalent syndicate.

But there was a rub even for the syndical organizations. Except in rare and minor instances, they were not permitted to name the occupant of the position directly, although they had the right to suggest a list of prospective candidates from which the President of the Republic or the minister would choose. This, of course, gave authority groups a certain discretionary power to reward loyalty and quiescence and to play one nominating confederation off against another. This has not hurt employers much, because of the larger number of posts available and the existence of informal arrangements to divide them equitably. For workers, this has led to acrimonious struggles, especially over the lucrative positions in the Labor Court and Retirement Institute bureaucracies. As I noted above, this has been one of the factors preventing the formation of a united front of worker organizations.

As the decisional process has become increasingly technocratic and sectorial—beginning during the 1950's—this system of corporatist consultation concentrated in the major syndical confederations has become less and less viable. For one thing, the confederations have lost their strong leadership and have been dividing up their numerous representations between member federations, essentially between Rio de Janeiro and São Paulo. In spite of efforts to institutionalize some control over them, it has proved impossible to coordinate policy in these different organs or to bring sanctions to bear against representatives in various agencies that take differing postions. For example, most of the CNI's ostensible representatives really represent the views of the state federations or of individual syndicates rather than of industry as a whole. Furthermore, técnicos have been demanding increasingly specific and technical kinds of information and opinions that the industrialists in these

---

* One should not overlook the fact that state governments have created a similar panoply of consultative and administrative bodies and that private associations frequently participate in them.

councils are usually unable to provide. The result has been a tendency for consultation to bypass the more aggregative and less representative confederations, as the economic administrators seek more specifically qualified informants directly in the industrial syndicates, the new national private associations, and, in many cases, individual firms. Leaders and individuals associated with some of the better organized and more active private entities like the Brazilian Association for the Development of Basic Industries and the Brazilian Association of the Pharmaceutical Industry were quietly invited to participate and eventually given formal consultative membership in executive groups, planning councils, and working committees. Since the coup of 1964 this has become quite standard practice. Although nominations for interest representatives on the Consultative Council on Planning (CONSPLAN) are the prerogative of syndical confederations, participation in the new coordinating groups for sectorial planing will depend on the minister's discretion, and it appears that private associations and syndical ones will be given equal consideration. Similarly, in the new advisory groups attached to the National Monetary Council and to the Ministry of Industry and Commerce, there is no discrimination against private groups; indeed several of them have major positions. Thus the near-monopoly on formal consultative positions formerly enjoyed by the syndical organizations has definitely been broken. It appears that in the future consultants will be selected on other criteria than formal legal status. This threatens to upset the basic quid pro quo of corporatism and to introduce new elements of competition, uncertainty, and possibly aggressiveness into Brazilian interest politics.

Consultation is the principal arena within which the influence of organized interests is felt in the Brazilian political system. Associations, both private and syndical, are internally articulated primarily to act in this arena, and their leaders seem to feel that this is where they operate most effectively and legitimately. They sometimes appear to forego opportunities for exerting more energetic (and risky) kinds of pressure when doing so might jeopardize the delicate relations of mutual confidence upon which successful consultations are based. When guaranteed the privilege of prior consultation, most associations have adopted an essentially passive, wait-and-see attitude and have left the area of general policy initiation to the políticos, técnicos, and their intellectual allies and mentors. However it is not easy to assess relative influence of consultation. It is an arena in which positions are flexible, changes are incremental, sacrifices and benefits are linked in a series of decisions, and payoffs are frequently deferred or merely symbolic. To say that representative associations participating in this exchange are less influential than those initiating new proposals or blocking the proposals of others, though it is certainly true, is somewhat beside the point. What we can say is that, for better or for worse, for reasons of political culture, government policy, historical formation, and political expediency, Brazilian interest politics follows a semicorporatist pattern. To assess influence purely on the basis of standards of performance derived from the activities of autonomous, aggressive representative associations in liberalist-pluralist systems is unrealistic. In terms of the standards of performance Brazilian interest group leaders set for themselves, it appears that the leaders have most of their modest demands satisfied in the arena of consultation or in the closely related arenas of regulation and revision.

Approval and veto. The ability to gain the agreement and support of executive-military or legislative elites for measures they would otherwise oppose and the ability to compel these same decision-makers to block a measure they would otherwise support are usually considered the hallmarks of political influence. Associations, especially the major national confederations, appear to have more regular and effective access to the President and his immediate advisors and ministers than to the Parliament. Of course the special relationship of the confederational leaders with the national executive is by no means a unilateral upward influence; indeed, it may be used for downward manipulation. Nevertheless, associations have occasionally single-handedly obtained executive or legislative approval for measures benefiting their clients. Certainly the clearest and most important case of this was President Dutra's backing for the SESI and SESC taxes of 1946. As I noted above, these measures had a crucial impact in the configuration of postwar Brazilian interest politics and came as a direct result of group pressures upon the President. On the legislative side perhaps the most clear-cut case was the *municipalistas'* constitutional amendment transferring the land tax to their jurisdiction.* According to interviews, associations' publications, and newspaper accounts, there have been virtually hundreds of such group measures approved by executive or legislative elites, although most of these have been of minor importance in terms of global policy configuration.

Even if alone they have a limited capacity to force approval, representative associations can be valuable potential allies and annoying opponents for political, administrative, and intellectual elites. The usual posture of organized groups, syndical and private, is one of diffuse support for executive decision-makers. A President, governor, or other high offi-

---

* Despite this Pyrrhic victory, the municípios' share of total tax revenues has declined from 8.2 percent in 1940 to 7.0 percent in 1960.

cial upon taking office can be assured of a flood of congratulatory telegrams from confederations, federations, syndicates, and other associations proclaiming their profuse willingness to collaborate. This is symbolically reinforced by periodic *homenagens* (honorary banquets). At times this sort of approval can have more than symbolic importance. Representative associations in the crucial period between Kubitschek's election and inauguration (1954–55) made numerous announcements to the effect that the country had its legally elected president. Even the commercial associations, known for their neo-liberalism and their support for the UDN (which was trying to prevent Kubitschek's taking office on the "constitutional" ground that he had not obtained a simple majority) joined the campaign "for the calming of spirits."[16] At other crucial junctures, national executives have solicited organized group support for initiatives. Kubitschek's defiance of International Monetary Fund pressures for an austerity policy met with the substantial and well-publicized approval of major interest associations. Similarly, his decision to establish a regional development agency in the Northeast (SUDENE) and to build Brasília were given a favorable (although less enthusiastic) public endorsement. João Goulart's Minister of Planning, Celso Furtado, made extensive efforts to sell class associations on the merits of his Three-Year Plan. A perusal of internal documents of the CNI revealed that many of these appeals for approval or support are much less public and consist simply of requests that the organization not protest or that it moderate its protest. In this way, and in a style typical of conciliation politics, the CNI might agree to go along with an "illegal" minimum salary increase or with the granting of an end-of-the-year salary bonus, provided appropriate assurances were given on limiting future workers' demands or on providing the necessary public credit.

One reason the approval of representative associations is so important to administrative and political elites is that aroused associations can do much to impede unfavorable policy outcomes. Several theorists have suggested that in general "interest groups are more at ease in acting to conserve acquired positions than in developing new ones; they are more ready to defend rights they believe menaced than to confront new problems."[17] Myron Weiner, Lucian Pye, and Fred Riggs have observed that in developing polities, interest groups tend to act as protective associations—"directed toward preventing government from pursuing some course of action."[18] Brazil is no exception to either of these generalizations. Most group demands are negative or restrictive, and associations have been noticeably more successful at vetoing than at initiating or approving policies.

The most consistently successful veto campaign has been that aimed at preventing any substantial modification in the syndical system itself. Despite repeated initiatives for repealing the *impôsto sindical* and for investigating some of the shady advantageous arrangements between authority groups (like the Labor Ministry and the welfare institutes) and syndical leaders, the basic rules of the game have hardly changed since they were "consolidated" under the Estado Novo. Threat after threat has been parried; several investigations have been filed away quietly. Employers' syndicates have been even more successful in vetoing all menaces to the main source of their financial strength, the SESI and SESC funds. The key to success in these opposition campaigns lies in the ability of the threatened groups to mobilize a wider coalition, usually on the grounds that the initiative violates constitutional practice or threatens to alter the existing political balance radically. In some instances, however, organized group pressures have been successfully directed toward preventing certain provisions of the 1946 Constitution from becoming effective, for example workers' participation in profits and the right to strike.[19] They have also been directed against executive initiatives that did not involve direct threats to the Constitution. For example, when at the end of the Estado Novo Getúlio Vargas decreed a comprehensive antitrust law aimed at restricting exorbitant postwar profit-taking, his interest advisors, Lodi of the National Confederation of Industry and Daudt d'Oliveira of the Federation of Commercial Associations, led the opposition on the grounds that the initiative was "contrary to moral and economic order." Vargas hesitated and postponed the measure, and two months after he was deposed the threat was rescinded. Similarly, sporadic government attempts to impose monetary and credit stabilization policies in 1953–54, 1954–55, 1958–59, 1961 and 1963 met with organized group resistance. None of these programs were successful, although it would be an exaggeration to give representative associations full credit for the negative outcomes.

During "normal periods," in which tactics of conciliatory politics were used to meet most interest conflict, the obstructive capacity of organized groups was rarely exercised. And when on occasion it was attempted, authority groups were able to co-opt the dissenting groups or otherwise bring them into line. But as these conditions of mutual responsiveness broke down in the 1960's, both political and interest actors became increasingly intransigent. Organized group pressures mounted and severely impaired Goulart's policy of basic reforms, especially agrarian reform, which needed constitutional revision in order to escape the requirement for cash payment. Interest parties effectively immobilized the Parliament, forcing the President to resort to threats of extraordinary measures and to request for special powers; these measures were even more intransigently opposed by both workers' and employers' associations.

Nathaniel Leff, in his monograph on economic policy-making in Brazil, arrived at similar conclusions regarding the limited influence of interest groups and cited several cases in which they were incapable of blocking measures contrary to their interests. However, two of the major examples he uses to illustrate his conclusions are somewhat misleading and, frankly, self-serving. First, he "proves" the weakness of employers' interest groups on the grounds that they "were not able to stand in the way of the large expansion in the government's controls and regulation or to curb its direct investment and production activities."[20] This suggests (1) that employers perceived themselves as locked in a zero-sum struggle with public authorities such that any additional resources allotted to the latter were taken at the expense of the former, and (2) that the private sector, regardless of the conflict over material resources, must have some sort of "natural" ideological antagonism toward government participation and interference in economic life. Certainly, one can find examples of both of these conditions in the pronouncements of syndical and private employers' groups. But on balance one would have to admit that industrialists' associations, in particular, did *not* see things this way. The government's developmental strategy minimized zero-sum calculations. Traditional clientelistic payoffs, credits and attractive incentives for the private industrial sector, and subsidies, price supports, and market controls for coffee growers, sugar planters, and maté producers were maintained—some even expanded—at the same time that the amount of resources channeled into government enterprises rose even more.[21] Ideologically, Brazilian industrialists had long since made their peace with direct public intervention. Simonsen, who was able to foresee the climate of government intervention, sought to convince the members of his sector not to reject it dogmatically, but to adapt to it: "In Brazil economic weakness and instability has led us to adopt a series of partial plannings and interventions by the state, always demanded by the producers in difficulty and almost always later condemned by these same people. . . . It is not a question of choosing between the presence and the absence of interventionism, but rather between good and bad interventionism."[22] The statements of succeeding conventions of industrialists, beginning in 1943, contain minor reservations about specific interventions mixed with major demands for more —stipulating that they be "supplementary, orienting, and auxiliary."[23] One must not overlook the fact that the enormous expansion of the government's interventionist role developed incrementally and, in large measure, unintentionally. Not until the end of the Goulart regime did these accumulated instruments seem to pose a threat to the basic principles of the economic system, namely the regime of private property and the existing distribution of benefits. Indeed, until then, state intervention had served to reinforce these principles, not to threaten them. As long as direct institutional confrontation was avoided and the policies adopted worked to their benefit, why should the industrialists have mounted a strong organizational protest? Would it not be more likely to expect that they would not attempt to prevent the expansion of direct government participation and intervention in the economy but would instead adopt Simonsen's conciliatory, nondogmatic point of view? It is not surprising, then, that a survey of industrialists' attitudes in 1962 showed quite strong support for the constitutional provision legitimating public economic intervention (56 percent in favor). Industrialists also seemed to agree that the government should, in principle, exercise direct entrepreneurial activities.[24] When the 136 interviewed industrialists were asked, "Have the direct entrepreneurial activities of the government exercised up to now contributed to the economic development of the country?" only 14 percent responded negatively.[25]

Leff's second "proof" of these groups' impotence was their inability to organize an effective protest against the incursion of foreign industrial capital and, more specifically, their failure to prevent the promulgation and, later, the extensive use of Instruction 113 of SUMOC.[26] This Instruction, instituted during the interim regime of Café Filho in 1955, permitted the importing of machinery at a favorable exchange rate in cases where the seller assumed a cruzeiro capital participation in the enterprise using the machinery, rather than payment in foreign exchange.[27] The measure decidedly discriminated in favor of foreign investors. The supposed compensating provisions designed to benefit national investors remained "no more than a hope of justice, forgotten on a page of the *Diário Official.*"[28] To obtain favored treatment a proposed investment had to be approved as desirable for the economy of the country, an approval that was decided by the Foreign Trade Section of the Bank of Brazil (CACEX) and in which the CNI was given consultative participation. Leff's point is that despite "panic" and "violent protest" on the part of domestic industrialists, the policy held firm; and when the government changed it, it did so largely for reasons of its own and not because of group pressures. Although my general conclusions are rather similar, again I believe that the example is badly chosen and that it overstates the case. Although there certainly are elements of nationalist reserve regarding the role of foreign investments in the ideology of Simonsen and Lodi, this issue has badly divided domestic industrialists and threatened to isolate them from their other "productive class" allies.[29] The formal statements on the issue of foreign capital made by the "Plenary Reunions of Industry" sponsored by the CNI in 1953, 1955, 1957, and 1960 waver and meander inconsistently. The Fourth Reunion failed even to make a statement directly on the issue, presumably because of internal differences. The campaign against Instruction 113 was led and conducted virtually single-handedly by FIESP and its member syndicates.[30] The CNI remained rather quiet on the issue; in fact, in 1958 it sponsored an international conference intended to attract foreign industrial capital! The one time a specific campaign was conducted coordinating various industrialists' associations, including the CNI, it was directed against the American Can Company, and the industrialists were successful in preventing the application of Instruction 113. The attitudinal evidence backs up the evidence of institutional uncertainty and indecision. In the survey mentioned above, industrialists' opinions on the Instruction were very divided: 38 percent found it "predominantly unfavorable," 32 percent gave mixed answers, and 30 percent thought it was "predominantly favorable." Asked whether they thought it had favored national development, 58 percent said yes.[31] Even if, as Leff argues (accurately, I believe), this understates the extent of opposition to the measure since hostility was greatest among the largest and most powerful firms, these firms are not the ones that dominate most of the state industrial federations; certainly they are not the ones that dominate the CNI, as I explained above. When this issue shifted in 1961 to the control of profit remittances, the industrialists again demonstrated their fundamental division and ambiguity. State federations took opposing positions. At one point, FIESP found itself in the rather embarrassing position of having taken a public stand against the Celso Brant Remêssa de Lucros bill and having the newspapers expose a secret letter it had sent out supporting the measure.[32] Within the CNI, the conflict between FIESP and FIEGA was ironed out only after a special mixed commission of representatives from both federations drafted a compromise bill designed to replace the Celso Brant proposal.[33] Much to the disappointment of nationalist intellectuals,[34] the anticipated confrontation between a militant national bourgeoisie and foreign imperialist interests with their domestic lackeys failed to materialize.

My point in discussing Leff's two examples is not to refute his conclusions, which in fact concur with those I have reached myself, but simply to note that they do not constitute adequate test cases. In both the expansion of government interventionism and the increase in foreign direct investment, industrialists and their leaders were unsure about where their true interests lay. Therefore, the fact that their representative associations were unable to veto government initiatives on these issues is hardly surprising. In order to test the preventive capacity of a representative association or a coalition of them, one must select an issue of contention in which the actors' interests are obvious to them; only in such cases will associations be willing to commit their resources to an attempt to veto unfavorable authoritative action. In fact, there have been enough examples of fully committed but fruitless veto campaigns for us to conclude that few associations possess this capacity. It is hardly necessary to castigate them for not being successful in a campaign they never undertook.

Regulation, revision, and renegotiation. As it is used here, "regulation" refers to a process whereby administrative elites translate (and in so doing, transform) an authoritatively approved law or decree into a set specific, practicable instructions. Revision and renegotiation involve a series of decisions whereby government controls and incentives in a given policy area are continually subjected to reassessment in the light of changing demands and supports by some government agency. Both stages are integral parts of the Brazilian policy process, and although they are not subjected to much publicity or study, they are extremely important foci for interest conflict and concord. Moreover, they are important manifestations of those traits of the operational code that stress the desirability of avoiding a definitive point of closure and of procrastinating as long as possible. Authority groups can use regulation to grant privately what they have refused publicly; through revision they can sustain the co-optation of interests by keeping alive the hope that it is still possible to obtain a favorable decision. In both cases the general configuration of policy lies firmly in the hands of public authorities, although in its specific implementation the distinction between public and private may break down.

In many ways these processes are similar to that of consultation, except that the latter occurs before an authoritative approval, whereas the former occurs after the decision has been made and is about to be implemented. For this reason, inferences about associational effectiveness in the forums of revision and regulation are difficult to make. Some of the same general rules hold, however. Effectiveness seems to rest on a carefully cultivated climate of mutual respect and mutually accorded legitimacy, on the quality of the association's information and the personal prestige of its leader, and, to a certain extent, on the association's willingness to moderate its demands in accordance with some consensual public interest. Here the associations have an extra foot in the door, since implementation of many policy measures depends on the active and voluntary support of the affected parties. Open refusal to cooperate, recourse to semilegal means of avoidance, or simple passive resistance can render government initiatives ineffective or raise the cost of implementation to prohibitive levels. Whereas a bill can be drafted "in a closet," with a minimum amount of information, to be applied it often requires not only more accurate information, but also the active collaboration of the persons affected. Arriving at a mutually satisfactory arrangement with a well-organized and authentic representative association lowers costs and risks considerably for administrative elites, who otherwise would have to deal with a dispersed and heterogeneous clientele. Thus when an association leader can claim to represent his *classe* and also ensure that his negotiated commitments will be accepted by it, he is in an influential position in the regulating and revising forums.

Physically, these forums are the same as those for consultation: working groups, ad hoc committees, permanent councils, executive groups, and planning and executive commissions. Virtually every important bill that comes from Congress or the presidency is turned over to some temporary or permanent group for regulation. Over time almost all functional major interests have had permanent agencies assigned to them for the constant revision and renegotiation of policy.[35] The discretionary authority these agencies have over the transformation of legislation and the subsequent course of public policy in their respective sectors varies, of course, but my impression is that it is substantial. The major check on their sectorial discretion comes not from legislative authorities or even from the President, but from the competing claims of other administrative agencies and from the mild coordinating activities exercised by finance and planning officials. The extent of this discretion was indirectly illustrated by an aside that I heard several times during interviews with leaders of employers' associations. In excusing their inactivity in the legislative forum, they would mention the general problems of operating in an environment of "demagogic populism" and add that, in any case, the "real" decisions were not made there. "We can afford to take a defeat in the Congress, because when it comes to regulating the bill, we have good contacts."[36]

A case study. Let me end my discussion of the policy-making process by following briefly the interaction between a single representative association and its authority groups from issue to outcome. Reform of the banking system had been a signal in the policy environment for some time, and any extensive changes in the rules of the game were bound to affect the private investment societies. Since 1962 these had been organized into the Association of Credit, Investment, and Finance Companies (ADECIF), under the leadership of a particularly dynamic Rio businessman. ADECIF did not initiate the reform measures; in fact its founding came in response to a tax reform bill initiated by técnicos. Repeatedly during 1963 ADECIF found itself on the defensive against "surprising" administrative regulations and legislative proposals. It fought back with lengthy technical "memorials" to SUMOC, lobbying activity in Brasília, and, in November and December of 1963, a full-scale public opinion campaign in conjunction with other banking and commercial associations against Carvalho Pinto's austerity and loan policies. After Pinto's downfall early in 1964 and during the increasingly "radical" trend of the Goulart regime, ADECIF moved into a position of open opposition to the government. Many of the more vociferous political opponents of the regime were invited to its weekly luncheons, where they gave fiery speeches and made barely concealed references to the impending coup. Immediately following the coup, ADECIF began to reorganize itself for exerting a different type of influence. "The times have changed, . . . and now our duty is to present to the government, which desires our collaboration, concrete and profound proposals—unlike in the past, when the government at best only tolerated our collaboration."[37] A system of permanent and temporary committees was established; ministers and higher civil servants were invited to honorary dinners, and invitations began to come in from the government for participation in working groups and drafting committees.

Despite its conciliatory position and its initial success in reestablishing access, ADECIF's troubles were far from over. The new "revolutonary" authorities had two immediate economic objectives: to reduce the rate of inflation and to improve the sources of government revenue. Both of these goals conflicted with the extensive sale of *letras de câmbio* (bills of exchange), the principal merchandise of the investment societies. The *letras* were manifestly inflationary, in that they promised a certain sum of money for future delivery at high monthly rates of return calculated on the anticipated intervening inflation. They were also normally made out to an anonymous bearer and thus were used as a convenient means for avoiding taxes. The monetary authorities were therefore bent upon eliminating, or at least curbing, the market in *letras de câmbio*, and the administration's proposed banking reform was definitely perceived as unfavorable to ADECIF's interests. Despite the association's opposition to the program, it agreed to proceed in "a technical, not a polemical manner" and sent a long and detailed "Exposition of Motives" to executive and legislative authorities.[38] Meanwhile, the regime, after brief and perfunctory formal consultations, had sent the Capital Markets Bill on to

Congress. A delegation of ADECIF leaders went to Brasília for an extended period of personal legislative lobbying. They had mixed success, losing in the *Câmara* and gaining in the *Senado*. Despite considerable fear of intervention and bureaucratic controls, pressures by members for a more aggressive stance, opposition by other representative associations, and some divisive tactics by individual firms making isolated appeals, the leadership remained calm and the *classe* united. The final compromise version was "great improved," and most of the favorable Senate amendments were accepted.*

The regime was adamant, however, and técnico-inspired executive vetos reinstated some of the original "objectionable" provisions. ADECIF was faced with a major tactical decision. The law set a very high minimum capital limit (five billion cruzeiros) on registered investment banks. Only foreign firms and a few national ones could possibly meet it. It also required that holders of the *letras* be identified. The ADECIF leaders knew that these were both issues with considerable potential for mobilizing public opinion. Moreover, they had both the necessary funds and access to mass media. But they also observed that "the law still depends on its regulation," and that regulation involved hearings before the consultative commissions attached to the National Monetary Council.[39] ADECIF (and its sister organization from São Paulo, ACREFI) had been given seats on three of these. In fact, one of its vice-presidents was to become the president of the crucial Capital Markets Commission. The choice was not without risk; it involved the future prosperity, if not the survival, of this line of business. In addition, as the members observed, "the men of this government have good intentions, but other governments will come, and so will other politicians."[40] To make matters even more uncertain, one of the government-appointed members of the National Monetary Council was a paulista banker from one of the few national concerns that could raise the high minimum capital.

ADECIF chose moderation. Its leaders apparently calculated that they had sufficient influence and that administrative authorities had enough decisional discretion to make a mutually satisfactory compromise possible. So, instead of widening the audience and bringing pressure to bear at a higher, more political level, they toned down their protest and offered to collaborate "practically and objectively." As one of its leaders said in the interview, "After all, we have to live with Dênio [the President of the Central Bank] for the rest of the year."[41] The gamble, if there ever was one, paid off. Although they did not receive complete

---

* The ADECIF cause was helped by the outbreak of the Mannesman Steel case, a scandal involving the parallel market.

satisfaction and had to accept a substantial degree of government control as well as a few new taxes, the credit, finance, and investment societies found their legal status and economic position consolidated, even
enhanced. ADECIF subsequently played an important role in consultations and revisions of stock market and tax reforms.

Of course, ADECIF is no ordinary representative association, and
thus this is not a typical case of exercise of influence. With a high
rate of member participation and social interaction, good technical resources, independent and voluntary financing, and authoritative leadership, ADECIF has an unusual edge in its exchanges with authority
groups. Moreover, it operates in a lucrative field where firms pay high
salaries and can attract better qualified personnel than the government.
But the case does illustrate clearly the central role of regulation, revision, and renegotiation in Brazilian policy-making. So central is this
stage that it colors the entire interaction process, inhibiting associations
from making aggressive moves or appeals to a wider public and reinforcing their propensity for consensual collaboration and acceptance of incremental successes. The discretion of administrative officials in the implementation of approved decisions varies according to policy sector,
but it appears sufficiently great to modify the behavior of interest actors
and to afford them one of their prime targets for exerting influence.

The Reaction to Impotence

Of course, not all associations accept this limited role voluntarily and
exclusively. For the frustrated, recourse from this consensual but lop-
sided transaction is possible, though costly and a bit risky. The essence
of this tactical recourse is to appeal to or threaten a wider public than
would normally or habitually be concerned with the matter.[42] For those
representative associations that can afford it, the usual response to a
lack of response on the part of authority groups is to engage in public
relations campaigns. Such attempts are no novelty in Brazilian interest
politics. One of the first concerns of the CIB when it was founded in
1933 was to set up a propaganda department "to enlighten public opinion by means of pamphlets, newspaper articles, and conferences."[43]
Funds of the SESI were used extensively for this purpose until the dis-
closures of 1953–54. However, large-scale public relations campaigns,
especially of the "institutional promotion" type, have become common
only in the last decade.[44] As Table 13.9 shows, civic associations engage
in a great deal of propagandizing, as might have been anticipated. Private employers' associations are slightly more likely to have actually engaged in a campaign than their syndical equivalents, and yet they are
also more likely to report not having done so. The paradox is explained

TABLE 13.9
INCIDENCE OF PUBLIC RELATIONS CAMPAIGNS

Type of association	Yes, and could cite a campaign	Yes, but could cite no campaign	No	No answer, Don't know
Employers'				
Syndical ($N = 27$)	18.6%	33.3%	[11.1%]	37.0%
Private ($N = 38$)	28.9	[10.6]	34.2	26.3
Workers' ($N = 21$)	[14.3]	[4.8]	42.9	38.2
Liberal-				
professional ($N = 10$)	[20.0]	40.0	[10.0]	30.0
Civic ($N = 11$)	54.5	[9.1]	0.0	34.4

NOTE: Rows may not add to 100 because of rounding.

by the fact that so many employers' syndicates think the tactic of public relations is fruitful although they have not yet used it. This may be because it is illegal to use *impôsto sindical* funds for propagandizing, and members must volunteer to raise large sums of money. For many syndicates of employers and liberal professionals, the will is greater than the wherewithal. For workers' syndicates the tactic seems out of reach. To date the most extensive public relations efforts have been produced by the specialized private associations: ABDIB, in favor of protection and preferential purchase arrangements for the national capital goods industry,[45] ABIF, against the threat to nationalize the pharmaceutical industry, and ABC, against the importation of refined copper. In all three cases, subsequent government policy was favorable, although of course the public relations efforts were not totally responsible for the outcomes.

For less well-organized and well-financed groups, the easiest way to enlarge their audience is to conduct a *marcha* (march), *passeata* (parade), or *comício* (public rally). This is a frequent tactic for interest or attitude groups composed of a relatively small number of militants who believe that their cause is backed by a great many latent or potential supporters. Hence one finds a "March with God and Against the High Cost of Living" organized by a housewives' organization, a "March with God and in Favor of Students Who Can't Get into the University" run by a group of parents, and even a "March of the Rosary for Peace and Tranquility in the Household" threatened by an association of sugar plantation owners. In 1958 the coffee growers' associations of Paraná organized a "March of Production" (this one in automobiles, not on foot), which was blocked by army troops on the grounds that it was "capable of disrupting public order and imposing upon the government measures that would be prejudicial to the country."[46] In general, such demonstrations are signs of impotence and marginality. A major exception, however, was the famous "March of the Family with God for Freedom," in which perhaps 500,000 paulistas turned out to demonstrate against the Goulart regime. Organized, as I have noted, by women's civic associations with the help of numerous employers' organizations, especially the Brazilian Rural Society, it has been credited by some with providing the civilian *cobertura* for the military coup that followed less than two weeks later. By contrast, two years later the principal organizers of the Marcha, dissatisfied with the ensuing policies of the "revolutionary" regime, held a second march, the "March of Silence," which drew no more than sixty participants and the complete indifference of authorities.[47]

The next step in this process of escalating group protest would appear to be a refusal to cooperate with authority groups. In practice, this is done by withdrawing representatives from existing committees, councils, or working groups, by withholding information, or by refusing to appoint members to newly established consultative posts in cases where government policy has become so unfavorable that the group refuses to associate with it. This is not a particularly common tactic in Brazilian interest politics, although, especially in the areas of price control and agrarian reform, both of the latter types of resistance have been used.

Another tactic of interest protest, even less public and more difficult to assess, is corruption, or the subversion or buying out of elected or administrative officials. Many of the practices I have discussed above might in some political cultures be considered corrupt, but in a system of political realism, such as Brazil's, they are considered normal adjustments to the exigencies of the situation. The outright buying of votes and support is, however, a definite violation of the rules of the game. Consequently, it is not easy to gather conclusive evidence on it. Some of the more "inside-dopesterish" descriptions of the polity tend to place a great deal of emphasis on the role of payoffs and kickbacks of various sorts, and I have been treated to some fairly convincing descriptions of how the method works. Nevertheless, my impression is that representative associations do not use this tactic on any massive scale. It is simply not possible, least of all for representative associations, to buy major policy changes. Occasionally, they will raise a *caixinha* (literally, a little box) for the purpose of pushing through or blocking a given policy measure. For example, in 1960 it became openly publicized that the Federation of Rural Associations of the State of São Paulo had raised a *caixinha* (by taxing its members informally ten cruzeiros per hectare) to finance a campaign against the state's impending agrarian reform bill. (FARESP protested that there was nothing illegitimate about this and that the funds were to go to a public relations campaign.)[48] But most informants felt that such tactics were risky for associations and that they were much more likely to be used by individual firms.*

The next step in the escalation of protest is the threat of violence. In its mildest and most institutionalized form, this involves strikes and lockouts. As we have seen, most of the conflict between workers and employers is handled indirectly—channeled through the labor court system and the conciliatory offices of the Ministry of Labor. Strikes tend to be infrequent, short-lived and oriented around immediate economic objectives. Controversies involving working conditions and recognition of bargaining rights have often been resolved "from above" by the Labor Code, and until the early 1960's work stoppages for purposes of political support or general class solidarity were rare.[49] Lockouts are also rather rare, and, as Jorge Miglioli indicates, they are more often directed against authority groups than against workers.[50] Most of these breakdowns are decided upon by the local syndicates, although there are occasional spontaneous, "wildcat" strikes. Under Goulart, peak associations, federations, and confederations engaged fairly often in this sort of protest.[51] Nevertheless, observers agree that most strikes and other forms of work stoppage—at least since 1930—have been peaceful and respectful of the rather restrictive legal proscriptions. Although on occasion troops have been called out and violence used to suppress such protests—most commonly against student strikes, for some reason—this is an accidental consequence, neither intended nor welcomed by the strikers themselves. Nor have associations been active in instigating or organizing riots or acts of sporadic violence. With the possible exception of the few rural workers' organizations that began encouraging land seizures in 1963, they have been very obviously reluctant to adopt such illegal strategies.

There is one final recourse for associations whose interests or attitudes have been threatened by authority groups: they can engage in

---

* The general opinion also seems to be that foreign-owned enterprises resort to these tactics most often. These companies are also demonstrably the largest investors in public relations. This suggests that their relative lack of success in dominating national representative associations, combined with the cautiousness of the foreign chambers of commerce, has prevented their using the usual consultative, regulative, and revisory channels. Thus the less orthodox channels of public relations and corruption are all that are open to them.

In 1963 two congressional investigations were held to investigate the activities of *grupos de pressão*—one into the activities of IBAD and IPÊS and the other into the activities of the various leftist student and worker organizations. Both came up with convincing evidence on massive financing of associational activity by both private parties and authority groups, but both failed to show any causal link between this financial hanky-panky and public policy outcomes.

conspiratorial activities to overthrow those authorities. As the climate of mutual confidence and its accompanying conciliatory political style disintegrated during the Goulart regime, interest and attitude groups of all types began to participate in conspiratorial activities. The leaders of many employers' associations widely believed that workers' organizations, especially the semilegal Commando Geral dos Trabalhadores, were conspiring to establish a revolutionary "syndicalist republic," although conclusive evidence has never been presented. This partly accounts for the counterrevolutionary efforts of the employers. Conservative elites were constantly urging them to oppose the regime more rigorously and to link up with the military.[52] Civil-military contacts were made, a good many of them through the offices of IPÊS in São Paulo.[53] Leaders of paulista employers' associations began secretly meeting with representatives of the state government. It was widely reported that leaders of rural associations were encouraging and coordinating the purchase of arms. On the day before the Goulartist *comício* of May 13, 1964, the Confederation of Commercial Associations launched a direct attack on the President's "subversive" activities, talked of arming to resist them, and suggested the creation of a "General Command of the Productive Classes." A similar fiery session occurred in the Commercial Association of São Paulo on the day before the coup broke out openly. During the coup itself, representative associations served as communications and mobilization headquarters.[54] In a personal interview, one of FIESP's executives claimed that it had collected one and a half billion cruzeiros (over a million dollars) for the cause and that it had supplied vast amounts of food, clothing, and transportation for the military forces.[55] The Federation of Industries of Minas Gerais has made similar, if not so substantial, claims.[56] Important as this activity might have been materially and spiritually, however, it was not decisive. The coup of 1964 was primarily a military affair.[57] In fact, no conspiracy or illegal attempt to seize power in Brazilian history has been primarily the product of representative associations.* In most cases, associations have been reluctant and startled spectators rather than enthusiastic participants.

But it is true that the Goulart regime experienced a marked rise in the importance of all these unorthodox means for expressing associational demands: public relations campaigns, *marchas, passeatas,* and *comícios*, refusal to cooperate, corruption, strikes, riots, sporadic violence, and conspiracy. Since the installation of the military regime in

---

* A possible exception might be the short-lived sergeants' revolt of September 1963, in which the leaders of a noncommissioned officer's association and some workers' leaders played a prominent role.

April 1964, except for public relations campaigns, which seem to have become a standard device of Brazilian employers, the use of these tactics has declined, and the interaction between representative associations and authority groups has returned to its normal pattern of conciliatory dependency.

A General Assessment of Influence

The evidence on influence from all three perspectives—reputational, situational, and inferential—is roughly concordant and thus permits sweeping but, I believe, reliable generalizations. Brazilian representative associations do not have the capacity to determine policy outcomes at the national level. No single organized group or coalition of organized groups dominates interest politics. Those specialized, relatively autonomous subsystems of influence within which organized groups have been able to control outcomes in their favor (*clientelas*) have been and are being subordinated to more general policy considerations. There is no evidence that, globally speaking, associational influence has risen consistently with development. In fact, there is evidence that the influence of industrialists' interest groups has even declined with industrialization.[58] The influence of workers appeared to have been increasing steadily since the 1950's, but it was always dependent upon the benevolence of authority groups, and hence was highly vulnerable, as the events following the 1964 coup proved conclusively. That of employers and liberal professionals has varied even more unevenly. The current influence of a few civic associations seems the product more of present political circumstances than of any long-term trend toward large-scale voluntary citizen participation and organization.

Representative associations have not been remarkably successful in determining which neglected problems are to become privileged issues for public debate and government deliberation. Most issues are selected for treatment simply because they are imposed upon policy-makers by manifest physical necessity (floods, droughts, power failures, etc.) or because of obvious economic pressures like the persistent crisis in the balance of payments. How these issues are treated seems to be more a function of the survival instinct of the professional politicians, the nationalist ideology of intellectuals, and the theoretical assessments of economic administrators than of the signaling efforts of organized interest and attitude groups. Issues that have been raised and handled creatively—autonomously and innovatively—have rarely been the result of organized pressures generated by the affected parties.[59] The efforts of Brazilian representative associations to influence public policy are, by and large, reactive, or in response to the initiative of other actors; defensive, or devoted to the retention of previously granted rights and benefits; and incremental, or aimed at introducing favorable modifications through consultation, negotiation, regulation, and revision. Rarely have associations embarked upon directive, offensive, and global campaigns for the acquisition of new privileges or status. Even more rarely have such campaigns been fruitful.[60]

As we have seen, there are a great many factors explaining why representative associations have had to accept this limited role. First are those relating to the pattern of political culture. A history of paternalism and patrimonialism has made association leaders and followers ready to leave initiation to higher authorities and to regard the government as the supreme *patrão* of the society. Differentiated private social groups feel no spontaneous sense of collective, societal responsibility. The strength and prevalence of family and friendship ties further weakens the consciousness of functionally specific groups and lowers the level of voluntary participation in formal associations. The historically weak role of political indoctrination and formal doctrines has left most social groups without a distinctive ideology. "Historical opportunism" dominates the behavior of associations, deprives them of ideological consistency and of militancy, and leaves them to operate out of pure empiricism and pragmatism. The interelite norms of nonviolence, procrastination, and co-optation produce a pervasive faith in *diálogo*, or the ability to solve problems and disputes by negotiated compromise. Associations will maintain this *diálogo* even when their obvious material interests are being violated. Given the tendency of the policy process to avoid definitive points of closure, they can always hope that by maintaining the posture of collaboration and moderation they will eventually be able to cash in on it.

Second are those factors relating to the corporatist pattern of government policy toward associability. There can be no doubt that the financial dependency of most interest groups upon the federal and state governments tends to inhibit their aggressiveness in pushing demands. Most of the syndical organizations depend on the *impôsto sindical*, employers' confederations and federations are very tied to their SESI, SESC, SENAI, and SENAC receipts, and many ostensibly private entities are dependent upon various official subsidies and loans. Government threats to cut these off, to make collection difficult, or even to examine closely how they have been spent are usually enough to ensure a collaborative posture. Interference in associational elections has been a more or less constant feature of Brazilian corporatism, giving rise to the *pelego*, whose professional task is that of maintaining moderation in group conflict for workers, employers, and liberal professionals. Government control over syndical recognition can be used to reward friends and punish recalcitrants. In addition, a vast gamut of personal incentives may be offered to or withheld from class leaders, ranging from patronage for self and relatives, to prestigious official service abroad, to low-cost credit and subsidies for their firms. An association leader who plays the game properly can parlay his position into economic, social, and even political fortune. Only a few leaders do this, but there are enough so that such "sell-outs" are a matter of public comment and a source of member disillusionment. Finally, the very existence of this set of incentives has divided the system of interest representation into two parts, at least for employers and liberal professionals: the syndical and the private associations. Although they occasionally work side by side, often they represent rather different interests, and it is sometimes unclear who is speaking for whom. In other instances, and this has particularly been the case with merchants and landowners, the two hierarchies have been in more or less constant conflict. The result has been a weakening of one of the supposed strengths of the corporatist system, unity of representation. Moreover, the official *enquadramento* system, with its distinctive hierarchies of representation, discourages and often even prohibits the formation of interassociational fronts. Many of these functionally distinct peak associations compete for the same institutional and personal privileges. The "productive classes," the middle sectors, and the workers find it difficult and hazardous to create lasting class coalitions. They may converge now and then to defend a single measure, but permanent class alliances, even those sanctioned and supported by authorities, have been strife-ridden, short-lived, and largely ineffective.

Third are those factors relating to the pattern of emergence. Representative associations are relative newcomers to the Brazilian policy process, reflecting the fact that the social groups they represent have themselves only recently acquired differentiated status and interests and are still quite heterogeneous in background and objective.[61] Most important, these organized groups appeared on the scene after, not before, the creation of a government bureaucracy. In fact, as we have seen, they were in part a creation of that bureaucracy. Associations that existed before 1930, especially the commercial associations and the rural societies, never managed to adjust to the changed rules of modern Brazilian politics and have acted, at least until as recently as 1964, as perpetual outsiders.* One might say those formed under the corporatist aegis have, also until recently, adjusted to the new rules all too well

---

* The reign of João Daudt d'Oliveira in the Rio Commercial Association is a definite exception to this rule.

and consequently have lost their capacity for autonomous action. The latest modification of the emergence pattern, the creation of independent private associations, has some far-reaching implications for the future role of organized interests, but they are too recent to have developed a distinctive style and operational code of their own. Although the generalization is hazardous because the number of exceptions nearly outweighs the number of confirmations, one might say that at this point the old groups are too alienated to understand the changes in Brazilian interest politics, the middle-aged groups are too co-opted to act independently, and the new groups are too uncertain and inexperienced to play an effective role. To these factors should also be added the fact that associability is still a relatively concentrated phenomenon. Only São Paulo and Guanabara have enough consciousness of purpose to succeed at influencing decisions at the national level, and yet both the national Congress and the peak associations usually have a predominance of members from areas where group consciousness and associability is still embryonic and the style of politics is still familistic and clientelistic. Typically, the less developed states fear the aggressiveness and sense of purpose of the more developed states and resist their leadership. These regionalist controversies, rooted in the unevenness of development and associability, weaken the position of national groups, which are often dominated by leaders from "unrepresentative" states.*

Fourth are those factors relating to the pattern of group interaction. The major source of the weakness of associational influence is the enormous, if poorly coordinated, economic power of the federal government. One of my Brazilian friends remarked to me, when I mentioned that industrialists did not seem to have much control over policy, "What can you expect? After all, most of them are concessionaries of state favors." This may be somewhat exaggerated—there are, after all, important sources of independent entrepreneurial skill and financial strength in the Brazilian industrialist sector—but it does reflect the prominent position of authority groups, both as consumers of products and services and as distributors of credit. It also explains why associations are reluctant to invest in aggressive assaults on and confrontations with government policies or even government intentions. For they have a very limited capacity for threatening the status or tenure of political and administrative elites. Their role in the election, selection, deposition, and ad-

---

* For example, the CNI president elected during Goulart's term was from Maranhão (eighteenth among twenty-two states in industrial production, fifteenth in industrial employment). The CNC president at that time was from Santa Catarina (tenth in commercial turnover). Its current president is from Rio Grande do Norte (nineteenth in commercial turnover).

vancement of these elites hardly matches the latter's ability to reward and punish. This disparity in the ability to affect each other's future is compounded by a growing disparity in their respective command of technical information and expertise.

There is another debilitating factor about which one can only speculate. For a businessman or industrialist to operate in the chaotic, over-bureaucratized, and inflationary environment of contemporary Brazil, he must resort to certain semilegal procedures (*jeitos*) in his dealings with authority groups, just as syndical organizations must occasionally ignore some of the more restrictive provisions of the CLT. As a result, he is exceedingly vulnerable. Even if authority groups are reluctant or unable to bring the economic weight of the state to bear, they can usually threaten individual firms or representative associations with disclosure, prosecution, or other legal sanctions. Faced with the prospect of having to pay up overdue welfare contributions, comply with minimum wage requirements, or explain why he did not file an income tax return, many an aggrieved and potentially aggressive industrialist is likely to reassess his position. So are syndicates when authorities threaten to inquire about where their funds are being banked or how they have been spent. The result is an added contribution to the generally defensive posture of both individual and collective interest actors.

The fact that the principal interlocutor of representative associations is the public administration has a somewhat paradoxical effect on their influence. On the one hand, the dispersion, the overlap, and the competition among agencies give them some assurance that they can find a "friend in court" and increase their potential for exerting defensive and obstructive influence, although it makes coodinated positive action more difficult.[62] On the other hand, the existence of a fairly homogeneous nucleus of técnicos—recruited by merit, in agreement on the general objectives of economic policy, and entrenched in horizontal, polyfunctional financial and planning agencies—definitely inhibits the capacity of associations for initiating new and specific measures designed to benefit themselves.

FOURTEEN

Conclusion: Development, Interest Politics, the "System," and Its Transformation

THE "ART OF ASSOCIATION" has increased with the development of Brazilian society. The number, coverage, and density of associational forms of interest expression have all expanded. During the period examined in detail (1930–65), complex networks linking groups at the local, state, and national levels have emerged and become institutionalized, contributing to the nationalization of political life. At the same time, the scope of associational activity has become more functionally specific. Interaction with authority groups has increased significantly and has tended to follow more and more institutionalized channels, despite the persistence of particularistic nexuses and personalistic styles of demand-making. These efforts are markedly concentrated upon executive authorities and bureaucratic agencies, bypassing party structures, the electoral system, and the legislative process. These findings were largely anticipated by my original working hypotheses.

The most challenging findings, however, are those concerning *indeterminate* relations between development and associability, findings that in effect involve the confirmation of null hypotheses. First, the structural transformation of Brazilian society has *not* led to the formation of autonomous, aggressive, and highly interactive interest groups articulating competitive, alternative demands. Indeed, there are only very faint and very belated signs of a relationship between development and pluralism. Second, these changes do *not* seem to have produced cohesive, multifaceted coalitions of associations along mutually exclusive and totally antagonistic lines. The Brazilian case calls into question orthodox assumptions about the relationship between industrialization and polarized class conflict. Third, despite the conclusive evidence on the general increase in associability, there is *no* such evidence of an increase in the influence these groups have upon public policy-making. In short, "pressure-group predominance" may not be the inevitable component of political modernity that it is often thought to be.

In the foregoing text, these puzzling outcomes of the emergence and interaction processes have (rather surreptitiously) been "explained away" by reliance upon the two intervening clusters of variables, political culture and public policy toward associability. It has been shown that, with few exceptions, the attitudes and expectations of interest group leaders and the efforts and intentions of authoritative elites have been both mutually supportive and temporally consistent. Their combined effect has certainly had a major impact in altering the development-associability pattern.

Nevertheless, I became dissatisfied with this explanation of the apparently deviant pattern. Summary comparison with other Latin American countries, such as Argentina, Chile, and Mexico, at roughly similar stages of societal development but with different historical patterns of policy and values, seemed to turn up some very similar outcomes. I have also become increasingly dissatisfied with the way in which the major independent variable, development, has been operationalized. Is it not possible that, in confining myself to quantitative, linear projections of multivariate trends, I have overlooked certain qualitative relationships between the component subprocesses of development, such as the interaction and timing of urbanization, bureaucratization, and industrialization? Perhaps a more imaginative juxtaposition of these factors might contribute to a better understanding of the pattern of associational response. I have therefore decided to end on a note of uncertainty and speculation about two general themes: (1) the qualitative nature of the developmental process and its relationship to the pattern of organized group response, and (2) the direct and indirect consequences of this response for the political system and for the future development of Brazilian society.

The Brazilian Pattern of Development

As used in this study, "development" is a universal (though historically delimited) concept, referring to a process of structural transformation in the division of labor brought on by greater differentiation and specialization and involving increased reliance on scientific technology and inanimate sources of power. As such, it can be used comparatively in a wide variety of societal contexts. However, I have also argued that it is composed of numerous subprocesses. The pattern of component subprocesses gives to a particular society a distinctive developmental syndrome; most important, it has a strong impact upon the formation of new social groups and upon the distribution of initiative and influence within and between these groups. The result is the emergence of different patterns of group identity, interest, and antagonism.

As the result of some reflection and reading on the general configuration of Brazilian development,[1] I have become more and more convinced that the pattern in that country (and, by inference, in several other Latin American countries) differs in certain fundamental aspects from the "classical" developmental syndrome of Northwestern Europe and North America. Development in Brazil is *not* a simple replication of what has happened in the already developed societies. Brazilian society (or polity for that matter) is not simply "further behind" on the same predetermined multivariate regression line. Only a new or modified regression equation involving a different weighting and timing of what are otherwsie universal variables is likely to predict the Brazilian (or, for that matter, the Latin American) variation in outcome.

If I am right in these speculations, the political consequences of development predicted by the major theorists of the classical pattern of structural transformation are not likely to materialize—at least not when and how they have been predicted. Pluralism, polarization, and pressure-group predominance are predictions of just such an order.

At several points in preceding chapters, I noted that the empirically observable pattern of differentiated interests and attitudes is not a sufficient guide to the pattern of associational emergence. What seemed to provide the necessary and sufficient condition was an element of entrepreneurship triggered by actual or anticipated conflict with other latent or organized interests. Interest conflict, or better its perception, served as the midwife of associability. Because of a variety of factors, the developmental process in Brazil in its initial stages has followed a nonantagonistic pattern—a sort of constantly expanding-sum game in which the existing system of economic, social, and political relationships has not faced a set of internal contradictions that it could not resolve by incremental adjustment. Those major interest and class conflicts that propelled the classical model of development to ever higher levels of investment and productivity—for example between traditional rural (feudal) and commercial-industrial (capitalist) elites, between bourgeoisie and proletariat, even between private and public control over production and allocation, failed to crystallize in Brazil. Instead, the principal stimuli for technological and institutional innovation have come from outside the system: shifts in export capacity, the terms of trade, and foreign capital flows.

This nonantagonistic, nonrevolutionary, externally penetrated pattern has had a number of political consequences. Most critically, there has been no dramatic confrontation between the *ancien* and the *nouveau régimes*; no single "modernizing elite" has succeeded in capturing the political apparatus and imposing its distinctive model of society. Instead, there has been a process of continuous accommodation whereby previous power holders have made concessions to new power contenders without losing their original privileges and perquisites. Likewise, the newcomers have respected these establishmentarian rights and have not tried to eliminate them, even when they have had the power to do so. Brazil is a prime example of what Charles Anderson has called "a political museum."[2] The two consequences of this "sedimentary" rather than "metamorphic" pattern of development of particular importance to this study are (1) the absence of any global challenge to or transformation of the role of authority groups and their subsequent wide degree of autonomy from organized control by class or sectorial interests, and (2) the absence of any major interest conflict that might have galvanized organizational energies, eliminated certain associations from contention, and established some definite hierarchy of influence or dominant ruling interest coalition. Let us now examine the subprocesses of structural change in order to understand how related policies have contributed to such a divergent developmental syndrome.

Urbanization. The urbanization of Brazil preceded its industrialization by many years and has subsequently continued at a higher rate.[3] By 1920, six cities already had populations exceeding 100,000. Unlike urbanization in Europe, which was closely related to the rapid absorption of large masses of factory labor, in Brazil it was the product of higher rates of population growth in rural areas and massive internal migration drawn, in particular, by the early marked disparity in living standards between town and country.[4] Employment in cities grew primarily as a result of commercialization, as the cities became entrepôts in the increasing integration of Brazil into the world economy. A sizable urban middle class developed and grew accustomed to relatively high incomes and living conditions, which they proved increasingly capable of protecting politically.

Bureaucracy. The urban expansion of the late nineteenth and early twentieth centuries, coupled with almost one hundred years of formal political independence, brought on the creation and consolidation of what was, by European standards, a prematurely large public bureaucracy. These administrative and political structures long antedate the accelerated differentiation of the contemporary period. They provided traditional ruling groups with relatively flexible institutions for protecting their existing privileges and also for co-opting emerging protest movements. As we have seen, the Estado Cartorial was developed during this period as an explicit strategy for using public employment as an accommodative device. Celso Furtado observes:

The institutional framework of the country . . . has always been relatively advanced, at least from a formal point of view. Brazilians have always had a fine opinion about their country and in elaborating its constitutions they were concerned more with keeping up with more advanced countries than with the social reality and degree of evolution of national structures. This form of alienation had its historical advantages, for in moments of crisis it was always possible to find solutions in elements of the institutional structure that had remained a dead letter, without *regulamentação*.[5]

Premature bureaucratization was also to have an important impact on one of the system's main policy outputs, chronic inflation. It virtually guaranteed inefficient and irrational performance of government services as well as a persistent budget deficit. Most important, however, was the creation of an enormous, complex, and largely parasitic social organization, the state, as a more or less autonomous stratum with corporate interests and objectives of its own, very difficult to dismantle (without the use of large-scale violence) or even to control in the interests of a single modernizing elite.[6]

Industrialization. A certain amount of industrialization in light consumer goods had accompanied the earlier urbanization process, but the major impetus came as the result of exogenous and essentially fortuitous factors: two world wars and a prolonged depression in the developed economies. The disruption in foreign trade, especially by the dramatic collapse of exchange earnings following 1929, shifted the focus of the economy to internal markets and investment and gave Brazilian industrialization its most distinctive rationale: import substitution.[7] Compared with the massive displacement of artisan production, the continuous enlargement of markets through competition, and lower prices for consumers (all of which were present in the classical model), import substitution was relatively painless. Few artisans were displaced, the market already existed, and the previous external suppliers had been conveniently removed. Being presented as it were with a guaranteed, captive market (sustained in the 1930's by government subsidies to the coffee sector) and with prices determined exogenously, the new domestic producers were under few pressures to rationalize or even consistently improve productivity. Benefiting mutually from these oligopolistic or near monopolistic conditions, domestic producers subsequently devoted most of their efforts to retaining their privileged condition. The linked crises in foreign trade, along with the gradual deterioration in Brazil's terms of trade, facilitated their task. Hence, seemingly irrational, uneconomical, and patrimonial managerial practices persisted, and these have had an important dampening effect upon labor protest.[8]

External dependence. Perhaps the most obvious effect the external context has had upon Brazilian development is Brazil's almost complete dependence upon imported technology. This twentieth-century technology is vastly more capital-intensive. Thus it has become possible for a late-developing economy to attain relatively high levels of productivity without employing large masses of workers.[9] As a consequence, industry's share of gross national income rises impressively while industrial employment tends to stagnate or even decrease. Gláucio Soares also points out that the new technology means large, even gigantic, firms with a much greater component of administrative, nonmanual personnel swelling the ranks of the *mesoi*—already unusually large as the result of premature urbanization and the expansion of public bureaucracies.[10] "Thus, that which was a belated effect of industrialization in Western Europe and the United States, . . . the formation of large service sectors, . . . manifests itself from the start of industrialization in Latin America"[11] and in so doing radically alters the balance of potential influence between different class actors. Whether for purposes of partisan appeal, bloc voting, mass demonstration, or revolutionary upheaval, the industrial working class in late-developing countries is outnumbered by these admittedly heterogeneous *mesoi*, especially in the strategically placed administrative centers.

But the influence of external factors has worked in more direct ways upon the polity. As we have seen, the issue of the role of foreign capital has badly divided many associations and fragmented many potential alliances that might otherwise have played a more assertive political role. On the other hand, I have commented that these large foreign interests were conspicuously absent from the normal channels of national interest expression, preferring to work through other means: foreign chambers of commerce (to a very limited extent), diplomatic circles, individual contacts, large-scale public relations campaigns, electoral lobbies like IBAD, and, it has been rumored, covert payment to public officials for services rendered. Their aggressive presence within the interest associational structure would have given it an alien image and thus incited popular resentment. (The commercial associations have long suffered from this.) Their cautious absence contributes to the general impression that entrepreneurial associations do not articulate the "real" interests at stake. (The Confederação Nacional da Indústria certainly illustrates this dilemma.) Either way, the sheer magnitude of the foreign presence in Brazil's economy helps rob its polity of an actor crucial to the classical or Marxist model of development: an active, self-confident "conquering bourgeoisie."[12]

Structural dualism. Although the collapse of agricultural export earnings did provide the major impulse to sustained development, the industrialization, urbanization, and bureaucratization of Brazilian society have neither produced nor been accompanied by a definitive break with the rural sector.[13] On the contrary, dependent as these processes have been upon foreign exchange earnings available only through the export of primary products, the emerging elites not only abstained from reforming that sector of the economy, they even intensified previous policies designed to subsidize and protect the privileges of rural landowners and their urban commercial and financial allies. The failure of this antagonism to materialize can also be explained in part by intersectorial capital flows from the rural to the urban sector and by the underlying persistence of rural-urban familistic ties.[14]

The simultaneous existence of such different forms of social organization, labor remuneration, technological skill, authority, and productive relations between a mercantilistic and stagnant rural sector and a capitalistic and dynamic urban sector has been termed structural dualism. Whether it is perceived as a complete gap or discontinuity between "open" and "closed" components[15] or as an asymmetric, exploitive, "internal colonialist" nexus between metropolis and satellite,[16] its existence clearly affects the pattern of emerging political conflict. The more or less intact persistence of traditional modes of production and authority in rural areas provides a steady outflow of migrants, an inexhaustible labor pool for the relatively few jobs created by industrialization. This of course tends to lessen the bargaining power of labor and elevate rates of return on capital—despite reduced market size caused by the lack of rural purchasing power. The persistence of such a vast differential in wages and working conditions also acts to inhibit the emergence of a sense of deprivation and, consequently, of group or class consciousness. Normally, the increase in the demand for agricultural products caused by higher urban standards of living could be expected to set off disruptive changes in rural areas, already weakened by massive out-migration. In Brazil this potential interest conflict has been largely avoided by a continuous expansion of the area cultivated. Initially, import substitution industrialization operates within "captive" markets and does not depend upon income or property redistribution for enlarged markets.

In summary, then,

Industrialization [in Brazil] can continue forward without any effect on agricultural salaries and without affecting significantly the profitability of the export sector; thus, there exists no incompatibility between the advance of substitutive industrialization and the recuperation of the export sector when favorable conditions occur in external markets, as became evident in Brazil during the 1950's, when a great expansion in coffee production was accomplished at the same time that substitutive industrialization reached high rates of growth.[17]

Rapid economic growth and inflation. Two "output characteristics" were crucial in avoiding (or at least postponing) the emergence of fundamental interest conflicts during the initial transformation process: rapid economic growth and inflation. The high growth rate, accompanied by high rates of profit, ensured that decisions on resource allocation would take place in an expanding-sum context. This undoubtedly helped convince actors that advantages accruing to one social group would not automatically entail losses to others—that public policies could benefit all concerned. The sense of expanding opportunity and unbounded optimism produced by high, cumulative rates of growth also probably caused some actors not directly and favorably affected to defer their gratifications and to accept greater short-term sacrifices.[18] It also meant a steady expansion of government revenues, some of which could be diverted into strategic co-optive, paternalistic payoffs to disfavored social groups and geographic regions.

Consistently high but controlled rates of inflation probably had an even greater effect on conflict avoidance. Beyond its economic impact of increasing the level of profits, ensuring the rapidity of investment, and diverting resources to the industrial sector, inflation has the supreme political virtue of obfuscating the distribution of benefits—"permitting one to give favors with one hand and withdraw them with the other, ... [which] confuses the workers, making them unable to distinguish their own interests."[19] Associational actors, especially those representing salaried groups, are compelled to concentrate on immediate economic demands and to bargain almost constantly. This tends to divert their attention from long-range organizational and more comprehensive class goals. Like Alice, they are forced to run just to stay in the same place.[20] Better placed or better organized groups can simply pass the increases in cost on to their captive consumers.[21] One of the major political consequences of rampant (but relatively controlled) inflation is growth of the role and autonomy of authority groups. Not only are their perennially unbalanced budgets an important contributor to the process, but through their control of exchange rate, credit, and wage policies they can determine its distributional effects. Through "demagogic" wage and welfare increases, on the one hand, and liberal credit policies at negative exchange rates, on the other, the state can in effect keep Peter and Paul simultaneously content. All this is predicated on a constantly expanding GNP and relatively moderate inflation. Should the former plummet and the latter skyrocket, this "all winners–no losers" style of rule is likely to become rapidly inviable.

Associational consequences. Early urbanization and bureaucratization, delayed industrialization through import substitution and over-mechanization, dependence upon foreign technology and capital, stagnation in the rural sector and structural dualism, and sustained high rates of growth and inflation have combined to produce a pattern of interest conflict and public policy quite different from that of its classical forerunners. Newly differentiated social groups have not attained the sort of awareness of distinctive corporate interests and values that might have caused them to mobilize organizationally and to challenge the hegemony of ruling groups. Brazil simply did not pass through a series of "stages of development," each characterized by the domination of a different cohesive elite. Of course, patterns of recruitment to and control over authority groups have changed substantially over time, but not because any single elite ruled exclusively, exhausted its "historical potential," and then was replaced by a new, more "progressive" one. Brazil has not experienced an anti-Western, anticolonial, antitraditional, antimercantilistic, anticapitalist, or anti-imperialist revolution; moreover, one finds little evidence of these major "contradictions" having engendered massive organizational protests.

Of conflict, of course, there has been plenty in Brazilian society, but not along the monolithic, polarized lines of cleavage predicted by the "classical" developmental syndrome. *More often than not it has involved opposition between sectors of the same class,* whether defined by property, status, or power. Caio Prado Junior has brilliantly captured the heterogeneous origin and syncretic nature of this ruling class in his recent essay on the Brazilian revolution:

Thus there formed in Brazil, during the course of the last century, the rudiments of an urban bourgeoisie that sheltered foreigners of the most varied origin in the country, along with Brazilians of the greatest chronological diversity in terms of their family tradition. All this bourgeoisie, so heterogeneous from the point of view of national origin and antiquity of its past in Brazil, is nevertheless perfectly homogeneous with respect to the nature of its business and interests and in the essential manner in which they are conducted. It must be noted that this bourgeoisie, emerging but already consolidated by the end of the century, developed and progressed without economic, social, or political obstacles of any size, except for those determined by the relative poverty and primitiveness of the country and the low cultural level of its population. But it did not encounter, as did Europe emerging from feudalism or the African and Asian countries, the obstacle of noncapitalist structures organized in a system and according to values incompatible with or adverse to capitalism.

... The integration of the Brazilian ... system, as well as the economic progress that accompanies, conditions, and drives it, is expressed through the emergence of a rapidly rising bourgeoisie, which, though constituted like any bourgeoisie of sectors with diverse interests, ... forms essentially a homogeneous and cohesive class that is not internally rent by irreducible contradictions or oppositions. This also applies inclusively, even especially, one might say, to the relations between the agrarian and industrial sectors, which, far from opposing each other, are linked together and support each other in many essential circumstances. ... There is ... no special difference at all between agricultural entrepreneurs and those of other economic activities. Between landowners and property owners in general, as well as between industrialists and merchants, one can find the whole gamut of political opinion—from conservatives to those more or less tolerant of popular rights and aspirations. ... When our businessmen dedicated to agriculture become reactionaries and retrogrades, it is not because they are large rural proprietors. Neither do industrial activities and occupations make individuals, under Brazilian conditions, more open and tolerant of social reforms. One finds them in all sectors of the Brazilian bourgeoisie, rural as well as urban. Distinctions in this regard are based on personal, not socioeconomic or class, criteria.[22]

Having obtained a certain hegemony or measure of effective participation in public policy without sustained effort of their own or implacable resistance on the part of previous power holders (and, one should add, without having deprived them of their sources of influence), the emergent propertied elites had no incentive to assert distinctive values and goals. Nor did they have a strong incentive to form and sustain large, aggressive, and broadly aggregative "class" associations. The working classes did not provide any. Relatively small in numbers,[23] heterogeneous in origin, "artificially" privileged in wages and working conditions owing to state paternalism, not radically alienated by having been dispossessed from previous artisan activities or threatened with submergence by a virtually inexhaustible migrant labor supply—they could hardly be expected to have posed a serious threat. Without such perceptions of conflicting interests to serve as a catalyst, only the paternalistic largess of the government and the offer of important ancillary commercial and advisory services—factors making membership almost involuntary—made it possible for larger associations to form and persist.[24]

Another contradiction that had a major impact on the patterns of associational emergence and interaction in the Western democracies but that has failed to materialize with equivalent intensity in Brazil is conflict over the role of the state in promoting and controlling economic development. As it turned out, all three potentially competitive elite groups—the rural landowners, the export commercial and financial intermediaries, and the industrialists—needed the support of state funds.

As long as a deal could be struck that guaranteed agricultural sub-sidies, developed a basic service infrastructure, left foreign trade in private hands, provided a minimum of protection against competitive imports and some cheap public credit, and shifted the payment for these policies to other groups, there was likely to be no serious resis-tance to an expansion of authority group functions—orthodox ideologi-cal rhetoric to the contrary notwithstanding. This, of course, was the ingenious package deal that Vargas put together during the 1930's—a logroll that has aptly been termed "the socialization of losses and the division of spoils."[25] Caio Prado Junior contends that this hybrid com-promise between the public and private sectors, "this more or less illicit enrichment at the cost and on the account of public power not only reaches exceptional proportions in comparison with the normal and ordinary forms of capitalist accumulation, but . . . has become a system that one can consider consecrated and institutionalized." He argues that this forms a distinctive route to economic modernization, a new developmental syndrome he calls "bureaucratic capitalism," distinct from the liberal or socialist model, a sort of privatized version of "state capitalism."[26] This discretionary control over state favors in turn facili-tates a populist alliance with middle-sector and working-class groups, especially those depending upon public employment.

The empirical evidence, then, is strong that authority groups have called the shots on how and which groups could organize and what de-mands they could make once they were established. But how did au-thorities get away with it—especially without a cohesive, monolithic ruling party to back them up? The answer to this challenging question lies, as I have intimated above, in the relatively nonantagonistic, non-zero-sum pattern taken by early development in Brazil and in the rather autonomous role authority groups can play under such conditions of elite heterogeneity and disorganization. Let us now look first at the political system that has emerged from this bureaucratic capitalist developmental syndrome.

O Sistema

I have argued at several points in this study that, despite the substan-tial, accelerated, and asynchronous structural transformations, the ex-treme range of internal variance, the frequency of unscheduled exec-utive changes, and of course the omnipresent confusion and seeming aimlessness of the political process, the patterns of attitudinal predis-positions, group interaction, and policy-making in Brazil have remained quite regular, consistent, and predictable. In sum, beneath the obviously (and often superficially) kaleidoscopic aspects of Brazilian politics lies a system. The System—*"o sistema,"* in the local jargon—is concrete rather than analytic; it is "a complex of experiences which are related in a distinctive and seemingly necessary way to each other."[27] Such a system is not exclusively in the mind of the observer, invisibly conditioning responses and applying homeostatic corrections. Rather, it is real, and it is perceived by the enculturated elite actors themselves, who generally seek consciously to preserve it. Its needs consist in a set of structural relationships and value expectations that condition and limit behavior, thereby making it mutually predictable. Possibly no actor or observer knows or understands the entire system in all its complexity.[28] Even the most agile performers come into contact with only restricted portions of it. Perhaps by listing only a few of the many jargonistic phrases used to refer to these partial relationships and structures one can give an idea of the complexity of the whole: *coronelismo, bacharelismo, populismo, desenvolvimentismo, clientelismo, Estado Cartorial, empreguismo, peleguismo, sindicalismo, filhotismo, pactualismo, transigência, conciliação, regulamentação, rotary, igrejinha, cúpula, panelinha, groupão, vôto de Cabresto, cabo eleitoral, cabide de emprêgo, verba pessoal, verba de representação, caixinha, subsídio, dispositivo, cobertura, projeção, promoção pessoal, pistolão, homen de confiança, testa-de-ferro, prévia,* and, of course, *jeito.*

Analysis of such a hybrid system is complicated by the tendency of most contemporary classification schemes to use dichotomous categories or polarized continua. The Brazilian variant is clearly neither totalitarian nor pluralist-democratic. The intermediary types suggested by such theorists as Edward Shils, James Coleman, and Gabriel Almond are no more helpful. They tend to be constructed, often illogically and inconsistently, from extraneous variables[29] and treated as imperfect, transient political forms, lucky enough to have escaped totalitarianism, but lacking the economic development, legitimacy, or effectiveness to become stable democracies. Since one of my major observations was precisely the extraordinary tenacity of these interdependent structures in spite of considerable environmental transformation, these teleological or heterostatic stereotypes would not do. I needed a model stressing certain unique, relatively stable, and interrelated characteristics of an intermediary system that was neither pluralist nor mobilizational, yet had some features of both.

So, fortunately, did Juan Linz for his analysis of Spain. His originality and inventiveness in the construction of a model of a stable "authoritarian regime" provided the sort of standard I needed.[30] The Brazilian system conforms in its broad outline to Linz's model, although it deviates sufficiently in certain aspects to suggest classification as a possible subtype, which I shall call "populist," or "semicompetitive." What, then, are the principal interrelated characteristics of an authoritarian system?

Elite heterogeneity. Unlike the totalitarian regime, which enforces a high degree of uniformity in ideology, style, career patterns, and social origins, the authoritarian variant recruits from a diversified base and generally is tolerant of a wide variety of interests and opinions. The basic ruling strategies consist of the absorption and accommodation of preexisting elite groups and the co-optation and manipulation of emerging ones. Unlike the strategies of the democratic regime, they do not involve open, public competition or periodic elections. Interelite competitiveness in an authoritarian setting characteristically involves greater repression, although the accent is on manipulation. It does not, however, normally involve the physical elimination of one's opponent or of his sources of power. In short, authoritarian rule depends on the institutionalization of an equilibrium of forces between existing competitive elites. It also must use restrictive criteria for the incorporation of new competitive elements, not to mention repressive force against intransigent dissidents.

Clearly the Brazilian case conforms to this basic characteristic of authoritarian rule. The pattern of development, induced by external crises and resolved by a non-zero-sum policy compromise, resulted in a coexistence of contending elites, rather than in domination by a sequence of different "modernizing" elites. Despite obvious differences in interest and attitude, the *sistema* was formed by sedimentation, not by metamorphosis. Intersectorial flows of capital and entrepreneurial talent, interelite family contacts, generalized fear of the enormous latent conflict potentiality of such a weakly integrated society, internal heterogeneity within the rural, commercial, industrial, and proletarian classes —all have helped seal the compromise. The success of this nonantagonistic pattern in turn ensured a continuity in the political culture and a reinforcement of those attitudes stressing conflict avoidance, dialogue, ideological flexibility, tolerance, and compromise.

There are two ways in which the Brazilian elite compromise differs from that of other authoritarian regimes. The first is the pervasive paternalism and personalism of elites and their considerable success in anticipating emerging conflicts and accommodating individual leaders before they can create independently organized protest movements. The second is the presence of an institutionalized keeper of the delicate balance of forces: the moderative power, as exercised originally by the Emperor and periodically since 1888 by the military.[31]

Relative autonomy of the state apparatus. Although this is not explicitly mentioned by Linz, it seems to be a logical derivative of elite heterogeneity. Unlike a totalitarian regime, where authority groups are fused with or dominated by a single party, or a democratic regime, where they are subordinated to a single class or distinctive coalition of private interests, an authoritarian regime is in a position to play off competing elites against each other. And because they are present everywhere, elective and administrative elites gain considerable autonomy and are relatively free to make initiatives and to pursue policies for their own advantage. Linz observes that authoritarian regimes are not arbitrary; indeed, they tend to place a great deal of emphasis on regular administrative and judicial procedures. "Given the nonideological character of much authoritarian politics, the emphasis on respectability and expertise, and the desire to co-opt elements of established society, a number of those assuming power will have had little previous involvement in politics."[32] In particular, this plus the historical persistence of legal and administrative forms confers special influence upon lawyers and civil servants. "This preoccupation with procedure ultimately becomes an important factor in the constant expansion of a state of law, with an increase in predictability and opportunities for legal redress for grievances. At the same time, it may prevent political problems from being perceived as such, irreducible to administrative problems and not soluble by legislation. Legal procedures are often seen . . . as an adequate equivalent of more collective, political expression of interest conflicts."[33]

Again, Brazil conforms to the general syndrome. Oliveiros Ferreira finds these to be the major characteristics of the *sistema*: its lack of accountability to organized, independent social groups, its self-serving corruption, and its domination by civilian and military bureaucracies. He also points out—as have numerous other observers—that Brazilian political life is permeated with a "bureaucratic ethos."[34] We have found this reflected primarily in the reported patterns of interaction: the associations' concentration on the public administration, their legalistic orientation, and their lack of initiative and general helplessness vis-à-vis government agencies.

Two characteristics of the Brazilian state apparatus seem unique, and both are related to its early bureaucratization and the absence of any major confrontation leading to a redefinition and restructuring of its role. First, despite marked tendencies toward centralization (especially concentration of financial and material resources in the hands of the federal government), the decision-making process remains quite unarticulated and free from unified control. Individual actors and agencies seek out and maintain autonomous particularistic relationships of mutual support and exploitation with local elites and influential persons (*clientelismo*). Second, despite the emergence of isolated, performance-oriented technocratic elites in the 1950's, employment in most public administration continues to be based on considerations of co-optive patronage and familistic opportunism (*empreguismo, cartorialismo, filhotismo*). Only after the coup of 1964 did something like a pure authoritarian bureaucracy appear with its accent on political neutrality, expertise, social and political engineering, and paramilitary command systems based on an alliance of officers and technocrats.[35]

The absence of a militant ruling ideology and the coexistence of several principles of legitimacy. Authoritarian regimes are sharply differentiated from totalitarian ones by their lack of a single, elaborate, and coherent set of norms and goals defining the relationship between state and society. Characteristically, an authoritarian regime is guided by a loose, nondoctrinaire, nonutopian, but nevertheless distinctive "mentality." Generally this mentality is supported and promoted by the state, although it may itself derive from such outside sources as social Catholicism. It is not, however, exclusive. These regimes frequently find it prudent—even necessary, given their heterogeneous composition—to permit the expression of competing ideologies, provided they do not lead to the organization of mass movements of opposition. Linz observes that authoritarian rule is compatible with a wide variety of leadership styles and rests on a mixture of legitimizing formulae. "Regimes may come to power as de facto authorities with little legitimacy and then develop some charismatic appeal, but they end in a mixture of legal, charismatic, and traditional authority."[36]

The discussion of Brazilian political culture highlighted just these qualities: an absence of rigid doctrine; the weakness of conscious attempts at indoctrination by authority groups; the lack of congruence between levels of the enculturation process, leading to cynicism and opportunism; the preference for short-term improvisations (*jeitos*) over long-term deferred payoffs and for pragmatism over dogmatism; and the coexistence of democratic and authoritarian, of equalitarian and elitist, of cosmopolitan and nationalist, of liberal and corporatist, and of secular and religious ideals. Yet, at the same time, Brazil has had an amazingly homogeneous distribution of these apparently contradictory principles among fully-enculturated participants. Perhaps the most distinctive quality of the Brazilian variant is precisely this juxtaposition of political styles and goals.[37] Continuity has been sustained by persistent infusions of paternalism, co-optation, and anticipated reaction. As a result, primary emphasis and responsibility are given to the legal and administrative machinery of the state for the regulation of social conflict and the sponsorship of social improvements, and spontaneous conflicts between group forces are regarded with suspicion or outright alarm. This desire for controlled change from above is crucial to the authoritarian corporatist response to development.

Lack of extensive and intensive political mobilization of the population. Both totalitarian and pluralist regimes place a great deal of emphasis on their high rates of citizen participation in political organizations. Indeed, their legitimacy rests on this mystique of extensve and intensive citizenship. The authoritarian regime is more modest. "Rather than enthusiasm or support, the regime often expects—even from officeholders and civil servants—passive acceptance, or at least that they refrain from public antigovernment activity."[38] This, Linz observes, is related to the regime's limited legitimacy: the great mass of the population consists of "parochials," or at best "subjects" who are unconcerned with legitimizing formulas. Hence they tend to obey out of "a mixture of habit and self-interest."[39]

Brazil deviates importantly from this characteristic of the authoritarian regime. As I have noted, it passed almost imperceptibly from colony to empire to republic to dictatorship and back to republic without great crises and therefore without a need for large-scale political mobilization. However, there was an increased use of populist electoral strategies,* owing to a combination of structural factors, especially the creation of a large urban mass weakly regimented into the industrial labor force or poorly organized into intermediary political associations, plus the persistence of the ideals of democratic competitiveness and a prudent reluctance on the part of elites to resort to overtly repressive policies.[40] In the early 1960's, competitive bidding for popular support led to a mobilization of hitherto parochial elements of the population and to a growing disparity between the plebiscitary offices of President and certain governors and the clientilistic roles of deputy and senator. This "direct pact with the masses," although it permitted elite groups to retain their authoritarian control of the political process,[41] led to severe interelite strains, temporarily resolved in 1964 by a military coup and a return to pure authoritarian rule under military tutelage. If "degrees of mobilization might be the most useful criteria by which to distinguish subtypes of authoritarian regimes,"[42] then the Brazilian *sistema* before 1964, with its comparatively greater competitiveness and need to appeal to the masses for support, might better be called populist.

---

* The electorate, made up of only 1.5 percent of the total population in 1922, grew dramatically to 13.4 percent in 1945 and 19.1 percent in 1960. This, however, was still low relative to other Latin American countries at an equivalent level of social and economic development.

A single-party system. One of the characteristic structural traits of authoritarian regimes is the dominant position of a single, omnibus, official party, although, as Linz observes, its monopoly on recruitment, ideology, and policy-making is often more formal than real. "A considerable part of the elite has no connection with the party and does not identify with it. Party membership creates few visible advantages, and imposes few, if any, duties."[43] In keeping with the heterogeneity of the elite, the party recruits broadly, but selectively. In keeping with the diversity of ideologies and formulas for legitimacy, indoctrination is not taken seriously and members are rarely expelled for unorthodox attitudes. In keeping with the restricted political mobilization, the party does not penetrate many spheres of social life, nor does it control the public bureaucracy. Rather, it "becomes only one more element in the power pluralism; one more group pressing for particular interests; one more channel through which divergent interests try to find access to power; one more recruiting ground for elite members."[44]

Brazil again deviates from the pure authoritarian model in the direction of less formal organization and greater competitiveness. During the system's formative period (1937–45), Getúlio Vargas chose to rule without even the formal support of a single, governing party. He relied instead on the state bureaucracy and a complex network of personal loyalties and reciprocal interests. Not until the "redemocratization" of 1945, long after the *sistema* had captured the principal posts of political power, did he begin to consider party organization. He sponsored the simultaneous creation of not one but two separate parties: the PSD, composed of professional politicians, federal and state bureaucrats, rural local notables, and a smattering of industrialists; and the PTB, composed of Welfare Institute and Labor Ministry bureaucrats, *pelegos*, some urban local notables, a few progressive industrialists, and large landowners. The alliance of these two dominated Brazilian politics during the postwar period, surviving even Vargas' suicide in 1954. They could almost be considered a single party, were it not for their competitiveness at the local and state levels. Despite their common parentage, however, the coalition began to degenerate, largely because of demagogic populist bidding for the urban mass vote, and especially over the prospect of enfranchising illiterates. It was weakened first by the opposition victory of Quadros in 1960, then by the split over Goulart's succession, and finally by his "basic reform" policies. The uncertainty this created over presidential succession in 1965 was one of the prime causes of the 1964 coup.

The apparent Brazilian exception actually confirms Linz's observation. A stable authoritarian regime does require at least loose one-party dominance, or the presence of a dominant coalition, if any degree of political competitiveness is to be permitted. Otherwise, it must devote much of its resources to either the repression of competitiveness or the manipulation of its results. Given the heterogeneity of elite interests, the persistence of democratic ideals, and the juxtaposition of legitimacy principles and increasing political mobilization, this would have been an expensive alternative in Brazil. Only a military-dominated regime like the one set up by the 1964 coup could afford such a costly policy and return to the pure authoritarian syndrome.

Limited pluralism. Pure totalitarian regimes do not permit the existence of intermediary associations that are not created by and dependent upon authority groups. Pure pluralist regimes, by contrast, insist upon the spontaneous creation and formal independence of such associations from public agencies. Authoritarian regimes, as we have seen, lie between the two. They may either co-opt and regiment preexistent associations (a policy I have called natural corporatism), sponsor and encourage the formation of new ones (artificial corporatism), or both. Under either "artificial" or "natural" circumstances, there is no rigid synchronization (*gleichschaltung*) of all groups to the goals of authority groups or to a movement. Nor is there extensive use of them to control all areas of social life or to inculcate regime values and goals. This follows from the regime's heterogeneity, limited citizen mobilization, and ideological weakness. Conversely, such a type of pluralism stops short of the liberal variety by placing restrictions on open, public competition between interests, by controlling the conditions of association formation and expression, and by channeling all conflicts through the mediative offices of the state. The nature of representation in such systems is also different, being less controlled by leaders' constituencies. "In authoritarian regimes the men who come to power reflecting the views of various groups and institutions do not derive their position from the support of these groups alone, but from the trust placed in them by the leader, monarch, or 'junta,' who certainly takes into account their prestige and influence."[45]

Linz does not argue that limited pluralism is the single most important component of the authoritarian syndrome. It is presented merely as one of a series of interrelated elements. However, since he discusses it first and most extensively, and since he has devoted a major proportion of his empirical research to patterns of group formation and activity, one might infer that the way a regime responds to the increase in the art of association concomitant with social and eonomic development provides the most significant clue, not only to its classification, but also to the pattern of its political development.

This, I would argue, is the case in Brazil. When Oliveiros Ferreira refers repeatedly to the Syndical Tax as the cornerstone of the *sistema,* he means of course that it provides the primary support for a limited pluralist or corporatist system of interest representation, which itself provides the primary structural support for the *sistema.* This decision by existing elites to tolerate, sponsor, and encourage but also to control, channel, and manipulate associational forms of interest expression came long before the late 1930's and early 1940's, when the authoritarian regime was institutionalized. As we have seen, these policies of institutionalized intervention and co-optation are accepted as legitimate and natural. The continuous operation of such a system appears to have been successful in inculcating supportive values and in creating a body of surprisingly like-minded interest representatives whose accountability, at best, is divided between their formal constituency and the confidence placed in them by authority groups.

In spite of the finding that associational activity has not come to dominate the process of public policy-making, the consequences of this corporatist or limited pluralist form of interest expression have been crucial for the larger political system. The sense of dependency and helplessness, the lack of rational interest or class consciousness, the expressions of deference and timidity, and the sheer disorganization—all characteristic of Brazilian interest politics—are in fact major contributors (along with the absence of a nationally organized party system) to the outstanding characteristic of the political system as a whole: namely, the autonomy of the professional political and administrative class. Relatively free from dependence upon organized special interests or classes, authority groups have been able to control the developmental process and its political consequences. Initiatives have either come from within their ranks or been imposed by forces from outside the system. They have not come from competitive interaction between dependent groups based on functional interests, ideological principles, regional loyalties, or class consciousness. As development proceeded, this professional political class was able to add to its legitimate monopoly over the means of collective violence (which it used only sparingly) various other means of social control. The state apparatus gradually absorbed the paternalistic service and welfare functions formerly provided by local notables, vastly increased them, and bestowed them upon grateful and as yet unaware and unorganized dominated groups. In this co-optative setting, the best these groups could do was to organize just well enough to protect the corporate rights and privileges bestowed upon them. So far, this has been their most important function: to protect themselves against policies that would impose the sacrifices inherent in the transformation of social, economic, and political structures, and to obtain marginal adjustments, special exemptions, and particularistic favors from new developmental policies. The sheer presence of such sponsored and subservient groups inhibits the emergence of either pluralist associations or totalitarian ones. Their influence also prevents the adoption by authority groups of certain basic reforms that could radically disturb the existing allocation of resources and benefits.

The failure of most formally organized interest groups to provide strongly backed, well-elaborated alternatives, accurate, well-documented information, and cohesive, reliable support for government policies forces authorities to look elsewhere for these indispensable inputs. And these needs become all the greater the more the state intervenes to control the production and allocation of resources, especially through comprehensive planning. The *políticos* and *técnicos* must turn, on the one hand, to influential individuals, firms, and local notables (a pattern I have called *clientelismo*) and, on the other hand, to diffuse movements of public opinion. Andrew Pearse sums up this peculiar setting in which decision-makers are especially responsive to the extremely particularistic, immediate claims of their cronies and clients and to the grandiose, vague, ideological, and symbolic demands of the people and the progressive forces:

In the Brazilian situation, populism is a predominant characteristic of the contemporary urban setting. The wealthy and influential classes see it as a question of maintaining their traditional privileges and authority in the face of constitutional democratic institutions, in the face of the dissolution of the system of direct dependency that an archaic rural style imposed on socioeconomic relations, in the face of that system's replacement by the independence without power of the urban worker, whose only connection with the center of power is his salary, and in the face of the breakdown of the social isolation of the rural population caused by the rapid development of the means of communication and the raising of culture levels.

Whereas the middle groups receive benefits by being assigned to positions in the bureaucracy, . . . the masses received them through legislation defending work and by being admitted to medical assistance stations, sports clubs, religious groups, cults, etc. that are sustained by the intervention of populist leaders. . . . Populism does not encourage the establishment of collective interest groups or cooperative associations, and power is generally delegated downward rather than upward. Representatives are named, but rarely from below.[46]

Such a system is doubly vulnerable. Because of the elites' desire to appear modern and democratic, they are exceedingly sensitive to external models and ideas, especially to advanced standards of economic, political, and administrative practice. But, lacking reliable and stable linkages with much of the formal citizenry, they are also very vulnerable to the claims of those who purport to speak for the inchoate masses—the mass media owners and spokesmen, the intellectuals, and, of course, the "popular" leaders.

The weaknesses of the Brazilian populist, semicompetitive authoritarian regime emerged most clearly in the early 1960's, as most of the factors that had earlier contributed to its nonantagonistic development pattern began to exhaust themselves. Urbanization increased far beyond the economy's capacity to absorb new manpower, creating a swelling marginal and manipulatable mass; the terms of trade declined markedly, reducing the capacity to import new machinery and raw materials for industry; the impulse originally provided by easy import substitution faded; the rate of economic growth lagged; inflation skyrocketed; peripheral regions became more and more aware of their growing disparity with the urban centers. It became less feasible every day to maintain the fiction of a non-zero-sum decisional process with payoffs in protection, privileges, subsidies, services, jobs, and welfare for all.

Given, however, the strong commitment to formal competitiveness —regular, democratic elections (with restricted participation) and freedom of opinion expression (for those with access to the media)—it was only a matter of time before the increasing elite antagonisms began to spill over into increasingly demagogic appeals, particularly into threats to organize and enfranchise previous nonparticipants. The competition centered on the office of the President of the Republic, which was converted from a conciliatory mediator of status quo interests into a protagonist for basic reforms. The result was an institutional deadlock at the center of the *sistema*: the President was increasingly vulnerable to the pressures of a disorganized populace and was backed by a highly articulate but self-deluded set of progressive intellectuals, whereas the legislative and administrative elites were backed by their conservative patrons and local notables.

Speculations about System Transformation

The coup of 1964 put an end, at least temporarily, to this disintegration and paralysis of the *sistema*. Numerous "subversive" organizations were abolished or driven underground; strict corporatist controls were reinstated by authorities over urban labor groups and extended to cover students' associations; the newly formed rural syndicates were purged and cautious attempts taken to organize that sector from above; permanent controls were installed over freedom of expression on grounds of national security; candidates and already elected representatives were deposed; contests for public office were more or less openly rigged; and, most important, the election of the President was made indirect. In essence, these policies have purged the system of its populist and semicompetitive aspects, making it conform more closely to the stable authoritarian regime described by Linz.

But is it likely to remain stable? Although I have stressed the continuity and amazing adaptability of the former *sistema*, such a regime is inevitably threatened by the more logically consistent and morally satisfying ideologies on either side of it. The appeal of rapid, autonomous development through the mobilization of mass support behind a militant and revolutionary party, on the one hand, and the appeal of a long-standing aspiration for liberal democracy through open political competition, on the other, make the authoritarian response seem immoral, wasteful, sluggish, prosaic, and far too unimaginative. Disgruntled intellectuals and disillusioned young people pose a more or less constant challenge to its assimilative capacities. Let me speculate, with the aid of theory and historical hindsight, on the internal dynamics, tensions, and contradictions of such a hybrid form of rule and about the tendencies that might lead it to develop into another type of regime.

Pluralist democracy as an outcome. Apologists, domestic and foreign, for the present military-controlled authoritarian regime insist on its transitional nature. Despite its extraconstitutionality and repressiveness, the coup of 1964 and the ensuing government were hailed as a victory for liberal democracy and the open society. After a period of tutelage, during which the *sistema* would be thoroughly dismantled by means of a rationalization of political and administrative procedures, Brazil would emerge "purified" and capable of assuming its long awaited place as a full-fledged pluralist democracy.

Self-justification and wishful thinking aside, certain trends in the semicompetitive, populist system that existed before the coup seemed to indicate such an evolution. As I have observed, the extent, variety, and density of associational participation had been increasing faster than the processes of structural differentiation (except, significantly, that of urbanization). Coverage was being extended (granted, through corporatist strategies) to previously unorganized sectors, especially to rural workers. Autonomy and combativeness seemed also to be on the rise. Employers were founding and voluntarily supporting an increasing variety of private entities. Workers' organizations seemed to be escaping slightly from ministerial tutelage and were occasionally even taking actions against the explicit will of authority groups. Electoral participation was rising. The many various personalistic and clientelistic parties were beginning to give way to broader-based (but often equally personalistic) alliances with more distinctive programs. It was rumored that something approaching a national bourgeoisie was forming. In league with other progressive forces, it would seize control of the state, implant its developmental project upon the country, provide the definitive break with traditionalist values and structures that had been lacking to date, and lead Brazil on the path toward a "classical" industrialist-capitalist order.[47]

Mobilization from the left as an outcome. Other observers of the same events interpreted them quite differently. In the rapidly increasing exposure to mass media, in the burgeoning and disproportionate rates of urbanization, in the massive rural out-migration, in the "favelization" of cities, in the unstable and limited integration of the population into productive occupations, in the rise in popular expectations, and in the uncertainty generated by accelerated inflation they saw the conditions leading to mass vulnerability. In the rising antagonism between elites, in the paralysis of government decision-making, in the rapid expansion and increased polarization of the electoral process, and in the collapse of the party system they saw excessive elite accessibility. In short, they saw the ingredients for the emergence of a mass society.[48] "Brazilian democracy thus radically differs from the Western traditional model [after 1945]. The most outstanding difference is that in this mass democracy the State has immediate contact with all its citizens. Indeed, all the important organizations functioning as mediators between the State and the individual are really entities annexed to the State itself rather than effectively autonomous organizations."[49] In addition to this weakness in intermediate associability, the individual citizen tended to relate himself in an isolated and personal manner to populist political leaders. All political life tended to concentrate increasingly on national political offices, national policy, and national issues. The President had become an omnipotent and omniscient national patron from whom all benefits flowed and in whom all expectations were lodged.[50] The expanding tendency to base legitimacy exclusively upon undifferentiated popular support seemed to indicate a corrosion or collapse of the former mixed patrimonial-legal-rational order.

Tocqueville, Talmon, Arendt, and Kornhauser, among others, have argued that such a mass society-polity is exceedingly vulnerable to totalitarianism; that is to say, it is difficult to sustain limited authoritarian rule under such conditions. It is therefore but a short step to predicting the demise of the *sistema* and its conversion by an ideologically dedicated, revolutionary nationalist elite into a mobilization system. Indeed, the seizure of power by the military and the subsequent repression of opposing intellectuals and popular leaders were legitimated on the grounds that such a system transformation was imminent in 1964.

Mobilization from the right as an outcome. An alternative outcome to the transformation of the *sistema* was not seriously considered and examined until after the 1964 coup. Brazil has very clearly followed "the route from the preindustrial to the modern world" that Barrington Moore, Jr. has called "capitalist and reactionary." Such a development pattern is based on the coalition of "a commercial and industrial class which is too weak and dependent to take power and rule in its own right and which therefore throws itself into the arms of the landed aristocracy and the royal bureaucracy, exchanging the right to rule for the right to make money."[51] These "conservative modernizers through revolution from above" are capable of generating and absorbing considerable structural change in the economic and social arenas. As Moore observes, they may experience a prolonged period of conservative and even authoritarian rule and acquire "certain democratic features: notably a parliament with limited powers. Their history may be punctuated with attempts to extend democracy which, toward the end, succeeded in establishing unstable democracies (the Weimar Republic, Japan in the twenties, Italy under Giolitti)."[52]

From the preceding description of the *sistema*, it is obvious that Brazil fits this syndrome, even down to Moore's description of its political consequences:

On the other hand, the political consequences from dismounting the old order from above are decidedly different. As they proceeded with conservative modernization, these semiparliamentary governments tried to preserve as much of the original social structure as they could, fitting large sections into the new building wherever possible. The results had some resemblance to present-day Victorian houses with modern electrical kitchens but insufficient bathrooms and leaky pipes hidden decorously behind newly plastered walls.[53]

Such makeshift regimes can carry out major transformations from above. The *sistema* in Brazil can be credited with the establishment of a strong central authority, the unification of a partly rationalized administrative system, the elaboration and enforcement of a more or less uniform code of law, the elimination of most artificial internal barriers to trade, the creation of a new set of national symbols and the shift of loyalties from an exclusively parochial to a national level, the transfer of resources from traditional to modern sectors (especially from agriculture to industry), the resistance against complete penetration by foreign interests, the dissemination of new literary and technical skills and the establishment of something approaching a national educational system, the promotion of a national network of communication and transportation, and the promulgation and partial enforcement of an extensive set of social welfare policies. Even if none of these transformations resulted "from below," they form quite a list of accomplishments.

Nevertheless, Moore's historical observation is that "ultimately, the makeshifts collapsed." "Eventually, the door to fascist regimes was

opened by the failure of these democracies to cope with the severe problems of the day and reluctance or inability to bring about fundamental
structural changes."[54] On these logical and historical grounds, fascism
or a totalitarian-mobilization system of the right becomes the likely
outcome of a populist, semicompetitive regime. The elites disintegrate.
Their accessibility, with the availability of the masses, results in a seizure
of power—not by a nationalist elite mobilizing the masses for the goal
of fundamentally restructuring property relationships, but by a military-
bureaucratic or petty-bourgeois elite bent upon mobilizing the middle
and upper groups to defend their privileges and property.[55]

Conclusion. None of these three alternative outcomes—pluralist democracy, revolutionary mass society, or mobilization from the right—
is entirely compelling. All still seem logically possible, but none seems
especially probable. This is another way of saying that the options are
still open in Brazil. As long as the pattern of fundamental polariza-
tions of interest and attitude (urban-rural, precapitalist-capitalist, cen-
ter-periphery, nationalist-imperialist, bourgeoisie-proletariat, *mesoi-
lumpen*, civil-military, black-white) remains fluid and noncumulative,
it is exceedingly difficult to predict the conditions under which a confrontation will be forced and a transformation of the system will occur.

Clearly, those who predicted the collapse of the *sistema* and the
emergence of a new liberal order overestimated the extent to which the
resurgence of associational activity and spread of associational coverage meant greater autonomy, a rejection of previous corporatist forms
of representation, or both. The party system remained disorganized; it
was not replaced by a simple and well-defined set of partisan structures.
Most important, the new "revolutionary" elites after 1964 were not ready
to dismantle completely and definitively the structure of the previous
system and to turn the social and political initiative over to autonomous,
private associations. In fact, the new authority groups did just the opposite; they took all possible steps to support the structure of authoritarian rule from above.

Those who foresaw the emergence of a leftist totalitarian regime
vastly overestimated the ideological coherence of the radical populists
and the degree of mass availability. Simplified applications of mass society arguments overlook such important factors as the persistence of
traditional values that keep political actors from regarding themselves
as "abstract and self-sufficing individuals," as social and political equals
possessing their own independent interests and attitudes. Furthermore,
they fail to notice Brazil's vast number of less formal intermediary
bodies—cliques, *panelinhas*, "rotaries," patron-client dyads, clubs, sects,
and cults—which give the individual actors a sense of "proximate re-

lation to society." When called upon in March 1964 by embattled elements of the radical elite, the masses proved not so available and easy
to mobilize after all.

In retrospect, the least seriously considered outcome, fascism or rightist mobilization, seems the most likely. A counterrevolutionary alliance
of traditionalists and threatened middle-sector groups backed a military
seizure of power, and there have been serious pressures from so-called
"hard-line" elements threatening to transform the shaky, makeshift system into a mobilized, rightist one. Protracted dictatorship, unpopular
policies of economic austerity, and favoritism to foreign interests led
to rising opposition during the regime of Castelo Branco (1964–67) and
especially during the shorter reign of Costa e Silva (1967–69). The abolition of traditional political parties, increasingly strict controls on representative associations, and sporadic restrictions on the mass media
atrophied legitimate channels of interest expression and drove much
of this activity underground. Eventually, in 1968–69, militant, well-
organized urban guerrilla bands began to operate in São Paulo and
Rio. The Church began increasingly to take on representational functions as one of the few societal institutions not controlled or manipulated
by central authorities and therefore free to voice popular opposition.
Faced with a succession of crises, the military rulers responded each
time with more and more repressive measures, until thorough censorship, arbitrary search and seizure, preventive detention, forced dis-
missals, and torture had become commonplace. By 1969 Brazil seemed
to be moving inexorably beyond the boundaries of a "merely" authoritarian political system.

There were signs, however, that the country might not break with its
authoritarian tradition and might stop short of becoming Latin America's
first full-blown fascist or rightist mobilizational system. The ambitions and aspirations of "hard-line" military elements were periodically
checked by more "liberal" factions, although not without serious concessions in the areas of police and security affairs. Promises were made
concerning the halting of torture, although nothing was said regarding
arbitrary arrest. No monolithic ruling party has been created, although
the regime has continued to use coercion as a means for ensuring the
majority status of the government party (ARENA). Existing representative associations have not been "harmonized" (*gleichgeschaltet*) in the
name of a single ideology under a unified command, although controls
over leadership selection and interest expression have been intensified.
Purges have spared much of the administrative class, although few sur-
vivors of the former political class are left. The legislative process has
been revived, although only after a long moratorium, and elections have

not been completely abolished, although they have been "depopularized" by being made indirect and by controls over nominations. Most of all, some freedom of opinion expression has been respected, although censorship continues.

Several factors mentioned by Barrington Moore as operative in the cases of Italy, Germany, and Japan seem to impede the transformation of Brazil's authoritarian system into a fascist one. In terms of political culture, Brazil lacks a glorious military tradition, a cult of blood, honor, and violence, an ingrained respect for hierarchy, a rigid obedience to legal norms, and a romantic tradition idealizing the virtues of the simple peasant, preindustrial, precapitalist life. More important, Brazilian elites do not see themselves as surrounded by hostile, territorially ambitious neighbors and have no irredentist demands to press upon them. Finally, it is hard to imagine how a military and industrial establishment so dependent upon foreign expertise and material could seriously consider (or survive) the sort of aggressive autarkic foreign policy that has been the hallmark of previous totalitarian-fascist regimes.

In the absence of demonstrably crystalized and irreversible forces propelling it into any of the three possible outcomes, the most likely prognosis is that the *sistema* will persist. This does not necessarily mean that it will stagnate or even remain stable. The dynamic of the system, its capacity to generate and absorb change, must be seen in the light of the tension between two trends: the rising demands from an increasing variety of social groups who are ever more conscious of their specific interests and gradually more autonomous in their organization; and the varying capacity of those in positions of public authority for capturing, manipulating, repressing, and conceding those interests.[56] So far, the authorities have been able to anticipate and frustrate most of the demands and to protect the existing distribution of privilege and power. Through paternalism and co-optation, newly emergent representative associations have been converted from potentially aggressive promoters of new demands and hence challengers of the status quo to protectors of already acquired special interest and supporters of the status quo. In short, they have been incorporated before they could learn the skills of opposition. As long as this corporatist pattern of interest politics remains politically and economically viable (and we have seen that it has deep roots in the country's political culture), it is difficult to imagine what internal forces could break the cycle of alternation between semicompetitive populist rule (*democradura*) and repressive, technocratic military rule (*dictablanda*)—both within the general confines of an authoritarian system.

APPENDIX

A *Methodological Comment*

THE IRREGULARITY of published documentation and census data, the absence of relevant secondary treatments, and the necessity for obtaining data on actor perceptions led me to rely heavily on written questionnaires and oral interviews. First, while teaching was tying me down, I tried a mailed questionnaire. On the basis of the 1961 syndical census, telephone directories of the six major cities, and newspaper accounts (the paid announcements for annual meetings proved especially useful, particularly given the great inaccuracy of the telephone directories), I arrived at an estimated universe of 250 nationally relevant representative associations. Relevance was decided, tentatively, on the basis of the association's formal title, the functional importance of the sector purportedly represented, or both. Thus the Brazilian Rural Society was included, although most of its members are from São Paulo; likewise the Association of the Cacao Industry of Bahia was included, since all production of that commodity is concentrated in that area. In March 1965 a nine-page, 38-item questionnaire was mailed to the sample, with a covering letter from the Instituto de Ciências Sociais da Universidade do Brasil. Questions focused on background data on the associations, patterns of interaction with authority groups, and some attitudes. Fifty-nine responses were received, of which slightly over one-half came from employers' associations. Given the uncertainty of the mails, the fact that several questionnaires were returned (opened) with notes saying that the associations had been closed by *policia política* or that they had been denounced in the immediate aftermath of the Camelot scandal, the response rate was rather good. In any case, the completed questionnaires provided important preliminary information for the next stage of research.

An extensive series of personal interviews was then conducted with leaders of representative associations in Rio de Janeiro, São Paulo, Belo

Horizonte, Londrina, and Salvador da Bahia. (There was not enough time for the interviews planned for Pôrto Alegre and Recife.) In all, 149 interviews were held with elected and appointed officials of 108 different associations. Many were arranged through intermediaries—personal friends and previous respondents—but a substantial proportion were conducted "cold," with only a prior telephone conversation. I even discovered a few national associations by accident—for example, by reading their names in building directories.

A standard interview schedule with 53 items was used for all associational respondents. A brief introduction was given explaining the nature of the project ("to determine the relationship between your association and the process of national development") and assuring the respondent of anonymity ("Your answers, along with those of other associational leaders, will be coded, punched into cards, and processed electronically"). With very few exceptions, the leaders proved cooperative, informative, and frank—not only by answering the questions and numerous probes about their associations and by filling in the Likert-scaled political culture questionnaires, but also by offering further documentation and by suggesting other leaders to contact. And although they were often difficult to locate or to tie down to a specific hour, once the interviews began their patience and willingness to submit to a fixed schedule of questions was impressive. There were only three cases in which an interview was either denied or impossible to arrange. The sessions ranged from a twenty-minute "quickie" to a three-and-one-half-hour marathon. The average interview took approximately one hour and fifteen minutes. Because of the limited time available to busy interest leaders (especially in São Paulo), the full schedule occasionally had to be cut short; hence the relatively high numbers of "Don't know's" and "Inappropriate's" in the distributions.

My original estimate of the universe (250) proved too small. Subsequent information from newspapers and the reputational influence item in the mailed questionnaire kept expanding the number. By my most recent estimate, I would say there are approximately 350 nationally relevant representative associations currently active in Brazil. At the time interviewing began, however, I was too unsure of the universe to draw a representative sample, and it would have been impossible for me to interview one person in every known national association. Nevertheless, I feel that the sample chosen generally represents the existing structures and prevailing attitudes in Brazilian interest politics at the national level in 1965–66. In Table A.1 I have juxtaposed my post-factum estimate with the number of interviews actually conducted by means of "stratified opportunity sampling."

The principal focus of the interview sample was upon industrial interests. Not only were all the major general and specialized associations covered, but in several of them, more than one interview was conducted,

TABLE A.1
DISTRIBUTION OF INTERVIEWS CONDUCTED AND ESTIMATED NUMBER OF
NATIONALLY RELEVENT REPRESENTATIVE ASSOCIATIONS, BY TYPE

Type of association	Number of interviews conducted (N=149)	Number of associations involved in interviews (N=108)	Estimated number of associations in 1966[a] (N=350)
Employers'			
Industrial	54		
Commercial	19		
Rural	10		
Service	7		
Mixed	2		
TOTAL	92	65	150
Workers'			
Industrial	6		
Commercial	7		
Rural	5		
Service	9		
Mixed	3		
TOTAL	30	21	70
Liberal-professional	12	10	65
Civic	14	11	25
Religious	1	1	40

[a] These figures probably include a number of organizations of dubious existence or marginal national relevance. It is not unknown for a spokesman to exaggerate his importance by referring to his leadership position in a nonexistent association.

so that both elected and administrative personnel in both Rio and São Paulo could be heard. A considerable number of second interviews and informal conversations with leaders and lower-level employees have not been included in the above total, even though many insightful generalizations and colorful details came from these less structured inquiries. A large number of the formal and informal interviews were conducted with the leaders of the National Confederation of Industry (CNI) and with leaders of the state federations of industry attending the CNI's Council of Representatives.

As Table A.2 shows, the number of elected and administrative leaders interviewed was almost equal. I usually expressed no preference for one type or the other. When prior knowledge of an association seemed to indicate that either its president or its executive secretary was likely to be the more knowledgeable informant, an interview with him was specifically requested. Otherwise, the choice was left to the association. There was, however, a noticeable tendency for the leadership, once approached for an interview, to direct me toward the best informed source. The slightly higher proportion of administrators interviewed in

TABLE A.2
NUMBER OF INTERVIEWS, BY TYPE OF LEADER

Type of association	Elected Leaders (N=79)	Administrative Leaders[a] (N=70)
Employers'	42	50
Workers'	14	16
Other	23	4

[a] Includes ten government-appointed intervenors.

the employers' groups is a reflection of their more bureaucratized nature compared with the workers' groups.

Table A.1 shows an underrepresentation of workers' organizations and professional and religious associations and a marked concentration on employers' and civic associations. This was intentional. The leadership of workers' syndicates had been extensively purged after the 1964 coup, and government controls on their selection had not yet been lifted when the interviews were conducted in 1965 and early 1966. This was even more the case for national federations and confederations. Twenty percent of those actually interviewed were appointed by the government, and a number of others could hardly be called the voluntary choice of their sectors. Liberal-professional and religious groups were shortchanged because many of them, though national in scope, appeared to be politically quiescent and exclusively concerned with either technical or charitable activities. Strictly speaking, this may not have been the case: some of the associations might well have been politically active in obscure policy-making contexts that were not scrutinized. In any case, with five or six exceptions, at least one interview was held with each of the most prominent national organizations, including those in the underrepresented categories.

I also held unstructured interviews with some thirty federal congressmen (mostly deputies) in Brasília in order to find out how the "other side" felt about the efforts of associations to influence their deliberations. I then conducted 38 interviews, this time following a fixed schedule, with higher civil servants in Rio, including at least one respondent in each of the major ministries and commodity institutes. In both cases cooperation was excellent.

Two samples were used primarily as control groups. The political culture questionnaire, which terminated the interview with interest representatives, was pretested on a group of 44 students from the University of Brazil in Rio who were applying for fellowships at the Instituto de Ciências Sociais. From 37 items, the final schedule was pared down to 26. (These items appear in Questionnaires Alpha and Beta, pp. 399 and 400.) In São Paulo, thanks to Professor J. V. Freitas Marcondes, I had

English Translation of Questionnaire Alpha

Statement	I agree		I disagree	
	Very much	A little	Very much	A little
1. To be happy one should do as others wish, even if it means not expressing one's own ideas.	( )	( )	( )	( )
2. The son of a worker does not have much opportunity to get into one of the liberal professions.	( )	( )	( )	( )
3. In general, life is better in small cities, because everyone knows everyone else.	( )	( )	( )	( )
4. When looking for a job, one should find a place near one's parents, even if this means losing a good opportunity.	( )	( )	( )	( )
5. People in large cities are cold and hard to get to know; it is difficult to make new friends.	( )	( )	( )	( )
6. Making plans only brings unhappiness, because plans are so difficult to realize.	( )	( )	( )	( )
7. These days, as things are, an intelligent person should worry about the present without bothering about what should happen tomorrow.	( )	( )	( )	( )
8. It doesn't make much difference whether the people elect one candidate or another, because nothing is going to change.	( )	( )	( )	( )
9. You can have confidence only in those you know well.	( )	( )	( )	( )
10. One must have good relations with influential people in order to progress in one's profession.	( )	( )	( )	( )
11. Obedience and respect for authority are the most important virtues a child has to learn.	( )	( )	( )	( )
12. There are two types of people in the world, the weak and the strong; and the latter will always run things.	( )	( )	( )	( )

ENGLISH TRANSLATION OF QUESTIONNAIRE BETA

Statement	I agree		I disagree	
	Very much	A little	Very much	A little
1. The political decisions in this country are always made by a small and closed group, and the average citizen never has much influence.	( )	( )	( )	( )
2. People are born into social groups, each one of which has different capacities; for this reason, people should have different duties and rights.	( )	( )	( )	( )
3. The government should help persons from less favored classes enter into occupations of higher prestige.	( )	( )	( )	( )
4. Religion is a force indispensable for social harmony.	( )	( )	( )	( )
5. Religious authorities should not interfere in the political life of the country.	( )	( )	( )	( )
6. Brazilians can do anything as well as foreigners.	( )	( )	( )	( )
7. Foreign capital brings only benefits to the country.	( )	( )	( )	( )
8. Brazil should be independent of other countries regardless of the cost.	( )	( )	( )	( )
9. In politics it is better to compromise than to fight.	( )	( )	( )	( )
10. Controversies should never be resolved by violence.	( )	( )	( )	( )
11. It is not worth the trouble to debate with people whose ideas are very different from your own.	( )	( )	( )	( )
12. More fortunate social groups have the duty to look after the well-being of the less fortunate.	( )	( )	( )	( )
13. The government should act as arbitrator between employers' associations and workers' syndicates in the interest of social harmony.	( )	( )	( )	( )
14. The political process would be better if the representatives were elected by their occupational groups rather than by parties.	( )	( )	( )	( )

an opportunity to administer the questionnaire to a group of 31 trainees at the Instituto Cultural do Trabalho. These trainees came from 14 of the 23 states in Brazil, and most of them were active in the lower echelons of workers' syndicates. Thus I was provided with a generational, geographical, and status contrast to the older, higher-status respondents in the leadership of national representative associations.

The data from all these interviews, as well as the aggregate census data on Brazilian states used in the statistical analysis in Chapter 7, are available to interested scholars upon request from the International Data Library and Reference Service at the University of California in Berkeley. Another set of duplicate cards and a codebook have been sent to the Instituto de Ciências Sociais da Universidade do Brasil for use by Brazilian scholars.

NOTES

Notes

For complete authors' names, titles, and publication data for works cited in short form, see the Bibliography, p. 471.

Chapter One

Epigraph: Alexis de Tocqueville, *Democracy in America* (New York: Vintage, 1954), II, 118.

1. It has, however, inspired much theoretical disquisition and at least one attempt at a secondary analysis. See Huntington; Kornhauser. Tocqueville was primarily concerned with the process whereby traditional solidarity groups were weakened and the consequent need for secondary political associations to replace them. Huntington's treatment is similar, although he places greater emphasis on the institutionalization of government structures than on the formation of non-authoritative political associations. Kornhauser's concern is more static; it is with the conditions of modern political groups most conducive to mass politics.

2. "Indeed, political organization often precedes large-scale economic change and may be an important factor in whether or not there is a large-scale economic change." Myron Weiner, "Political Integration and Political Development," *The Annals*, Mar. 1965, pp. 63–64.

3. Smelser, p. 41. This is a rather specialized use of the concept of integration, equivalent to structural recombination. Subsequently in this study, structural differentiation will be used to refer to both aspects of this contrapuntal process.

4. Riggs, "Reflections," p. 14. In later writings he has preferred the term "diffraction." See Riggs, *Administration*, p. 23.

5. Lucian Pye, *Politics, Personality, and Nation Building* (New Haven, Conn., 1962), pp. 4, 62. This monograph on Burma is something of a case study in frustrated development—of differentiation outrunning integration—apparently because of problems of normative adjustment.

6. This conceptualization of successful development owes a great deal to S. N. Eisenstadt's "Modernization: Growth and Diversity," *América Latina*, IX, 1 (Jan.–Mar. 1966), 34–58. See also W. E. Moore, *Social Change* (Englewood Cliffs, N.J., 1963), p. 11.

7. Emile Durkheim, *Professional Ethics and Civic Morals* (Glencoe, Ill., 1958), p. 64.

8. Fred Riggs, "Bureaucrats and Political Development: A Paradoxical View," in J. LaPalombara, ed., *Bureaucracy and Political Development* (Princeton, N.J., 1965), p. 139.

9. Lucian Pye, in *Communications*, p. 16, makes a similar point: "The realm of politics, as generally thought of, consists of two rather different forms of activities, involving different structures. These are, on the one hand, the domain of administration and formal government and, on the other hand, the political processes of the society which permeate in a diffuse fashion the entire society and provide the fundamental framework of the polity. Thus political development must involve both the strengthening of formal government and the establishment of mechanisms for giving coherence to the polity as a whole."

10. Silvert, p. 19.

11. Reinhard Bendix, *Nation-Building and Citizenship* (New York, 1964), p. 15. Weber labels them "politically-oriented corporate groups" and "political corporate groups" in Weber, pp. 141–43. In this study they will be called political groups and authority groups, respectively.

12. Emile Durkheim, *De la Division du Travail Social* (Paris, 1962), p. xxxvi.

13. "Older nations have been built upon the myth that if each seeks his own interests, the interests of all will be served; new countries are trying to be built upon the myth that if each strives to get ahead in government and politics, the public good will be served." Pye, *Communications*, p. 3.

14. G. A. Almond and J. S. Coleman, eds., *The Politics of the Developing Areas* (Princeton, N.J., 1960), p. 23.

15. See S. N. Eisenstadt, "Patterns of Political Leadership and Support," in *Representative Government and National Progress* (Ibadan, Nigeria, 1959), pp. 3 et seq.; the essays by C. Geertz and L. Fallers in C. Geertz, ed., *Old Societies and New States* (New York, 1963), pp. 105–219; B. Hoselitz, "Tradition and Economic Growth," in R. Braibanti and J. J. Spengler, eds., *Tradition, Values, and Socio-Economic Development* (Durham, N.C., 1961).

16. See Riggs, "Reflections," p. 56.

17. Weiner, p. 221.

18. Lewis Coser, *The Functions of Social Conflict* (London, 1956), pp. 38, 68, 76.

19. Tocqueville defined the political association as "l'adhésion publique que donne un certain nombre d'individus à telles ou telles doctrines et dans l'engagement qu'il contractent de concourir d'une certain façon à les faire prévaloir." *Oeuvres Complètes*, Tome I, Vol. I (Paris, 1961), 185.

20. "The rate of segmentation of the support structure can be expected to vary inversely with differentiation." David Easton, "Political Anthropology," in B. J. Siegel, ed., *Biennial Review of Anthropology: 1959* (Stanford, Calif., 1959), p. 246. "The rate of association formation may serve as an index of the stability of a society and their number may be used as an index of its complexity." Truman, p. 57.

21. "The initial response is a trial-and-error type of reaching for many kinds of integration at once." Smelser, p. 81.

22. Samuel Eldersveld, "American Interest Groups: A Survey of Research and Some Implications for Theory and Method," Ehrmann, pp. 180–81.

23. See Weiner, *passim.*

24. Neil MacDonald, *The Study of Political Parties* (New York, 1955), p. 86. These observations have been confirmed empirically by recent American studies on party identification. See esp. A. Campbell et al., *The American Voter* (New York, 1960), pp. 117–67.

25. For the original source of this functional distinction between interest articulation and interest aggregation, see Almond and Coleman, *The Politics of the Developing Areas.* For a later reformulation, see G. Almond and G. B. Powell, *Comparative Politics: A Developmental Approach* (Boston, 1966), pp. 98–127. In this latter work, the authors note that aggregation is not institutionally specialized and that it "can occur at many points in the political system." Given the ubiquity of this function, it will hardly serve as the only distinguishing characteristic of party.

26. Truman, p. 33.

27. "Associating personalities present only special facets of themselves to one another." R. H. Cooley, R. C. Angell, and L. J. Carr, *Introductory Sociology* (New York, 1933), p. 214.

28. Weber, p. 141.

29. Riggs, *Administration,* pp. 164–73.

30. For an excellent monograph on the role of such voluntary associations, see Kenneth Little, *West African Urbanization* (London, 1965). See also Fred Riggs, "Interest and Clientele Groups," in Joseph Sutton, ed., *Problems of Politics and Administration in Thailand* (Bloomington, Ind., 1962), pp. 153–91.

31. "Wherever communal barriers can be bridged over and a functionally specific association created to which all communities can be attracted, associational rather than clect-like patterns appear. . . . The organization of clects is a natural counterpart of polycommunalism." Riggs, *Administration,* pp. 171, 172.

32. Douglas Ashford, "National Organizations and Political Development in Morocco," *Il Politico,* July 1963, p. 360.

33. Coser, p. 80. See also Ralf Dahrendorf, *Class and Class Conflict in Industrial Society* (Stanford, Calif., 1959), pp. 206–18.

34. For example, the most recent descriptive survey of North American interest groups daringly concludes that "interest groups have a good possibility of success if they: (1) draw their membership from a high-ranking social strata, (2) espouse goals not in conflict with societal values, and (3) are accorded legitimacy by those in a position to make authoritative decisions." Zeigler, pp. v-vii.

35. The nature of interest group research may be changing. See Eckstein for an excellent example of a systematic conceptual apparatus combined with a self-conscious and modest attempt at verification. See also LaPalombara.

36. For critiques from this perspective, see J. LaPalombara, "The Utility and Limitations of Interest Group Theory in Non-American Field Situations," in N. W. Polsby et al., eds., *Politics and Social Life* (Boston, 1963), pp. 642–54; Roy C. Macridis, "Groups and Group Theory," in R. C. Macridis and B. Brown, eds., *Comparative Politics* (Homewood, Ill., 1964), pp. 139–44. Three of the most recent monographs on interest group activity outside the United States have all stressed the role of political culture (or "attitudes") and government policy as important determinants. See Eckstein; LaPalombara; Weiner.

37. The other side of the process occurs when, as Tocqueville observed, primary groups like the family and local authorities become incapable of resolving conflict and providing needed services alone. They are forced to appeal beyond their own customs and resources to some outside authority. For an interesting case study of this process of group transformation, see Robert E. Anderson and Gallatin Anderson, "Voluntary Associations and Urbanization: A Diachronic Analysis," *American Journal of Sociology*, LXV (1958), 265–73.

38. For a discussion of this theme in the context of a developed welfare-conscious polity, see Samuel H. Beer, "Pressure Groups and Parties in Britain," *American Political Science Review*, L (1956), 1–23. See also Eckstein, p. 16. "As governments become more intensely involved in the control or guidance of the nation's economic system, the complex nature of the ensuing decisions requires that administrative agencies assume much of the burden." Zeigler, p. 78.

39. Riggs, *Administration*, p. 74

40. For a discussion of the combined impact of interaction rate (significance) and functional specificity, see Wallace S. Sayre and Herbert Kaufman, *Governing New York City* (New York, 1960), pp. 78–80.

Chapter Two

1. Castro, p. 196. For an excellent English treatment, see Wagley, "Brazilian Revolution."

2. See Neil J. Smelser, *Social Change and the Industrial Revolution* (Chicago, 1959), *passim*.

3. On the impact of these boom-and-bust export cycles upon Brazilian society and cultural values, see Normano.

4. See B. J. Hoselitz, "La Estratificación Social y el Desarrollo Económico," *América Latina*, VII, 1 (Jan.–Mar. 1964), 8–9.

5. The literature on the assimilation of immigrants in Brazil is substantial. In addition to the work of E. Willems on the Germans and H. Saito on the Japanese, see Diégues Júnior, *Imigração*, for an excellent summary. See also E. Willems, "Immigrants and their Assimilation in Brazil," in Smith and Marchant, pp. 209–25.

6. The Brazilian case does not fit perfectly the "cross-cutting" model suggested above. To some extent increased occupational differentiation has reinforced preexisting racial and ethnic stratification. Roger Bastide concludes that "industrialization has played a double role in Brazil. On the one hand, it has intensified prejudice and given sharper forms to discrimination at the beginning of industrial growth, when the blacks first became competitors with the whites. On the other hand, in periods of prosperity and rapid economic development, it has tended to make social tensions predominate over racial tensions." "The Development of Race Relations in Brazil," in Guy Hunter, ed., *Industrialization and Race Relations* (London, 1965), p. 26. See also R. A. Metall and M. Paranhos da Silva, "Equality of Opportunity in a Multi-Racial Society: Brazil," *International Labour Review*, XCIII, 5 (1966), 477–508.

7. For a discussion of these problems, see T. Pompeu Accioly Borges and Gustaaf Loeb, "Desenvolvimento econômico e distribuição da população ativa," in Bernstein, pp. 27–40.

8. See Brasil, IBGE, *Análise Crítica de Resultados dos Censos Demográficos* (Rio, 1956).

9. See Accioly Borges and Loeb. See also Accioly Borges, "Estratificação."

10. Brasil, IBGE, *Anuário Estatístico—1965*, p. 35.

11. Other statistical computations of occupational stratification show a more even pattern of industrial employment. The Joint Brazil–United States Economic Commission Report of 1953 claimed a steady climb of 3.8% in 1920 to 9.5% in 1940 to 13.1% in 1950 in those employed by industrial firms. Nonetheless, the 1960 figures show only 12.3%, or a drop of 0.8%, in this category. Joint Brazil–United States Economic Commission, p. 291. These data were based upon an unspecified "rearrangement of demographic census data." In a more recent article, Isaac Kerstenetsky offers yet another set of figures. According to him, the proportion of the population engaged in industry rose from 8.9% in 1940 to 12.9% in 1950 and then declined to 12.7% in 1960. "Aspectos do desenvolvimento da economia brasileira," *Revista Econômica do Jornal do Brasil*, Feb. 10, 1966.

12. For an extended discussion of social stratification in pre-1930 Brazil stressing the relative lack of change in occupational diversification from Independence (1889) until 1940, see J. Camillo de Oliveira Torres, "A Estructura da sociedade brasileira," in *Estratificação Social no Brasil* (São Paulo: Difusão Européia do Livro, 1965), pp. 178–214. Oliveira Torres concludes, "The fact is that the 'social fan' is opening in Brazil and that in the place of compact, slightly differentiated groups, today we have a greater variety of classes and activities offering an extraordinary richness of tones and hues." The quotation is from p. 205.

13. "Whatever the reason, there can be little doubt that an economy, to lift itself to higher income levels, must and will first develop within itself one or several regional centers of economic strength. This need for the emergence of 'growing points' or 'growth poles' in the course of the development process means that international and interregional inequality of growth is an inevitable concomitant and condition of growth itself." Hirschman, *Strategy*, pp. 183–84.

14. See Werner Baer, "Regional Inequality and Economic Growth in Brazil," *Economic Development and Cultural Change*, XII, 3 (Apr. 1964). For specific treatments of the Northeast problem, see Furtado, *A Pre-Revolução Brasileira*; Furtado, *Dialética*; Hirschman, *Journeys*; S. Robock, *Brazil's Developing Northeast* (Washington, D. C., 1963).

15. Furtado, *Economic Growth*, p. 22.

16. "The data reveal two important facts. First, that an important structural change took place, i.e. a marked rise of industry's share in the national product and probably a relative decline in the importance of agriculture. Second, it is also clear that industry can be considered as the dynamic or pace-setting sector of the economy." Baer, *Industrialization*, p. 72.

17. Slawinski, pp. 163–87, esp. Table III.

18. Celso Furtado, "Political Obstacles to Economic Growth in Brazil," in Veliz, p. 150.

19. For the average number of workers per establishment, see Brasil, IBGE, *Anuário Estatístico—1953* and *Anuário Estatístico—1964*. Comparative figures on employment in artisan establishments are difficult to obtain. If we assume that "Zero to Five occupied" is equivalent to "One to Four employed" per firm, then the share of employment dropped from 12.2% to 11.3% during the 1950's. The value of production declined even more, from 12.5% to 7.3% (at current prices). Brasil, IBGE, *Censo Industrial* 1950 and 1960.

20. It is difficult to extend the time series to include data from 1940 and earlier. For a discussion of the changes between 1940 and 1950, see "Evolução," pp. 49–59.

21. Baer, *Industrialization*, pp. 76–77.

22. Lopes, *Sociedade*, p. 148. This book contains an excellent comparison of two factories stressing the way such traditional, paternalistic norms inhibit worker recourse to "outside" interest representatives such as the local sindicato.

23. With the possible exception of 1965, when for conjunctural reasons industrial production remained stagnant or actually declined. See "A Economia Brasileira 1965," *Desenvolvimento e Conjuntura*, X, 2 (Feb. 1966), 5–106; *Conjuntura Econômica*, XX, 2 (Feb. 1966), 27–34.

24. Bendix, p. 211.

25. Corrected data from Borges, "Estratificação," p. 95, were used. Straight census data would have shown an increase to 49.1% in salaried employees, owing to underreporting of female rural employment.

26. Bendix, p. 221 *et seq.*

27. See Bertram Hutchinson, "Class Self-Assessment in a Rio de Janeiro Population," *América Latina*, VI, 1 (Jan.–Mar. 1963), 56–57. See also G. A. D. Soares, "Classes sociais, strata sociais e as eleições presidenciais de 1960," *Sociologia*, XXIII (1961), 217–38.

28. Slawinski, p. 179. See also D. Lambert, "L'Urbanisation accelerée de l'Amérique Latine et la formation d'un secteur tertiaire refuge," *Civilisations*, XV, 2, 3, 4.

29. The inclusion of liberal professions may seem strange. In Brazil, a very high percentage of doctors, economists, engineers, and architects work part time for the government and for other administrative agencies, even though their predominant activity (hence, their census classification) is in private practice. See Vieira da Cunha, p. 110. For an excellent discussion of the importance of multiple job holding among government employees, see Iutaka, pp. 126–30.

30. See Soares, "A nova industrialização."

31. Vieira da Cunha is the most comprehensive empirical investigation to date of the expansion of the civilian and military bureaucracies. See esp. "estudos sôbre a burocracia civil e militar," pp. 110–75.

32. For an interesting discussion of the political role of government employees in a small town of the interior, see José Murilo de Carvalho, "Barbacena: a familia, a política e uma hipôtese," *Revista Brasileira de Estudos Políticos*, XX (Jan. 1966), 125–93. Over one-third of the eligible electorate were federal, state, or municipal employees!

33. Iutaka, p. 130.

34. Pinto, p. 222.

35. G. B. Siegel, "Administration, Values and the Merit System in Brazil," in Daland, *Perspectives*, pp. 1–11. See also other essays in this volume.

36. Ianni, "Desenvolvimentos Patológicos da Burocracia," in *Industrialização*, pp. 27–37.

37. See Cardoso, *Empresário*, pp. 95–158. See also M. W. Vieira da Cunha, "Resistência da Burocracia as Mudânças Sociais, no Setor Público, e no Setor Privado," in *Resistências a Mudânça* (Rio: CLAPCS, 1960), pp. 204–5.

38. Ianni, *Industrialização*, p. 29.

39. "Conditions were not created within the public sector to enable it to prepare itself institutionally for the exercise of its new functions, the administrative machinery growing tumultuously under the pressure of irreversible situations." Furtado, *Dialética*, p. 124.

40. Geiger. By census definition, urban population consists of those living in *sêdes municipais* (county seats). If some size threshold were imposed, the urban percentage would decrease. For example, were it settlements over 2,000, only 30.8% of the 1950 population would have been urban, as opposed to 36.2% "officially" urban. Detailed 1960 figures are not yet available.

41. Smith, in *Brazil: People and Institutions*, pp. 144–57, notes that 16.5% of the population of Rio had migrated there during the ten years prior to 1950, and that 23.8% of the município of São Paulo had arrived during the same period.

42. *Ibid.*, pp. 597–99.

43. Bazzanella, p. 7.

44. Frank Bonilla expressed this well when he referred to the *favela* as "the rural slum within the city." "Rio's Favelas," *American Universities Field Staff Report*, VII, 2 (Oct. 1960).

45. In his excellent study of Rio's *favelas*, Carlos Alberto de Medina concludes that "the major part of the *favelados* are people whose employment is characterized by the predominance of manual labor, demanding a very low educational level. Normally, they are unskilled or semiskilled workers, but have considerable professional experience." *A Favela e o Demagogo* (São Paulo: Martins, 1964), p. 66.

46. Deutsch, p. 494. For an interesting premonition of Deutsch's concept and an application of it to Imperial and Republican Brazil, see Oliveira Vianna's discussion of *circulação* in *Evolução*.

47. Deutsch, pp. 499–500.

48. Deutsch, p. 513, "Notes to Table III-B."

49. For the argument that the "myth" of impending mobility in Brazil has impeded the formation of working-class consciousness and organization, see F. H. Cardoso, "Proletariado e mudança social," *Sociologia*, XXII, 1 (1960); A. Touraine, "Industrialisation et conscience ouvrière à São Paulo," *Sociologie du Travail*, III, 4 (1961), 77–95.

50. S. Kuznets, "Quantitative Aspects of the Economic Growth of Nations: Distribution of Income by Size," *Economic Development and Cultural Change*, XI (Jan. 1963). He places the period of widening inequality in the United States "from about 1840 and particularly from 1870." Tocqueville left the United States some ten years prior to this period.

51. Brasil, Ministério do Planejamento e Coordenação Econômica, *Programa de Ação Econômica do Govêrno 1964–1966*, 2nd ed. Documentos EPEA No. 1 (May 1965), p. 39.

52. General price index rose from 53 in 1947 (base year 1953) to 5215 in January 1966. The cost of living index for Guanabara rose from 56 to 5657 during the same period; for São Paulo it rose to 5483. *Conjuntura Econômica*, XX, 2 (Feb. 1966).

53. See "O novo salário mínimo," *Desenvolvimento e Conjuntura*, V, 11 (Nov. 1961), 43.

54. Baer, *Industrialization*, pp. 123–24.

55. Brasil, Presidência da República, p. 20.

56. Havighurst and Moreira, p. 103.
57. Hutchinson, "Class Self-Assessment in a Rio de Janeiro Population," p. 230.
58. Hutchinson, *Mobilidade.*
59. *Ibid.,* pp. 218–19.
60. *Ibid.,* pp. 221–22. For an extended discussion, see Hutchinson, "Urban Social Mobility."
61. Hutchinson, "Urban Social Mobility," p. 55.
62. In a comparison between São Paulo, Montevideo, and Buenos Aires, Hutchinson concludes that, although differences in the age composition of the samples make definitive comparisons impossible, "while between Buenos Aires and Montevideo there is no significant difference in the general social mobility rate, when changes in opportunity are left out of account the São Paulo structure is slightly less permeable." "Social Mobility Rates," p. 18. On the greater importance of "structural mobility" in São Paulo, see Table 9 on p. 16.

Chapter Three

1. For the pioneering formulation of the concept, see Gabriel Almond, "Comparative Political Systems," *Journal of Politics,* XVIII (1956), 391 et seq. See also S. H. Beer and A. B. Ulam, eds., *Patterns of Government* (New York, 1962), pp. 32–44; Almond and Verba; Pye and Verba.
2. For the concept of enculturation, see M. J. Herskovits, *Man and His Works* (New York, 1950).
3. According to Lucian Pye, "In no society is there a single uniform political culture, and in all polities there is a fundamental distinction between the culture of the rulers or power holders and that of the masses." Pye and Verba, pp. 525–26.
4. According to Sidney Verba, "It may be that political beliefs are sharply discontinuous from or in some way inconsistent with other beliefs. . . . A more usual situation would be the one in which the formal values stressed in the political realm were not consistent with those stressed in other areas of social life." *Ibid.,* p. 524. See also pp. 553–54.
5. Robert Scott emphasizes "the difficulties inherent in building a congruent relationship between a political culture and the political structures when both are being affected by change . . . but at different rates." *Ibid.,* p. 334. See also Almond and Verba, p. 20.
6. Not all members of the political system complete the full course. *Parochials* whose "frequency of orientation to specialized political objects . . . approaches zero" do not complete the first stage; *subjects* who perceive the differentiated system and orient themselves only to its "output aspects" make it only as far as the second; *participants* who are aware of "both the input and output aspects of the system" complete the full course and graduate as politically enculturated actors. Almond and Verba, pp. 11–26.
7. Robert Scott mentions "the three stages of the political socialization process: basic socialization, political socialization and political recruitment." Pye and Verba, pp. 348–49. My conceptual scheme is a revision and expansion of his suggestive but incomplete remarks.
8. Phyllis Peterson, "Brazil," in Martin Needler, ed., *Political Systems of Latin America* (Princeton, N.J., 1964). Bonilla, "Brazil" also contains a discussion of Brazilian political culture.

9. Some of the more important essays have been: Joaquim Nabuco, "O Espírito do Nacionalidado na História do Brasil," *Discurso e Conferências nos Estados Unidos* (Rio: Aguilar, 1911), pp. 121–37; Affonso Celso, *Porque Me Ufano do Mau Pais* (Rio: Livraria Garnier, 1901); Cunha; Torres; Oliveira Vianna, *Populações*; Oliveira Vianna, *Evolução*; Amado, *Grão*; Amado, *A Chave;* Paulo Prado; Bomfim; Freyre, *Masters*; Freyre, *Mansions*; Buarque de Holanda; Melo Franco; Azevedo Amaral; Tavares de Sá; Azevedo; Duarte; Leal; Vianna Moog; Freyre, *Ordem* and *New World*. Two excellent summaries of the literature are Moreira Leite; and Rodrigues, *Aspirações*. The latter contains a good working bibliography of accounts by foreign travelers. A useful anthology is Menezes.

10. Amado, *Grão*, p. 166.

11. Rodrigues, p. 41.

12. Buarque de Holanda, *passim*, stresses this theme. See also Freyre, *New World*; Duarte.

13. For the best statement of this interpretation, see Diégues Júnior, *Regiões*.

14. Bomfim stresses the Amerindian heritage; Freyre, *Masters*, gives the most extensive discussion of the African contribution.

15. Wagley, *Introduction*, p. 1.

16. Melo Franco, p. 6.

17. Amaral, p. 248.

18. Wagley, p. 2.

19. "Gibt es einen brasilianischen Volkscharacter?," *Staden Jahrbuch* (São Paulo), VII/VIII (1959–60), 149.

20. Oliveira Vianna, *Instituições*, I, 217–18. See also Oliveira Vianna, *Instituições*, I, 374; II, 430.

21. Freyre, *Masters*, p. 31.

22. Tavares de Sá, p. 8.

23. Freyre, *Masters*, p. 189.

24. *Ibid.*, pp. 36, 169.

25. See the observations of H. Koster, a foreigner who became a *senhor de engenho* in Pernambuco, in Oliveira Vianna, *Instituições*, I, 326. See also Buarque de Holanda, p. 103.

26. Oliveira Vianna, *Populações*, I, 239.

27. In Brazil, compadre relations are established not only at baptism, but also at a wide variety of other occasions: confirmation, marriage, and even certain feast days. See Oliveira Vianna, *Instituições*, I, 270 et seq.; Wagley, *Introduction*, pp. 190–92.

28. Wagley, in *Introduction*, pp. 199–200, reports respondents in recent anthropological research who were capable of naming up to five hundred relatives. See also Diégues Júnior, pp. 58–61, on the familistic social order.

29. Freyre, *Mansions*, p. 94.

30. "The patriarchal system still impregnates the minds of Brazilians, even when they are no longer able to live it out." Tavares de Sá, p. 10.

31. E. Willems, "The Structure of the Brazilian Family," *Social Forces*, XXXI, 4 (May 1953), 345. For another discussion of continuity in the Brazilian family, see Wagley, pp. 198–204. Antônio Candido, "The Brazilian Family," in Smith and Marchant, pp. 291–312, places a greater accent upon change than upon continuity.

32. Rosen, "Achievement Syndrome," p. 350.

33. *Ibid.*, p. 348.

34. Buarque de Holanda, p. 199. This author had already summarized the political consequences of this privatization and personalization of the public: "[Brazilians] consider perfectly normal the acquisition of certain types of personal favors through individuals with whom they have affective or friendly relations and do not understand that a person who has a certain public position stops giving to friends and relatives favors dependent on that position." *Ibid.*, p. 189.

35. Oliveira Vianna, *Instituições*, I, 358.

36. See Torres. Alberto Torres was perhaps the first to link these themes with a nationalist appeal. For an earlier but more strictly literary discussion, see the many writings of Sylvio Romero.

37. Bonilla, p. 206. See also Duarte. Nestor Duarte was the originator of this theme. Oliveira Vianna argues that originally the purpose of the patriarchal clan was not primarily religious, economic, ideological, or military, but political—to protect and insulate the local group from arbitrary rule by the colonial power (*"A necessidade de defêsa contra a anarquia branca"*). See Oliveira Vianna, *Populações*, I, 204 et seq.

38. "Privatism and personalism . . . do not remain confined in these local primary structures—this is a central point in our political psychology. . . . They have deep reflections, reaching the higher elites and giving the tone to the spiritual atmosphere surrounding the formation and functioning of the provincial and Imperial regimes." Oliveira Vianna, *Instituições*, I, 333.

39. Duarte, p. 231. Frank Bonilla also cites this statement.

40. Freyre, *Masters*, p. 159.

41. Oliveira Vianna, as cited in Duarte, p. 96. See also the distinction made between *"zonas de ação direta do Govêrno"* and *"zonas de ação amortecida"* in Lambert, p. 247.

42. Nestor Duarte shrewdly argues that, because of, first, the similarity in family structure and, second, the absence of "general and comprehensive sentiments" produced by such a structure, neither Portugal nor the Empire had to confront any "large movements of social action or reaction." Secessionist movements never materialized. See Duarte, p. 89. In fact, the Empire succumbed without a struggle as a consequence of the success of what was the only movement of "general and comprehensive sentiment" it had to face: the Abolitionist Movement.

43. Freyre, *New World*, p. 5.

44. "The Secret Instructions of Viceroy Lavrádio to his Successor," in Burns, *Documentary History*, p. 146.

45. In interviews, the most frequently mentioned specific trait associated with the *bondade do nosso povo* was his "extraordinary patience." "The indolence and the passivity of the populace facilitated the preservation of the political and social unity of the enormous territory." Prado, p. 200.

46. Freyre, *New World*, p. 265.

47. Alberto Rangel, ed., *No Rolar do Tempo* (Rio: José Olympio, 1937), p. 22.

48. Freyre, *New World*, p. 5.

49. Tavares de Sá, p. 137, calls this the "Fique Rico" complex. This is a major theme in Prado.

50. Melo Franco, pp. 139–42.

51. Rosen, "Achievement Syndrome," p. 352. See also Torres, p. 42.

52. See Buarque de Holanda; Freyre, *New World*, pp. 39–66.

53. Buarque de Holanda, p. 273.

54. Not all Brazilian commentators agree on the existence or frequency of "cordiality." Vianna Moog denies its importance, except as a manipulative device or as a means for restraining aggressive impulses. He argues that "to the Brazilian, . . . man is generally evil unless he is proved otherwise." Vianna Moog, pp. 207, 226.

55. Oliveira Vianna, *Populações*, I, 237–43.

56. Freyre, *New World*, p. 162.

57. From *mazombo*, the son of a Portuguese born in Brazil, equivalent to *criollo* in Spanish. Even today the term is synonymous with somber, taciturn, and ill-tempered. See Vianna Moog.

58. Cruz Costa, p. 5.

59. Freyre, *Ordem*, I, 119, notes that a "deep feeling of insecurity" followed upon the disappearance of slavery and monarchy. The loss of these orienting institutions and a growing disillusion with republicanism may have been in part responsible for the acute malaise of the early twentieth century.

60. See Gilberto Freyre's personal confession in the introduction to *The Masters and the Slaves*.

61. Abreu, as cited in Prado, p. 132.

62. "The Secret Instructions of Viceroy Lavrádio to His Successor," in Burns, *Documentary History*, p. 146. For a virtually identical description given two hundred years later, see Lambert, p. 230.

63. Freyre, *New World*, p. 81.

64. Freyre, *Mansions*, p. 19.

65. Wagley, *Introduction*, p. 107.

66. Rosen, "Achievement Syndrome," p. 352. An interesting comment on the personalization of authority is the widespread propensity for Brazilians to refer to popular leaders by their first names or by nicknames. It is hard to imagine a Mexican, for example, calling his president Gustavo, much less Adolfito. For an excellent speculative essay on the origins and consequences of Brazilian paternalism and patrimonialism, see Hutchinson, "Patron-Dependent Relationship."

67. Amado, *Grão*, p. 156.

68. As cited in Oliveira Vianna, *Populações*, I, 229.

69. It is not true that Independence was gained completely without the shedding of blood, however. See Rodrigues, *Conciliação*.

70. Oliveira Vianna, *Instituições*, I, 392. For the importance of the Empire on the consolidation of a sense of community and a distinctive political style, see *ibid.*, pp. 379–85; Faoro, pp. 163–98; Mercadente.

71. Torres, p. 84. Sometimes Torres appears to confuse lack of national consciousness with lack of a national policy or sense of national destiny on the part of the elites.

72. Oliveira Vianna, *Instituições*, II, 513. See also Amaral, p. 161.

73. Harris, pp. 179, 206.

74. Pye and Verba, p. 533.

75. Tavares de Sá, p. 242.

76. Moreira Leite, *passim*. The chapter on national stereotyping among paulistano schoolchildren has been removed from the revised second edition of *O Carácter Nacional Brasileiro* (São Paulo: Pioneira, 1969).

77. Morais, pp. 38–39.

78. Florestan Fernandes, "Como muda o Brasil," *Cadernos Brasileiros*, VIII, 3 (May–June 1966), 32.

79. Rosen, "Achievement Syndrome." See also Rosen, "Socialization."

80. Joseph Kahl, "Urbanização e mudanças ocupacionais no Brasil," *América Latina*, V, 4 (Oct.–Dec. 1962), 21–30.

81. This is often coupled with the remark "They are slow to revolt; therefore, easy to govern." Cynically, one could argue that this probably correct association of traits explains why elites have not devoted more effort to raising the level of general political consciousness. See Anísio Teixeira, "Revolução o educação," *Revista Brasileira do Estudos Pedagógicos*, XXXIX, 90 (Apr.–June 1963), 4.

82. In the expressive words of the poet Mário de Andrade, [our] "elites flirt with ideologies by telegram." The quotation is from Cruz Costa, p. 252.

83. *Ibid.*, p. 3. This book is an excellent treatment of this theme, emphasizing the pragmatic nature of the modification process.

84. Frank Bonilla, "A National Ideology for Development: Brazil," in Silvert, p. 233.

85. Moreira, p. 35. For a discussion of the impact of the Jesuit schools as well as a comprehensive history of education in Brazil, see Azevedo, pp. 325–526.

86. "*O Correio Brasilense* of Hipólito da Costa, edited in London, was the principal vehicle through which untraveled Brazilians received their political instruction, if not their notions of the outside world." Amado, *Grão*, p. 15.

87. Anísio Teixeira, "Valores proclamados o valores reais nas instituições escolares brasileiras," *Revista Brasileira do Estudos Pedagógicos*, XXXVII, 86 (Apr.–June 1962), 63. Azevedo Amaral, *A Aventura Política do Brasil* (São Paulo: Companhia Editôra Nacional, 1937), pp. 173–74, suggests another reason for the weak role of political ideas in Brazilian history. How, he asks, could one expect to inherit a strong set of ideological beliefs from Portugal, a nation that has never created "a sufficiently viable political ideology"?

88. Teixeira, p. 64.

89. Azevedo, p. 376.

90. *Ibid.*, pp. 389–90.

91. Amaral, as quoted in Azevedo, pp. 414–15. For a more comprehensive treatment of positivism, see João Cruz Costa, *O Positivismo na Republica* (São Paulo: Companhia Editôra Nacional, 1956).

92. See Leôncio Martins Rodrigues, *Conflito*, pp. 115–56.

93. See Astrojildo Pereira, *Formação do Partido Communista Brasileiro* (Rio: Vitória, 1962).

94. For representative expressions of concern, see José Verissimo, *A Educação Nacional* (Belem: Tavares Cardoso, 1895); and A. Carneiro Leão, *O Brasil o a Educação Popular* (Rio: Jornal do Commercio, 1917).

95. Azevedo, p. 428. According to him, in some states, including Bahia and Pernambuco, there was probably a regression in literacy rates during the republican period.

96. K. Silvert, "The Strategy of the Study of Nationalism," in Silvert, p. 18.

97. Alberto Torres is a fascinatingly original, if uneven, thinker. For example, he argued that in new nations, nationalism played a different role than in already formed ones, where it was merely a "morbid exaggeration of patriotism." In new nations, with a "young people," it was necessary to create a

sense of national consciousness "artificially" and "rationally." Torres, pp. 27, 148.

98. See Cruz Costa, p. 240.

99. On this movement and its ideology, see John Wirth, "Tenentismo in the Brazilian Revolution of 1930," *Hispanic American Historical Review*, XLIV, 2 (May 1964), 161–79; Robert J. Alexander, "Brazilian Tenentismo," *Hispanic American Historical Review*, XXXVI, 2 (May 1956), 229–42.

100. Moreira, p. 90.

101. For a representative discussion of the educational aims of the period, see Humberto Grande, *A Pedagogia no Estado Novo* (Rio: Grafica Guarany, 1941). Education is described on p. 65 as "the vigorous social process that conscious people use to reconstruct their nationality in molds superior and better adjusted to their nature." See also Burns, *Nationalism*, pp. 84–85.

102. See M. A. Caldas Barbosa, "A Organização da Juventude Brasileira," *Estudos e Conferências*, No. 4 (1940), pp. 57–70. Alzira Vargas do Amaral Peixoto, Getúlio's daughter, mentions that she held up this project for two years by placing it deliberately in her bottom desk drawer. Vargas do Amaral Peixoto, pp. 349–51.

103. The most important sources are Campos; Azevedo Amaral, *O Estado Autoritário e Realidade Nacional* (Rio: José Olympio, 1938); Octavio de Faria, *Machiavel e o Brasil* (Rio: Civilização Brasileira, 1933); Oliveira Vianna, *Problemas de Direito Corporativo*; Oliveira Vianna, *Direito do Trabalho*; Oliveira Vianna, *Problemas de Organização*; A. B. Cotrim Noto, *Doutrina e Formação do Corporativismo* (Rio: A. Coelho Branco, 1938); Niemeyer.

104. In addition to his works noted above, see Oliveira Vianna, "Condições."

105. This "official" corporatism should not be confused with Catholic corporatism, inspired by *Rerum Novarum* and *Quadragesimo Anno*. These furnished the guiding principles for the Catholic revival movement (*Ação Católica, Centro Dom Vital*) of the 1920's and 1930's. Although similar, the two corporatisms clashed on the issue of syndical unity versus syndical pluralism. See Alceu Amoroso Lima, *Política; idem, O Problema do Trabalho*, 2nd ed. (Rio: Agir, 1956). This ideological current is far from exhausted, and corporatist proposals designed "to overcome the class struggle by the installation of an organic order uniting employers and workers" continue to appear from time to time. See J. P. Galvão de Sousa, "Do princípio do subsidiariadade ao corporatismo," *Digesto Econômico* (Mar.–Apr. 1963), pp. 78–92; Goffredo Tellos Junior, "Linheamentos do uma Democracia Auténtica para o Brasil," *Convivium*, II, 5 and 6 (July–Aug. and Sept. 1964). For a modified, contemporary version, see Bastos de Avila.

106. For a stinging criticism of the Bill for the failure of the federal government to meet its responsibility for the creation of an "integrated national consciousness," see Jaime Abreu, "Anacronismo educacional da classe dominante brasileira," *Revista Brasileira de Estudos Pedagógicos*, XXXV, 82 (Apr.–June 1961), pp. 6–14.

107. N. Sucupira, "A nova disciplina organização social o política brasileira," *Educação e Ciencias Sociais*, VII, 19 (Jan.–Apr. 1962), 112.

108. Delegado de Carvalho, *Organização Social e Política Brasileira* (Rio: Fundo de Cultura, 1963); Theobaldo Miranda Santos, *Organização Social e*

Político do Brasil (São Paulo: Companhia Editôra Nacional, 1963). There is a Catholic text by J. C. Oliveira Torres which I have not read.

109. For a comprehensive discussion of ISEB, see Frank Bonilla, "A National Ideology for Development: Brazil," in Silvert, pp. 232–64.

110. For the earlier period, the most important sources are Jaguaribe, "Crise,"; *idem, Nacionalismo; idem, Desenvolvimento*; Guerreiro Ramos, *O Problema Nacional do Brasil*, 2nd ed. (Rio: Editôra Saga, 1960). Mendes, *Nacionalismo*, though published later, probably belongs in this period.

111. The most important work of this period is the monumental, but nearly incomprehensible, Vieira Pinto.

112. Frank Bonilla, "A National Ideology for Development: Brazil," in Silvert, p. 239.

113. See "Número especial sôbre a segurança nacional," *Revista Brasileira de Estudos Políticos*, July 1966.

114. Usually referred to as "the Sorbonne," the group of army officers around the Escola, headed by Marshal Castelo Branco, played a key but belated role in the 1964 military takeover and occupied many of the command posts and important offices in the succeeding regime. See Carlos Castelo Branco, "Da conspiração a revolução," in *Os Idos de Março e a Queda em Abril* (Rio: José Alvaro, 1964), pp. 279–306. President Castelo Branco's successor, General Costa e Silva, though not usually linked with the Sorbonne group, has proclaimed that his administration will be faithful to its ideology. *Jornal do Brasil*, July 21, 1966. For the accusation by an army colonel that ISEB was "an authentic base of operation for the Communist Party," see *O Estado de São Paulo*, July 8, 1965.

115. See IPÊS, *Declaração de Princípios* (Rio, 1963). The more militant São Paulo branch of IPÊS played the more active role in the coup of 1964. However, the Rio group received a substantial number of important government posts. In 1964, the two became separate entities. There is a certain overlap of personnel between IPÊS-GB and ESG. For a detailed study based on interviews and focusing on IPÊS-GB, see Norman Blume, "Pressure Groups and Decision-Making in Brazil," *Studies in Comparative International Development*, III, 11 (1967–68).

116. IPÊS-SP, *Esquema do Planejamento* (São Paulo, 1965).

117. IPÊS-GB, *Estatutos* (Rio, 1964), p. 11.

118. Bonilla, "Brazil," p. 217.

119. Paulo Freire, "Escola primaria para o Brasil," *Revista Brasileira de Estudos Pedagógicos*, XXXV, 82 (Apr.–June 1961), 15–32.

120. The "revolutionary" regime is, however, showing a renewed interest in civic indoctrination through the school system. Interestingly, the Escola Superior de Guerra, the Liga de Defêsa Nacional, and the Campanha de Educação Cívica are collaborating in the planning of the new program. See *Jornal do Brasil*, July 27, 1966.

121. Free, pp. 24–33.

122. Bonilla, "A National Ideology for Development: Brazil," in Silvert, pp. 262–63.

123. This, of course, is an indirect confirmation of Cruz Costa's major theme —that all foreign ideas, however manifestly idealistic, have been accepted eclectically, applied pragmatically, and "always linked to action." Cruz Costa, pp. 272–77.

124. Free, p. 36.
125. *Ibid.*, p. 34. One should stress, however, that "avowed nationalists" are a concentrated group: metropolitan, better educated, and from a higher status.
126. For this important conceptual distinction, I am indebted to Kalman Silvert and Frank Bonilla. See esp. "Introduction: The Strategy of the Study of Nationalism," in Silvert.
127. Free, p. 39.
128. *Ibid.*, p. 40.
129. Bonilla, "Brazil," pp. 210–11.
130. *Ibid.*, p. 211.
131. *Ibid.*, pp. 211–12.
132. "Our people are completely indifferent to forms of government." Oliveira Vianna, *Evolução*, p. 311.
133. Harris, p. 103. See also Vianna Moog, p. 131, for similar observations, juxtaposing high expectations with a low sense of responsibility and efficacity. Oliveira Vianna, in *Populações*, II, 387, argued that Brazilians lacked *consciência nacional*, but were aware of "the omnipotence of the state, . . . [of] its immeasurable capacity for doing good and evil."
134. Alceu Amoroso Lima, "Considerações sôbre a crise Brasileira" (unpublished, 1964).
135. José Honório Rodrigués, in *Conciliação*, pp. 11–107, argues that this policy of conciliation "had as its principal objective the smoothing out of divergencies between dominant groups, rather than concession of benefits to the people" and that "conciliation and lack of conciliation, bloody and unbloody history, have alternated in the Brazilian historical process, although it is correct and just to affirm that the examples of conciliation predominate."
136. Melo Franco, p. 230. Melo Franco is a member of a very prominent "political family" from Minas Gerais.
137. Oliveira Vianna, *Evolução*, p. 270.
138. The quotation is from Buarque de Holanda, p. 168. "In Brazil man would have to conquer nature by feeling his way, temporizing, detouring, distrusting, wriggling, tricking, biding his time, waiting for opportunities, developing subtleties." Vianna Moog, p. 223.
139. Oliveira Vianna argues that this is particularly true of the southern Brazilian. *Populações*, I, 423. Recently there was an instance of attempted murder on the floor of the Parliament (a senatorial bystander was killed.) The opponents were Northeasterners. The state of Alagoas, for example, has something of a national reputation for endemic political violence.
140. Amado, *Chave*, pp. 122–23.
141. Oliveira Vianna, *Evolução*, pp. 322–23.
142. Lambert, p. 273.
143. *Ibid.*, p. 273. For a suggestive attempt at a theory of Brazilian corruption linking it with high rates of vertical mobility, anomie, familism, inflation, structural bottlenecks, and presidentialism, see José Arthur Rios, "Consideração sôbre a corrupção," *Cadernos Brasileiros*, No. 32 (Nov.–Dec. 1964), pp. 5–13.
144. Horowitz, p. 92.
145. The quotation is from Henriques.
146. Bonilla, "Brazil," p. 213.

147. See Jaguaribe, "Crise," for an excellent extended discussion of this use of the government mechanism as an employment agency and favor-granting machine. Jaguaribe called this the "Estado Cartorial," and the term has stuck.

148. Joaquim Nabuco described the Imperial electoral system as follows: "The moderative power can call whomever it pleases to organize the cabinet; this person calls the elections because he has to; this election provides him with a majority. That is the representational system of our country." The quotation is from Cunha, p. 295.

149. See Pedreira, pp. 35–62.

150. Pinto, pp. 236–37, argues that this is a common trait of all unequally developing societies.

151. See Henriques, pp. 16–17, 101. This book is a very biased attack on Vargas's career up to the establishment of the Estado Novo. Nevertheless, it does provide valuable insights into the code and style of Brazil's most successful politician and the writer and inspirer of most of the contemporary codebook.

152. Morais, p. 119.

153. This is the major theme of Phyllis Peterson's essay on Brazilian political culture in Needler.

154. *Cobertura* (coverage) is one of the most frequently used terms in Brazilian political jargon and refers to mutually accorded support. No policy innovation is made without prior negotiation of the requisite *cobertura*. For a fascinating case showing the "mutuality" of the process, see Mauro Borges, *O Golpe em Goiás* (Rio: Civilizaçao Brasileira, 1965), pp. 21–23.

155. See Hélio Jaguaribe, "O Moralismo e alienação das classes médias," *Cadernos do Nosso Tempo*, No. 2 (1954), pp. 15–19. For the UDN's historical links with the liberals, see José Honório Rodrigues, *Conciliação*, pp. 11–12, 100.

156. See Pedreira, pp. 112–14. The phrase "historical opportunism" is Pedreira's.

157. "A pronounced love of fixed forms and generic laws that [attempt to] circumscribe a difficult and complex reality . . . is one of the most constant and significant aspects of the Brazilian character." Buarque de Holanda, p. 220.

158. For a highly amusing description of this demagogic style, see Kellemen, pp. 107–12.

159. Paulo Prado, p. 214.

160. Melo Franco, p. 217.

161. As Hirschman notes, it combines the mechanical notion of "Yankee ingenuity" and the personal one of "*se débrouiller*." Hirschman, *Journeys*, p. 325.

162. Roberto Campos, "A Sociologia do jeito," *O Senhor*, July 1960.

163. Kellemen, pp. 11–12.

164. Vianna Moog, p. 212.

165. Freyre, *Ordem*, p. xxxv.

166. The classical discussion of this concept is Leal. See also Lambert, pp. 252–55; João Camillo de Oliveira Torres, "O coronelismo, sua genêse o suas formas de ação," *Estatificação Social do Brasil* (São Paulo: Difusão Européia do Livro, 1965), pp. 82–140.

Chapter Four

1. Oliveira Vianna, *Problemas de Direito Sindical*, pp. vi–vii.

2. Joseph Kahl, *The Measure of Modernism* (Austin, Texas, 1968). I am indebted to Gláucio Soares for calling my attention to this work when it was still unpublished. He suggested some modifications and a number of new items for the other scales. He is, of course, not responsible for my use or misuse of them.

3. Gláucio D. A. Soares and Loreto Hoecker, "El mundo de la ideologia: la función de las ideas y la legitimidad de la política estudiantil," *Aportes*, No. 5 (July 1967), pp. 101–22.

4. This conforms with Kahl's finding that education influenced modernism more than location. He found that rural-provincial respondents were as modernist as their city equivalents once they had completed at least a secondary-school education. Kahl, pp. 45–71.

5. For evidence that suggests that the national identification of Brazilian managers is higher than that of skilled workers or slum-dwellers, but lower than that of other stratified samples in Argentina and Chile, see K. H. Silvert, "National Values, Development and Leaders and Followers," *International Social Sciences Journal*, XV, 4 (1963), 565–68. Unfortunately, the table says nothing about the sampling procedure, the number of respondents, or the exact wording of the questions. For additional details, see K. H. Silvert and F. Bonilla, *Education and the Social Meaning of Development: A Preliminary Statement* (New York: American Universities Field Staff, 1961, mimeo.).

6. See Torcuato di Tella, "Populism and Reform in Latin America," in Veliz, pp. 47–74.

Chapter Five

Epigraph: Oliveira Vianna, *Problemas de Direito Sindical*, p. 48.

1. The variables are adapted from Weber, pp. 35–38. Weber uses the awkward terms "autonomy-heteronomy" and "autocephalousness-heterocephalousness."

2. International Labour Office, p. 178. The prevision was contained in Article 72, paragraph 8, along with other fundamental liberties.

3. For a discussion of the law, its background, and its consequences, see Freitas Marcondes.

4. *Ibid.*, p. 45.

5. See Mauríco de Lacerda, *Evolução Legislativa do Direito Social Brasileiro* (Rio: Servico de Documentação, MTIC, 1960); Paul de Carvalho Neto, "Um Precursor do direito trabalhista brasileiro," *Estudos Sociais e Políticos*, No. 24 (Belo Horizonte, 1964).

6. Article 34, line 38, of the 1926 Constitutional Revision.

7. Everado Dias, in his memoirs of this period, claims that "from 1903 to 1930, not a sindicato enjoyed a regular life free from police intervention." Dias, p. 20. The partisans of the Aliança Liberal in 1930 accused the outgoing President Washington Luis of having said, "The social question is a simple case for the police," and the new Minister of Labor claimed that the Revolution found the workers in "the most complete and painful anarchy." Leôncio Martins Rodrigues notes, however, that assemblies continued to be held and

newspapers published and distributed, and that "the violence exerted against the working movement was more sporadic and disorganized than generalized and constant." Rodrigues, *Conflito*, p. 139. Whatever the actual extent of physical repression, it was not enough for the workers' movement to acquire a strong tradition of struggle and mutual solidarity.

8. Paula R. Lopes, p. 493; Oliveira Vianna, *Direito*, pp. 65–66.

9. Dias, pp. 216 et seq. Oliveira Vianna seems to be admitting this when he says that the técnicos of the new Labor Ministry were more engaged in systematizing the customary law that regulated employer-worker relations than in creating a new code. *Instituições*, I, 15–17.

10. Moraes Filho, *Problema*, p. 210. This book is an excellent study of the historical and legal evolution of Brazilian syndicalism.

11. Paula R. Lopes, p. 493.

12. Getúlio Vargas shortly after assuming power, as cited by Segadas Viana, p. 30.

13. Moraes Filho, *Problema*, pp. 217–18.

14. Leôncio Martins Rodrigues, *Conflito*, p. 159. See also Moraes Filho, *Problema*, pp. 220–21.

15. Actually, the system of interest representation has three legal categories: the recognized sindicatos; the *associacões professionais*, which aspire to become sindicatos but lack some of the legal prerequisites (these are very few in number); and the *entidades civís,* which are too heterogenously composed or unwilling to become syndicalized. See Oliveira Vianna, *Preblemas de Direito Sindical*, pp. 107 et seq.

16. Oliveira Vianna, as cited in Ranulpho Pinheiro Lima, *A Representacão Professional no Brasil* (Rio: Irmão Pongetti, n.d.), pp. 18–19, 86. See also Oliveira Vianna, *Idealismo*, pp. 259–60.

17. For critical comments on the performance of the *deputados classistas*, see the editorials of the *Jornal do Brasil*, in Ranulpho Pinheiro Lima, pp. 63–76, and those of the *Correio da Manhã*, May 4 and 5, 1934. Both stressed that the syndical elections for representatives were "tumultuous" and subjected to heavy government interference and that, subsequently, the class deputies contributed little to the debates, hesitated to express any opposition to the regime, and loyally followed the President's lead.

18. Moraes Filho, *Problema*, p. 226. In 1942 the Church, through the National Confederation of Catholic Workers, announced its support of the government's *sindicalismo único*. Segadas Viana, p. 33.

19. Moraes Filho, *Problema*, pp. 229–30.

20. *Ibid.*, p. 241.

21. Article 138. As Moraes Filho points out, this is virtually a word-for-word translation of Declaration III of Mussolini's *Carta del Lavoro*. Moraes Filho, *Problema*, pp. 243–44.

22. For an English translation, see *Consolidation of the Brazilian Labor Laws*.

23. Cesarino, *Direito Corporativo*, I, 7.

24. Beginning in the mid-1930's, the Ministry of Labor has conveniently supplied a "model pattern" for aspiring sindicatos. Most sindicato constitutions differ only in the title of the entity. For a "how to do it" manual with a list of the 14 separate documents needed to gain recognition and respective "model patterns," see Justo Guaranha, *Como Fundar Entidades Sindicais*

(Pôrto Alegre: Livraria Sulma, n.d.). Federations and confederations require 28 different documents.

25. The establishment of employment agencies is listed officially as a "privilege." Robert Alexander, p. 61, observes that charging the workers' sindicatos with the provision of numerous social services was a way of compensating them for their loss of collective bargaining functions. The duties and "spheres of action" of the employers' sindicatos are less clearly defined under the CLT than those of workers' sindicatos, and not so loaded with social charges.

26. The items of legitimate expense are detailed (Art. 592) and tied to a variety of welfare services. No provision is made for the accumulation of revenue in strike funds. Neuma Aguiar Walker, in "The Organization and Ideology of Brazilian Labor," in Horowitz, p. 244, observes that, owing to high rates of inflation, saving for this purpose is almost impossible. The CLT prohibits sindicatos from engaging in profit-making activities.

27. Oliveira Vianna, *Problemas de Direito Sindical*, p. 115.

28. Moura Brandão Filho, pp. 75–76, citing Oliveira Vianna, argues that the Code's drafters intended the federations to become a second control mechanism over the syndicates for the "installation of discipline and order." He further notes that these dispositions never took effect.

29. FIESP, *Relatório–1930*, pp. 11–12.

30. "This would have made difficult the unity of thought [at the state level]. . . . Thus the government of São Paulo, if it wanted to consult the industrialists of various categories, would have had to go to Rio to confer with the National Confederation of Industry." Cesarino, *Direito Corporativo*, I, 18.

31. See FIESP, *A Constituição de 37 e Organização Corporativa Sindical*, São Paulo, 1940; Oliveira Vianna, *Problemas de Direito Sindical*, pp. 21–81.

32. Oliveira Vianna, *Problemas do Direito Sindical*, pp. 87–96.

33. See José Albertino Rodrigues, "Estrutura," p. 7.

34. Oliveiros S. Ferreira, "A Pedra angular do 'Sistema': o impôsto sindical," *O Estado de São Paulo*, Aug. 11, 1963; *idem*, "O Sindicalismo diante do estado," *Temas e Problemas* (São Paulo), III (1965), 13–14.

35. Neuma Aguiar Walker, in "The Organization and Ideology of Brazilian Labor," in Horowitz, p. 244, reports that the government can legally freeze the syndicate's account in the event of a strike, although none of the union leaders interviewed reported that their accounts had been so closed. It is very important that the Ministry can and does use the excuse of financial irregularities to close down syndical accounts. All syndicate funds over a certain amount are supposed to be deposited in the Banco do Brasil.

36. "The Social Syndical Fund is a powerful instrument for the subversion of the syndicates and a perpetual source of the most grotesque scandals. The contributions of the workers, along with those of the employers, land in badly guarded coffers and constitute a powerful and terrible economic arm. Most of it is consumed in accounting artifices and criminal liberalities. . . . It would be easy to find in the meanders of the Commission for the Syndical Tax thousands of passages for Europe, bills from banquets, fictitious receipts, payment orders without proven credit, etc." Fernando Ferrari, in *Congresso Brasileiro para a Definição das Reformas de Base* (São Paulo, mimeographed, Jan. 20–26, 1963), III, 6, 14. This "secret budget" of the Labor Ministry has been repeatedly attacked and "investigated" (by Congress in 1959, by Quadros in 1961). Its ostensible function was "to promote the syndical spirit, develop the

government's syndical orientation, organize courses in syndical administration, and offer collaboration to the syndicates." (Decree No. 5, 199, 1943). It pursued these vague but suggestive objectives apparently by granting subsidies to entities and personal favors to their leaders. See *Diário Carioca,* Sept. 25, 1951; *Estado de São Paulo,* July 7, 1959.

37. In 1957 the Ministry announced new instructions for improving the syndical tax, claiming that the practice had become widespread for employers to pocket the money they collected. The newspapers interpreted this as part of an attempt by Goulart, then Vice-President, to gain control of the workers' associations. *O Jornal,* July 7, 1959. In 1963, when Goulart was President, a pseudo-syndical tax was initiated whereby a fixed percentage of certain newly negotiated wage increases was to go directly to the syndicate, not to the worker. These contracts were rescinded after the 1964 coup.

38. Ministério do Trabalho e Previdência Social, *Relatório da Comissão Instituida pela Portaria No. 439/65 de 24 de agosto de 1965* (mimeographed). The author would like to thank Dona Natércia Silveira Pinto da Rocha for her assistance in obtaining this document. Not only has the tax been maintained, but it has been extended to cover rural syndicates.

39. Each congressman receives a personal budget—currently (in 1965) about $25,000—which he can give to the "social service" entities he chooses. Some of this money finds its way to representative associations. The *Estado de São Paulo,* which has been waging a campaign against such subsidies, occasionally publishes lists of benefited entities—a good number of which are fictitious. A congressional commission discovered 800 such "phantom entities" in a single survey. *Jornal do Brasil,* May 19, 1966.

40. For an "Illustrative Latin American (Brazilian) Collective Bargaining Agreement" in English, see *Industrial and Labor Relations Review,* XVII, 3 (Apr. 1964), 421–25.

41. Many have suggested that the employers deliberately prolong the process, since inflation constantly decreases the real cost of final indemnities. See Rodrigues, *Estrutura,* p. 10.

42. However, Lowy and Chucid, p. 157, indicate that 70.2% of the metallurgical union leaders studied thought the Labor Courts favored the *patrões,* 23.2% said they were impartial, and only 6.4% found them favoring the workers.

43. José Albertino Rodrigues, "Estrutura," p. 9. In an informal interview, Dona Alzira Vargas do Amaral Peixoto observed that the innovation of Labor Courts with "class representatives" provided the major incentive for the creation of employers' sindicatos. The innovation forced the recalcitrant employers to band together to protect their interests before these courts.

44. "These choices are submitted to the most varied interference on the part of economic and political powers, even including the high clergy." José Albertino Rodrigues, "Estrutura," p. 10. My own interviews confirmed these remarks informally.

45. The national confederations of industry and of commerce, for example, have such gentlemen's agreements. Interview, Rio, Dec. 6, 1965.

46. Interview, Rio, Sept. 14, 1965.

47. See Marcondes Machado.

48. Rodrigues, *Conflito,* p. 185.

49. Law No. 4,725 (July 13, 1965).

50. Oliveira Vianna, *Problemas de Organização,* p. 75.

51. See Marta Cardoso, *Sindicatos Rurais na Federação* (São Paulo: Imprensa Oficial do Estado, 1941).

52. Law No. 2,656 (Nov. 26, 1955). See "Subvenções a associações rurais," *Gleba,* II, 1 (Jan. 1956), p. 8.

53. As cited in Moraes Filho, *Problema,* p. 259.

54. This became Article 559 of the CLT. Oliveira Vianna excused the exception, noting that since Brazil was so poor in cooperative spirit existing associations must be used where possible. He even admitted that many of these "non-syndicalized" entities were more influential and representative of their categories than the syndicates. Oliveira Vianna, *Problemas de Direito Sindical,* pp. 123–24.

55. Oliveira Vianna, *Idealismo,* p. 201.

56. *Ibid.,* p. 211.

57. For the ideology behind corporatist representation, see Campos, p. 49; Oliveira Vianna, *Direito do Trabalho,* p. 92 et seq.

58. The CLT itself was studied by such an ad hoc commission, and employer groups were successful in obtaining certain concessions. See "Exposition of Motives of the Minister of Labor, Industry, and Commerce," *Consolidation of the Brazilian Labor Laws,* pp. 4–20.

59. For an excellent study of the role of this Council in the establishment of a national steel industry, see Wirth.

60. For a study of the dominance of industrial interests over the Textile Executive Commission, see Stein.

61. One of Celso Furtado's most important themes is that these acts of "economic defense" through product valorization, especially in coffee, resulted unintentionally in a strengthening of internal markets at the same time export earnings were dropping. The result was a powerful impetus for import substitution in manufactures. Any study of the Institutes must take into account these latent functions, as well as the manifest ones. See Furtado, *Economic Growth,* pp. 193–224.

62. Oliveira Vianna, *Problemas de Direito Sindical,* p. 64, note 44.

63. Pontes de Miranda, *Comentários a Constituição* (Rio: Imprensa Nacional, 1947), IV, 65–66.

64. Moraes Filho, *Problema,* pp. 273–79. For a similar view, see Themistocles Brandão Cavalcanti, *A Constituição Federal Comentada* (Rio: Freitas Bastos, 1948), II, 62.

65. Moraes Filho, *Problema,* p. 279. The minor changes listed gave slightly more autonomy to the syndicates in their electoral processes and reinforced the prohibition against party activity.

66. Stanley Hoffmann has argued that the corporatism of the Vichy regime was instrumental in upsetting the "atomism" of the prewar French society and in creating new intermediary associations. The Resistance preserved and continued many of these and thereby set the stage for a more pluralistic, organized system of interest representation. "Paradoxes of the French Political Community," in S. Hoffmann et al., *In Search of France* (Cambridge, Mass., 1963), pp. 21–59.

67. Telles, p. 40, claims that "the directories of over four hundred syndicates were removed." As of June 21, 1950, three years later, some 234 were still under intervention. *Diário de Notícias,* July 13, 1950.

68. *Notes on Labor Abroad*, Aug. 1950, p. 32.

69. Several projects comprehensively revising the CLT were presented from 1949 to 1953, and long debates were held, especially on their syndical provisions. In 1962 Evaristo de Moraes Filho drafted a comprehensive *Projeto de Codigo de Trabalho*, which would have maintained a more limited form of syndical unitarism, greatly reduced ministerial controls, gradually extinguished the *impôsto sindical*, permitted the creation of union centrals, and eliminated the preestablished *enquadramento*. Although several forums and national congresses discussed this and other reform projects, no important modifications were made. See *Anais do Forum de Debates Lindolfo Collor*, May 1–7, 1963 (Rio: n.pub., 1963); *Congresso Brasileiro para a Definição das Reformas de Base*, Jan. 20–26, 1963 (São Paulo: mimeo., 1963).

70. *Notes on Labor Abroad*, Mar. 1951, p. 14.

71. A Catholic writer claims that there are three types of *pelego*, all dependent upon the *impôsto sindical*: the yellow *pelego*, or government bureaucrat; the red *pelego*, or party agent; and the blue *pelego*, "an unauthentic democrat in the camouflaged service of the patronal syndicates." He places 1957 as the high point of yellow *pelegismo*, with the red variety increasing in importance until it represented some 70% of all the leadership cadres. See Faria.

72. Fernando Henrique Cardoso, "Proletariado no Brasil: situação e comportamento social," *Revista Brasilense*, No. 41 (May–June 1962), p. 118.

73. The "revolutionary" Labor Minister said of his predecessor's use of the office: "From an organ responsible for social equilibrium, it was transformed into an instrument of worker agitation. Instead of promoting the accommodation and mutual understanding of workers and employers, it was made the agent of a dangerous class struggle." *Jornal do Brasil*, Dec. 3, 1965. "The Ministry of Labor itself was transformed into a house without an owner, with the [Minister's] cabinet always jammed with people who, although not part of it, upset the ambience by giving orders, making exigent demands, sending spurious representations, menacing, and coercing." *Jornal do Brasil*, Dec. 8, 1965.

74. For a discussion of this bill and its antecedents, see Price.

75. Goulart vetoed the requirement that one-tenth of the respective class was needed to form a sindicato. The formal limit was set at 50 members. A later *portaria ministerial* exempted members from necessary proof of professional identity and the syndicate from publishing a convocation notice. As an experienced rural leader noted, "It will mean the fabrication en masse of phantom syndicates." José Rotta, "Sindicalização rural: mais uma portaria ministerial," *O Estado de São Paulo*, July 28, 1963.

76. Price, p. 69. The Ministry's Goal No. 7 was "civil and electoral registration of three million new voters."

77. SUPRA, Departamento de Promoção e Organização Rural, *Plano Geral de Organização Sindical Rural*, Nov. 1963.

78. *O Estado de São Paulo*, Apr. 7, 1965. This would have meant 435 out of a total of 2,900. Since very few patronal syndicates were intervened (the National Confederation of Industry and the Syndicate of Textile Manufacturers of São Paulo being the only prominent cases), the figure represents more than one-fourth of the workers' syndicates and certainly more than that in terms of members affected. Virtually all the worker federations and confederations had their leaderships deposed. "Política sindical," *Correio da Manhã*,

June 7, 1964. Elsewhere the Minister reported that 584 separate investigations were made: 28% concerning subversion, 13% concerning embezzlement, 23% concerning a mixture of the two, and 36% for causes yet unknown. *Manchete,* No. 695, Aug. 14, 1965. Several of my mailed interviews were returned with inscriptions scrawled on envelopes such as "Office closed by Social and Political Police," and "This association has been closed by the police since March 31, 1964."

79. MTPS, Serviço de Documentação, *Extinção da CIS e CTOS e Reestructuração de Orgãos do Ministério do Trabalho e Providência Social,* 1965, pp. 1–2.

80. These instructions, which applied to both workers' and employers' syndicates, included a minutely detailed set of bureaucratic controls over the elections. Rather surprisingly, illiterates were allowed for the first time to vote in syndical elections. In fact, these are the only elections in Brazil where they are permitted to vote. For a detailed criticism of the new electoral rules, see "O Progresso econômico e as eleições sindicais," *O Estado de São Paulo,* Apr. 4, 1965.

81. It was reported that 72% of the intervened unions had been "liberated" by the end of 1965. *O Estado de São Paulo,* Dec. 31, 1965.

82. See "O Sindicalismo pátrio e suas reformações (I–III)," *O Estado de São Paulo,* Apr. 28–May 2, 1965.

83. "The [impending] administrative reform will not create a Welfare Ministry. . . . One reason [against it] is that it would completely deplete the actual Ministry of Labor, which has already had almost all its other functions absorbed by the Ministry of Planning." *Visão,* Nov. 11, 1966, p. 9. The Ministry of Industry and Commerce was split off from the Ministry of Labor in the mid-1950's.

84. "A Nova imagem do trabalhismo," *Revista Econômica do Jornal do Brasil,* Feb. 10, 1966. The influential and conservative *O Estado de São Paulo* irreverently baptized the *novo trabalhismo "neopeleguismo."* Feb. 13, 1966. For a critique from another perspective, see Ianni, *Colapso,* p. 208.

Chapter Six

1. Helvécio Xavier Lopes, as cited in Segadas Viana, pp. 24–25. See also Oliveira Vianna, *Direito,* p. 66.

2. This poses an interesting challenge to Marxist-oriented social scientists. Class conflict, as measured by open encounters between broad interest coalitions, actually declined with industrialization—at least until the 1960's. For an intelligent treatment of this theme stressing not only mitigating factors in the social composition of the actors (immigration, rural-urban migration, and social mobility) but also the self-conscious role of public authorities in institutionalizing conflict, see Ianni, *Industrialização,* esp. pp. 21–22, 74.

3. Freyre, *Masters,* pp. 200–201.

4. Buarque de Holanda, p. 62.

5. *Ibid.,* p. 226.

6. These brotherhoods are the direct historical descendants of the early guilds. Community studies by anthropologists and sociologists testify to their continued existence and vitality in the interior, where they are frequently stratified according to race as well as occupation. See the account in Oracy Nogueira, *Família e Communidade* (Rio: Centro Brasileiro de Pesquisas Edu-

cacionais, 1962), pp. 309–31. According to Freyre, slaves were permitted from an early date to organize such societies. Nor is their significance confined to small, interior cities. In response to my written query on reputational influence, several leaders of national associations listed certain brotherhoods and charitable organizations. I did not, however, follow up this lead to discover what interests are articulated by these groups.

7. Abreu, pp. 230–40. Article 179 of the Constitution of 1934 formally abolished the privileges of *"corporações de ofício."*

8. Buarque de Holanda, p. 30 et seq.

9. Leroy-Beaulieu defines the "antique" type of association as "regulated, forcing together into more or less inflexible cadres all the individuals in a determined occupation." The modern association, by contrast, is an "open one, to which men subordinate themselves by free choice and from which they can withdraw without prior authorization." *Précis d'Economie Politique*, 13th ed. (Paris: Librairie C. Delagrave, 1910), pp. 182–83. For a discussion of the failure of such antique associations to become modern ones in Peru, see Payne, p. 41.

10. Simão, *Sindicato*. This is the most comprehensive historical and sociological account of pre-1930 workers' organizations and their gradual conversion into semiofficial entities.

11. Moraes Filho, *Problema*, p. 182. Fernando Henrique Cardoso, however, discusses a strike occurring in 1886 among hatworkers in São Paulo, in which a Centro Socialista played a key bargaining role. "Le Prolétariat brésilien: situation et comportement social," *Sociologie du Travail*, III, 4 (Oct.–Dec. 1961), 56–58. Telles, p. 18, reports that "one of the first organized struggles" occurred among typographical workers as early as 1858. See also Simão, *Sindicato*, pp. 99–151, for a detailed breakdown of strikes in São Paulo from 1888 to 1930.

12. International Labour Office, *Industrial and Labour Information*, Nov. 17, 1930.

13. For a description of the Encilhamento and its impact on the Brazilian economy, see Bello, pp. 72–76.

14. See Rodrigues, *Conflito*, pp. 148–54.

15. For historical treatments with lists of active organizations and their publications, see Dias, passim, esp. pp. 243–305; Telles, pp. 17–34; A. Bastos, *Prestes e a Revolução* (Rio: Editorial Calvino, 1946); Hermínio de Linhares, *Contribuição a História das Lutas Operárias no Brasil* (Rio: Baptista de Souza e Cia. Editôres, 1955).

16. Dias, pp. 253–55.

17. Hermínio de Linhares, as cited by Leôncio Martins Rodrigues, *Conflito*, p. 125.

18. The attendance figures are from Dias, pp. 277–78. Moraes Filho, *Problema*, pp. 194–95, lists only 57 associations. Among the 71 were regional federations from Rio, São Paulo, Minas Gerais, Rio Grande do Sul, and Alagoas.

19. Evaristo de Moraes Filho, "Sindicatos e lutas operárias," in "400 Anos memoráveis," Caderno No. 20, *Jornal do Brasil*, Dec. 16, 1965.

20. Leôncio Martins Rodrigues, *Conflito*, pp. 104–12.

21. For a recent detailed treatment of the revolution, see Hélio Silva, *1930 —A Revolução Traida* (Rio: Civilização Brasileira, 1966). *Correio da Manhã*, Oct. 5, 1930, carried a manifesto of support for President Washington Luis

from a number of the major workers' associations exactly one week before he was deposed by the Aliança Liberal forces.

22. Rodrigues, *Conflito*, p. 115.

23. See Waldemar Mattos, *Panorama Econômico da Bahia 1800–1960* (Salvador da Bahia: n. pub., 1960).

24. Rio (1834), Recife (1839), Maranhão (1854), Paraiba (1858), Pará (1864), Amazonas (1871), Sergipe (1872), and Pelotas (1873). Oswaldo Benjamin de Azevedo, "Comércio Carioca—Sua Função Regional e no Ámbito Nacional," *Revista CNC* (Rio), Oct. 1961, pp. 11–26. The Commercial Association of São Paulo was not founded until 1894.

25. See Edward O. Corwin, "Associações comerciais brasileiras," in *A Missão Cooke no Brasil* (Rio: Fundação Getúlio Vargas, 1949), p. 350.

26. Interview, Salvador da Bahia, Dec. 30, 1965.

27. For an official history of the Associação Comercial do Rio de Janeiro, see Endes Barros, *A Associação Comercial no Império e na República* (Rio: O Cruzeiro, 1959).

28. From 1846 to 1847 Irineu Evangelista de Souza, the "Barão e Visconde de Mauá," was its president; the Association frequently refers to itself as the Casa de Mauá" in an attempt to link its name and reputation with this extraordinary industrial and railroad entrepreneur of the nineteenth century. A. Marchant, *Viscount Mauá and the Empire of Brazil* (Berkeley, Calif., 1965).

29. According to Barros, pp. 89–90, the Association as such never came out against slavery, owing to the heavy representation of rural aristocrats on its board of directors. In fact, an 1884 "representation" to Parliament protested the existing manumission laws. Individual members of the Association did, however, play an active role in the Abolition Movement.

30. Apparently there was some resistance on the part of local associations to accepting the hegemony of Rio, and the Commercial Association of São Paulo was not on the list of founders. *Ibid.*, p. 136.

31. Oliveira Vianna, *Idealismo*, p. 239.

32. Amado, *Eleição*, p. 48.

33. Berman, p. 34. The records show that the tax on industry and professions (most of which was paid by small merchants and artisans) for 1886–87, was paid by 2,631 Brazilians, 8,240 Portuguese, and 1,024 others. Luz, p. 58.

34. *Correio da Manhã*, Nov. 5, 1930.

35. *Ibid.*, Dec. 4, 1930.

36. Freyre, *New World*, p. 91.

37. These were the stated purposes of the Sociedade Fluminense Agrícola, founded in 1854. The oldest of these was the Sociedade de Agricultura da Bahia (1832).

38. For a list of the "services performed" from 1897 to 1929, see Luis Amaral, I, 285–86. See also "Associativismo rural no Brasil," *Gleba*, III, 87 (July 1962), 25–28.

39. The SRB is in part a social club, and admission is by approval of the directorate and by payment of a large fee. Its numbers have consequently remained small. According to Luis Amaral, I, p. 285, "The Brazilian Rural Society—very brilliant and academic, and responsible for real services, although it is a bit courtly and platonic—[has given] more profit to the National Telegraph Service than to agriculture."

40. Sociedade Rural Brasileira (São Paulo), *Annaes*, 1920.
41. *Correio Paulistano*, June 26, 1954.
42. *Revista Sociedade Rural Brasileira* (São Paulo), Apr. 1936, p. 17.
43. Sociedade Rural Brasileira, *Annaes*, 1935.
44. *Jornal do Commercio* (Rio), Aug. 8, 1956.
45. As cited in Normano, p. 89.
46. Humberto Bastos, *Pensamento*, pp. 97–98. See also Luz, pp. 46–48, for more evidence on internal conflicts.
47. Luz, p. 43 et seq.
48. My description of the activities of the Associação Industrial rests on the excellent monograph of Nícia Vilela Luz. Her account is based on the Annual Reports of the Association, its newspaper, *O Industrial*, and other press accounts of the period. *Ibid.*, p. 50 et seq. The textile manufacturers, who were the most active and articulate of the early industrialists, are studied with great thoroughness in Stein, *The Brazilian Cotton Manufacture*.
49. Luz, p. 52.
50. Luz observes that agricultural interests were never opposed to industrialization—so long as it happened gradually and without aggravating their own capital and manpower problems. She notes, however, that commercial importing interests (presumably through the Commercial Association) worked effectively and surreptitiously in the back corridors with executive authorities or the commissions named to review tariff policy. *Ibid.*, pp. 55, 57. For a discussion of the ideological position of the Associação Industrial, see pp. 61–64.
51. Cited in Bastos, *Pensamento*, p. 28. For a discussion of the ideology of the CIB's first president, Serzedelo Correa, see Luz, pp. 73–77.
52. For a discussion of the complicated process of tariff revision during this period, see Luz, pp. 96 et seq. Luz, politically a very sensitive author, demonstrates how in this period the tariff became an "anarchic" and "unorthodox" compromise between commercial, rural, industrial, and government interests. None got the full measure of its demands. Most of the protection came not from high rates, but through the back door, so to speak, in the form of a gold quota on tariff payments and a stabilized underevaluation of the exchange rate. The former met the government's need for fiscal revenues, the latter the export interests of the coffee planters. Both pleased industrialists—all in a nearly classic case of the Brazilian propensity for "plastic," "unorthodox," "seemingly irrational" solutions that are subject, of course, to constant revision.
53. *Ibid.*, pp. 149–50, 155.
54. An official of the Federation of Industries of the State of São Paulo showed me a photograph of the Centro's first directorate and commented that only one man in the picture was a *quatrocentão*—a member of the paulista four-hundred-year aristocracy—and that he had never amounted to anything. However, the directory contained the cream of Brazilian large industry: F. Matarazzo, R. Simonsen, J. Street, H. Lafer, and J. Ermírio de Moraes. Only the last was not of immigrant origin, and he was a migrant from Pernambuco. Luis Amaral commented bitterly, "Alone, the Centro das Indústrias, led almost exclusively by foreigners, with Brazilians as figureheads, has accomplished more than the millions of agriculturalists with all their barons and social clubs." Amaral, Luis, I, 215.
55. *Jornal do Comércio* (Rio), June 3, 1928. For a different assessment of Simonsen, see Warren Dean, *The Industrialization of São Paulo* (Austin,

Texas, 1969), pp. 143–45. This monograph, which appeared after the above was written, contains an excellent, detailed description of the differentiation of commercial and industrial interests in São Paulo in the late 1920's.

56. "The Commercial Association, which does not distinguish between the interests of industry, agriculture, and commerce, because there is no reason to disassociate them, cannot lend its unqualified applause to the noteworthy speech by the talented boy" *Jornal do Comércio* (Rio), June 7, 1928. The speaker also accused Simonsen of disloyalty, pointing out that most of the industrialists had begun as merchants.

57. *Folha da Manhã* (São Paulo), June 16, 1928.

58. See Finer; A. Potter, *Organized Groups in British Politics* (London: Faber and Faber, 1961), pp. 25–43. Both authors note that a rigid distinction between the two types is hard to maintain. In terms of our conceptual scheme, both are representative associations if they are permanently organized, secondary groups. To the extent that promotional or attitude groups espouse very broad programs of change and tend to mobilize intensely committed recruits, they can be called movements.

59. See Azevedo, pp. 439–40.

60. For example, the total industrial worker population for 1920 has been estimated at 293,637. Pereira, p. 136. I have argued that there is little evidence of a sharp increase in industrial employment in the 1920's. If I accept the tentative figure 11,500 for membership in 1930 and double the 1920 figure to include transport, communications, and commercial workers, I obtain a very rough density figure of 2 per 100.

Chapter Seven

1. The Labor Ministry tallies before 1952 were rather erratic and often geographically incomplete: 1935, 1936, 1938, 1944, 1945, 1946. Also, because the number of nonreporting syndicates was not disclosed, it is impossible to introduce corrections. Since 1952, data on the number, type, location, functional scope, membership, circulation of library books, number of students and schools maintained, and amount of *impôsto sindical* collected are regularly available in the *Anuário Estatístico*. The material is gathered through the mail by the Service for Labor and Welfare Statistics (SEPT) of the Labor Ministry. In 1961, a more detailed Syndical Census was taken; it made data on every individual syndicate public for the first time. Serviço de Estatística da Previdência e Trabalho, *Cadastro Sindical Brasileiro, 1961–1962*.

2. For a similar observation that the pattern of syndicalism in the 1930's was reflecting not social reality, but political opportunism, see Segadas Viana, p. 27.

3. *América en Cifras—1965* reports the total membership for workers in 1964 as 2,053,788, citing as a source the *Directory of Labor Organizations: Western Hemisphere* (Washington, D.C., 1964). This is about what my corrected totals show, although U.S. government estimates in the past have been much higher than the official Brazilian totals. For example, the study by the Senate Subcommittee on American Republic Affairs of the Committee on Foreign Relations, *Latin American Relations* (Washington, D.C., 1960), p. 77, credits Brazil with 2,536,000 unionized workers, double the corrected estimates in Figure 5. Union Panamericana, Instituto Interamericano de Estatística, *América en Cifras—1965*, "Situación Social," p. 159.

4. A recent Brazilian congressional investigation confirms these findings. It concluded that "Only 20 percent of the [presumably urban] workers are syndicalized." *O Estado de São Paulo*, Aug. 25, 1968. Actually, this density strikes me as quite high, especially when one considers that some rather large categories of urban dwellers are ineligible for membership (civil and military government employees, for example). One is reminded that syndicates routinely report "registered members," not just those who are currently paying dues in addition to the syndical tax. Therefore registered members who have changed professions, left town, or died may still be carried on the rolls.

5. See my "Latin American Aggregate Data Bank," unpublished, University of Chicago, 1968. For an extended discussion of the quality and analytical utility of this type of data, see my "New Strategies for the Comparative Analysis of Latin American Politics," *Latin American Research Review*, IV (summer 1969), 83–106. Ted Gurr, in an independent attempt at quantifying trade union membership in comparable terms, has used data for a different time period (1952–61) and has introduced a different control variable (percent in nonagricultural employment). According to his calculations, the Brazilian performance is better than that of Chile, Uruguay, Peru, and Colombia. He credits Brazil with a unionized population of 2,687,000 and a density of 40%! Irving Louis Horowitz, using an unspecified source and controlling for percent "workers," calculates a density of 26% for 1950—again higher than my estimates. This places it ahead of Uruguay, Colombia, and Peru, but behind Paraguay. See Ted Gurr, "New Error Compensated Measures for Comparing Nations," *Research Monograph No. 25* (Princeton, N.J., 1966), pp. 101–6; I. L. Horowitz, "Electoral Politics, Urbanization and Social Development in Latin America," in G. H. Beyer, ed., *The Urban Explosion in Latin America* (Ithaca, N.Y., 1967), p. 233.

6. Marvin Olsen, "Multivariate Analysis of National Political Development," unpublished, Indiana University, 1967. For another indicator of this variable, see Jack Gibbs and Walter Martin, "Urbanization, Technology and the Division of Labor," *American Sociological Review*, XXVII (Oct. 1962), 667–77.

7. The Brazilian Rural Confederation, alone among the major interest associations, attempted to discover the causes for the very low density of participation in rural associations. A series of research monographs disclosed that, although the coverage of such associations had extended so far that almost every município in the areas studied had one, the average membership was declining and use of its services was quite low. When queried about the motivations for participation, respondents gave a variety of reasons having to do with welfare and commerce. The least frequently given reason was "struggle for . . . class interests." The major conclusion of the series was that "the development of rural associability is strictly linked to the level of technological progress reached by the agricultural activity of each region." This rather neatly supports my differentiation hypothesis. "Agricultura e associativismo rural no Rio Grande do Sul," *Revista Brasileira dos Municípios*, XV (1957/58), 24–30. See also "Agricultura e associativismo rural no Estado da Bahia," *Revista Brasileira dos Municípios*, XIV (1953/54), 25–36; "Associativismo e desenvolvimento do município," *Revista Brasileira dos Municípios*, XIV (1953/54), 1–6; "Agricultura e associativismo rural: Maranhão," *Gleba*, Suplemento No. 6 (June 1961).

8. A recent study of workers' syndicates in the municipality of São Paulo challenges these conclusions, which are based on aggregate national statistics. Syndical leaders were asked how many workers were eligible to join their syndicates and how many members had paid their dues in the past month. The two reported figures were used to calculate a "rate of syndicalization." The category I found to be least syndicalized (land transport workers) the São Paulo study found to be most syndicalized. Bank workers were close behind, and workers in communications and publicity were third. It is not possible to determine whether the discrepancy with national statistics is due to the different structure of syndical membership in the city of São Paulo or to the different method used in gathering data. Rabello, pp. 141–44.

9. According to Rabello's questionnaire, it had 40,000 paid-up members in 1964. According to the Syndical Census of 1961, it had 71,163 registered members. *Cadastro Sindical Brasileiro—1961*, p. 154. Its annual report for that same year claimed that it had increased its membership by 13,763 and had a total of 90,905. *Revista de Estudos Sócio-econômicos* (São Paulo), I, 7 (Mar.–Apr. 1962), 56.

10. See Alexander, p. 77.

11. *O Estado de São Paulo*, May 26, 1968. The survey was conducted by a professional polling firm (IBOPE) and commissioned by the Costa e Silva regime. No information on the nature of the sample was given.

12. *Correio da Manhã*, Mar. 27, 1966.

13. Interview, São Paulo, Mar. 17, 1966. The AMB had 19,000 members, and 7,153 physicians were in syndicates as of 1963. It is unknown to what degree these figures overlap.

14. The National Union of Civil Servants (UNSP) has claimed 300,000 adherents. One of its current leaders reported that the 1964 "revolution" had adversely affected it. He reported numerous requests from government employees for statements to the effect that they had not been members as protection against dismissal. Interview, Rio, Aug. 20, 1965.

15. See Martins Alonso, "O nosso sindicato," *Jornal do Brasil*, Jan. 4, 1967.

16. For the original discussion of this fallacy, see W. S. Robinson, "Ecological Correlations and the Behavior of Individuals," *American Sociological Review*, XV (1950), 351–57. For a recent restatement incorporating the comments of Menzel, Goodman, Arrow, Duncan, and Davis, see Raymond Boudon, "Propriétés individuelles et propriétés collectives: un problème d'analyse écologique," *Revue Française de Sociologie*, IV, 3 (July–Sept. 1963), 275–99. See also Erwin K. Scheuch, "Cross-National Comparisons Using Aggregate Data: Some Substantive and Methodological Problems," in R. Merritt and S. Rokkan, eds., *Comparing Nations* (New Haven, Conn., 1966), pp. 131–68.

17. Robinson, p. 357.

18. Scheuch, "Cross-National Comparisons," and Ralph Retzlaff, "The Use of Aggregate Data in Comparative Political Analysis," *Journal of Politics*, XXVII (Nov. 1965), 797–817. For an excellent and detailed discussion of estimates of error in international census data, see Bruce Russett et al., *World Handbook of Political and Social Indicators* (New Haven, Conn., 1963), pp. 2–4, 15–257 *passim*.

19. The correlation of cinema attendance with newspaper circulation is .82; its correlation with radio audience is .77. Russett, p. 275.

20. K. Deutsch, J. D. Singer, and K. Smith, "The Organizing Efficiency of Theories: The N/V Ratio as a Crude Rank Order Measure," *The American Behavioral Scientist*, IX, 2 (Oct. 1962), 32.

21. See H. Blalock, *Social Statistics* (New York, 1960), pp. 326–58.

22. The partial correlations and multiple regression equations were made using the MESA 85 program at the University of Chicago Computation Center.

Chapter Eight

1. Rabello, p. 68. In particular, 57% of the industrial workers' syndicates were municipal in scope.

2. Although in 1965 the Public Works Contractors' Syndicate had 205 members out of an estimated 912 eligible firms, the active members tended to be the larger firms engaged in road building, and no special efforts were being made to interest all those eligible in joining. Interview, Rio, Sept. 12, 1965. One analogous sector missing from the list, the shipbuilding industry, is presently organized into a single syndicate covering Rio de Janeiro only. Since the few major firms in this industry are all concentrated in that area, no demand for national syndicate status has been made, although there are plans to this end. Interview, Rio, Sept. 2, 1965.

3. Informants had different ideas about the reasons for the split. I am indebted to Sr. Humberto Dantas, Secretary General of FIESP since 1944, for permitting me to examine documents and an unpublished manuscript of his discussing this period.

4. In the early 1930's, FIESP actively assisted in the creation of other state federations, especially in Rio Grande do Sul and Minas Gerais, "with the objective of organizing a national confederation." *Relatório de 1933*. FIESP was also active in converting its sectorial "committees" into syndicates during the same period. As a rule, federations do not themselves play an active role in stimulating the formation of member syndicates, once enough (five) have been created to guarantee their existence. In fact, there is a negative incentive against this, since the federation receives directly the syndical tax contributions of workers or employers in categories not yet syndicalized. On the other hand, since each syndicate has one vote in the council of representatives of its federation, electoral factions may sponsor the creation of new "drawer syndicates" (*sindicatos de gaveta*) or the subdivision of existing ones as a means of consolidating their position or undermining that of their opponents. Such an organizational tactic, used by both employers' and workers' groups, depends usually on the connivance or active cooperation of the Labor Ministry.

5. The *Relatórios* of the Associação Comercial of São Paulo for 1943 and 1944–45 report "an intimate interrelationship" with the new Federation of Commerce and a syndicalization campaign in the interior of the state.

6. Tariff revision was again an issue and may well have precipitated the founding of the CIB. In his "Plan of Action," Horácio Lafer proposed that the Confederation immediately establish a "Statistics Department to show the value of industry, its role in the development of agriculture and cattle raising, its contribution to public tax funds, to the interests of the working classes, [and] . . . to the approximation and greater interrelationship between the diverse states of the country, and finally, its undeniable and decisive participation in the Brazilian economy." He also proposed a "Propaganda Depart-

ment . . . to seek out a direct and permanent contract with influential persons."
CIB, *Circular*, No. 5, Apr. 27, 1933.

7. CIB, *Relatório* 1937, p. 17.

8. For a description of the relationship between Vargas and Lodi, I am indebted to the observations of Dona Alzira Vargas do Amaral Peixoto in an informal conversation.

9. Roberto Simonsen was the leading proponent of postwar economic planning. The following quotation succinctly sums up the man, his ideas, and his style. "In Brazil, economic weakness and instability have led us to adopt a series of partial planning experiences and state interventions, always demanded by the producers in difficulty and almost always later condemned by the same producers. It is a question of choosing not between the presence and absence of interventionism, but rather between good and bad interventionism." *A Planificação da Economía Brasileira* (São Paulo: n. pub., 1944), pp. 11–12.

10. CIESP, *Circular*, No. 54, 1946.

11. CIESP, *Circular*, No. 49, 1946.

12. *Decreto-Lei*, No. 9, 403, June 25, 1946. A detailed account of the events leading up to the signing of the SESI decree was given to me by one of Simonsen's close collaborators. Checking his information against that from other interviews and mimeographed circulars of the time, I have concluded that the measure did originate among the FIESP-CIESP leaders, with Simonsen providing the intellectual inspiration and Dias de Figuereido providing the personal contact with General Dutra. Several months after the SESI decree, the latter became Minister of Labor, Industry, and Commerce.

13. The best document on the original objectives of Simonsen and SESI is the symposium on "Educação Social," *Arquivos do Instituto de Direito Social*, VI, 3 (Mar. 1947). I am indebted to Professor J. V. Freitas Marcondes, who helped organize the original course on "social education," for his own direct observations and for access to personal documents such as the above. Among other participants in the course was Jânio Quadros. For a brief history of SESI and the argument that it follows a Catholic *solidarista* line, see Mário G. Reis, "O segundo aniversario do serviço social da indústria," *Síntese Política Econômica Social* (Rio), Apr.–June 1966, pp. 5–35.

14. At one point, Simonsen even toyed with the idea of giving workers' organizations some institutionalized voice in the control of SESI. Interview, São Paulo, Apr. 25, 1966.

15. Assis Chateaubriand, "O olho do comércio," in Rui Gomes de Almeida, *Idéias e Atitudes* (Rio: José Olympio, 1965), p. xviii. For more biographical information on Daudt, see *Revista das Classes Produtoras*, Oct. 1965.

16. For a short "official" history of the CNC, see Confederação Nacional do Comércio, *CNC: Vinte Anos de Lutas pelo Brasil* (Rio, 1966).

17. The SSR was suppressed in 1963 despite protests from the CRB. Meinberg complained that "No President of the Republic had really understood the SSR and considered it in good faith." *Gleba*, VIII, 89 (Sept. 1962), 21. See also *Gleba*, VIII, 90 (Nov. 1962), 7–9. One possible reason for the reluctance of authority groups to turn over full control of the SSR to the CRB might have been the numerous scandals involving SESI and SESC. Industrial leaders opposed the creation of the SSR largely because it diminished SESI revenues from such rural industries as sugar, cacao, and lumber.

18. "We cannot afford to be neglectful in this hour when rural workers

are organizing in syndicates . . . . We must create the instruments that will permit a dialogue between the two classes, a precondition for social peace." CRB, *Boletim de Imprensa*, No. 45 (Mar. 23, 1965).

19. Moreover, the agency supervising the agrarian reform movement, SUPRA, was also charged with providing the incentives for syndicalization. In 1954, the CRB had strenuously protested Goulart's earlier attempt to syndicalize rural workers, and their report to the National Security Council probably contributed to Goulart's removal as Labor Minister under military pressures. See *A Lavoura* (Rio), Mar.–Apr. 1954. *A Lavoura* is the official journal of the SNA, the Rio affiliate of the CRB.

20. *O Estado de São Paulo*, Nov. 30, 1963.

21. *Diario de Notícias*, May 8, 1966. São Paulo, with 71 associations, and Minas Gerais, with 61, led the conversion parade. Conversion is voluntary but the Confederation has warned that henceforth the government will deal only with recognized syndicates and will no longer give subsidies to rural associations. All will have to pay the syndical tax. CRB, "Sindicalização rural," *Boletim de Imprensa*, No. 1 (1965).

22. Formerly the tax was to have been based on registered capital (90% of Brazilian farms have no registered capital). Law No. 4,755 altered it, tying it to the amount of land tax paid. *Jornal do Comércio*, Oct. 27, 1965. Interview, Rio, Oct. 1, 1965. The syndical tax receipts for the CNA in 1965 were only 81,900,000 cruzeiros, or $40,000.

23. The role of INDA, like that of the former "subversive" SUPRA, in sponsoring and controlling the extension of syndicalization to the rural sector looms very important. It finances regional and national congresses, and it intends to hold indoctrination courses for rural leaders. CRB, *Boletim de Imprensa*, No. 126 (Aug. 16, 1965). The present regime is no more willing than the deposed one to let such potentiality develop spontaneously. Sponsored associability seems to have an inescapable political logic of its own.

24. For a detailed but biased (pro-Communist) account of this Congress, see Telles, pp. 39, 255–72. For a different, also biased perspective, see Robert Alexander, *Organized Labor in Latin America* (Glencoe, Ill., 1965), p. 78.

25. There is evidence that the newly founded commercial employers' confederation (CNC) assisted at the birth of the CNTC. I found no such evidence of a CNI role in sponsoring the creation of the CNTI, but it is not inconceivable. I was, however, given a detailed account of SESI's role in sponsoring workers' organizations at the local and state levels during this period in São Paulo and the Northeast. Interview, Rio, Dec. 2, 1965. Interview, São Paulo, Apr. 25, 1966.

26. Leôncio Martins Rodrigues, one of the few Brazilian sociologists to devote serious empirical attention to the syndical movement, has stressed that the success of the Communists was due primarily to their capacity for dedicated and honest work at the grass roots and not to ideological conviction. He notes, in fact, that the Communists toned down the revolutionary collectivist aspects of their beliefs and adopted the generally pro-capitalist ideology of "national-developmentalism." "The syndicalism that reemerged in the last few years did not attempt to base its actions in defense of the proletariat on the theme of class struggle and the fight against private property; it did not reject capitalist society; rather, it attempted to expand and better [worker] participation within such a competitive society. The 'agitation' and

'politicization' of recent years was accompanied by a decline in socialist ideology. . . . Nationalism replaced Marxism." Rodrigues, *Conflito*, pp. 191–92.

27. For accounts of these meetings, see Telles, *passim*.

28. The Second National Syndical Conference in 1959 seems to have been principally an electoral rally for Marechal Lott. *Ibid.*, pp. 83–86.

29. ORIT and ICFTU officials seem to have played an important role in inspiring, and perhaps even in drafting, the manifesto. The newspapers noted that representatives of ORIT and ICFTU were present, and the text specifically reaffirms the Confederations' solidarity with the "free" international trade union movement. *Correio da Manhã*, May 1, 1960, and *O Estado de São Paulo*, May 3, 1960.

30. *O Estado de São Paulo*, May 28, 1960.

31. Telles, p. 111. Oliveiros S. Ferreira has interpreted this period in the development of the Brazilian labor movement as the moment at which the workers, "overcoming the economic-corporative phase of class consciousness, pose the problem of the syndicate's role before the state and Party—the problem of the relationship between syndicalism and political society." *O Estado de São Paulo*, July 31, 1960.

32. For a partisan commentary, see Antônio Chamorro, "O III Congresso Nacional dos Trabalhadores," *Revista Brasilense*, 31 (Sept.–Oct. 1960), pp. 72–84.

33. José Albertino Rodrigues, "II Congresso Sindical dos Trabalhadores do Estado de São Paulo," *Revista Brasilense*, 29 (Mar.–June 1960), pp. 73–78.

34. *O Estado de São Paulo*, May 29, 1963. The "research" was directed by Padre Veloso of the National Confederation of Workers' Circles, a Catholic organization; 221 syndicates were classified as "Communist," 204 as "fellow-traveling," 589 as "democratic," and 453 as "unclassifiable." The states in which the various CGT-affiliated pacts and councils were proportionately strongest were Pernambuco (71%), Pará and Piauí (61%), Maranhão (59%), Guanabara (47%), and Rio de Janeiro (40%). See also Faria.

35. *O Estado de São Paulo*, May 6, 1964.

36. President Goulart was quoted as saying "The General Workers' Command is the highest organ of the Brazilian working class." *O Estado de São Paulo*, Sept. 24, 1963. Goulart's support was not given unconditionally, however. For an account of his attempts to control it by playing one group off against another, see Peralva, "Esquerda."

In a study of opinions of paulistano trade union leaders, 56.4% stated that they considered the creation of a workers' central necessary, 28.2% considered it unnecessary, and 15.4% did not respond. Of these same leaders, however, 45% claimed not to belong to any of the existing centrals. Freitas Marcondes, *Radiografia*, pp. 78–80. This study covered 81% of the syndicates in the municipality of São Paulo.

37. Its president was the president of the CNTC. The MSD was heavily supported by the ORIT and the ICFTU. It was also linked politically to Carlos Lacerda, then Governor of Guanabara. *O Estado de São Paulo*, Aug. 21, 1962. See also Peralva, "Esquerda."

38. Peralva, "Esquerda." For a discussion of this Autonomist faction, see also Adalgisa Nery, *Retrato sem Retoque* (Rio: Civilização Brasileira, 1963), pp. 150–61; *Jornal do Brasil*, May 26, 1963.

39. After two years of activity, the ICT had graduated 2,477 syndical leaders from its short course and 182 from its full course. These trainees came from every state in the country. The ICT also has a branch office in Recife for training rural leaders. Instituto Cultural do Trabalho, *Dois Anos de Atividades* (São Paulo, 1965).

40. Berman, p. 36.

41. Interview, Rio, Sept. 25, 1965. The CBTC accepts members who are not Roman Catholic, but the informant observed that they are reluctant to join. Were the estimate of 500,000 members correct, this would mean that every third syndicalized worker is a *circulista*. This is very doubtful. Possibly the figure includes the family of the member, since the *circulista* ideology places considerable stress on a comprehensive social and moral approach to workers' problems.

42. *O Estado de São Paulo*, July 23, 1961.

43. See *A Primacia do Trabalho sobre o Capital*, 2nd ed. (São Paulo: Frente Nacional do Trabalho, 1962).

44. For a description of AP's role in the first elections in the National Confederation of Agricultural Workers, see L. D. Therry, "Dominant Power Components in the Brazilian University Student Movement Prior to April, 1964," *Journal of Inter-American Studies*, VII, 1 (Jan. 1965), 34–41.

45. For a case study showing the transformation from "rubber-stamp" syndicalism into radical activism, see Wilson Reis, *Notas de um Dirigente Sindical* (Rio: Gráfica Editôra São Francisco, 1965). The organization in question is the Syndicate of Telegraph Workers in Rio.

46. The actual president of AC-Rio, Amaral Osório, as quoted in *Jornal do Comércio*, Dec. 16, 1965.

47. Associação Comercial do Rio, *Relatório—1963*. The CACB total is inflated by the inclusion of a large number of foreign associations loosely affiliated with the Brazilian commercial associations by way of the Federation of Foreign Chambers of Commerce in Brazil (whose president is also the president of AC-Rio and CACB).

48. The desirable formula for interest group representation was, as one would expect, one of the thorniest issues. The 1957 *Plenário* supported syndical unity on grounds of "historical tradition and the chaos and anarchy that would result from sudden plurality." No stand was taken on the syndical tax. *Revista da Associação Comercial do Rio de Janeiro*, Feb. 10, 1957, pp. 17–18. At the 1961 meeting, apparently not attended by syndical associations, corporatism was declared incompatible with democracy. *Jornal do Brasil*, Jan. 18, 1962.

49. *O Estado de São Paulo*, Apr. 1, 1964.

50. For a representative manifesto, see *O Estado de São Paulo*, Mar. 9, 1961. CONCLAP-Rio's opposition to Getulian politics can be demonstrated by their eight suggestions for the new Guanabara State Constitution: (1) no more than 50% of the budget should be spent on administrative costs; (2) no state employee should earn more than a State Secretary; (3) no subventions should be granted to newspapers; (4) state services should be provided through private firms; (5) rigid control should be maintained over all budget expenditures; (6) qualification for public employment should be determined by competition only, and promotion should be on the basis of merit; (7) no man should be able to place relatives on the public payroll; and (8) no public

salary should be more than ten times the minimum salary. *O Estado de São Paulo*, Nov. 20, 1960. To an orthodox, liberal North American these may seem "normal" demands; to Brazilians they have revolutionary implications.

51. *O Estado de São Paulo*, Mar. 11–13, 1964.

52. For a brief historical sketch of ABDIB, see *Visão*, May 21, 1965, and *O Estado de São Paulo*, June 6, 1965.

53. See the articles cited above in note 52. However, the Association's principal demand, enhanced protection against imports of foreign equipment, was not satisfied until the early 1960's and then only as the indirect result of measures designed to alleviate balance of payment difficulties. See Nathaniel Leff, *The Brazilian Capital Goods Industry* (Cambridge, Mass., 1968).

54. *Jornal do Brasil*, Dec. 10, 1965; interview, Rio, Aug. 11, 1965.

55. *Correio da Manhã*, Aug. 29, 1965. Judging from a list of the 50 Rio members, the clubs attract almost exclusively the larger chain and department stores.

56. Interview, Rio, Aug. 22, 1965.

57. Interview, São Paulo, Apr. 9, 1966.

58. ADECIF was studied in some detail to provide a basis of comparison between private and syndical entities on such dimensions as internal process, channels of access, and patterns of intergroup relations. I would like to thank Sr. Marcus Mello for his patient cooperation. He is, of course, in no way responsible for the conclusions I have drawn from the data.

59. ADECIF, *Ata* (Acts of the weekly meeting), Apr. 22, 1965. This is perhaps one of the most competitive sectors of contemporary Brazilian commerce and banking. The rate of both the creation of new firms and the demise of old ones is high. ADECIF's success suggests that the degree of commercial competition among members is at least not an overpowering deterrent to policy coordination. The relative activity and strong stands taken by ACADE, an association representing the competitive electrical appliance dealers, is another case in point. One could advance the contrary hypothesis: competition is conducive to a high rate of intragroup interaction, which in turn is conducive to greater collaboration vis-à-vis outsiders.

60. The NTC grew out of a National Congress of Truckers held in 1960. Those who called the congress were surprised at the large turnout, and they became convinced that a more permanent form of collective representation was possible in a sector that previously had been marked by bitter competition. The preexistent syndicate was the São Paulo Truckers' Syndicate, which had been dominated for years by a single man "who uses the position to perpetuate himself in office and his links with the government to finance his personal business ventures." This same man dominates the National Federation of Truckers and the National Confederation of Land Transport (CNTT). The opposition managed to capture control of the São Paulo syndicate in 1961, but in order to take over the CNTT, it must first organize new syndicates and federations. Since this is a lengthy process (and depends upon ministerial support), the opposition decided in 1963 to form a national private association as an alternative. They have since been so successful that their interest in capturing the CNTT has diminished. Interview, São Paulo, Mar. 17, 1966.

61. *ABERT: Orgão de Divulgação* (Rio), I, 2 (July 1964), 5.

62. Diva Benevides Pinho, *Dicionário de Cooperativismo* (São Paulo: Uni-

versidade de São Paulo, Faculdade de Filosofía, Ciências e Letras, 1962), pp. 41–42.

63. This is not accidental. At one time they were linked. See Diva Benevides Pinho, *Sindicalismo e Cooperativismo* (São Paulo: Instituto Cultural do Trabalho, 1964), pp. 81–95.

64. As of 1964, there were 5,865 cooperatives and 27 federations; 2,156 were engaged in animal husbandry or agricultural production; 1,627 were consumer cooperatives. *UNASCO* (São Paulo), V, 60 (July 1965), 29.

65. Its role is severely limited by the fact that the most numerous categories —physicians, lawyers, and journalists—do not participate. Only accountants and dentists are active in it. Attempts have been made at organizing a broad, more politicized, front of professionals and intellectuals, but they have failed or been suppressed. In October 1963, a General Command of Intellectual Workers was founded with a strong radical manifesto. Designed to cooperate with the other leftist, semilegal peak associations in a united front, it grouped journalists, professors, students, and "progressive" factions from other professional associations. See H. Cony, *O Ato e o Fato* (Rio: Civilização Brasileira, 1965), for the manifesto. A much milder form of group representation was initiated in Rio Grande do Sul in 1964 with the founding of the Association of University-Trained Liberal Professionals. It has since spread to Rio. As yet, however, no single entity speaks collectively for the middle sectors.

66. Interview, Rio, Aug. 27, 1965; interview, Rio, Feb. 3, 1966.

67. "To obtain [public] employment, one, two, or three jobs became the only, or almost the only, means of subsistence for the physicians, who were continually losing their liberality [i.e., their self-employed status]." *Jornal da AMB*, Sept. 19, 1965. Also, interview, São Paulo, Mar. 17, 1966.

68. *Jornal da AMB*, Apr. 20, 1964. The AMB is a member of the World Medical Association and has frequent contacts with the American Medical Association, upon which it is more or less modeled. Its policy line has been more moderate and compromising than that of the AMA—as befits the political culture—and has directed its efforts not to abolishing or curtailing welfare medicine, but to ensuring certain freedoms for physicians within the system. One of its strongest desires is to get the whole welfare system transferred from the Labor Ministry to the Health Ministry, which it rightly perceives as more friendly to the interests of physicians.

69. One informant claimed that there were 156 of these entities in Guanabara alone. Interview, Rio, Aug. 20, 1965.

70. Lei No. 1,711, Oct. 28, 1952.

71. This was a major demand at the Fourth (1962) and Fifth (1966) National Congresses of Public Servants. A bill to this effect was introduced in Congress in 1963 and was supported by the Minister of Labor. See *Jornal do Brasil*, Sept. 26, 1963.

72. "Three-quarters of the first-year students [at the University of São Paulo] came from upper-middle and middle-class families, and a little more than a sixth from the lower-middle class." B. Hutchinson, "A Origem sócio-econômica dos estudantes universitários," *Mobilidade e Trabalho*, p. 150.

73. For an extensive discussion of the structural variables affecting Brazilian student behavior, see Marialice M. Foracchi, *O Estudante e a Transformação da Sociedade Brasileira* (São Paulo: Companhia Editôra Nacional, 1965), pp. 220 et seq. For a historical analysis, see Poerner. Limited survey research indicates strong support for political activism on the part of student

organizations. See Sulamita de Brito, "O Radicalismo estudantil," *Cadernos Brasileiros*, 35 (May–June 1965), p. 71.

74. Some associations of students from individual faculties go back much further. Poerner, pp. 43–107, locates one in the Academia de São Paulo as early as 1833. A Federation of Brazilian Students was founded in 1901.

75. Thirty congresses have been held to date. For a rather biased but factually accurate description of the factional conflict in UNE, see Leonard D. Therry, "Dominant Power Components in the Brazilian University Student Movement Prior to April 1964," *Journal of Inter-American Studies*, VII, 1 (Jan. 1965). See also *O Estado de São Paulo*, July 27, 1963, for a discussion of the caucus system of decision-making at UNE congresses.

76. "UNE, as well as being an entity for the revindication of more privileges for the students, should also be a movement, an organ for the manifestation of the political thought of students concerning the great problems that afflict our country and the people of our land." *Relatório 1958–1959*, as cited in Sonia Seganfreddo, *UNE: Instrumento de Subversão* (Rio: Edições GRB, 1963), pp. 48–54.

77. Lei No. 4,464—often called the "Lei Suplicy."

78. *Correio da Manhã*, Aug. 29, 1965. In an "unofficial" plebiscite, 81% of the students in Rio, 91% in São Paulo, 90% in Minas Gerais, and 82% in Rio Grande do Sul rejected the Suplicy Law. In São Paulo, 95% of the students voted. See also *Correio da Manhã*, Sept. 5, 1965.

79. In May 1966 the DNE received a 310,000,000-cruzeiro (approximately $150,000) grant for a "campaign to enlighten the public on the objectives of the DNE." *Jornal do Brasil*, May 26, 1966. The Suplicy Law regulates the representation of students on university councils and thus makes sure that there will be loyalist directories. Opposing associations were ejected from those councils to which student organization had already gained formal access. The new DNE was also granted a monopoly on the issuance of student cards.

80. According to a Congressional Inquiry in 1963, the UNE had received 23 million cruzeiros in 1962 and 113 million in 1963 plus assorted funds for expenses of the annual congresses, for its "Popular Culture Movement," and for participation in the World Youth Festival. In a Military Inquiry (IPM) after the "Revolution," it was "proved" (though documentary proof was never made public) that the UNE had received money from various Eastern European embassies. *O Globo*, June 30, 1965; *O Estado de São Paulo*, July 1, 1965.

81. *Jornal do Brasil*, Aug. 1, 1965.

82. *Ibid.*, July 30, 1966; July 31, 1966; and Oct. 14, 1966. In September 1966 a wave of student strikes broke out in Rio and Minas Gerais. The UNE claimed to be coordinating the protest. *Correio da Manhã*, Sept. 21, 1966; *Jornal do Brasil*, Sept. 24, 1966.

83. *Jornal do Brasil*, July 14, 1967.

84. *Ibid.*, Jan. 28, 1964.

85. The emergence of Peasant Leagues in the Northeast is another typical case of this pattern. See Galjart.

86. For a discussion of these groups, see Pearse. Of course, the communitarian associations are not limited to lower-class communities. The Sociedade Amigos da Cidade of São Paulo, for example, is a very upper-status association. Brazil also has numerous Rotary and Lions Clubs.

87. These amount to a very substantial sum and are granted at all levels

of government and by almost all types of authorities. The plurality of sources combined with the laxity of budgetary controls results in frequent allegations of corruption. A congressional investigation into the matter discovered some 800 fictitious entities receiving aid in only six states. *O Estado de São Paulo,* Sept. 6, 1966. At the state level, the Guanabara Secretary for Social Services recently discovered that 293 of 912 subsidized organizations were "phantoms" and thereby saved one billion cruzeiros (slightly less than $500,000). *Jornal do Brasil,* Dec. 3, 1966.

88. Interview, Rio, Feb. 25, 1965.

89. In addition to the six, 21 had applications pending. See Mascarenhas.

90. Accounts of the evolution of the Peasant Leagues are found in Julião; F. Novaes Sodre, *Quem é Francisco Julião?* (São Paulo: Edição pela Redenção Nacional, 1963); Fonseca; Barreto; Callado, *Tempo de Arraes*; Antônio Callado, *As Indústrias de Seca e os "Galileus" de Pernambuco* (Rio: Civilização Brasileira, 1960).

91. The first *Ligas Camponêsas* in the Northeast were created by the Communist Party in the 1940's and had disappeared by 1945. From the start, the landowners sought to associate the new form of workers' association with these Communist precedents. See Barreto, pp. 110, 130. For Julião's testimony, see Fonseca, pp. 42–43.

92. Andrade, pp. 245–47; M. Meira, "Nordeste: as sementes de subversão," *O Cruzeiro* (Rio), Nov. 11, 1961.

93. "We believe that the peasants who are best fitted for the revolutionary struggle are not the ones who have nothing but their labor to sell, but the *arrendatários* who rent the land from the most backward landowners and pay their excessive rent either in cash, in kind or in labor. The sharecroppers are easier to organize. They had some security, a little money and were aware of the value of their labor. They could never afford to rent a plot of the size they were able to cultivate. The promise of land can turn them into soldiers of the revolution. They are indeed the weakest link in the system. As for the others, they were wretched semi-nomads without any security or awareness of the value of their labor. They can become revolutionaries only in a later stage." Francisco Julião, as quoted in Michel Bosquet, "Is Brazil at the Brink?" *Atlas,* XII (July 1966), pp. 20–21.

94. F. Borges, pp. 254–55.

95. The verbal radicalism of Julião, amplified by the fears of conservatives and the alarmist reports of foreign journalists, tended to overshadow the fundamentally legalist nature of the Ligas Camponêsas and the role of traditional and provincial intellectuals in "orienting" the movement. For an article that accents the paternalist, legalist, and careerist nature of its leadership, see Anthony Leeds, "Brazil and the Myth of Francisco Julião," in Joseph Maier and Richard W. Weatherhead, eds., *Politics of Change in Latin America* (New York, 1964), pp. 190–204.

96. "In the cities they have their headquarters. In the cities the peasants meet. And in the cities they receive the support and solidarity of workers, students, and intellectuals and even of such authorities as some prefects and judges." Fragmon Borges, p. 254.

97. Callado, *Tempo de Arraes,* p. 58.

98. For example, the largest and most active of the Peasant Leagues, that of Sapé, Paraíba, had 14,000 members and a leadership quite independent

from that of Julião. See *Jornal do Brasil*, July 4, 1965. The Leagues did provide, however, a sufficient basis for a few meteoric political careers. Julião's vote rose from 497 in 1954 to 3,216 in 1958 to 16,266 in 1962. In the later election he was elected to the Federal Congress.

99. For the "Declaration" of the Congress, see Julião, pp. 81–87.

100. Also, his rapid ascent seems to have convinced Julião of the imminent nature of revolution, and his program became correspondingly more radical. The Tiradentes Revolutionary Movement (MRT) became the radical complement to the Ligas Camponêsas. On the factional strife, see *Jornal do Brasil*, Nov. 19, 1961.

101. See Mascarenhas, pp. 23–24. For a discussion of Communist influence in Pernambuco and Paraíba, see Callado, *Tempo de Arraes*; Price.

102. See Julieta Calazans, *Cartilha Sindical do Trabalhador Rural*, as cited in Price, pp. 47–50.

103. Julião insisted that the syndicates by no means replaced the leagues and encouraged his followers to join both. He had, however, only very caustic comments for the Catholic syndicates. See his "Letter from Recife" in Irving Horowitz, ed., *Revolution in Brazil*, pp. 49–50. In spite of this, "The Leagues are everywhere, but the syndicates are devouring them. And, unlike the syndicates, the Leagues do not have an identity-card—that magic charm of Brazilian culture." Callado, *Tempo de Arraes*, p. 59.

104. For an insider's views on this political juggling, see Jurema, p. 237. Jurema was Goulart's Minister of Justice and a native of Paraíba.

105. João Pinheiro Neto, then Minister of Labor, as cited in George W. Bemis, *From Crisis to Revolution: Monthly Case Studies* (Los Angeles: International Public Administration Center, USC, 1964). The fact that it was not generally perceived as a conservative move or that the Goulart regime failed to keep it under control is, of course, beside the point. Among other conflict institutionalizing provisions, the Statute provided for an extensive network of Arbitration Councils (Articles 151 and 152).

106. These figures are from a SUPRA report cited in Price, p. 88.

107. *O Estado de São Paulo*, Mar. 3, 1964. In an interview with a high official in the rural syndical movement I was told that at its climax 1,600 syndicates and 29 federations had been recognized. This would mean that 1,300 syndicates were recognized during December 1963–March 1964!

108. The extent of this violent repression is not ascertainable. The only widely publicized case was the murder of a shoemaker in Governador Valadares (Minas Gerais) who had been leader of the local Liga. For an account of the postrevolutionary violence in Paraíba, see *Jornal do Brasil*, July 4, 1965.

109. Interview, Rio, Jan. 28, 1966.

110. Interview, Rio, Sept. 11, 1965. At the joint suggestion of CONTAG and CRB, the "revolutionary" Minister of Labor issued a directive permitting the formation of "eclectic" syndicates, made up of all the rural workers or employers of a given município. Under Goulart's directive they were to have been divided into five occupational sub-categories. The new directive, although it reduces their total potential numerical strength, probably makes rural syndicates easier to form and gives them a wider financial base. The present CONTAG leadership regards this as one of its most significant victories.

111. The commission works slowly and cautiously. Reportedly it had a

backlog of 1,419 requests for recognition. Many of these were presumably from employers' syndicates. *Correio da Manhã*, May 13, 1966. For the norms governing recognition, see *Portaria No. 71*, Ministério do Trabalho e Previdência Social, Feb. 2, 1965.

112. In Pernambuco, Fathers Melo and Crespo have repeatedly complained that the local ministerial delegate was in league with the sugar industrialists and was constantly harassing their attempts to enforce legal compliance. See *Jornal do Brasil*, Mar. 9, 1965, July 25, 1965; *Correio da Manhã*, Aug. 18, 1965; *Jornal do Brasil*, Nov. 28, 1965; *Correio da Manhã*, Dec. 2, 1965; *Jornal do Brasil*, Dec. 30, 1965, Feb. 27, 1966, June 5, 1966.

113. "Father Crespo recognized that the top leadership had shown themselves willing to support rural syndicates; however, those at the base were acting in an exactly contrary manner. Thus, whereas sectors of the army and police in the capital declare that the demands of the syndicates must be respected, the police detachments in the interior put pressure on both leaders and followers at the slightest sign of activity." *Jornal do Brasil*, Nov. 28, 1965.

114. Some of these local immigrant associations are nationally affiliated, e.g. the Federation of Portuguese Associations of Brazil and the Israelite Confederation of Brazil. For an extended discussion of the comparatively high rate of associability among immigrants and the role of these as instruments of assimilation, see Diégues Júnior, *Imigração*, pp. 268–77.

115. See Fernandes, *Integração*; Bastide and Fernandes; Thales de Azevedo, *Les Elites de Couleur dans une Ville Brésilienne* (Paris: UNESCO, 1953); Fernando Henrique Cardoso and Octávio Ianni, *Côr e Mobilidade Social em Florianópolis* (São Paulo: Companhia Editôra Nacional, 1960); Fernando Henrique Cardoso, *Capitalismo e Escravidão: O Negro na Sociedade Escravocrata do Rio Grande do Sul* (São Paulo: Difusão Européia do Livro, 1962); Octávio Ianni, *As Metamorfoses do Escravo* (São Paulo: Difusão Européia do Livro, 1962); René Ribeiro, *Religião e Relações Raciais* (Rio: Ministério da Educaçao e Cultura, 1956); Artur Ramos, *Negro*; Donald Pierson, *Negroes in Brazil* (Chicago, 1942); Wagley, *Race*.

116. Fernandes, *Integração*, esp. II, 1–95.

117. *Ibid.*, p. 5.

118. *Ibid.*, p. 8.

119. *Ibid.*, p. 35 et seq. See also Ramos, *O espírito*.

120. Roger Bastide even reports that a "Service for the Protection of the Brazilian Negro" similar to the "Service for the Protection of the Indian" was once proposed. Bastide and Fernandes, p. 239.

121. For a suggestive, preliminary exploration of this theme, I am indebted to Bolivar Lamounier's unpublished manuscript, "Race and Class in Brazilian Politics," UCLA, Jan. 1966.

122. Bello, p. xvi.

123. *Ibid.*, p. 5.

124. The Bishops of Northeastern Brazil have been a particularly active and independent group. In 1961 they launched the Movement for Basic Education (MEB) and the drive for rural syndicalization at their Second Regional Conference. For an account of the "Natal Movement," see David Mutchler, "Roman Catholicism in Brazil," *Studies in Comparative International Development*, I, 8 (1965).

125. And, apparently, considerable internal dissension. There was an open

split after the 1963 Manifesto, and it was eventually announced that the Manifesto represented the position not of the entire CNBB, but only of its Central Commission. *Jornal do Brasil*, May 3, 1963; *O Estado de São Paulo*, May 4, 1963. The 1962 Manifesto had the courage to castigate "the higher organs of the productive classes" for not seeking to correct exploitive practices. *Correio da Manhã*, July 17, 1962. For factionalism within the CNBB, see Mutchler, "Roman Catholicism in Brazil" (cited in Note 124 above).

126. *Jornal do Brasil*, Nov. 12, 1965; *Jornal do Brasil*, May 13, 1966. Helping in the elaboration of this plan and providing the CNBB and the CRB with more reliable information on the ecological and sociological setting of Church activity is the Center for Religious Statistics and Social Research (CERIS). See Alfonso Gregory, *A Igreja no Brasil* (Louvanim: FERES, 1965); Gustavo Pérez, Alfonso Gregory, and François Lepargneur, *O Problema Sacerdotal no Brasil* (Bruxelles: FERES, 1966). Whereas, as we have seen, association leaders in general seem to resent political activity on the part of religious authorities, recent research conducted at the request of the CNBB and the CRB among a sample in Greater São Paulo indicates the reverse may be true among the general populace. Although 60% of those who called themselves Catholics never go to church, all but 9.5% of those interviewed agreed that "the action of religious authorities should not be limited to its specific area." *O Estado de São Paulo*, Sept. 1, 1968.

127. *Jornal do Brasil*, Dec. 22, 1966.

128. *O Estado de São Paulo*, June 4, 1964. In addition to forcing the Church to close down some of its social action programs, the revolutionary elites also imprisoned several priests and accused two archbishops (Dom Helder Câmara in Olinda and Dom Newton de Almeida Batista in Brasília) of Communism. As late as January 1967, it was reported that secret police agents (DOPS) were attending meetings of the Social Action Secretariat of the CNBB. *Jornal do Brasil*, Jan. 25, 1967.

129. For an extended discussion of this transformation, see Cândido Mendes de Almeida, *Momento dos Vivos* (Rio: Tempo Brasileiro, 1967).

130. See Bastos de Avila. Fernando Bastos de Avila is ACDE's ecclesiastic assistant.

131. *Jornal do Brasil*, June 26, 1966. It is too early to judge whether the coup of 1964 will result in the permanent resurgence of Catholic conservatism. It has certainly stimulated its revival within the Church and outside it in such entities as the Brazilian Society for the Defense of Tradition, Family, and Property (TFP). Coincidentally, there has been a reemergence of native fascist movements. The *Jornal do Brasil* of Jan. 15, 1967, carried a lengthy article on the open revival of the Integralista party in Rio de Janeiro. These native fascists met again the following year in Jaú (São Paulo) under the guise of the "Second National Concentration of Cultural Centers"; they marched in the streets and sang "Avante," their hymn of the 1930's. *O Estado de São Paulo*, Aug. 27, 1968.

132. See Márcio Moreira Alves, "Os Católicos," *Correio da Manhã*, Mar. 9, 1965. For an example of "progressive" Catholic thought, see Paulo de Tarso, *Os Cristãos e a Revolução Social* (Rio: Zahar Editôres, 1963); Pe. Aloisio Guerra, *A Igreja Está Com o Povo?* (Rio: Civilização Brasileira, 1963). The most thoughtful and balanced account of the Church's recent political and social ferment is Emanuel de Kadt, "Religion, the Church and Social Change

in Brazil," in Cláudio Veliz, ed., *The Politics of Conformity in Latin America* (London, 1967), pp. 192–220.

133. See Yves de Oliveira, *Que é Municipalismo?* (Rio: Associaçao Brasileira de Municípios, 1959).

134. Interview, Rio, Jan. 19, 1966. The ABM was actually founded by técnicos. Its first president was Rafael Xavier, director of the Brazilian Institute of Geography and Statistics (IBGE). This connection with the administrative reform movement is maintained through the work of a sort of sui generis technical assistance group, the Brazilian Institute for Municipal Administration (IBAM).

135. In the words of a well-informed observer, "The ABM has become a political trampoline." Interview, Rio, Jan. 18, 1966.

136. Celso Mello de Azevedo, ed., *Cartas Municipalistas* (Rio: Associação Brasileira de Municípios, 1959); *Problemas e Reivindicações Fundamentais dos Municípios* (Rio: DASP, Serviço de Documentação, 1964).

137. Interview, Rio, Jan. 19, 1966.

138. See Frank P. Sherwood, *Brazil's Municipalities* (Los Angeles, n.d.); Donald L. Larr, "The Politics of Local Government Finance in Brazil," *Interamerican Economic Affairs*, XII, 1 (Summer 1959), 21–37. For case studies in municipal politics, see the various issues of the *Revista Brasileira de Estudos Políticos*. See also Leal.

139. As the well-informed observer remarked, "The ABM is bound to be one of the most influential groups in Brazilian political life. All politicians must at least say they support municipalism, even if they don't. This is their political base. They can't oppose municipalism any more than they can oppose motherhood." Interview, Rio, Jan. 18, 1966.

140. It was accused of financing IPÊS's operation clandestinely, but this was never conclusively proven. It was alleged that the National Commercial Confederation (CNC) was used as the locale for IBAD reunions. Students at the Superior War School (ESG) and members of CONCLAP were prominent participants. *Política e Negócios*, Oct. 14, 1963. It appears, however, that IBAD had much less active member participation than IPÊS, CONCLAP, or ADESG and served more as a conduit for funds to other "democratic" associations and individuals. See Paulo Ayres Filho, "The Brazilian Revolution," in N. Bailey, ed., *Latin America: Politics, Economics, and Hemispheric Security* (New York, 1965), pp. 139–60.

141. See Dutra; *O Estado de São Paulo*, June 13, 1963, June 20, 1963, June 30, 1963, Aug. 21, 1963, Aug. 28, 1963, and Sept. 28, 1963; *Correio da Manhã*, May 30–Sept. 10, 1963.

142. See the testimony as reported in the *Correio da Manhã*, Aug. 1, 1963, Aug. 8, 1963, Aug. 9, 1963, and Aug. 23, 1963. The five billion figure comes from Dutra, p. 17. Two respected conservative spokesmen with considerable experience in fund-raising testified that it would be impossible to raise so much money from national sources alone. *Correio da Manhã*, Aug. 22, 1963, and Aug. 30, 1963. Participation of foreign governments or firms was never proven. The president of IBAD refused to name the 126 national firms he said contributed to the slush fund. *Correio da Manhã*, Sept. 27, 1963. It is widely believed and vigorously denied that the sums came from the cruzeiro surplus accumulated by US PL480 wheat sales to Brazil.

143. Paid announcement, *Correio da Manhã*, Sept. 6, 1963.

144. For lack of information—since they have been disbanded or forced underground—I will not discuss the numerous leftist attitude groups. For a general discussion of Communism in Brazil, see Rollie Poppino, *Communism in Latin America* (Glencoe, Ill., 1964). For an intriguing personal account, see Peralva, *Retrato*.

145. The Society's leader is a professor at the Catholic University of São Paulo and coauthor (along with the Archbishop of Diamantima and the Bishop of Campos) of a very widely distributed book attacking agrarian reform. The Society is not an official Catholic organization. In fact the Church hierarchy has officially disassociated itself from the Society's views. *Jornal do Brasil*, June 19, 1966.

146. The Brazilian Federation for Feminine Progress apparently still exists. It was modeled on the League of Women Voters of the United States, but has not performed the same political tasks. In 1929 it sponsored the foundation of the Brazilian Association for University Women, which currently has some 300 members. As one of the leaders of the latter said, "The trails are open today. It is no longer an adventure. . . . Women can defend their rights through professional associations and syndicates." Interview, Rio, Sept. 27, 1965. Except for sporadic attempts to legalize divorce, they have been politically quiescent. The "System" has absorbed them.

147. Interview, São Paulo, Apr. 1, 1966.

148. Interview, São Paulo, Apr. 23, 1966. Incidentally, the bus for the registration campaign was furnished by SESI of São Paulo. UCF, and to a lesser extent MAF, have received funds and orientation from IPÊS–São Paulo. IPÊS and UCF are joint sponsors of the Campaign for Civic Education.

149. CAMDE's first public meeting was held in the auditorium of *O Globo*. Since then, it and other conservative newspapers have given full and free coverage to CAMDE's activities. The idea to create CAMDE (in 1962, shortly before the elections) came from three men: a parish priest from the upper-middle-class suburb of Ipanema, a geologist closely linked to IPÊS, and an army general in the intelligence service (SNI). They argued convincingly that the Army was undermined by "the vice of legalism," that it would move only if "legitimized" by some civilian force, and that the middle-class and upper-class women were the most concerned and easily mobilized group of civilians. The immediate cause was to prevent a "leftist," Santiago Dantas, from becoming Prime Minister. Interview, Rio, Sept. 28, 1965.

150. Another important institution in the organization of the Marcha was the Council of Democratic Entities (CED), which functions as a peak association for a wide variety of specialized, professionally based "democratic" associations. For a detailed account of the march and the entities that participated in it, see Rodrígues Matias, "Marcha da Família com Deus pela Liberdade" (São Paulo: n. pub., 1964). See also *O Estado de São Paulo*, Mar. 19, 1965, and Mar. 19, 1966.

151. See Stacchini. The leader of one of these associations informed me that they had been fully apprised of the military conspiracy three months before the fact.

152. Interview, Rio, Sept. 28, 1965.

153. Truman, p. 51.

154. The total receipts for SESI in 1966 were estimated at one hundred billion cruzeiros, or fifty million dollars. Of this, about one-half consists of

income from the 2% tax and the other half comes from the sale of services. Reis, p. 30.

155. In São Paulo there are some interesting exceptions to this generalization. Through *convênios*, or agreements, the SESI services are channeled through workers' syndicates. Nonetheless, the control over resources stays with FIESP and is used selectively to reward "deserving" syndical leaders. Interview, São Paulo, Apr. 18, 1965. Apparently, some SESC funds are also dispensed in collaboration with commercial workers' syndicates. Interview, São Paulo, Mar. 23, 1966. The general pattern is that of unilateral dispensation without reference to the corresponding worker syndicate.

Introduction to Part III

1. Harry Eckstein, *Pressure Group Politics*, p. 27.

Chapter Nine

1. Juarez Rubens Brandão Lopes, *Sociedade*, p. 58.

2. For supporting evidence, see Aziz Simão, "Industrialisation et syndicalisme au Brésil," *Sociologie du Travail*, III, 4 (Oct.–Dec. 1961), 66–76; Alain Touraine, "Industrialisation et conscience ouvrière à São Paulo," *Sociologie du Travail*, III, 4 (Oct.–Dec. 1961), 77–95. See also Leôncio Martins Rodrigues, *Conflito*, pp. 94–98. A recent survey conducted during a statewide "encounter" of paulista workers' leaders confirms this. It first asked the assembled representatives what the objectives of their syndicates should be. Of the 228 respondents, 32% stated that political ends should be foremost, 19% opted for welfare functions, 15% chose interest-oriented demands, and 26% gave mixed responses. However, when asked what attracted most members to their syndicates, 59% admitted that social welfare payoffs were of prime importance, 23% thought that workers joined for the promotion of class interests, and only 8% mentioned political motives as the major factor. "Características sócio-econômicas dos participantes do primero encontro dos trabalhadores do Estado de São Paulo," *DIESE em Resumo* III, 4/5 (Aug.–Sept. 1968), 10–14. Ministerial authorities, incidentally, watched this meeting very closely and repeatedly warned of its "subversive" nature.

3. For the accusation that leaders actually impede new recruitment for fear of diluting their control and that opposing groups (as well as authorities) seek to have massive numbers of outsiders enrolled just prior to elections, see L. R. de R. Puech, "Evolução do sindicalismo no Brasil," *Revista de Estudios Sócio-Econômicos*, I, 7 (Mar.–Apr. 1962), 10. See also Leôncio Martins Rodrigues, *Conflito*, p. 56. Rabello's research disclosed that of 33 municipal syndicates only two maintained branch offices. Six of the statewide syndicates had them, but even these could hardly be called locals. Rabello, pp. 68–69. In the survey cited in note 2 above, the leaders were asked to name the major obstacles to recruitment of new members; 49% blamed the nature of the Brazilian worker (his "low intellectual level," the absence of class or group consciousness, financial and temporal problems, lack of knowledge about syndicalism, etc.), 25% felt that the syndicates themselves were at fault, and another 25% argued that "political obstacles" of various sorts were of paramount importance. "Características sócio-econômicas," pp. 14–17.

4. Leôncio Martins Rodrigues has studied this through the archives of the Regional Labor Delegation in São Paulo. He discovered that only a small per-

centage of registered members were eligible to vote, i.e. had paid their dues, and that elections were held with from 10% to 20% of the enrolled workers in such major categories as printing, metalworking, textiles, and construction. Rodrigues, *Conflito*, p. 93.

5. Cardoso, *Empresário*, pp. 163–64.

6. *Ibid.*, p. 134.

7. Cardoso also notes that a younger generation with a different mentality is beginning to gain control of both syndicates and federations. *Ibid.*, p. 165.

8. Interview, Rio, Feb. 28, 1966.

9. Although the above account rests on interviews with several of the parties involved, some of the maneuvers were reported in the newspapers of the period. See esp. *Correio da Manhã*, Sept. 30–Oct. 3, 1964. Pressure was put upon several state representatives by their respective governors, one of whom was quoted as saying "Castelo will not intervene in the elections, but he would be very pleased if Macedo were elected."

10. However, external groups, including, of course, authority groups at the highest level, do interfere with these elections. IBAD was even accused of corrupting the Military Club elections in 1962. In 1965, as a contest between supporters of Castelo Branco and Costa e Silva was shaping up, it was resolved by means of a primary (*prévia*), and finally only a single ticket was run. In the past, however, there have been some monumental electoral battles in the Military Club. The Naval and Aeronautical Clubs are much less interesting in this and other respects. Naval and Air officers are eligible to join the Military Club and vote in its elections, but few of them have ruled it. See Gerardo Majella Bijos, *O Clube Militar e Seus Presidentes* (Rio: n. pub., 1960). For a personal account of the contest during the 1950's, see Sodré, *Memórias*, p. 295 et seq.

11. For one of the best summaries of Brazilian pluralism, see Diégues Júnior, *Regiões, passim*. For a shorter statement, see Manuel Diégues Júnior, *O Brasil e os Brasileiros* (São Paulo: Livraria Martins, 1964).

12. Authority groups have cleverly exploited the divisive tendencies. Unlike the positions on other consultative councils in the Brazilian administration, those on the administrative junta of the Brazilian Coffee Institute (IBC) are elective. The competition between the associations for these offices institutionalizes the divergence in interests and methods. For expressions of discontent with the government's coffee policy, see Sálvio Pacheco de Almeida Prado, *Dez Anos na Política do Café* (São Paulo: Editôra Jornal dos Livros, 1965).

13. Interview, São Paulo, Apr. 2, 1966; interview, São Paulo, Mar. 3, 1966. This theme was discussed at the National Congress of Coffee Growers, Londrina, Paraná, Apr. 14–15, 1966.

14. One leader reported, "The first thing they [the government] asked me after I founded [the association] was whether or not I wanted a subsidy." Interview, São Paulo, Apr. 25, 1966.

Chapter Ten

1. See Baer, *Industrialization*, pp. 79–82, for a matrix of economic policy-making and a discussion of institutional proliferation and goal incompatibilities. Another major study of Brazilian policy-making observed similarly: "However, from the above, one should not draw the absolute conclusion that

a rational process of economic policy-making existed. It probably still [in 1964] is a long way from the moment when there might be a perfect coherence and integration of the ends pursued and the means used. Until now it has not been possible to implant a centralized process of decision-making that could confer satisfactory internal coherence on economic policy decisions. . . . Many pieces of economic policy are loose; contradictory objectives are simultaneously adopted; policy instruments are used without taking into account their side effects." "Quince Años," p. 153.

2. The president of the Getúlio Vargas Foundation recently announced that the total government share (including mixed enterprises) of gross national consumption was nearly 44% in 1964. *Jornal do Brasil,* Mar. 4, 1966.

3. Werner Baer argues convincingly that inflation alone causes a transfer of resources from private consumption to private and public investment, and especially to the latter. Hence inflation seems likely to increase the politicization of representative associations regardless of qualitative changes in the nature of government policy.

4. The author of "Quince Años" suggests two reasons for this. First, the disparity in development between regions, their imperfect integration, different aspirations, and political structures made polycentrism politically expedient, if not mandatory. Second, the original simplicity of economic problems and their vulnerability to external influences made policy-making essentially a "reactive" pursuit that did not require a coordinated administrative structure. These conditions have rapidly changed, however, and there is now a greater need for new instruments of coordination and decisional centralization. In fact, as we shall see, coordination and centralization have been very important since the 1964 coup.

5. Most of the autarchies, "mixed governmental enterprises," regional *superintendências,* institutes, *fundos,* and *Caixas* receive either a constitutionally or a legally alloted fixed percentage of tax revenues, total budget receipts, or export sales. It has been estimated that in 1964, 42.3% of the total federal budget was "tied-down" in this manner! Although the government does not always honor its statutory commitment, the arrangement does afford these agencies considerable decisional autonomy. For a discussion of the impact of earmarking on policy-making, see Hirschman, *Journeys,* pp. 74–77, 80, 92–93.

6. Inflation, one of the most manifest and persistent of Brazil's problems, is both externally imposed and internally exacerbated. See Baer, *Industrialization,* for an excellent discussion of its causes.

7. Although centralized interelite violence is relatively rare, Brazil rates high on a global "Incidence of Internal War" index for Latin America. Only Cuba, Argentina, and Bolivia score higher. Most of Brazil's "internal war" consists of rioting (27 of 49 cases). Harry Eckstein, *Internal War: The Problem of Anticipation* (Washington, D.C., 1962), as cited in I. Horowitz, "The Military Elites," in Seymour M. Lipset and Aldo Solari, eds., *Elites in Latin America* (New York, 1967), p. 151.

8. One of the immediate causes of President Goulart's deposition was his attempt to promulgate two "radical" decrees, one nationalizing privately owned oil refineries, the other expropriating a narrow strip of land along federal highways. See James W. Rowe, "Revolution or Counterrevolution in

Brazil? Part II: From 'Black Friday' to the New Reforms," *American University Field Staff, Reports Service*, East Coast South America Series, XI, 5 (1964).

9. Luis Barbosa, "Vinte mil atos, leis e decrêtos em três anos," *Jornal do Brasil*, Caderno Especial, Mar. 13, 1970. The article goes on to note that the previous average annual flow of executive proposals to Congress (1960–63) was slightly fewer than 60. An article in the same paper two months earlier (Jan. 10, 1967) claimed that the legislature had passed 848 laws since the coup. Since the last few months of the session were absorbed with regime-sponsored legislation, one can safely assume that over 80% of its production was inspired by the executive branch.

10. *Jornal do Brasil*, Jan. 10, 1967.

11. Under the current system, bills sponsored by the President follow a special *tramite*, or process. They are considered by explicitly convened joint committees and rapidly passed to the floor, where they usually pass unamended. Private member bills must follow the normal, more cumbersome *tramite* involving approval by two or three parliamentary committees. See Norman Blume, "Pressure Groups and Decision-Making in Brazil," *Studies in Comparative International Development*, III, 11 (1968), p. 206.

12. Inflation, as usual, deforms the decisional process. It makes imperative and routine the need for special credits, which are controlled by the Ministry of Finance, and supplementary appropriations, which are passed retroactively by Congress at the end of the year. See "Quince Años," p. 188.

13. For an analysis of this bargaining and a description of one such fiefdom, the Superintendency of the São Francisco River, see Hirschman, *Journeys*, pp. 77 et seq.

14. Article 10 of the First Institutional Act. The new Constitution makes such actions partially subject to judicial review. This executive prerogative was used, for example, just before the 1965 indirect gubernatorial elections and again just before the inauguration of the new President on March 15, 1967, to remove "undesirables" and to ensure a smooth and "loyal" transition.

15. For valuable information on the role of the National Security Council in an earlier period, see Wirth.

Chapter Eleven

1. Brazil has at least some of the characteristics of three of Dahl's five patterns of leadership. The descriptive literature stresses the central role of the President at the summit of a hierarchy of influence ("executive-centered coalition"), but ignores or underplays the limitations imposed upon him by the necessity for constant bargaining. The findings from the pattern of associational attention suggest a great deal of decentralization and dispersion of decisional autonomy with relatively few points of hierarchic concentration ("independent sovereignties with spheres of influence"). When indirect access is considered, important communication hubs and foci of decisional concentration emerge more clearly: the Presidency, of course; the Bank of Brazil; the Ministry of Finance; and, more recently, the Ministry of Planning. The mutual interdependence of these centers, plus the independent "moderating power" of the military high command, more closely resembles what Dahl calls a "coalition of chieftains." At the national elite level, there is definitely no "covert

integration by economic notables" or "rival sovereignties fighting it out," although these two patterns do seem prevalent at the local levels. Robert Dahl, *Who Governs?* (New Haven, Conn., 1961), pp. 184 et seq.

2. See, for example, Phyllis Peterson, "Brazil: Institutionalized Confusion," in Martin Needler, ed., *Political Systems of Latin America* (Princeton, N.J., 1964).

3. This is an important point. The deputies for whom associational activity was the most salient were the most critical of the actual performance of these associations. Several mentioned that both workers' and employers' syndicates were plagued by self-serving oligarchies of *pelegos* and were much too submissive toward the President and the ministries. Others complained of overly "personalistic" leadership and a general lack of a "spirit of association." Interviews, Brasília, July 6, 1965; July 7, 1965; July 8, 1965. It would be misleading to interpret this disillusionment with current performance as a global rejection of specialized interest representation. I found very little evidence of the latter in any of the groups studied.

4. Interview, Brasília, May 8, 1965.

5. The crucial legislative role is as the rapporteur of a bill, whose decision is rarely overridden. Interview, Brasília, July 7, 1965. One informant stated that the unwritten code prohibited appointing "interested parties" as *relatores* and that "We all know pretty well what each other's interests are." Interview, Brasília, July 8, 1965. This rule is not followed invariably, however. The *relator* of the crucial 1957 tariff reform bill was Brasílio Machado Neto, the well-known leader of the São Paulo Federation of Commerce and the National Confederation of Commerce.

6. As one deputy put it, "Economic power and political power have been increasingly seeking each other out." Interview, Brasília, July 6, 1965. Most of this seeking out has involved individual firms and individual deputies. The massive effort of IBAD in the 1962 elections was a rare example of a collective effort.

7. Interview, Brasília, July 8, 1965.

8. This was confirmed in an interview with a national business leader who was also a federal deputy. He claimed that his *vida associativa* had greatly hurt his *carreira política*, in spite of his attempts at segmenting them. On the one hand, it had given him a "sectorial image" that harmed him electorally; on the other hand, he found it difficult to explain to his *companheiros da classe* why he could not support all their demands in the Congress. Interview, Rio, Feb. 28, 1966.

9. The latter effort was, in a sense, forced on the system by ideological polarization and was not very effective. No similar attempt was made during the 1965 and 1966 elections, although observers have claimed that, new legal prescriptions notwithstanding, these elections were marked by a massive infusion of economic power into the electoral process. "Dinheiro e Voto," *Jornal do Brasil*, Oct. 30, 1966. This editorial places the cost of a congressional campaign in Goiás at approximately 20,000 dollars for incumbents and 50,000 dollars for a challenger. Most campaigns were said to cost much more.

10. Interview, Brasília, July 8, 1965.

11. Interviews, Brasília, July 8, 1965. Incidentally, all those interviewed were PTB or PST deputies.

12. Interview, Brasília, July 8, 1965. As a PSD deputy put it, "They don't have any appreciation for the power of legislation."

13. Interview, Brasília, July 6, 1965.

14. *Correio da Manhã*, Nov. 20, 1965. The original executive draft had 37 articles.

15. Deputies were rather critical of the *pareceres* they received. One deputy shrewdly pointed out that the associations were organized to appeal to bureaucrats, not politicians. Therefore, the *pareceres* tend to be too dry, statistical, rational, and specialized. Few groups take the trouble to adopt a human, interpretive, and interpersonal style. He noted that government employees' associations and, to a limited extent, workers' syndicates are well received because they lack technical prowess and rely instead on a more direct, personal appeal. Interview, Brasília, July 6, 1965. Other deputies complained that the *pareceres* were too unimaginative, too timid (especially in taking a position against the executive), and much too slow in appearing, even when opinions were solicited. On the other end, the men in charge of the legislative research departments complained bitterly about the difficulty of keeping up with the enormous flood of bills, all of which had only thirty days to clear the Congress at that time.

16. This is the source of another weakness in access. As one deputy pointed out in detail, representatives from states "with a political tradition," e.g. Minas Gerais and Bahia, dominate the proceedings of the Câmara. They are more likely to be professional, clientelistic politicians. The more interest-oriented deputies are amateurs by comparison and do not devote full attention to parliamentary politics. Interview, Brasília, July 8, 1965.

17. The Congress has no advisory staff or reference service of its own. The deputies themselves rarely possess the technical skills necessary for informed decision-making in an increasingly rationalized environment. They are aware of this "gap," and proposals have been put forth for such a service. See Sérgio Magalhaes, *Problemas do Desenvolvimento Econômico* (Rio: Editôra Civilização Brasileira, 1960), p. 2. The information emanating from representative associations has not been sufficiently consistent, authoritative, or digestible to fill the gap; in fact, the tendency on the part of association leaders is to regard the gap as a serious impediment to their efforts to influence legislators rather than as a potentially exploitable resource.

18. One association, that of National Trucking Companies (NTC), claims (unofficially) the distinction of having been the only group in Brazil during the Castelo Branco dictatorial regime to have successfully overridden a presidential veto. It organized a massive caravan to Brasília for the purpose. Interview, São Paulo, Mar. 17, 1966.

19. See John D. Martz, *Acción Democrática* (Princeton, N.J., 1966); Payne; Torcuato di Tella, *El Sistema político argentino y la clase obrera* (Buenos Aires: EUDEBA, 1965); Robert E. Scott, *Mexican Government in Transition*, 2nd ed. (Urbana, Ill., 1964).

20. See J. P. Galvão de Sousa, "O Significado político do corporativismo," *Digesto Econômico* (São Paulo), Mar. 1951, p. 13.

21. Phyllis Peterson, "Brazilian Political Parties: Formation, Organization and Leadership, 1945–1959," unpublished, University of Michigan, 1962.

22. The deal (proposed by the CNTI) would have involved syndical control over the selection of candidates and formal direct participation by sindi-

cato, federação, and confederação leaders in the local, state, and national directories of the party. It was consciously modeled on the British Labour Party. For the text of the proposal and a critical commentary, see Telles, pp. 178–205. All Brazilian parties have a multiclass composition, however. Soares, in a study of carioca voter preference prior to the 1960 presidential elections, showed that, although UDN preference declined consistently with declining socioeconomic status and PTB preference rose (somewhat less consistently), both drew support from throughout the stratification system. Interestingly, in the "manual supervisory" and "skilled manual" categories—the ones with the highest rate of syndicalization—UDN preference was substantial (in the first stratum it was higher than PTB preference), and the proportion of those voting for minor parties or without any party preference was also high. "Classes sociais strata sociais e as Eleições presidenciais de 1960," *Sociologia* (Sept. 1961).

23. For a discussion of what strategy of influence the syndicates should adopt vis-à-vis the party machines, see Victorio Martorelli, "Sindicalismo e política partidária," *Revista Brasilense*, XVIII (July–Aug. 1958), 139–44. Martorelli concludes that they should run candidates in several parties, and that those elected should thereafter band together at the parliamentary level.

24. *O Estado de São Paulo*, Feb. 16, 1966. It was not possible to ascertain if this practice was followed in the composition of state and local directories.

25. There are, as always in Brazil, exceptions. For example, just prior to the 1965 Guanabara gubernatorial election, Carlos Lacerda, the outgoing governor, announced a freeze on the number of taxicab permits. He was rewarded shortly thereafter with the distribution of a flood of handbills supporting "his" candidate and signed by the president of the Syndicate of Autonomous Taxicab Drivers. Presumably, this is a flagrant infraction of the Consolidated Labor Laws. For evidence of electoral activism on the part of the Petroleum Workers' Syndicate, see Nelson de Souza Sampaio, "Bahia," in T. Cavalcanti and R. Dubnic, eds., *Comportamento Eleitoral no Brasil* (Rio: Fundação Getúlio Vargas, 1964), p. 38.

26. Singer, "Política," pp. 74–75. For suggestive discussion of the *cabo eleitoral* and other types of professional politicians, see pp. 71–77. See also José Arthur Rios, "El Pueblo y el político," *Política* (Caracas), VI (Feb. 1960), 12–36.

27. SESI, in particular, has been frequently attacked as a source of "electoral corruption." In its earlier period, when it was wholeheartedly devoted to mitigating the Communist threat (1945–48), the charges were probably justified. I was given a detailed account of how these funds were used in the Northeast to support non-Communist workers' syndicates and, concomitantly, the PTB's electoral campaign. Interview, Rio, Dec. 9, 1965. Since then its direct electoral role seems to have diminished, although in 1963 some 100 million cruzeiros of SESI funds were allotted for financing Goulart's plebiscite campaign.

28. *Revista CNC* (July–Aug. 1962).

29. I would like to thank Dr. Bento Ribeiro Dantas, then president of the CIRJ, for his cooperation in making these unpublished data available to me.

30. In the 1934 elections, it ran directly as a party and carried the entire state of Ceará. *Jornal do Brasil*, Sept. 6, 1959.

31. The *Diário de Notícias*, Sept. 17, 1950, noted somewhat ironically

that the LEC Manifesto of that year did not condemn Getúlio Vargas in spite of his "anti-Catholic past and the fact that he had a son named Luther." Café Filho, his running-mate, was denounced because of his support of divorce legislation.

32. *O Estado de São Paulo*, Sept. 5, 1962, and Sept. 23, 1962. For discussions of ALEF's role in the 1962 Congressional elections, see Nelson de Souza Sampaio, "Bahia," and José Arthur Rios, "Guanabara," in Cavalcanti and Dubnic, *Comportamento Eleitoral no Brasil*, pp. 26–27, 39–40, 145–49. These also contain interesting information on the activities of IBAD.

33. Interview, Brasília, July 6, 1965.

34. Interview, Brasília, July 7, 1965.

Chapter Twelve

1. Merle Kling, in "Toward a Theory of Power and Political Instability in Latin America," *Western Political Quarterly*, IX, 1 (Mar. 1956), argues that this is the case throughout Latin America.

2. Hélio Jaguaribe, "The Dynamics of Brazilian Nationalism," in Veliz, p. 168. For an excellent case study of this system at the local level, see Harris.

3. Hélio Jaguaribe has discussed this concept in several publications. In addition to the one cited in note 2, see Jaguaribe, "Crise," pp. 123 et seq. Here he attempts to explain the 1930 revolution in terms of the inability of the *Cartorial* system to expand public employment sufficiently and to maintain an adequate level of public salaries, and the 1945 deposition of Vargas in terms of the transformation of this parasitic middle class into something approaching a bourgeoisie.

4. Jaguaribe, *Condições*, p. 23.

5. For a theory of Brazilian history based on the emergence of a bureaucratic stratum, see Faoro. In their salary campaigns, the civil servants' associations often claim to represent the largest occupational category in the country—1,400,000 strong!

6. One should not assume that because of the technological expansion of administrative processes the old patterns of recruitment and performance have disappeared or even become the exception. Two of the few empirically minded students of Brazilian public administration have tried to explain, not how decisions were made, but how—given the predominance of nepotism, favoritism, absenteeism, and corruption and the lack of supervision, education, specialized training, and motivation—anything got decided at all in public agencies! They discovered, incidentally, that minimal services were performed by a small core, or "workhorse group," but they could not explain why or how this group emerged, since there were no apparent positive incentives for taking such initiatives. John Rood and Frank Sherwood, "The 'Workhorse' Group in Brazilian Administration," in Daland, *Perspectives*, pp. 47–56.

7. Ianni, *Estado*, p. 189.

8. See Baer, *Industrialization*, p. 78.

9. "Quince Años," p. 186.

10. Celso Furtado, "Political Obstacles to Economic Growth in Brazil," in Veliz, p. 158. Consider, for example, the following editorial from *Jornal do Brasil* requesting that the incoming President break with past political tradition: "It is worthwhile to remind President Costa e Silva that there exists an

extensive second level of government decision-making, . . . the part of the civil service that in settled and organized countries remains almost unaltered when the government changes and that in Brazil is automatically renovated. . . . In Brazil, as far as departments, institutes, and, even more seriously, autarchies are concerned, the most varied and usually the least sensible criteria for selecting leaders prevail. There is, in the first place, the criterion of nepotism, familism, and cronyism. There is also the criterion of political coreligion and even the geographical criterion, as when the government discovers that some state has not yet received any post. Thus, agencies are distributed like dessert—Cacao, Sugar, and Coffee." Feb. 26, 1967. Costa e Silva did not follow the advice.

11. My generalizations about the técnicos and the sources of their influence are based on interviews with both association leaders and técnicos themselves. On the general role of economic administrators in policy-making in Latin America and limitations on that role, see Hirschman, *Journeys*, and Charles W. Anderson, *Politics and Economic Change in Latin America* (Princeton, N. J., 1967).

12. He also appointed many more military officers to these posts than had his predecessor. Several observers have argued that the revolution of 1964 very dramatically enhanced the influence of the técnicos in administrative decision-making. For the first time, they were appointed on merit alone and were given substantial autonomy. See Mendes de Almeida, "Sistema." A recent public opinion poll showed surprisingly strong support for técnico appointments. Some three hundred persons in five major cities were asked: "In your opinion, should the future cabinet be composed of persons linked to the people by political interests or by técnicos without any political link to the people?" The majority in four of the cities favored the técnicos (Belo Horizonte was the exception). See *Manchete*, No. 177 (Mar. 11, 1967).

13. A survey of Brazilian entrepreneurs disclosed that 43% of those interviewed had received long-term or medium-term loans from state sources, and 71% had received short-term loans. See Richers et al.

14. However, "the paulistas present themselves best and maintain a good technical level." Interview, Rio, Feb. 16, 1966. Joseph LaPalombara has pointed out that in the Italian case superior control over the sources of information is a key variable in determining the relations of influence between representative associations and authority groups. In Brazil the associations seem to depend more on the government for information than vice versa.

15. Interview, Rio, Feb. 10, 1966.
16. Interview, Rio, Feb. 16, 1966.
17. Interview, Rio, Feb. 10, 1966.
18. Interview, Rio, Feb. 10, 1966.
19. Interview, Rio, Feb. 14, 1966.
20. Interview, Rio, Feb. 10, 1966.
21. Interview, Rio, Feb. 14, 1966.
22. Interview, Rio, Feb. 17, 1966.

23. "Ministries and organizations of the vertical type are more accessible to organized interests than horizontal ones." Meynaud, p. 277.

24. An indirect confirmation of this was the frequently expressed resentment against associations that either refused to collaborate or preferred to take their cases directly and immediately to another forum. The expectation

is that they should first deal directly with the administrative unit involved and exhaust all possibilities for conciliation at that level. Administrators cited case after case in which they had invited direct associational participation in the earliest stages of policy drafting and in the final stages of regulation in order to avoid a "misunderstanding." For description of a similar custom in British politics, see Finer, pp. 21–22.

25. Interview, Rio, Feb. 14, 1966.

26. Interview, Rio, Jan. 31, 1966.

27. A young economist in one of the executive groups claimed, "The trouble with these associations is that they don't have technical advisory staffs to orient their members." Interview, Rio, Feb. 14, 1966. Thus the function of the association is not to represent preexisting opinion, but to reform it.

28. As one informant in the Sugar and Alcohol Institute put it, differentiating between regional styles and organizational strengths, "Those from the North plead for help and those from the South negotiate for assistance." Interview, Rio, Feb. 8, 1966.

29. There have been cases of direct indication, especially at the state level. One came to light in 1966 when the Governor of São Paulo, Ademar de Barros, asked FARESP to suggest a man for Secretary of Agriculture and later reneged and appointed a político to fulfill a political commitment. *O Estado de São Paulo*, Mar. 24, 1966. According to this account, the Governor had given the FARESP president a blank, signed act of nomination and told him "any name would do." At the federal level, such interventions are less common. When the Ministry of Industry and Commerce was first broken off from that of Labor, the CNI and the CNC were invited to nominate candidates for the posts of Secretary of Industry and Secretary of Commerce, respectively. Interview, Rio, Dec. 10, 1965. During the Goulart period, workers' syndicates and their semilegal peak associations threatened strikes on several occasions in attempts to influence the composition of cabinets. As I mentioned above, a number of judicial and consultative posts are filled by indication of workers' and employers' syndicates.

The selection of ministers and higher administrators—despite the gradual "technification" noted above—still involves a delicate regional balancing act and certain posts seem to acquire a regional *coloração*. For example, the Ministry of Agriculture almost invariably goes to someone from the southern states. These are also the states that dominate the affairs of the CRB. The last two Ministers of Industry and Commerce have been men identified with São Paulo, one a prominent member of the directory of the Commercial Association, the other the president of the CNI and a former member of the FIESP directory. In these cases, the regionalist and functionalist criteria seem to combine to ensure selection. In neither case would one be justified in asserting that the CRB, the AC-São Paulo, or the CNI "indicated" the minister.

30. LaPalombara, p. 343.

31. Gordon, pp. 13, 23–24.

32. Interview, Rio, Dec. 22, 1965.

33. Interview, Rio, Nov. 30, 1965. As one industrial leader remarked, it was very difficult during the presidency of Goulart for the productive classes to gain access to the closed circle of drafting técnicos, but the long period of discussion in the Congress gave them ample opportunity to defeat, delay, or modify executive initiatives. Since the coup, with the 30-day and 45-day

restrictions imposed on congressional deliberation, influence, if it is to be expected at all, must be exerted directly in the executive branch or on the "studious bureaucrats." Interview, Rio, Feb. 26, 1966.

34. The following quote from the president of the Confederation of Commercial Associations of Brazil is rather typical: "Here is the great lacuna of this government: the lack of dialogue with the entrepreneurial class. . . . It seems to us that economic and financial matters would achieve greater authenticity if they were preceded by an understanding with the entrepreneurial forces. . . . We feel patriotic enough to be able to collaborate in the elaboration of projects and plans that now are the privilege of a group of técnicos with recognized theoretical competence but with little experience with reality. . . . If we sometimes lack excellent technical skill, we have more than enough experience and knowledge of applied problems. It disturbs us to know that we are suspected of being incapable of going beyond immediate interests and considering problems in a broad social perspective." *Manchete,* No. 718 (Jan. 22, 1966).

35. Interview, Rio, Aug. 18, 1965.

36. One even went so far as to say that attempts to influence the legislature were a waste of time. All that really matters can be handled in the *regulamentação*. Interview, Rio, Jan. 26, 1966.

37. LaPalombara, p. 262. The *clientela* is not to be confused with the more omnibus concept of *clientelismo* used above. As used by LaPalombara, "clientela" refers specifically to a relationship between two or more highly organized actors. Below I shall refer to this as an "associational clientela" to distinguish it from the more diffuse, personalistic, and factionalistic variety.

38. This definition of clientele is from Herbert Simon et al., *Public Administration* (New York, 1950), p. 461. Relevant examples in Brazil would be found in the coal, iron ore, petroleum distribution, and perhaps the shipbuilding, cacao processing, pharmaceuticals, automobiles, machinery, and electrical equipment sectors.

39. LaPalombara, p. 293.

40. For example, SUMOC, the monetary authority, was reported as having had 16 different directors in 15 years. Augusto Cesar Carvalho, "Equilíbrio financeiro, missão do Banco Central," *Jornal do Brasil,* Oct. 30, 1966. The same article notes that the director of the Mexican Central Bank has had the job for twenty years.

41. Prado Júnior in *Revolução*, brilliantly analyzes the failure of the Left in terms of its exclusive preoccupation with the long-term demands and its overlooking of the immediate short-term desires for better salaries and working conditions.

42. Various subterfuges are used to circumvent the legal requirement that all federal public employee appointments be made by *concurso* (examination). It has been estimated by various authorities that only from 10 to 17% have obtained their positions by competition. See Celso Lafer, "Politics, Administration and Development," unpublished, Cornell University, Apr. 1967, p. 94, and the sources cited therein. Some agencies, e.g. the Bank of Brazil and Itamaratí (the Foreign Ministry) have been recruiting by merit for some time. Others have been doing so since they were formed. One frequently finds "graduates" of these agencies loaned out on request to other government organs.

43. *Jornal do Brasil,* Dec. 16, 1966.

44. Both statements can be found in full in Burns, *Documentary History,* pp. 369, 376.

45. See Hambloch. Hambloch was perhaps the first to argue that the republican President was the historical heir to the monarchic tradition of concentration and personalization of power. See also João Camillo de Oliveiro Torres, *O Presidencialismo no Brasil* (Rio: Edições O Cruzeiro, 1962); Afonso Arinos de Mello Franco, *Evolução da Crise Brasileira* (São Paulo: Companhia Editôra Nacional, 1965), pp. 142–66. For the argument that institutionalized personalist power is a standard syndrome of Latin American politics, see Jacques Lambert, *Amérique Latine* (Paris: Presses Universitaires de France, 1963), pp. 376–402.

46. See Rood and Sherwood.

47. Decision-making at the state level is similarly centralized. Hélio Betrão, who attempted to rationalize the Guanabara administration, reported that the Governor had to sign an average of more than 50 *processos* a day. For a hospital to purchase a single drug, 47 transactions and signatures were involved, including that of the Governor. "Decentralização, democracia, liberdade e eficiência," *Jornal do Brasil,* Feb. 1, 1966. A side product of this propensity is the proliferation of agencies directly subordinate to the presidency. From a high of over 100 in 1960, the number has declined in recent years. For example, the production institutes and executive groups were brought within the orbit of the Ministry of Industry and Commerce, and the regional development agencies were subordinated to the new Ministry of the Interior.

48. Brazilian politicians, administrators, and interest leaders have, from my observations, a veritable mania for information and are inexhaustible and incorrigible gossips and rumormongers. An indispensable adjunct to any major ministry or agency is its own *serviço de informações* (espionage network). Since the coup a special militarily controlled service, the SNI, reporting directly to the President, has been created alongside the preexisting civilian service. To my astonishment, a number of interviewees openly admitted that as a matter of patriotic duty they were SNI informants and that they reported regularly on the internal activities of their respective associations. Goulart's last Minister of Justice argues that the transfer of the presidency to Brasília contributed greatly to the success of the coup by cutting off the President from important sources of confidential information. Jurema, pp. 31–37. The creation of the SNI and the reorganization of the presidency have presumably corrected this deficiency.

49. According to count, there were 3,749 assorted acts of "official" punishment (loss of mandate, removal of political rights, expulsions, etc.) during Castelo Branco's term of office. *Jornal do Brasil,* Mar. 12, 1967.

50. This, for example, was the case for an incumbent candidate for the presidency of the CNI in 1962, who had sought to lead a broad employer's front in opposition to Goulart. Interview, Rio, Nov. 20, 1965.

51. During certain periods of the Goulart regime, particularly from January to April 1964, workers' leaders had regular and intimate access to the President. From an insider's account, however, it appears that there was no predominance of one or the other party; rather, there was a great deal of mutual exploitation and suspicion. See Maia Netto, *Brasil—Guerra Quente na América Latina* (Rio: Civilização Brasileira, 1965), pp. 147–55.

52. Many intermediaries may be used for this purpose: state governors,

congressmen, ministers, bishops, etc. Especially important are the President's personal advisors. These tend to specialize in different interest sectors and may, as under Goulart, even get a formally specialized title, e.g. "syndical advisor." These gatekeepers are prime targets, important in the upward transmission of demands and the downward transmission of "imperative coordinations." In an interview I asked one of Goulart's advisors who handled relations with industrialists how the Goulart regime had managed to keep most of the industrialists' associations in line with the President's policies. He denied that it was necessary to apply formal sanctions such as threat of intervention or selective retention of credit from the Bank of Brazil. He explained: "Catholics no longer argue that Hell is fire and brimstone. According to modern theology, it is the absence of the presence of God. We have learned from this. All that is necessary is to threaten them with the absence of the presence of the President. No more dinner invitations, private plane rides, informal conversations, or places on ILO delegations. Those who collaborate are not deprived of this presence—and most do collaborate." Interview, Rio, Dec. 9, 1965.

53. *Jornal do Brasil*, Feb. 9, 1967. The editorial comments that this demonstrates "the rubble of technicism and petty politics" into which his regime had fallen, "the fantastic and unwholesome symbiosis of the Executive with the Legislature" (1966 audiences amount to an average of four for each of the 475 members of Congress), and the "figurative . . . and frightening" marginalization of students and workers.

54. *Estado de São Paulo*, July 11, 1965. Also, I would like to thank Dr. Luiz Navarro de Britto, Deputy Chief of the Civil Household of the Presidency, for providing me with unpublished data on the President's correspondence.

55. The following example illustrates how the process works. In early 1966 the government announced its intention of transferring a number of imported items from the "special" to the "general" tariff category, thereby increasing potential competition with nationally manufactured goods. The industrialists protested and tried to take the issue directly to the President. They were rebuffed and informed that Castelo Branco would not have a "dialogue" with them because they had representatives on the Council for Tariff Policy (CPA), where the decision would be made. Of course the industrialists knew this and had come directly to the President precisely because they also knew they had little chance of prevailing in the prescribed arena. See *Jornal do Brasil*, Feb. 19, 1966.

56. Jurema, pp. 58–59. A similar point could be made regarding the second Vargas administration from 1950 to 1954. Such a doubling up of roles leaves the President too exposed to group conflict and leads to a steady erosion of support from both sides with the danger of military intervention.

Chapter Thirteen

1. Two recent studies by North Americans have assimilated these syndromes. Leeds is little more than a jargonized version of the "informal-irrational-particularistic-corruptible" model based on a very limited sample. Leff is a serious study that concludes with something approaching the "formal-rational-universalistic-incorruptible" model. This latter study is an important and original contribution to an understanding of economic policy-making in

Brazil and has influenced my thinking and evaluation in the following parts of this chapter.

2. Leff is quite aware of this. He even hints at possible cyclical shifts between "technocratic-austere" and "political-corrupt" styles of rule. Leff, p. 101. Leeds seems to argue for the exclusivity of his "model."

3. Robert Dahl, *Who Governs?* (New Haven, Conn., 1961), p. 330.

4. Interview, Rio, Feb. 10, 1966.

5. Interview, Rio, Feb. 16, 1966.

6. Truman, pp. 264 et seq.

7. For a discussion of the importance of "fixed channels of access in the bureaucracy," see LaPalombara, p. 391.

8. "The stronger an organization's relations . . . the less public notice it arouses, and, conversely, . . . fuss, noise, mass lobbying and similar demonstrations are often an indication of failure." Finer, p. 54.

9. "In Brazil there is a well-known tendency for professional and social groups to promote themselves by referring to their indispensability for the maintenance of the entire society." M. Vieira da Cunha, "Resistência da burocracia às mudanças sociais no setor público e no setor privado," in *Resistências à Mudança* (Rio: Centro Latinamericano de Pesquisas em Ciências Sociais, 1960), p. 202.

10. "The general lines of Simonsen's ideas constitute the basis for the economic orientation of the Brazilian governments that followed." Jacy Montenegro Magalhães, "Os Organismos sindicais dos empregadores e o desenvolvimento econômico do Brasil," *CNI-Notícias* (Jan.–Feb. 1958), p. 13.

11. Interview, Rio, Dec. 9, 1965.

12. Interview, Rio, Jan. 13, 1966.

13. On this point, see "Quince Años," pp. 185 et seq. See also the writings cited above by Furtado, who appears to have originated this theme of "industrialization without an industrialization policy," and the historical evidence presented in Skidmore, pp. 41–47, 69, 71, 185.

14. See esp. Grant McConnell, *Private Power and American Democracy* (New York, 1966).

15. Ianni, *Estado*, pp. 59–60. Stein, *Brazilian Cotton*, pp. 81 et seq., argues convincingly that the link between industrial interests and state patronage was forged much earlier—in the first years of the Republic, 1890–92—and was merely an extension of practices already prevalent in agriculture. As for the Estado Novo, he observes that "years of practice before 1930 in consulting with the chief executive and congressional committees prepared industrialists' associations for active collaboration in the formulation of governmental policy under Vargas, and the mutual acceptance of the concept of the corporative state, with its emphasis upon state intervention and planning, . . . so close to the thinking of many Brazilian industrialists, made the collaboration more effective." *Ibid.*, p. 136.

16. See Rui Gomes de Almeida, *Idéias e Atitudes* (Rio: José Olympio, 1965), pp. 79 et seq.

17. Ehrman, p. 563.

18. Weiner, p. 216.

19. The right to strike was regulated in a restrictive manner by President Dutra in 1946, just prior to the drafting of the Constitution. According to one account, the content of the decree was an executive approval of a measure

initiated and drafted by a committee of employers' representatives. See "Editorial," *Digesto Econômico*, Mar. 1946, p. 20. The right to strike was reinterpreted in 1964, again restrictively.

20. Leff, p. 52.

21. The author of "Quince Años" observes that, while public credit grew an average of 8.3% a year, private credits expanded at a rate of 5.3% a year.

22. Roberto Simonsen, *A Planificação da Economia Brasileira* (São Paulo: n. pub., 1944), pp. 11–12. For a discussion of the ideological dispute surrounding Simonsen's ideas, see Almeida Magalhães.

23. See Ianni, *Estado*, pp. 100 et seq. See also Cardoso, *Empresário*, pp. 166 et seq.

24. Richers, pp. 127, 62.

25. *Ibid.*, p. 64. For a general summary of responses that show the favorable attitude of industrialists toward measures of government stimulus or control, see pp. 197–99.

26. *Leff*, p. 61 et seq.

27. Gordon and Grommers, pp. 19–20.

28. *Desenvolvimento e Conjuntura*, July 1957, p. 50, as cited in Gordon and Grommers, p. 42.

29. According to an article in the New York *Herald Tribune* of Apr. 6, 1958, of twelve developed and underdeveloped countries polled, Brazil had the lowest proportion (14%) of respondents who regarded foreign private investment as "bad" for the country. As cited in W. B. Dale, *Brazil: Factors Affecting Foreign Investment* (Menlo Park, Calif., 1958).

30. For the most articulate statement of FIESP's position, see Manoel de Costa Santos, *Os Investimentos Estrangeiros no Brasil* (FIESP: Forum Roberto Simonsen, 1958). Costa Santos is the president of the large and well-organized Syndicate of the Electric and Electronic Industry of the State of São Paulo and of the Brazilian Association of the Electric and Electronics Industry.

31. Richers, pp. 19–20, Tables 7-B and 7-C.

32. *Correio da Manhã*, Dec. 10, 1961. See also G. de Paiva, "A Rêmessa de lucros e os investimentos estrangeiros," *Digesto Econômico*, Jan.–Feb. 1962, pp. 8–15.

33. See *Desenvolvimento e Conjuntura*, Apr. 1962, pp. 135–40. The final bill did meet with the approval of the CNI, and, in July 1964, when the revolutionary government discussed the possible revocation of the Profit Remittance Law, the CNI supported its retention—to no avail. *Desenvolvimento e Conjuntura*, July 1964, pp. 25–34.

34. See esp. Prado Júnior, *Revolução*.

35. As one interest leader whose association enjoys a particularly advantageous clientela with its "regulatory agency" said to me, "We have our commission; coffee has its institute; automobiles have their executive group. The ideal would be for every interest to have its own agency within the government." Interview, Rio, Aug. 17, 1965.

For the liberal professions, the most crucial issue is the *regulamentação* of the profession itself. This stipulates the conditions required for obtaining the title and the privileges attached to it. Many of the middle-sector associations owe their existence to the fight for a favorable *regulamentação*. Usually this includes provisions for the creation of a professional *ordem* or *conselho* to revise and supervise subsequent policy. Not all professions have been successful in this quest. In 1966, the sociologists saw their attempt at regulation vetoed by the President of the Republic.

36. Interview, Rio, Aug. 25, 1965.

37. ADECIF, *Ata*, Apr. 16, 1964.

38. ADECIF, *Ata*, Apr. 30, 1965. The language of the Exposition illustrates the cautious, conciliatory style of opposition: "It is difficult ... to disagree without being badly interpreted, to suggest without running the risk of being charged with exclusive defense of its interest .... From the start, we want to praise the government's effort, *but ....*" (Italics mine.)

39. ADECIF, *Ata*, July 15, 1965.

40. ADECIF, *Ata*, June 10, 1965.

41. Interview, Rio, Sept. 9, 1965.

42. For an insightful discussion of this as a general tactic of interest politics, see E. E. Schattschneider, *The Semi-Sovereign People* (New York, 1960).

43. CIB, *Circular*, No. 5 (Apr. 27, 1933).

44. Interestingly, several respondents to my written reputational influence question cited McKann-Erickson and J. Walter Thompson as among the twelve most influential representative associations in Brazil. For a polemic but informative discussion of the role of North America advertising techniques and companies from a nationalist point of view, see Genival Rabelo, *O Capital Estrangeiro na Imprensa Brasileira* (Rio: Civilização Brasileira, 1966). This business sector is quite well organized and has several representative associations: the Brazilian Association of Advertisers (ABA), the Brazilian Association of Advertising Agencies (ABAP), the Brazilian Association for Propaganda (ABP), and the Paulista Association for Propaganda (APP).

45. For a brief discussion of this campaign and its results, see Leff, *The Brazilian Capital Goods Industry*.

46. *Correio da Manhã*, Oct. 18, 1958.

47. *Folha de São Paulo*, Mar. 20, 1966.

48. *O Estado de São Paulo*, Oct. 22, 1960, and *Correio Paulistano*, Oct. 20, 1960.

49. The best summary treatment of strikes is Rodrigues, *Conflito*, pp. 51–102. Unfortunately, no systematic and reliable statistics on strikes are available, although DIESE has been collecting information on the state of São Paulo since 1961. See its *Revista de Estudos Sócio-Econômicos* (Jan. 1962) and "Balanço Trabalhista Sindical do Ano de 1965," (mimeographed, Jan. 1966). See also Miglioli. Miglioli records the following political strikes: railway workers in 1891 in support of the Navy revolt against Marshal Deodoro, a general strike in 1918, a general strike in Recife in 1961 in support of SUDENE, a petroleum workers' strike in favor of a nationalist director for Petrobras in 1962, and two national general strikes in that same year in support of Goulart. An attempt at a general strike in opposition to the coup of 1964 failed.

50. Miglioli, pp. 32–34.

51. *Ibid.*, pp. 80–81.

52. Consider, for example, the following editorial from *O Estado de São Paulo*, Sept. 24, 1963: "Most recently, the productive classes have sinned by their own excessive prudence in their demonstrations concerning national political events .... These [the executive, legislative, and judiciary] are not the

only reserves we should mobilize for the collision that is coming soon: other responsible forces must hear the anguished appeal, because to them the nation has freely entrusted the task of defending it."

53. For a somewhat exaggerated account of IPÊS's counterrevolutionary activities, see Philip Siekman, "When Executives Turned Revolutionaries," *Fortune* LXX, 3 (Sept. 1964), 147 et seq. One of IPÊS's leaders has given a more balanced account playing down its role in military plotting and arms purchasing. Paulo Ayres Filho, "The Brazilian Revolution," in Norman A. Bailey, ed., *Latin America: Politics, Economics, and Hemispheric Security* (New York, 1965), pp. 239–60.

54. This was no new role for the FIESP, which, in collaboration with the Institute of Engineering, organized the mobilization of industrial resources for the paulista uprising of 1932. See Clovis de Oliveira, *A Indústria e o Movimento Constitucionalista de 1932* (São Paulo: Serviço de Publicações do Centro e da Federaçao das Indústrias do Estado de São Paulo, 1956).

55. Interview, São Paulo, Apr. 21, 1966.

56. *O Estado de São Paulo*, Apr. 2, 1964.

57. The literature on the coup is enormous. For the basis of the above conclusion, see esp. Stacchini.

58. Evidence for this assertion has been presented at several points in the text. For a particularly striking contrast, compare my account of the contemporary difficulties of industrialists with the description in Stein, *Brazilian Cotton*, pp. 81–184, of the activities of textile manufactures from the proclamation of the Republic until the 1940's.

59. "The movements for apparent reform in Brazil have almost always come from the top down; they were of intellectual, not sentimental, inspiration." Buarque de Holanda, *Raízes*, p. 234.

60. Coffee is an excellent example of this observation. Unevenly organized, badly divided internally, and long dependent upon government subsidies, the coffee growers were unable to prevail upon the authorities for parity price treatment, for a devalued currency, or for the end of export taxation. However, they were successful in preventing a major revision of coffee policy, and some 10 to 20% of total annual gross investment continues to go into accumulating coffee inventories and sustaining prices. For a more detailed treatment, see Leff, pp. 9–34. See also A. Delfim Netto, *O Problema do Café no Brasil* (São Paulo: Faculdade de Ciências Econômicas e Administrativas, USP, 1959).

61. The lack of class consciousness on the part of both propertied and working strata has been the subject of extensive comment and some empirical research. For important treatments of this theme, see Cardoso, *Empresário*, pp. 159 et seq.; Ianni, *Industrialização*, pp. 93 et seq.

62. See Meynaud, p. 274; La Palombara, p. 370.

Chapter Fourteen

1. The intellectual parentage of these speculations is difficult for me to trace. They owe a great deal to the influence of Furtado, especially his *Dialética* and his more recent *Subdesenvolvimento*, and to Prado Júnior, *Revolução*. The theoretical writings of ECLA have also contributed a great deal, especially *The Process of Industrial Development in Latin America* (New York: United Nations, 1966), E/CN.12/716/Rev.1. See also Cardoso and

Reyna; Soares, "A nova industrialização"; Luciano Martins, "Formação do empresariado industrial no Brasil," *Revista Civilização Brasileira*, 13 (May 1967), pp. 91–132.

2. Charles Anderson, *Politics and Economic Change in Latin America* (Princeton, N.J., 1967), pp. 87 et seq.

3. See Bazzanella.

4. Furtado, "Political Obstacles to Economic Growth in Brazil," in Veliz, p. 155. I might add that, unlike Europe, where emigration was an important factor in sustaining a relative balance between urbanization and employment opportunities, Brazil lacked this safety valve and was, in fact, attracting large numbers of European immigrants, most of whom settled in cities.

5. Furtado, *Dialética*, pp. 129–30.

6. The best historical analysis of the creation of this *estamente burocrático* is Faoro.

7. See Conceição Tavares, "Growth and Decline." See also Maria da Conceição Tavares, "Substituição de importações e desenvolvimento econômico na América Latina," *Dados*, I (1966), 115–40. Since writing this chapter, I have found in Albert O. Hirschman, "The Political Economy of Import-Substituting Industrialization in Latin America," *The Quarterly Journal of Economics*, LXXXII, 1 (Feb. 1968), 18, an interesting confirmation of my speculations. Hirschman, after observing that "the import-substituting process is far smoother, less disruptive, but also less learning-intensive than had been the case for industrialization in Europe, North America, and Japan," advances a slightly different argument about why this process debilitates group consciousness on the part of entrepreneurs: "The newly established industries may not act at all as the entering wedge of a broad industrialization drive. The high customs duties on their outputs, combined with low (or negative) duties on their inputs, could almost be seen as a plot on the part of the existing powerholders to corrupt or buy off the new industrialists, to reduce them to a sinecured, inefficient, and unenterprising group that can in no way threaten the existing social structure."

8. Cardoso, in *Empresário*, pp. 121 et seq., investigates these "premodern" practices of "modern" industrial firms and argues quite convincingly that, despite their abstract *wertirrationalitaet*, given the context of business decision-making in Brazil they are definitely *zweckrational* and not simply the product of a cultural lag. See also J. Lopes, *Sociedade*.

9. Furtado, in *Subdesenvolvimento*, p. 98, argues that in the Brazilian case the tendency for capital intensity, or "overmechanization," was especially great owing to artifically high wages in the industrial sector (caused by co-optive state welfare policies) and to certain exchange policies making imports of capital equipment artificially cheap.

10. Soares, "A nova industrialização," p. 35.

11. Cardoso and Reyna, p. 14. Another characteristic of Brazilian industrialization is its very great geographic concentration. In a federalist system this predominance of a single state (São Paulo alone has about 40% of the national industrial product) tended to reduce the potential political impact of the industrial bourgeoisie.

12. Again, after drafting my original remarks, I have found support in the recent work of Albert Hirschman. In "How to Divest in Latin America, and Why," *Essays in International Finance* (Princeton University), No. 76

(Nov. 1969), p. 7, he suggests that foreign businessmen probably act too timidly, depriving "the policy-makers of the guidance, pressures, and support they badly need to push through critically required development decisions and policies amid a welter of conflicting and antagonistic interests." He then observes that such a situation also has "a debilitating and corroding effect on the rationality of official economic policy-making for development. For, when newly arising investment opportunities are largely or predominantly seized upon by foreign firms, the national policy-makers face in effect a dilemma: more development means at the same time less autonomy."

13. See Florestan Fernandes, "Crescimento econômico e inestabilidade política no Brasil," *Revista Civilização Brasileira*, 11–12 (Dec. 1966–Mar. 1967), pp. 17 et seq.

14. Many authors have suggested that this coexistence of objectively antagonistic forces must be rooted in a network of familistic or economic interconnections. See, for example, Sodré, *História da Burguesia*, pp. 271 et seq.; Prado Júnior, *Revolução*, pp. 106–8. Luciano Martins, in "Formação do empresário industrial," shows substantial flows of entrepreneurial talent in and out of the industrial sector from services and finances, but little from the agricultural sector. Other studies have shown contemporary industrialists to be predominantly of immigrant origin. Maurício Vinhas de Queiroz, "Grupos econômicos," *Revista do Instituto de Ciências Sociais*, II, 1 (Jan.–Dec. 1965), 47 et seq., and Luis Carlos Besser Pereira, "Origins sociais e étnicas do empresariado paulista," *Revista de Administração de Emprêsas*, 11 (June 1964). Queiroz also disclosed that "35% of the national economic groups own agricultural enterprises."

15. See Lambert, and Furtado, *A Pre-Revolução Brasileira*. For reflections on Latin America as a whole, see S. N. Eisenstadt, *Modernization: Protest and Change* (Englewood Cliffs, N.J., 1966), pp. 87 et seq., and the works cited therein.

16. See Andre Gunder Frank, *Capitalism and Underdevelopment in Latin America* (New York, 1967), and the works cited therein.

17. Furtado, *Subdesenvolvimento e Estagnação*, pp. 82–83.

18. See Free for survey data on the very high degree of optimism of the Brazilian populace in the early 1960's.

19. Furtado, *Dialética*, p. 84.

20. The process is circular and cumulative. Inflation inhibits the associational consolidation of disfavored groups, especially of consumers, and this in turn permits greater concentration of benefits for the better organized, favored groups. Some Brazilian employers seem to have been aware of this vicious circle, as the following quote from a CNI official indicates: "In Brazil, instead of reacting against any lowering of their real salary [the workers] oppose its fall only beyond certain limits. . . . Thus the conclusion is that, given the behavior of the Brazilian proletariat, chronic inflation can cause an increase in savings even over a long term. This is not valid under European conditions, but should be accepted for Brazil and probably for all of Latin America." *Estudos Econômicos*, 1954, pp. 117–18. In an unevenly developed society with such disparities in associational capacity, inflation is not only probable (in the well-entrenched struggle to protect existing privilege), but profitable (given the associational weakness of the disorganized masses).

21. In the Fundação Getúlio Vargas' study on entrepreneurial behavior,

48% reported that they responded to inflationary increases in costs by readjusting prices. Only 11% claimed they would rationalize production to cut costs. Richers, p. 184.

22. *A Revolução Brasileira*, pp. 178–80. I might add that my evidence from the political culture questionnaire supports his contention that attitudinal responses are related more to personal than to class characteristics.

23. According to ECLA data, whereas over 50% of the urban population in Great Britain, Italy, Austria, and other early developers is employed in industry, only 36% in Brazil was so occupied in 1920, and the proportion has declined steadily since. It was 27% in 1960. *The Industrial Development of Latin America*, pp. 36–37.

24. After writing these lines, my attention was called to Mancur Olson, *The Logic of Collective Action* (Cambridge, Mass., 1965), p. 2. By logical analysis, he demonstrates that "rational, self-interested individuals will not act to achieve their common or group interests" by participation in large associations, "unless there is coercion to force them to do so or unless some separate incentive . . . is offered to the members of the group individually." He also notes that, for smaller associations, collective action is a more rational strategy. Perhaps this helps explain the greater dynamism of the more recently formed and functionally specific associations noted above.

25. Luciano Martins, "Aspectos políticos da revolução brasileira," *Revista Civilização Brasileira*, 2 (May 1966), pp. 23 et seq.

26. Prado Júnior, *Revolução*, p. 192. See also the developmental models in Jaguaribe, *Desenvolvimento*.

27. Carl J. Friedrich, *Man and His Government* (New York, 1963) p. 24.

28. Oliveiros S. Ferreira, political columnist for the prestigious *O Estado de São Paulo*, has written most about *o Sistema*. Jaguaribe's developmental models are also formalized presentations of parts of it. As Ferreira himself states, "The fact that we affirm the real existence of the *Sistema* does not mean that its components (groups and individuals) have an expressed consciousness of belonging to it. Only when one of its vital parts is threatened does the organism react as a whole, and in this reaction one sees manifested the solidarity of the parts with the whole and vice versa." "Uma caracterização do Sistema—1," *O Estado de São Paulo*, Oct. 17, 1965.

29. See A. L. Kallenberg, "The Logic of Comparison," *World Politics*, XIX, 1 (Oct. 1966) 69–82. I confess that at one point I attempted to extrapolate two of David Apter's system types, but found it difficult to construct a hybrid model of a "conciliatory modernizing autocracy." His speculations about a "neo-mercantilist system," though suggestive and germane, are not complete and precise enough. See his *Politics of Modernization* (Chicago, 1965), pp. 37, 224–25, 396–97, 412–20.

30. Juan Linz, "An Authoritarian Regime: Spain," in Erik Allardt and Yrjo Littunen, eds., *Cleavages, Ideologies and Party Systems* (Helsinki, 1964), pp. 291–342. See also L. Coser, "Prospects for the New Nations: Totalitarianism, Authoritarianism or Democracy?," in L. Coser, ed., *Political Sociology* (New York, 1966), pp. 247–71.

31. Linz, pp. 317–19, does observe that authoritarian regimes, with their limited basis of popular support, have more need for potential force, and this places the army in a privileged position. It is usually accorded complete autonomy in managing its own affairs and may also control a variety of other po-

litical and administrative posts. Linz notes, however, that such regimes tend to regard military men rather ambiguously, and to pursue policies of depoliticization and professionalization. These comments apply fully to the Brazilian case, where the crisis in the system caused military elites to eschew their former temporary "order-restoring" role in favor of that of semipermanent tutor.

32. *Ibid.*, p. 325.

33. *Ibid.*, p. 327.

34. Oliveiros S. Ferreira, "A nação sem projeto," *O Estado de São Paulo,* Nov. 21, 1965.

35. See Mendes de Almeida, "Sistema."

36. Linz, p. 320.

37. Linz, p. 301, hypothesizes that "the more traditional an authoritarian regime is, or the greater the role of the military and civil servants, the more important 'mentalities' become in understanding the system, and the more a focus on ideologies . . . may be misleading."

38. *Ibid.*, p. 304.

39. *Ibid.*, p. 323.

40. "This urban population, having no definite stratification to give it stability and bereft of a class or group consciousness that would enable it to act as a coherent whole, came to represent the new decisional factor in the Brazilian political struggle." Furtado, "Political Obstacles," p. 156.

41. "The danger of populism derives from its effect in provoking a redistribution of income in favor of certain groups and to the detriment of others. . . . Thus it constitutes a powerful arm in the hand of one faction of the ruling class against others." Furtado, *Dialética*, p. 83.

42. Linz, p. 304.

43. *Ibid.*, p. 312.

44. *Ibid.*

45. *Ibid.*, p. 300.

46. Pearse, "Algunas características de la urbanización en Rio de Janeiro," in Hauser, pp. 204–5.

47. Perhaps the best examples of this "projective" type of analysis are to be found in the earlier writings of Jaguaribe: *Nacionalismo,* and *Desenvolvimento.* See also Sodré's *Historia da burguesia* and his *Raizes Históricas do Nacionalismo Brasileiro* (Rio: ISEB, 1960).

48. See Francisco C. Weffort's "State and Mass in Brazil," *Studies in Comparative International Development,* II, 12 (1966), and his "Política de Massas," in Ianni et al., *Política e Revolução no Brasil* (Rio: Civilização Brasileira, 1965); Antônio Octávio Cintra and Fabio Wanderley Reis, "Política e desenvolvimento: o caso brasileiro," *América Latina,* IX, 3 (July–Sept. 1966), 52–74; Celso Furtado, *Diagnosis of the Brazilian Crisis* (Berkeley, Calif., 1965), p. xxiv.

49. Weffort, "State and Mass," p. 190.

50. See Kornhauser, p. 75 et seq., in which he specifies as basic conditions of the mass society model (1) the weakness of intermediary relations, (2) the isolation of primary relations, and (3) the centralization of national relations.

51. Barrington Moore, Jr., *Social Origins of Dictatorship and Democracy* (Boston, 1966), p. 437. I am reminded of the conclusion in Cardoso, *Empresario,* p. 168, that "the entrepreneur [in Brazil] not identifying himself with

the government, in part because he is not objectively linked with it, gains the maximum benefit from being in the economically dominant class without quite being in the dominant political stratum."

52. Moore, *Social Origins*, p. 438.

53. *Ibid.*

54. *Ibid.*

55. For a discussion of possible "Nasserist," "colonial-fascist," or "right nationalist" alternatives, see Mendes de Almeida, "Sistema," pp. 28–29; and Hélio Jaguaribe, "Brazil: A Political Analysis," (unpublished, Cambridge, Mass., 1966), pp. 46 et seq. Perhaps the most explicit formulation of the possible structures and policies of such a regime are to be found in the writings of Oliveiros S. Ferreira: "Organizar o povo e salvar a nação," *O Estado de São Paulo*, May 2, 1965; "Revolução institucional," *O Estado de São Paulo*, May 23, 1965; "Representação revolucionária," *O Estado de São Paulo*, Apr. 18, 1965.

56. Presumably it is this sort of capacity for controlled accommodation that led David Apter to advance the proposition that "modernizing autocracies and neo-mercantilist societies are optimal political forms for long-term modernization, in particular, for the conversion from the 'early' to the 'late' stages of the process." *Politics of Modernization*, p. 40.

Bibliography

Only those works that have been cited at least twice in the notes and a few others considered of special relevance are included.

Brazilian Public Documents

Centro Industrial do Brasil. O Brasil: Suas Riquezas, Suas Indústrias. Rio: M. Orosco & Cia., 1909. Vol. III.

Conselho Nacional de Estatística. Produção Industrial Brasileira—1958.

Directoria Geral de Estatística. Recenseamento do Brasil—1920.

IBGE. Anuário Estatístico do Brasil 1937/38—1966. Rio, 1939–67.

———— Censo Comercial—1950, 1960.

———— Censo Industrial—1940, 1950, 1960.

———— Recenseamento Geral—1940, 1950.

———— Censo Demográfico, Resultados Preliminares. Série Especial, Vol. II, 1960.

Presidência da República. Three-Year Plan for Economic and Social Development, 1963–1965.

Serviço de Documentação, Ministério do Trabalho, Indústria e Comércio. Organização Sindical Brasileira, Rio, 1954.

Serviço de Estatística da Previdência e Trabalho, Ministério do Trabalho e Previdência Social. Cadastro Sindical—1961. Rio, 1962.

———— Relatório Anual—1944. Rio, 1945.

———— Relatório de 1949. Rio, 1950.

———— Relatório de 1950. Rio, 1951.

———— Relatório de 1954. Rio, 1955.

———— Relatório Anual—1956. Rio, 1957.

———— Sinopse do Relatório de 1946. Rio, 1947.

———— Sinopse do Relatório de 1947. Rio, 1948.

Other Works

Abreu, João Capistrano de. Capítulos da História Colonial: 1500–1800. 3rd ed. Rio: Sociedade Capistrano de Abreu, 1934.

Abreu Ramos, Plínio de. Como Agem os Grupos de Pressão? Rio: Civilização Brasileira, 1963.

Accioly Borges, T. Pompeu. "Estratificação e mobilidade social no Brasil," *Desenvolvimento e Conjuntura*, Year II, No. 10 (Oct. 1958), pp. 93–104.

Alexander, Robert. Labor Relations in Argentina, Brazil, and Chile. New York: McGraw-Hill, 1962.

Almeida, José Américo, et al. A Revolução de 31 de Março: 2º Aniversário. Rio: Biblioteca do Exército, 1966.

Almeida Magalhães, João Paulo de. Controvérsia Brasileira sôbre o Desenvolvimento Econômico. Rio: Edição de Desenvolvimento e Conjuntura, 1961.

Almond, Gabriel A., and Sidney Verba. The Civic Culture. Boston: Little, Brown, 1965.

Amado, Gilberto. A Chave de Salomão e Outros Estudos. Rio: José Olympio, 1947.

———— Eleição e Representação. 2nd ed. Rio: Irmãos Pongetti, 1946.

———— Grão de Areia e Estudos Brasileiros. Rio: José Olympio, 1948.

Amaral, Azevedo. O Brasil na Crise Atual. São Paulo: Companhia Editôra Nacional, 1938.

Amaral, Luis. História Geral da Agricultura Brasileira. 2nd ed. São Paulo: Companhia Editôra Nacional, 1958. 2 vols.

Amoroso Lima, Alceu. Política. 4th ed., rev. Rio: Livraria Agir, 1956.

Andrade, Manuel Correia de. A Terra e o Homen no Nordeste. São Paulo: Editôra Brasilense, 1963.

Azevedo, Fernando de. Brazilian Culture. New York: Macmillan, 1950.

Baer, Werner. "Brazil: Inflation and Economic Efficiency," *Economic Development and Cultural Change*, XLI, 4 (July 1963), 395–406.

———— Industrialization and Economic Development in Brazil. Homewood, Ill.: Irwin, 1965.

Baklanoff, Eric N., ed. New Perspectives of Brazil. Nashville, Tenn.: Vanderbilt University Press, 1966.

————, ed. The Shaping of Modern Brazil. Baton Rouge: Louisiana State University Press, 1969.

Barreto, Lêda. Julião, Nordeste, Revolução. Rio: Civilização Brasileira, 1963.

Bastide, Roger. Brazil: Terra de Contrastes. 2nd ed. São Paulo: Difusão Européia do Livro, 1964.

————, and Florestan Fernandes. Brancos e Negros em São Paulo. 2nd ed. São Paulo: Companhia Editôra Nacional, 1959.

Bastos, Humberto. A Marcha do Capitalismo no Brasil: Ensaio de Interpretação 1500–1940. São Paulo: Livraria Martins, 1944.

———— O Pensamento Industrial no Brasil. São Paulo: Livraria Martins, 1952.

Bastos de Avila, Fernando, S.J. Neo Capitalismo, Socialismo, Solidarismo. Rio: Editôra Agir, 1963.

Bazzanella, Waldemiro. "Industrialização e urbanização no Brasil," *América Latina*, VI, 1 (Jan.–Mar. 1963), 3–27.

Bello, José Maria. A History of Modern Brazil: 1889–1964. Stanford, Calif.: Stanford University Press, 1966.

Bendix, Reinhard. Work and Authority in Industry. New York: Harper, 1956.

Berman, Albert H. Industrial Labor in Brazil. Washington: U.S. Office of the Coordinator of Inter-American Affairs, 1944.

Bernstein, E. M., et al. Contribuições à Análise do Desenvolvimento Econômico. Rio: Editôra Agir, 1957.

Bomfim, Manoel. O Brasil na História. Rio: Livraria F. Alves, 1930.

Bonilla, Frank. "Brazil," in James Coleman, ed., Education and Political Development. Princeton, N.J.: Princeton University Press, 1965.

Borges, Fragmon. "O Movimento camponês no nordéste," *Estudos Sociais*, No. 15 (Dec. 1962).

Buarque de Holanda, Sérgio. Raízes do Brasil. 3rd ed., rev. Rio: José Olympio, 1956.

Burns, E. Bradford. Nationalism in Brazil: A Historical Survey. New York: Praeger, 1968.

————, ed. A Documentary History of Brazil. New York: Knopf, 1966.

Callado, Antônio. Tempo de Arraes: Padres e Communistas ra Revolução sem Violência. Rio: José Alvaro Editôra, 1964.

Campos, Francisco. O Estado Nacional. 3rd ed. Rio: José Olympio, 1941.

Cardoso, Fernando H. Empresário Industrial e Desenvolvimento Econômico no Brasil. São Paulo: Difusão Européia do Livro, 1964.

————, and José L. Reyna. "Industrialização, estructura ocupacional e estratificação social na América Latina," *Dados*, No. 2/3 (1967), pp. 4–31.

"Carta da paz social," *O Observador Econômico e Financeiro*, Year X, No. 120 (Jan. 1946), pp. 15–16.

Carvalho Ribeiro, Augusto Barbosa de. Organização Sindical Brasileira. São Paulo: Magalhaes, 1952.

Castro, Josué de. "A revolução social brasileira," *Revista Brasileira de Ciências Sociais*, II, 2 (July 1962), 196–215.

Cesarino Júnior, A. F. Direito Corporativo e Direito do Trabalho: Soluções Práticas. São Paulo: Livraria Martins, 1940–42. 2 vols.

———— Direito Social Brasileiro. 5th ed. Rio: Livrarias Freitas Bastos, 1963. 2 vols.

Conceição Tavares, Maria, et al. "The Growth and Decline of Import Substitution in Brazil," *Economic Bulletin for Latin America*, IX, 1 (Mar. 1964), 1–60.

Consolidation of the Brazilian Labor Laws. Rio and São Paulo: American Chamber of Commerce in Brazil, n.d. The edition used was brought up to date as of February 1960. The latest Brazilian edition is A. Campanhole, ed., Consolidação das Leis do Trabalho e Legislação Complementar, 13th ed., revised and brought up to date as of June 1966. São Paulo: Editôra Atlas, 1966.

Cooke, Morris L. Brazil on the March: A Study in International Cooperation. New York: McGraw-Hill, 1944.

Cruz Costa, João. A History of Ideas in Brazil. Translated by Suzette Macedo. Berkeley: University of California Press, 1964.

Cunha, Euclydes da. À Margem da História. Pôrto: Livraria Chardron, 1926.

Daland, Robert T. Brazilian Planning. Chapel Hill: University of North Carolina Press, 1967.

————, ed. Perspectives of Brazilian Public Administration. Rio de Janeiro and Los Angeles: The Brazilian School of Public Administration and the School of Public Administration, USC, June 1963.

Debrun, Michel. "Nationalisme et politiques du développement au Brésil" (deuxième partie), *Sociologie du Travail*, VI, 4 (Oct.–Dec. 1964), 351–80.

"Desenvolvimento recente do sindicalismo no Brasil," *Boletim do DIEESE*, Year I, No. 10 (Jan. 1961).

Deutsch, Karl. "Social Mobilization and Political Development," *American Political Science Review*, LV, 3 (Sept. 1961).

Dias, Everardo. História das Lutas Sociais no Brasil. São Paulo: Editôra Edaglit, 1962.

Diégues Júnior, Manuel. Imigração, Urbanização e Industrialização. Rio: Centro de Pesquisas Educacionais, 1964.

────── Regiões Culturais do Brasil. Rio: Centro Brasileiro de Pesquisas Educacionais, INEP, MEC, 1960.

Duarte, Nestor. A Ordem Privada e a Organização Política Nacional. São Paulo: Companhia Editôra Nacional, 1939.

Dulles, John W. F. Vargas of Brazil. Austin: University of Texas Press, 1967.

Dutra, Eloi. IBAD. Sigla da Corrupção. Rio: Civilização Brasileira, 1963.

Eckstein, Harry. Pressure Group Politics. Stanford, Calif.: Stanford University Press, 1960.

Ehrman, H., ed. Interest Groups on Four Continents. Pittsburgh, Pa.: University of Pittsburgh Press, 1958.

"A estratificação e mobilidade social na cidade do Rio de Janeiro a luz dos dados censitários e da estatística da renda nacional," *Desenvolvimento e Conjuntura*, Year V, No. 9 (Sept. 1961).

"Evolução da mão-de-obra brasileira (II)," *Conjuntura Econômica*, Year X, No. 8 (Aug. 1956).

Falcão, Waldemar. O Ministério do Trabalho: Realização Integral do Govêrno Getúlio Vargas. Rio: Departamento de Imprensa e Propaganda, 1941.

Faoro, Raymundo. Os Donos do Poder. Pôrto Alegre: Editôra Globo, 1958.

Faria, Octavio de. "Sindicalismo novo," *Síntese*, No. 22 (Apr.–June 1964), pp. 23–38.

Fernandes, Florestan. A Integração do Negro na Sociedade de Classes. São Paulo: Dominus Editôra, 1965. 2 vols.

────── Sociedade de Classes e Subdesenvolvimento. Rio: Zahar, 1968.

Ferreira, Oliveiros S. As Forças Armadas e o Desafio da Revolução. Rio: GRD, 1964.

Ferreira Lima, Heitor. Evolução Industrial de São Paulo. São Paulo: Livraria Martins, 1954.

Finer, S. E. Anonymous Empire. London: Pall Mall Press, 1958.

Fonseca, Gondim da. Assim Falou Julião. São Paulo: Editôra Fulgor, 1963.

Free, Lloyd. Some International Implications of the Political Psychology of Brazilians. Princeton, N.J.: Institute of International Social Research, 1961.

Freitas Marcondes, J. V. First Brazilian Legislation Relating to Rural Labor Unions, Monograph No. 20. Gainesville: University of Florida Press, 1962.

────── Radiografia da Liderança Sindical Paulista. São Paulo: Instituto Cultural do Trabalho, 1964.

Freyre, Gilberto. The Mansions and the Shanties. Translated by Harriet de Onís. New York: Knopf, 1963.

────── The Masters and the Slaves: A Study in the Development of Brazilian Civilization. Translated by S. Putnam. New York: Knopf, 1946.

────── New World in the Tropics. New York: Knopf, 1959.

────── Ordem e Progresso. Rio: José Olympio, 1959. 2 vols.

Furtado, Celso. Desenvolvimento e Subdesenvolvimento. Rio: Fundo de Cultura, 1961.

────── Dialética do Desenvolvimento. Rio: Fundo de Cultura, 1964.

——— The Economic Growth of Brazil. Berkeley: University of California Press, 1965.

——— A Pre-Revolução Brasileira. Rio: Fundo de Cultura, 1962.

——— Um Projeto para o Brasil. Rio: Editôra Saga, 1968.

——— Subdesenvolvimento e Estagnação na América Latina. Rio: Civilização Brasileira, 1966.

———, ed. Brasil: Tempos Modernos. Rio: Editôra Paz e Terra, 1968.

Galjart, Benno. "Class and 'Following' in Rural Brazil," *América Latina*, VII, 3 (July–Sept. 1964), 3–24.

Geiger, Pedro Pinchas. Evolução da Rêde Urbana Brasileira. Rio: Centro Brasileiro de Pesquisas Educacionais, 1962.

Gordon, Lincoln, and E. Grommers. U.S. Manufacturing Investment in Brazil. Cambridge, Mass.: Harvard University Press, 1962.

Guilherme, Wanderley. Introdução ao Estudo das Contradições Sociais no Brasil. Rio: ISEB, 1963.

Guimarães, Alberto Passos. Inflação e Monopólio no Brasil. Rio: Civilização Brasileira, 1963.

Hambloch, Ernest. His Majesty the President of Brazil. New York: Dutton, 1936.

Harris, Marvin. Town and Country in Brazil. New York: Columbia University Press, 1956.

Hauser, Philip M., ed. La Urbanización en América Latina. Paris: UNESCO, 1961.

Havighurst, R., and J. R. Moreira. Society and Education in Brazil. Pittsburgh, Pa.: University of Pittsburgh Press, 1965.

Henriques, Affonso. Vargas: o Maquiavélico. São Paulo: Palácio do Livro, 1961.

Hirschman, A. O. Journeys Toward Progress. New York: Twentieth Century Fund, 1963.

——— The Strategy of Economic Development. New Haven, Conn.: Yale University Press, 1958.

Horowitz, I., ed. Revolution in Brazil. New York: Dutton, 1964.

Huntington, Samuel. "Political Development and Political Decay," *World Politics*, XVII (Apr. 1965), 386–430.

Hutchinson, Bertram. "The Patron-Dependent Relationship in Brazil: A Preliminary Examination," *Sociologia Ruralis*, VI, 1 (1966), 3–30.

——— "Social Grading of Occupations in Brazil," *British Journal of Sociology* (1957), 176–89.

——— "Social Mobility Rates in Buenos Aires, Montevideo and São Paulo," *América Latina*, V, 4 (Oct.–Dec. 1962), 3–21.

——— "Urban Social Mobility Rates in Brazil Related to Migration and Changing Occupational Structure," *América Latina*, VI, 3 (July–Sept. 1963), 47–61.

———, et al. Mobilidade e Trabalho. Rio: Centro Brasileiro de Pesquisas Educacionais, 1960.

Ianni, Octávio. O Colapso do Populismo no Brasil. Rio: Civilização Brasileira, 1968.

——— Estado e Capitalismo. Rio: Civilização Brasileira, 1965.

——— Industrialização e Desenvolvimento Social no Brasil. Rio: Civilização Brasileira, 1963.

———— Raças e Classes Sociais no Brasil. Rio: Civilização Brasileira, 1966.

International Labour Office. "Brazil," in Freedom of Association, Vol. I (Geneva, 1930), pp. 175–86. In International Labour Office, Series and Reports, Series A (Industrial Relations), No. 32.

Iutaka, S. "Social Mobility and Differential Occupational Opportunity in Urban Brazil," *Human Organization*, XXIV (Summer 1965).

Jaguaribe, Hélio. Condições Institucionais do Desenvolvimento. Rio: ISEB, 1958.

———— "A crise brasileira," *Cadernos do Nosso Tempo*, No. 1 (Oct.–Dec. 1953), pp. 120–60.

———— Desenvolvimento Político e Desenvolvimento Econômico. Rio: Fundo de Cultura, 1962.

———— "As eleicões de 62," *Tempo Brasileiro*, Year I, No. 2 (Dec. 1962), pp. 7–38.

———— O Nacionalismo na Atualidade Brasileira. Rio: ISEB, 1958.

Joint Brazil–United States Economic Development Commission. The Development of Brazil. Washington, D.C.: GPO, 1953.

Julião, Francisco. Que São as Ligas Camponesas? Rio: Civilização Brasileira, 1962.

Jurema, Abelardo. Sexta-Feira 13. Rio: O Cruzeiro, 1964.

Kellemen, Peter. Brasil para Principiantes. 3rd ed. Rio: Civilização Brasileira, 1961.

Kornhauser, William. The Politics of Mass Society. New York: Free Press, 1959.

Kuznets, S., W. E. Moore, and J. J. Spengler, eds. Economic Growth: Brazil, India, Japan. Durham, N.C.: Duke University Press, 1955.

Lambert, Jacques. Os Dois Brasís. Rio: Centro Brasileiro de Pesquisas Educacionais, 1959.

LaPalombara, Joseph. Interest Groups in Italian Politics. Princeton, N.J.: Princeton University Press, 1964.

Leal, Victor Nunes. Coronelismo, Enxada e Voto. Rio: Livraria Forense, 1949.

Leeds, Anthony. "Brazilian Careers and Social Structure," *American Anthropologist*, LXVI, 6, Part I (Dec. 1964), 1321–47.

Leff, Nathaniel. Economic Policy-Making and Development in Brazil, 1947–1964. New York: Wiley, 1968.

Lipson, Leslie. "Government in Contemporary Brazil," *The Canadian Journal of Economics and Political Science*, XXII, 2 (May 1956), 183–98.

Loewenstein, Karl. Brazil under Vargas. New York: Macmillan, 1942.

Lopes, Júarez Rubens Brandão. Desenvolvimento e Mudança Social. São Paulo: Companhia Editôra Nacional, 1968.

———— "Étude de quelques changements fondamentaux dans la politique et la société bresiliennes," *Sociologie du Travail*, No. 3 (July–Sept. 1965), 238–53.

———— Sociedade Industrial no Brasil. São Paulo: Difusão Européia do Livro, 1964.

Lopes, Paula R. "Social Problems and Legislation in Brazil," *International Labour Review*, XLIV, 5 (Nov. 1941), 493–537.

Lowy, M., and S. Chucid. "Opiniões e atitudes de líderes sindicais metalúrgicos," *Revista Brasileira de Estudos Políticos*, XIII (1962), 132–69.

Luz, Nícia Vilela. A Luta pela Industrializacão do Brasil. São Paulo: Difusão Européia do Livro, 1961.

Marcondes Machado, Alexander. Trabalhadores do Brasil. Rio: Revista Judiciária, 1943.

Mascarenhas, João Antônio. "Levantamento dos sindicatos e associações de lavradores e empregados rurais existentes no pais," *Gleba*, Year VIII, No. 82 (Feb. 1962), 22–27.

Meister, Albert. "Cambio social y participación social formal en asociaciones voluntarias," *Desarrollo Económico*, II, 3 (Oct.–Dec. 1962), 5–18.

Melo Franco, Affonso Arinos de. Conceito de Civilização Brasileira. São Paulo: Companhia Editôra Nacional, 1936.

Mendes de Almeida, Cândido. Memento do Vivos. Rio: Tempo Brasileiro, 1966.

——— Nacionalismo e Desenvolvimento. Rio: Instituto de Estudos Afro-Asiáticos, 1963.

——— "Sistema político e modelos de poder no Brasil," *Dados* (Rio), No. 1 (second semester, 1966), 7–41.

Menezes, Djacir, ed. O Brasil no Pensamento Brasileiro. Rio: Centro Brasileiro de Pesquisas Educacionais, INEP, MEC, 1957.

Mercadente, Paulo. A Consciência Conservadora no Brasil. Rio: Editôra Saga, 1965.

Meynaud, Jean. Nouvelles Études sur les Groupes de Pression en France. Paris: Armand Colin, 1962.

Miglioli, Jorge. Como São Feitas as Greves no Brasil? Rio: Civilização Brasileira, 1963.

Moore, W. E. The Impact of Industry. Englewood Cliffs, N.J.: Prentice-Hall, 1965.

Moraes Filho, Evaristo de. "Aspirações atuais do Brasil: análise sociológica," *Revista do Instituto de Ciências Sociais*, Vol. I, No. 1 (1962), 19–66.

——— O Problema do Sindicato Único no Brasil. Rio: Editôra A. Noite, 1952.

Morais, Pessoa de. Sociologia da Revolução Brasileira. Rio: Editôra Leitura, 1965.

Moreira, Roberto. Educacão e Desenvolvimento no Brasil. Rio: Centro Latino-americano de Pesquisas em Ciências Sociais, 1960.

Moreira Leite, Dante. O Carater Nacional Brasileiro. São Paulo: Universidade de São Paulo, 1954. Faculdade de Filosofia, Ciências e Letras, Boletim: Psicologia, No. 7.

Moura Brandão Filho, Francisco de. Teoria e Prática da Organização Sindical do Brasil. Rio: Editôra Borsoi, 1961.

Needler, Martin, ed. Political Systems of Latin America. Princeton, N.J.: Van Nostrand, 1964.

Niemeyer, W. Movimento Sindicalista no Brasil. Rio: n. pub., 1933.

Normano, J. F. Brazil: A Study of Economic Types. Chapel Hill: University of North Carolina Press, 1935.

Oliveira, Franklin de. Revolução e Contra-revolução no Brasil. Rio: Civilização Brasileira, 1962.

Oliveira Campos, Roberto de. Economia, Planejamento e Nacionalismo. Rio: APEC Editôra, 1963.

Oliveira Vianna, F. J. de. "Condições antropogeográficas e estrutura sindical," in Anais do Primeiro Congresso Brasileiro de Direito Social, IV (São Paulo: Instituto de Direito Social, 1945), 27–52.

——— Direito do Trabalho e Democracia Social: O Problema da Incorporação do Trabalhador no Estado. Rio: José Olympio, 1951.

——— Evolução do Povo Brasileiro. 3rd ed. São Paulo: Companhia Editôra Nacional, 1938.

——— O Idealismo da Constituição. São Paulo: Companhia Editôra Nacional, 1939.

——— Instituições Políticas Brasileiras. 3rd ed., rev. Rio: José Olympio, 1955. 2 vols.

——— Populações Meridionais do Brasil. 5th ed. Rio: José Olympio, 1952.

——— Problemas de Direito Corporativo. Rio: José Olympio, 1938.

——— Problemas de Direito Sindical. Rio: M. Limonad Ltda., 1943.

——— Problemas de Organização e Problemas de Direção. Rio: José Olympio, 1952.

Payne, James. Labor and Politics in Peru. New Haven, Conn.: Yale University Press, 1965.

Pearse, Andrew. "Notas sôbre a organização social de uma favela do Rio de Janeiro," *Educação e Ciências Sociais*, Year III, Vol. III, No. 7 (Apr. 1958), 9–32.

Pedreira, Fernando. Março 31: Civís e Militares no Processo da Crise Brasileira. Rio: José Alvaro Editôra, 1964.

Peralva, Osvaldo. "A esquerda positiva nos sindicatos," *Jornal do Brasil*, Aug. 18, 1963.

——— O Retrato. Pôrto Alegre: Editôra Globo, 1962.

Pereira, Luiz. Trabalho e Desenvolvimento no Brasil. São Paulo: Difusão Européia do Livro, 1965.

Perreira, Osny Duarte. Quem Faz as Leis no Brasil? Rio: Civilização Brasileira, 1962.

Perreira de Queiroz, Maria Isaura. "Les classes sociales dans le Brésil actuel," *Cahiers Internationaux de Sociologie*, XXXIX (1965), 137–70.

——— "Mandonismo na vida política brasileira," in M. I. Perreira de Queiroz, C. Castaldi, E. T. Ribeiro, and C. Martuscelli, eds., Estudos de Sociologia e História. São Paulo: Editôra Anhembi, 1957.

Pinto, Luiz de Aguilar Costa. Sociologia e Desenvolvimento. Rio: Civilização Brasileira, 1963.

Poerner, Arthur José. O Poder Jovem. Rio: Civilização Brasileira, 1968.

Poppino, Rollie F. Brazil: The Land and People. New York: Oxford University Press, 1968.

Prado, Paulo. Retrato do Brasil. 4th ed. Rio: F. Briguiet, 1931.

Prado Júnior, Caio. História Economica do Brasil. São Paulo: Editôra Brasilense, 1961.

——— A Revolução Brasileira. São Paulo: Editôra Brasilense, 1966.

Price, Robert E. "Rural Unionization in Brazil." Unpublished ms. The Land Tenure Center, 310 King Hall, University of Wisconsin, 1964.

Pye, Lucian. Communications and Political Development. Princeton, N.J.: Princeton University Press, 1963.

——— and Sidney Verba. Political Culture and Political Development. Princeton, N.J.: Princeton University Press, 1965.

"Quince años de política económica en el Brasil," *Boletin Económico de América Latina,* IX, 2 (Nov. 1964).

Rabello, Ophelina. A Rêde Sindical Paulista. São Paulo: Instituto Cultural do Trabalho, 1965.

Ramos, Artur, "O espírito associativo do negro brasileiro," *Boletim do MTIC,* VII, 84 (Aug. 1941).

―――― The Negro in Brazil. Washington, D.C.: Associated Publishers, 1939.

Ramos, Guerreiro. A Crise do Poder no Brasil. Rio: Zahar, 1961.

―――― Mito e Verdade da Revolução Brasileira. Rio: Zahar, 1963.

Richers, Raimar, Claude Machline, Ary Bouzan, Ary R. Carvalho, and Haroldo Bariani. Impacto da Ação do Govêrno Sôbre as Emprêsas Brasileiras. Rio: Fundação Vargas, 1963.

Riggs, Fred. Administration in Developing Countries. Boston: Houghton Mifflin, 1964.

―――― "Reflections on Development." Unpublished ms., 1963.

Rodrigues, José Albertino. "Estrutura sindical brasileira," *Revista de Estudos Sócio-Econômicos,* Year I, No. 10–11 (Sept.–Dec., 1962).

―――― "Situação econômico-social da classe trabalhadora," *Revista de Estudos Sócio-Econômicos,* Year I, No. 1, 17–27.

Rodrigues, José Honório. Aspirações Nacionais: Interpretação Histórico-Política. São Paulo: Editôra Fulgor, 1963.

―――― Conciliação e Reforma no Brasil: Um Desafio Histórico-Cultural. Rio: Civilização Brasileira, 1965.

Rodrigues, Leôncio Martins. Conflito Industrial e Sindicalismo no Brasil. São Paulo: Difusão Européia do Livro, 1966.

―――――, ed. Sindicalismo e Sociedade. São Paulo: Difusão Européia do Livro, 1968.

Rose, Arnold M. Theory and Method in the Social Sciences. Minneapolis: University of Minnesota Press, 1954.

Rosen, Bernard C. "The Achievement Syndrome and Economic Growth in Brazil," *Social Forces,* XLII, 3 (Mar. 1964), 341–53.

―――― "Socialization and Achievement Motivation in Brazil," *American Sociological Review* XXVII (Oct. 1962), 612–24.

Segadas Viana, José de. O Sindicato no Brasil. Rio: Gráfica Olympia, 1953.

Siegel, Gilbert B. "The Strategy of Public Administration Reform: The Case of Brazil," *Public Administration Review,* XXXI, 1 (Mar. 1966), 45–55.

Silvert, K., ed. Expectant Peoples. New York: Random House, 1963.

Simão, Aziz. "Industrialização e sindicalização no Brasil," *Revista Brasileira de Estudos Políticos,* No. 13 (Jan. 1962).

―――― Sindicato e Estado. São Paulo: Dominus Editôra, 1966.

Simonsen, Roberto C. Alguns aspectos da política econômica mais conveniente ao Brasil no período de após-guerra. São Paulo: Sigueira, [1943?].

―――― Brazil's Industrial Evolution. São Paulo: Escola Livre de Sociologia e Política, 1939.

―――― Ensaios sociais, políticos e econômicos. São Paulo: FIESP, 1943.

―――― História Econômica do Brasil, 1500–1820. São Paulo: Companhia Editôra Nacional, 1937.

Singer, Paulo. Desenvolvimento e Crise. São Paulo: Difusão Européia do Livro, 1969.

———— "A Política das Classes Dominantes," in O. Ianni et al., Política e Revolução Social no Brasil. Rio: Civilização Brasileira, 1965.

Skidmore, Thomas E. Politics in Brazil, 1930–64: An Experiment in Democracy. New York: Oxford University Press, 1967.

Slawinski, Z. "Structural Changes in Employment within the Context of Latin America's Economic Development," *Economic Bulletin for Latin America*, X, 2 (Oct. 1965).

Smelser, Neil. "Mechanisms of Change and Adjustment to Change," in B. F. Hoselitz and W. E. Moore, eds., Industrialization and Society. The Hague: UNESCO-Mouton, 1963.

Smith, T. Lynn. Brazil: People and Institutions. 3rd ed. Baton Rouge: Louisiana State University Press, 1963.

————, and Alexander Marchant, eds. Brazil: Portrait of Half a Continent. New York: Dryden Press, 1951.

Soares, Gláucio D. Ary. "Alianças e coligações eleitorais: notas para uma teoria," *Revista Brasileira de Estudos Políticos*, No. 17 (July 1964), 95–124.

———— "Economic Development and Social Development." Unpublished ms., University of California, 1963.

———— "A nova industrializacão e o sistema político brasileiro," *Dados*, I, 2/3 (1967), 32–50.

Sodré, Nelson Werneck. História da Burguesia Brasileira. Rio: Civilização Brasileira, 1964.

———— História Militar do Brasil. Rio: Civilização Brasileira, 1965.

———— Introdução a Revolução Brasileira. Rio: Civilização Brasileira, 1963.

———— Memórias de um Soldado. Rio: Civilização Brasileira, 1967.

Stacchini, José. Março 1964: Mobilização da Audácia. São Paulo: Companhia Editôra Nacional, 1965.

Stein, Stanley J. The Brazilian Cotton Manufacture: Textile Enterprise in an Underdeveloped Area, 1850–1950. Cambridge, Mass.: Harvard University Press, 1957.

———— Vassouras. Cambridge, Mass.: Harvard University Press, 1957.

Tavares de Sá, Hernane. The Brazilians: People of Tomorrow. New York: John Day, 1947.

Telles, Jover. O Movimento Sindical no Brasil. Rio: Editorial Vitória, 1962.

Torres, Alberto. O Problema Nacional Brasileiro. Rio: Imprensa Nacional, 1914.

Truman, David. The Governmental Process. New York: Knopf, 1951.

Vargas do Amaral Peixoto, Alzira. Getúlio Vargas, Meu Pai. Pôrto Alegre: Editôra Globo, 1960.

Veliz, Claudio, ed. Obstacles to Change in Latin America. London: Oxford University Press, 1965.

Veloso, P. "Situação ideológica dos sindicatos," *Vozes* (July 1963), 537–40.

Vianna Moog, C. Bandeirantes and Pioneers. Translated by L. L. Barrett. New York: Braziller, 1964.

Vieira da Cunha, Mário. O Sistema Administrativo Brasileiro, 1930–1950. Rio: Centro Brasileiro de Pesquisas Educacionais, 1963.

Vieira Pinto, Alvaro. Consciência e Realidade Nacional. Rio: ISEB, 1960. 2 vols.

Wagley, Charles. "The Brazilian Revolution: Social Change since 1930," in

Richard Adams et al., Social Change in Latin America Today. New York: Vintage, 1960.

———— An Introduction to Brazil. New York: Columbia University Press, 1963.

———— "Regionalism and Cultural Unity in Brazil," *Social Forces*, XXVI, 4 (1948), 457–64.

————, ed. Race and Class in Rural Brazil. Paris: UNESCO, 1952.

Weber, Max. The Theory of Economic and Social Organization. Translated by T. Parsons. London: William Hodge, 1947.

Weiner, Myron. The Politics of Scarcity. Chicago: University of Chicago Press, 1962.

Wirth, John D. The Politics of Brazilian Development. Stanford, Calif.: Stanford University Press, 1970.

Wythe, George. Brazil: An Expanding Economy. New York: Twentieth Century Fund, 1949.

Zeigler, Harmon. Interest Groups in American Society. Englewood Cliffs, N.J.: Prentice-Hall, 1964.

Index

AABB (Athletic Association of the Bank of Brazil), 204
ABA (Brazilian Association of Advertisers), 463
ABAP (Brazilian Association of Advertising Agencies), 463
ABC [Brazilian Copper Association], 357
ABCOOP (Brazilian Alliance of Cooperatives), 203n
ABDIB, see Brazilian Association for the Development of Basic Industries
ABEOP (Brazilian Association of Public Contractors), 163
ABERT (Brazilian Association of Radio and Television Stations), 201–2
ABIEE, see Brazilian Association of the Electrical and Electronic Industry
ABIF, see Brazilian Association of the Pharmaceutical Industry
ABM, see Brazilian Association of Municipalities
ABP (Brazilian Association for Propaganda), 463
ABRAVE, see Brazilian Association of Authorized Automobile Dealers
Abreu, João Capistrano de, 139
ACADE, see Association of Dealers in Electrical Appliances
Ação Católica (Catholic Action), 149, 216–17
Ação Democrática Parlementar (ADP), 278
Ação Democrática Popular ([Popular Democratic Action], ADEP), 218–19

Ação Popular ([Catholic] Popular Action, AP), 193, 212
access, 125, 179, 198, 249, 255, 274, 293, 298n, 457; predictability of channels, 14; to interest groups, 17; survey question on, 96; guaranteed, 111, 116, 123, 180; changes in Brazilian pattern, 128, 223; to President of Republic, 257–58, 260, 301, 307, 310–14; to Congress, 265; Brazilian pattern of, 285, 313 (author's summary); defined, 324; distinguished from influence, 324–25; legitimacy of, 328–29; equality of, 329–30; too easy, 388, 390
Accioly Borges, T. Pompeu, 22
Acre, 118n, 181
ACREFI, 355
AC-Rio, see Commercial Association of Rio de Janeiro
AC-SP, see Commercial Association of São Paulo
ADCE, see Association of Catholic Business Managers
Additional Act of 1834, 60
ADECIF, see Association of Credit, Investment, and Finance Companies
ADEP, see Ação Democrática Popular
ADESG, 446
ADP (Parliamentary Democratic Action), 278
AFL-CIO, see American Free Labor Development Institute
age (as factor in study): 87–105 passim, 294